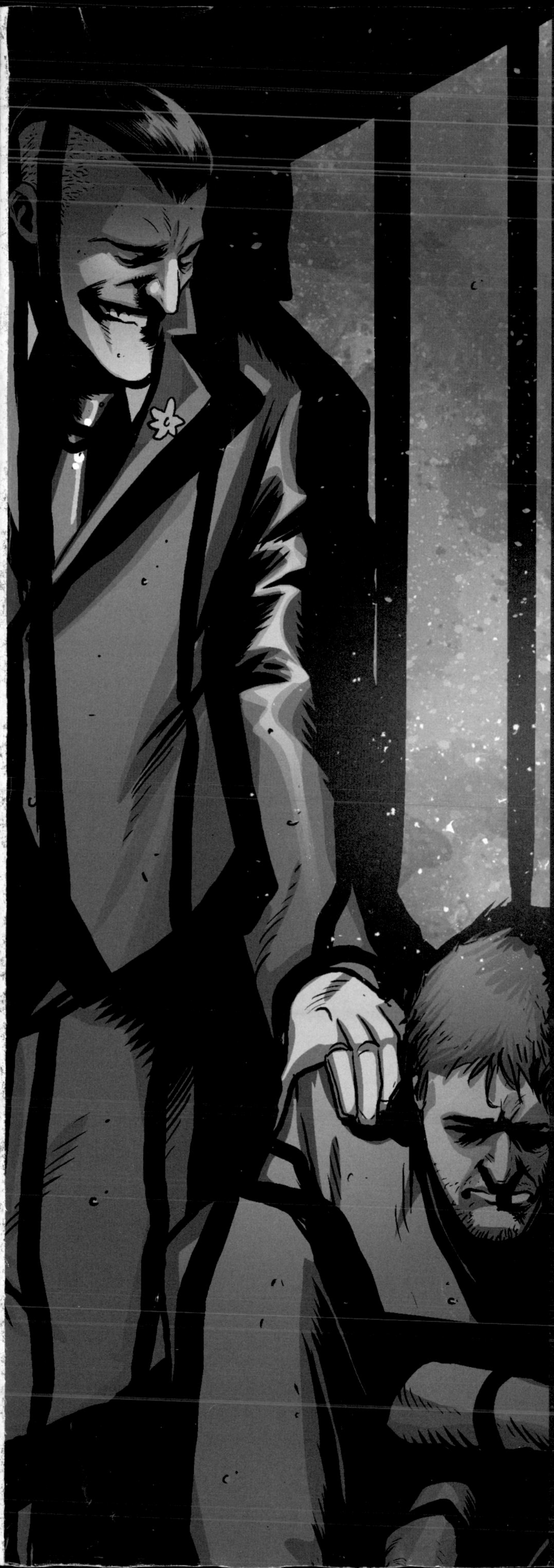

THE JOKER

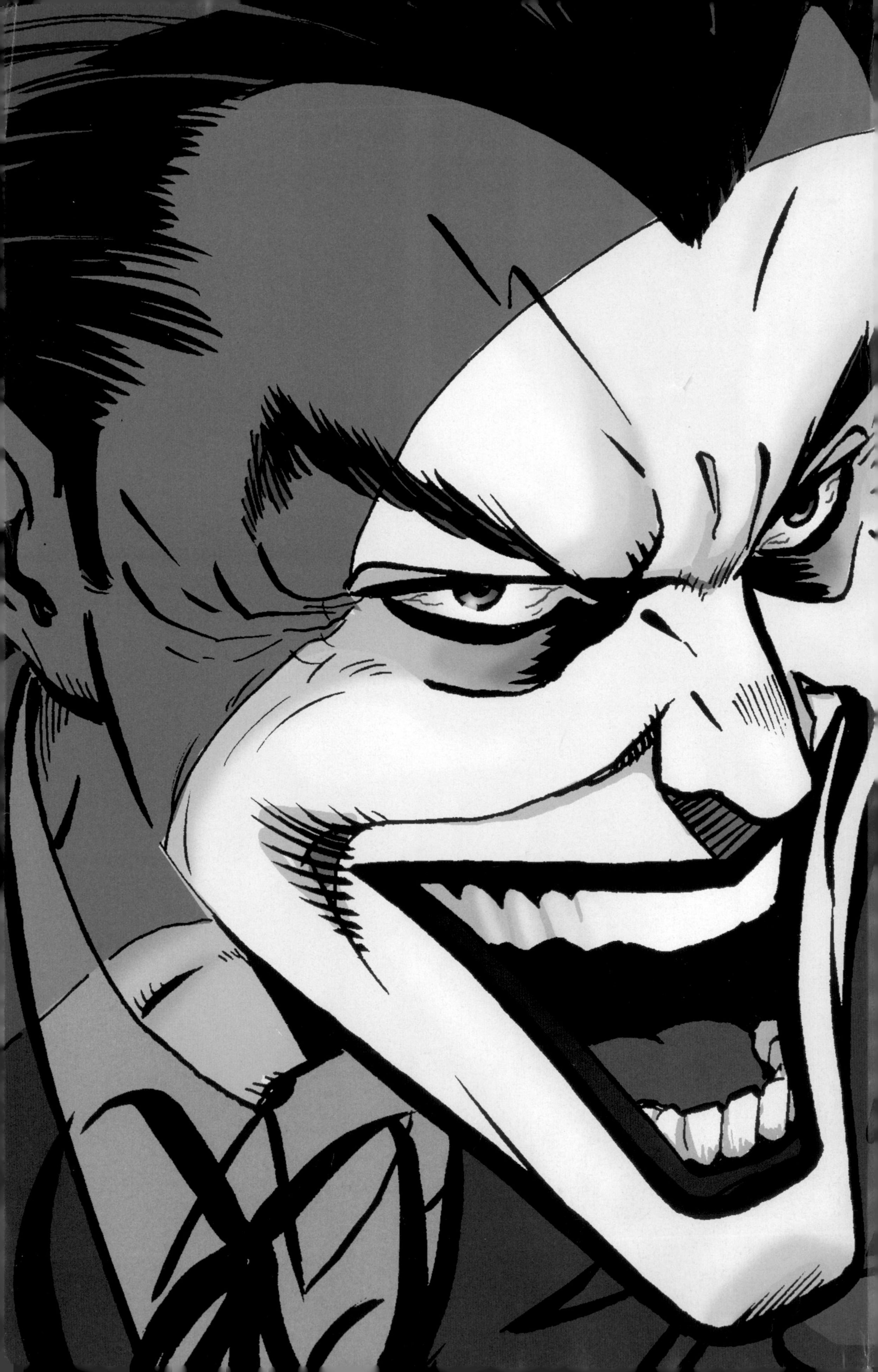

ENDGAME

COLLECTION COVER ARTIST
GREG CAPULLO

BATMAN CREATED BY
BOB KANE WITH **BILL FINGER**

SUPERMAN CREATED BY
JERRY SIEGEL & JOE SHUSTER
BY SPECIAL ARRANGEMENT WITH
THE JERRY SIEGEL FAMILY

ANARKY CREATED BY
ALAN GRANT
AND **NORM BREYFOGLE**

THE JOKER

CHRIS CONROY MARK DOYLE RACHEL GLUCKSTERN Editors - Original Series
REBECCA TAYLOR Associate Editor - Original Series
MATT HUMPHREYS DAVE WIELGOSZ Assistant Editors - Original Series
JEB WOODARD Group Editor - Collected Editions
STEVE COOK Design Director - Books
DAMIAN RYLAND Publication Design

BOB HARRAS Senior VP - Editor-in-Chief, DC Comics

DIANE NELSON President
DAN DIDIO and JIM LEE Co-Publishers
GEOFF JOHNS Chief Creative Officer
AMIT DESAI Senior VP - Marketing & Global Franchise Management
NAIRI GARDINER Senior VP - Finance
SAM ADES VP - Digital Marketing
BOBBIE CHASE VP - Talent Development
MARK CHIARELLO Senior VP - Art, Design & Collected Editions
JOHN CUNNINGHAM VP - Content Strategy
ANNE DEPIES VP - Strategy Planning & Reporting
DON FALLETTI VP - Manufacturing Operations
LAWRENCE GANEM VP - Editorial Administration & Talent Relations
ALISON GILL Senior VP - Manufacturing & Operations
HANK KANALZ Senior VP - Editorial Strategy & Administration
JAY KOGAN VP - Legal Affairs
DEREK MADDALENA Senior VP - Sales & Business Development
JACK MAHAN VP - Business Affairs
DAN MIRON VP - Sales Planning & Trade Development
NICK NAPOLITANO VP - Manufacturing Administration
CAROL ROEDER VP - Marketing
EDDIE SCANNELL VP - Mass Account & Digital Sales
COURTNEY SIMMONS Senior VP - Publicity & Communications
JIM (SKI) SOKOLOWSKI VP - Comic Book Specialty & Newsstand Sales
SANDY YI Senior VP - Global Franchise Management

THE JOKER: ENDGAME

DC Comics, 2900 West Alameda Ave., Burbank, CA 91505
Printed by RR Donnelley, Salem, VA, USA. 4/15/16. First Printing.
ISBN: 978-1-4012-6165-8

Library of Congress Cataloging-in-Publication Data

Snyder, Scott, author.
The Joker : Endgame / Scott Snyder, Brenden Fletcher, writers ; Dustin Nguyen, artist.
pages cm
ISBN 978-1-4012-6165-8
1. Graphic novels. I. Fletcher, Brenden, illustrator. II. Nguyen, Dustin, illustrator. III. Title.
PN6728.J65T95 2015
741.5'973—dc23
2015012140

PEFC Certified
Printed on paper from sustainably managed forests and controlled sources
PEFC/29-31-75
www.pefc.org

Cover by **RAFAEL ALBUQUERQUE**

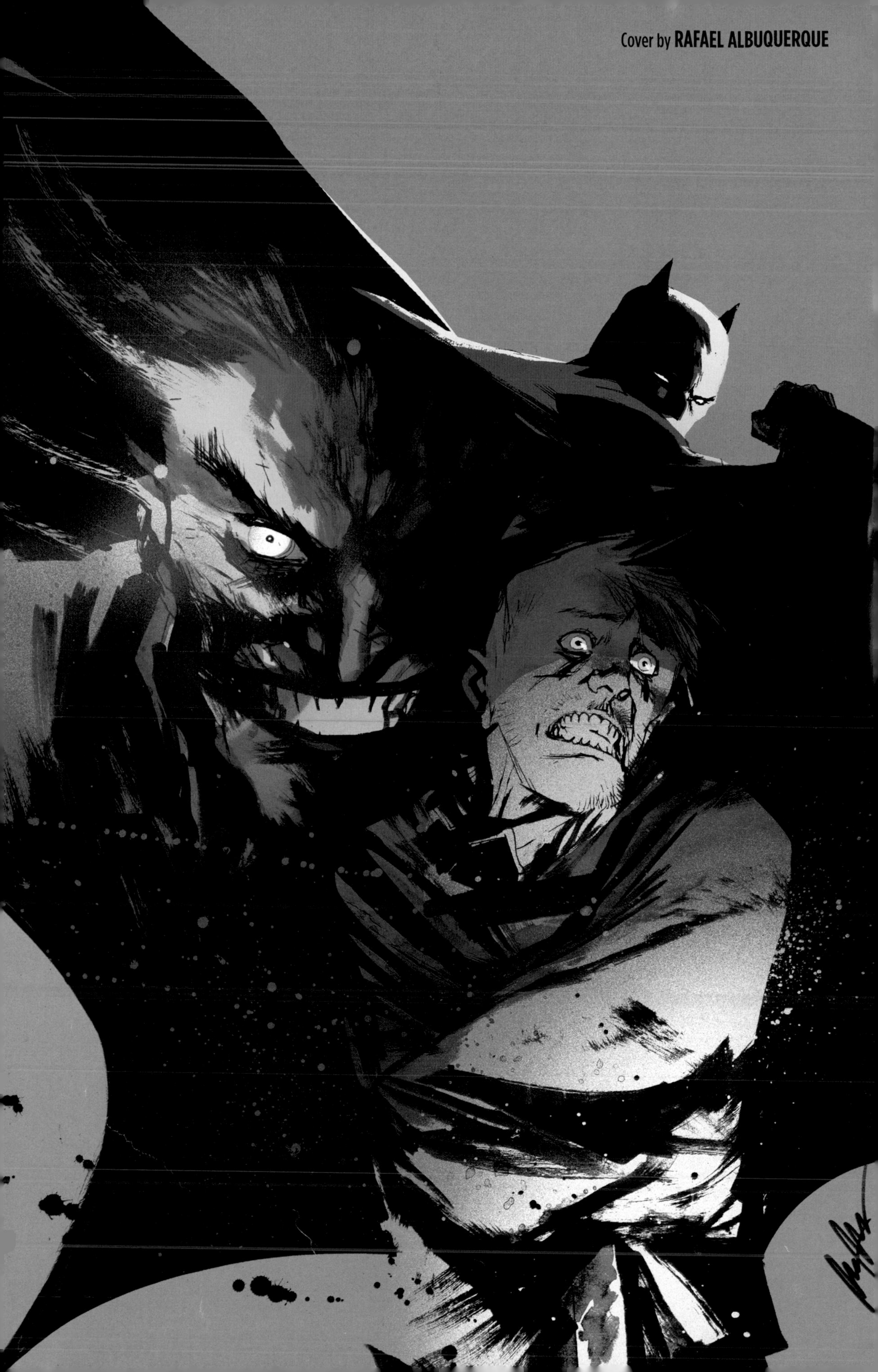

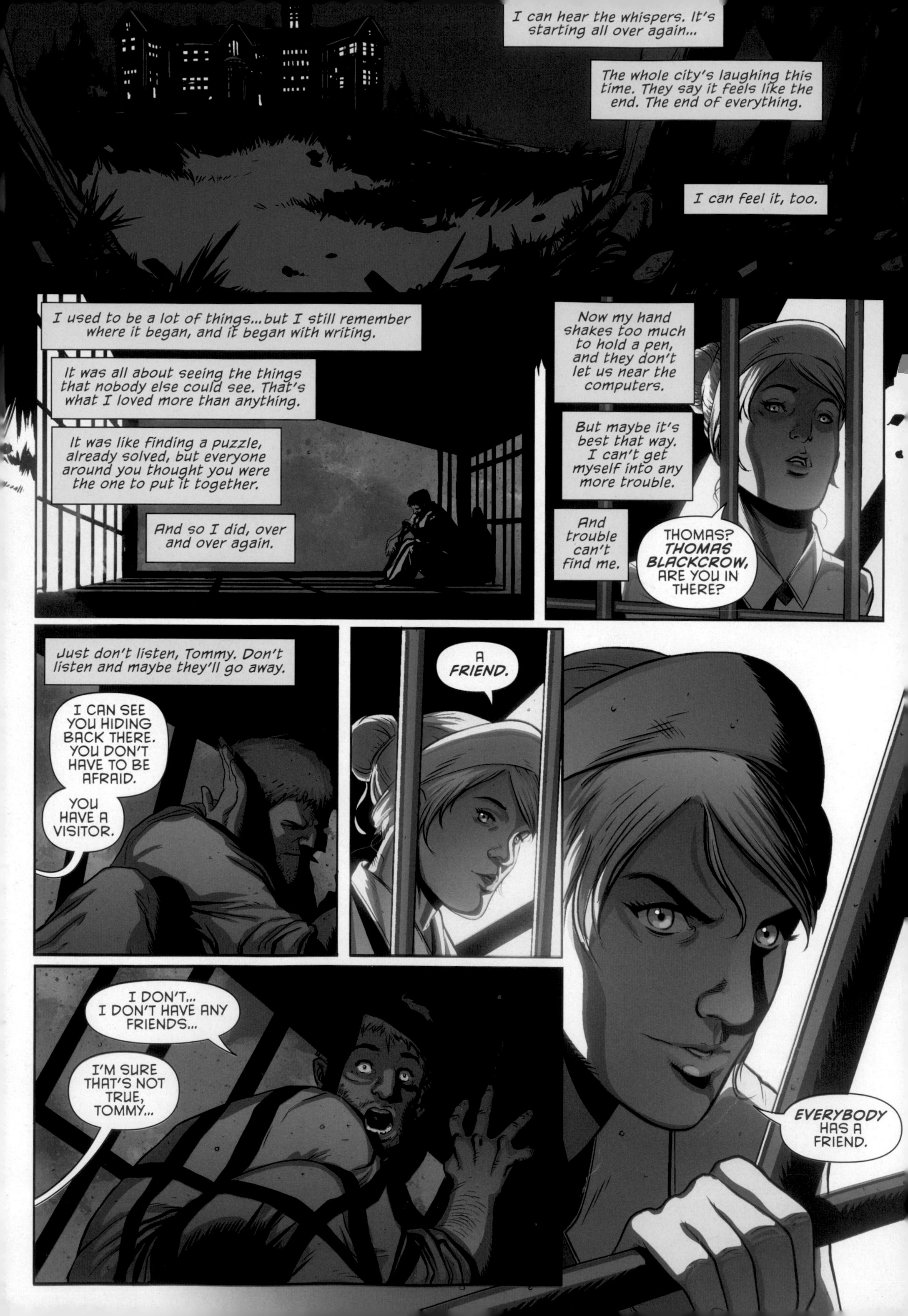

I can hear the whispers. It's starting all over again...
The whole city's laughing this time. They say it feels like the end. The end of everything.
I can feel it, too.
I used to be a lot of things...but I still remember where it began, and it began with writing.
It was all about seeing the things that nobody else could see. That's what I loved more than anything.
It was like finding a puzzle, already solved, but everyone around you thought you were the one to put it together.
And so I did, over and over again.
Now my hand shakes too much to hold a pen, and they don't let us near the computers.
But maybe it's best that way. I can't get myself into any more trouble.
And trouble can't find me.
THOMAS? THOMAS BLACKCROW, ARE YOU IN THERE?
Just don't listen, Tommy. Don't listen and maybe they'll go away.
I CAN SEE YOU HIDING BACK THERE. YOU DON'T HAVE TO BE AFRAID.
YOU HAVE A VISITOR.
A FRIEND.
I DON'T... I DON'T HAVE ANY FRIENDS...
I'M SURE THAT'S NOT TRUE, TOMMY...
EVERYBODY HAS A FRIEND.

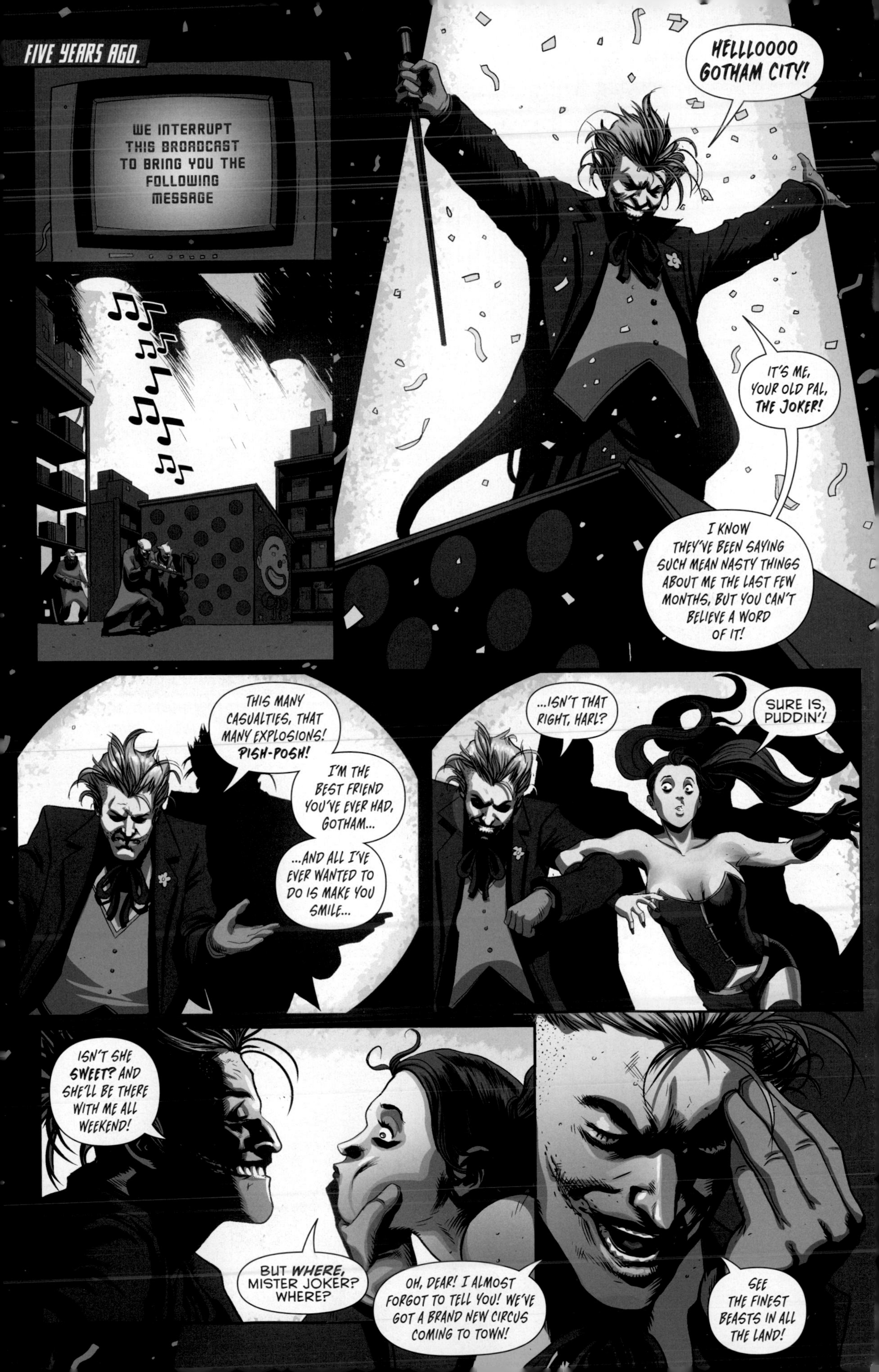
FIVE YEARS AGO.
WE INTERRUPT THIS BROADCAST TO BRING YOU THE FOLLOWING MESSAGE
HELLLOOOO GOTHAM CITY!
IT'S ME, YOUR OLD PAL, THE JOKER!
I KNOW THEY'VE BEEN SAYING SUCH MEAN NASTY THINGS ABOUT ME THE LAST FEW MONTHS, BUT YOU CAN'T BELIEVE A WORD OF IT!
THIS MANY CASUALTIES, THAT MANY EXPLOSIONS! PISH-POSH!
I'M THE BEST FRIEND YOU'VE EVER HAD, GOTHAM...
...AND ALL I'VE EVER WANTED TO DO IS MAKE YOU SMILE...
...ISN'T THAT RIGHT, HARL?
SURE IS, PUDDIN'!
ISN'T SHE SWEET? AND SHE'LL BE THERE WITH ME ALL WEEKEND!
BUT WHERE, MISTER JOKER? WHERE?
OH, DEAR! I ALMOST FORGOT TO TELL YOU! WE'VE GOT A BRAND NEW CIRCUS COMING TO TOWN!
SEE THE FINEST BEASTS IN ALL THE LAND!

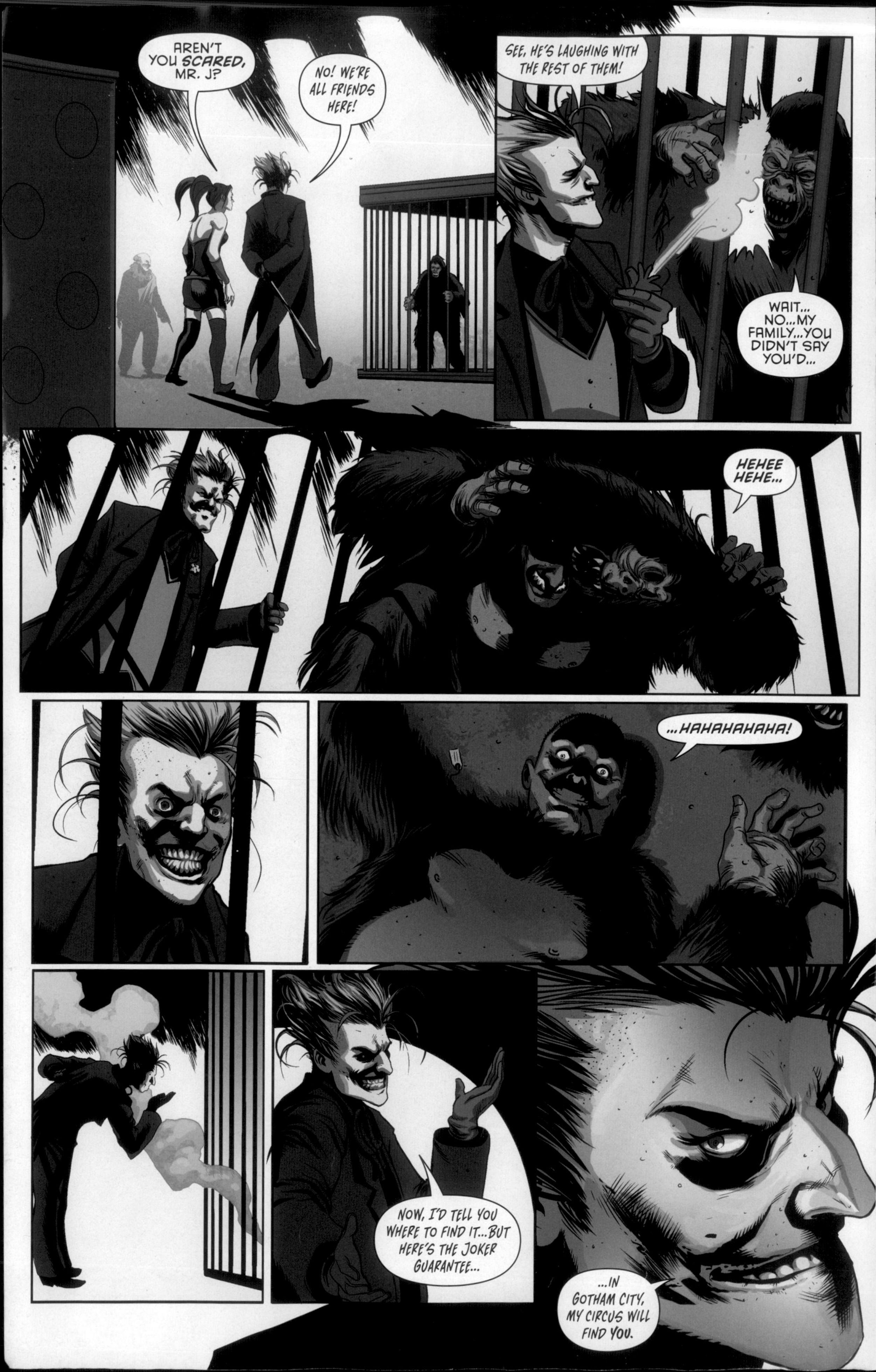
AREN'T YOU SCARED, MR. J?
NO! WE'RE ALL FRIENDS HERE!
SEE, HE'S LAUGHING WITH THE REST OF THEM!
WAIT... NO...MY FAMILY...YOU DIDN'T SAY YOU'D...
HEHEE HEHE...
...HAHAHAHAHA!
NOW, I'D TELL YOU WHERE TO FIND IT...BUT HERE'S THE JOKER GUARANTEE...
...IN GOTHAM CITY, MY CIRCUS WILL FIND YOU.

FRIENDS

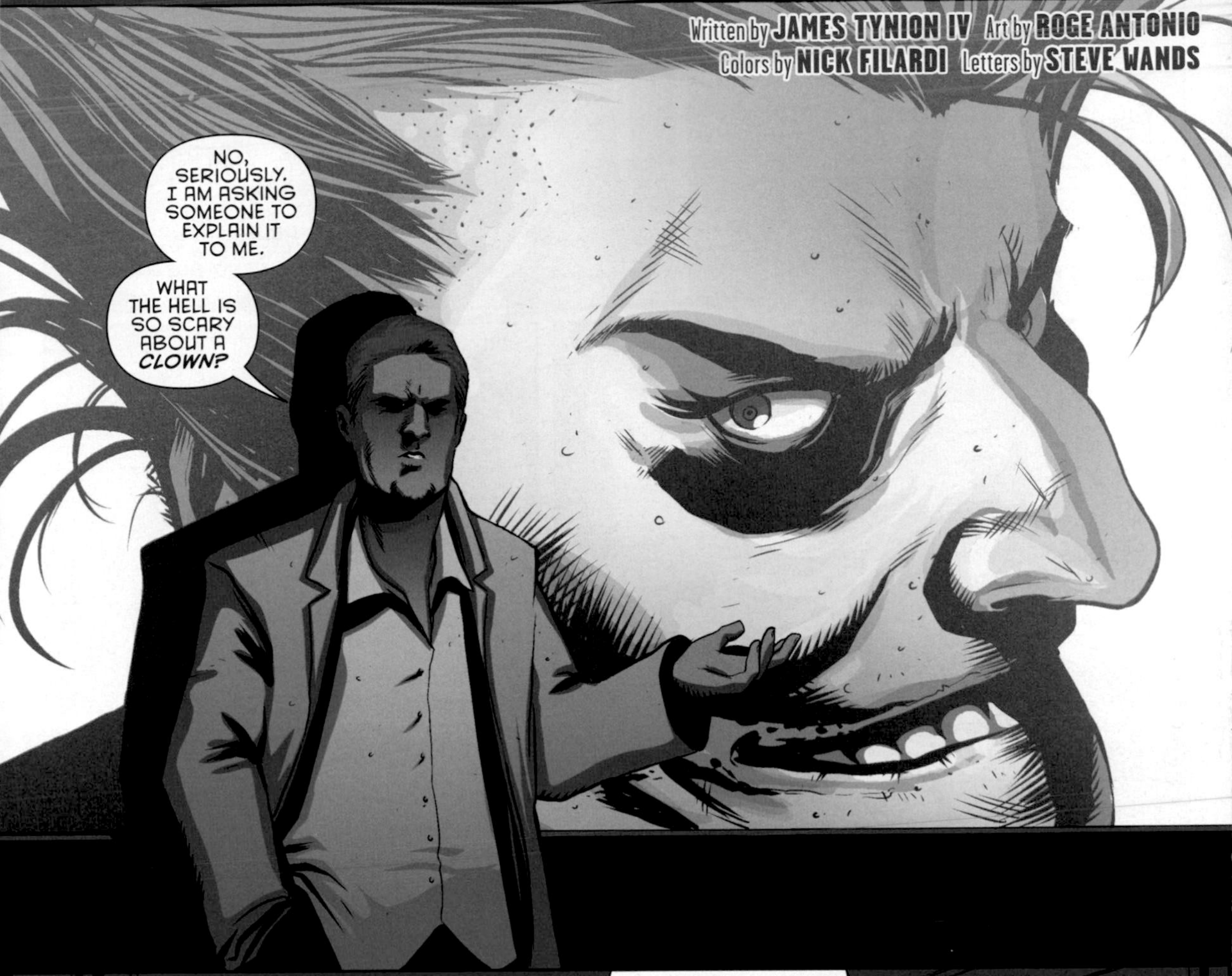

Written by JAMES TYNION IV Art by ROGE ANTONIO
Colors by NICK FILARDI Letters by STEVE WANDS
NO, SERIOUSLY. I AM ASKING SOMEONE TO EXPLAIN IT TO ME.
WHAT THE HELL IS SO SCARY ABOUT A *CLOWN?*

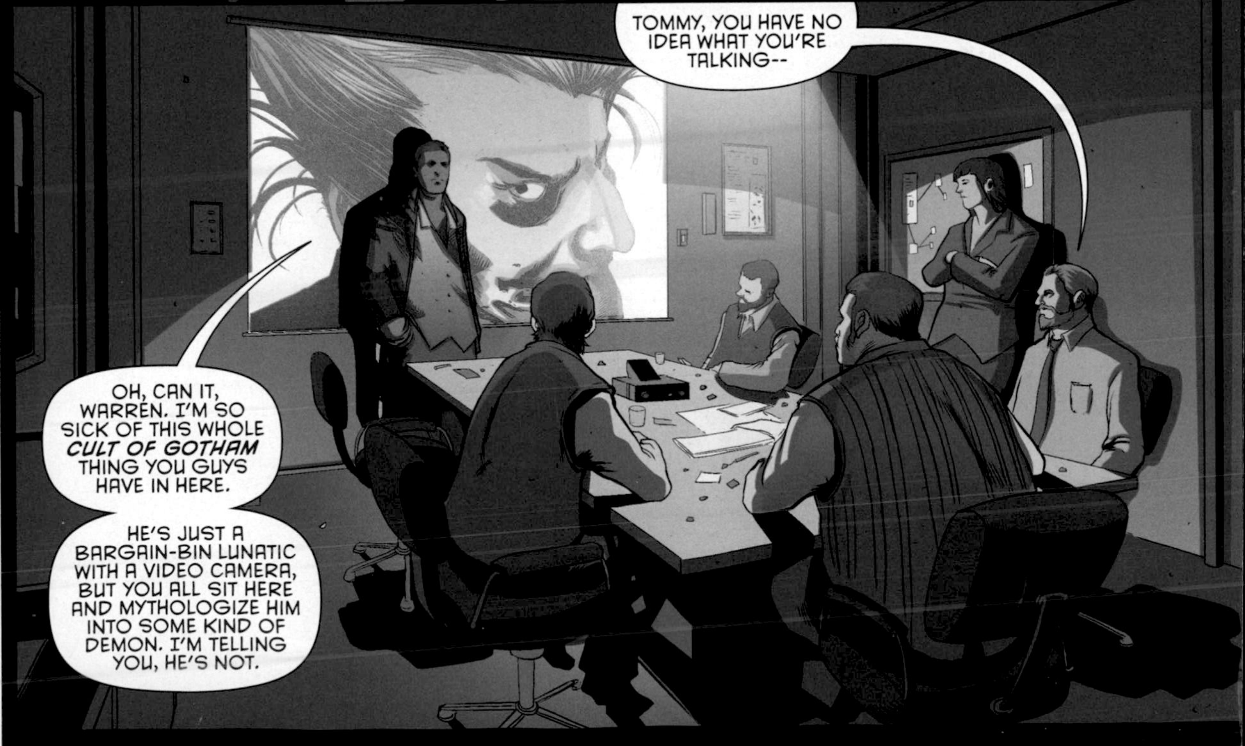

TOMMY, YOU HAVE NO IDEA WHAT YOU'RE TALKING--
OH, CAN IT, WARREN. I'M SO SICK OF THIS WHOLE *CULT OF GOTHAM* THING YOU GUYS HAVE IN HERE.
HE'S JUST A BARGAIN-BIN LUNATIC WITH A VIDEO CAMERA, BUT YOU ALL SIT HERE AND MYTHOLOGIZE HIM INTO SOME KIND OF DEMON. I'M TELLING YOU, HE'S NOT.

I'VE SAT DOWN AT A TABLE ACROSS FROM A GENERAL WHO ORDERED THE SLAUGHTER OF SIX HUNDRED OF HIS OWN PEOPLE.

ENTIRE VILLAGES BURNED. BODIES LEFT OUT TO ROT. CHILDREN.

THAT SCARED ME. *THIS* GUY IS A JOKE.

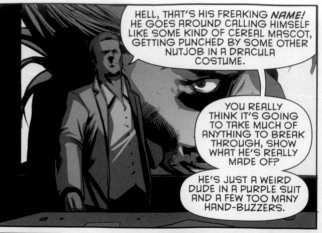

HELL, THAT'S HIS FREAKING *NAME!* HE GOES AROUND CALLING HIMSELF LIKE SOME KIND OF CEREAL MASCOT, GETTING PUNCHED BY SOME OTHER NUTJOB IN A DRACULA COSTUME.

YOU REALLY THINK IT'S GOING TO TAKE MUCH OF ANYTHING TO BREAK THROUGH, SHOW WHAT HE'S REALLY MADE OF?

HE'S JUST A WEIRD DUDE IN A PURPLE SUIT AND A FEW TOO MANY HAND-BUZZERS.

YOU'VE SPENT THE LAST FIVE YEARS AS A FOREIGN CORRESPON-DENT. YOU MISSED THE ZERO YEAR ENTIRELY. THIS CITY IS CHANGING...

OH GOD, NOT THIS CRAP AGAIN.

CHIEF, YOU CAN'T LET HIM DO THIS.

SHUT UP, THE LOT OF YOU.

WE HAVE AN OPPORTUNITY HERE TO GIVE THE PEOPLE A BETTER UNDERSTANDING OF THE SO-CALLED "CLOWN PRINCE OF CRIME" THAN THEY'VE EVER HAD BEFORE.

IF TOMMY'S THE ONLY ONE WHO WANTS THAT CHALLENGE? SO BE IT.

YOU REALLY THINK YOU'RE READY FOR THIS?

COME ON, WARREN...THIS IS YOUR OLD PAL TOMMY BLACKCROW. WHO DO YOU THINK YOU'RE TALKING TO?

AN *IDIOT.*

LOOK. I REALIZE WE DIDN'T END THINGS GREAT BEFORE I LEFT TOWN...BUT YOU DON'T HAVE TO WORRY.

I'M NOT GOING AFTER CRIME AS A WHOLE... THAT'S *YOUR* TERRITORY, I GET THAT.

OH, SHUT THE HELL UP BEFORE I GRAB YOU BY THE NECK AND TRY TO SHAKE THE EGO OUT.

JUST SERIOUSLY... TRY NOT TO GET *KILLED.*

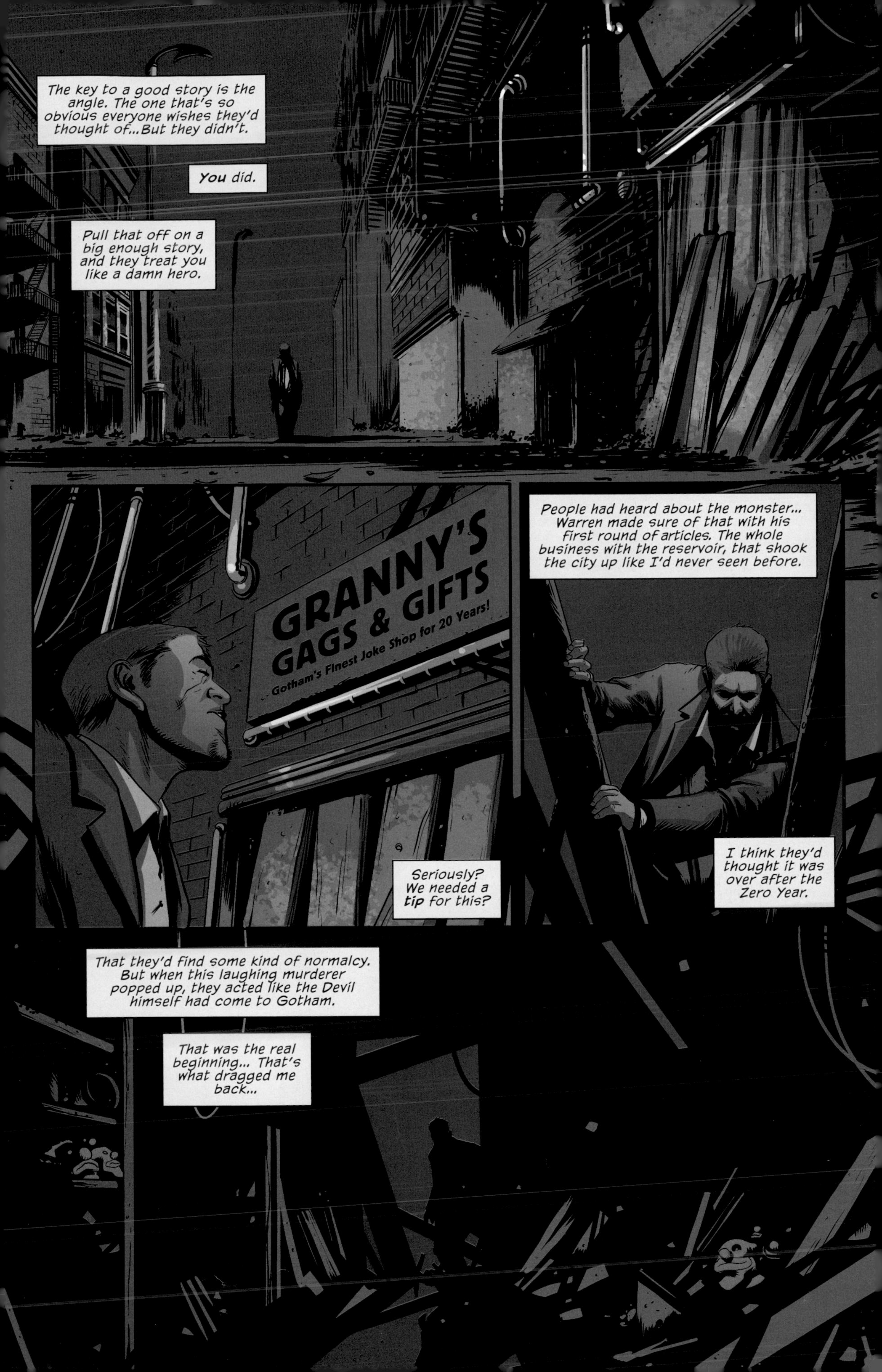
The key to a good story is the angle. The one that's so obvious everyone wishes they'd thought of...But they didn't.
You did.
Pull that off on a big enough story, and they treat you like a damn hero.
GRANNY'S GAGS & GIFTS
Gotham's Finest Joke Shop for 20 Years!
Seriously? We needed a tip for this?
People had heard about the monster... Warren made sure of that with his first round of articles. The whole business with the reservoir, that shook the city up like I'd never seen before.
I think they'd thought it was over after the Zero Year.
That they'd find some kind of normalcy. But when this laughing murderer popped up, they acted like the Devil himself had come to Gotham.
That was the real beginning... That's what dragged me back...

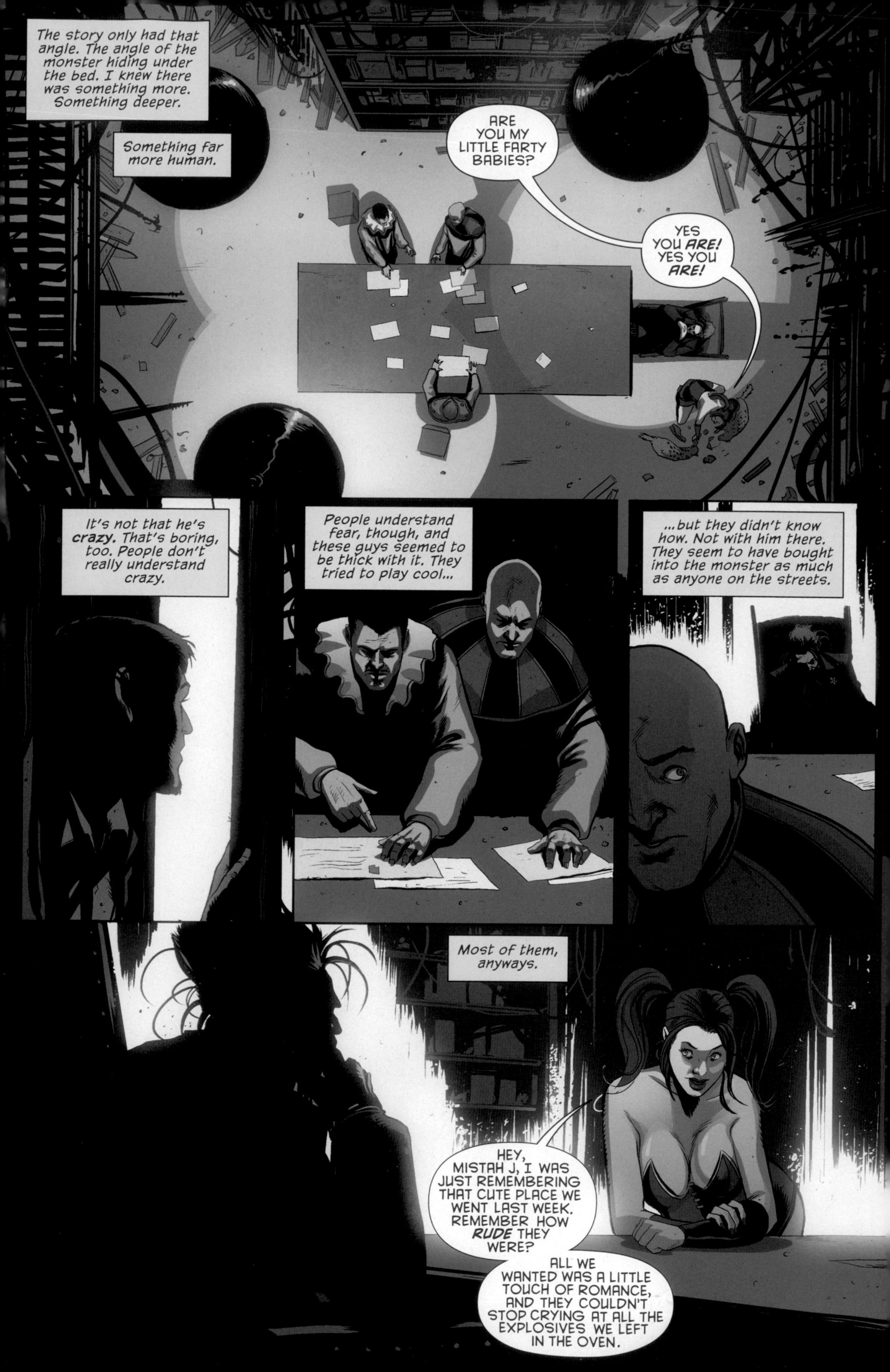
The story only had that angle. The angle of the monster hiding under the bed. I knew there was something more. Something deeper.
Something far more human.
ARE YOU MY LITTLE FARTY BABIES?
YES YOU ARE! YES YOU ARE!
It's not that he's crazy. That's boring, too. People don't really understand crazy.
People understand fear, though, and these guys seemed to be thick with it. They tried to play cool...
...but they didn't know how. Not with him there. They seem to have bought into the monster as much as anyone on the streets.
Most of them, anyways.
HEY, MISTAH J, I WAS JUST REMEMBERING THAT CUTE PLACE WE WENT LAST WEEK. REMEMBER HOW RUDE THEY WERE?
ALL WE WANTED WAS A LITTLE TOUCH OF ROMANCE, AND THEY COULDN'T STOP CRYING AT ALL THE EXPLOSIVES WE LEFT IN THE OVEN.

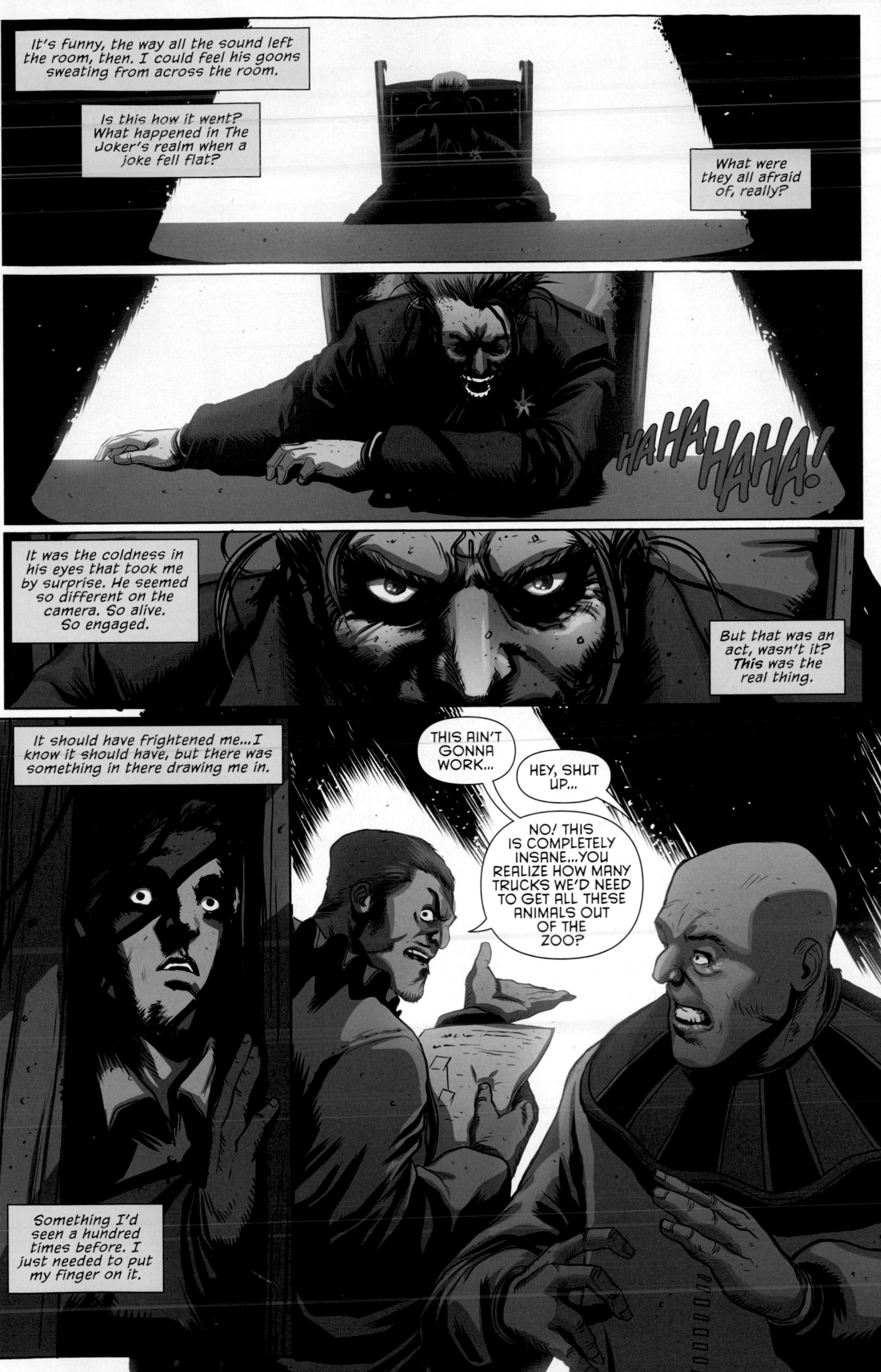
It's funny, the way all the sound left the room, then. I could feel his goons sweating from across the room.
Is this how it went? What happened in The Joker's realm when a joke fell flat?
What were they all afraid of, really?
HAHAHAHAHA!
It was the coldness in his eyes that took me by surprise. He seemed so different on the camera. So alive. So engaged.
But that was an act, wasn't it? This was the real thing.
It should have frightened me...I know it should have, but there was something in there drawing me in.
THIS AIN'T GONNA WORK...
HEY, SHUT UP...
NO! THIS IS COMPLETELY INSANE...YOU REALIZE HOW MANY TRUCKS WE'D NEED TO GET ALL THESE ANIMALS OUT OF THE ZOO?
Something I'd seen a hundred times before. I just needed to put my finger on it.

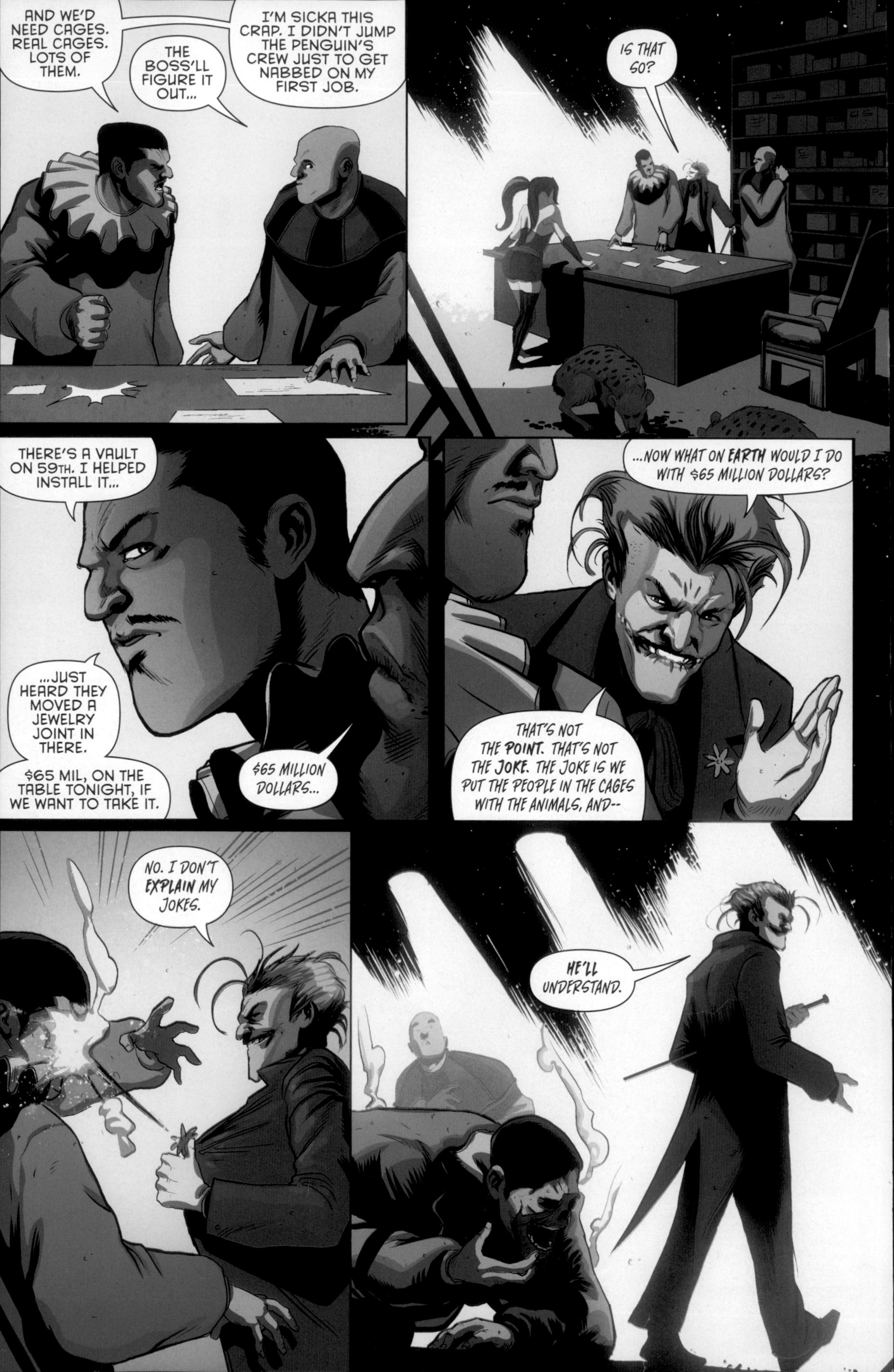
AND WE'D NEED CAGES. REAL CAGES. LOTS OF THEM.
I'M SICKA THIS CRAP. I DIDN'T JUMP THE PENGUIN'S CREW JUST TO GET NABBED ON MY FIRST JOB.
THE BOSS'LL FIGURE IT OUT...
IS THAT SO?
THERE'S A VAULT ON 59TH. I HELPED INSTALL IT...
...JUST HEARD THEY MOVED A JEWELRY JOINT IN THERE.
$65 MIL, ON THE TABLE TONIGHT, IF WE WANT TO TAKE IT.
$65 MILLION DOLLARS...
...NOW WHAT ON EARTH WOULD I DO WITH $65 MILLION DOLLARS?
THAT'S NOT THE POINT. THAT'S NOT THE JOKE. THE JOKE IS WE PUT THE PEOPLE IN THE CAGES WITH THE ANIMALS, AND--
NO. I DON'T EXPLAIN MY JOKES.
HE'LL UNDERSTAND.

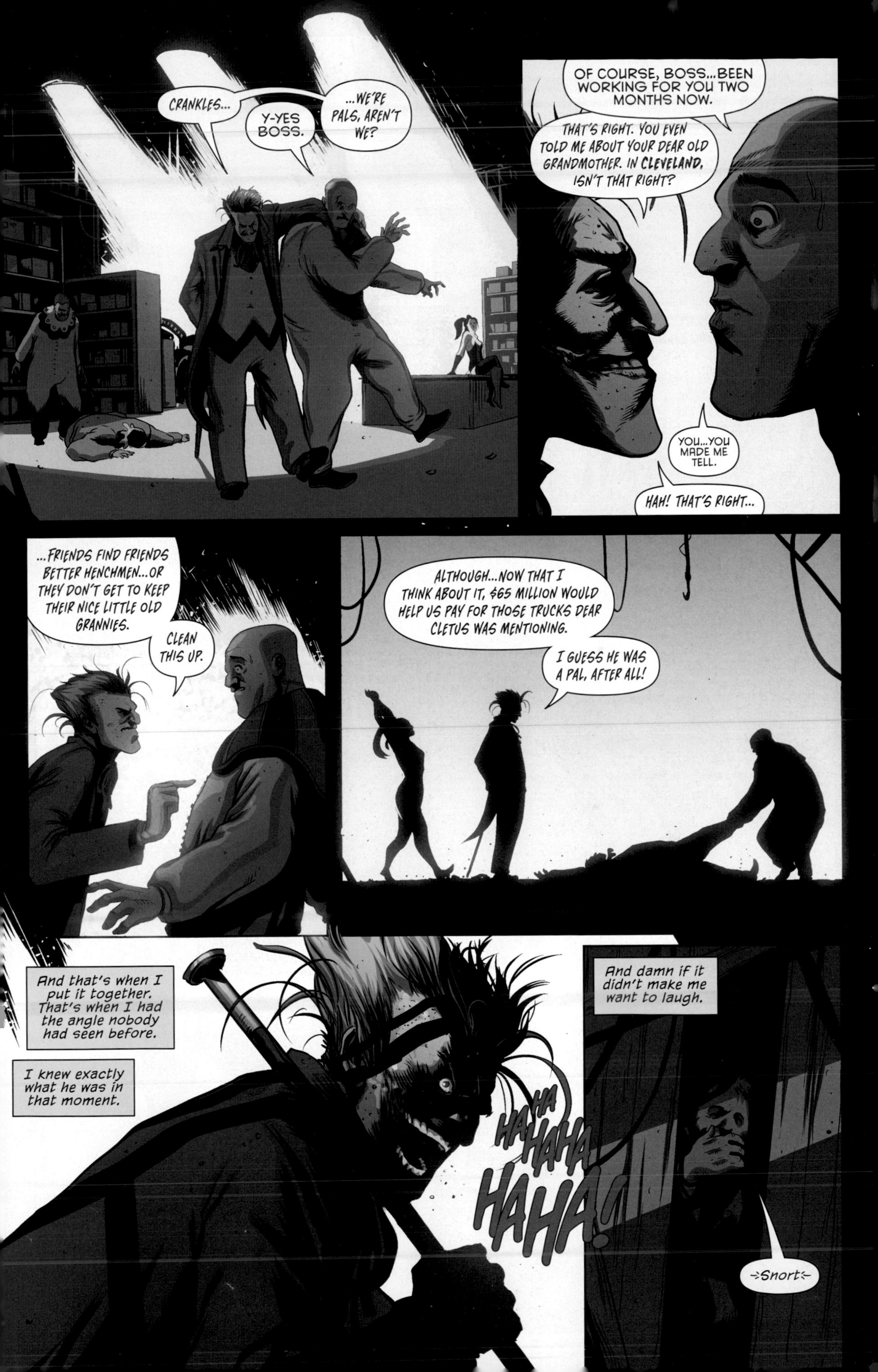
CRANKLES...
Y-YES BOSS.
...WE'RE PALS, AREN'T WE?
OF COURSE, BOSS...BEEN WORKING FOR YOU TWO MONTHS NOW.
THAT'S RIGHT. YOU EVEN TOLD ME ABOUT YOUR DEAR OLD GRANDMOTHER. IN CLEVELAND, ISN'T THAT RIGHT?
YOU...YOU MADE ME TELL.
HAH! THAT'S RIGHT...
...FRIENDS FIND FRIENDS BETTER HENCHMEN...OR THEY DON'T GET TO KEEP THEIR NICE LITTLE OLD GRANNIES.
CLEAN THIS UP.
ALTHOUGH...NOW THAT I THINK ABOUT IT, $65 MILLION WOULD HELP US PAY FOR THOSE TRUCKS DEAR CLETUS WAS MENTIONING.
I GUESS HE WAS A PAL, AFTER ALL!
And that's when I put it together. That's when I had the angle nobody had seen before.
I knew exactly what he was in that moment.
HAHAHAHAHAHA!
And damn if it didn't make me want to laugh.
Snort

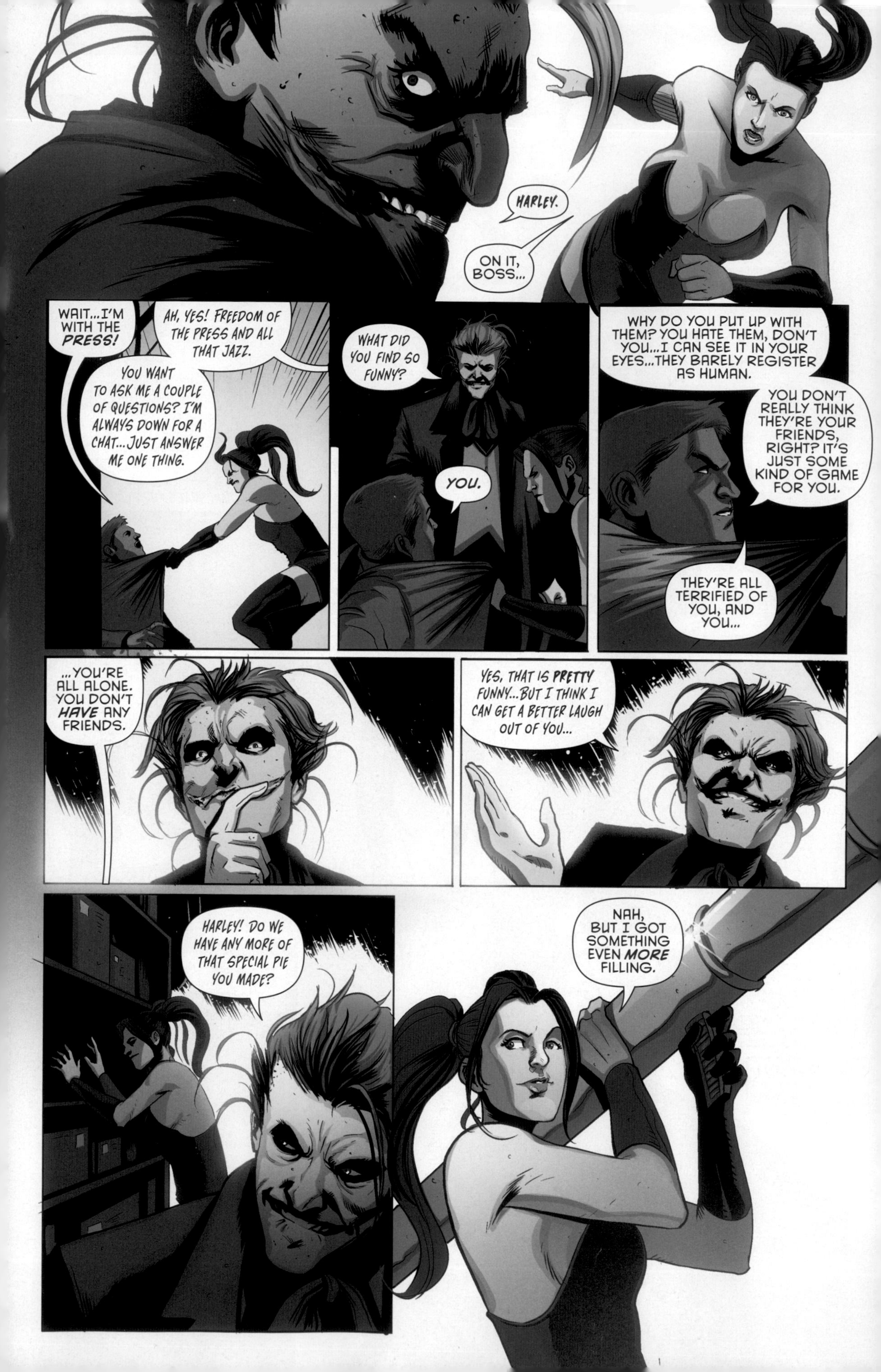
HARLEY.
ON IT, BOSS...
WAIT...I'M WITH THE *PRESS!*
AH, YES! FREEDOM OF THE PRESS AND ALL THAT JAZZ.
YOU WANT TO ASK ME A COUPLE OF QUESTIONS? I'M ALWAYS DOWN FOR A CHAT...JUST ANSWER ME ONE THING.
WHAT DID YOU FIND SO FUNNY?
YOU.
WHY DO YOU PUT UP WITH THEM? YOU HATE THEM, DON'T YOU...I CAN SEE IT IN YOUR EYES...THEY BARELY REGISTER AS HUMAN.
YOU DON'T REALLY THINK THEY'RE YOUR FRIENDS, RIGHT? IT'S JUST SOME KIND OF GAME FOR YOU.
THEY'RE ALL TERRIFIED OF YOU, AND YOU...
...YOU'RE ALL ALONE. YOU DON'T *HAVE* ANY FRIENDS.
YES, THAT IS **PRETTY** FUNNY...BUT I THINK I CAN GET A BETTER LAUGH OUT OF YOU...
HARLEY! DO WE HAVE ANY MORE OF THAT SPECIAL PIE YOU MADE?
NAH, BUT I GOT SOMETHING EVEN *MORE* FILLING.

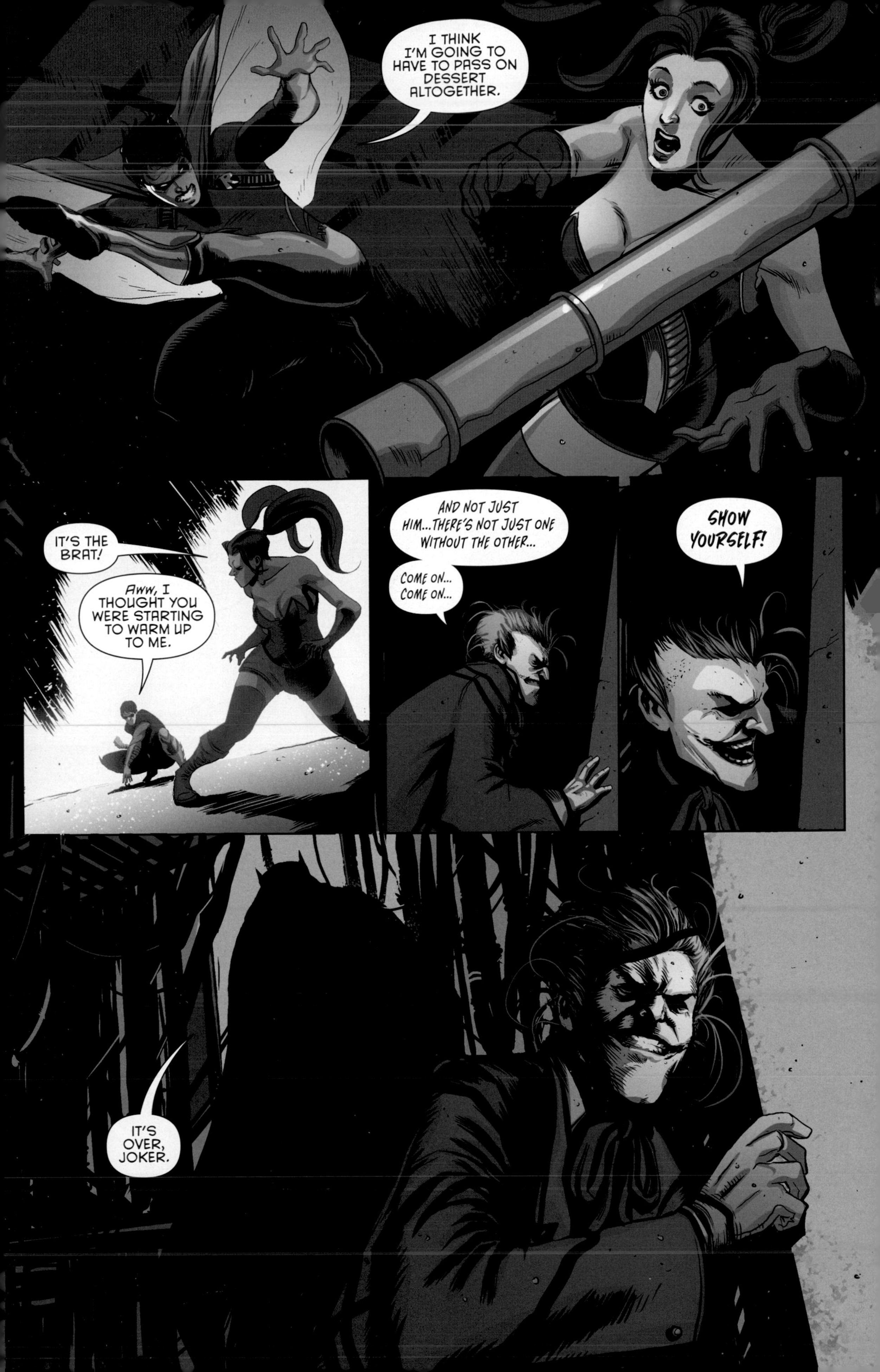
I THINK I'M GOING TO HAVE TO PASS ON DESSERT ALTOGETHER.
IT'S THE BRAT!
Aww, I THOUGHT YOU WERE STARTING TO WARM UP TO ME.
AND NOT JUST HIM...THERE'S NOT JUST ONE WITHOUT THE OTHER...
COME ON... COME ON...
SHOW YOURSELF!
IT'S OVER, JOKER.

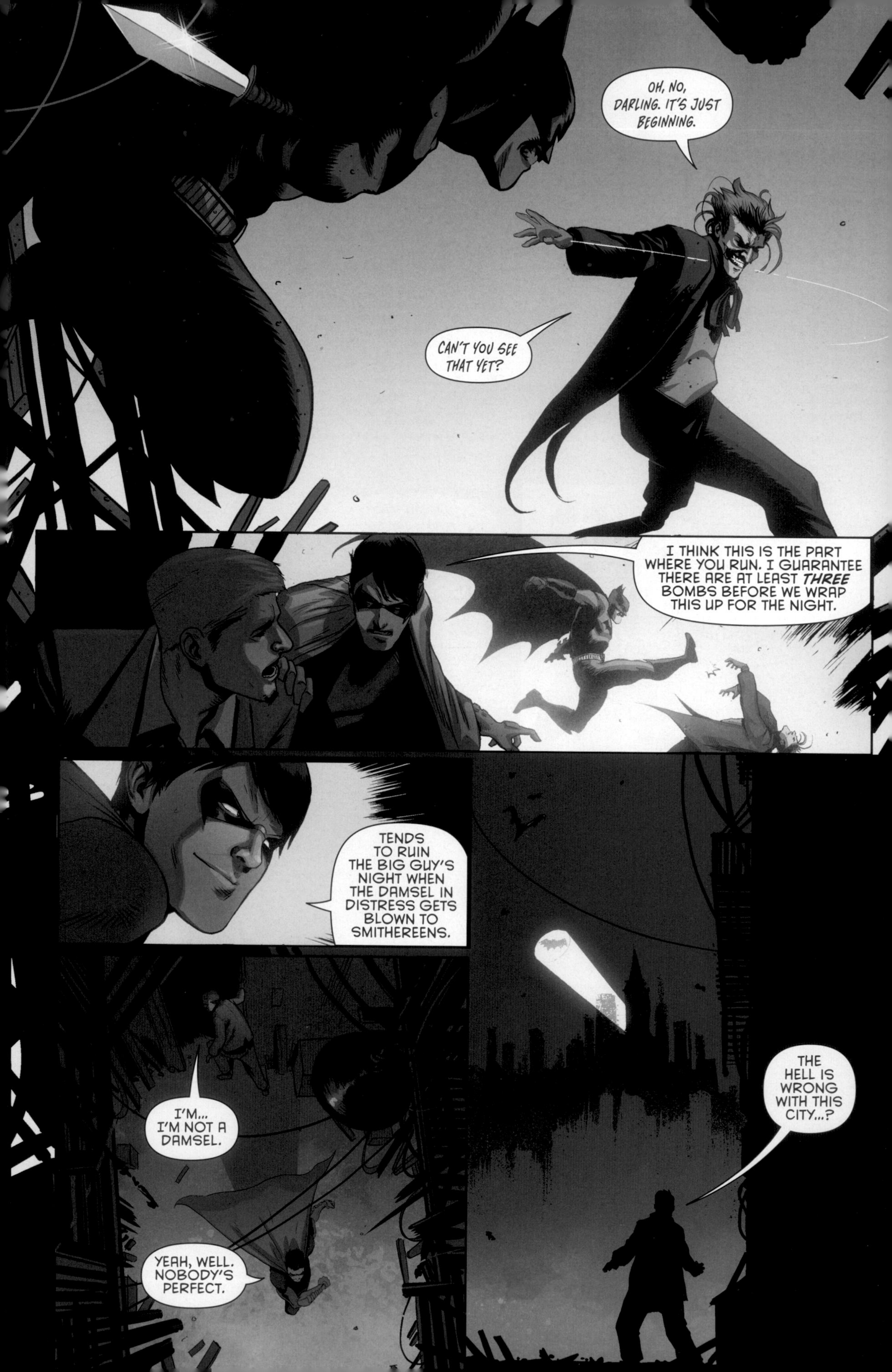
OH, NO, DARLING. IT'S JUST BEGINNING.
CAN'T YOU SEE THAT YET?
I THINK THIS IS THE PART WHERE YOU RUN. I GUARANTEE THERE ARE AT LEAST *THREE* BOMBS BEFORE WE WRAP THIS UP FOR THE NIGHT.
TENDS TO RUIN THE BIG GUY'S NIGHT WHEN THE DAMSEL IN DISTRESS GETS BLOWN TO SMITHEREENS.
I'M... I'M NOT A DAMSEL.
YEAH, WELL. NOBODY'S PERFECT.
THE HELL IS WRONG WITH THIS CITY...?

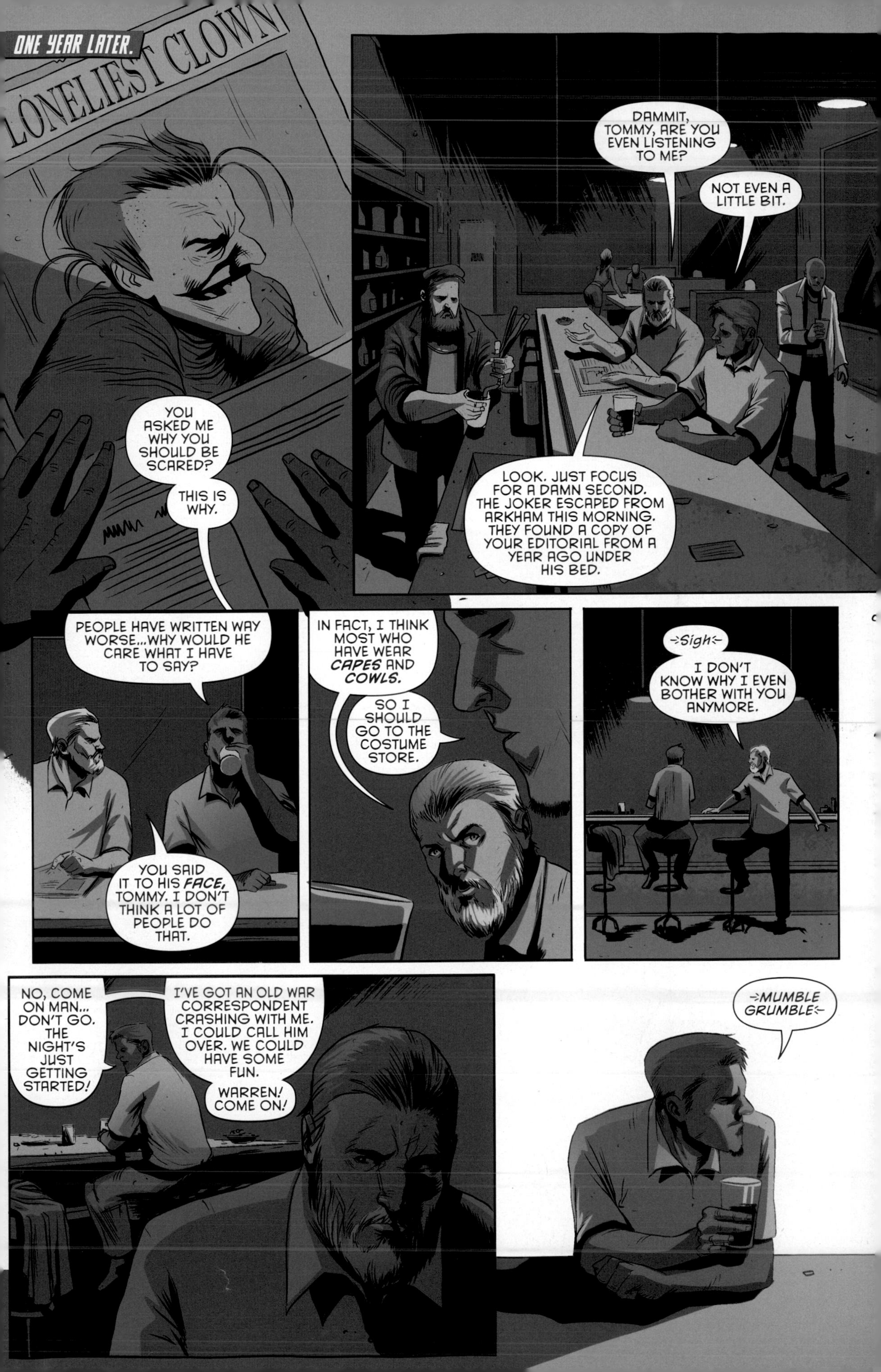
ONE YEAR LATER.
LONELIEST CLOWN
YOU ASKED ME WHY YOU SHOULD BE SCARED?
THIS IS WHY.
DAMMIT, TOMMY, ARE YOU EVEN LISTENING TO ME?
NOT EVEN A LITTLE BIT.
LOOK. JUST FOCUS FOR A DAMN SECOND. THE JOKER ESCAPED FROM ARKHAM THIS MORNING. THEY FOUND A COPY OF YOUR EDITORIAL FROM A YEAR AGO UNDER HIS BED.
PEOPLE HAVE WRITTEN WAY WORSE...WHY WOULD HE CARE WHAT I HAVE TO SAY?
YOU SAID IT TO HIS FACE, TOMMY. I DON'T THINK A LOT OF PEOPLE DO THAT.
IN FACT, I THINK MOST WHO HAVE WEAR CAPES AND COWLS.
SO I SHOULD GO TO THE COSTUME STORE.
Sigh
I DON'T KNOW WHY I EVEN BOTHER WITH YOU ANYMORE.
NO, COME ON MAN... DON'T GO. THE NIGHT'S JUST GETTING STARTED!
I'VE GOT AN OLD WAR CORRESPONDENT CRASHING WITH ME. I COULD CALL HIM OVER. WE COULD HAVE SOME FUN.
WARREN! COME ON!
MUMBLE GRUMBLE

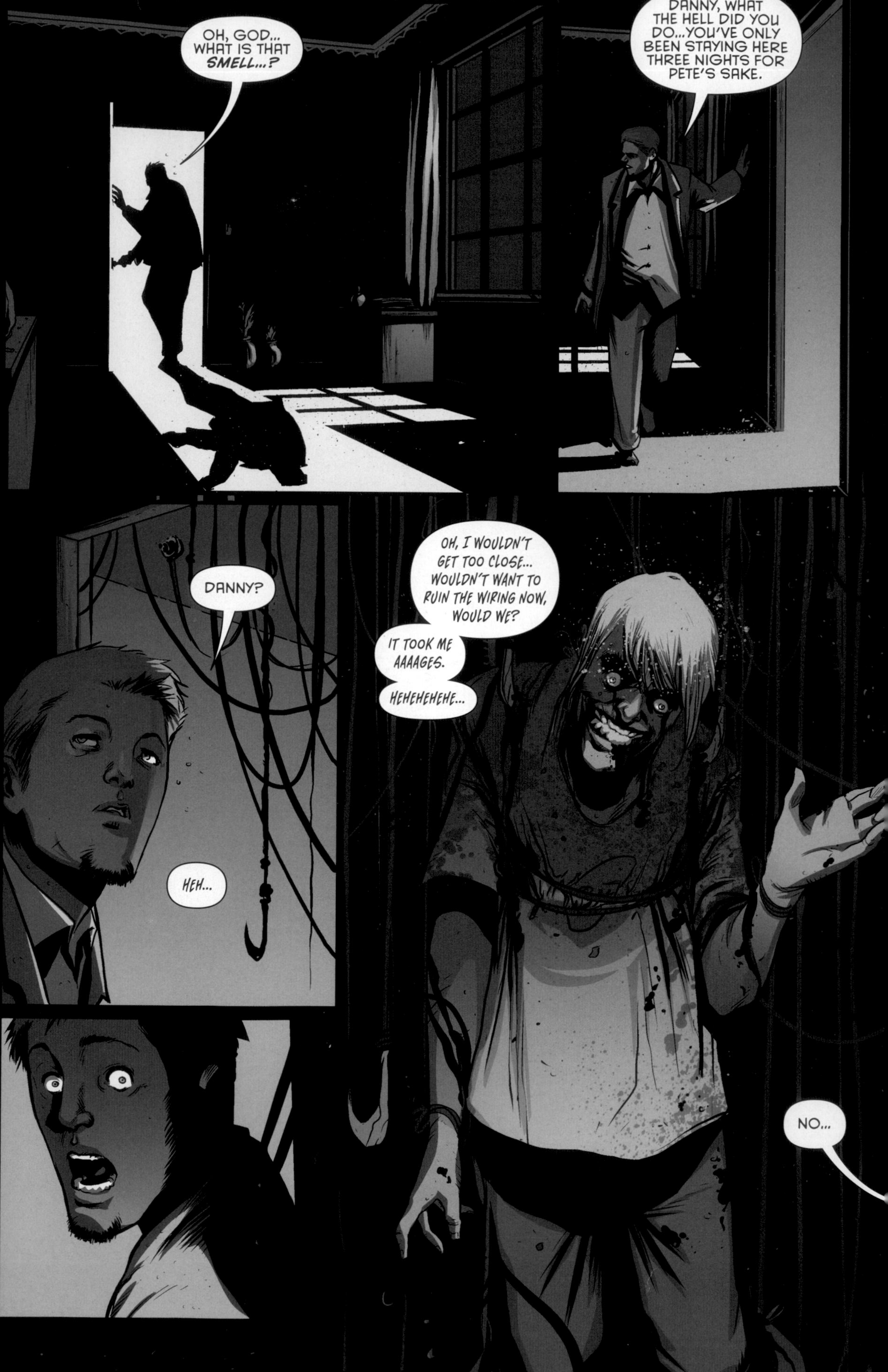
OH, GOD... WHAT IS THAT SMELL...?
DANNY, WHAT THE HELL DID YOU DO...YOU'VE ONLY BEEN STAYING HERE THREE NIGHTS FOR PETE'S SAKE.
DANNY?
OH, I WOULDN'T GET TOO CLOSE... WOULDN'T WANT TO RUIN THE WIRING NOW, WOULD WE?
IT TOOK ME AAAAGES.
HEHEHEHEHE...
HEH...
NO...

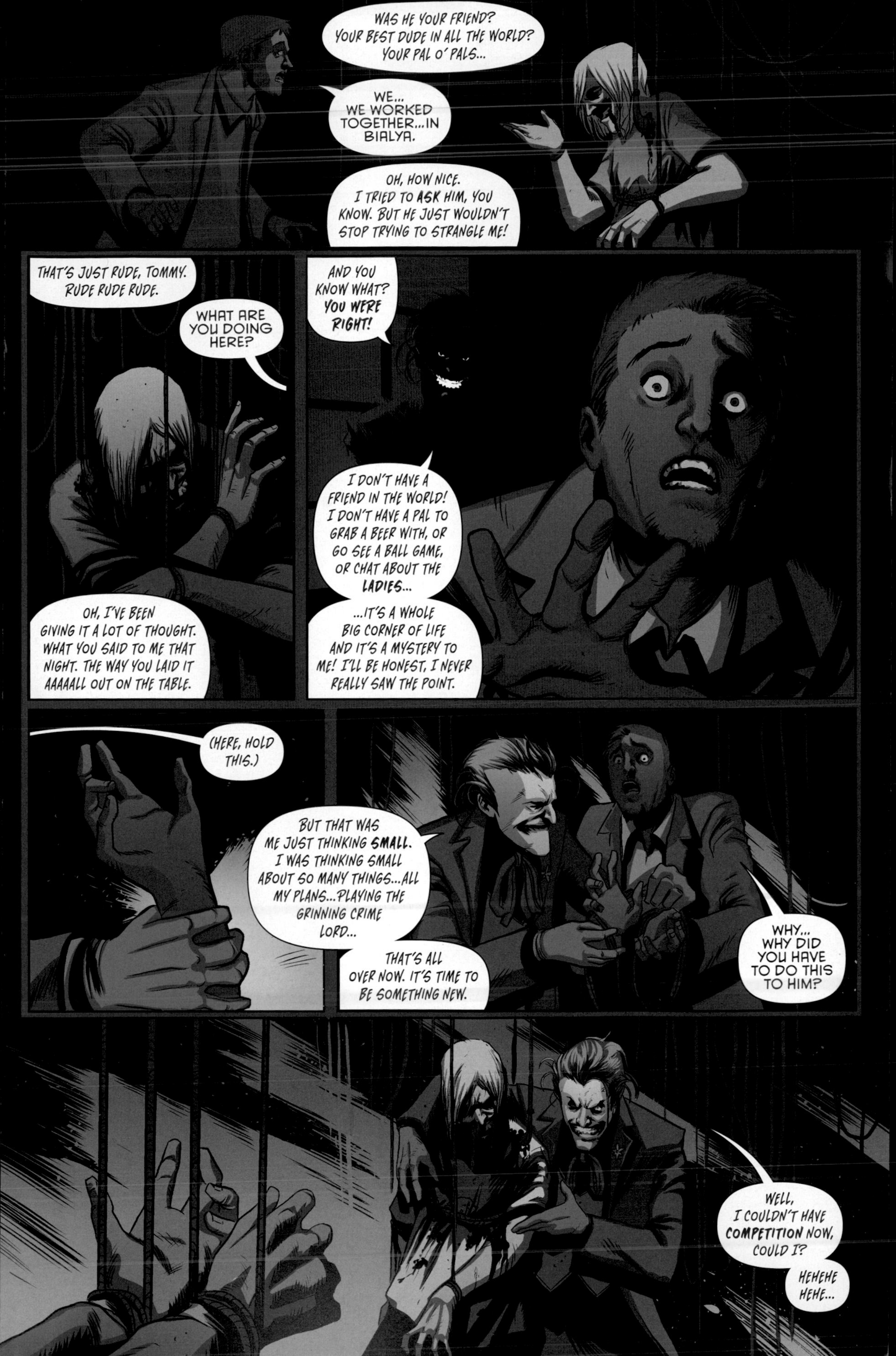
WAS HE YOUR FRIEND? YOUR BEST DUDE IN ALL THE WORLD? YOUR PAL O' PALS...
WE... WE WORKED TOGETHER...IN BIALYA.
OH, HOW NICE. I TRIED TO **ASK** HIM, YOU KNOW. BUT HE JUST WOULDN'T STOP TRYING TO STRANGLE ME!
THAT'S JUST RUDE, TOMMY. RUDE RUDE RUDE.
WHAT ARE YOU DOING HERE?
OH, I'VE BEEN GIVING IT A LOT OF THOUGHT. WHAT YOU SAID TO ME THAT NIGHT. THE WAY YOU LAID IT AAAAALL OUT ON THE TABLE.
AND YOU KNOW WHAT? **YOU WERE RIGHT!**
I DON'T HAVE A FRIEND IN THE WORLD! I DON'T HAVE A PAL TO GRAB A BEER WITH, OR GO SEE A BALL GAME, OR CHAT ABOUT THE **LADIES**...
...IT'S A WHOLE BIG CORNER OF LIFE AND IT'S A MYSTERY TO ME! I'LL BE HONEST, I NEVER REALLY SAW THE POINT.
(HERE, HOLD THIS.)
BUT THAT WAS ME JUST THINKING **SMALL**. I WAS THINKING SMALL ABOUT SO MANY THINGS...ALL MY PLANS...PLAYING THE GRINNING CRIME LORD...
THAT'S ALL OVER NOW. IT'S TIME TO BE SOMETHING NEW.
WHY... WHY DID YOU HAVE TO DO THIS TO HIM?
WELL, I COULDN'T HAVE **COMPETITION** NOW, COULD I?
HEHEHE HEHE...

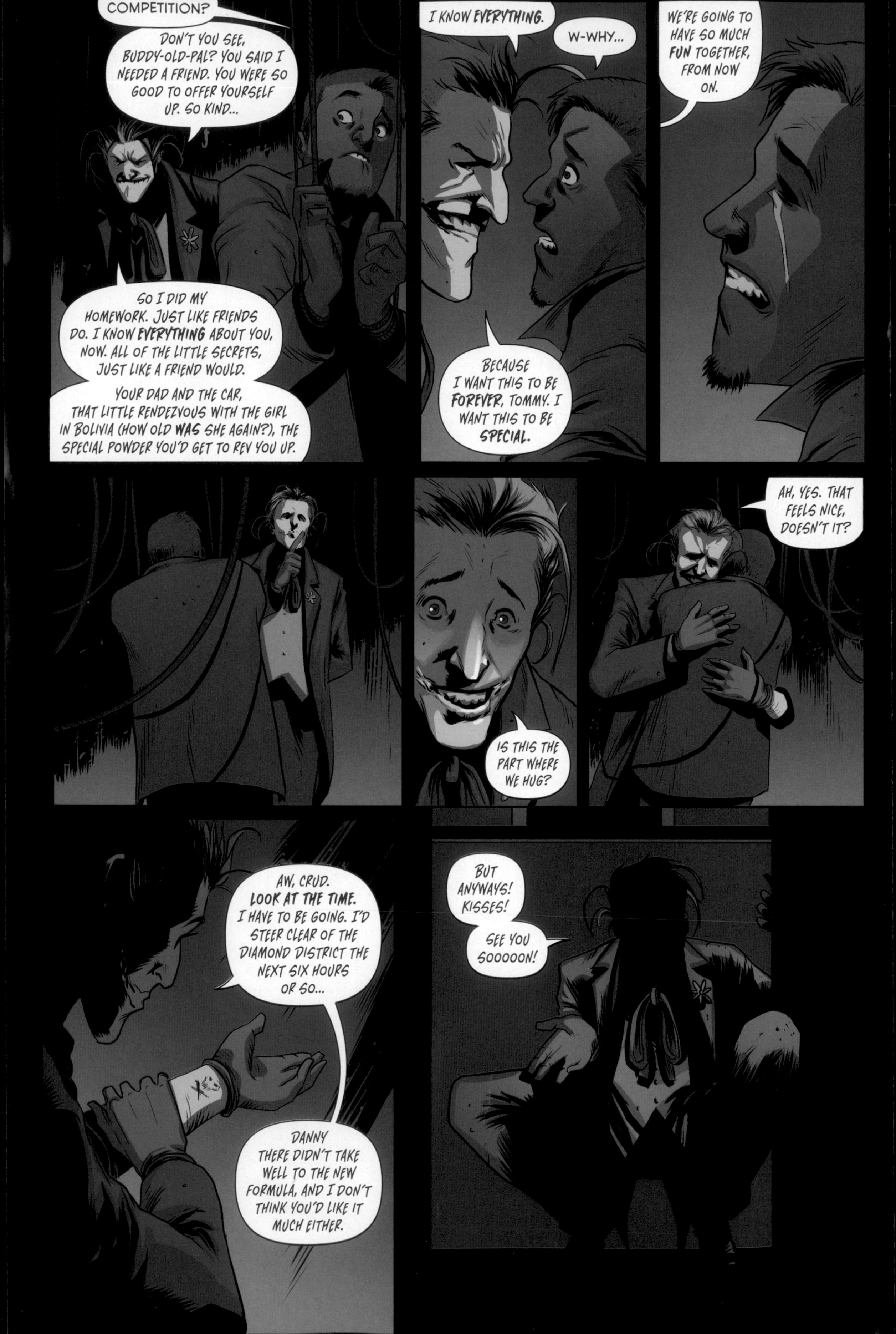
COMPETITION?
DON'T YOU SEE, BUDDY-OLD-PAL? YOU SAID I NEEDED A FRIEND. YOU WERE SO GOOD TO OFFER YOURSELF UP. SO KIND...
SO I DID MY HOMEWORK. JUST LIKE FRIENDS DO. I KNOW EVERYTHING ABOUT YOU, NOW. ALL OF THE LITTLE SECRETS, JUST LIKE A FRIEND WOULD.
YOUR DAD AND THE CAR, THAT LITTLE RENDEZVOUS WITH THE GIRL IN BOLIVIA (HOW OLD WAS SHE AGAIN?), THE SPECIAL POWDER YOU'D GET TO REV YOU UP.
I KNOW EVERYTHING.
W-WHY...
BECAUSE I WANT THIS TO BE FOREVER, TOMMY. I WANT THIS TO BE SPECIAL.
WE'RE GOING TO HAVE SO MUCH FUN TOGETHER, FROM NOW ON.
IS THIS THE PART WHERE WE HUG?
AH, YES. THAT FEELS NICE, DOESN'T IT?
AW, CRUD. LOOK AT THE TIME. I HAVE TO BE GOING. I'D STEER CLEAR OF THE DIAMOND DISTRICT THE NEXT SIX HOURS OR SO...
DANNY THERE DIDN'T TAKE WELL TO THE NEW FORMULA, AND I DON'T THINK YOU'D LIKE IT MUCH EITHER.
BUT ANYWAYS! KISSES!
SEE YOU SOOOOON!

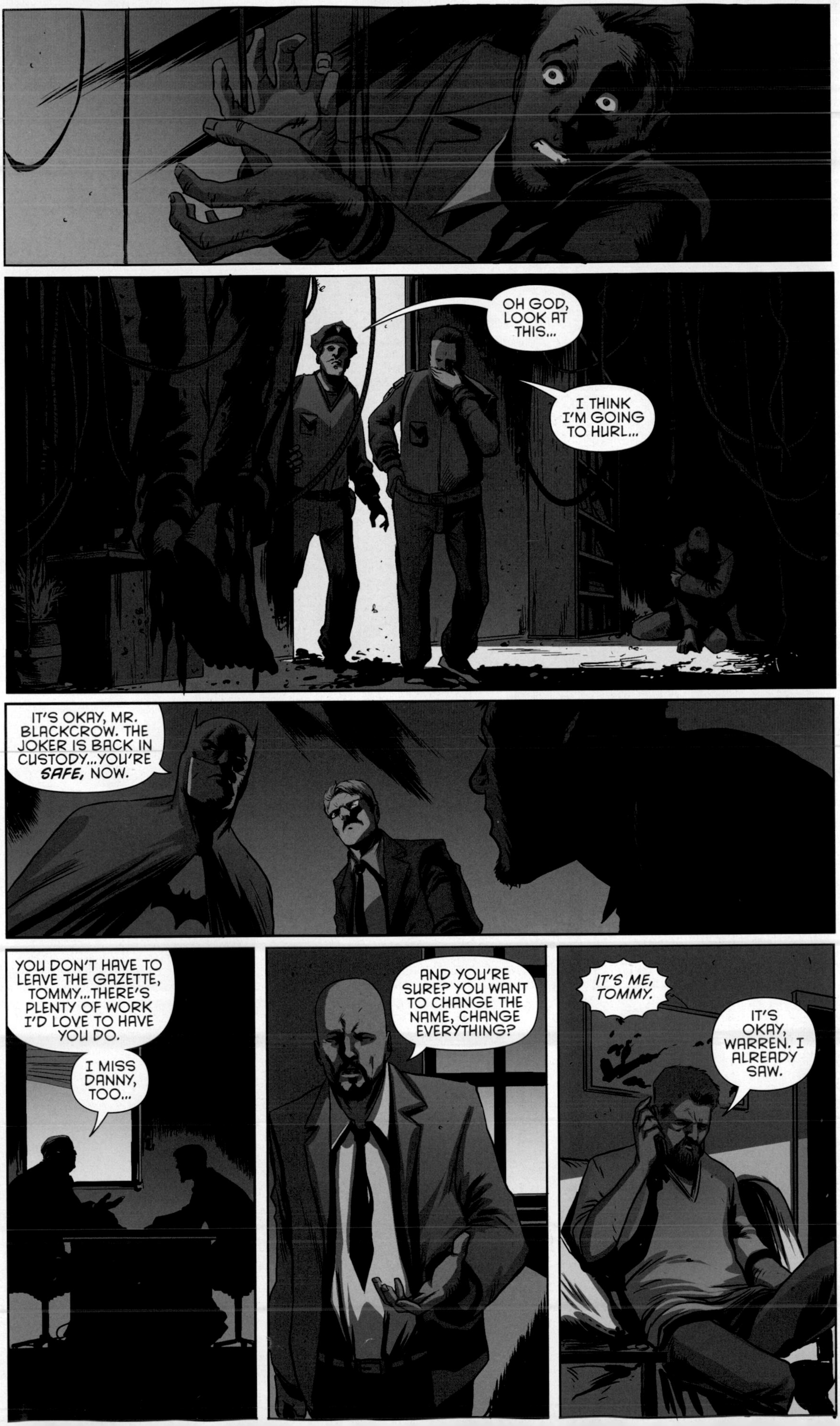
OH GOD, LOOK AT THIS...
I THINK I'M GOING TO HURL...
IT'S OKAY, MR. BLACKCROW. THE JOKER IS BACK IN CUSTODY...YOU'RE SAFE, NOW.
YOU DON'T HAVE TO LEAVE THE GAZETTE, TOMMY...THERE'S PLENTY OF WORK I'D LOVE TO HAVE YOU DO.
I MISS DANNY, TOO...
AND YOU'RE SURE? YOU WANT TO CHANGE THE NAME, CHANGE EVERYTHING?
IT'S ME, TOMMY.
IT'S OKAY, WARREN. I ALREADY SAW.

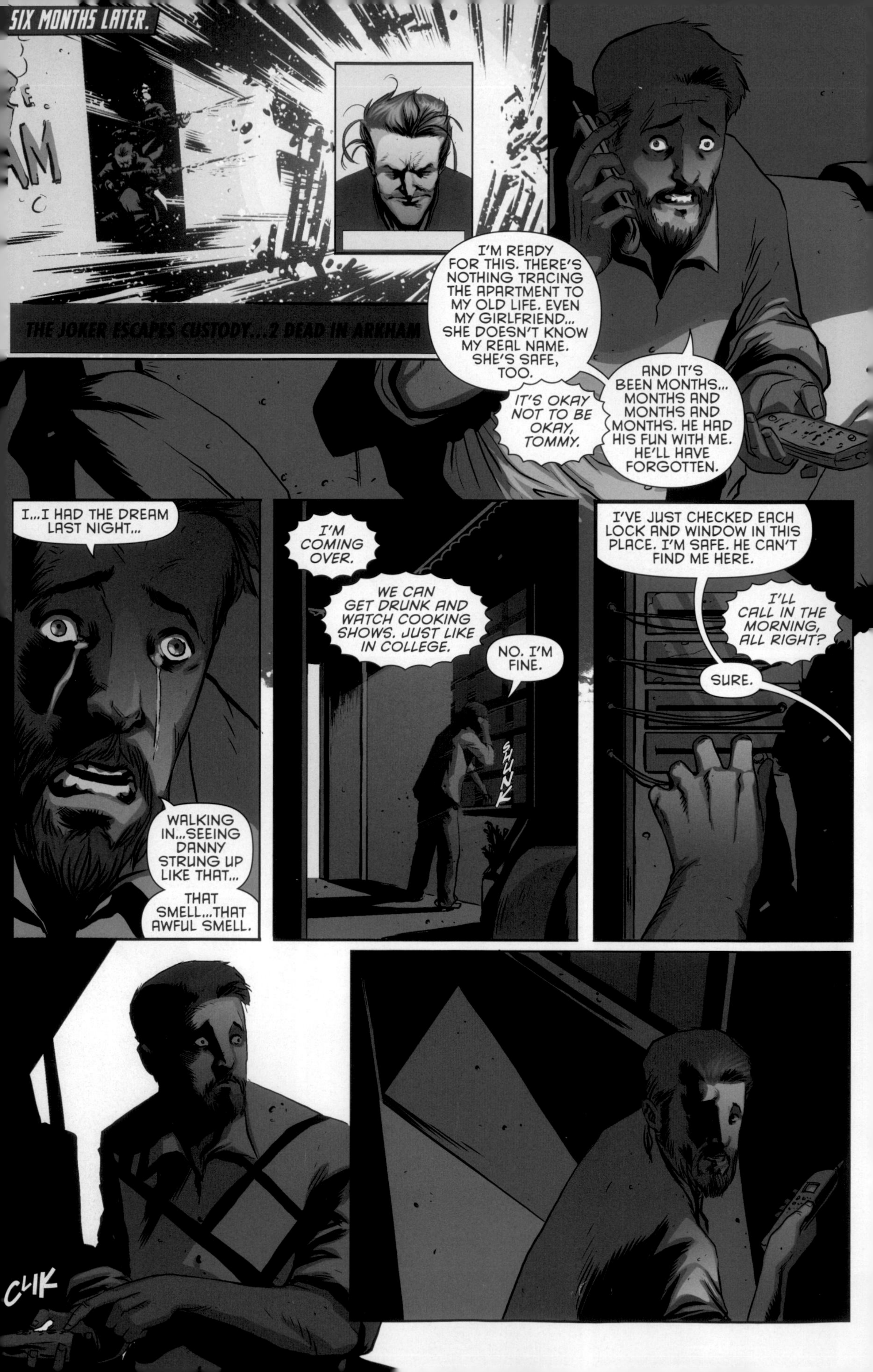
SIX MONTHS LATER.
THE JOKER ESCAPES CUSTODY...2 DEAD IN ARKHAM
I'M READY FOR THIS. THERE'S NOTHING TRACING THE APARTMENT TO MY OLD LIFE. EVEN MY GIRLFRIEND... SHE DOESN'T KNOW MY REAL NAME. SHE'S SAFE, TOO.
IT'S OKAY NOT TO BE OKAY, TOMMY.
AND IT'S BEEN MONTHS... MONTHS AND MONTHS AND MONTHS. HE HAD HIS FUN WITH ME. HE'LL HAVE FORGOTTEN.
I...I HAD THE DREAM LAST NIGHT...
WALKING IN...SEEING DANNY STRUNG UP LIKE THAT...
THAT SMELL...THAT AWFUL SMELL.
I'M COMING OVER.
WE CAN GET DRUNK AND WATCH COOKING SHOWS. JUST LIKE IN COLLEGE.
NO. I'M FINE.
SHUNK
I'VE JUST CHECKED EACH LOCK AND WINDOW IN THIS PLACE. I'M SAFE. HE CAN'T FIND ME HERE.
I'LL CALL IN THE MORNING, ALL RIGHT?
SURE.
CLIK

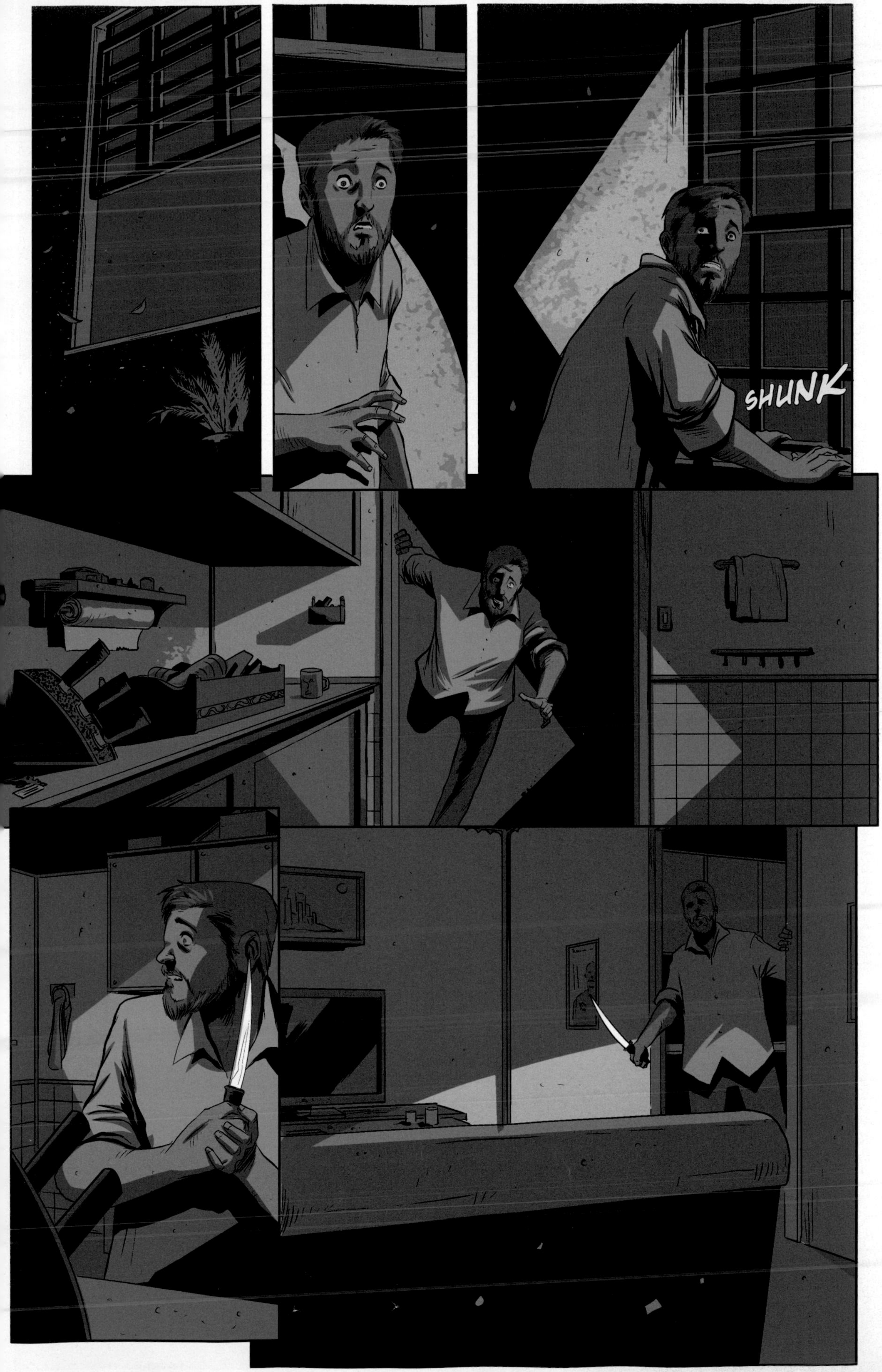
SHUNK

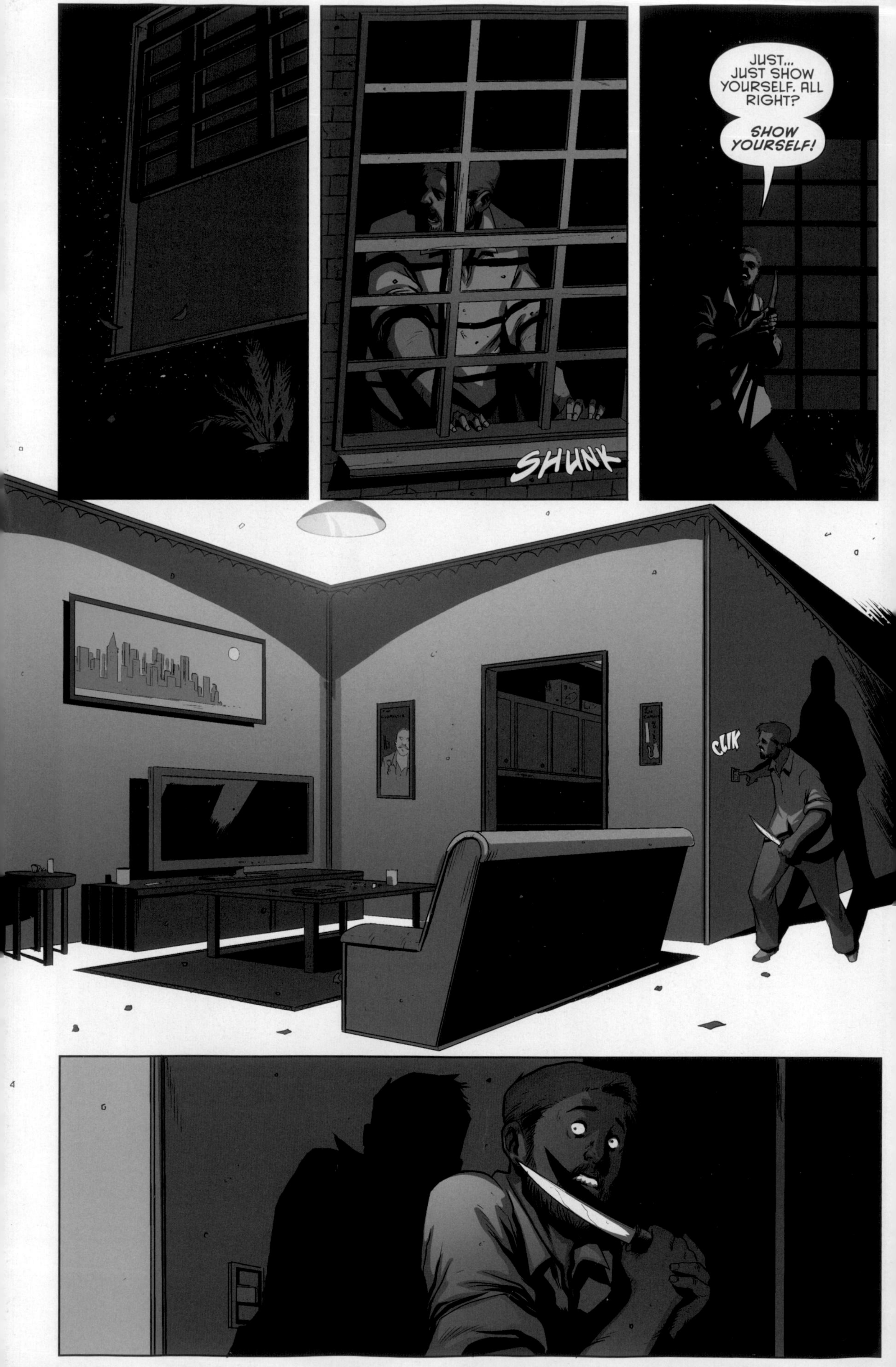
SHUNK
JUST... JUST SHOW YOURSELF. ALL RIGHT?
SHOW YOURSELF!
CLIK

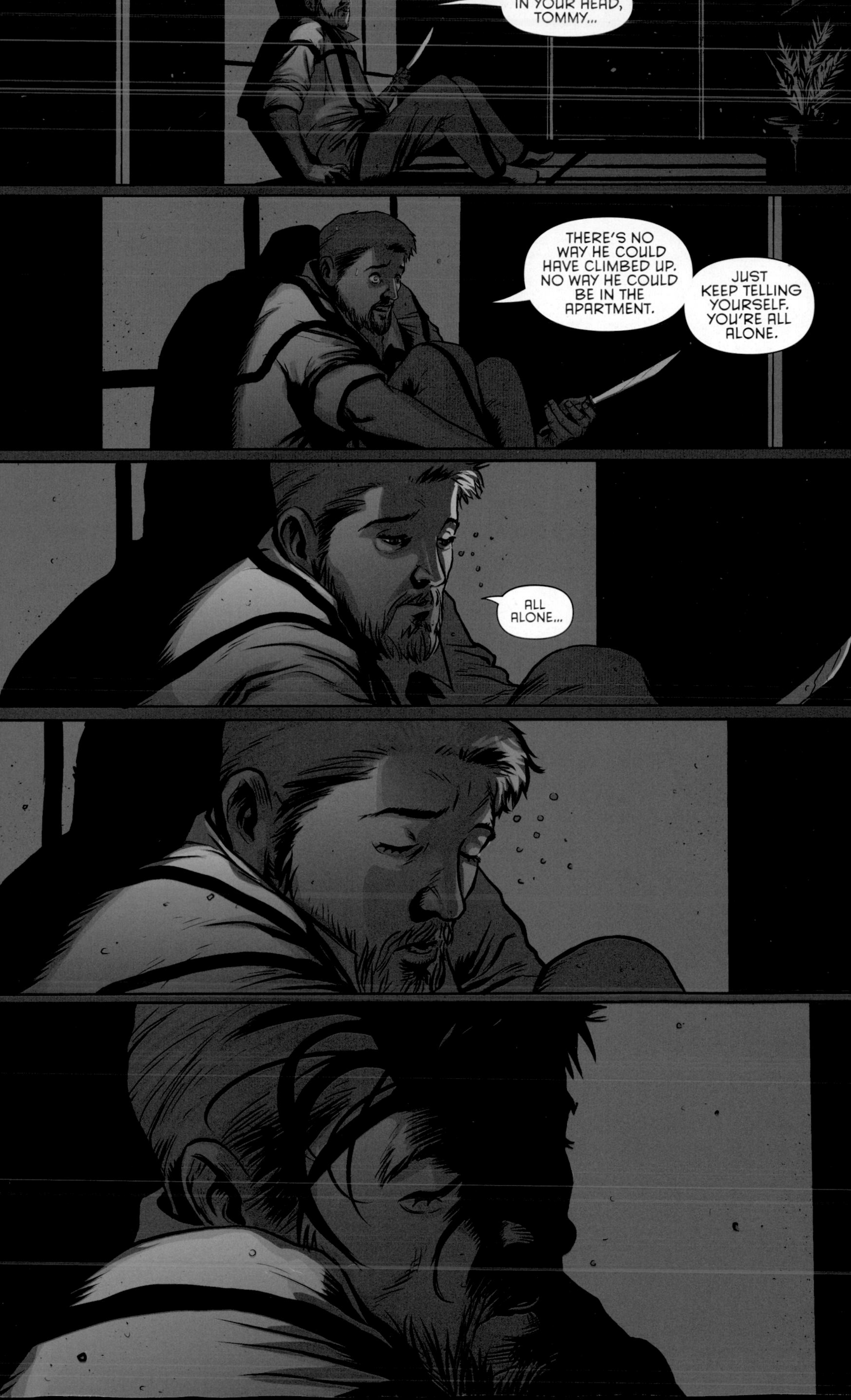
IN YOUR HEAD, TOMMY...
THERE'S NO WAY HE COULD HAVE CLIMBED UP. NO WAY HE COULD BE IN THE APARTMENT.
JUST KEEP TELLING YOURSELF. YOU'RE ALL ALONE.
ALL ALONE...

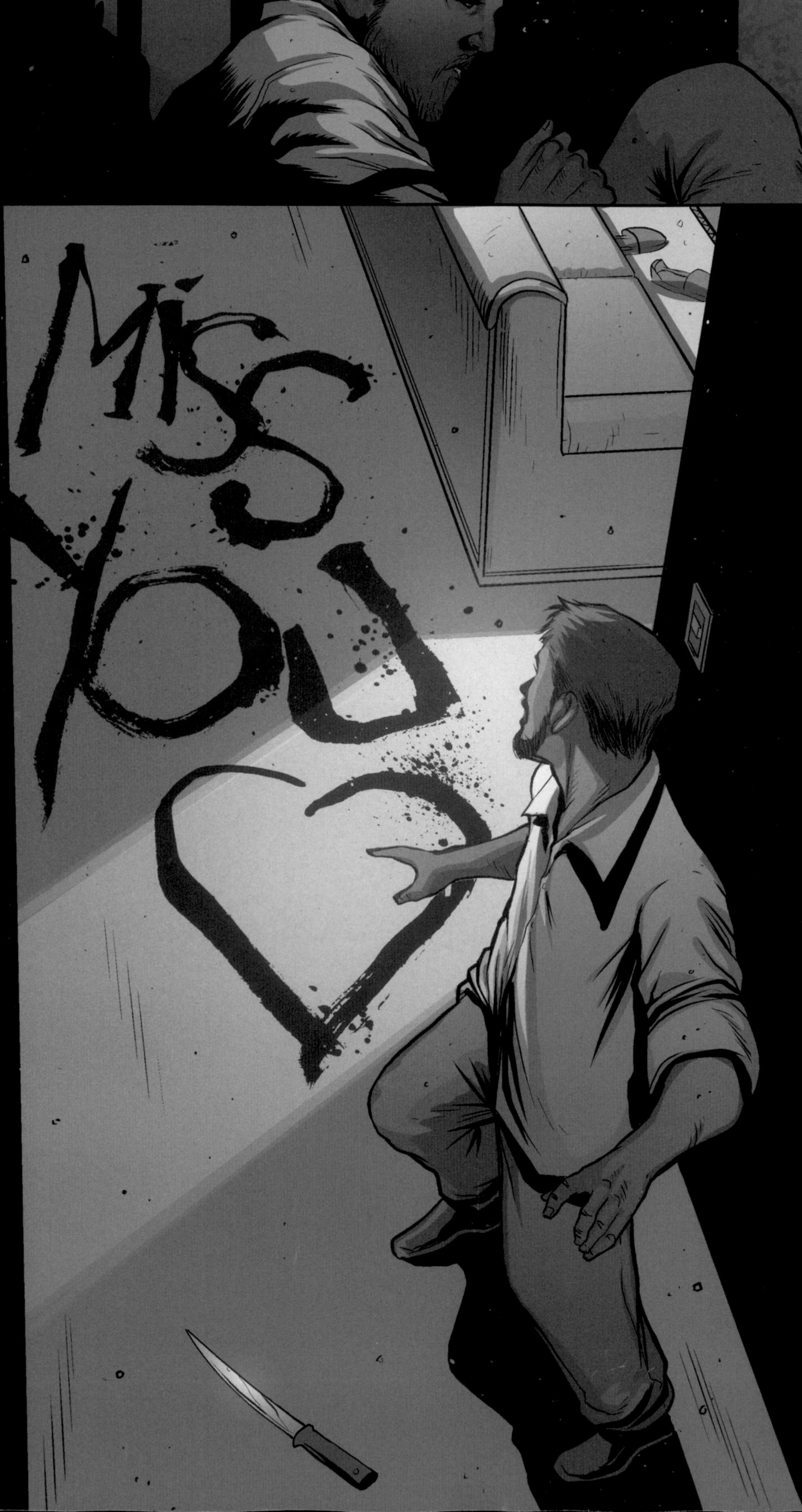
MISS YOU

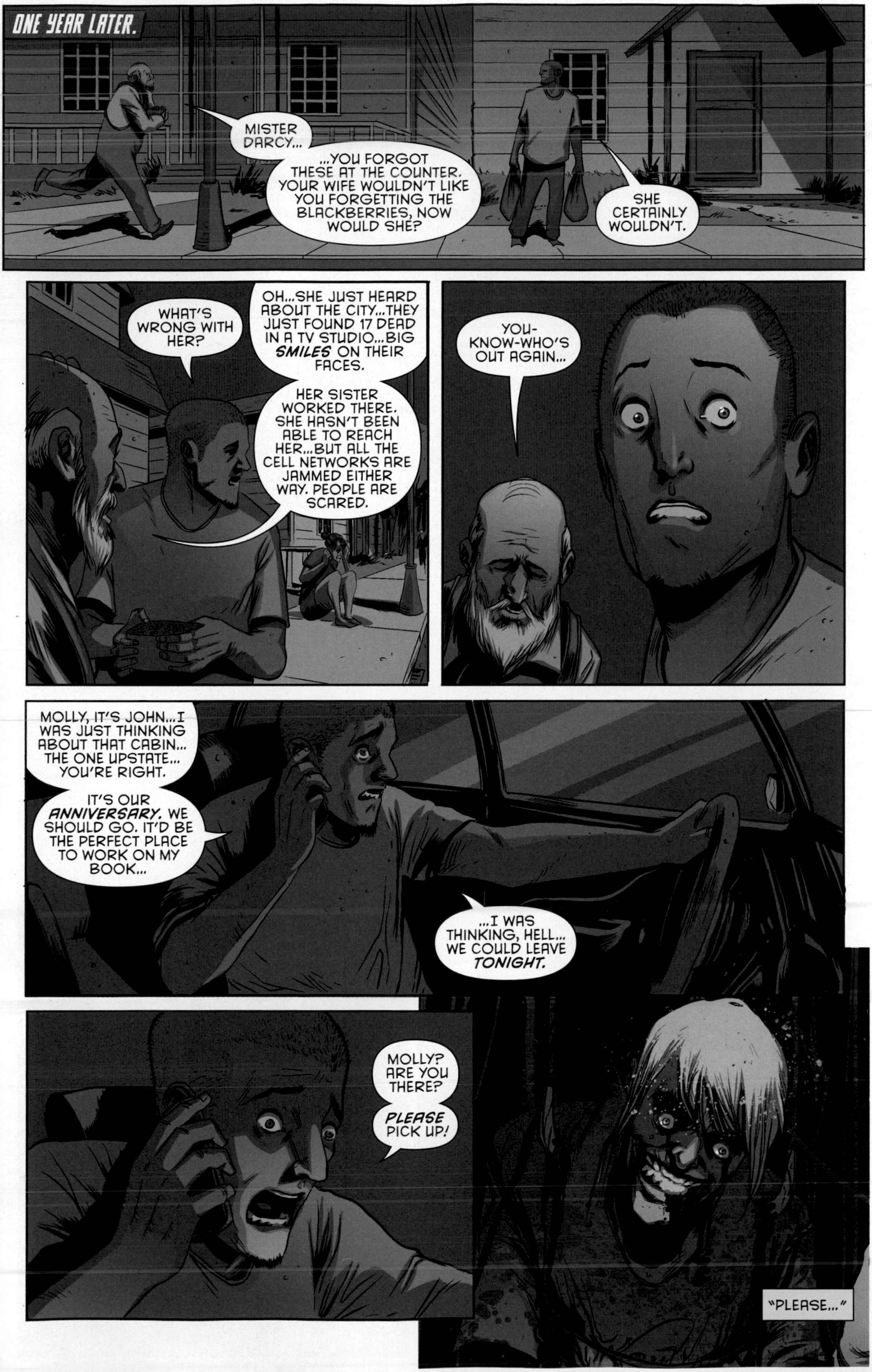
ONE YEAR LATER.
MISTER DARCY...
...YOU FORGOT THESE AT THE COUNTER. YOUR WIFE WOULDN'T LIKE YOU FORGETTING THE BLACKBERRIES, NOW WOULD SHE?
SHE CERTAINLY WOULDN'T.
WHAT'S WRONG WITH HER?
OH...SHE JUST HEARD ABOUT THE CITY...THEY JUST FOUND 17 DEAD IN A TV STUDIO...BIG SMILES ON THEIR FACES.
HER SISTER WORKED THERE. SHE HASN'T BEEN ABLE TO REACH HER...BUT ALL THE CELL NETWORKS ARE JAMMED EITHER WAY. PEOPLE ARE SCARED.
YOU-KNOW-WHO'S OUT AGAIN...
MOLLY, IT'S JOHN...I WAS JUST THINKING ABOUT THAT CABIN... THE ONE UPSTATE... YOU'RE RIGHT.
IT'S OUR ANNIVERSARY. WE SHOULD GO. IT'D BE THE PERFECT PLACE TO WORK ON MY BOOK...
...I WAS THINKING, HELL... WE COULD LEAVE TONIGHT.
MOLLY? ARE YOU THERE?
PLEASE PICK UP!
"PLEASE..."

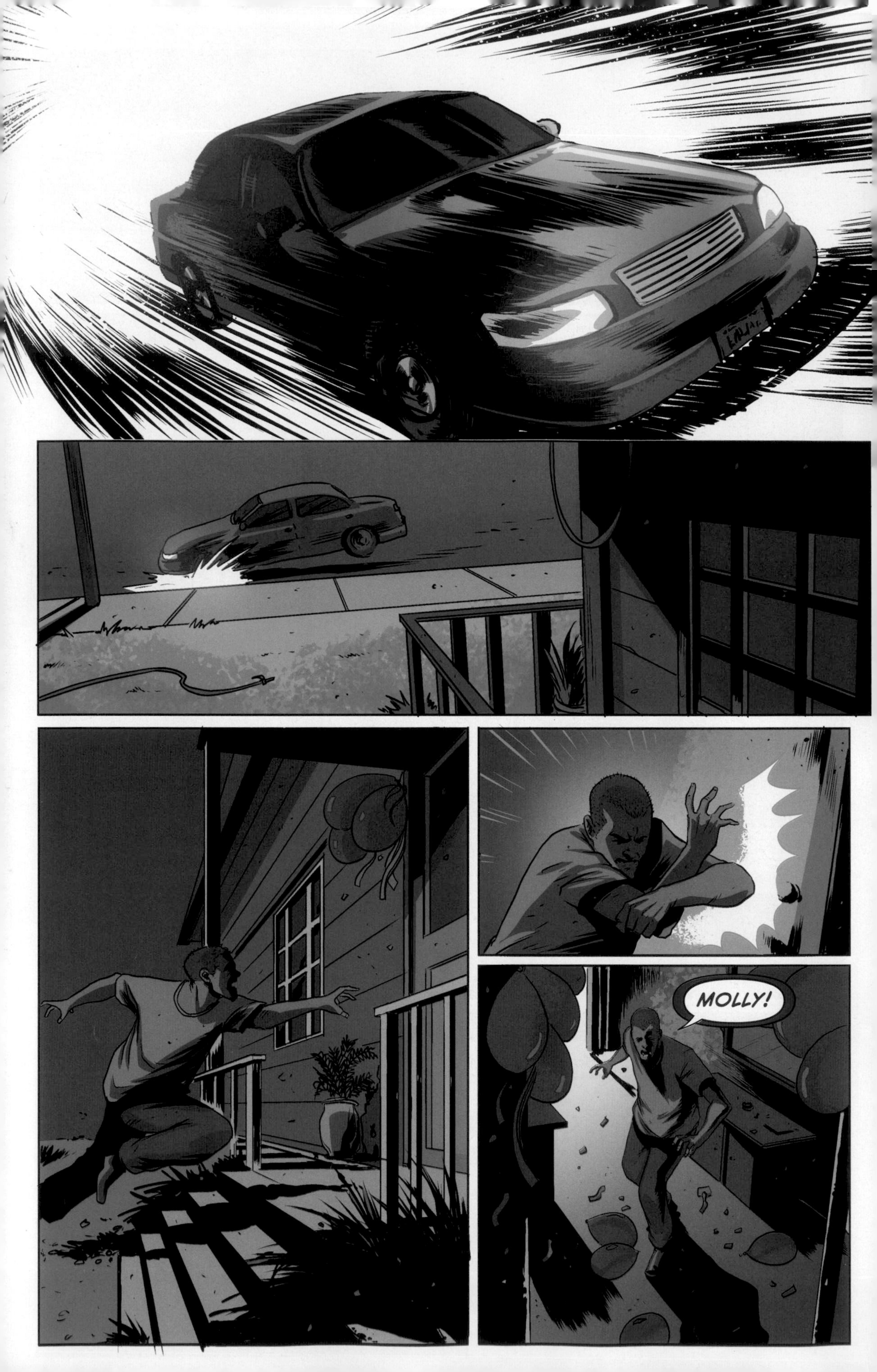
MOLLY!

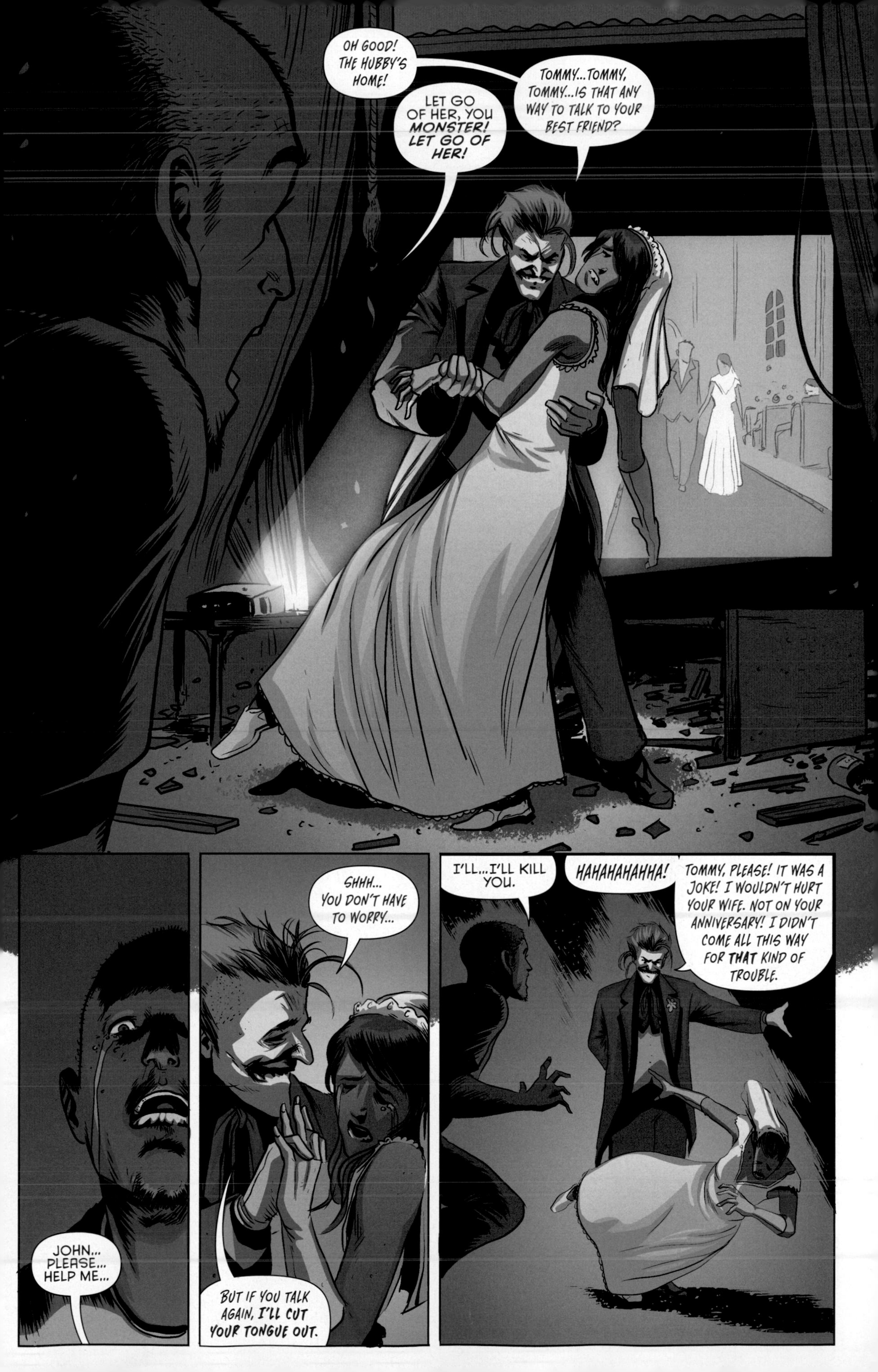
OH GOOD! THE HUBBY'S HOME!
LET GO OF HER, YOU MONSTER! LET GO OF HER!
TOMMY...TOMMY, TOMMY...IS THAT ANY WAY TO TALK TO YOUR BEST FRIEND?
JOHN... PLEASE... HELP ME...
SHHH... YOU DON'T HAVE TO WORRY...
BUT IF YOU TALK AGAIN, I'LL CUT YOUR TONGUE OUT.
I'LL...I'LL KILL YOU.
HAHAHAHAHHA!
TOMMY, PLEASE! IT WAS A JOKE! I WOULDN'T HURT YOUR WIFE. NOT ON YOUR ANNIVERSARY! I DIDN'T COME ALL THIS WAY FOR THAT KIND OF TROUBLE.

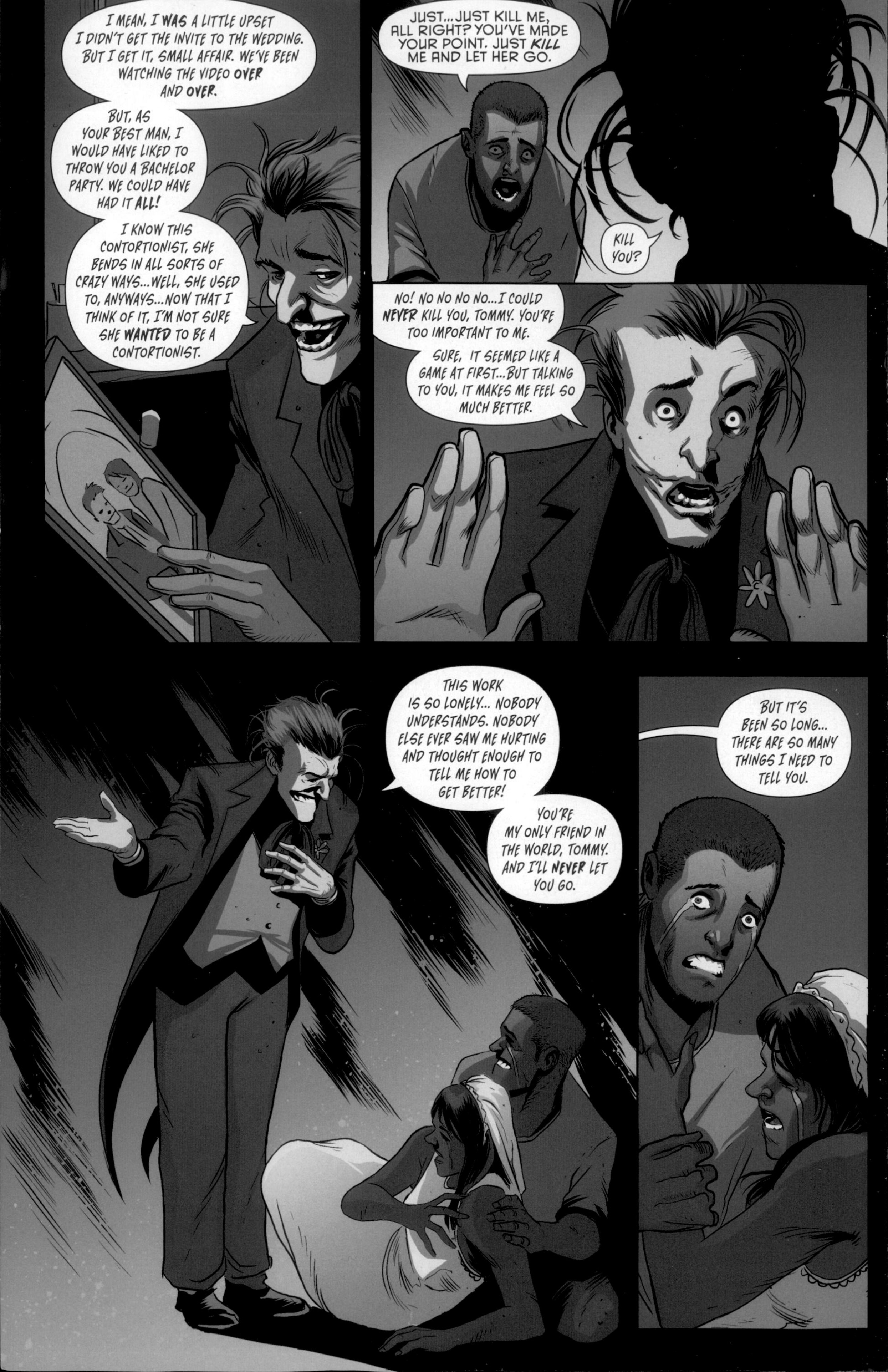
I MEAN, I WAS A LITTLE UPSET I DIDN'T GET THE INVITE TO THE WEDDING. BUT I GET IT, SMALL AFFAIR. WE'VE BEEN WATCHING THE VIDEO OVER AND OVER.
BUT, AS YOUR BEST MAN, I WOULD HAVE LIKED TO THROW YOU A BACHELOR PARTY. WE COULD HAVE HAD IT ALL!
I KNOW THIS CONTORTIONIST, SHE BENDS IN ALL SORTS OF CRAZY WAYS...WELL, SHE USED TO, ANYWAYS...NOW THAT I THINK OF IT, I'M NOT SURE SHE WANTED TO BE A CONTORTIONIST.
JUST...JUST KILL ME, ALL RIGHT? YOU'VE MADE YOUR POINT. JUST KILL ME AND LET HER GO.
KILL YOU?
NO! NO NO NO NO...I COULD NEVER KILL YOU, TOMMY. YOU'RE TOO IMPORTANT TO ME.
SURE, IT SEEMED LIKE A GAME AT FIRST...BUT TALKING TO YOU, IT MAKES ME FEEL SO MUCH BETTER.
THIS WORK IS SO LONELY... NOBODY UNDERSTANDS. NOBODY ELSE EVER SAW ME HURTING AND THOUGHT ENOUGH TO TELL ME HOW TO GET BETTER!
YOU'RE MY ONLY FRIEND IN THE WORLD, TOMMY. AND I'LL NEVER LET YOU GO.
BUT IT'S BEEN SO LONG... THERE ARE SO MANY THINGS I NEED TO TELL YOU.

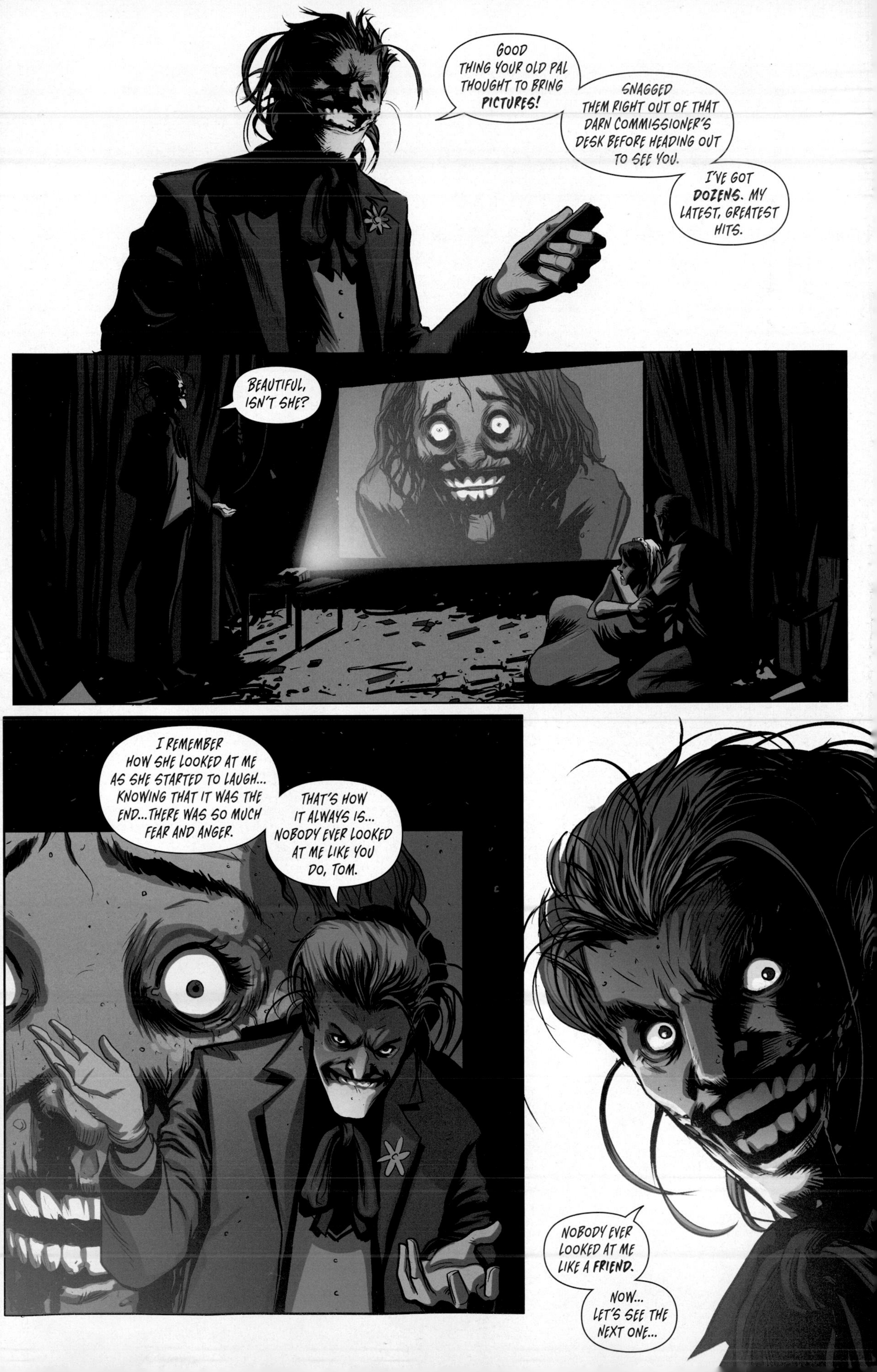
GOOD THING YOUR OLD PAL THOUGHT TO BRING **PICTURES!**
SNAGGED THEM RIGHT OUT OF THAT DARN COMMISSIONER'S DESK BEFORE HEADING OUT TO SEE YOU.
I'VE GOT **DOZENS.** MY LATEST, GREATEST HITS.
BEAUTIFUL, ISN'T SHE?
I REMEMBER HOW SHE LOOKED AT ME AS SHE STARTED TO LAUGH... KNOWING THAT IT WAS THE END...THERE WAS SO MUCH FEAR AND ANGER.
THAT'S HOW IT ALWAYS IS... NOBODY EVER LOOKED AT ME LIKE YOU DO, TOM.
NOBODY EVER LOOKED AT ME LIKE A **FRIEND.**
NOW... LET'S SEE THE NEXT ONE...

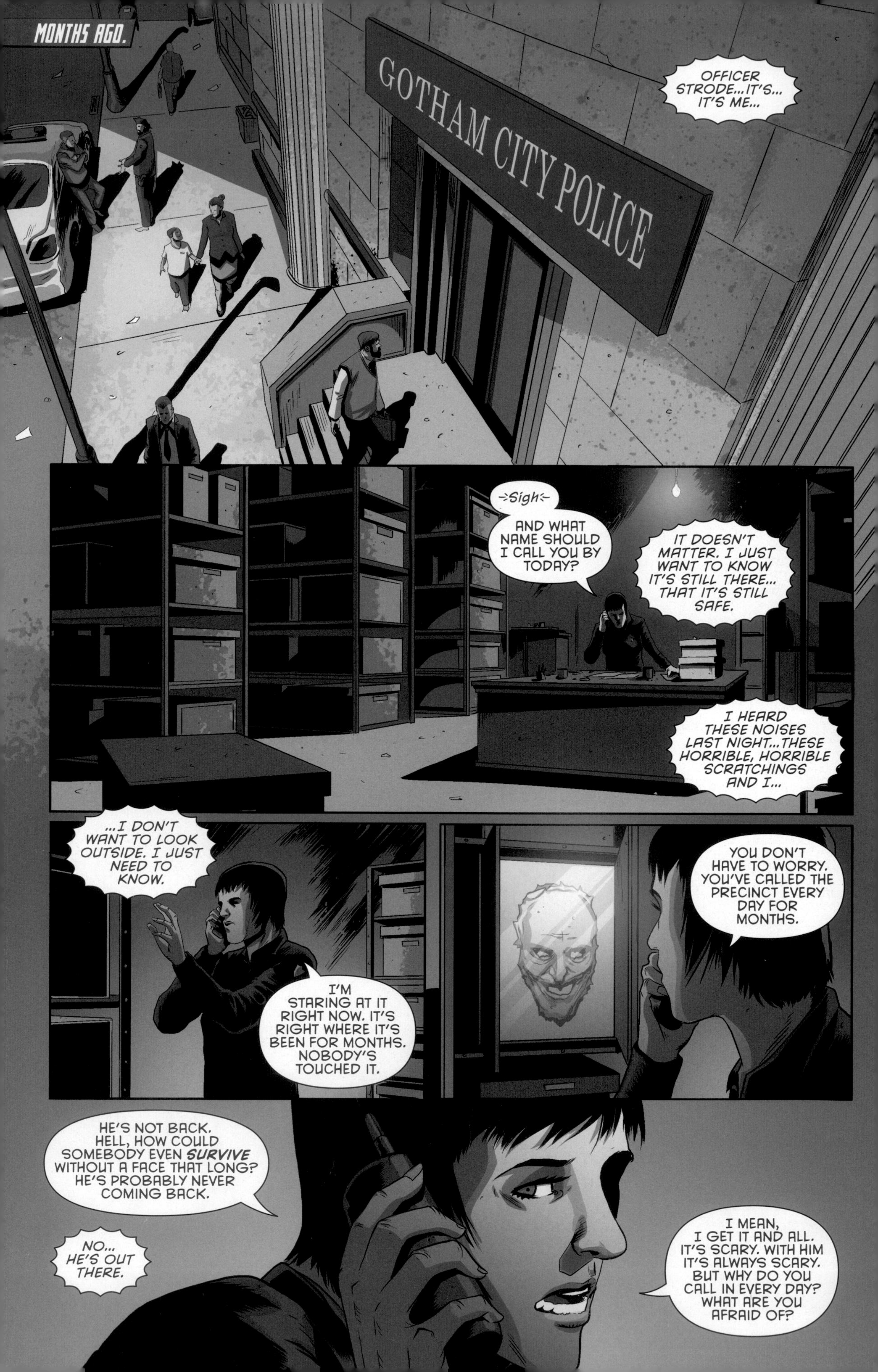
MONTHS AGO.
GOTHAM CITY POLICE
OFFICER STRODE...IT'S... IT'S ME...
~Sigh~
AND WHAT NAME SHOULD I CALL YOU BY TODAY?
IT DOESN'T MATTER. I JUST WANT TO KNOW IT'S STILL THERE... THAT IT'S STILL SAFE.
I HEARD THESE NOISES LAST NIGHT...THESE HORRIBLE, HORRIBLE SCRATCHINGS AND I...
...I DON'T WANT TO LOOK OUTSIDE. I JUST NEED TO KNOW.
I'M STARING AT IT RIGHT NOW. IT'S RIGHT WHERE IT'S BEEN FOR MONTHS. NOBODY'S TOUCHED IT.
YOU DON'T HAVE TO WORRY. YOU'VE CALLED THE PRECINCT EVERY DAY FOR MONTHS.
HE'S NOT BACK. HELL, HOW COULD SOMEBODY EVEN SURVIVE WITHOUT A FACE THAT LONG? HE'S PROBABLY NEVER COMING BACK.
NO... HE'S OUT THERE.
I MEAN, I GET IT AND ALL. IT'S SCARY. WITH HIM IT'S ALWAYS SCARY. BUT WHY DO YOU CALL IN EVERY DAY? WHAT ARE YOU AFRAID OF?

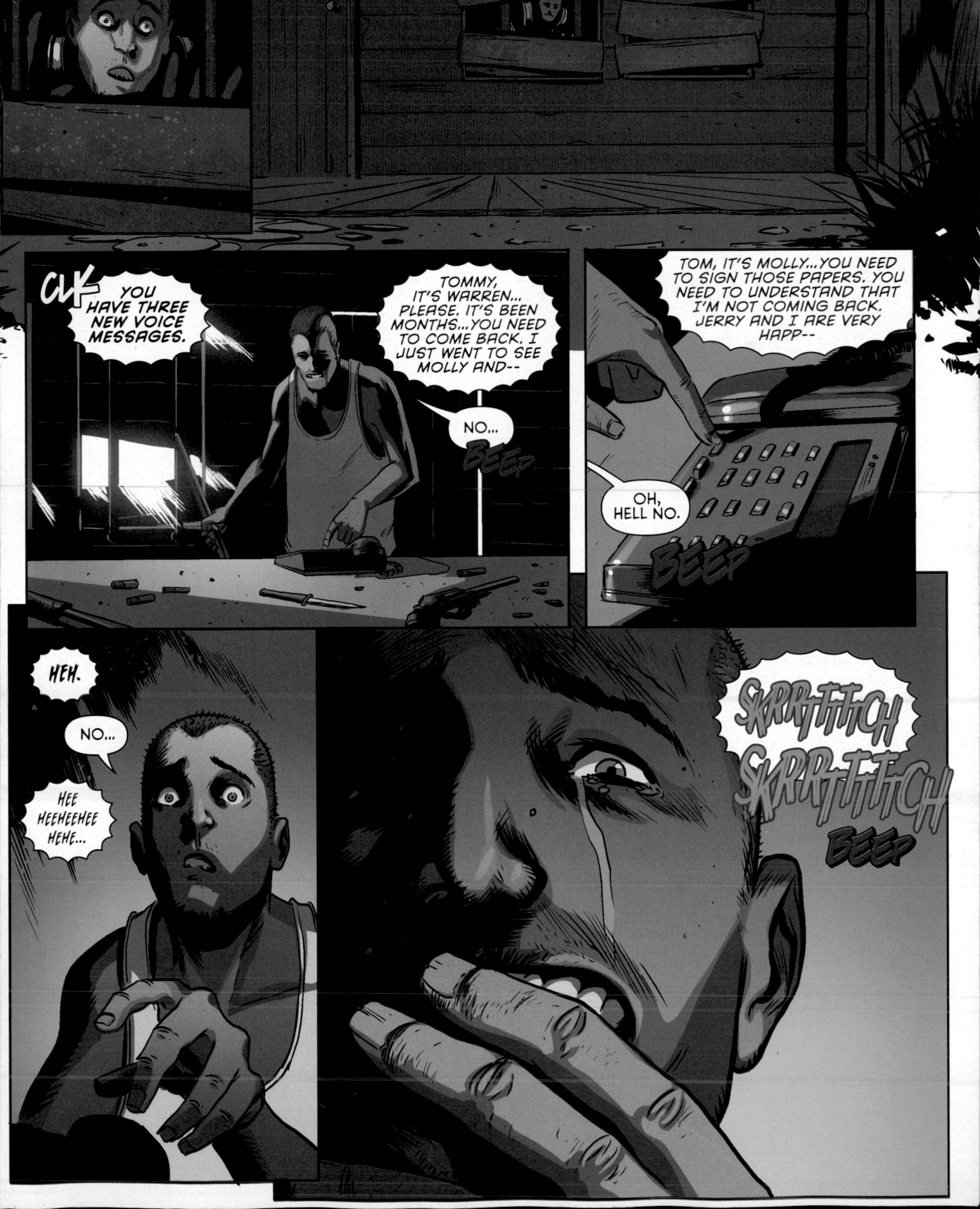
CLK
YOU HAVE THREE NEW VOICE MESSAGES.
TOMMY, IT'S WARREN... PLEASE. IT'S BEEN MONTHS...YOU NEED TO COME BACK. I JUST WENT TO SEE MOLLY AND--
NO...
BEEP
TOM, IT'S MOLLY...YOU NEED TO SIGN THOSE PAPERS. YOU NEED TO UNDERSTAND THAT I'M NOT COMING BACK. JERRY AND I ARE VERY HAPP--
OH, HELL NO.
BEEP
HEH.
NO...
HEE HEEHEEHEE HEHE...
SKRRTTTTTCH
SKRRTTTTTTCH
BEEP

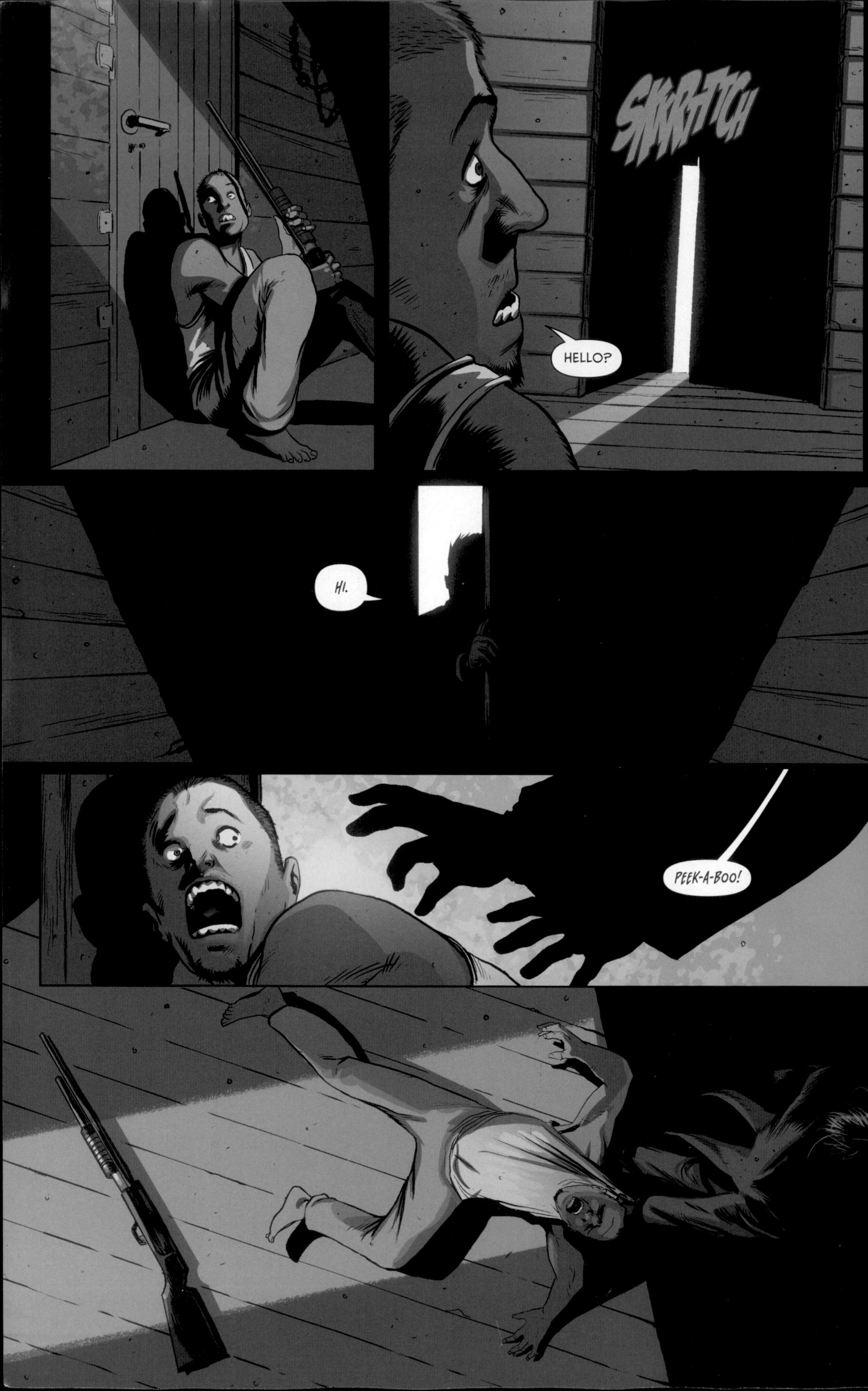
SKRRITCH
HELLO?
HI.
PEEK-A-BOO!

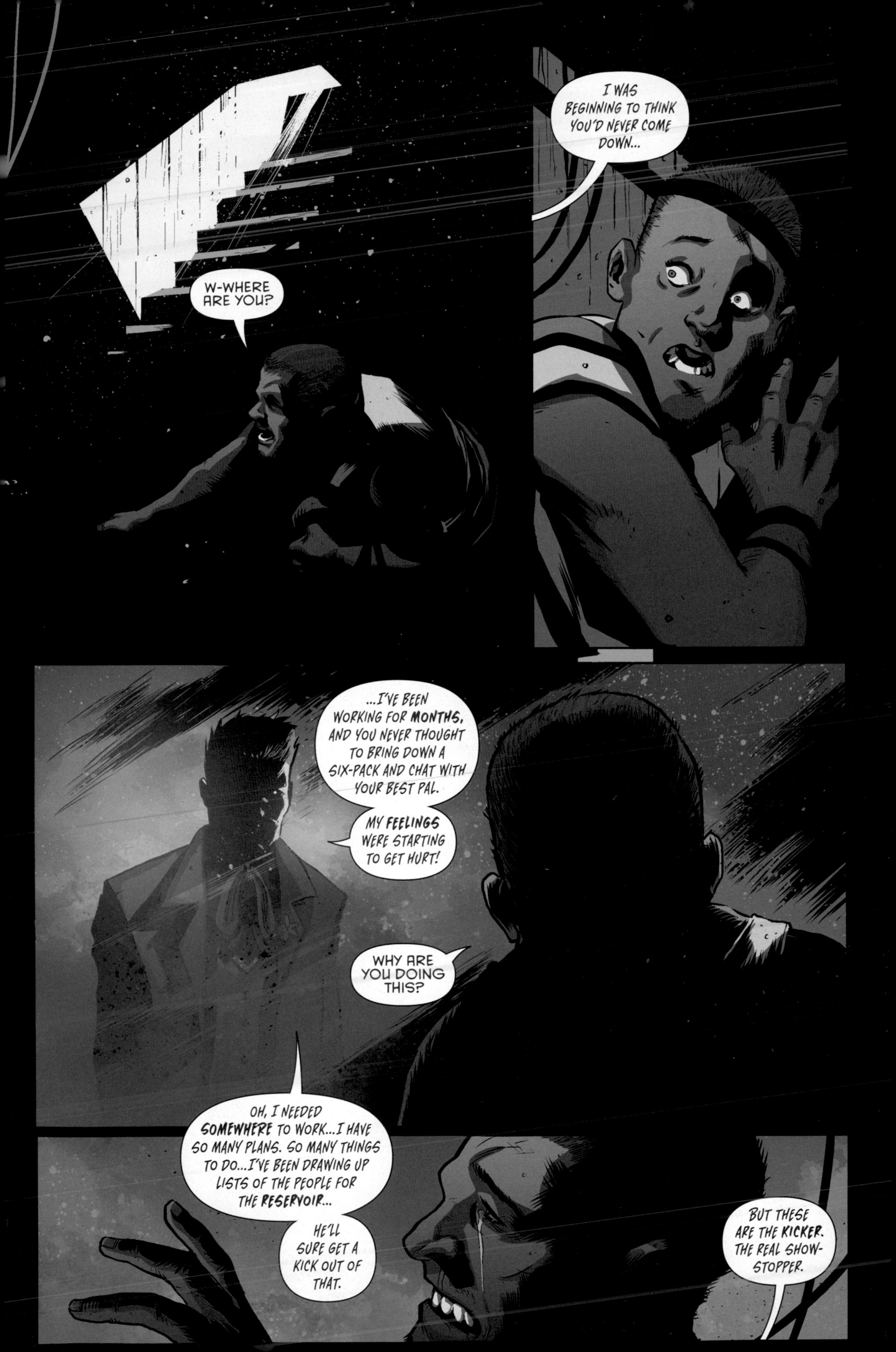
W-WHERE ARE YOU?
I WAS BEGINNING TO THINK YOU'D NEVER COME DOWN...
...I'VE BEEN WORKING FOR MONTHS, AND YOU NEVER THOUGHT TO BRING DOWN A SIX-PACK AND CHAT WITH YOUR BEST PAL.
MY FEELINGS WERE STARTING TO GET HURT!
WHY ARE YOU DOING THIS?
OH, I NEEDED SOMEWHERE TO WORK...I HAVE SO MANY PLANS. SO MANY THINGS TO DO...I'VE BEEN DRAWING UP LISTS OF THE PEOPLE FOR THE RESERVOIR...
HE'LL SURE GET A KICK OUT OF THAT.
BUT THESE ARE THE KICKER. THE REAL SHOW-STOPPER.

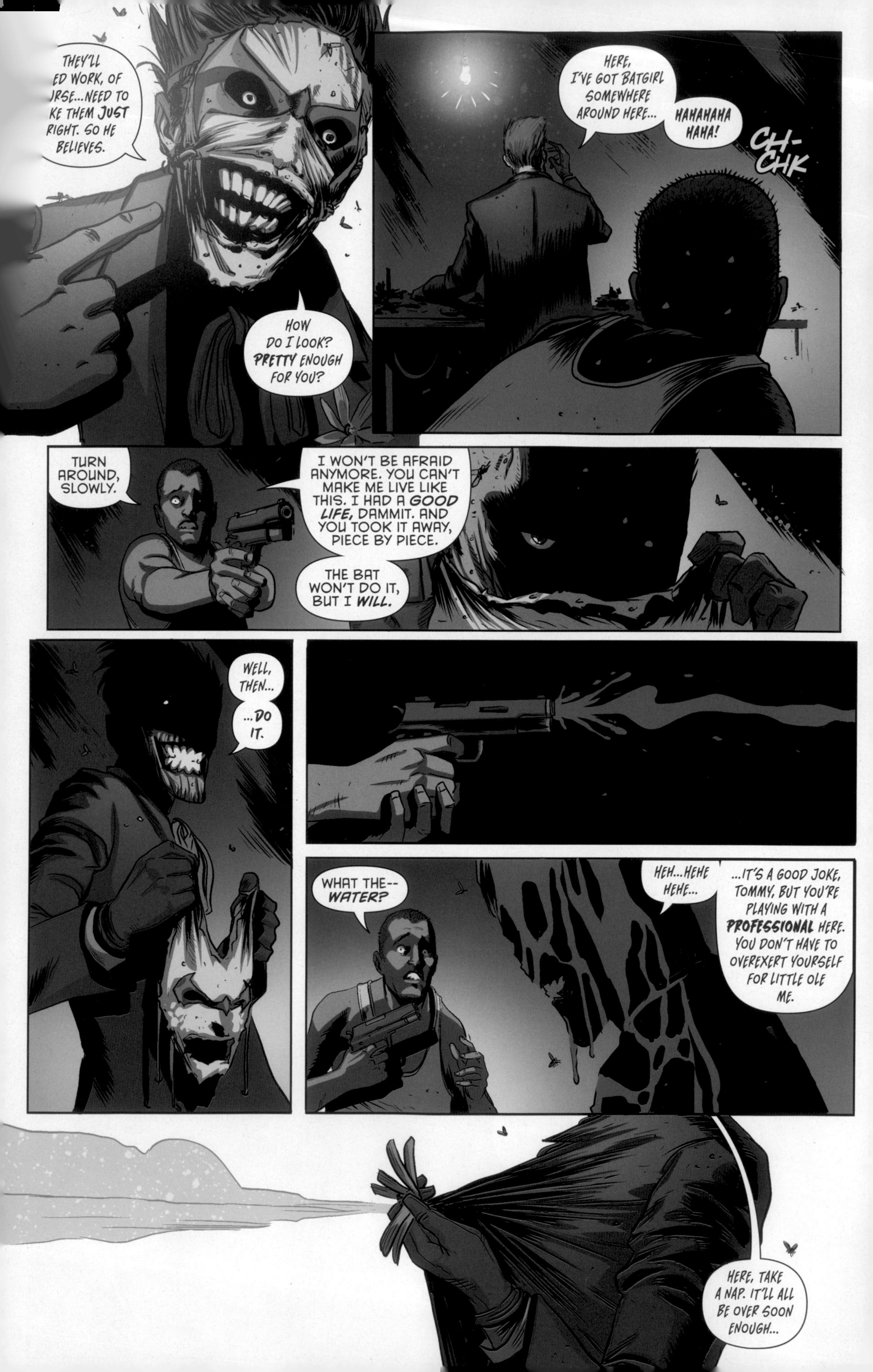
THEY'LL
ED WORK, OF
JRSE...NEED TO
KE THEM JUST
RIGHT. SO HE
BELIEVES.
HOW DO I LOOK? PRETTY ENOUGH FOR YOU?
HERE, I'VE GOT BATGIRL SOMEWHERE AROUND HERE...
HAHAHAHA HAHA!
CH-CHK
TURN AROUND, SLOWLY.
I WON'T BE AFRAID ANYMORE. YOU CAN'T MAKE ME LIVE LIKE THIS. I HAD A GOOD LIFE, DAMMIT. AND YOU TOOK IT AWAY, PIECE BY PIECE.
THE BAT WON'T DO IT, BUT I WILL.
WELL, THEN...
...DO IT.
WHAT THE-- WATER?
HEH...HEHE HEHE...
...IT'S A GOOD JOKE, TOMMY, BUT YOU'RE PLAYING WITH A PROFESSIONAL HERE. YOU DON'T HAVE TO OVEREXERT YOURSELF FOR LITTLE OLE ME.
HERE, TAKE A NAP. IT'LL ALL BE OVER SOON ENOUGH...

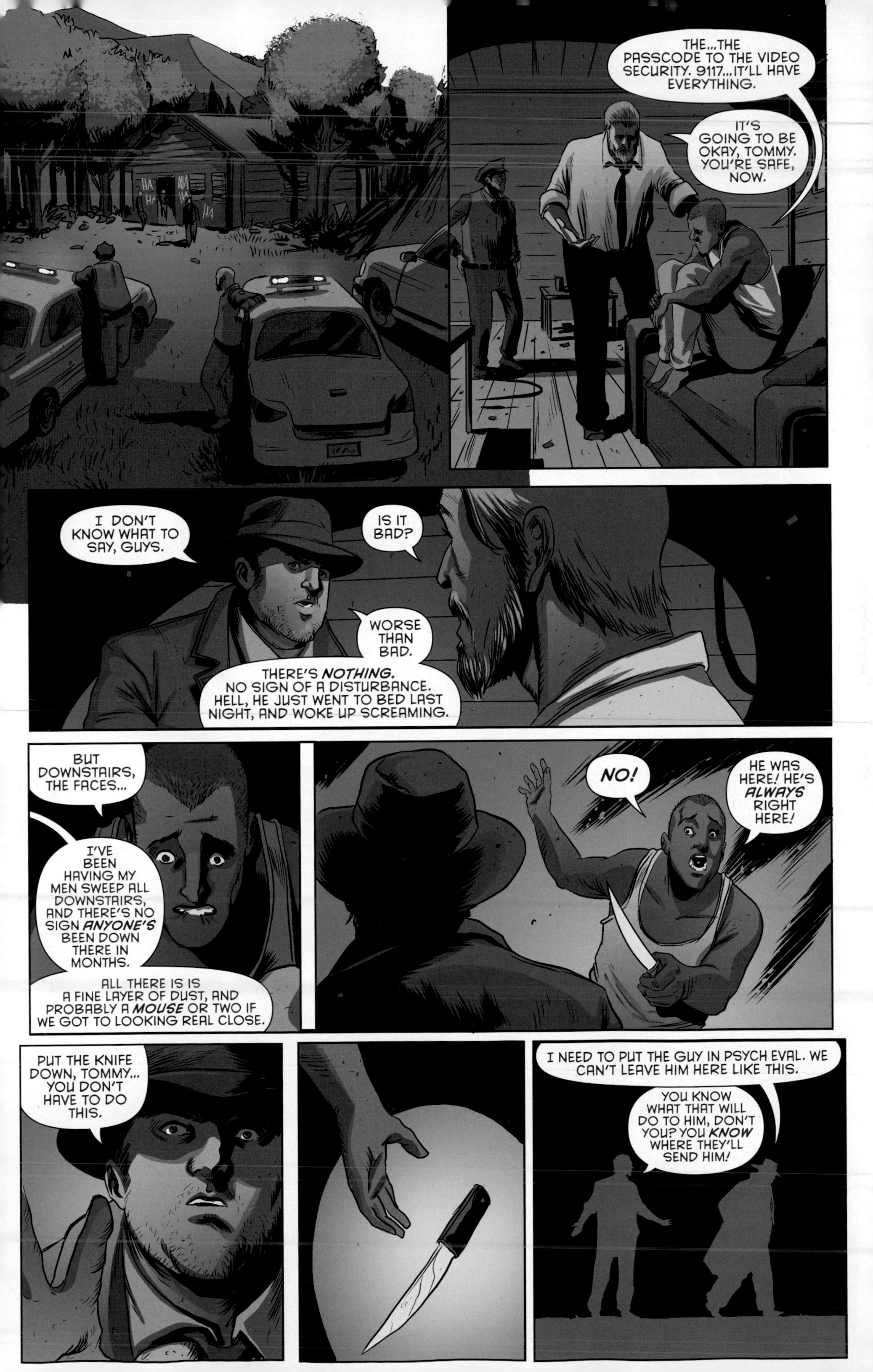
HA
HA
HA
HA
HA
THE...THE PASSCODE TO THE VIDEO SECURITY. 9117...IT'LL HAVE EVERYTHING.
IT'S GOING TO BE OKAY, TOMMY. YOU'RE SAFE, NOW.
I DON'T KNOW WHAT TO SAY, GUYS.
IS IT BAD?
WORSE THAN BAD.
THERE'S NOTHING. NO SIGN OF A DISTURBANCE. HELL, HE JUST WENT TO BED LAST NIGHT, AND WOKE UP SCREAMING.
BUT DOWNSTAIRS, THE FACES...
I'VE BEEN HAVING MY MEN SWEEP ALL DOWNSTAIRS, AND THERE'S NO SIGN ANYONE'S BEEN DOWN THERE IN MONTHS.
ALL THERE IS IS A FINE LAYER OF DUST, AND PROBABLY A MOUSE OR TWO IF WE GOT TO LOOKING REAL CLOSE.
NO!
HE WAS HERE! HE'S ALWAYS RIGHT HERE!
PUT THE KNIFE DOWN, TOMMY... YOU DON'T HAVE TO DO THIS.
I NEED TO PUT THE GUY IN PSYCH EVAL. WE CAN'T LEAVE HIM HERE LIKE THIS.
YOU KNOW WHAT THAT WILL DO TO HIM, DON'T YOU? YOU KNOW WHERE THEY'LL SEND HIM!

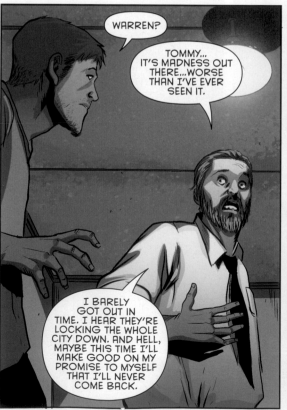

WARREN?

TOMMY... IT'S MADNESS OUT THERE...WORSE THAN I'VE EVER SEEN IT.

I BARELY GOT OUT IN TIME. I HEAR THEY'RE LOCKING THE WHOLE CITY DOWN. AND HELL, MAYBE THIS TIME I'LL MAKE GOOD ON MY PROMISE TO MYSELF THAT I'LL NEVER COME BACK.

I CAN STILL FEEL THE LAUGHTER RATTLING IN MY EARS...

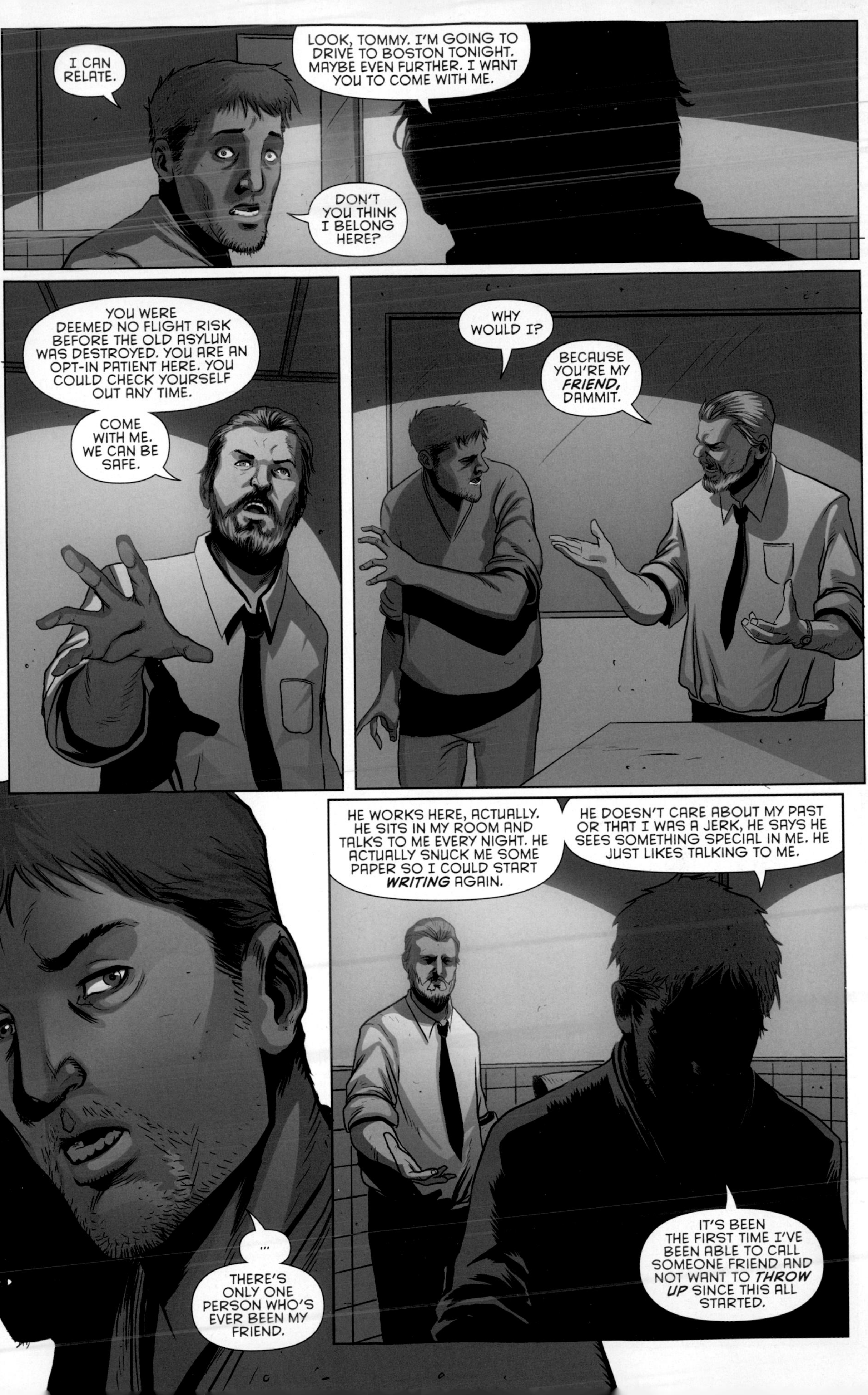

I CAN RELATE.
LOOK, TOMMY. I'M GOING TO DRIVE TO BOSTON TONIGHT. MAYBE EVEN FURTHER. I WANT YOU TO COME WITH ME.
DON'T YOU THINK I BELONG HERE?
YOU WERE DEEMED NO FLIGHT RISK BEFORE THE OLD ASYLUM WAS DESTROYED. YOU ARE AN OPT-IN PATIENT HERE. YOU COULD CHECK YOURSELF OUT ANY TIME.
COME WITH ME. WE CAN BE SAFE.
WHY WOULD I?
BECAUSE YOU'RE MY *FRIEND,* DAMMIT.
...
THERE'S ONLY ONE PERSON WHO'S EVER BEEN MY FRIEND.
HE WORKS HERE, ACTUALLY. HE SITS IN MY ROOM AND TALKS TO ME EVERY NIGHT. HE ACTUALLY SNUCK ME SOME PAPER SO I COULD START *WRITING* AGAIN.
HE DOESN'T CARE ABOUT MY PAST OR THAT I WAS A JERK, HE SAYS HE SEES SOMETHING SPECIAL IN ME. HE JUST LIKES TALKING TO ME.
IT'S BEEN THE FIRST TIME I'VE BEEN ABLE TO CALL SOMEONE FRIEND AND NOT WANT TO *THROW UP* SINCE THIS ALL STARTED.

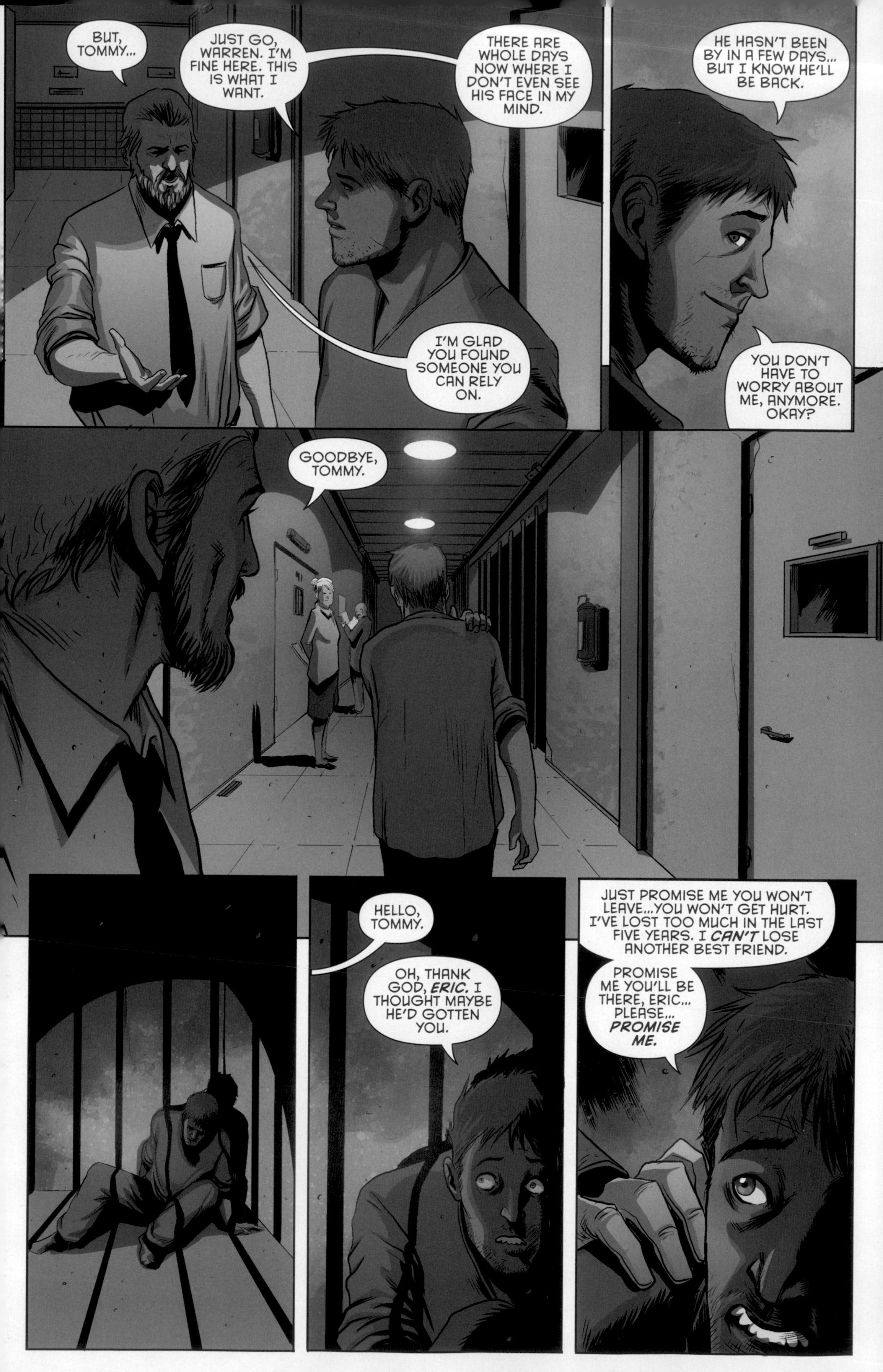
BUT, TOMMY...
JUST GO, WARREN. I'M FINE HERE. THIS IS WHAT I WANT.
THERE ARE WHOLE DAYS NOW WHERE I DON'T EVEN SEE HIS FACE IN MY MIND.
I'M GLAD YOU FOUND SOMEONE YOU CAN RELY ON.
HE HASN'T BEEN BY IN A FEW DAYS... BUT I KNOW HE'LL BE BACK.
YOU DON'T HAVE TO WORRY ABOUT ME, ANYMORE. OKAY?
GOODBYE, TOMMY.
HELLO, TOMMY.
OH, THANK GOD, ERIC. I THOUGHT MAYBE HE'D GOTTEN YOU.
JUST PROMISE ME YOU WON'T LEAVE...YOU WON'T GET HURT. I'VE LOST TOO MUCH IN THE LAST FIVE YEARS. I CAN'T LOSE ANOTHER BEST FRIEND.
PROMISE ME YOU'LL BE THERE, ERIC... PLEASE... PROMISE ME.

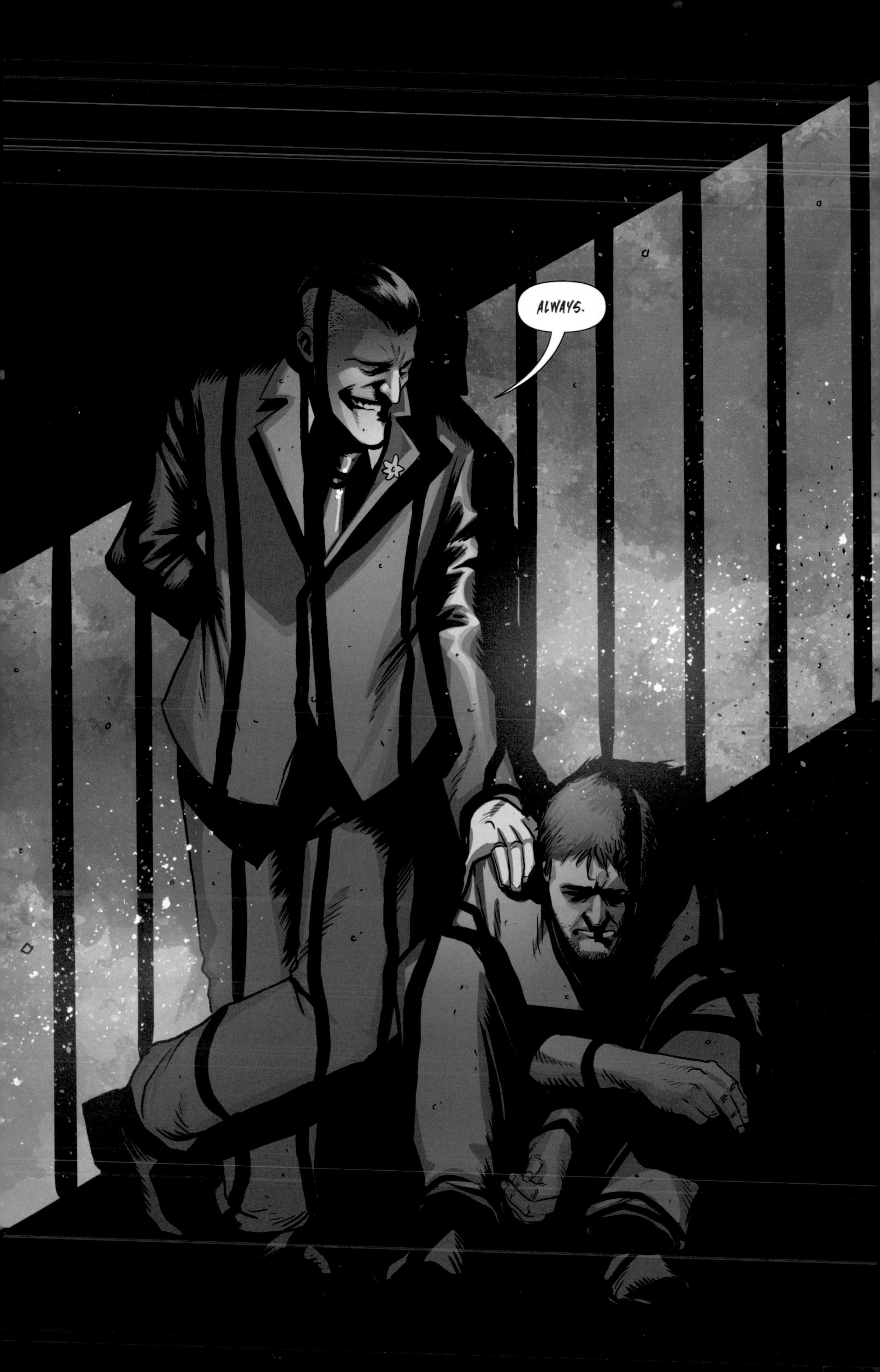
ALWAYS.

Cover by **GREG CAPULLO, DANNY MIKI** & **FCO PLASCENCIA**

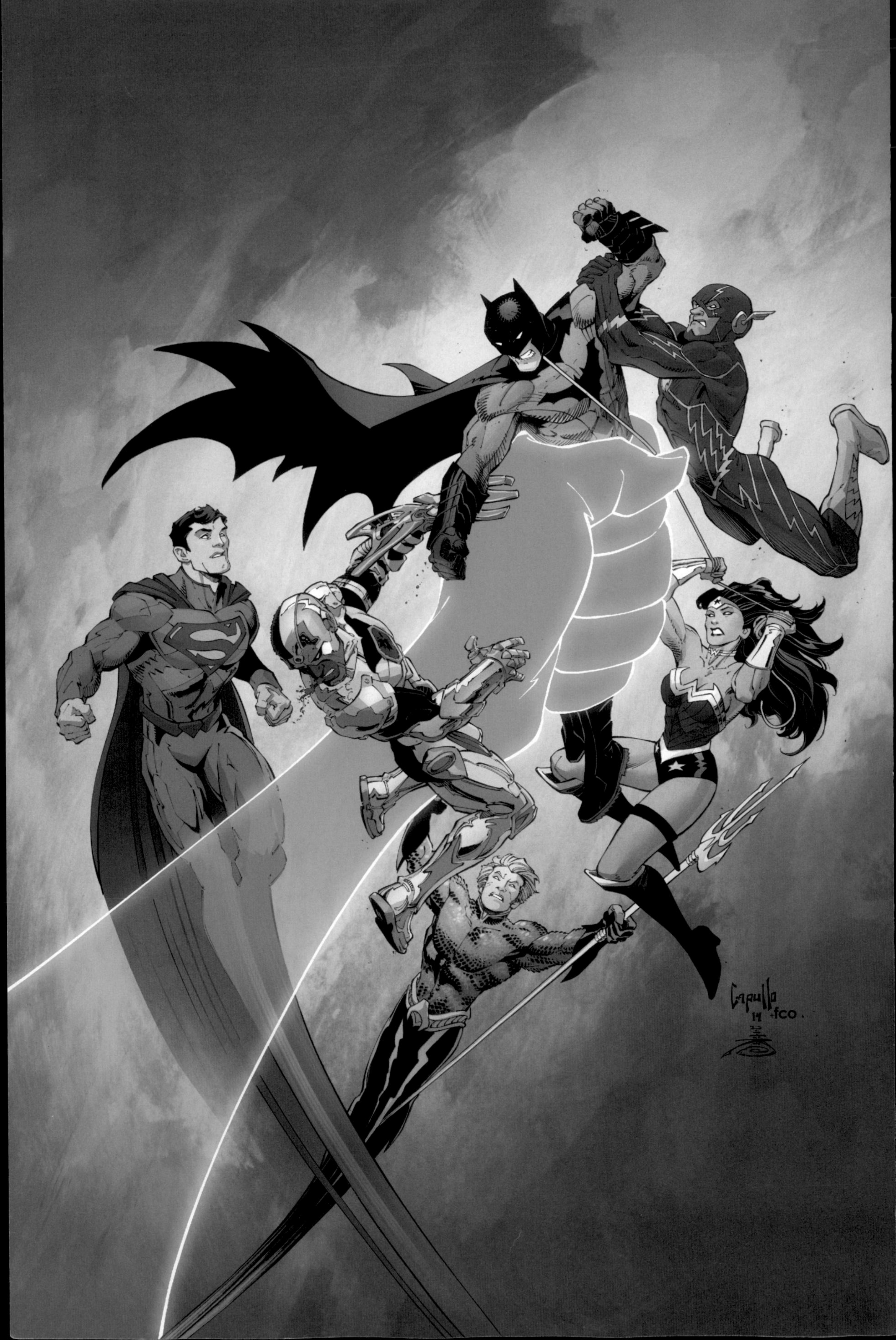

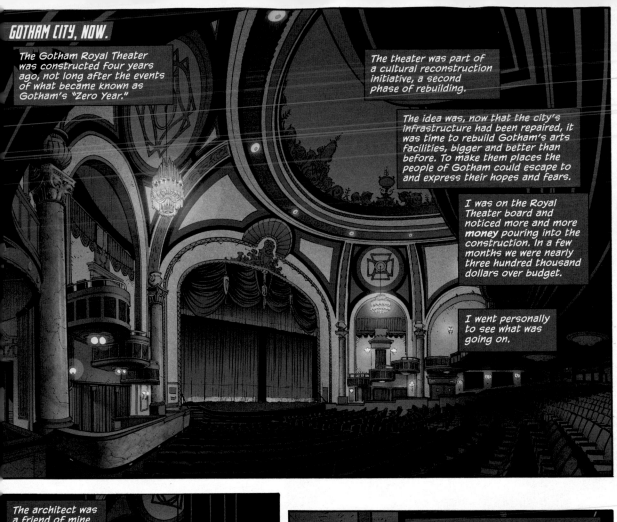

The Gotham Royal Theater was constructed four years ago, not long after the events of what became known as Gotham's "Zero Year."

The theater was part of a cultural reconstruction initiative, a second phase of rebuilding.

The idea was, now that the city's infrastructure had been repaired, it was time to rebuild Gotham's arts facilities, bigger and better than before. To make them places the people of Gotham could escape to and express their hopes and fears.

I was on the Royal Theater board and noticed more and more **money** pouring into the construction. In a few months we were nearly three hundred thousand dollars over budget.

I went personally to see what was going on.

The architect was a friend of mine named **Wade**. When I asked him about the money, he pointed up.

He'd constructed a special **harness** for the theater. They were doing Orestes, and, Wade explained, at the end of the play there was a "deus ex machina."

A moment when a god, Apollo, descends from the sky to save the characters from destruction.

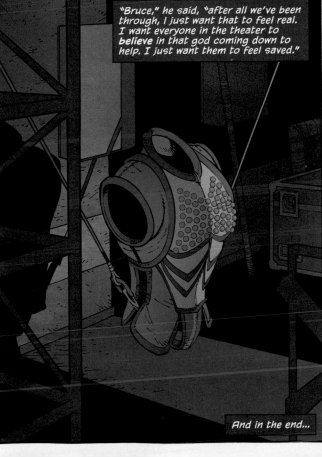

"Bruce," he said, "after all we've been through, I just want that to feel real. I want everyone in the theater to **believe** in that god coming down to help. I just want them to feel saved."

And in the end...

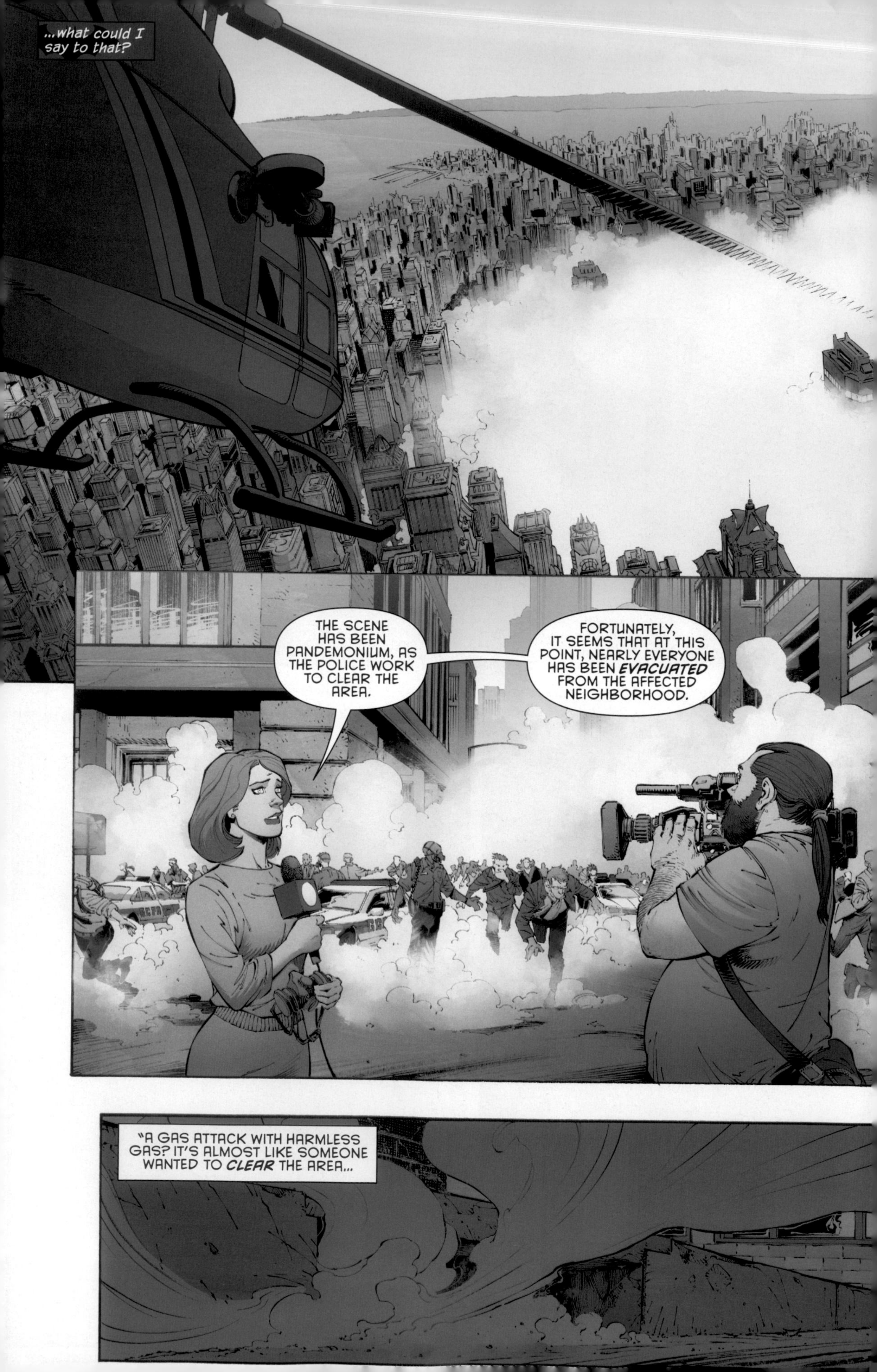
...what could I say to that?
THE SCENE HAS BEEN PANDEMONIUM, AS THE POLICE WORK TO CLEAR THE AREA.
FORTUNATELY, IT SEEMS THAT AT THIS POINT, NEARLY EVERYONE HAS BEEN EVACUATED FROM THE AFFECTED NEIGHBORHOOD.
"A GAS ATTACK WITH HARMLESS GAS? IT'S ALMOST LIKE SOMEONE WANTED TO CLEAR THE AREA...

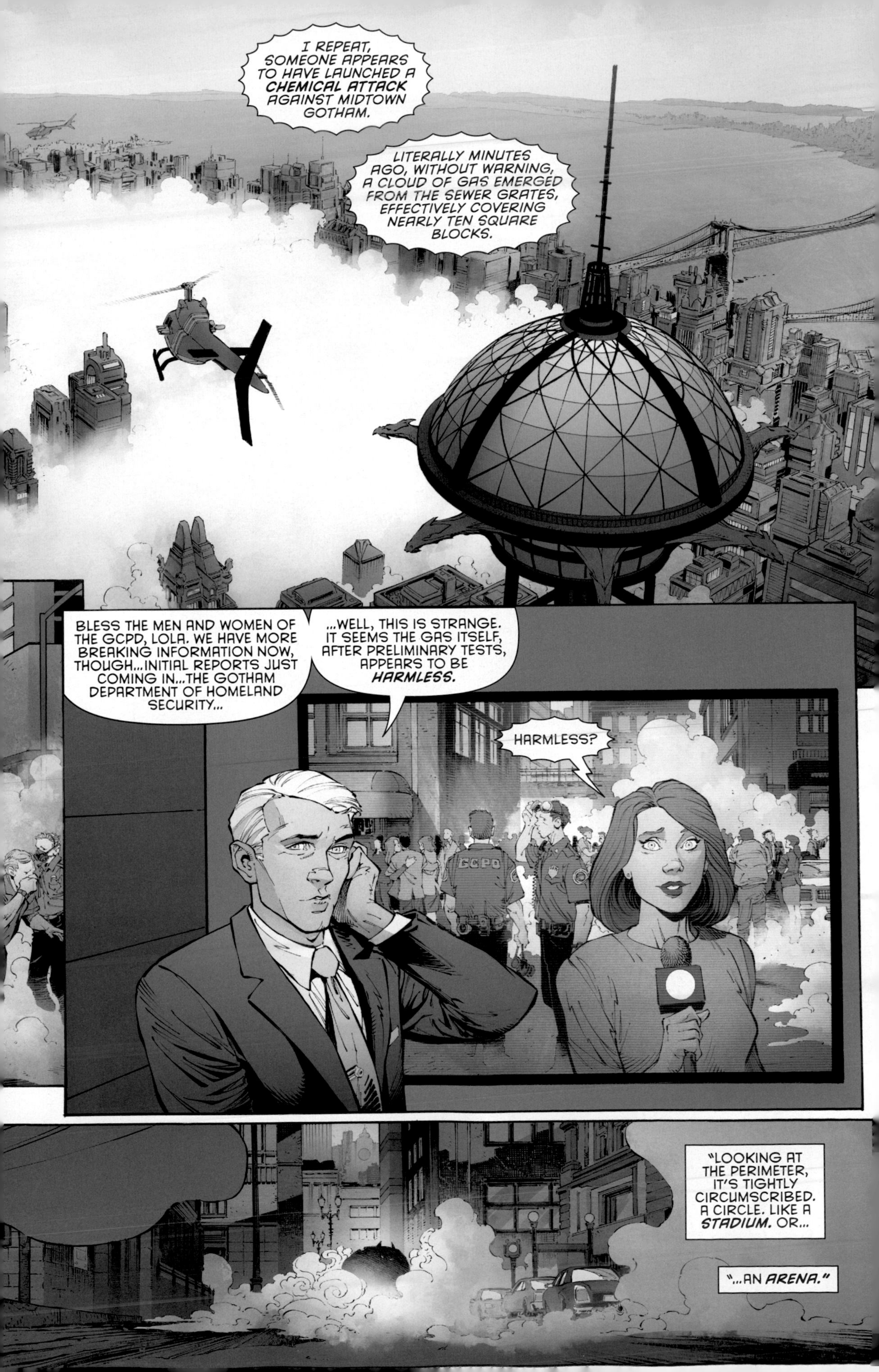
I REPEAT, SOMEONE APPEARS TO HAVE LAUNCHED A **CHEMICAL ATTACK** AGAINST MIDTOWN GOTHAM.
LITERALLY MINUTES AGO, WITHOUT WARNING, A CLOUD OF GAS EMERGED FROM THE SEWER GRATES, EFFECTIVELY COVERING NEARLY TEN SQUARE BLOCKS.
BLESS THE MEN AND WOMEN OF THE GCPD, LOLA. WE HAVE MORE BREAKING INFORMATION NOW, THOUGH...INITIAL REPORTS JUST COMING IN...THE GOTHAM DEPARTMENT OF HOMELAND SECURITY...
...WELL, THIS IS STRANGE. IT SEEMS THE GAS ITSELF, AFTER PRELIMINARY TESTS, APPEARS TO BE **HARMLESS.**
HARMLESS?
GCPD
"LOOKING AT THE PERIMETER, IT'S TIGHTLY CIRCUMSCRIBED. A CIRCLE. LIKE A **STADIUM.** OR...
"...AN **ARENA.**"

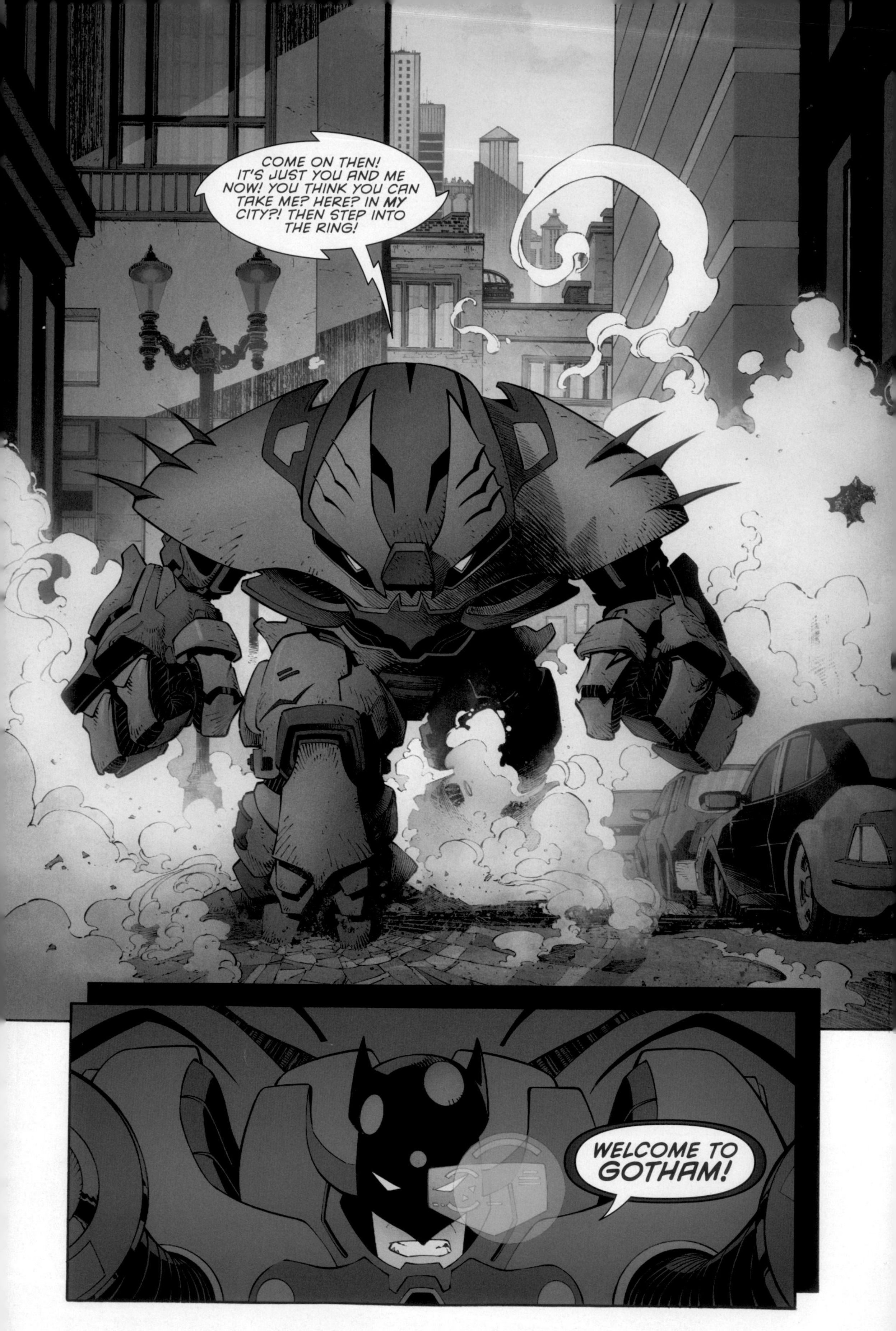
COME ON THEN! IT'S JUST YOU AND ME NOW! YOU THINK YOU CAN TAKE ME? HERE? IN MY CITY?! THEN STEP INTO THE RING!
WELCOME TO GOTHAM!

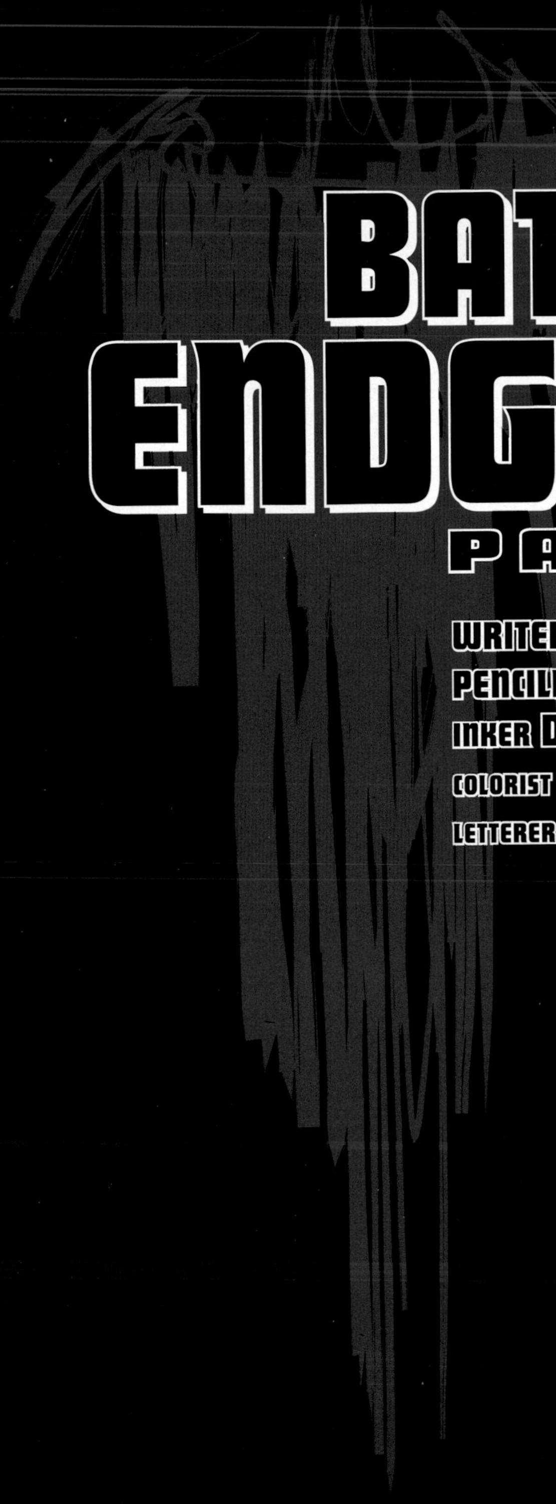

BATMAN: ENDGAME

PART ONE

WRITER SCOTT SNYDER
PENCILLER GREG CAPULLO
INKER DANNY MIKI
COLORIST FCO PLASCENCIA
LETTERER STEVE WANDS

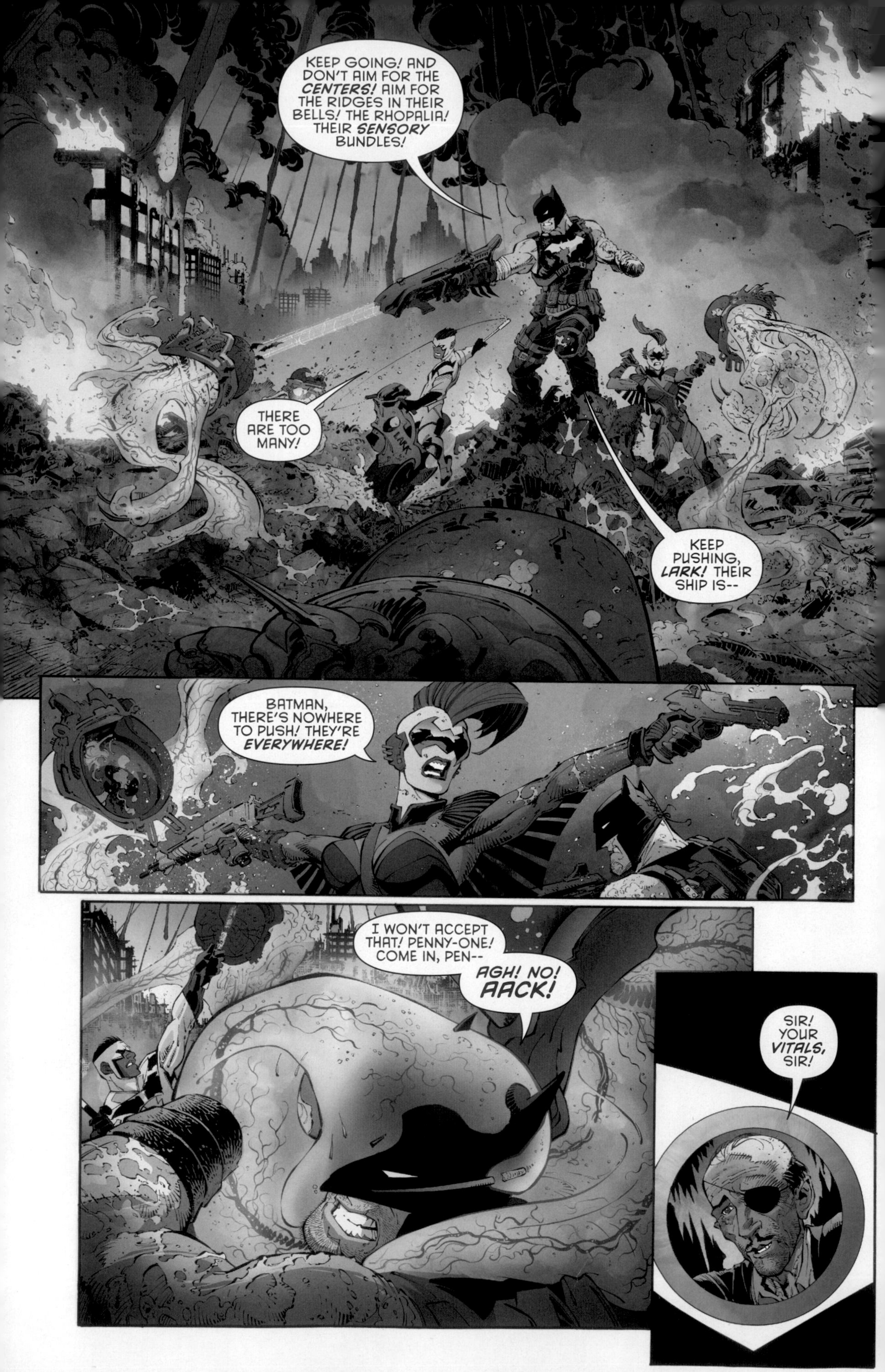
KEEP GOING! AND DON'T AIM FOR THE CENTERS! AIM FOR THE RIDGES IN THEIR BELLS! THE RHOPALIA! THEIR SENSORY BUNDLES!
THERE ARE TOO MANY!
KEEP PUSHING, LARK! THEIR SHIP IS--
BATMAN, THERE'S NOWHERE TO PUSH! THEY'RE EVERYWHERE!
I WON'T ACCEPT THAT! PENNY-ONE! COME IN, PEN--
AGH! NO! AACK!
SIR! YOUR VITALS, SIR!

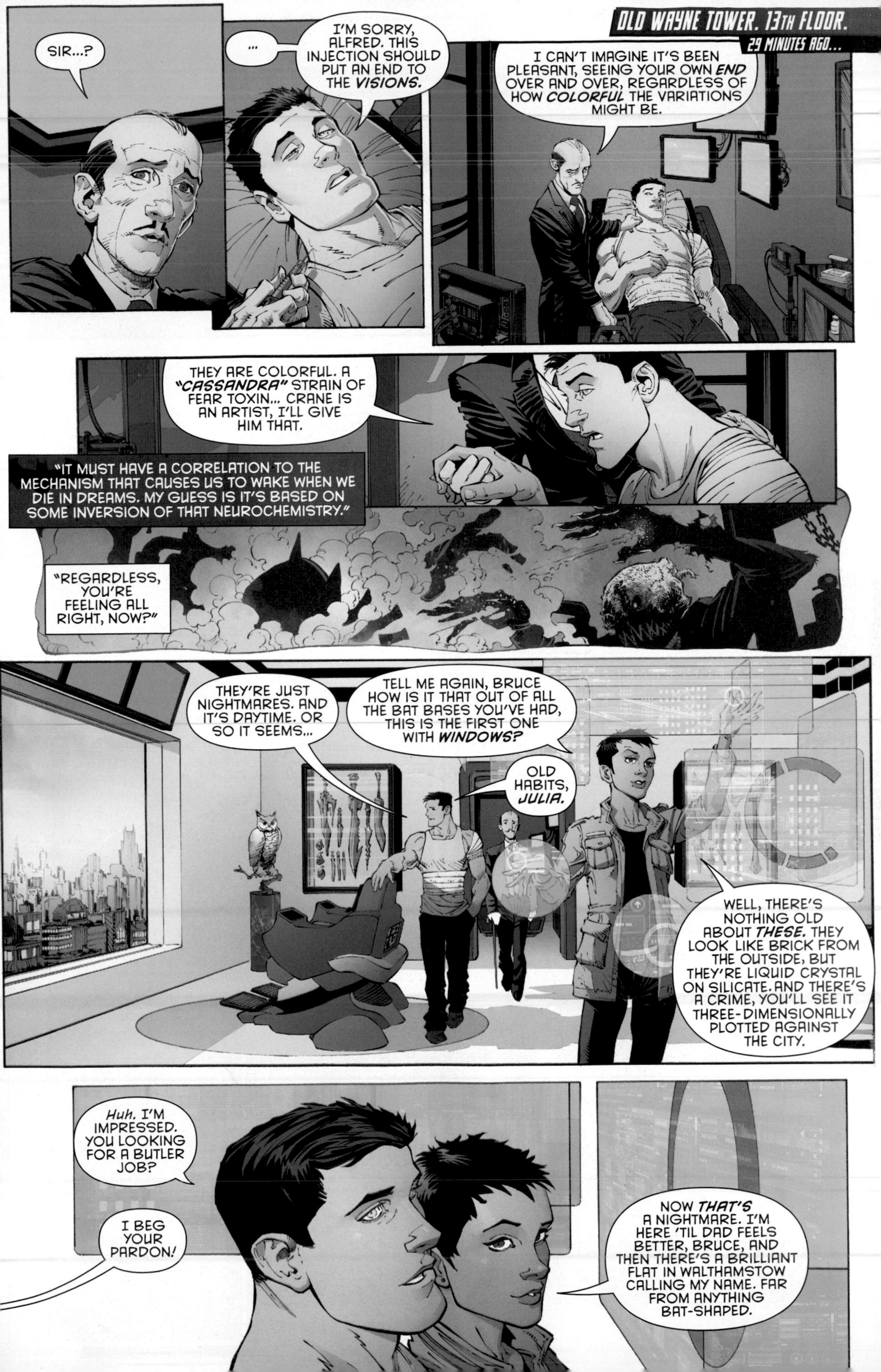
OLD WAYNE TOWER. 13TH FLOOR.
29 MINUTES AGO...
SIR...?
...
I'M SORRY, ALFRED. THIS INJECTION SHOULD PUT AN END TO THE *VISIONS.*
I CAN'T IMAGINE IT'S BEEN PLEASANT, SEEING YOUR OWN *END* OVER AND OVER, REGARDLESS OF HOW *COLORFUL* THE VARIATIONS MIGHT BE.
THEY ARE COLORFUL. A *"CASSANDRA"* STRAIN OF FEAR TOXIN... CRANE IS AN ARTIST, I'LL GIVE HIM THAT.
"IT MUST HAVE A CORRELATION TO THE MECHANISM THAT CAUSES US TO WAKE WHEN WE DIE IN DREAMS. MY GUESS IS IT'S BASED ON SOME INVERSION OF THAT NEUROCHEMISTRY."
"REGARDLESS, YOU'RE FEELING ALL RIGHT, NOW?"
THEY'RE JUST NIGHTMARES. AND IT'S DAYTIME. OR SO IT SEEMS...
TELL ME AGAIN, BRUCE HOW IS IT THAT OUT OF ALL THE BAT BASES YOU'VE HAD, THIS IS THE FIRST ONE WITH *WINDOWS?*
OLD HABITS, *JULIA.*
WELL, THERE'S NOTHING OLD ABOUT *THESE.* THEY LOOK LIKE BRICK FROM THE OUTSIDE, BUT THEY'RE LIQUID CRYSTAL ON SILICATE. AND THERE'S A CRIME, YOU'LL SEE IT THREE-DIMENSIONALLY PLOTTED AGAINST THE CITY.
Huh. I'M IMPRESSED. YOU LOOKING FOR A BUTLER JOB?
I BEG YOUR PARDON!
NOW *THAT'S* A NIGHTMARE. I'M HERE 'TIL DAD FEELS BETTER, BRUCE, AND THEN THERE'S A BRILLIANT FLAT IN WALTHAMSTOW CALLING MY NAME. FAR FROM ANYTHING BAT-SHAPED.

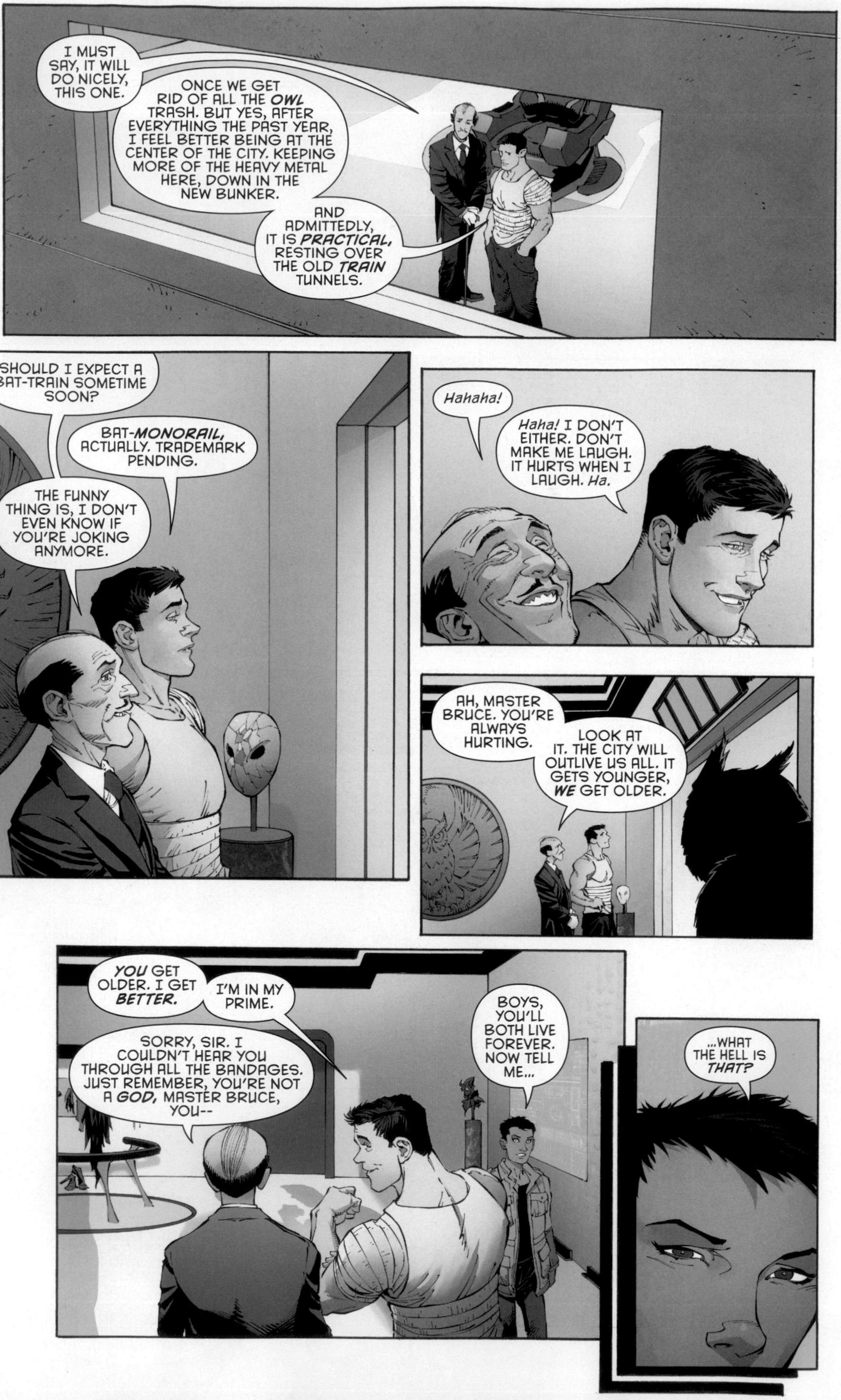
I MUST SAY, IT WILL DO NICELY, THIS ONE.
ONCE WE GET RID OF ALL THE OWL TRASH. BUT YES, AFTER EVERYTHING THE PAST YEAR, I FEEL BETTER BEING AT THE CENTER OF THE CITY. KEEPING MORE OF THE HEAVY METAL HERE, DOWN IN THE NEW BUNKER.
AND ADMITTEDLY, IT IS PRACTICAL, RESTING OVER THE OLD TRAIN TUNNELS.
SHOULD I EXPECT A BAT-TRAIN SOMETIME SOON?
BAT-MONORAIL, ACTUALLY. TRADEMARK PENDING.
THE FUNNY THING IS, I DON'T EVEN KNOW IF YOU'RE JOKING ANYMORE.
Hahaha!
Haha! I DON'T EITHER. DON'T MAKE ME LAUGH. IT HURTS WHEN I LAUGH. Ha.
AH, MASTER BRUCE. YOU'RE ALWAYS HURTING.
LOOK AT IT. THE CITY WILL OUTLIVE US ALL. IT GETS YOUNGER, WE GET OLDER.
YOU GET OLDER. I GET BETTER.
I'M IN MY PRIME.
SORRY, SIR. I COULDN'T HEAR YOU THROUGH ALL THE BANDAGES. JUST REMEMBER, YOU'RE NOT A GOD, MASTER BRUCE, YOU--
BOYS, YOU'LL BOTH LIVE FOREVER. NOW TELL ME...
...WHAT THE HELL IS THAT?

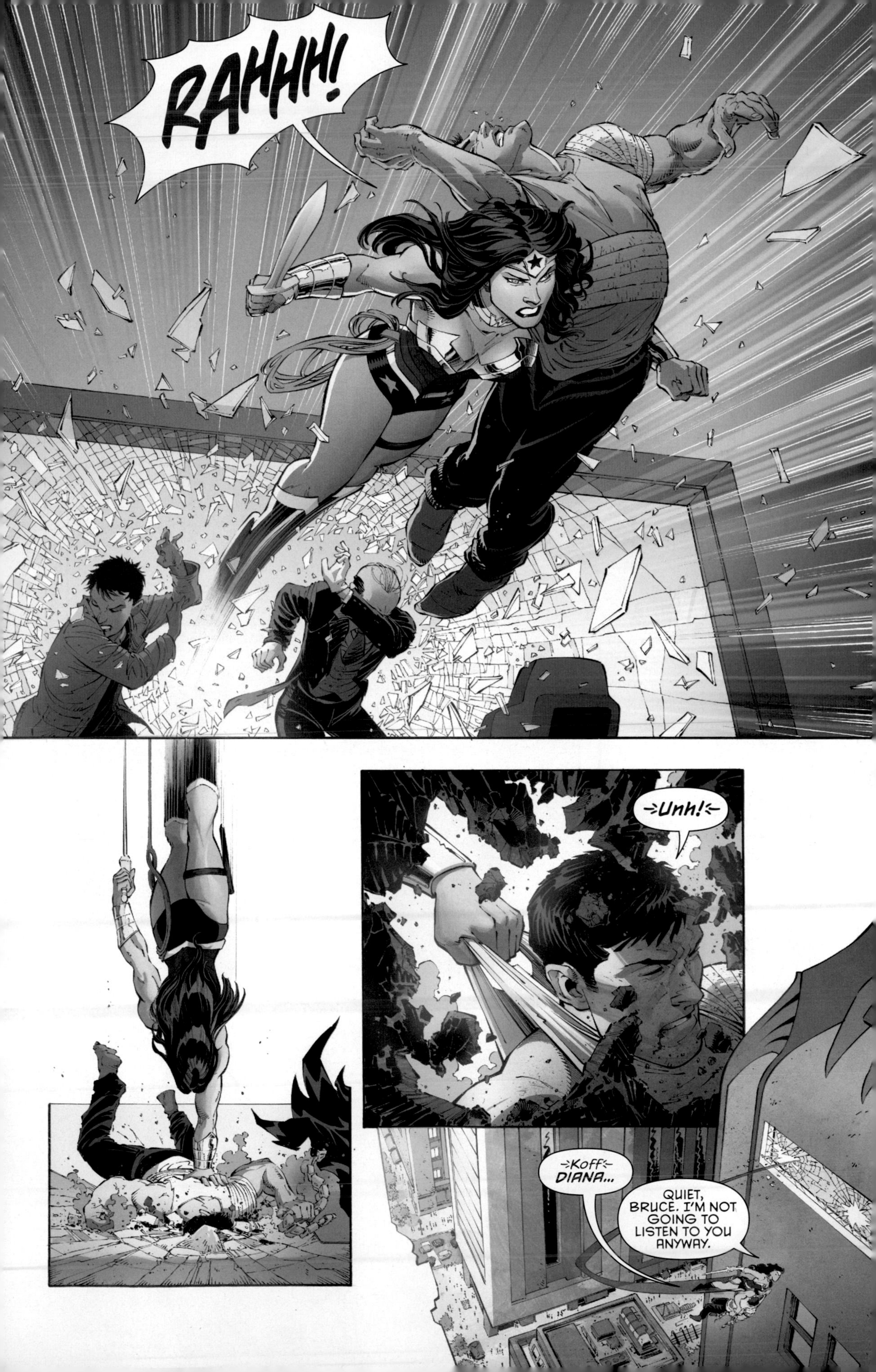
RAHHH!
Unh!
Koff
DIANA...
QUIET, BRUCE. I'M NOT GOING TO LISTEN TO YOU ANYWAY.

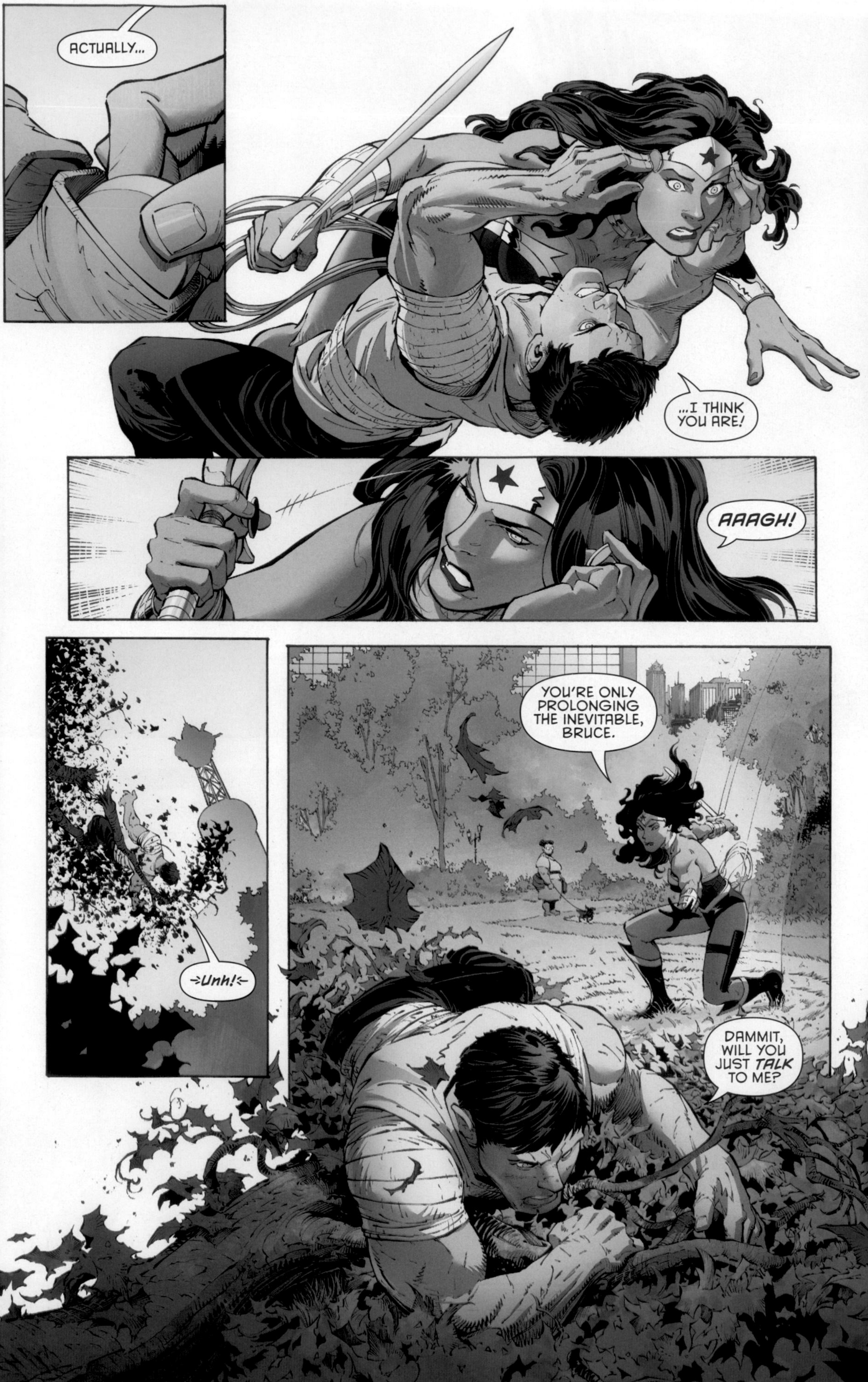
ACTUALLY...
...I THINK YOU ARE!
AAAGH!
~Unh!~
YOU'RE ONLY PROLONGING THE INEVITABLE, BRUCE.
DAMMIT, WILL YOU JUST TALK TO ME?

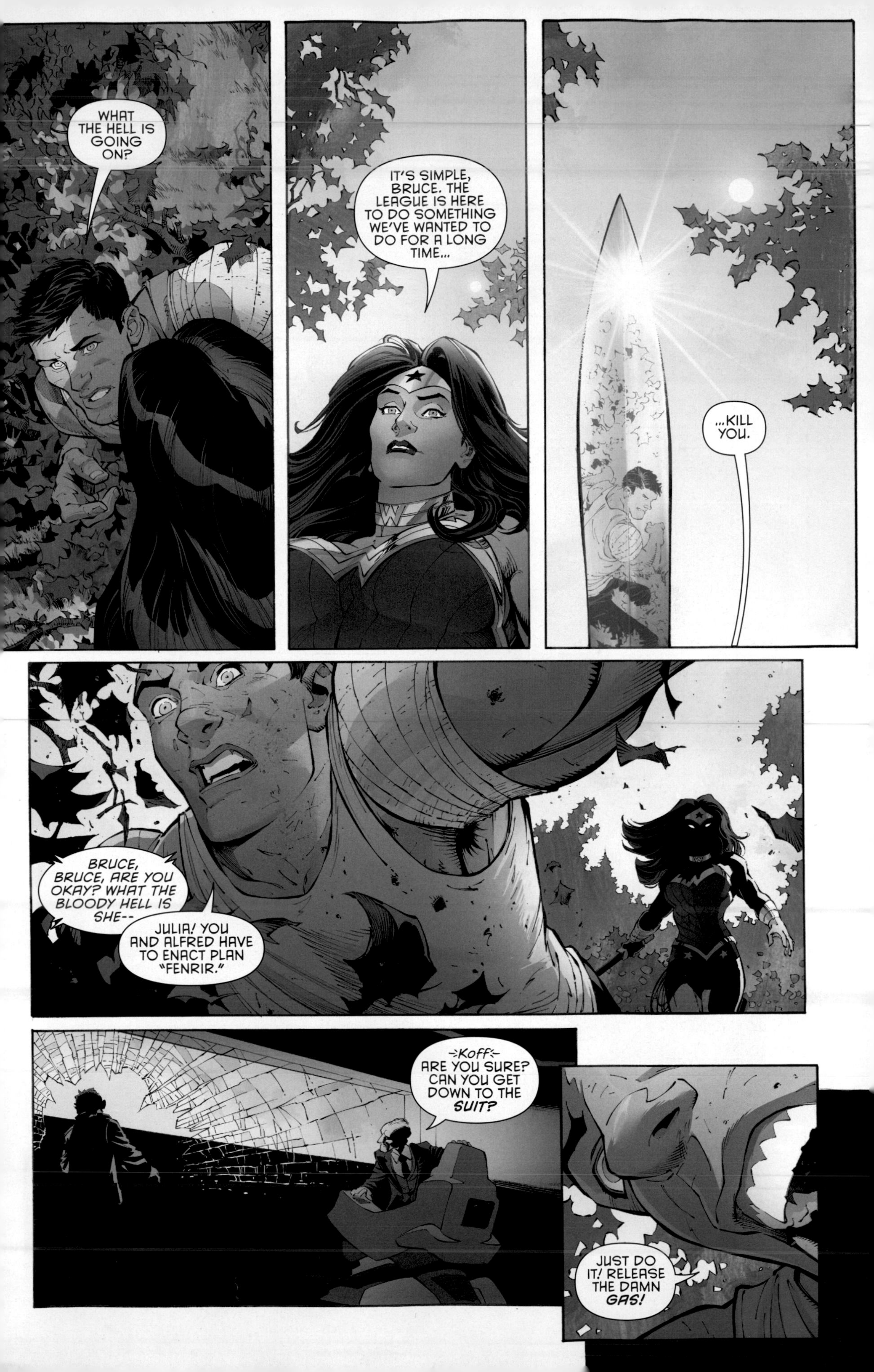
WHAT THE HELL IS GOING ON?
IT'S SIMPLE, BRUCE. THE LEAGUE IS HERE TO DO SOMETHING WE'VE WANTED TO DO FOR A LONG TIME...
...KILL YOU.
BRUCE, BRUCE, ARE YOU OKAY? WHAT THE BLOODY HELL IS SHE--
JULIA! YOU AND ALFRED HAVE TO ENACT PLAN "FENRIR."
-KOFF- ARE YOU SURE? CAN YOU GET DOWN TO THE SUIT?
JUST DO IT! RELEASE THE DAMN GAS!

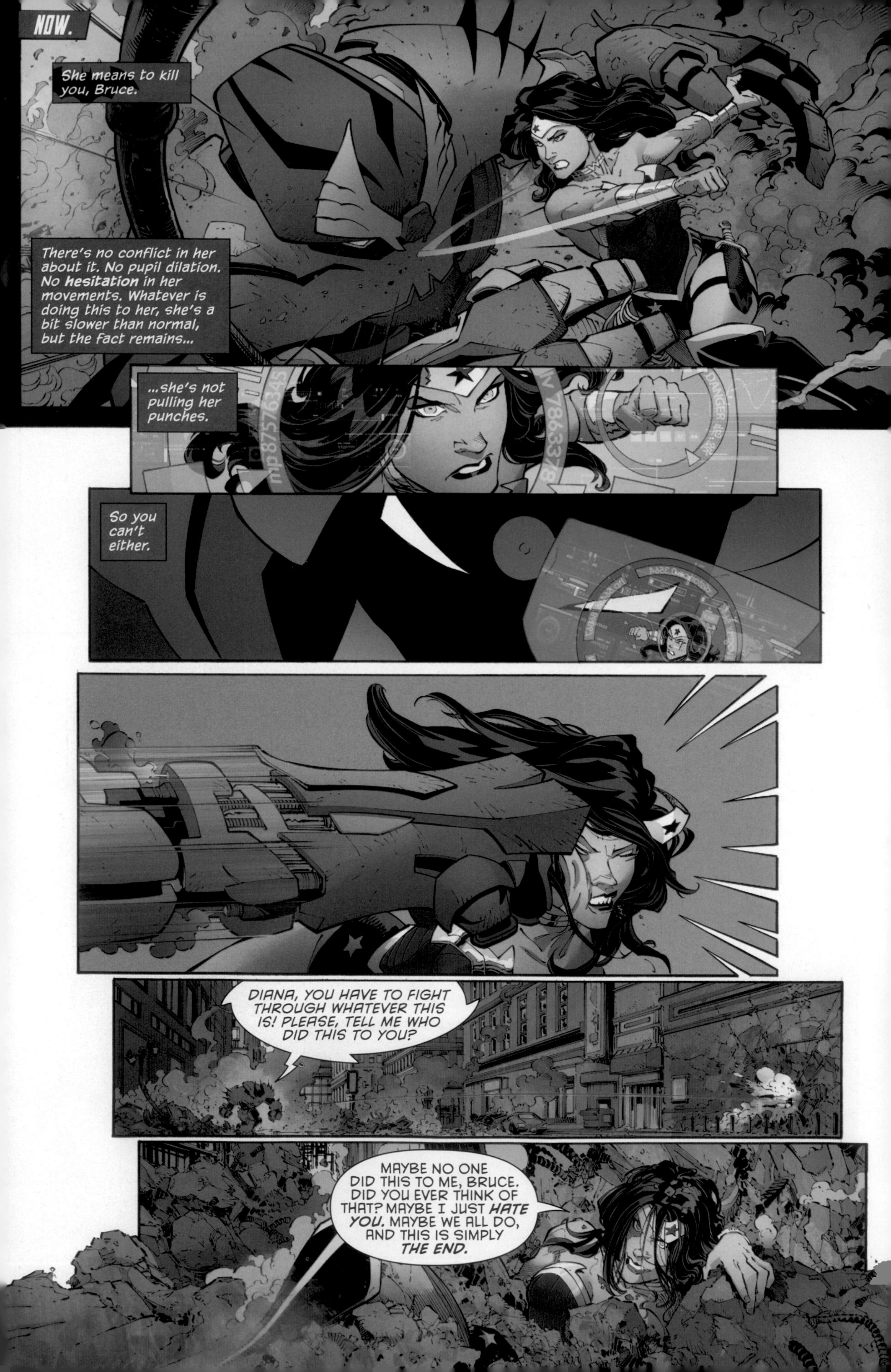
NOW.
She means to kill you, Bruce.
There's no conflict in her about it. No pupil dilation. No **hesitation** in her movements. Whatever is doing this to her, she's a bit slower than normal, but the fact remains...
...she's not pulling her punches.
So you can't either.
DIANA, YOU HAVE TO FIGHT THROUGH WHATEVER THIS IS! PLEASE, TELL ME WHO DID THIS TO YOU?
MAYBE NO ONE DID THIS TO ME, BRUCE. DID YOU EVER THINK OF THAT? MAYBE I JUST *HATE YOU.* MAYBE WE ALL DO, AND THIS IS SIMPLY ***THE END.***

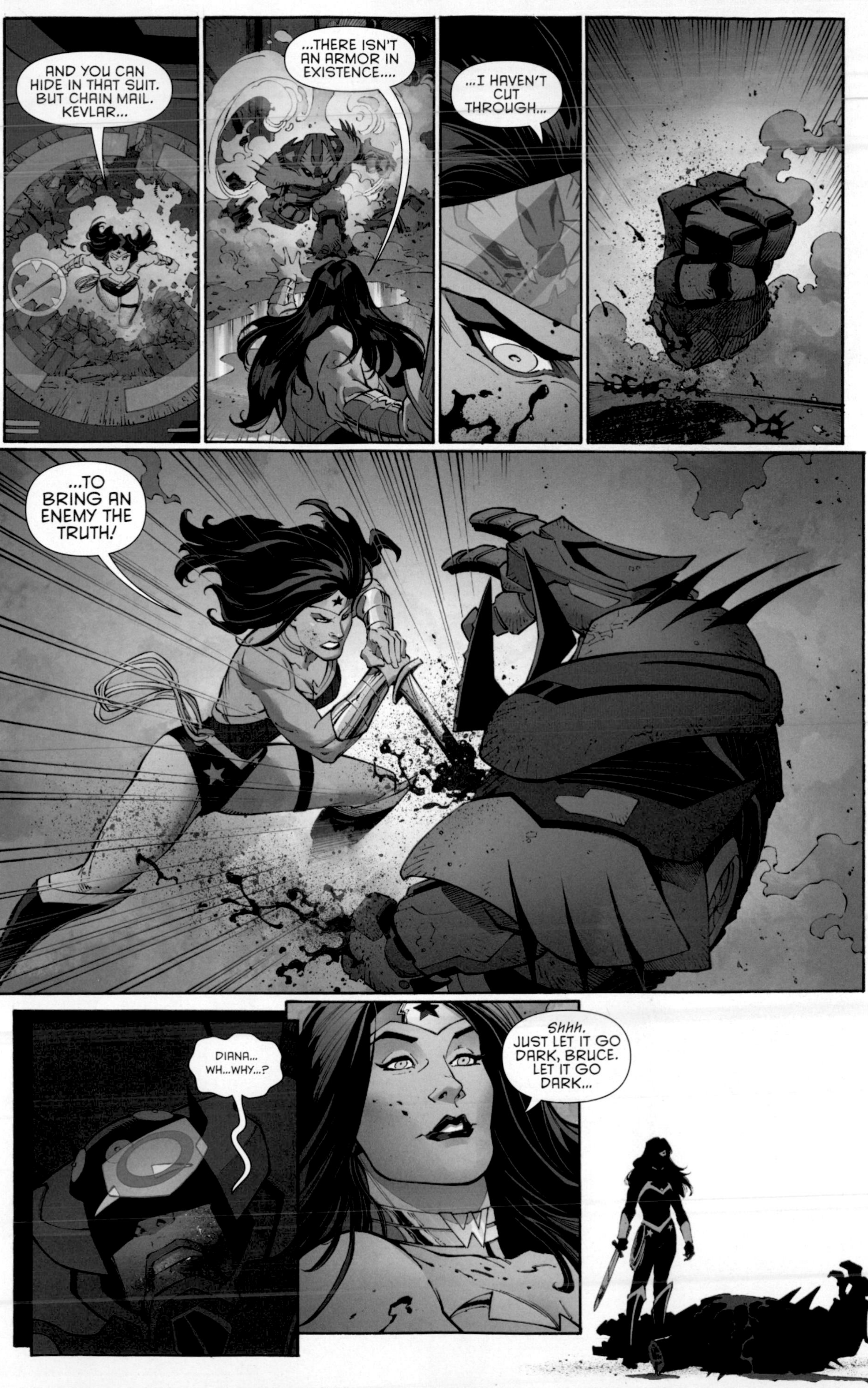
AND YOU CAN HIDE IN THAT SUIT. BUT CHAIN MAIL. KEVLAR...
...THERE ISN'T AN ARMOR IN EXISTENCE....
...I HAVEN'T CUT THROUGH...
...TO BRING AN ENEMY THE TRUTH!
DIANA... WH...WHY...?
Shhh. JUST LET IT GO DARK, BRUCE. LET IT GO DARK...

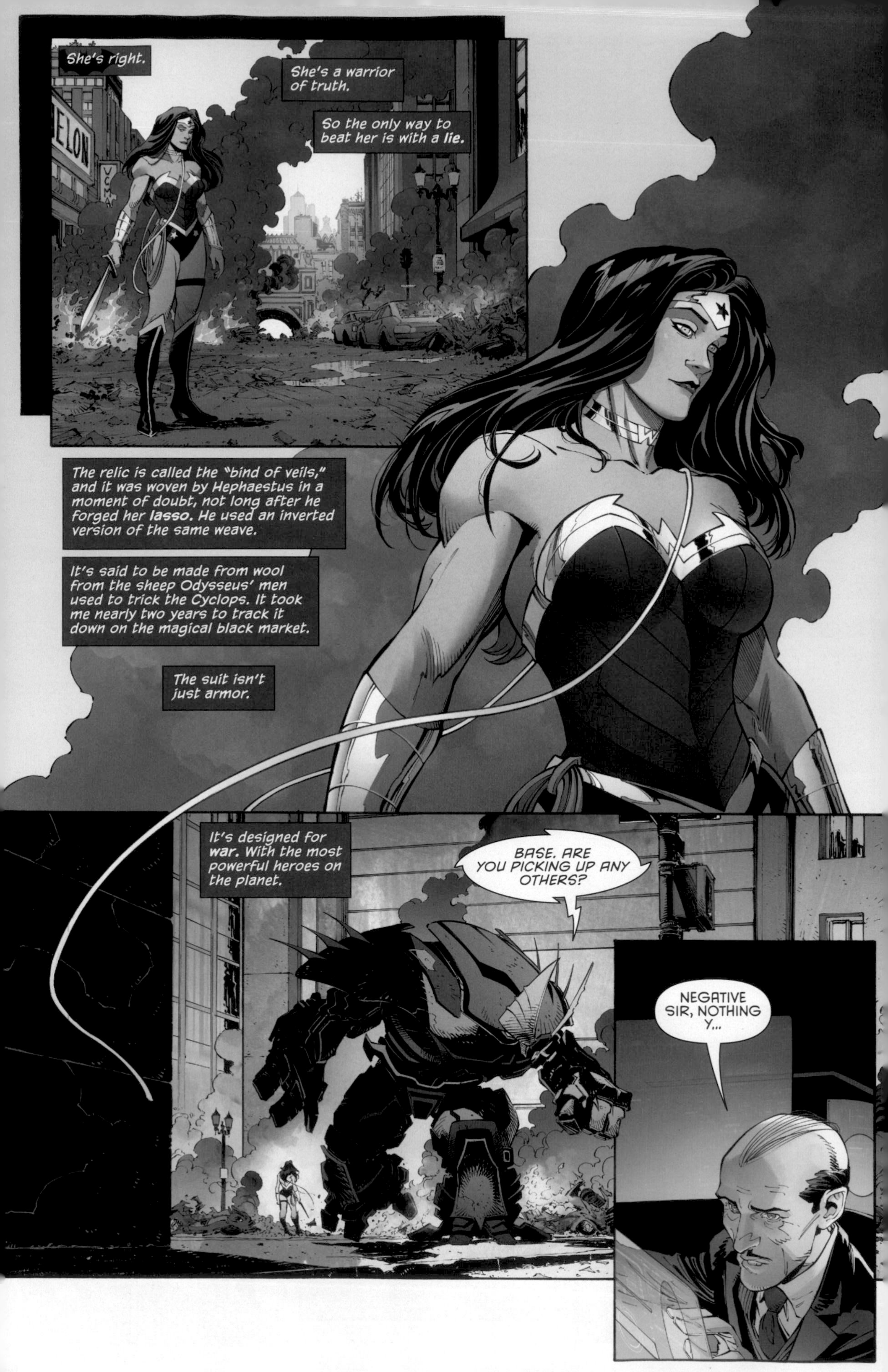
She's right.
She's a warrior of truth.
So the only way to beat her is with a **lie.**
The relic is called the "bind of veils," and it was woven by Hephaestus in a moment of doubt, not long after he forged her **lasso.** He used an inverted version of the same weave.
It's said to be made from wool from the sheep Odysseus' men used to trick the Cyclops. It took me nearly two years to track it down on the magical black market.
The suit isn't just armor.
It's designed for **war.** With the most powerful heroes on the planet.
BASE. ARE YOU PICKING UP ANY OTHERS?
NEGATIVE SIR, NOTHING Y...

"...YYYYYEEEEEE...

"...EEEEEE..."

"...EEEEEETTTTTTTTTT."

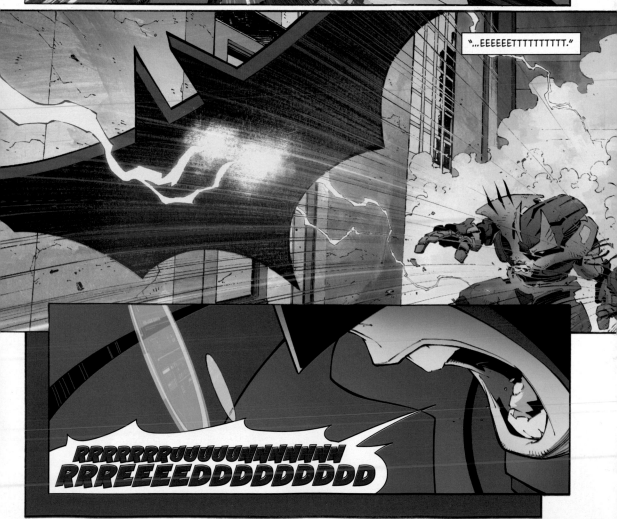

RRRRRRRUUUUUNNNNNNN
RRREEEEEDDDDDDDDD

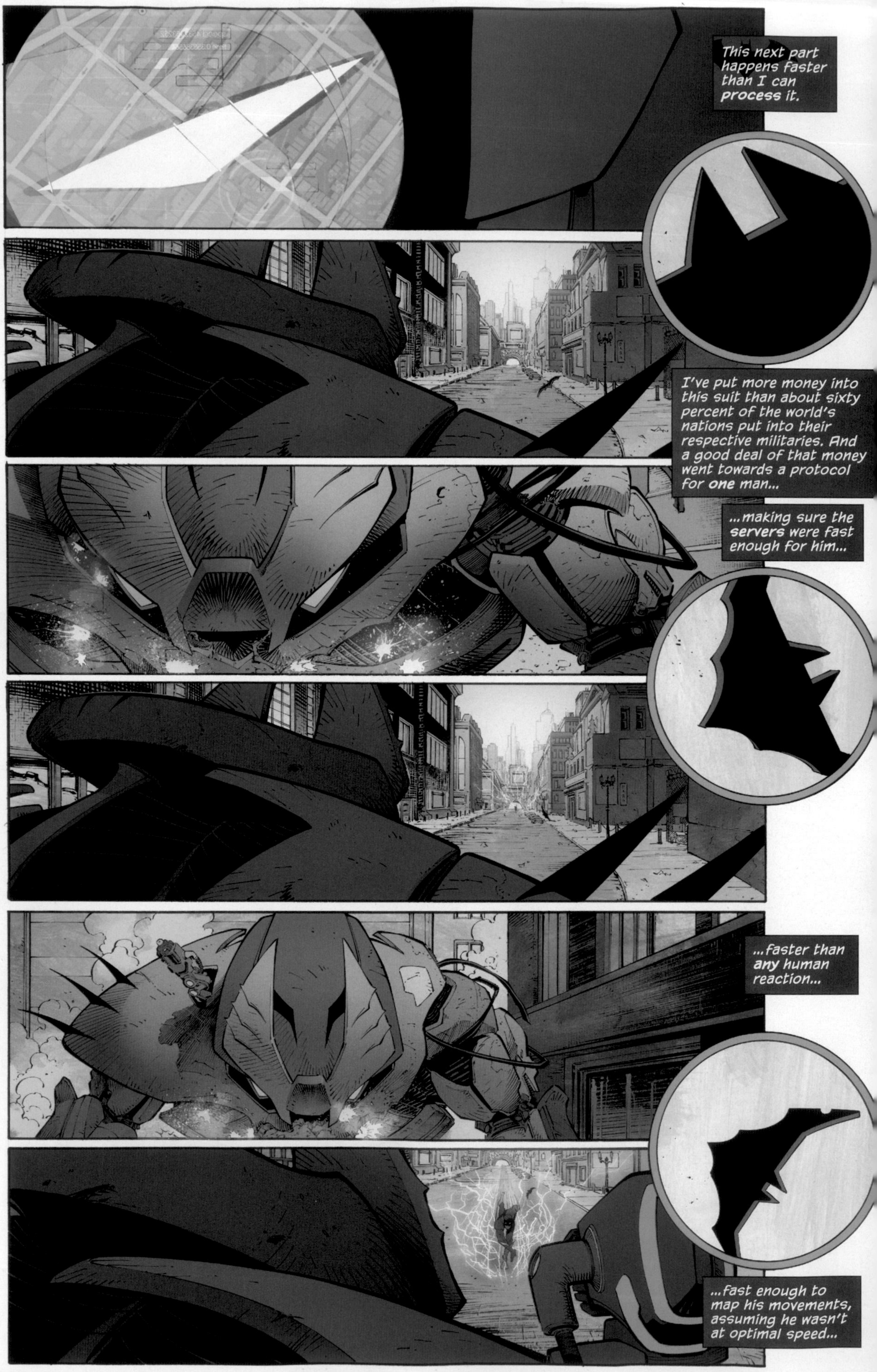
This next part happens faster than I can **process** it.
I've put more money into this suit than about sixty percent of the world's nations put into their respective militaries. And a good deal of that money went towards a protocol for **one** man...
...making sure the **servers** were fast enough for him...
...faster than **any** human reaction...
...fast enough to map his movements, assuming he wasn't at optimal speed...

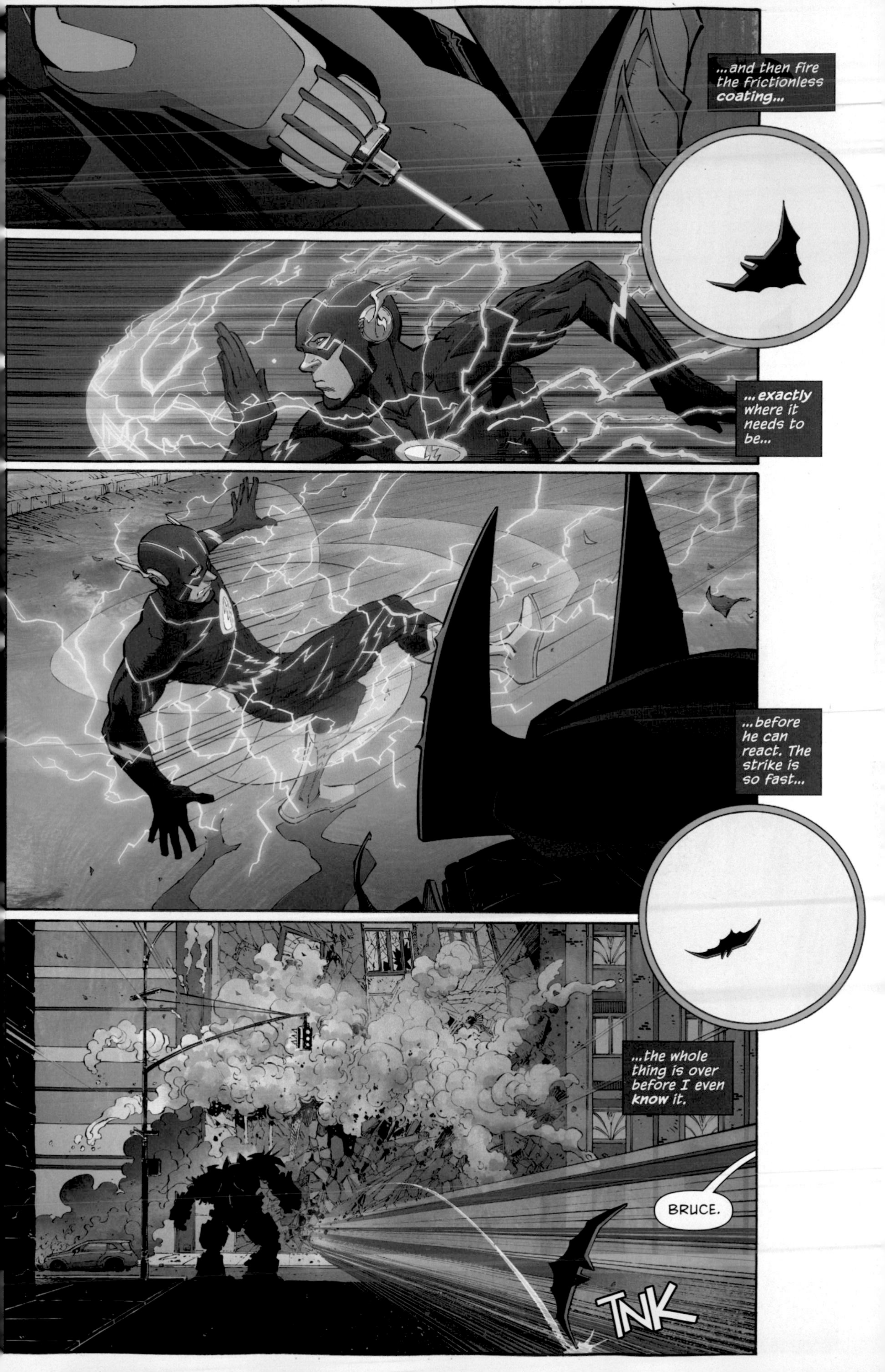
...and then fire the frictionless coating...
...exactly where it needs to be...
...before he can react. The strike is so fast...
...the whole thing is over before I even know it.
BRUCE.
TNK

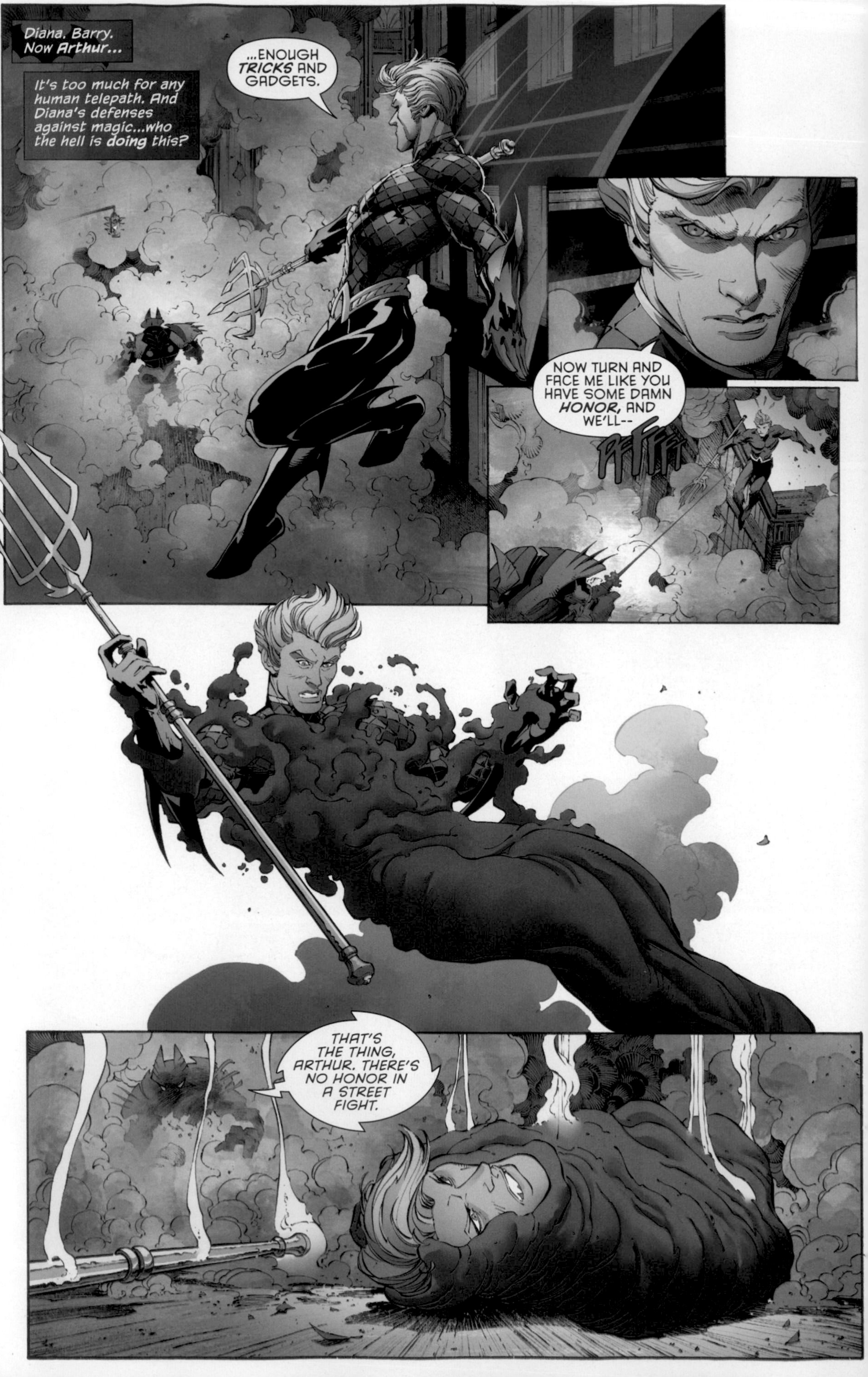
Diana. Barry. Now Arthur...
It's too much for any human telepath. And Diana's defenses against magic...who the hell is doing this?
...ENOUGH TRICKS AND GADGETS.
NOW TURN AND FACE ME LIKE YOU HAVE SOME DAMN HONOR, AND WE'LL--
THAT'S THE THING, ARTHUR. THERE'S NO HONOR IN A STREET FIGHT.

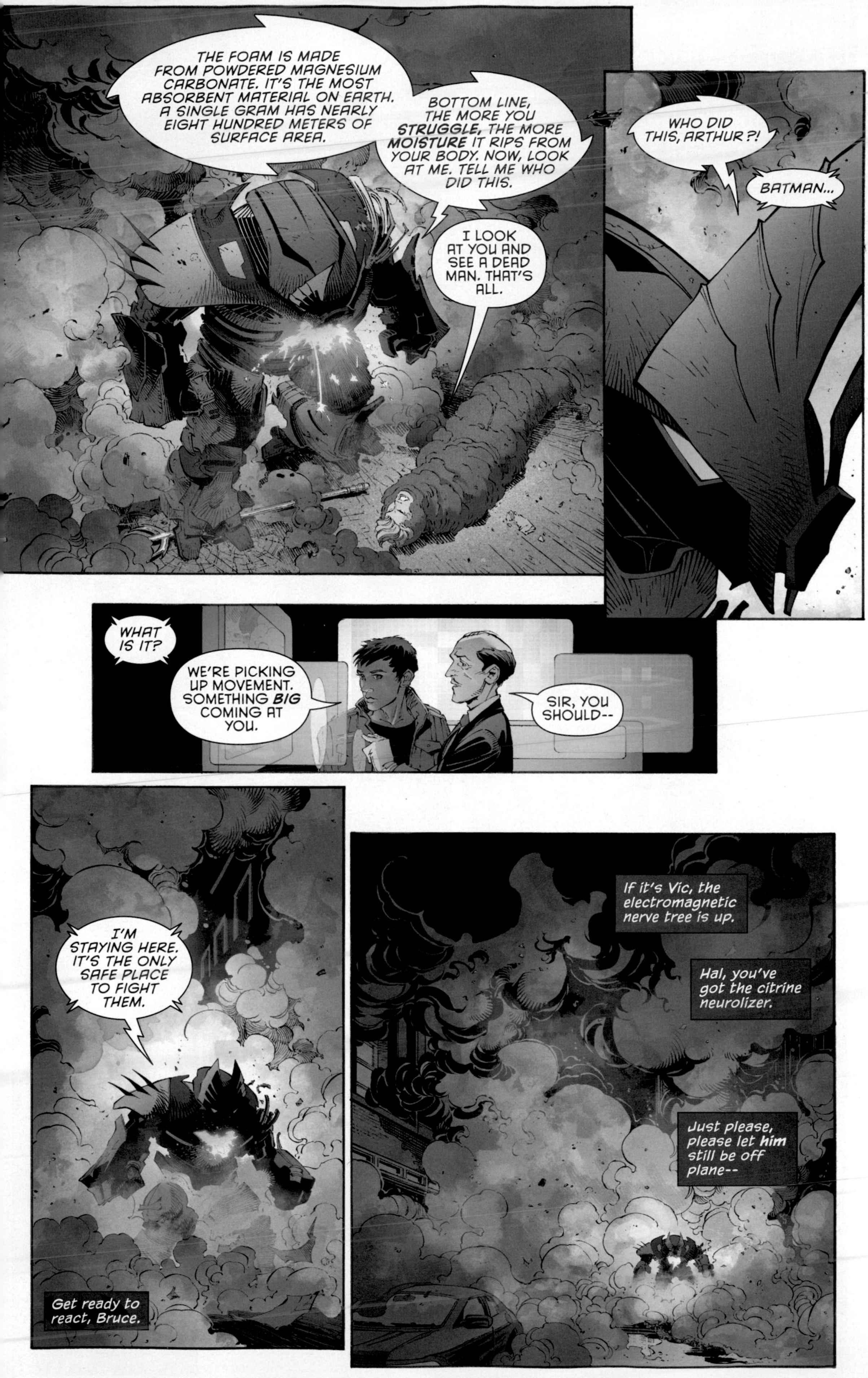
THE FOAM IS MADE FROM POWDERED MAGNESIUM CARBONATE. IT'S THE MOST ABSORBENT MATERIAL ON EARTH. A SINGLE GRAM HAS NEARLY EIGHT HUNDRED METERS OF SURFACE AREA.
BOTTOM LINE, THE MORE YOU STRUGGLE, THE MORE MOISTURE IT RIPS FROM YOUR BODY. NOW, LOOK AT ME. TELL ME WHO DID THIS.
I LOOK AT YOU AND SEE A DEAD MAN. THAT'S ALL.
WHO DID THIS, ARTHUR?!
BATMAN...
WHAT IS IT?
WE'RE PICKING UP MOVEMENT. SOMETHING BIG COMING AT YOU.
SIR, YOU SHOULD--
I'M STAYING HERE. IT'S THE ONLY SAFE PLACE TO FIGHT THEM.
Get ready to react, Bruce.
If it's Vic, the electromagnetic nerve tree is up.
Hal, you've got the citrine neurolizer.
Just please, please let him still be off plane--

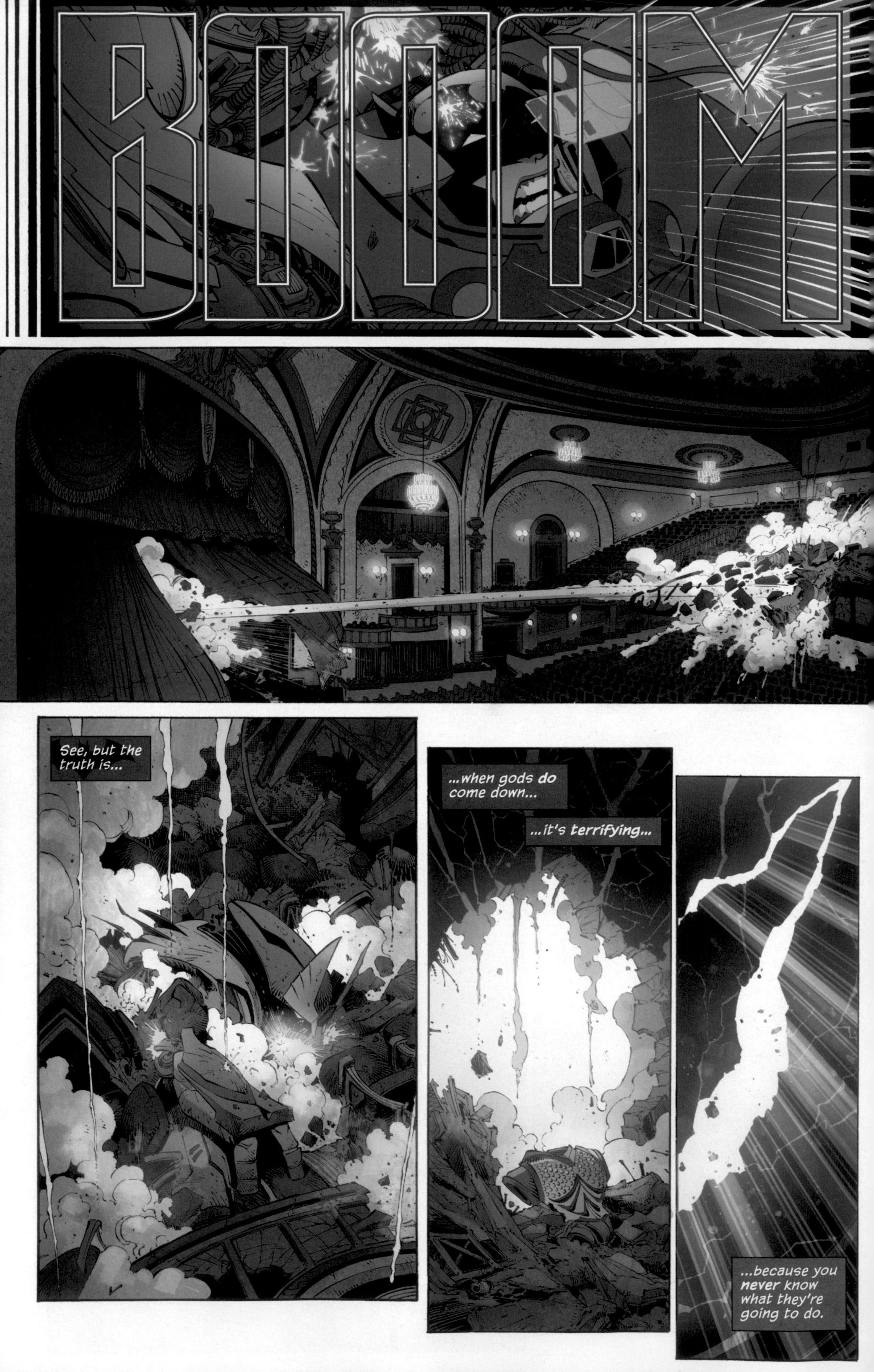
BOOOM
See, but the truth is...
...when gods do come down...
...it's terrifying...
...because you never know what they're going to do.

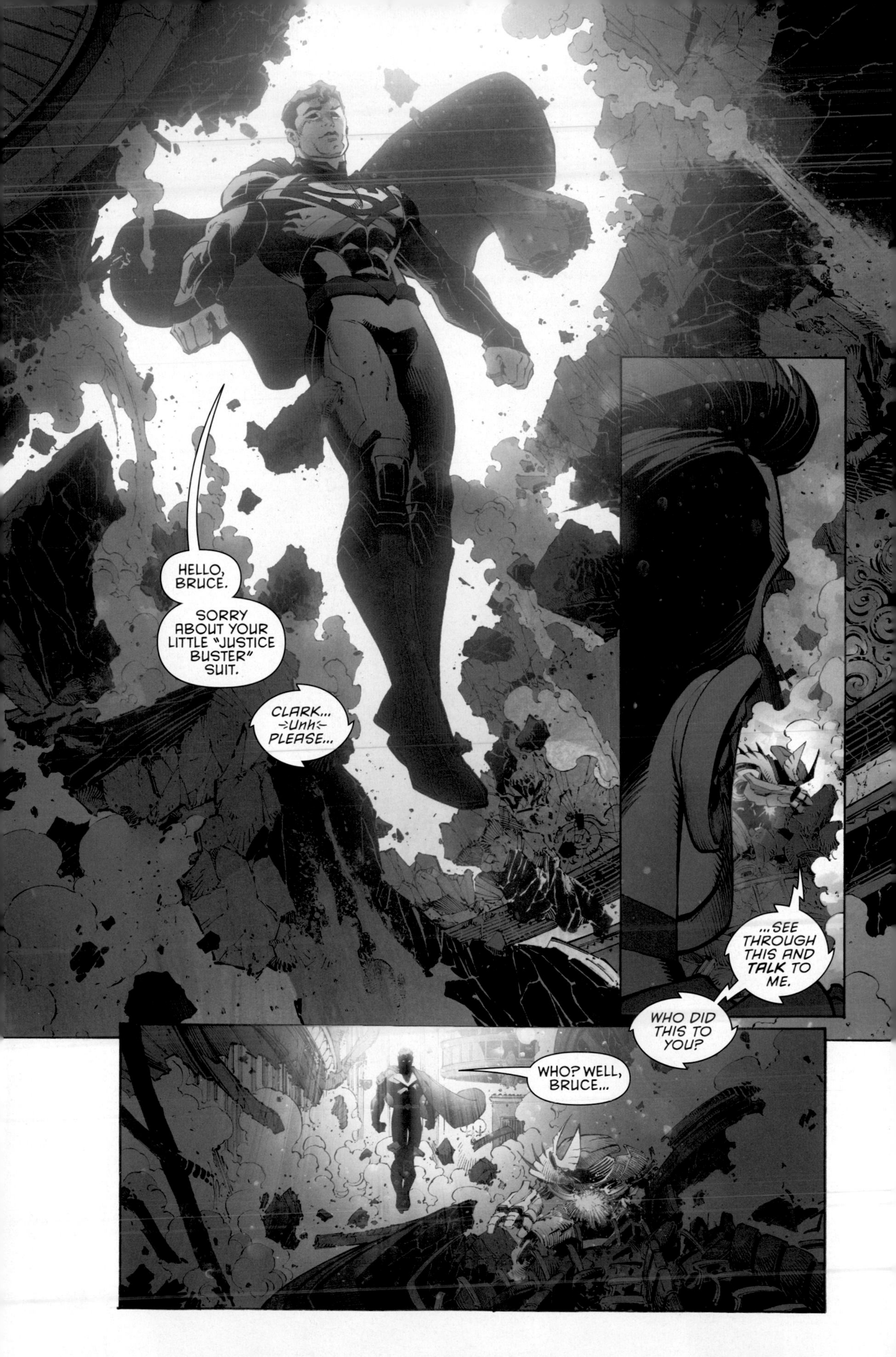
HELLO, BRUCE.
SORRY ABOUT YOUR LITTLE "JUSTICE BUSTER" SUIT.
CLARK... Unh PLEASE...
...SEE THROUGH THIS AND TALK TO ME.
WHO DID THIS TO YOU?
WHO? WELL, BRUCE...

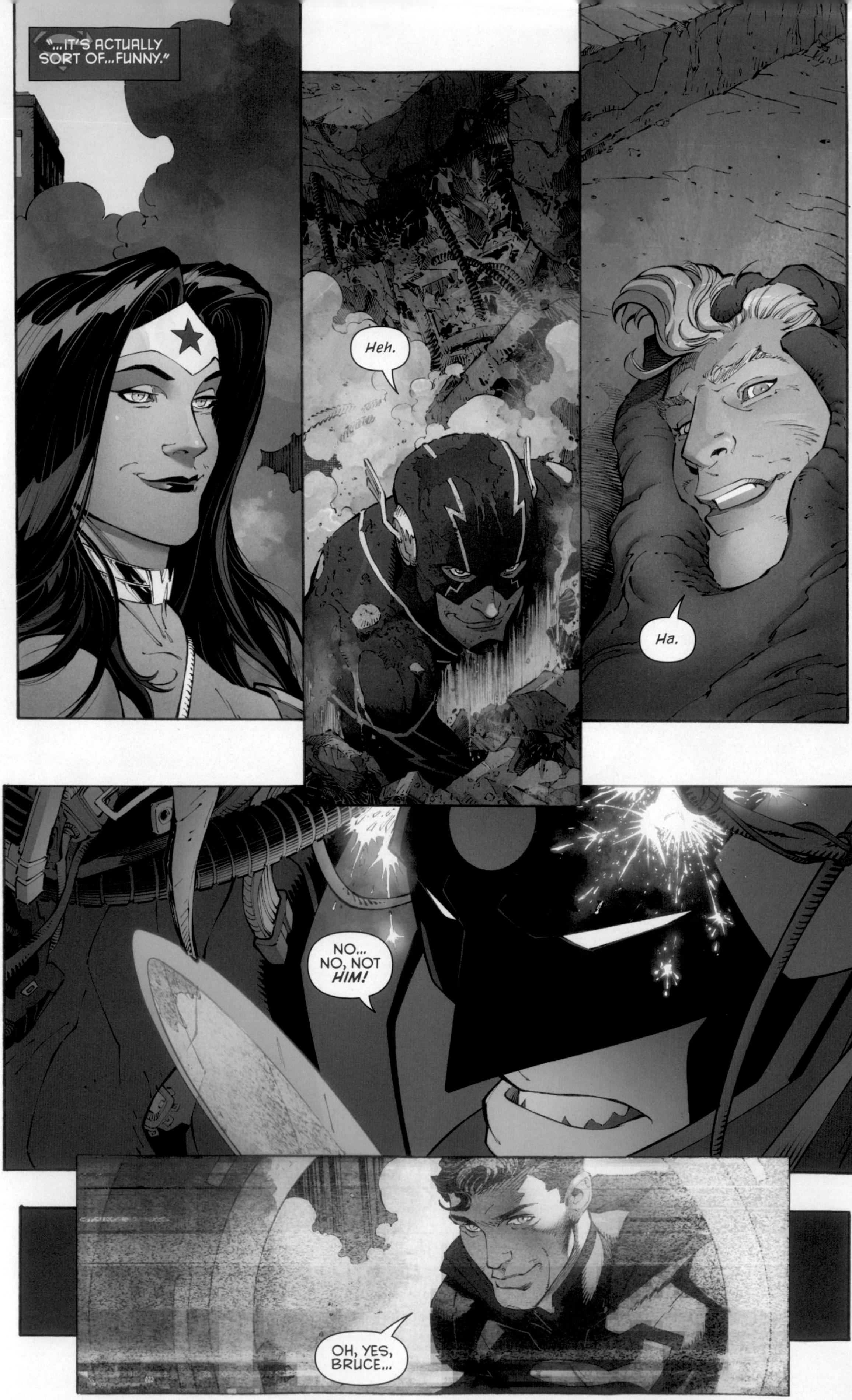
"...IT'S ACTUALLY SORT OF...FUNNY."
Heh.
Ha.
NO... NO, NOT *HIM!*
OH, YES, BRUCE...

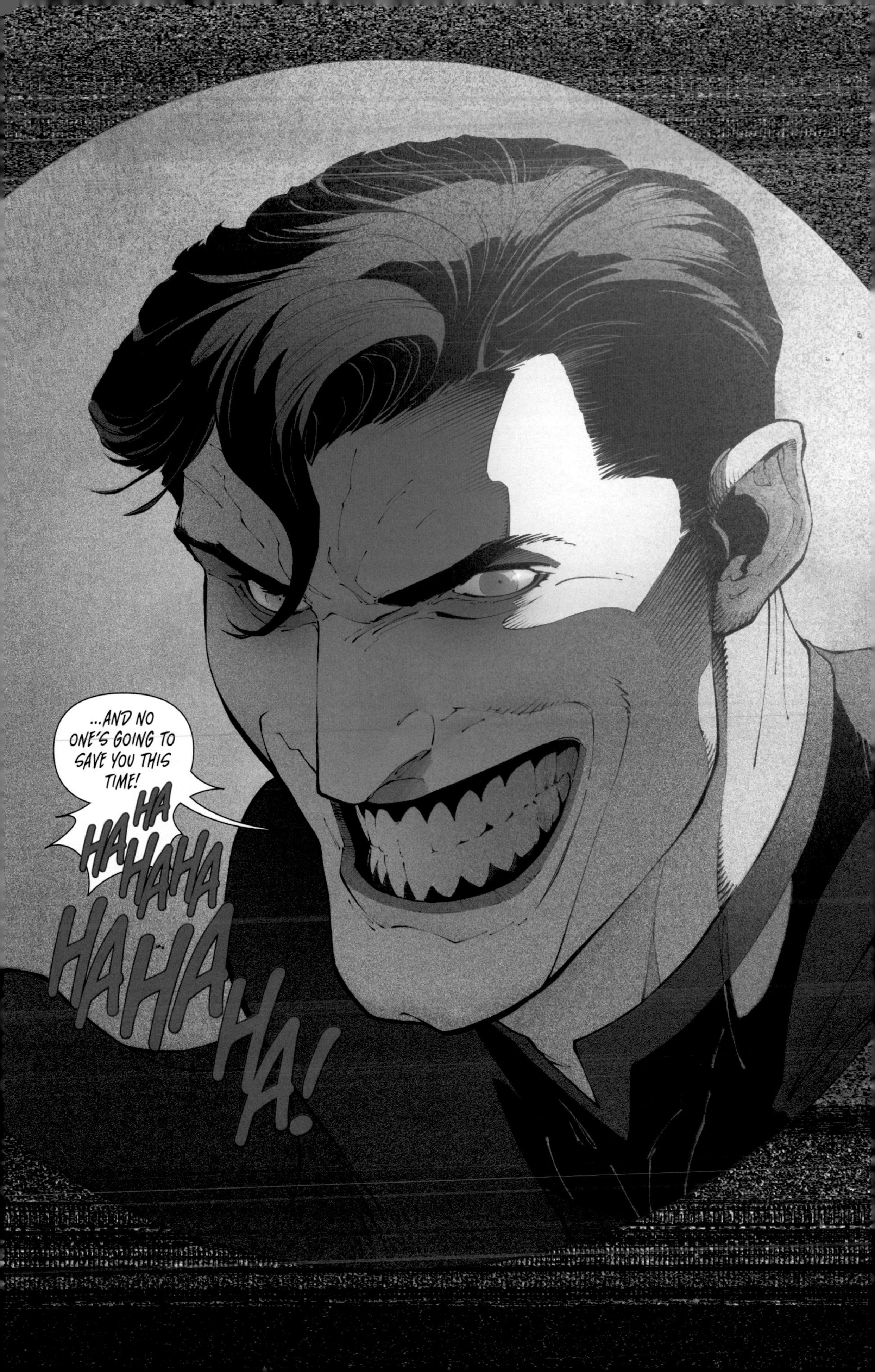
...AND NO ONE'S GOING TO SAVE YOU THIS TIME!
HA HA HAHA HAHA HA!

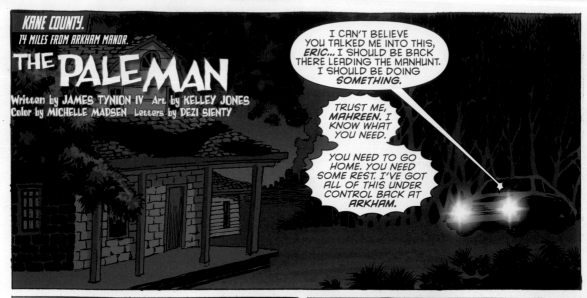

KANE COUNTY.
14 MILES FROM ARKHAM MANOR.

THE PALE MAN

Written by JAMES TYNION IV Art by KELLEY JONES
Color by MICHELLE MADSEN Letters by DEZI SIENTY

I CAN'T BELIEVE YOU TALKED ME INTO THIS, *ERIC*... I SHOULD BE BACK THERE LEADING THE MANHUNT. I SHOULD BE DOING *SOMETHING*.

TRUST ME, *MAHREEN*. I KNOW WHAT YOU NEED.

YOU NEED TO GO HOME. YOU NEED SOME REST. I'VE GOT ALL OF THIS UNDER CONTROL BACK AT *ARKHAM*.

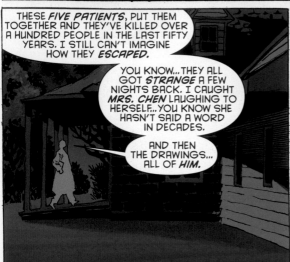

THESE *FIVE PATIENTS*, PUT THEM TOGETHER AND THEY'VE KILLED OVER A HUNDRED PEOPLE IN THE LAST FIFTY YEARS. I STILL CAN'T IMAGINE HOW THEY *ESCAPED*.

YOU KNOW... THEY ALL GOT *STRANGE* A FEW NIGHTS BACK. I CAUGHT *MRS. CHEN* LAUGHING TO HERSELF... YOU KNOW SHE HASN'T SAID A WORD IN DECADES.

AND THEN THE DRAWINGS... ALL OF *HIM*.

THE FIVE OF THEM HAVE NOTHING IN COMMON. THEIR ISSUES ARE SO DISTINCT. THEIR CELLS ARE NOWHERE NEAR EACH OTHER.

IT WAS *SNOW* WHO ADMITTED HE SAW SOMETHING. SAID HE HEARD A *STORY*. THAT THEY ALL DID. BUT HE WOULDN'T TELL ME WHAT.

KEPT SAYING, "NOT YET, NOT YET, NOT YET..."

I KNOW WHAT YOU'RE THINKING, MAHREEN, BUT IT'S *IMPOSSIBLE*. WE HAVE SECURITY LIKE ARKHAM HAS NEVER SEEN BEFORE AT THE MANOR, AND THERE'S NO SIGN OF ANY INTRUDERS.

AND HIM... THEY SAY HE'S *DEAD*. THERE'S NOTHING POINTING TO THE FACT THAT HE *COULD* BE BACK.

I WISH THAT MADE ME FEEL BETTER.

MORTON WALES

EPHRAM SNOW

MRS. CHEN

CORDELIA DOE

OKAY, I'M HOME. THAT'S WHAT YOU WANTED, RIGHT?

I'LL SLEEP FOR THREE HOURS, AND THEN I'LL BE BACK AT THE MANOR. WE NEED TO FIND THEM, ERIC. BEFORE THEY HURT ANYBODY.

W-WE DON' WANNA HURT NOBODY.

TH-THAT ISN'T WHAT THIS IS ABOUT.

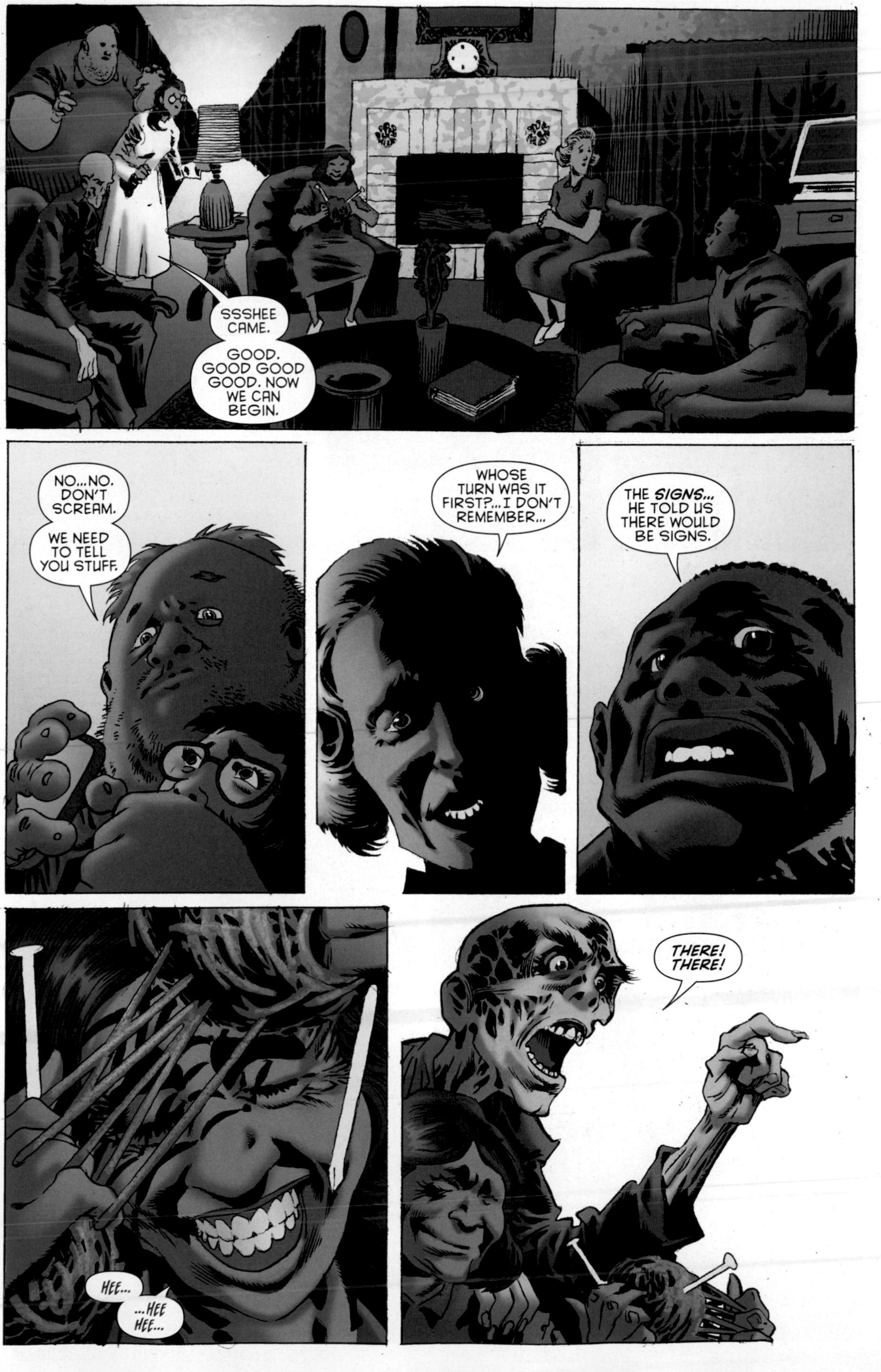
SSSHEE CAME.
GOOD. GOOD GOOD GOOD. NOW WE CAN BEGIN.
NO...NO. DON'T SCREAM.
WE NEED TO TELL YOU STUFF.
WHOSE TURN WAS IT FIRST?...I DON'T REMEMBER...
THE SIGNS... HE TOLD US THERE WOULD BE SIGNS.
HEE...
...HEE HEE...
THERE! THERE!

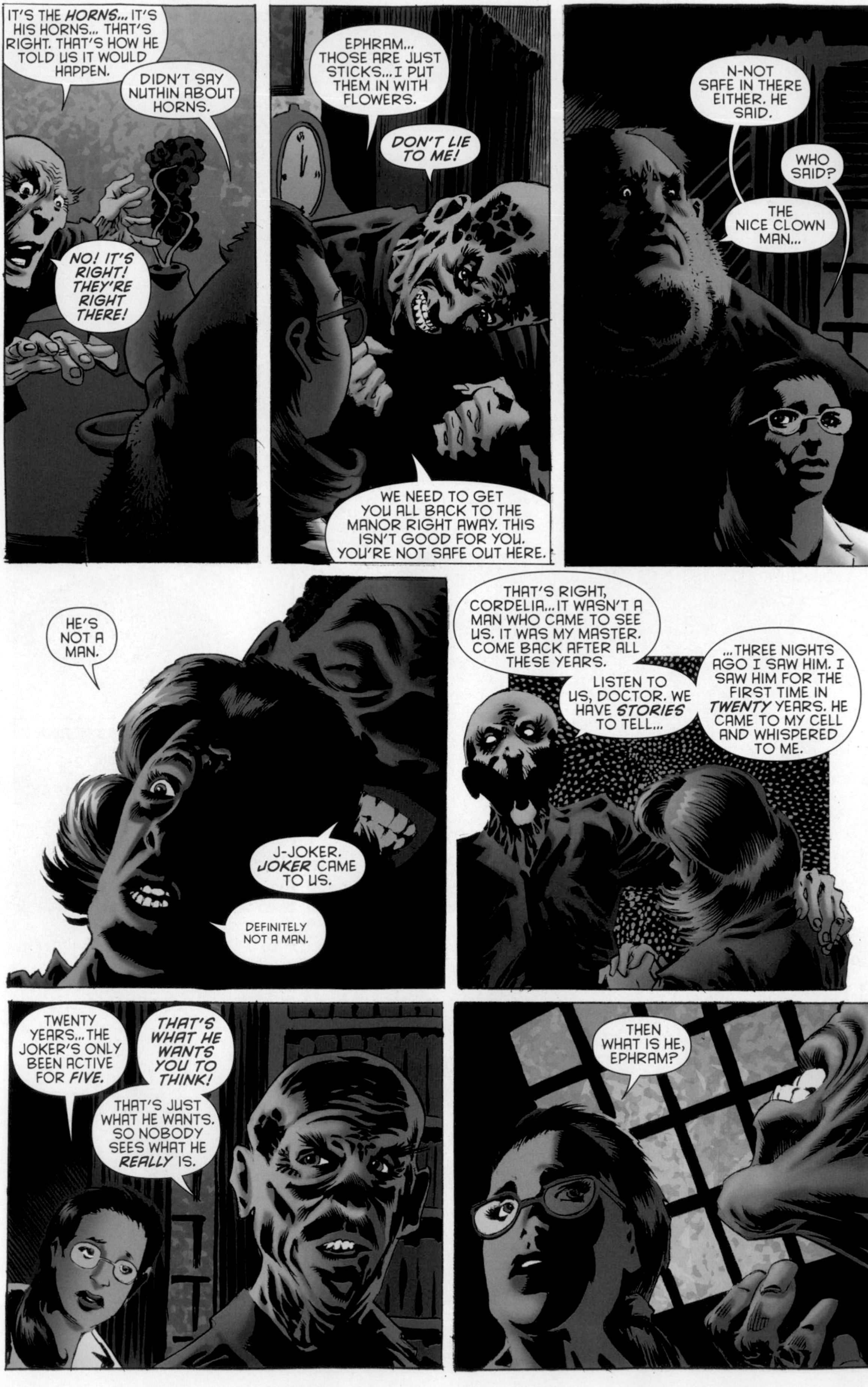

IT'S THE HORNS... IT'S HIS HORNS... THAT'S RIGHT. THAT'S HOW HE TOLD US IT WOULD HAPPEN.
DIDN'T SAY NUTHIN ABOUT HORNS.
NO! IT'S RIGHT! THEY'RE RIGHT THERE!
EPHRAM... THOSE ARE JUST STICKS... I PUT THEM IN WITH FLOWERS.
DON'T LIE TO ME!
WE NEED TO GET YOU ALL BACK TO THE MANOR RIGHT AWAY. THIS ISN'T GOOD FOR YOU. YOU'RE NOT SAFE OUT HERE.
N-NOT SAFE IN THERE EITHER. HE SAID.
WHO SAID?
THE NICE CLOWN MAN...
HE'S NOT A MAN.
J-JOKER. JOKER CAME TO US.
DEFINITELY NOT A MAN.
THAT'S RIGHT, CORDELIA... IT WASN'T A MAN WHO CAME TO SEE US. IT WAS MY MASTER. COME BACK AFTER ALL THESE YEARS.
LISTEN TO US, DOCTOR. WE HAVE STORIES TO TELL...
...THREE NIGHTS AGO I SAW HIM. I SAW HIM FOR THE FIRST TIME IN TWENTY YEARS. HE CAME TO MY CELL AND WHISPERED TO ME.
TWENTY YEARS... THE JOKER'S ONLY BEEN ACTIVE FOR FIVE.
THAT'S WHAT HE WANTS YOU TO THINK!
THAT'S JUST WHAT HE WANTS. SO NOBODY SEES WHAT HE REALLY IS.
THEN WHAT IS HE, EPHRAM?

"THE DEVIL.

"THE DEVIL HIMSELF.

"STILL REMEMBER THAT NIGHT, TWENTY YEARS AGO. IT GETS HAZY WHEN YOU MAKE ME TAKE THE PILLS, BUT IT'S STILL IN THERE.

"I FOUND A PATH THAT NEVER EXISTED BEFORE THAT NIGHT AND NEVER EXISTED AFTER.

"WASN'T LIKE IN THE STORYBOOKS.

"AND ON THAT PATH THERE WAS A CROSSROADS... AND HE CAME TO ME THERE. HE TOLD ME WHAT I NEEDED TO DO.

"WASN'T RED, WITH THE HORNS AND THE HOOVES...HE WAS *TALL* AND *PALE.*

"HE TOLD ME ABOUT THE GIRLS... THE GIRLS WHO HE NEEDED BACK. HE TOLD ME WHERE TO FIND THEM. THEIR SECRET PLACES.

"AND WHEN HE SMILED I COULD SEE *HELL* REFLECTED IN HIS CROOKED TEETH.

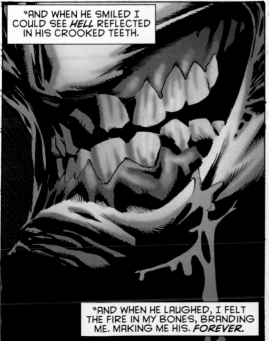

"AND WHEN HE LAUGHED, I FELT THE FIRE IN MY BONES, BRANDING ME, MAKING ME HIS. *FOREVER.*

"TOLD ME HOW TO *GIVE* THEM TO HIM."

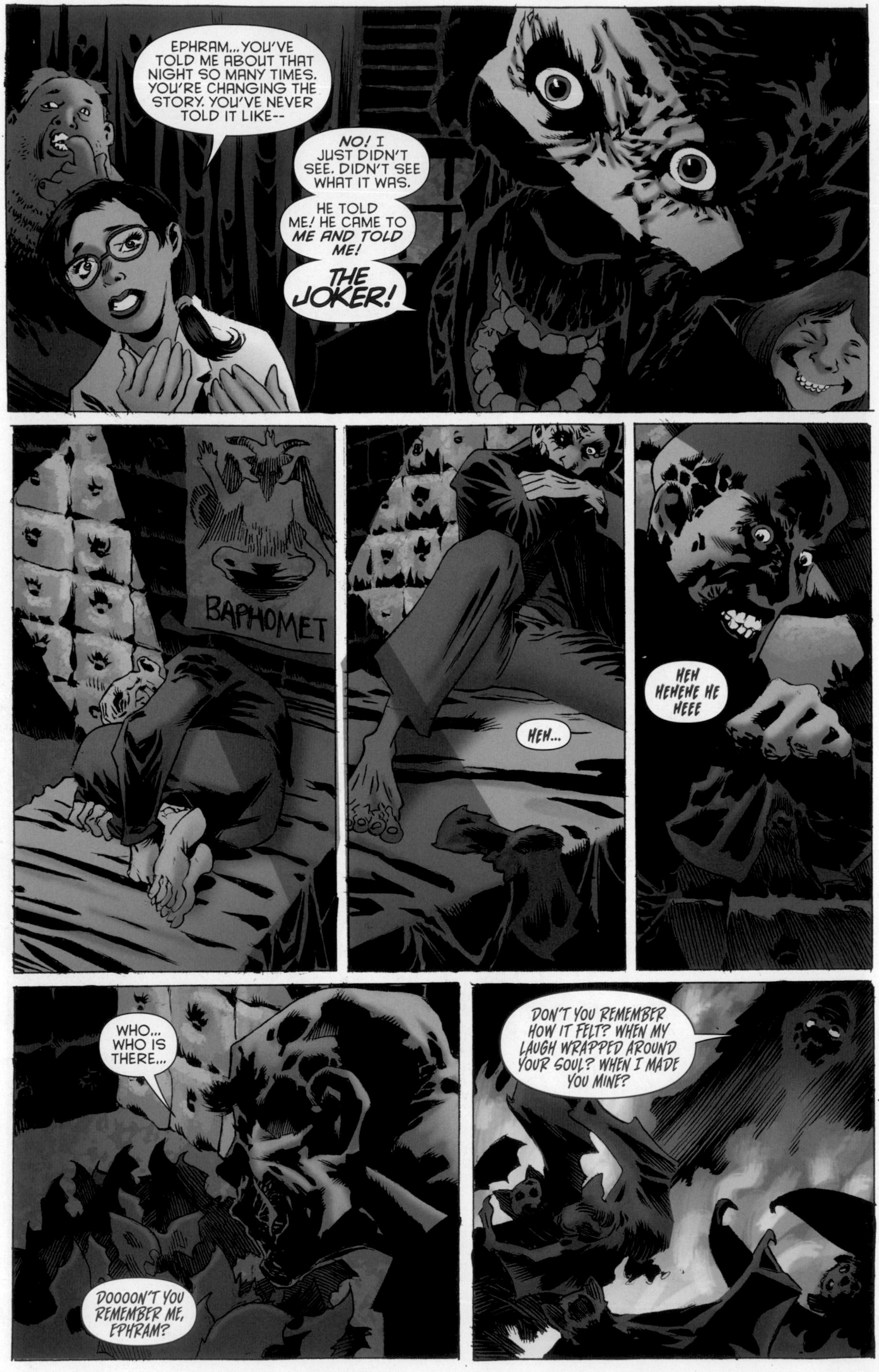
EPHRAM... YOU'VE TOLD ME ABOUT THAT NIGHT SO MANY TIMES. YOU'RE CHANGING THE STORY. YOU'VE NEVER TOLD IT LIKE--
NO! I JUST DIDN'T SEE. DIDN'T SEE WHAT IT WAS.
HE TOLD ME! HE CAME TO ME AND TOLD ME!
THE JOKER!
BAPHOMET
HEH...
HEH HEHEHE HE HEEE
WHO... WHO IS THERE...
DOOOON'T YOU REMEMBER ME, EPHRAM?
DON'T YOU REMEMBER HOW IT FELT? WHEN MY LAUGH WRAPPED AROUND YOUR SOUL? WHEN I MADE YOU MINE?

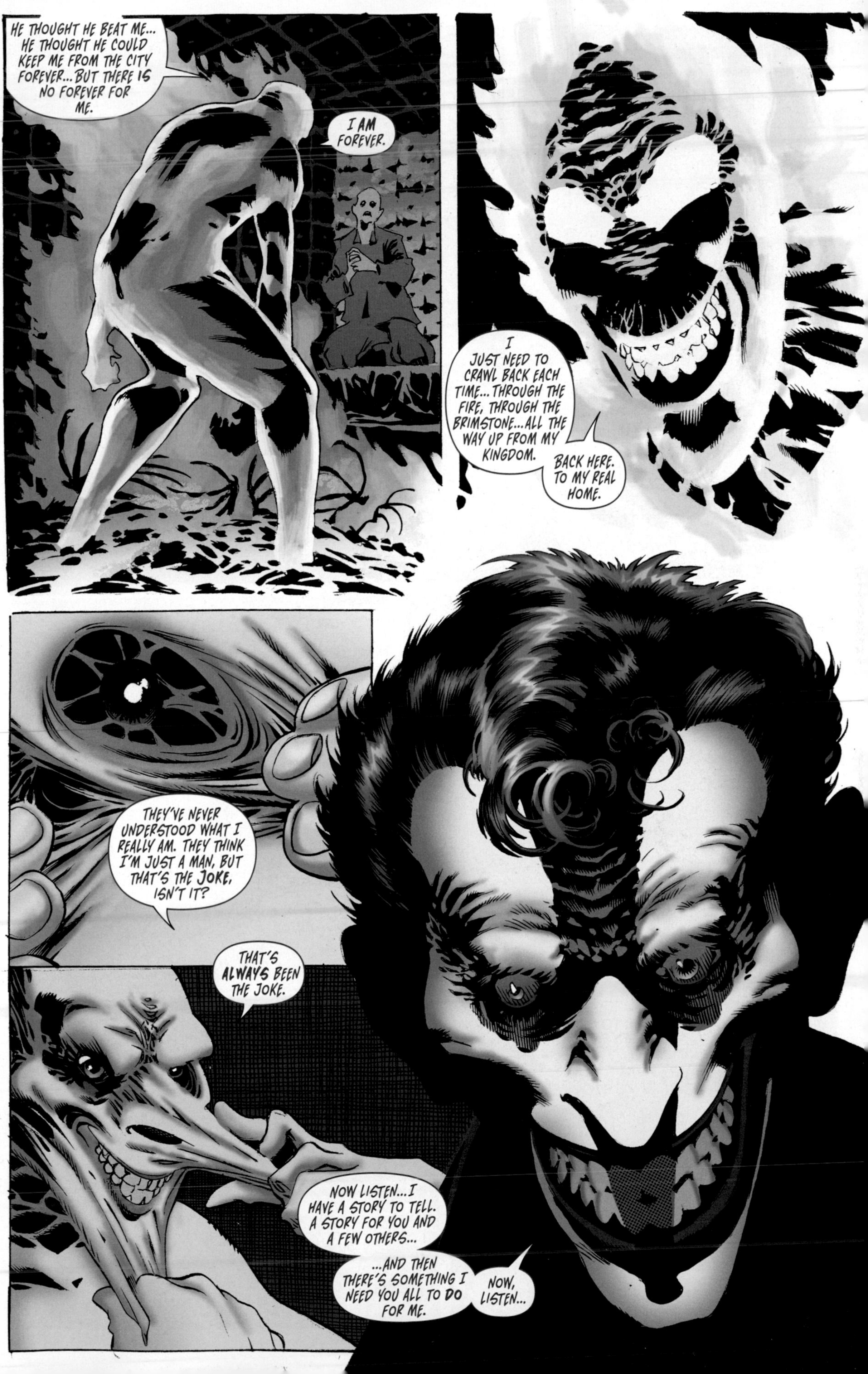
HE THOUGHT HE BEAT ME... HE THOUGHT HE COULD KEEP ME FROM THE CITY FOREVER... BUT THERE IS NO FOREVER FOR ME.
I AM FOREVER.
I JUST NEED TO CRAWL BACK EACH TIME... THROUGH THE FIRE, THROUGH THE BRIMSTONE... ALL THE WAY UP FROM MY KINGDOM.
BACK HERE. TO MY REAL HOME.
THEY'VE NEVER UNDERSTOOD WHAT I REALLY AM. THEY THINK I'M JUST A MAN, BUT THAT'S THE JOKE, ISN'T IT?
THAT'S ALWAYS BEEN THE JOKE.
NOW LISTEN... I HAVE A STORY TO TELL. A STORY FOR YOU AND A FEW OTHERS...
...AND THEN THERE'S SOMETHING I NEED YOU ALL TO DO FOR ME.
NOW, LISTEN...

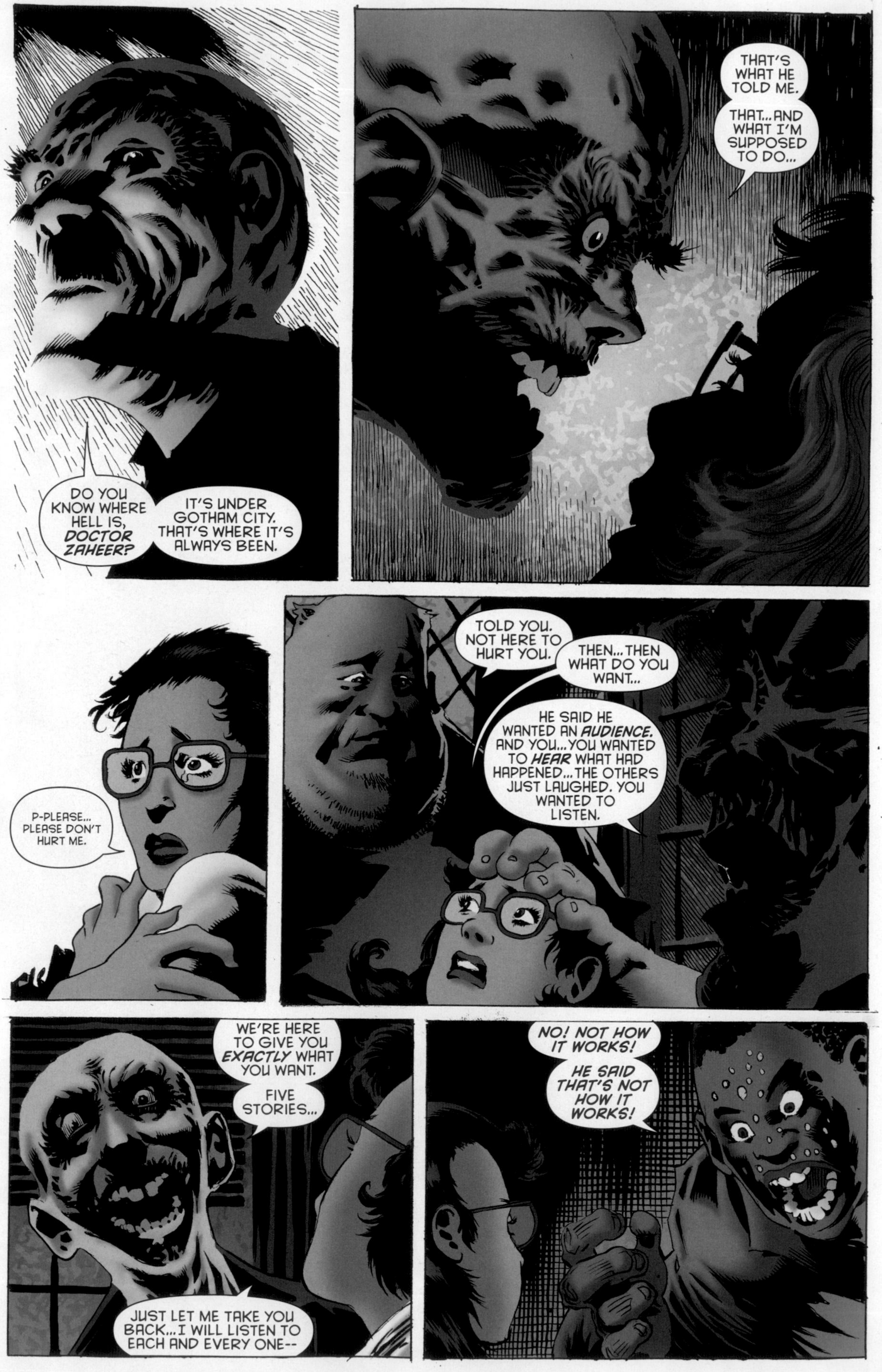
DO YOU KNOW WHERE HELL IS, DOCTOR ZAHEER?
IT'S UNDER GOTHAM CITY. THAT'S WHERE IT'S ALWAYS BEEN.
THAT'S WHAT HE TOLD ME.
THAT... AND WHAT I'M SUPPOSED TO DO...
P-PLEASE... PLEASE DON'T HURT ME.
TOLD YOU. NOT HERE TO HURT YOU.
THEN... THEN WHAT DO YOU WANT...
HE SAID HE WANTED AN AUDIENCE. AND YOU... YOU WANTED TO HEAR WHAT HAD HAPPENED... THE OTHERS JUST LAUGHED. YOU WANTED TO LISTEN.
WE'RE HERE TO GIVE YOU EXACTLY WHAT YOU WANT.
FIVE STORIES...
JUST LET ME TAKE YOU BACK... I WILL LISTEN TO EACH AND EVERY ONE--
NO! NOT HOW IT WORKS!
HE SAID THAT'S NOT HOW IT WORKS!

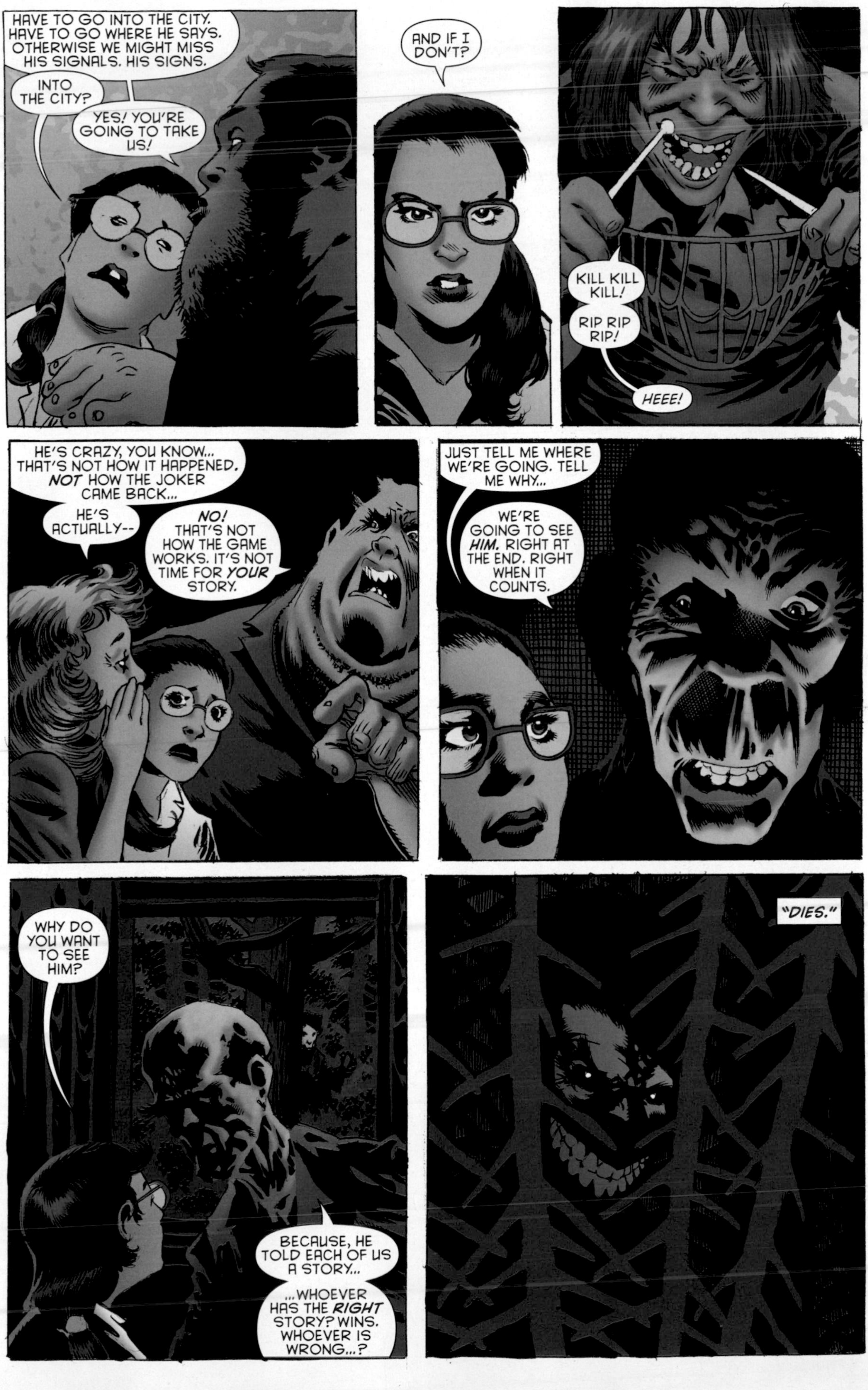
HAVE TO GO INTO THE CITY. HAVE TO GO WHERE HE SAYS. OTHERWISE WE MIGHT MISS HIS SIGNALS. HIS SIGNS.
INTO THE CITY?
YES! YOU'RE GOING TO TAKE US!
AND IF I DON'T?
KILL KILL KILL!
RIP RIP RIP!
HEEE!
HE'S CRAZY, YOU KNOW... THAT'S NOT HOW IT HAPPENED. NOT HOW THE JOKER CAME BACK...
HE'S ACTUALLY--
NO! THAT'S NOT HOW THE GAME WORKS. IT'S NOT TIME FOR YOUR STORY.
JUST TELL ME WHERE WE'RE GOING. TELL ME WHY...
WE'RE GOING TO SEE HIM. RIGHT AT THE END. RIGHT WHEN IT COUNTS.
WHY DO YOU WANT TO SEE HIM?
BECAUSE, HE TOLD EACH OF US A STORY...
...WHOEVER HAS THE RIGHT STORY? WINS. WHOEVER IS WRONG...?
"DIES."

Cover by **GREG CAPULLO, DANNY MIKI & FCO PLASCENCIA**

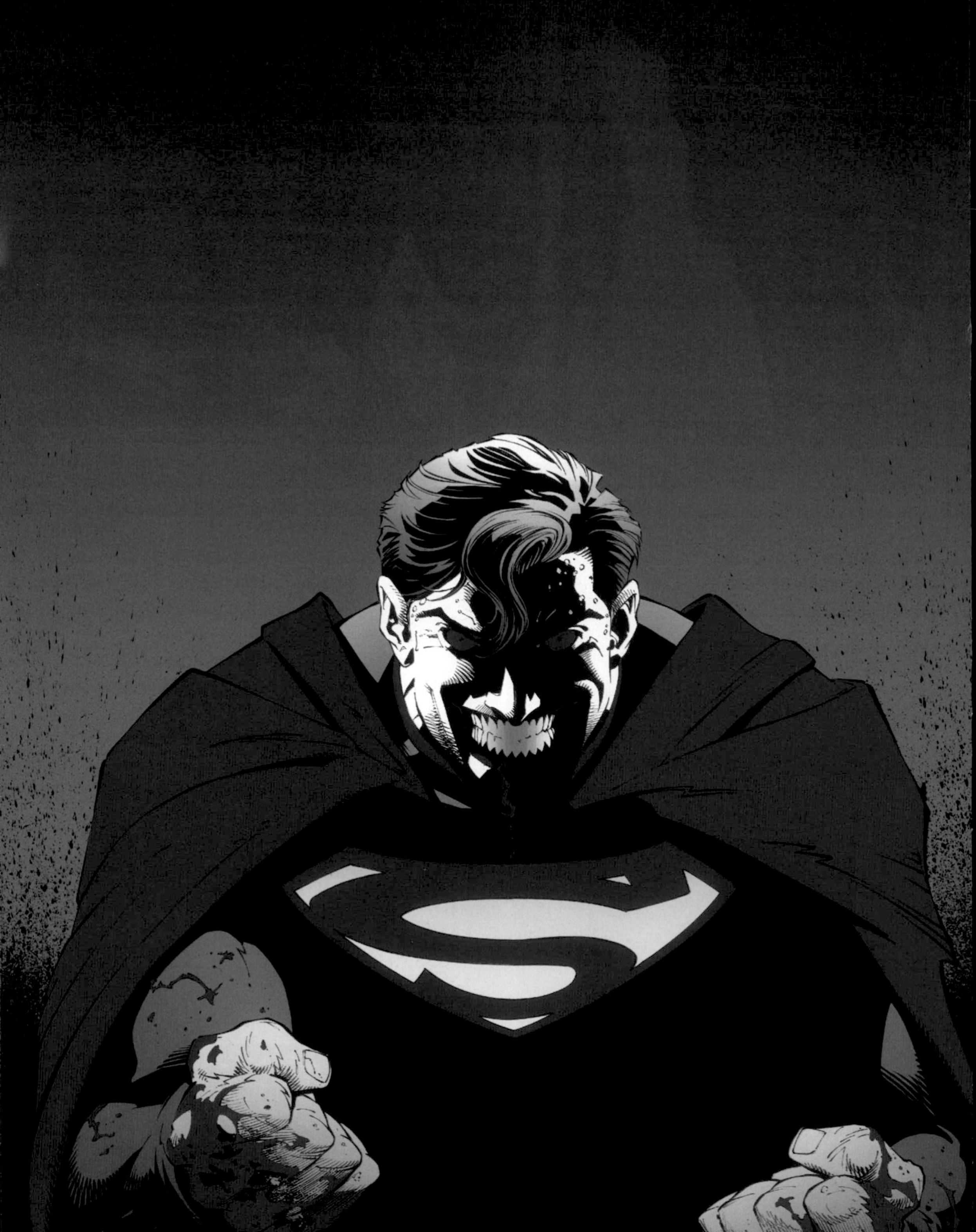

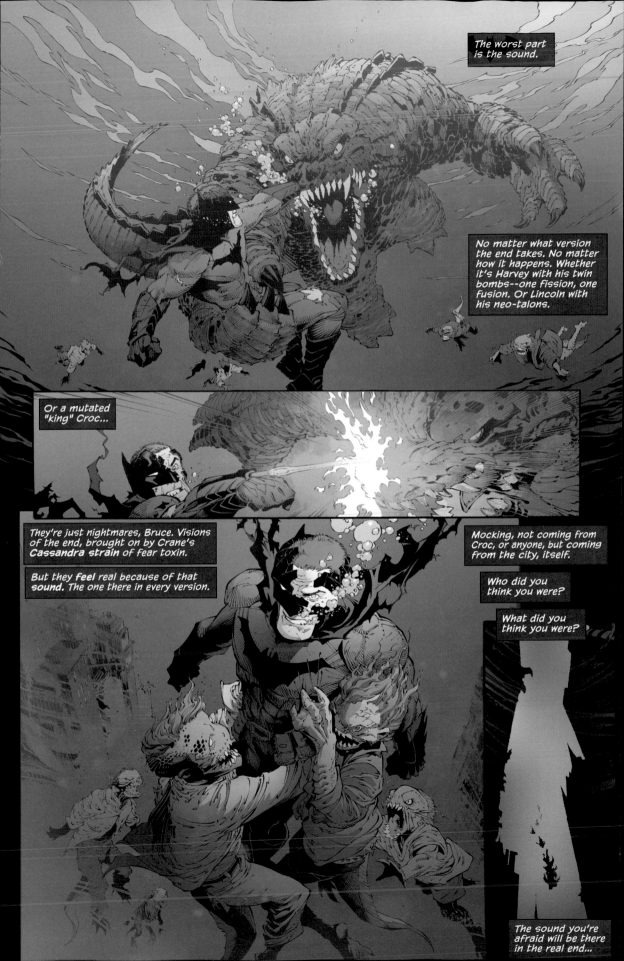

The worst part is the sound.

No matter what version the end takes. No matter how it happens. Whether it's Harvey with his twin bombs--one fission, one fusion. Or Lincoln with his neo-talons.

Or a mutated "king" Croc...

They're just nightmares, Bruce. Visions of the end, brought on by Crane's *Cassandra strain* of fear toxin.

But they *feel* real because of that *sound.* The one there in every version.

Mocking, not coming from Croc, or anyone, but coming from the city, itself.

Who did you think you were?

What did you think you were?

The sound you're afraid will be there in the real end...

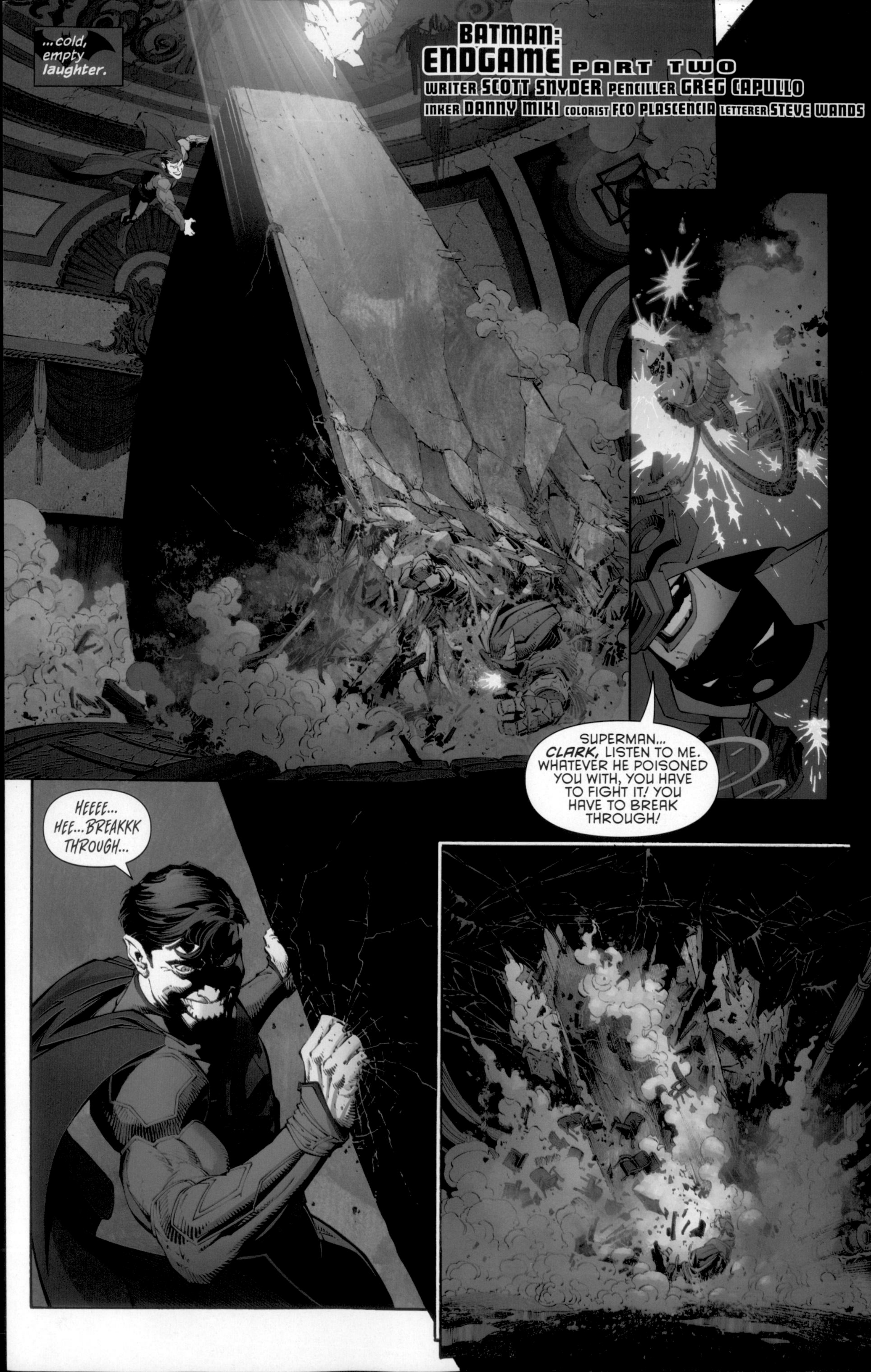
...cold, empty laughter.
BATMAN: ENDGAME PART TWO
WRITER SCOTT SNYDER PENCILLER GREG CAPULLO
INKER DANNY MIKI COLORIST FCO PLASCENCIA LETTERER STEVE WANDS
SUPERMAN... CLARK, LISTEN TO ME. WHATEVER HE POISONED YOU WITH, YOU HAVE TO FIGHT IT! YOU HAVE TO BREAK THROUGH!
HEEEE... HEE...BREAKKK THROUGH...

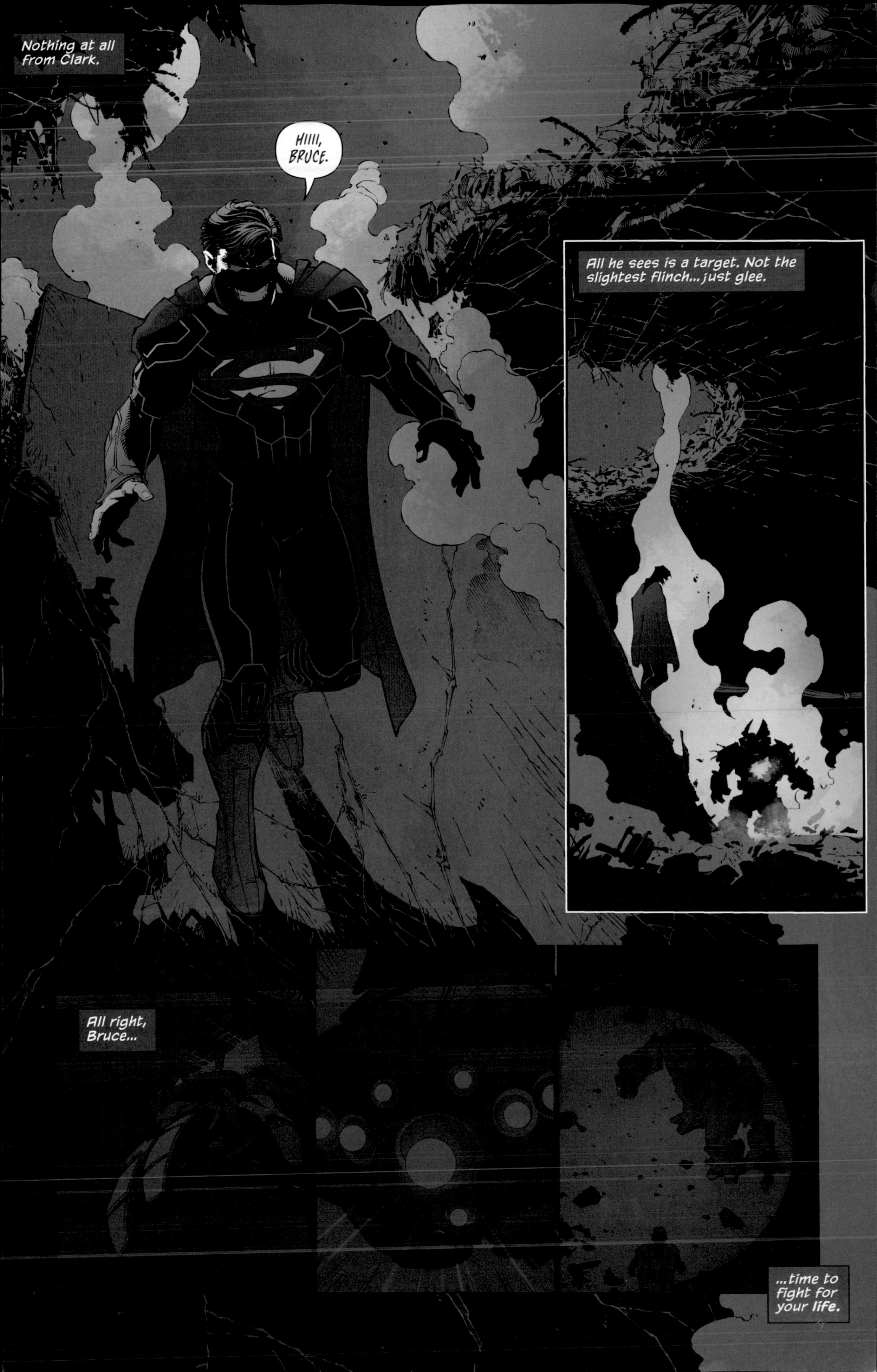
Nothing at all from Clark.
HIIII, BRUCE.
All he sees is a target. Not the slightest flinch... just glee.
All right, Bruce...
...time to fight for your life.

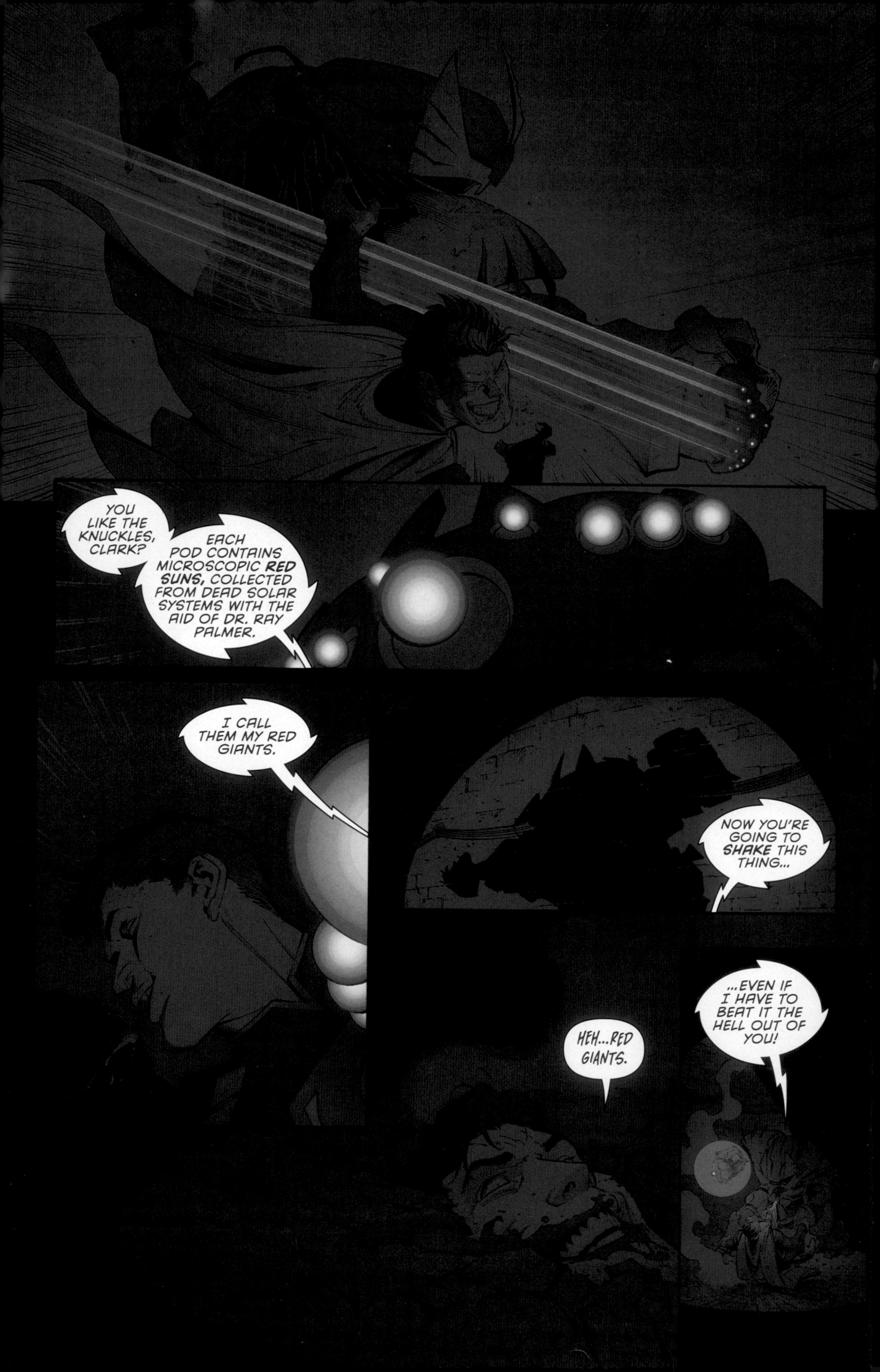

YOU LIKE THE KNUCKLES, CLARK?
EACH POD CONTAINS MICROSCOPIC **RED SUNS,** COLLECTED FROM DEAD SOLAR SYSTEMS WITH THE AID OF DR. RAY PALMER.
I CALL THEM MY RED GIANTS.
NOW YOU'RE GOING TO **SHAKE** THIS THING...
HEH...RED GIANTS.
...EVEN IF I HAVE TO BEAT IT THE HELL OUT OF YOU!

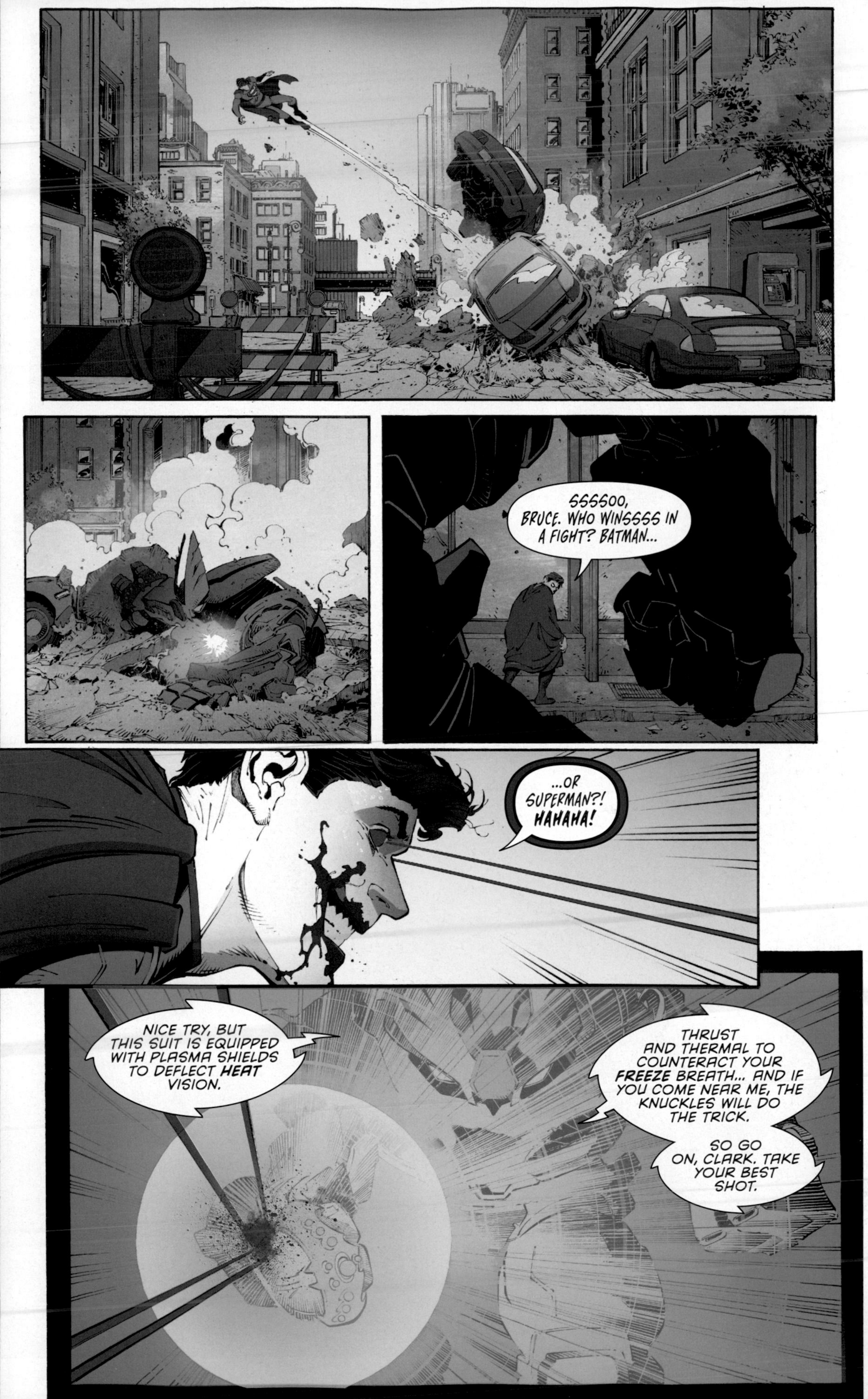
SSSSOO, BRUCE. WHO WINSSSS IN A FIGHT? BATMAN...
...OR SUPERMAN?! HAHAHA!
NICE TRY, BUT THIS SUIT IS EQUIPPED WITH PLASMA SHIELDS TO DEFLECT HEAT VISION.
THRUST AND THERMAL TO COUNTERACT YOUR FREEZE BREATH... AND IF YOU COME NEAR ME, THE KNUCKLES WILL DO THE TRICK.
SO GO ON, CLARK. TAKE YOUR BEST SHOT.

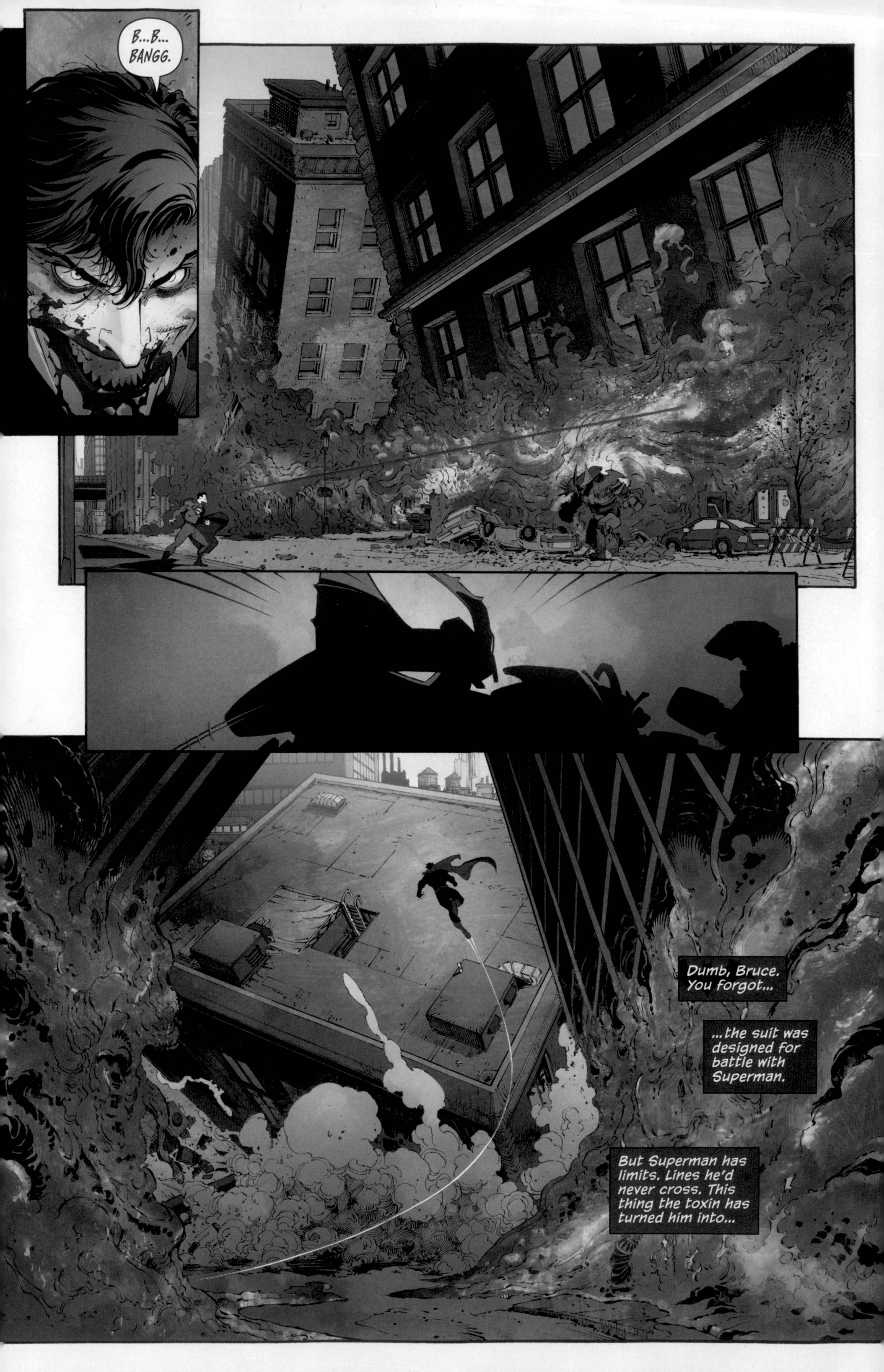

B...B... BANGG.
Dumb, Bruce. You forgot...
...the suit was designed for battle with Superman.
But Superman has limits. Lines he'd never cross. This thing the toxin has turned him into...

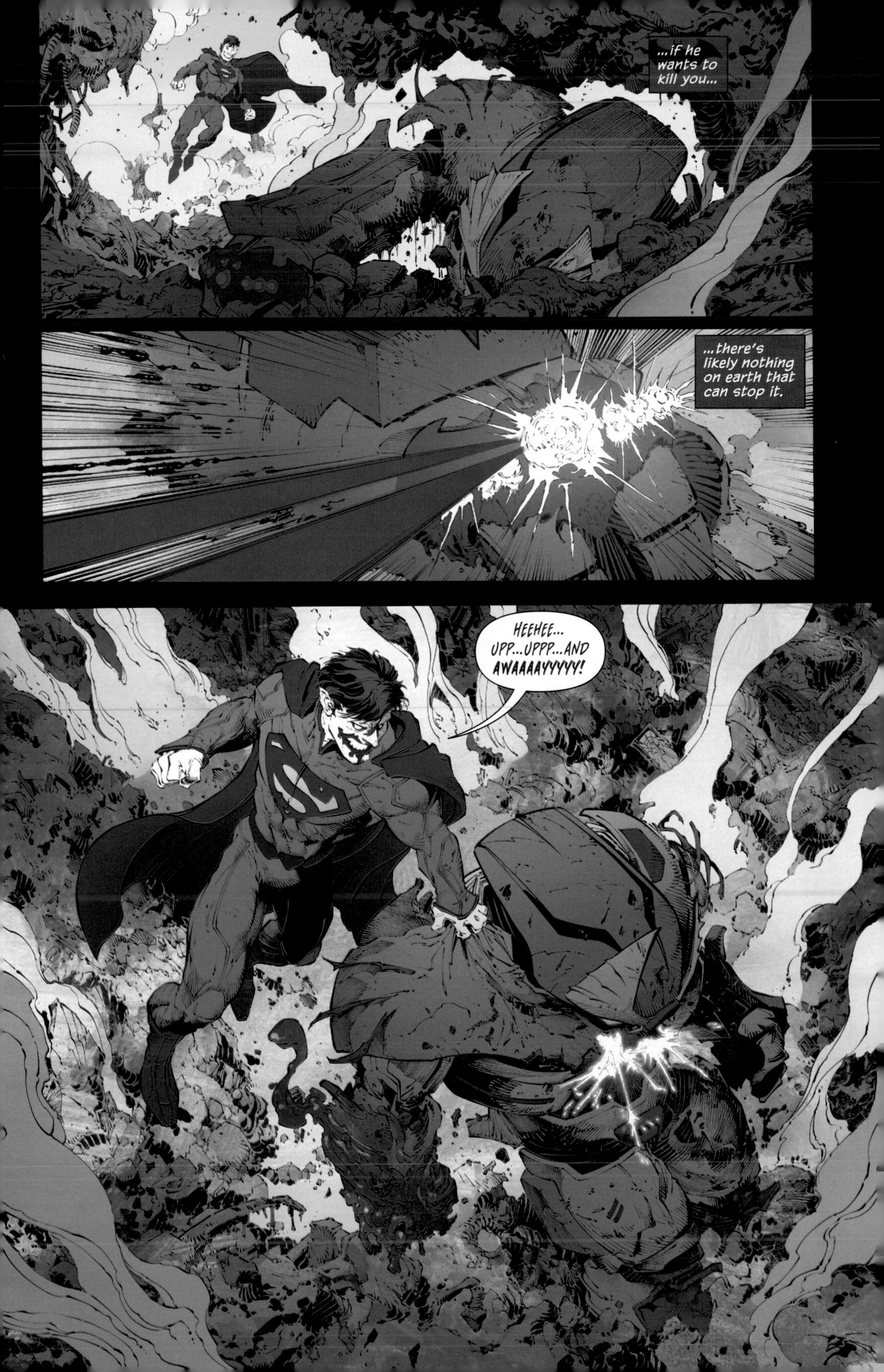
...if he wants to kill you...
...there's likely nothing on earth that can stop it.
HEEHEE... UPP...UPPP...AND **AWAAAAYYYYY!**

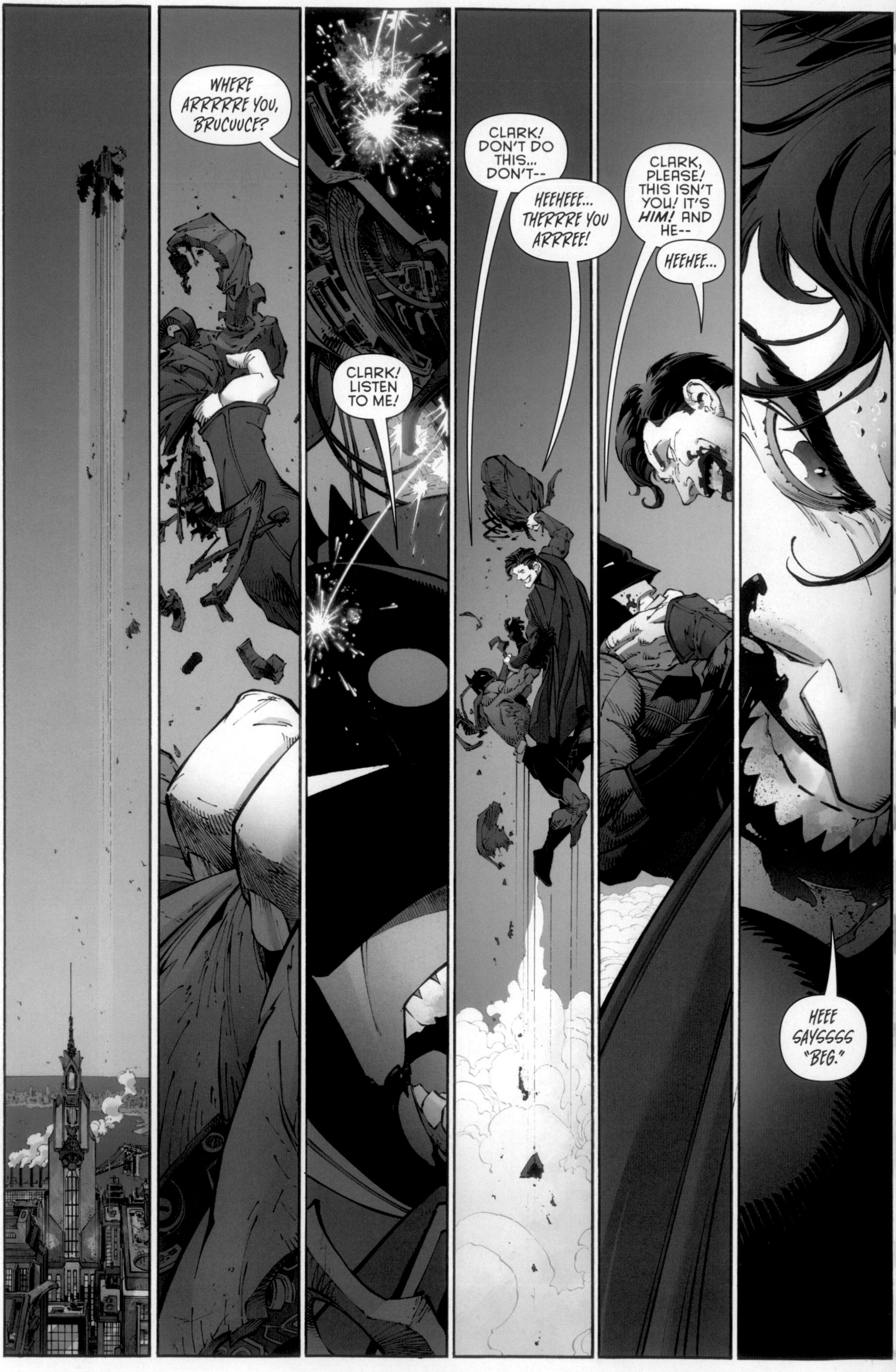
WHERE ARRRRRE YOU, BRUCUUCE?
CLARK! LISTEN TO ME!
CLARK! DON'T DO THIS... DON'T--
HEEHEEE... THERRRE YOU ARRRREE!
CLARK, PLEASE! THIS ISN'T YOU! IT'S HIM! AND HE--
HEEHEE...
HEEE SAYSSSS "BEG."

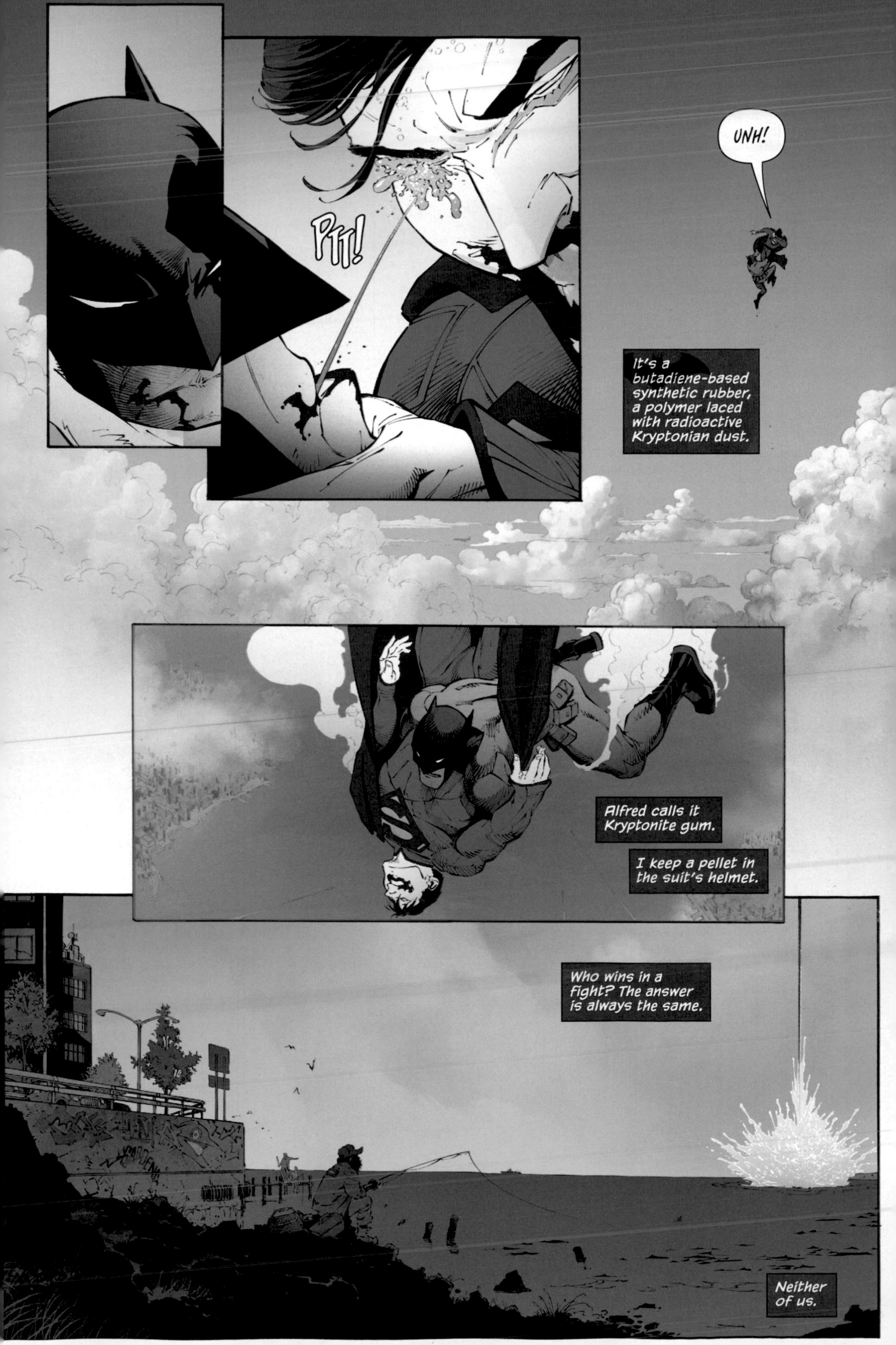
PTT!
UNH!
It's a butadiene-based synthetic rubber, a polymer laced with radioactive Kryptonian dust.
Alfred calls it Kryptonite gum.
I keep a pellet in the suit's helmet.
Who wins in a fight? The answer is always the same.
Neither of us.

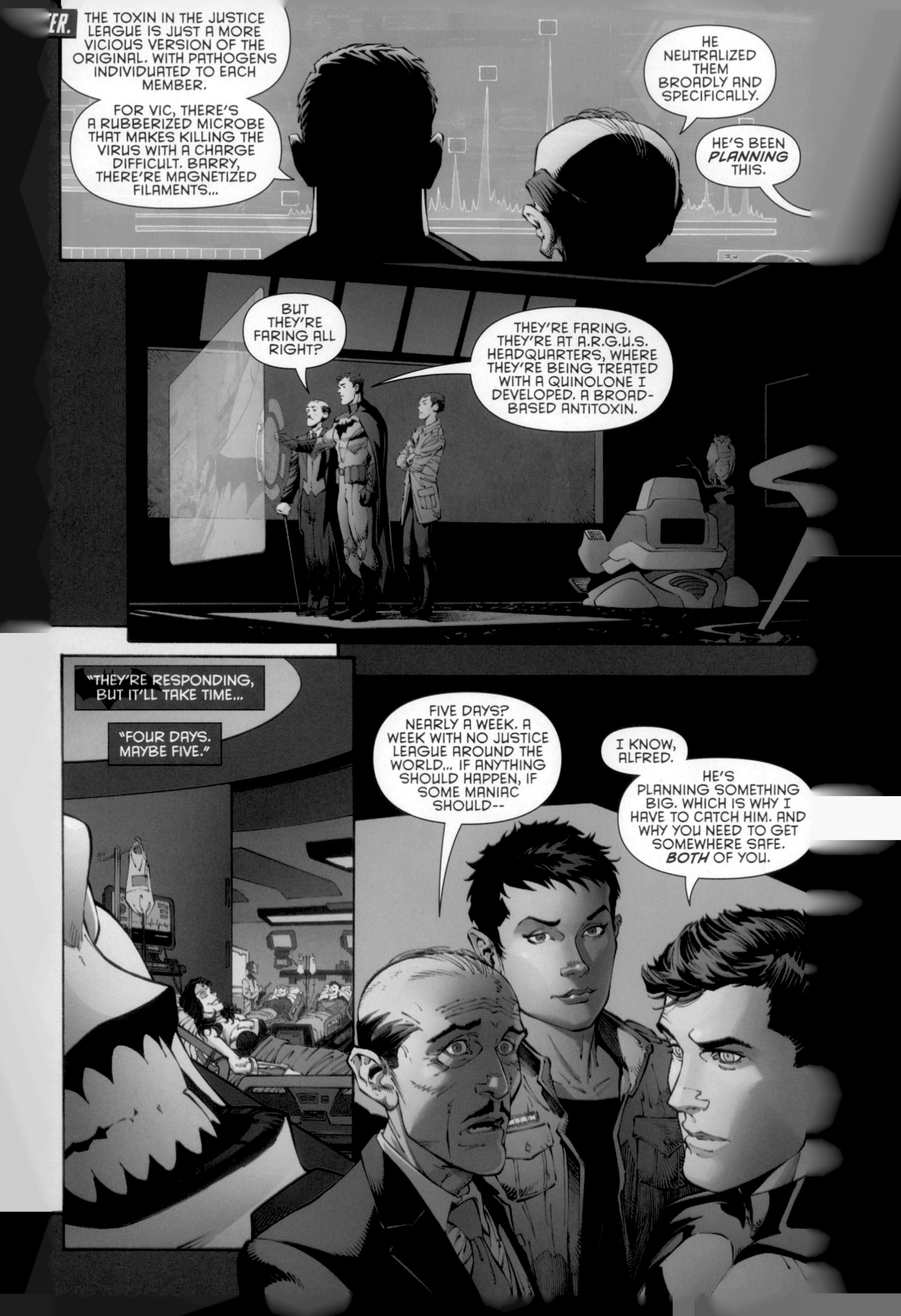
ER.
THE TOXIN IN THE JUSTICE LEAGUE IS JUST A MORE VICIOUS VERSION OF THE ORIGINAL. WITH PATHOGENS INDIVIDUATED TO EACH MEMBER.
FOR VIC, THERE'S A RUBBERIZED MICROBE THAT MAKES KILLING THE VIRUS WITH A CHARGE DIFFICULT. BARRY, THERE'RE MAGNETIZED FILAMENTS...
HE NEUTRALIZED THEM BROADLY AND SPECIFICALLY.
HE'S BEEN *PLANNING* THIS.
BUT THEY'RE FARING ALL RIGHT?
THEY'RE FARING. THEY'RE AT A.R.G.U.S. HEADQUARTERS, WHERE THEY'RE BEING TREATED WITH A QUINOLONE I DEVELOPED. A BROAD-BASED ANTITOXIN.
"THEY'RE RESPONDING, BUT IT'LL TAKE TIME...
"FOUR DAYS. MAYBE FIVE."
FIVE DAYS? NEARLY A WEEK. A WEEK WITH NO JUSTICE LEAGUE AROUND THE WORLD... IF ANYTHING SHOULD HAPPEN, IF SOME MANIAC SHOULD--
I KNOW, ALFRED.
HE'S PLANNING SOMETHING BIG. WHICH IS WHY I HAVE TO CATCH HIM. AND WHY YOU NEED TO GET SOMEWHERE SAFE. *BOTH* OF YOU.

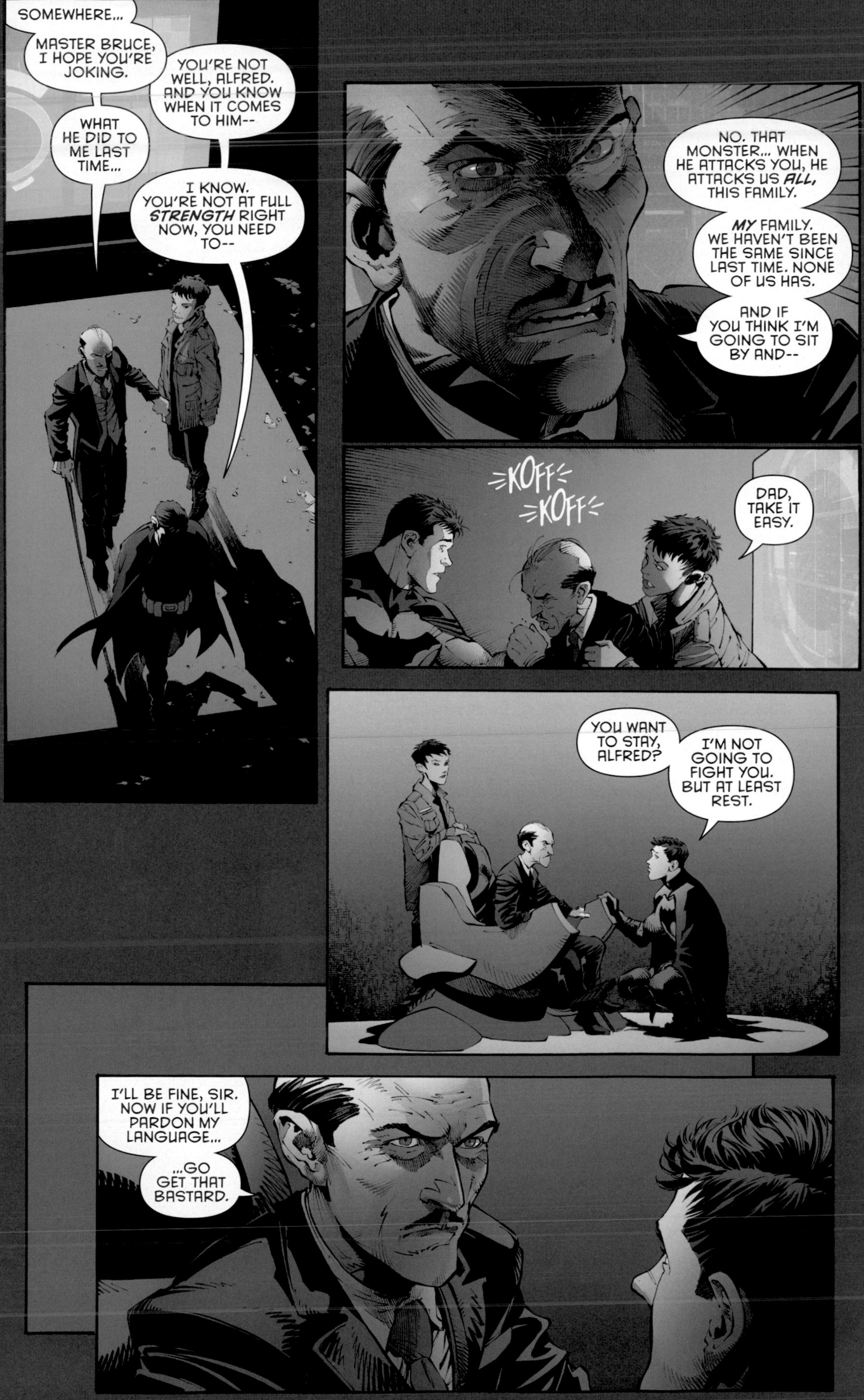
SOMEWHERE...
MASTER BRUCE, I HOPE YOU'RE JOKING.
WHAT HE DID TO ME LAST TIME...
YOU'RE NOT WELL, ALFRED. AND YOU KNOW WHEN IT COMES TO HIM--
I KNOW. YOU'RE NOT AT FULL STRENGTH RIGHT NOW, YOU NEED TO--
NO. THAT MONSTER... WHEN HE ATTACKS YOU, HE ATTACKS US ALL, THIS FAMILY.
MY FAMILY. WE HAVEN'T BEEN THE SAME SINCE LAST TIME. NONE OF US HAS.
AND IF YOU THINK I'M GOING TO SIT BY AND--
KOFF
KOFF
DAD, TAKE IT EASY.
YOU WANT TO STAY, ALFRED?
I'M NOT GOING TO FIGHT YOU. BUT AT LEAST REST.
I'LL BE FINE, SIR. NOW IF YOU'LL PARDON MY LANGUAGE...
...GO GET THAT BASTARD.

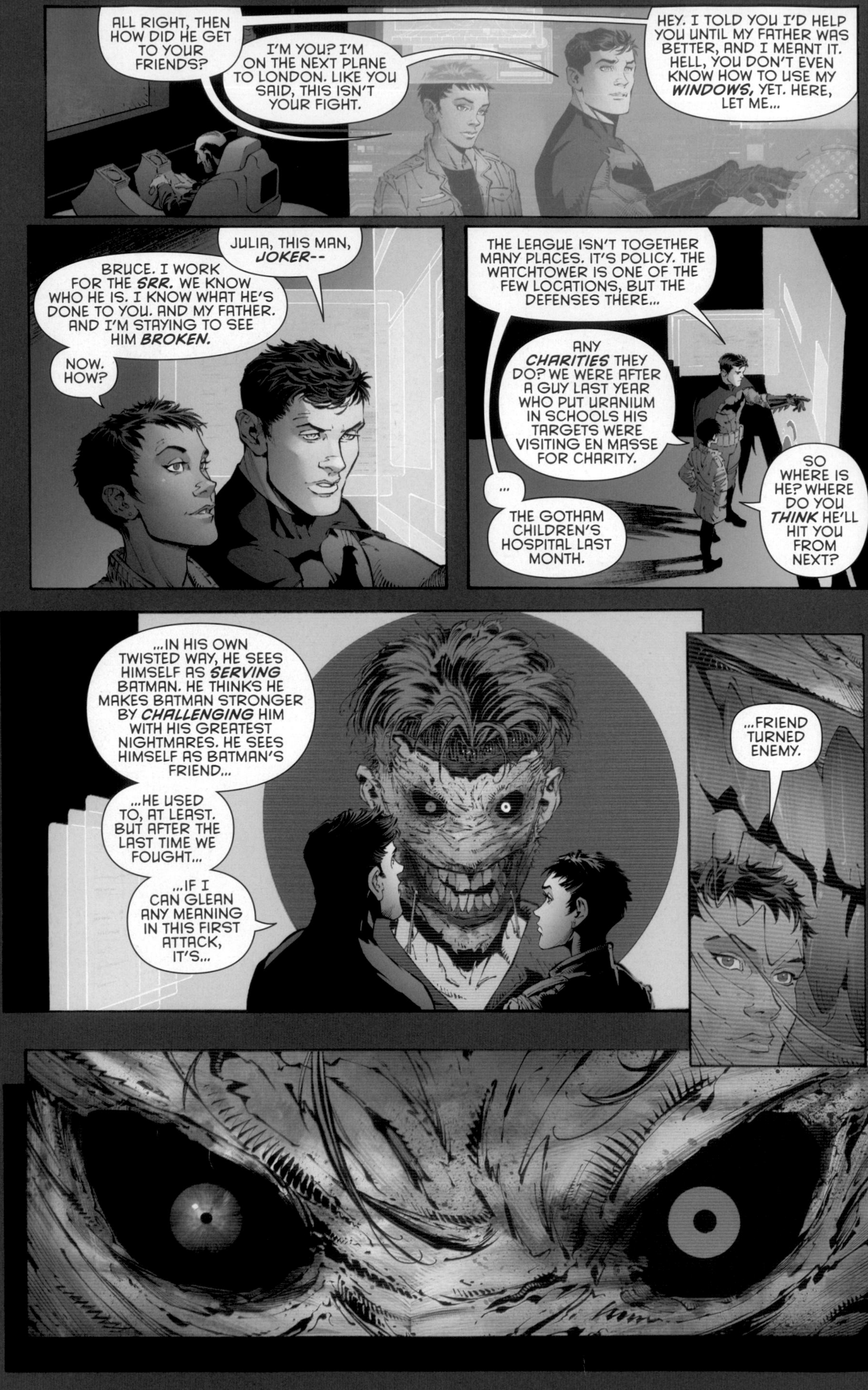
ALL RIGHT, THEN HOW DID HE GET TO YOUR FRIENDS?
HEY. I TOLD YOU I'D HELP YOU UNTIL MY FATHER WAS BETTER, AND I MEANT IT. HELL, YOU DON'T EVEN KNOW HOW TO USE MY WINDOWS, YET. HERE, LET ME...
I'M YOU? I'M ON THE NEXT PLANE TO LONDON. LIKE YOU SAID, THIS ISN'T YOUR FIGHT.
JULIA, THIS MAN, JOKER--
BRUCE. I WORK FOR THE SRR. WE KNOW WHO HE IS. I KNOW WHAT HE'S DONE TO YOU. AND MY FATHER. AND I'M STAYING TO SEE HIM BROKEN.
NOW. HOW?
THE LEAGUE ISN'T TOGETHER MANY PLACES. IT'S POLICY. THE WATCHTOWER IS ONE OF THE FEW LOCATIONS, BUT THE DEFENSES THERE...
ANY CHARITIES THEY DO? WE WERE AFTER A GUY LAST YEAR WHO PUT URANIUM IN SCHOOLS HIS TARGETS WERE VISITING EN MASSE FOR CHARITY.
...
THE GOTHAM CHILDREN'S HOSPITAL LAST MONTH.
SO WHERE IS HE? WHERE DO YOU THINK HE'LL HIT YOU FROM NEXT?
...IN HIS OWN TWISTED WAY, HE SEES HIMSELF AS SERVING BATMAN. HE THINKS HE MAKES BATMAN STRONGER BY CHALLENGING HIM WITH HIS GREATEST NIGHTMARES. HE SEES HIMSELF AS BATMAN'S FRIEND...
...HE USED TO, AT LEAST. BUT AFTER THE LAST TIME WE FOUGHT...
...IF I CAN GLEAN ANY MEANING IN THIS FIRST ATTACK, IT'S...
...FRIEND TURNED ENEMY.

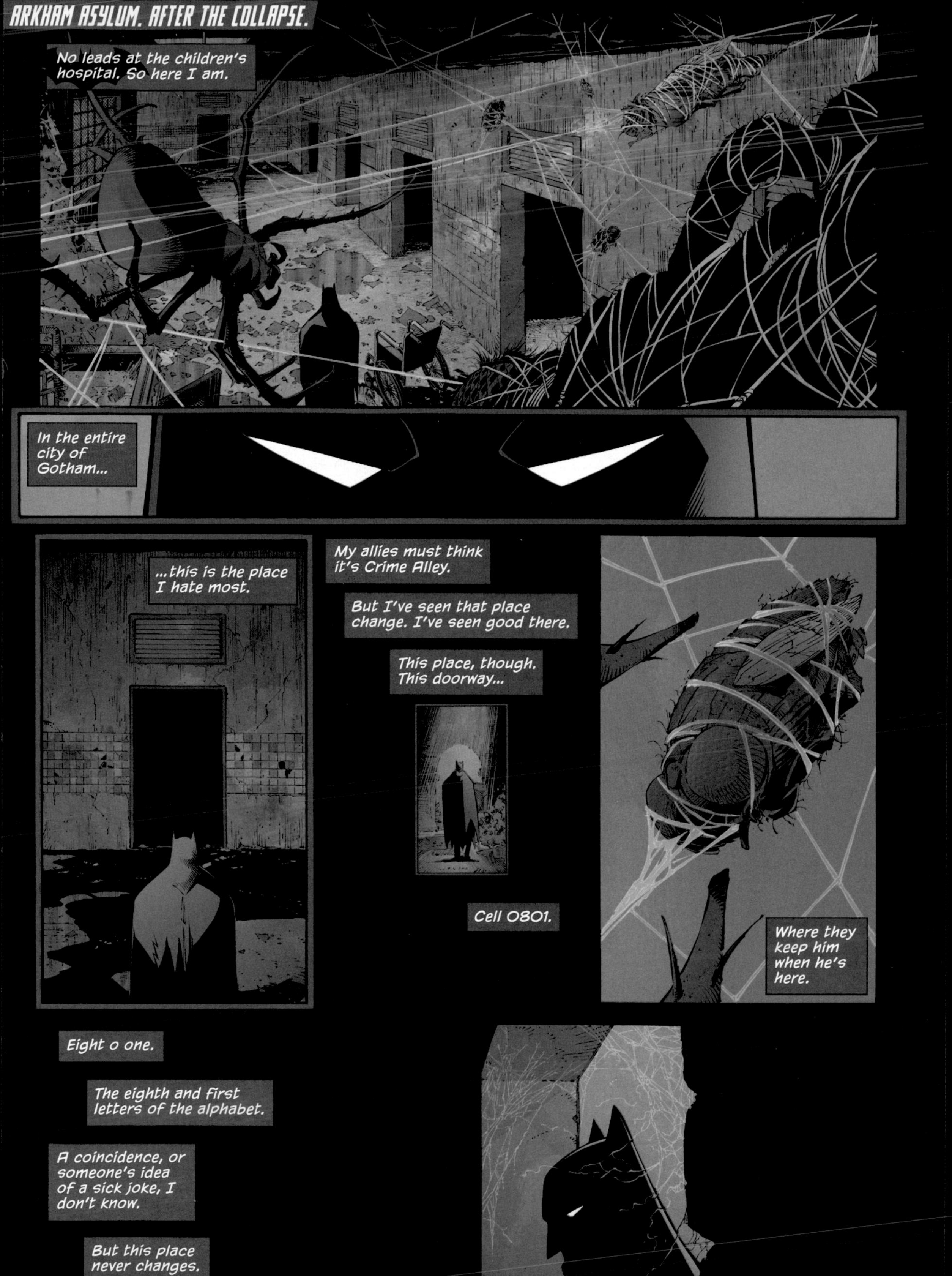
ARKHAM ASYLUM. AFTER THE COLLAPSE.
No leads at the children's hospital. So here I am.
In the entire city of Gotham...
...this is the place I hate most.
My allies must think it's Crime Alley.
But I've seen that place change. I've seen good there.
This place, though. This doorway...
Cell 0801.
Where they keep him when he's here.
Eight o one.
The eighth and first letters of the alphabet.
A coincidence, or someone's idea of a sick joke, I don't know.
But this place never changes.

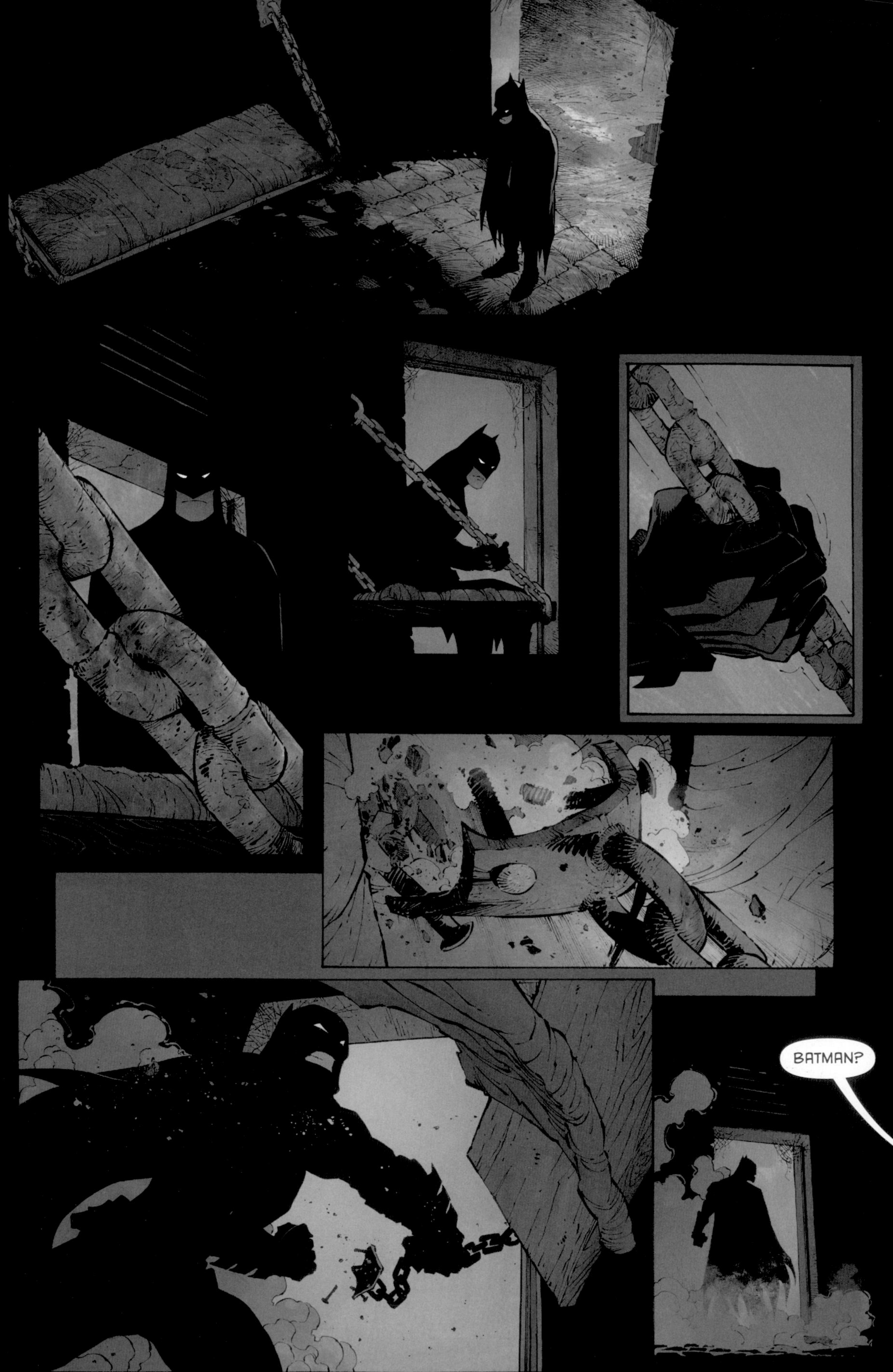
BATMAN?

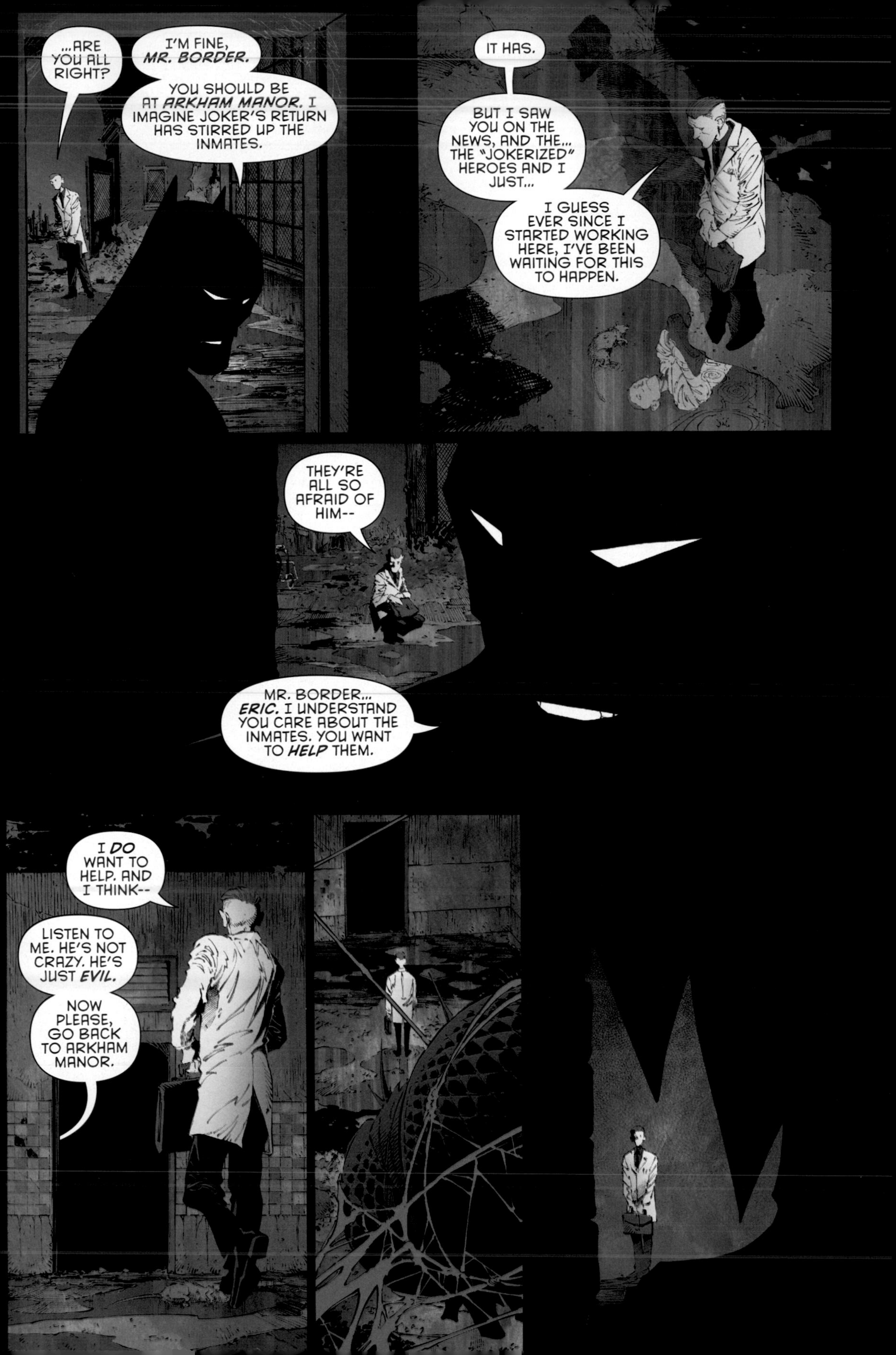
...ARE YOU ALL RIGHT?
I'M FINE, *MR. BORDER.*
YOU SHOULD BE AT *ARKHAM MANOR.* I IMAGINE JOKER'S RETURN HAS STIRRED UP THE INMATES.
IT HAS.
BUT I SAW YOU ON THE NEWS, AND THE... THE "JOKERIZED" HEROES AND I JUST...
I GUESS EVER SINCE I STARTED WORKING HERE, I'VE BEEN WAITING FOR THIS TO HAPPEN.
THEY'RE ALL SO AFRAID OF HIM--
MR. BORDER... *ERIC.* I UNDERSTAND YOU CARE ABOUT THE INMATES. YOU WANT TO *HELP* THEM.
I *DO* WANT TO HELP. AND I THINK--
LISTEN TO ME. HE'S NOT CRAZY. HE'S JUST *EVIL.*
NOW PLEASE, GO BACK TO ARKHAM MANOR.

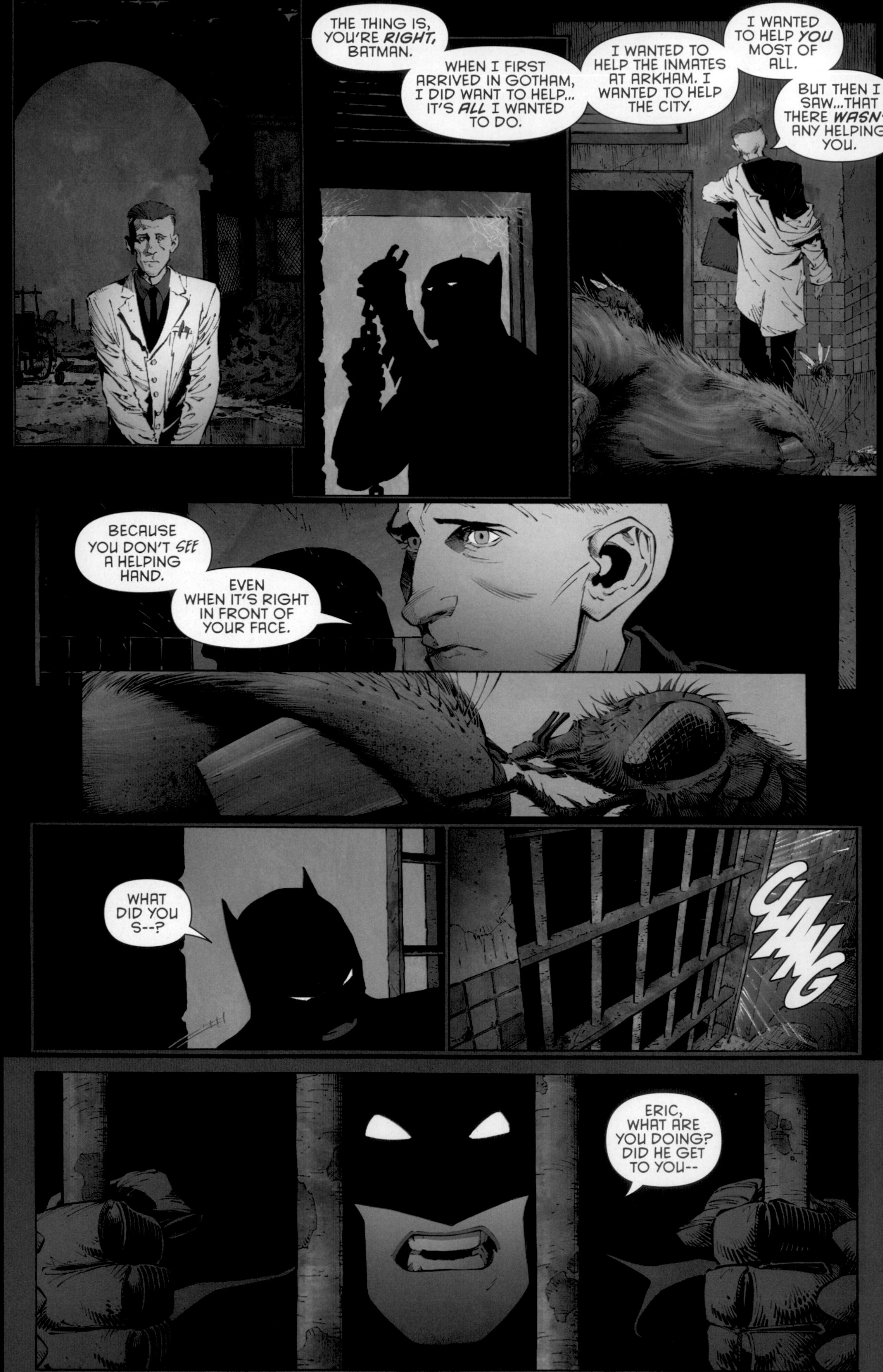
THE THING IS, YOU'RE RIGHT, BATMAN.
WHEN I FIRST ARRIVED IN GOTHAM, I DID WANT TO HELP... IT'S ALL I WANTED TO DO.
I WANTED TO HELP THE INMATES AT ARKHAM. I WANTED TO HELP THE CITY.
I WANTED TO HELP YOU MOST OF ALL.
BUT THEN I SAW...THAT THERE WASN'T ANY HELPING YOU.
BECAUSE YOU DON'T SEE A HELPING HAND.
EVEN WHEN IT'S RIGHT IN FRONT OF YOUR FACE.
WHAT DID YOU S--?
CLANG
ERIC, WHAT ARE YOU DOING? DID HE GET TO YOU--

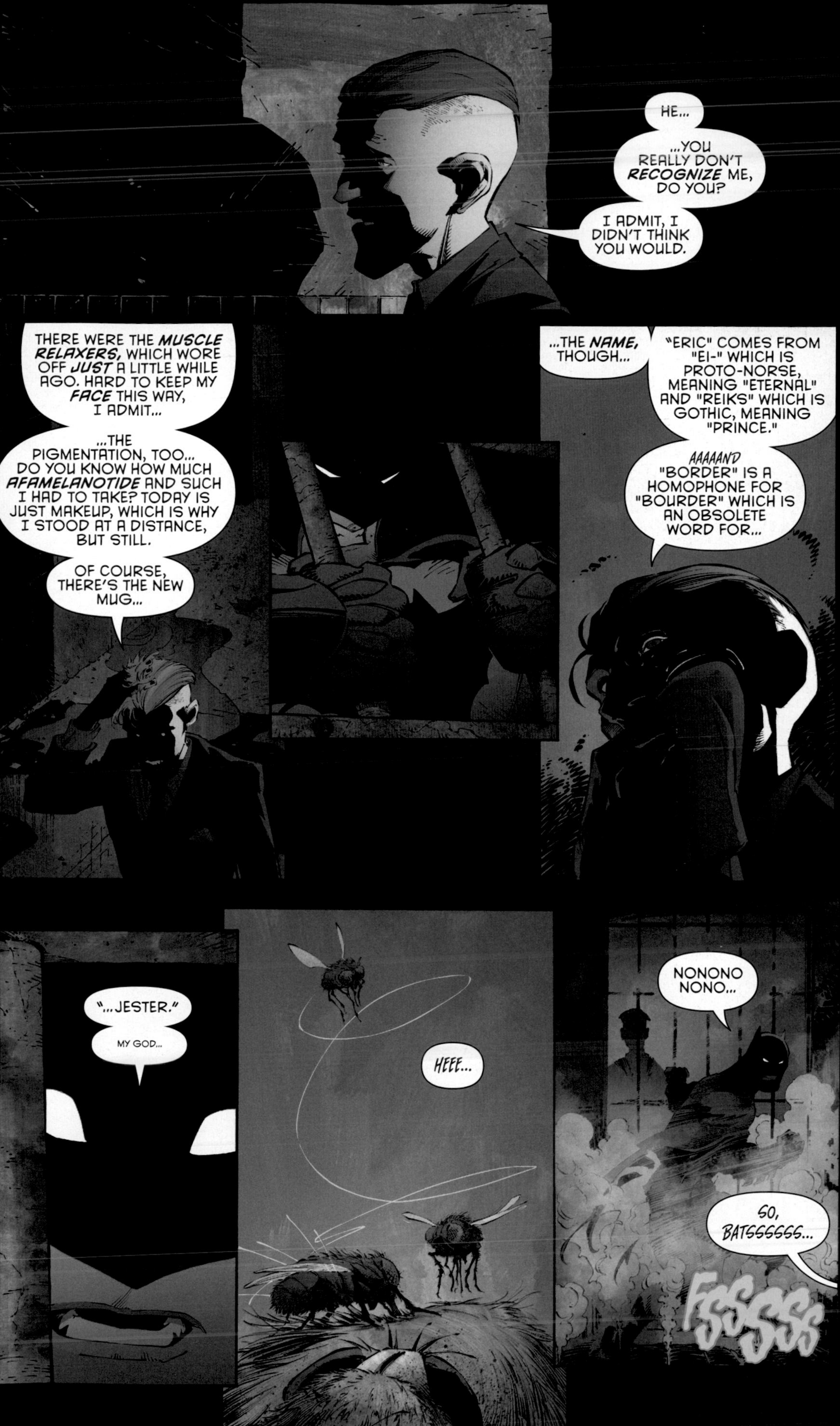
HE...
...YOU REALLY DON'T RECOGNIZE ME, DO YOU?
I ADMIT, I DIDN'T THINK YOU WOULD.
THERE WERE THE MUSCLE RELAXERS, WHICH WORE OFF JUST A LITTLE WHILE AGO. HARD TO KEEP MY FACE THIS WAY, I ADMIT...
...THE PIGMENTATION, TOO... DO YOU KNOW HOW MUCH AFAMELANOTIDE AND SUCH I HAD TO TAKE? TODAY IS JUST MAKEUP, WHICH IS WHY I STOOD AT A DISTANCE, BUT STILL.
OF COURSE, THERE'S THE NEW MUG...
...THE NAME, THOUGH...
"ERIC" COMES FROM "EI-" WHICH IS PROTO-NORSE, MEANING "ETERNAL" AND "REIKS" WHICH IS GOTHIC, MEANING "PRINCE."
AAAAAND "BORDER" IS A HOMOPHONE FOR "BOURDER" WHICH IS AN OBSOLETE WORD FOR...
"...JESTER."
MY GOD...
HEEE...
NONONO NONO...
SO, BATSSSSSS...
FSSSSS

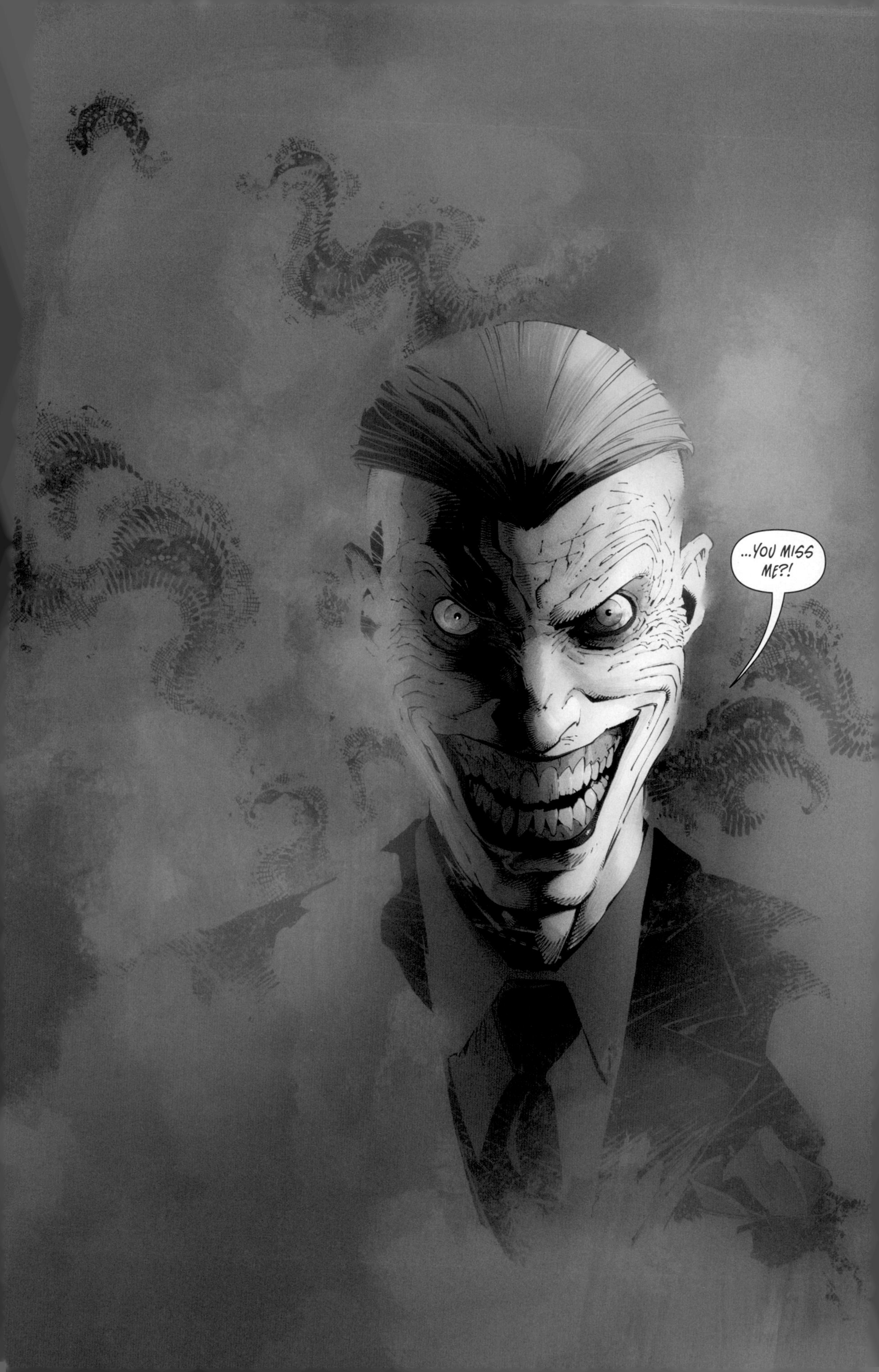
...YOU MISS ME?!

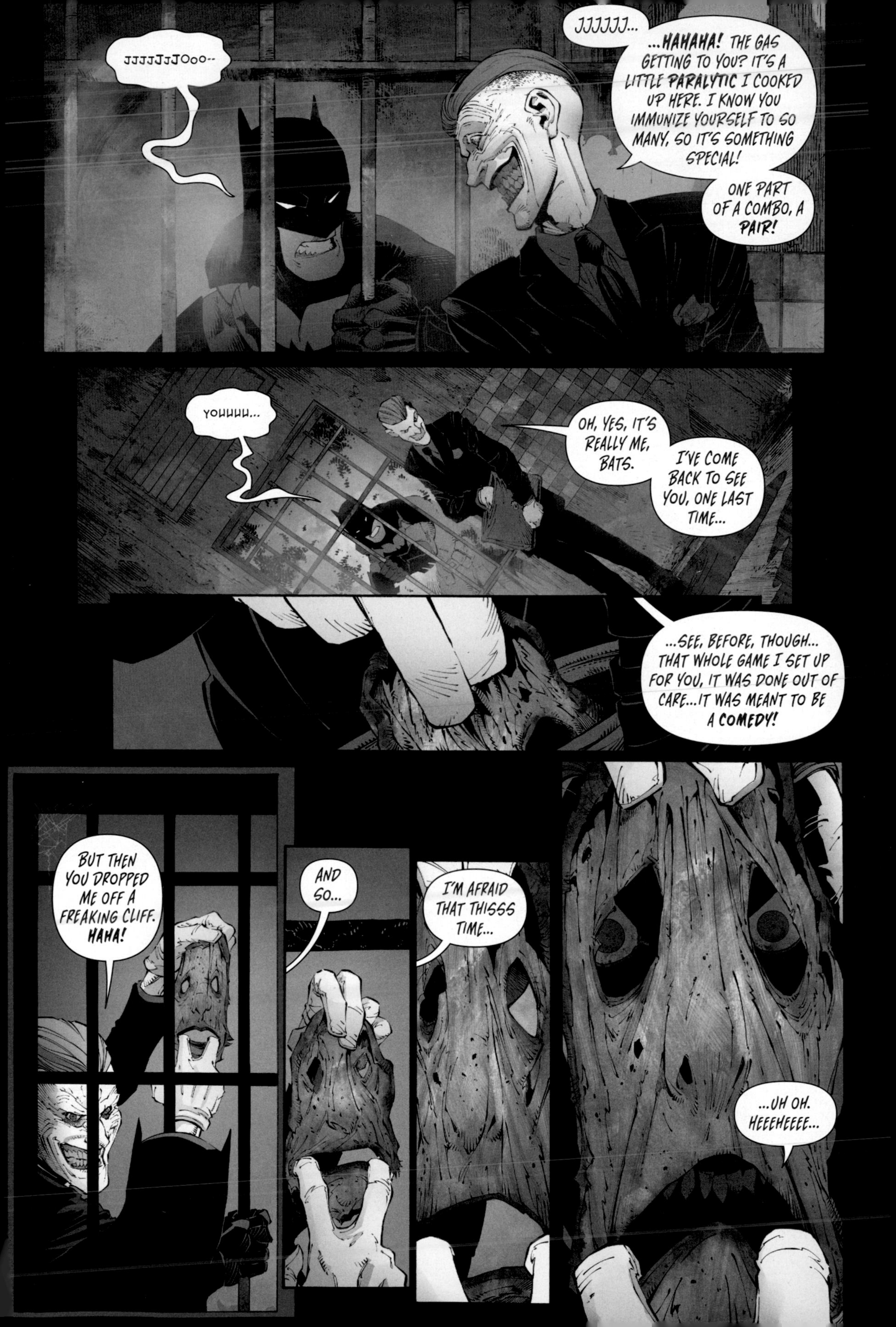

JJJJJJJOoo--
JJJJJ...
...HAHAHA! THE GAS GETTING TO YOU? IT'S A LITTLE PARALYTIC I COOKED UP HERE. I KNOW YOU IMMUNIZE YOURSELF TO SO MANY, SO IT'S SOMETHING SPECIAL!
ONE PART OF A COMBO, A PAIR!
YOUUUU...
OH, YES, IT'S REALLY ME, BATS.
I'VE COME BACK TO SEE YOU, ONE LAST TIME...
...SEE, BEFORE, THOUGH... THAT WHOLE GAME I SET UP FOR YOU, IT WAS DONE OUT OF CARE...IT WAS MEANT TO BE A COMEDY!
BUT THEN YOU DROPPED ME OFF A FREAKING CLIFF. HAHA!
AND SO...
I'M AFRAID THAT THISSS TIME...
...UH OH. HEEEHEEEE...

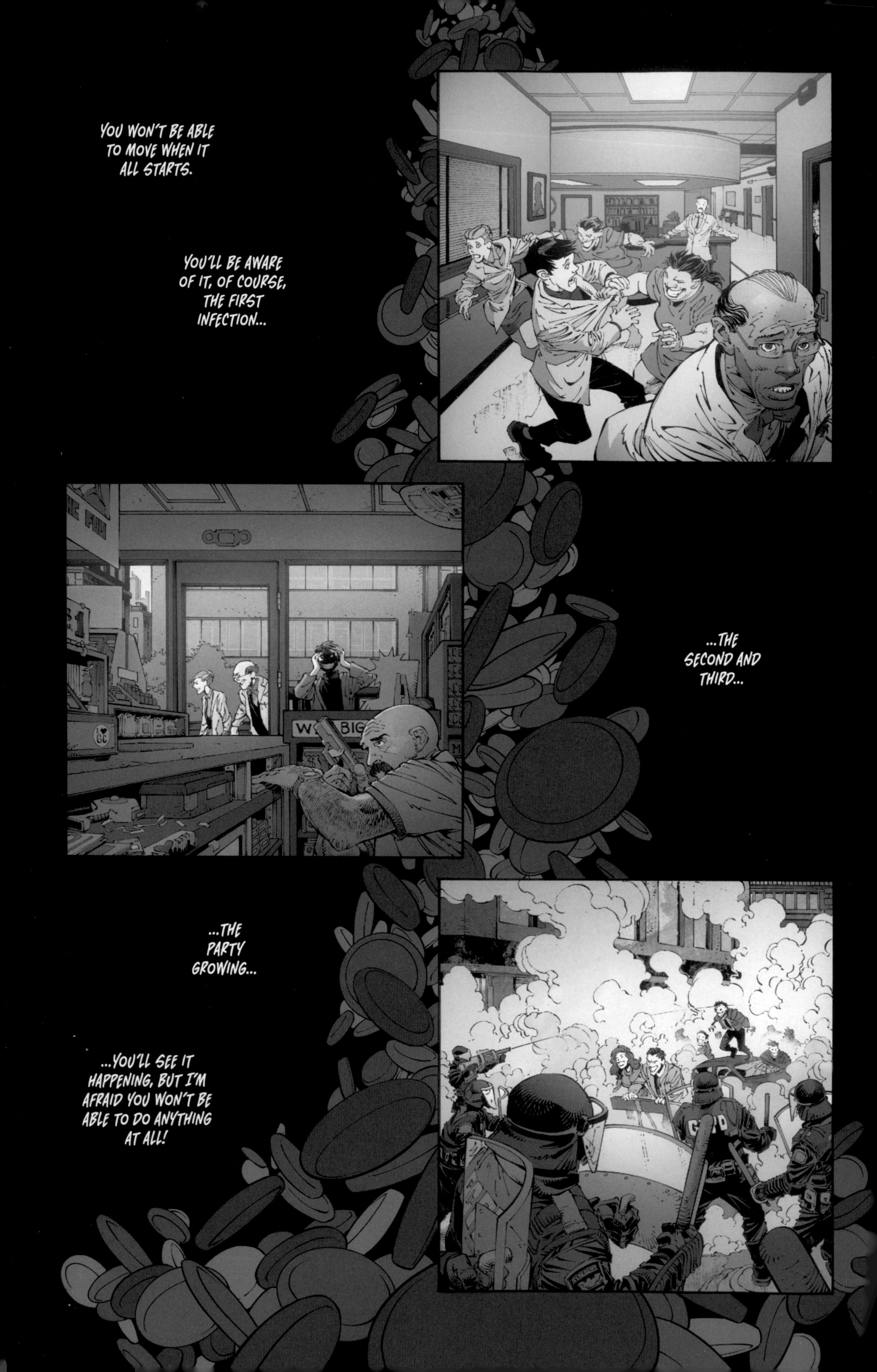
YOU WON'T BE ABLE TO MOVE WHEN IT ALL STARTS.
YOU'LL BE AWARE OF IT, OF COURSE, THE FIRST INFECTION...
...THE SECOND AND THIRD...
...THE PARTY GROWING...
...YOU'LL SEE IT HAPPENING, BUT I'M AFRAID YOU WON'T BE ABLE TO DO ANYTHING AT ALL!

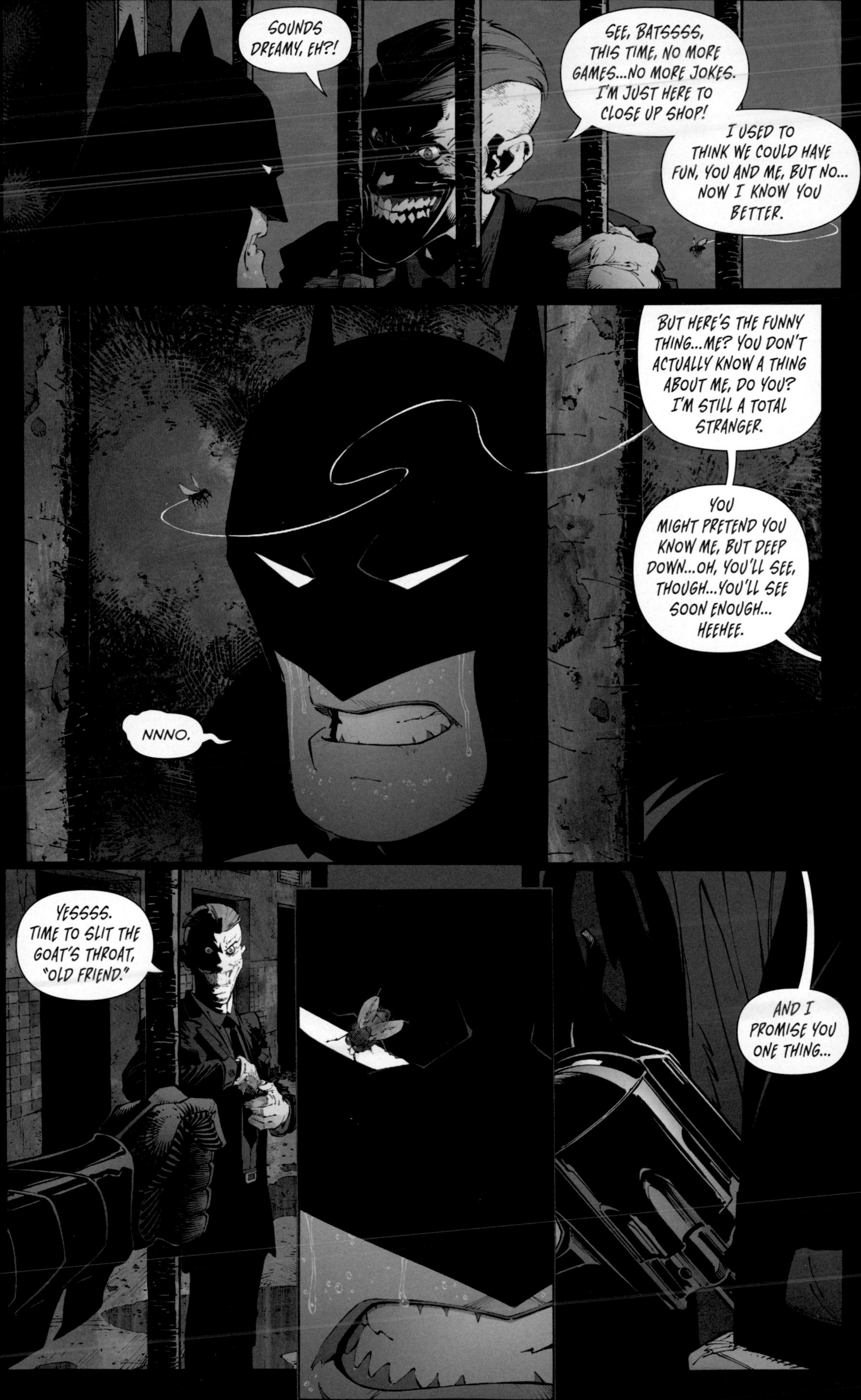
SOUNDS DREAMY, EH?!
SEE, BATSSSS, THIS TIME, NO MORE GAMES...NO MORE JOKES. I'M JUST HERE TO CLOSE UP SHOP!
I USED TO THINK WE COULD HAVE FUN, YOU AND ME, BUT NO... NOW I KNOW YOU BETTER.
BUT HERE'S THE FUNNY THING...ME? YOU DON'T ACTUALLY KNOW A THING ABOUT ME, DO YOU? I'M STILL A TOTAL STRANGER.
YOU MIGHT PRETEND YOU KNOW ME, BUT DEEP DOWN...OH, YOU'LL SEE, THOUGH...YOU'LL SEE SOON ENOUGH... HEEHEE.
NNNO.
YESSSS. TIME TO SLIT THE GOAT'S THROAT, "OLD FRIEND."
AND I PROMISE YOU ONE THING...

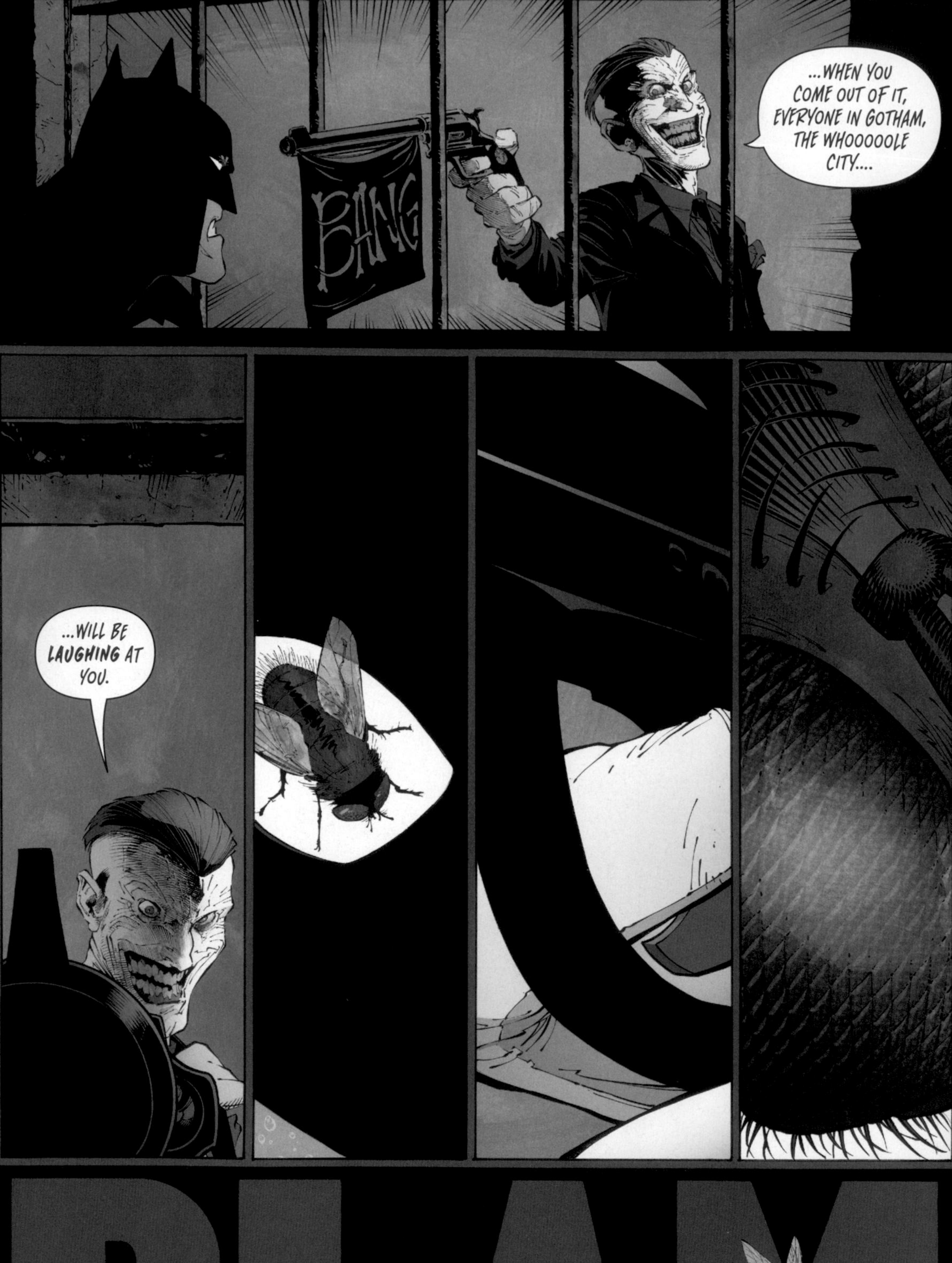
BANG
...WHEN YOU COME OUT OF IT, EVERYONE IN GOTHAM, THE WHOOOOOLE CITY....
...WILL BE LAUGHING AT YOU.

"IT'S JUST STRANGE, THE WAY A LAUGH ECHOES. FROM A DISTANCE, ALL PERSONALITY GETS STRIPPED AWAY. IT'S JUST THE NOISE...

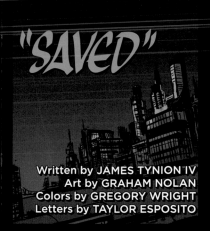

"SAVED"

Written by JAMES TYNION IV
Art by GRAHAM NOLAN
Colors by GREGORY WRIGHT
Letters by TAYLOR ESPOSITO

GREAT WALL
Chinese Restaurant

"...THOSE HIGH-PITCHED JOLTS OF SOUND. RIPPED AWAY FROM A PERSON. THIS FAR AWAY, IT STOPS SOUNDING NICE...IT STOPS SOUNDING *FUN*..."

...HERE, IT STARTS TO SOUND LIKE SCREAMING.

DEAR, SOME OF THOSE NOISES *ARE* SCREAMS.

Oh.

P-PLEASE...ARE YOU A *DOCTOR?* YOUR COAT...IT SAYS YOU'RE FROM *ARKHAM.*

I GOT *BIT.* ONE OF THEM BIT ME...

I'M SORRY... I CAN'T...I CAN'T HELP... THEY WON'T LET ME.

WHO BIT YOU?

ONE OF *THEM.* ONE OF THE ONES ON THE STREET. THEY...THEY WERE LAUGHING. SMILING.

HE'S BACK, ISN'T HE? *THE JOKER...*

...I THINK I'M *SICK.*

NO! CAN'T GET US SICK. NO NO NO...

...WE'RE ON A MISSION!

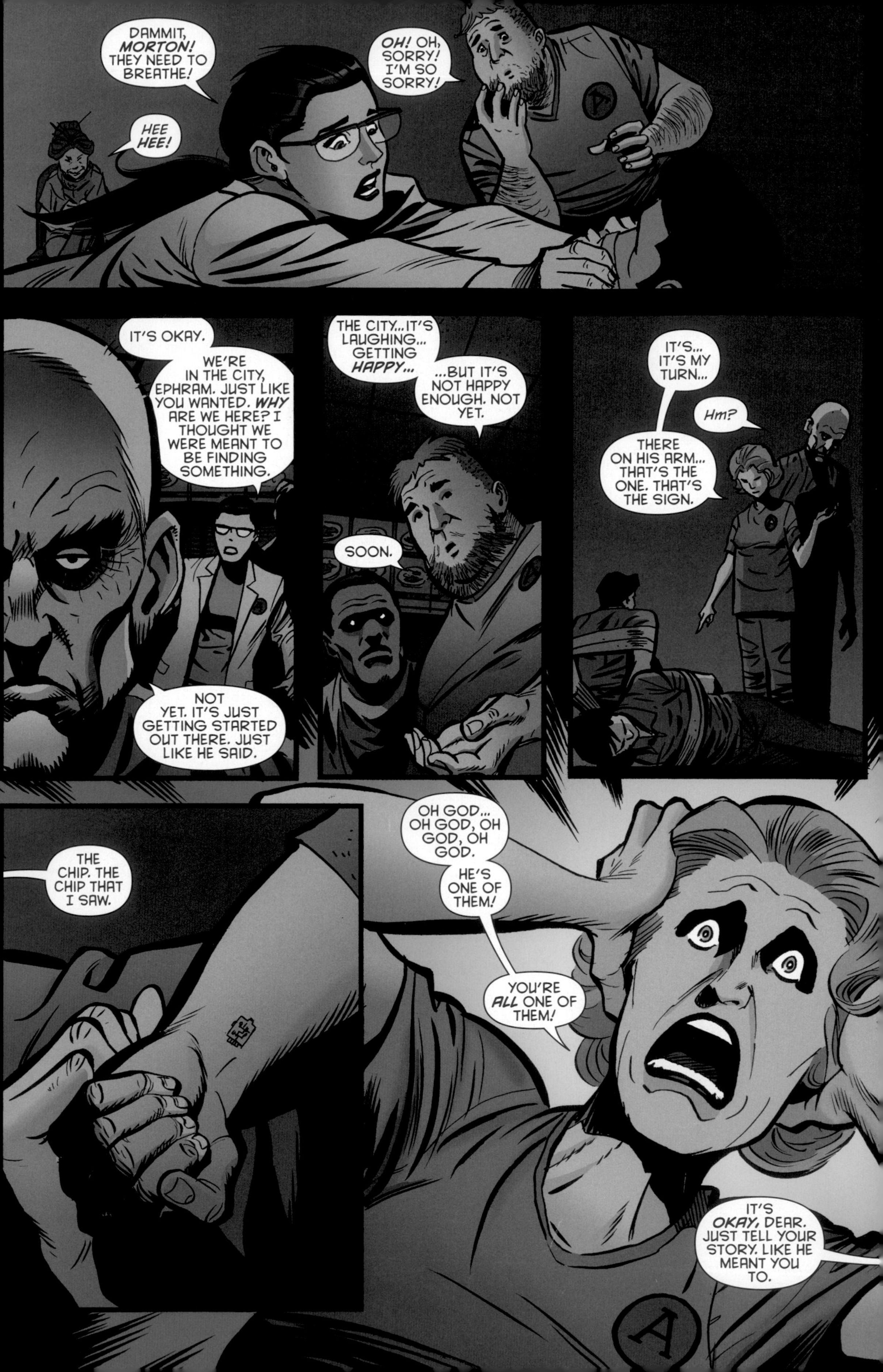
DAMMIT, MORTON! THEY NEED TO BREATHE!
OH! OH, SORRY! I'M SO SORRY!
HEE HEE!
IT'S OKAY.
WE'RE IN THE CITY, EPHRAM. JUST LIKE YOU WANTED. WHY ARE WE HERE? I THOUGHT WE WERE MEANT TO BE FINDING SOMETHING.
NOT YET. IT'S JUST GETTING STARTED OUT THERE. JUST LIKE HE SAID.
THE CITY... IT'S LAUGHING... GETTING HAPPY...
...BUT IT'S NOT HAPPY ENOUGH. NOT YET.
SOON.
IT'S... IT'S MY TURN...
Hm?
THERE ON HIS ARM... THAT'S THE ONE. THAT'S THE SIGN.
THE CHIP. THE CHIP THAT I SAW.
OH GOD... OH GOD, OH GOD, OH GOD.
HE'S ONE OF THEM!
YOU'RE ALL ONE OF THEM!
IT'S OKAY, DEAR. JUST TELL YOUR STORY. LIKE HE MEANT YOU TO.

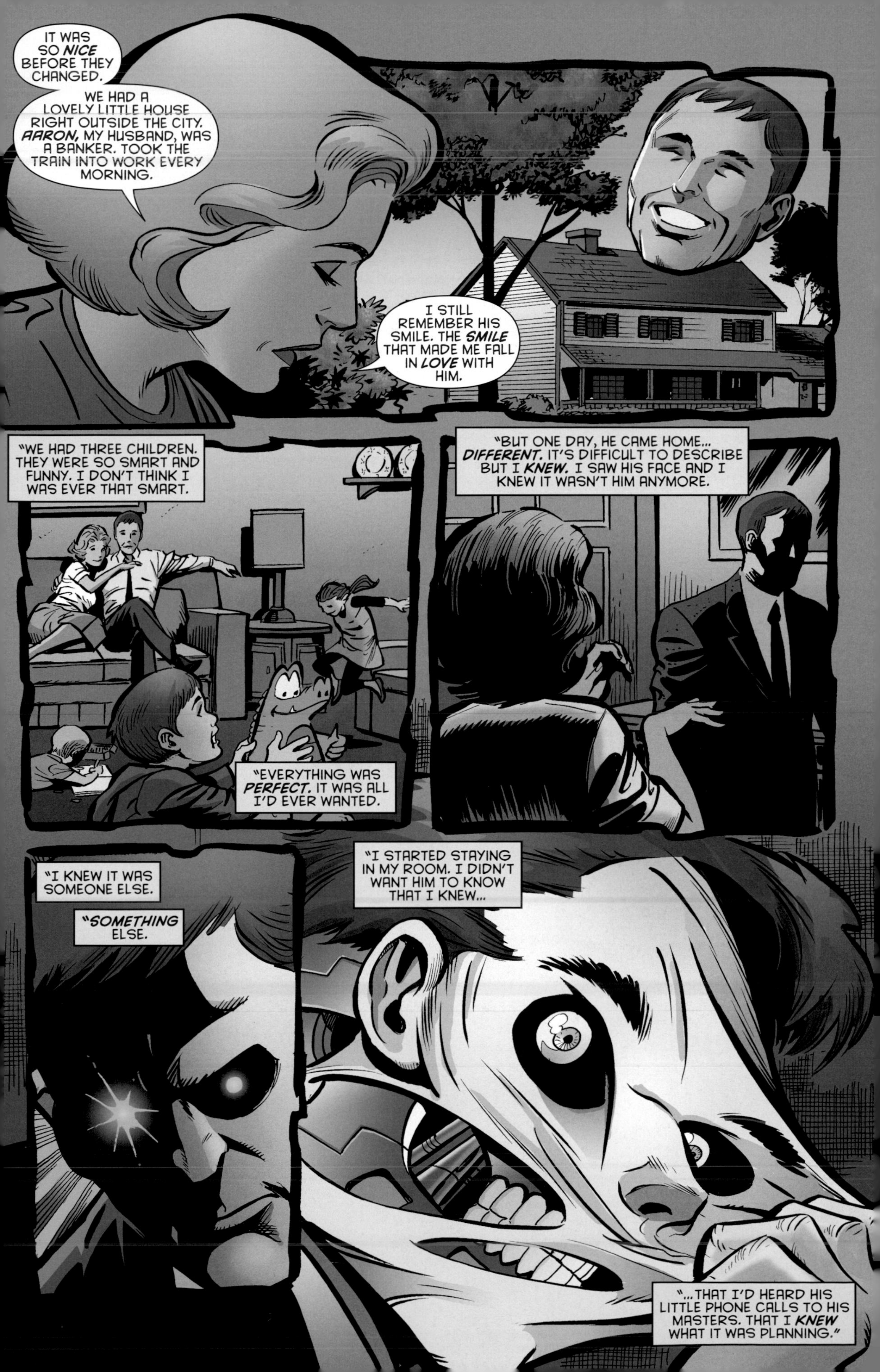
IT WAS SO NICE BEFORE THEY CHANGED.
WE HAD A LOVELY LITTLE HOUSE RIGHT OUTSIDE THE CITY. AARON, MY HUSBAND, WAS A BANKER. TOOK THE TRAIN INTO WORK EVERY MORNING.
I STILL REMEMBER HIS SMILE. THE SMILE THAT MADE ME FALL IN LOVE WITH HIM.
"WE HAD THREE CHILDREN. THEY WERE SO SMART AND FUNNY. I DON'T THINK I WAS EVER THAT SMART.
"EVERYTHING WAS PERFECT. IT WAS ALL I'D EVER WANTED.
"BUT ONE DAY, HE CAME HOME... DIFFERENT. IT'S DIFFICULT TO DESCRIBE BUT I KNEW. I SAW HIS FACE AND I KNEW IT WASN'T HIM ANYMORE.
"I KNEW IT WAS SOMEONE ELSE.
"SOMETHING ELSE.
"I STARTED STAYING IN MY ROOM. I DIDN'T WANT HIM TO KNOW THAT I KNEW...
"...THAT I'D HEARD HIS LITTLE PHONE CALLS TO HIS MASTERS. THAT I KNEW WHAT IT WAS PLANNING."

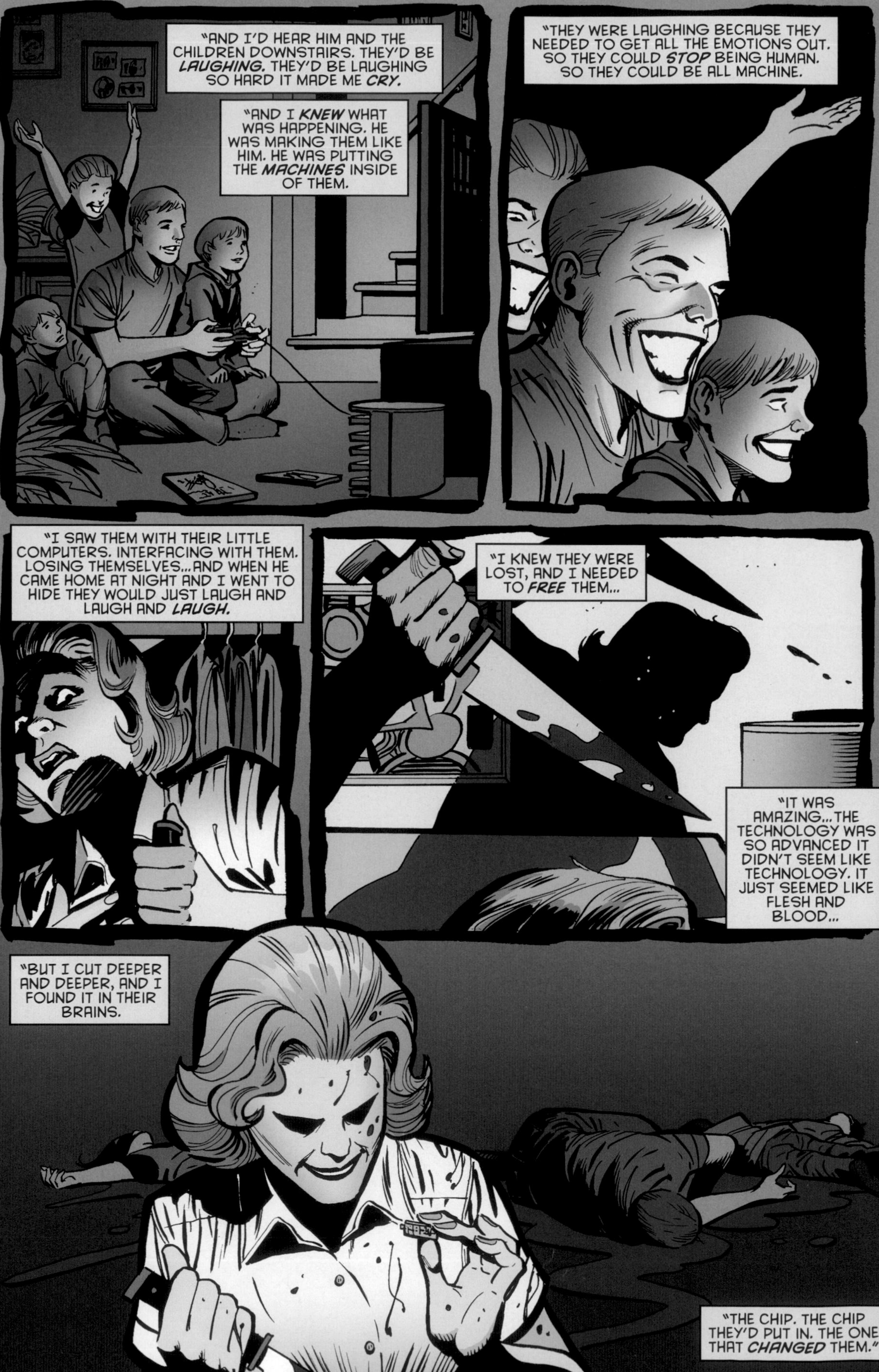
"AND I'D HEAR HIM AND THE CHILDREN DOWNSTAIRS. THEY'D BE LAUGHING. THEY'D BE LAUGHING SO HARD IT MADE ME CRY.
"AND I KNEW WHAT WAS HAPPENING. HE WAS MAKING THEM LIKE HIM. HE WAS PUTTING THE MACHINES INSIDE OF THEM.
"THEY WERE LAUGHING BECAUSE THEY NEEDED TO GET ALL THE EMOTIONS OUT. SO THEY COULD STOP BEING HUMAN. SO THEY COULD BE ALL MACHINE.
"I SAW THEM WITH THEIR LITTLE COMPUTERS. INTERFACING WITH THEM. LOSING THEMSELVES...AND WHEN HE CAME HOME AT NIGHT AND I WENT TO HIDE THEY WOULD JUST LAUGH AND LAUGH AND LAUGH.
"I KNEW THEY WERE LOST, AND I NEEDED TO FREE THEM...
"IT WAS AMAZING... THE TECHNOLOGY WAS SO ADVANCED IT DIDN'T SEEM LIKE TECHNOLOGY. IT JUST SEEMED LIKE FLESH AND BLOOD...
"BUT I CUT DEEPER AND DEEPER, AND I FOUND IT IN THEIR BRAINS.
"THE CHIP. THE CHIP THEY'D PUT IN. THE ONE THAT CHANGED THEM."

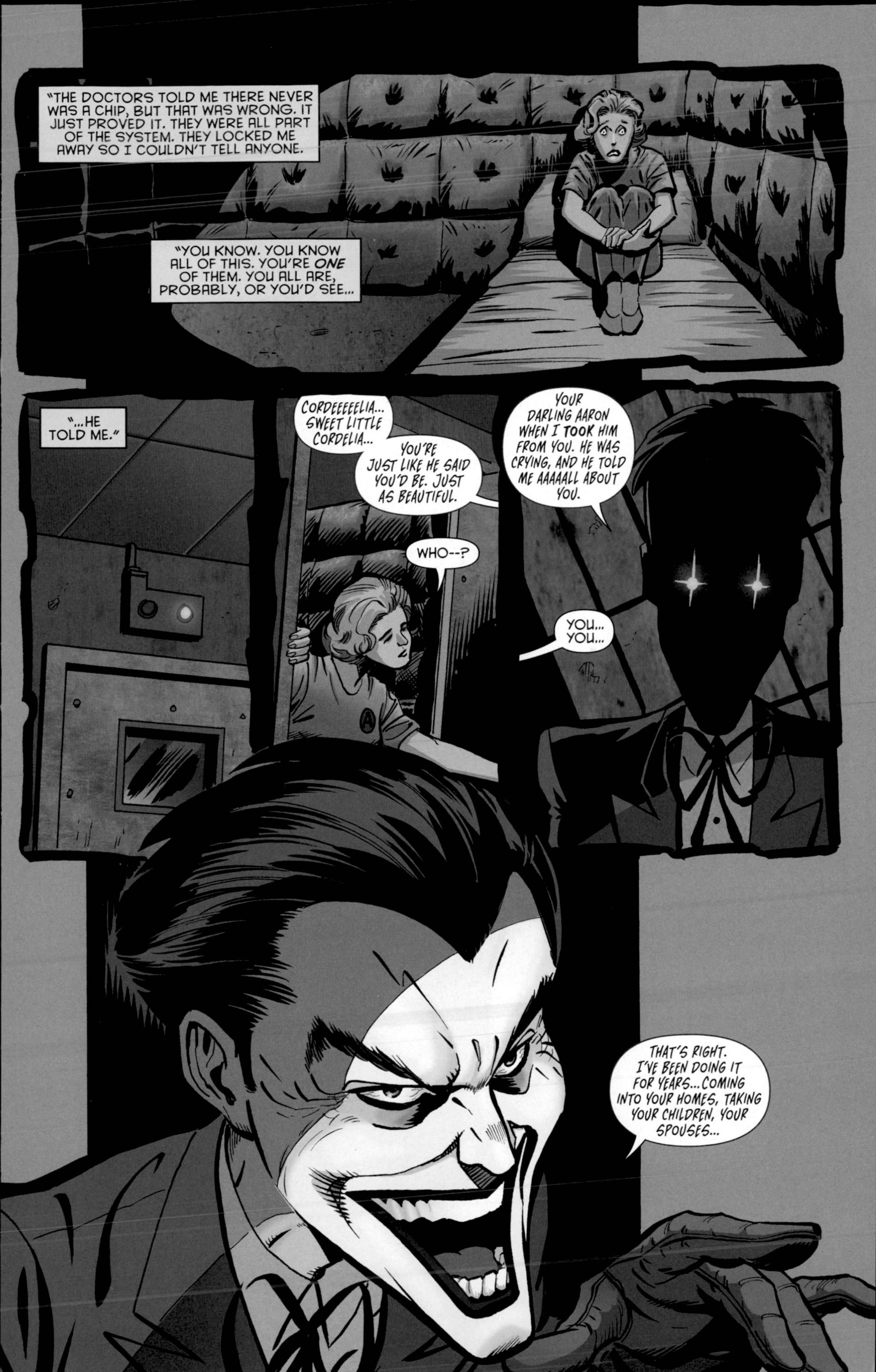
"THE DOCTORS TOLD ME THERE NEVER WAS A CHIP, BUT THAT WAS WRONG. IT JUST PROVED IT. THEY WERE ALL PART OF THE SYSTEM. THEY LOCKED ME AWAY SO I COULDN'T TELL ANYONE.
"YOU KNOW. YOU KNOW ALL OF THIS. YOU'RE ONE OF THEM. YOU ALL ARE, PROBABLY, OR YOU'D SEE...
"...HE TOLD ME."
CORDEEEEELIA... SWEET LITTLE CORDELIA...
YOU'RE JUST LIKE HE SAID YOU'D BE. JUST AS BEAUTIFUL.
YOUR DARLING AARON WHEN I TOOK HIM FROM YOU. HE WAS CRYING, AND HE TOLD ME AAAAALL ABOUT YOU.
WHO--?
YOU... YOU...
THAT'S RIGHT. I'VE BEEN DOING IT FOR YEARS... COMING INTO YOUR HOMES, TAKING YOUR CHILDREN, YOUR SPOUSES...

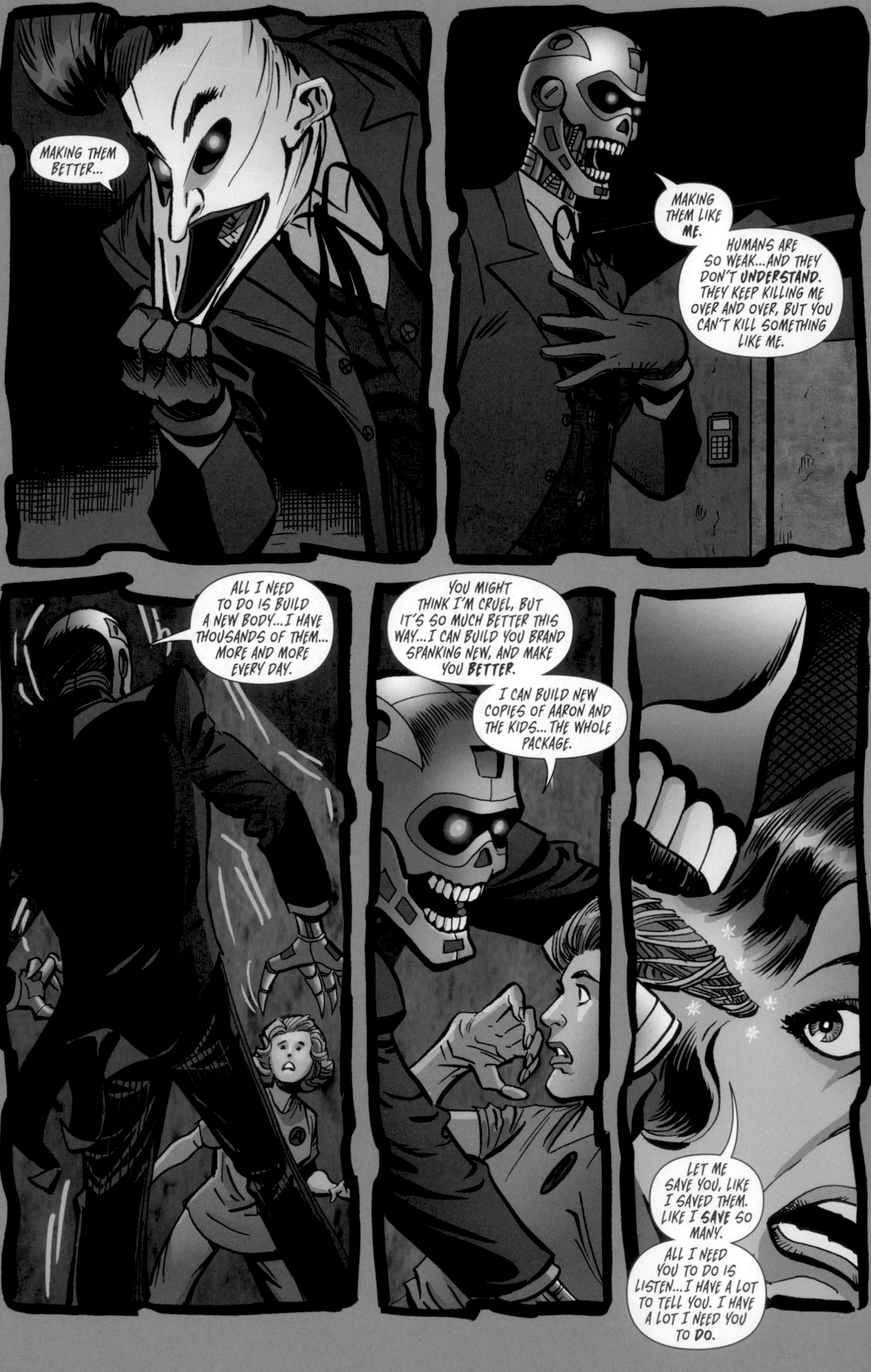
MAKING THEM BETTER...
MAKING THEM LIKE ME.
HUMANS ARE SO WEAK...AND THEY DON'T UNDERSTAND. THEY KEEP KILLING ME OVER AND OVER, BUT YOU CAN'T KILL SOMETHING LIKE ME.
ALL I NEED TO DO IS BUILD A NEW BODY...I HAVE THOUSANDS OF THEM... MORE AND MORE EVERY DAY.
YOU MIGHT THINK I'M CRUEL, BUT IT'S SO MUCH BETTER THIS WAY...I CAN BUILD YOU BRAND SPANKING NEW, AND MAKE YOU BETTER.
I CAN BUILD NEW COPIES OF AARON AND THE KIDS... THE WHOLE PACKAGE.
LET ME SAVE YOU, LIKE I SAVED THEM. LIKE I SAVE SO MANY.
ALL I NEED YOU TO DO IS LISTEN...I HAVE A LOT TO TELL YOU. I HAVE A LOT I NEED YOU TO DO.

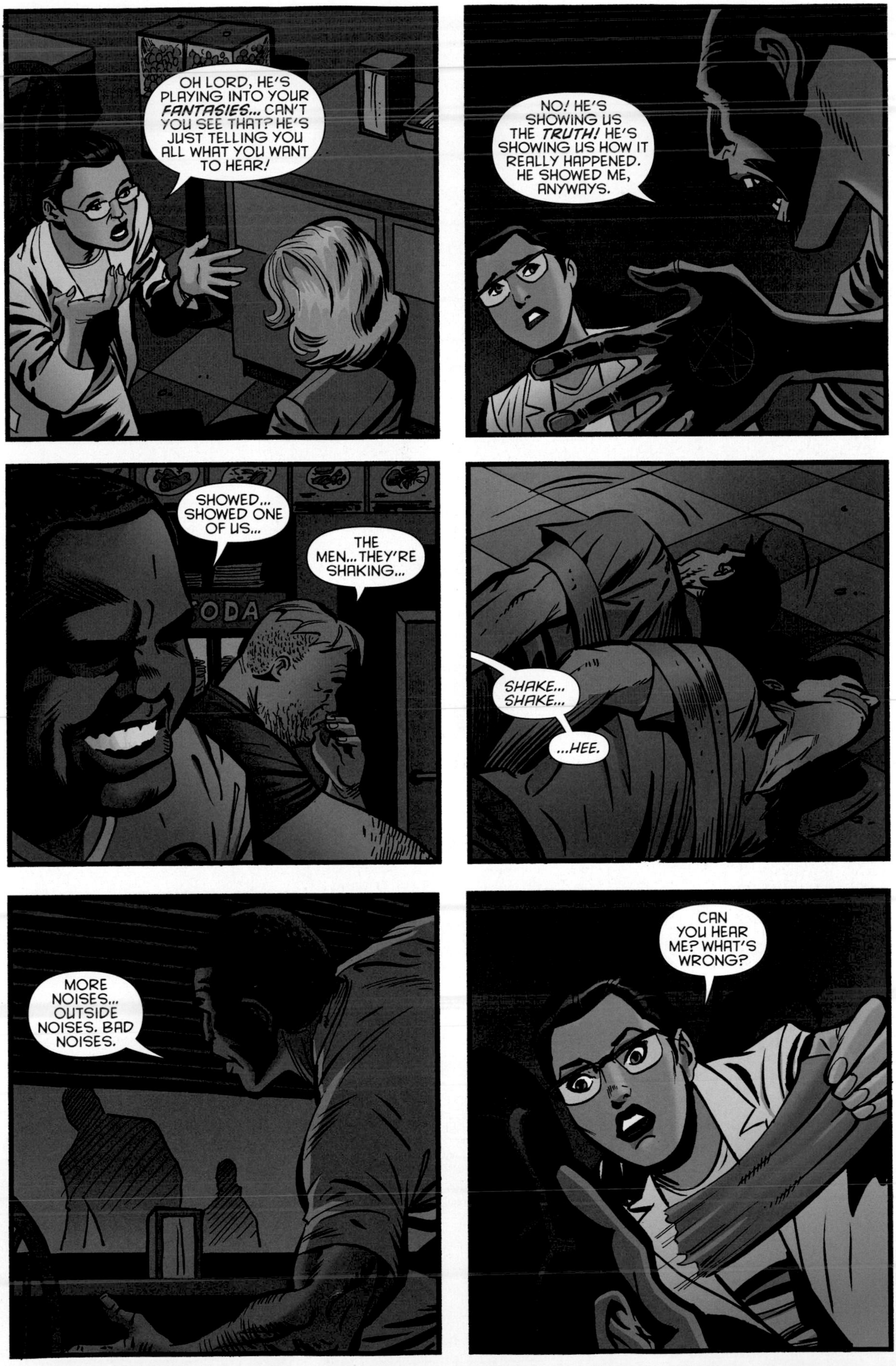
OH LORD, HE'S PLAYING INTO YOUR FANTASIES... CAN'T YOU SEE THAT? HE'S JUST TELLING YOU ALL WHAT YOU WANT TO HEAR!
NO! HE'S SHOWING US THE TRUTH! HE'S SHOWING US HOW IT REALLY HAPPENED. HE SHOWED ME, ANYWAYS.
SHOWED... SHOWED ONE OF US...
THE MEN... THEY'RE SHAKING...
SODA
SHAKE... SHAKE...
...HEE.
MORE NOISES... OUTSIDE NOISES. BAD NOISES.
CAN YOU HEAR ME? WHAT'S WRONG?

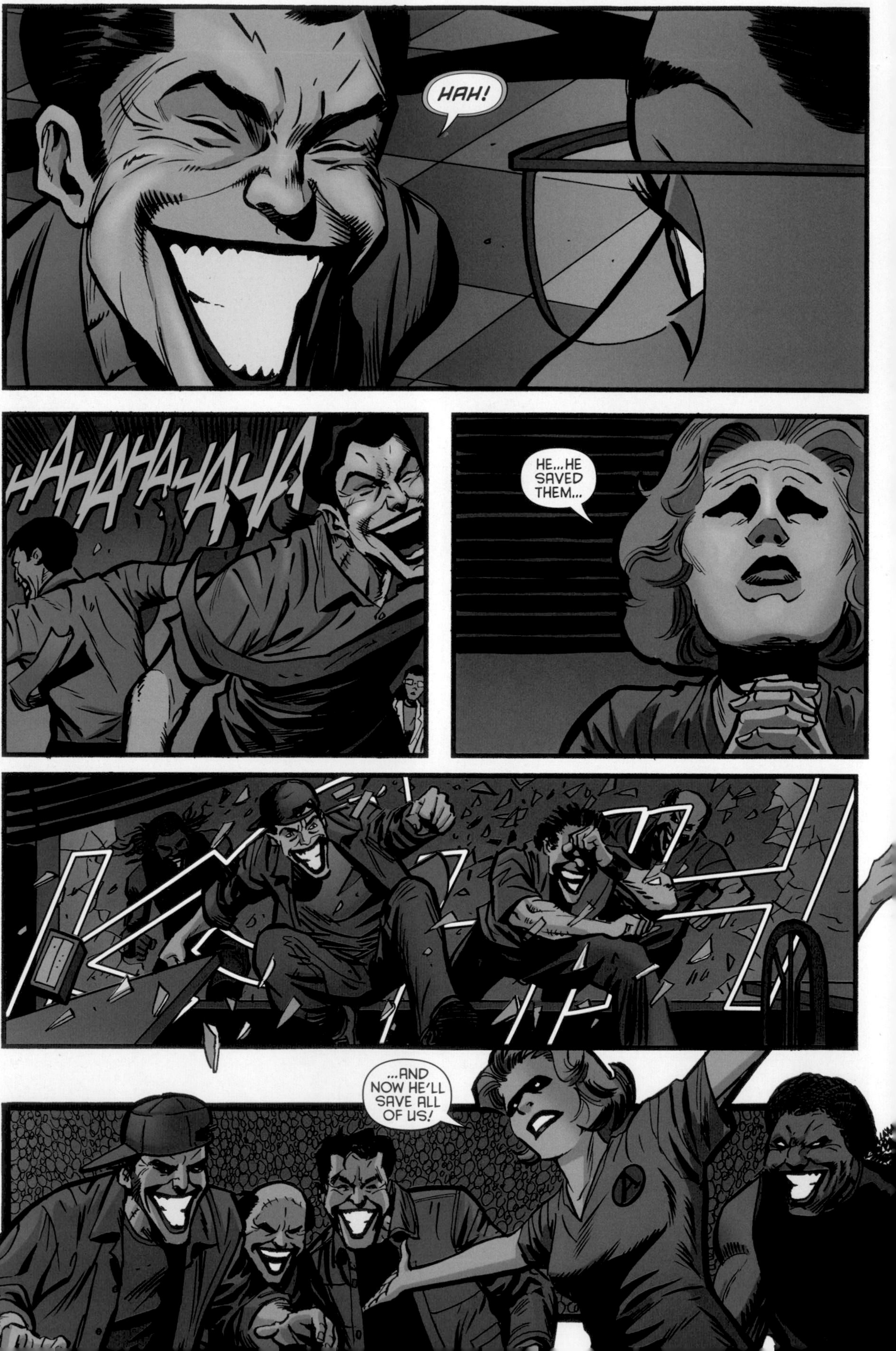
HAH!
HAHAHAHAHA
HE...HE SAVED THEM...
...AND NOW HE'LL SAVE ALL OF US!

Cover by **RAFAEL ALBUQUERQUE**

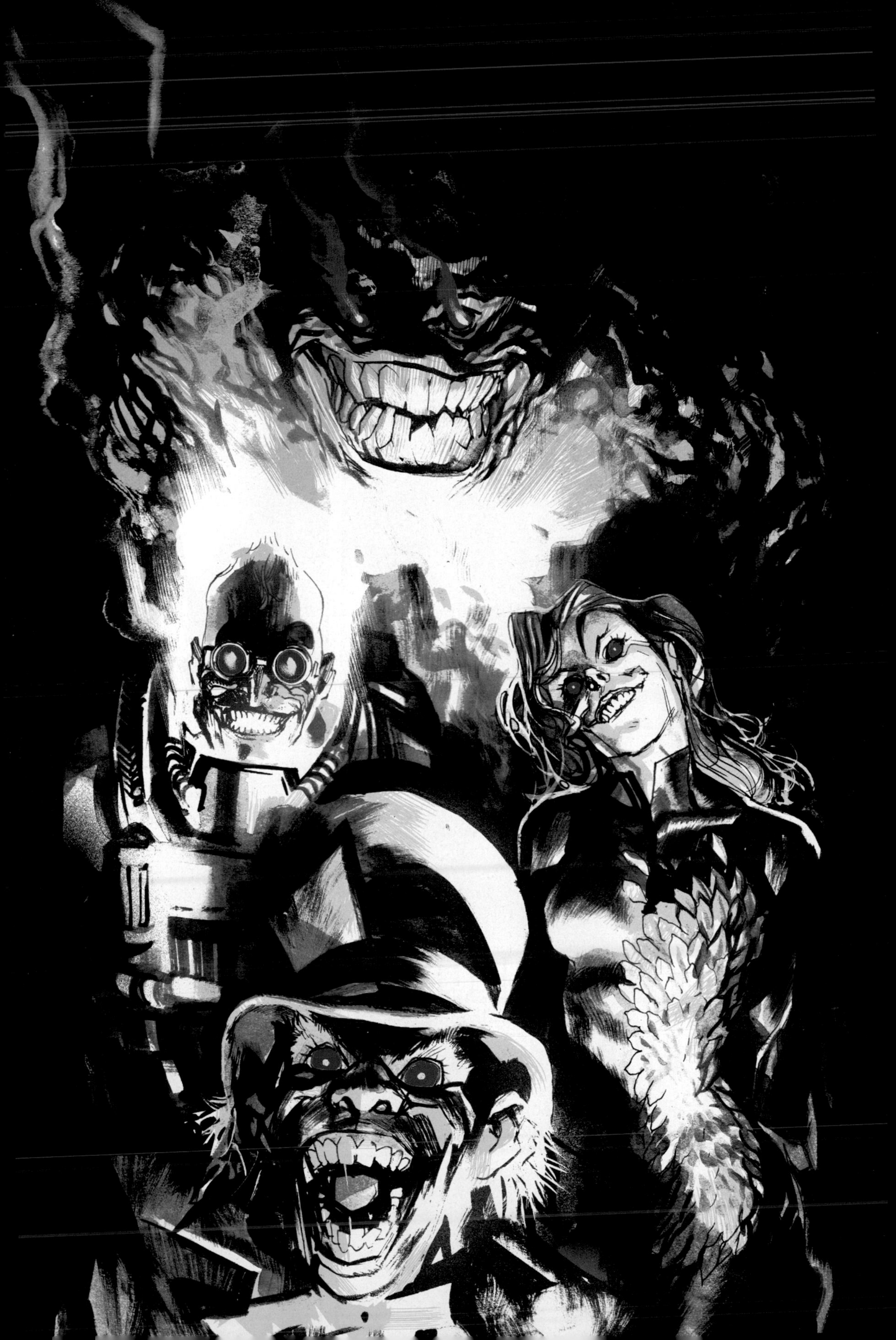

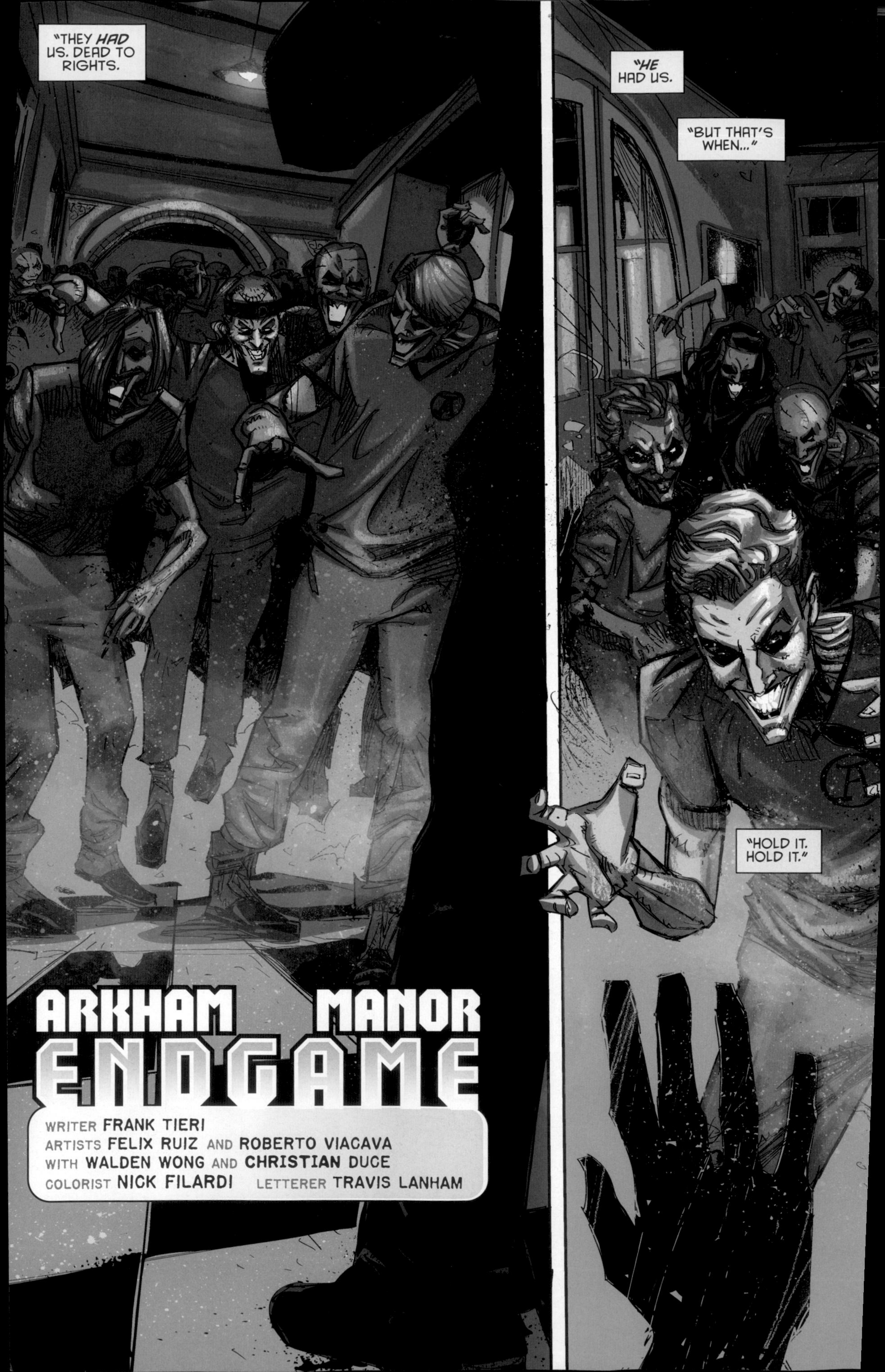
"THEY HAD US. DEAD TO RIGHTS.
"HE HAD US.
"BUT THAT'S WHEN..."
"HOLD IT. HOLD IT."
ARKHAM MANOR
ENDGAME
WRITER FRANK TIERI
ARTISTS FELIX RUIZ AND ROBERTO VIACAVA
WITH WALDEN WONG AND CHRISTIAN DUCE
COLORIST NICK FILARDI LETTERER TRAVIS LANHAM

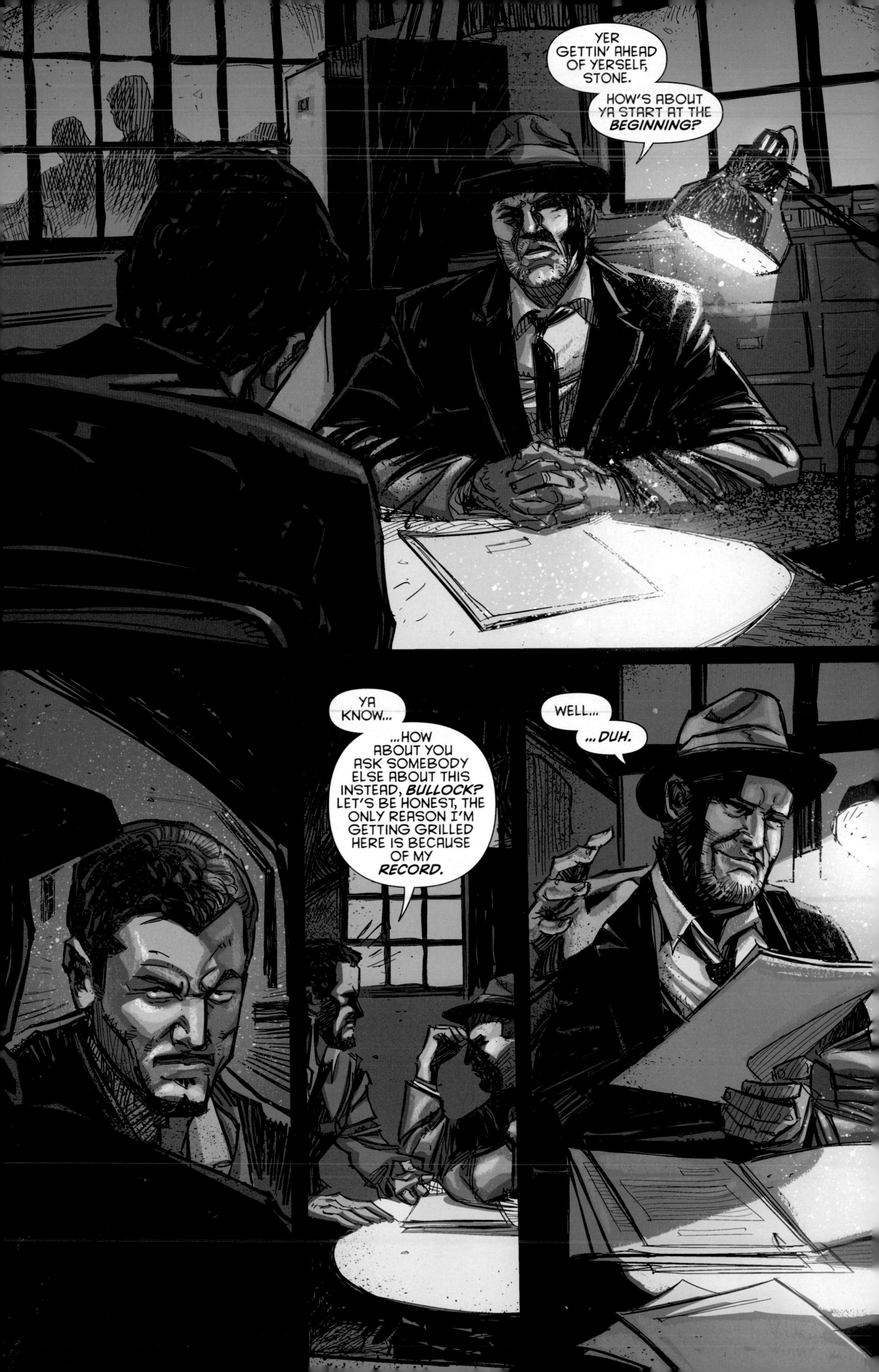
YER GETTIN' AHEAD OF YERSELF, STONE.
HOW'S ABOUT YA START AT THE BEGINNING?
YA KNOW...
...HOW ABOUT YOU ASK SOMEBODY ELSE ABOUT THIS INSTEAD, BULLOCK? LET'S BE HONEST, THE ONLY REASON I'M GETTING GRILLED HERE IS BECAUSE OF MY RECORD.
WELL...
...DUH.

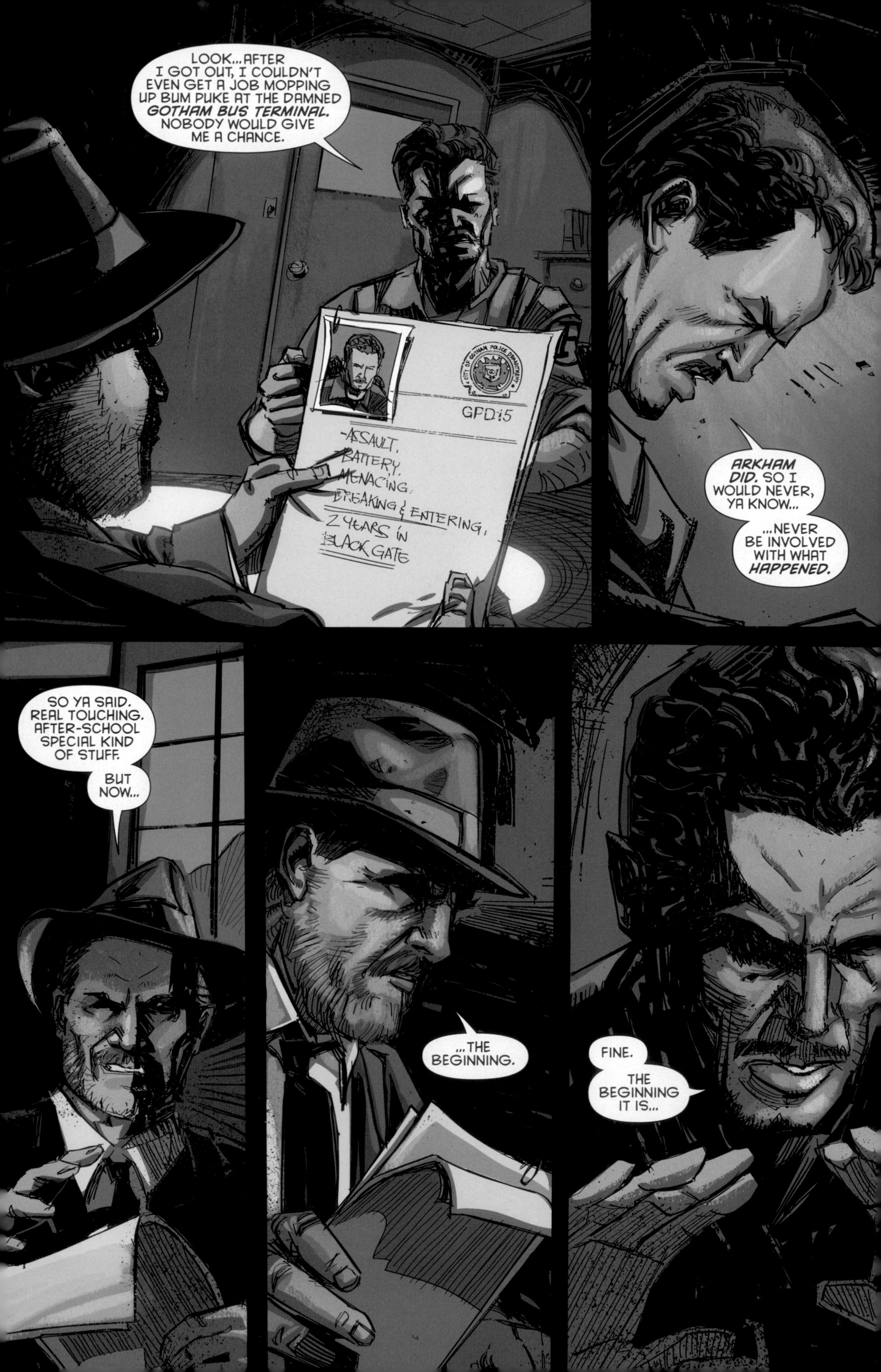
LOOK...AFTER I GOT OUT, I COULDN'T EVEN GET A JOB MOPPING UP BUM PUKE AT THE DAMNED GOTHAM BUS TERMINAL. NOBODY WOULD GIVE ME A CHANCE.
CITY OF GOTHAM POLICE DEPARTMENT
GPD15
ASSAULT, BATTERY, MENACING. BREAKING & ENTERING, 2 YEARS IN BLACK GATE
ARKHAM DID. SO I WOULD NEVER, YA KNOW...
...NEVER BE INVOLVED WITH WHAT HAPPENED.
SO YA SAID. REAL TOUCHING. AFTER-SCHOOL SPECIAL KIND OF STUFF.
BUT NOW...
...THE BEGINNING.
FINE.
THE BEGINNING IT IS...

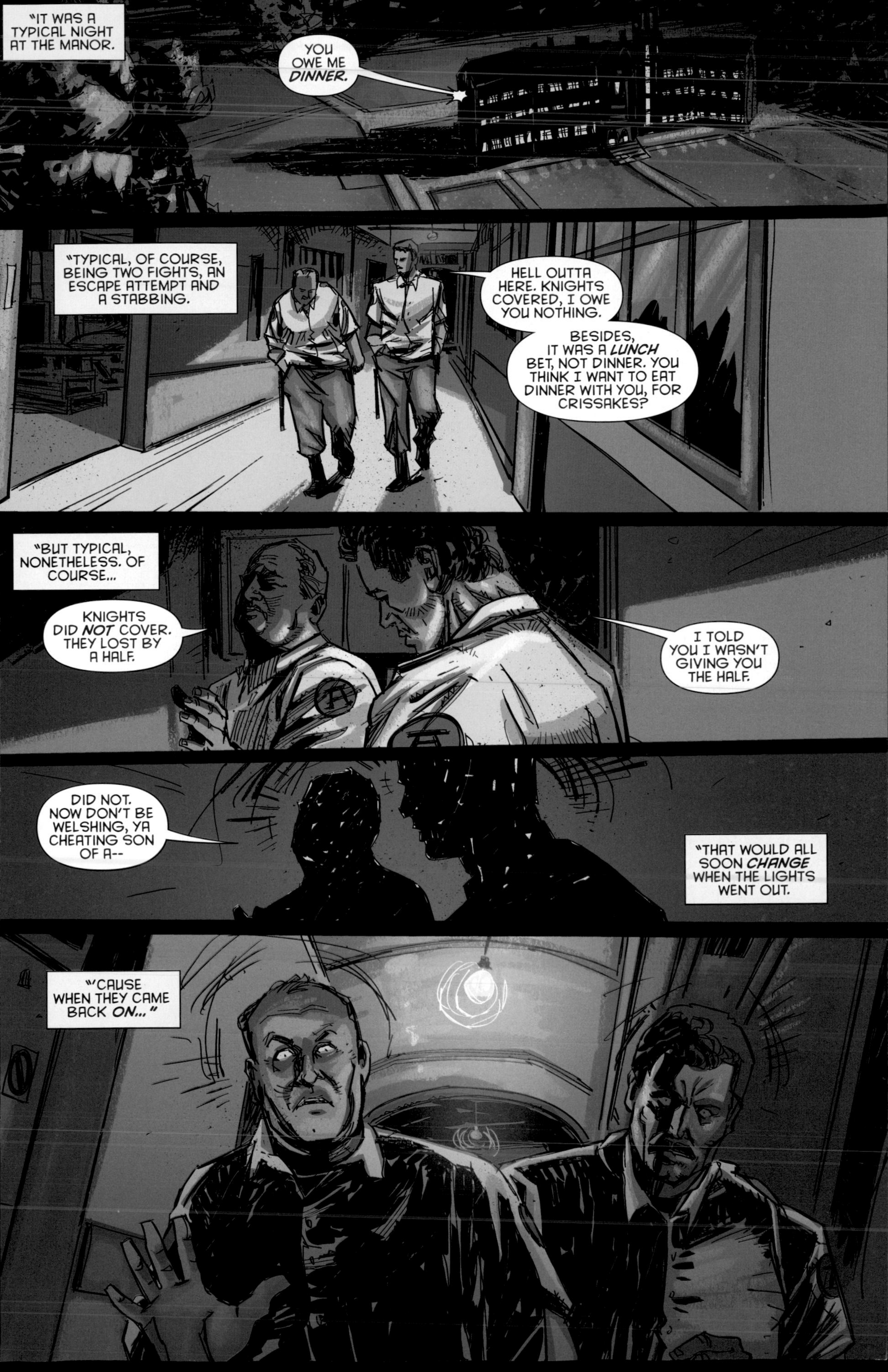
"IT WAS A TYPICAL NIGHT AT THE MANOR.
YOU OWE ME *DINNER.*
"TYPICAL, OF COURSE, BEING TWO FIGHTS, AN ESCAPE ATTEMPT AND A STABBING.
HELL OUTTA HERE. KNIGHTS COVERED, I OWE YOU NOTHING.
BESIDES, IT WAS A *LUNCH* BET, NOT DINNER. YOU THINK I WANT TO EAT DINNER WITH YOU, FOR CRISSAKES?
"BUT TYPICAL, NONETHELESS. OF COURSE...
KNIGHTS DID *NOT* COVER. THEY LOST BY A HALF.
I TOLD YOU I WASN'T GIVING YOU THE HALF.
DID NOT. NOW DON'T BE WELSHING, YA CHEATING SON OF A--
"THAT WOULD ALL SOON *CHANGE* WHEN THE LIGHTS WENT OUT.
"'CAUSE WHEN THEY CAME BACK *ON...*"

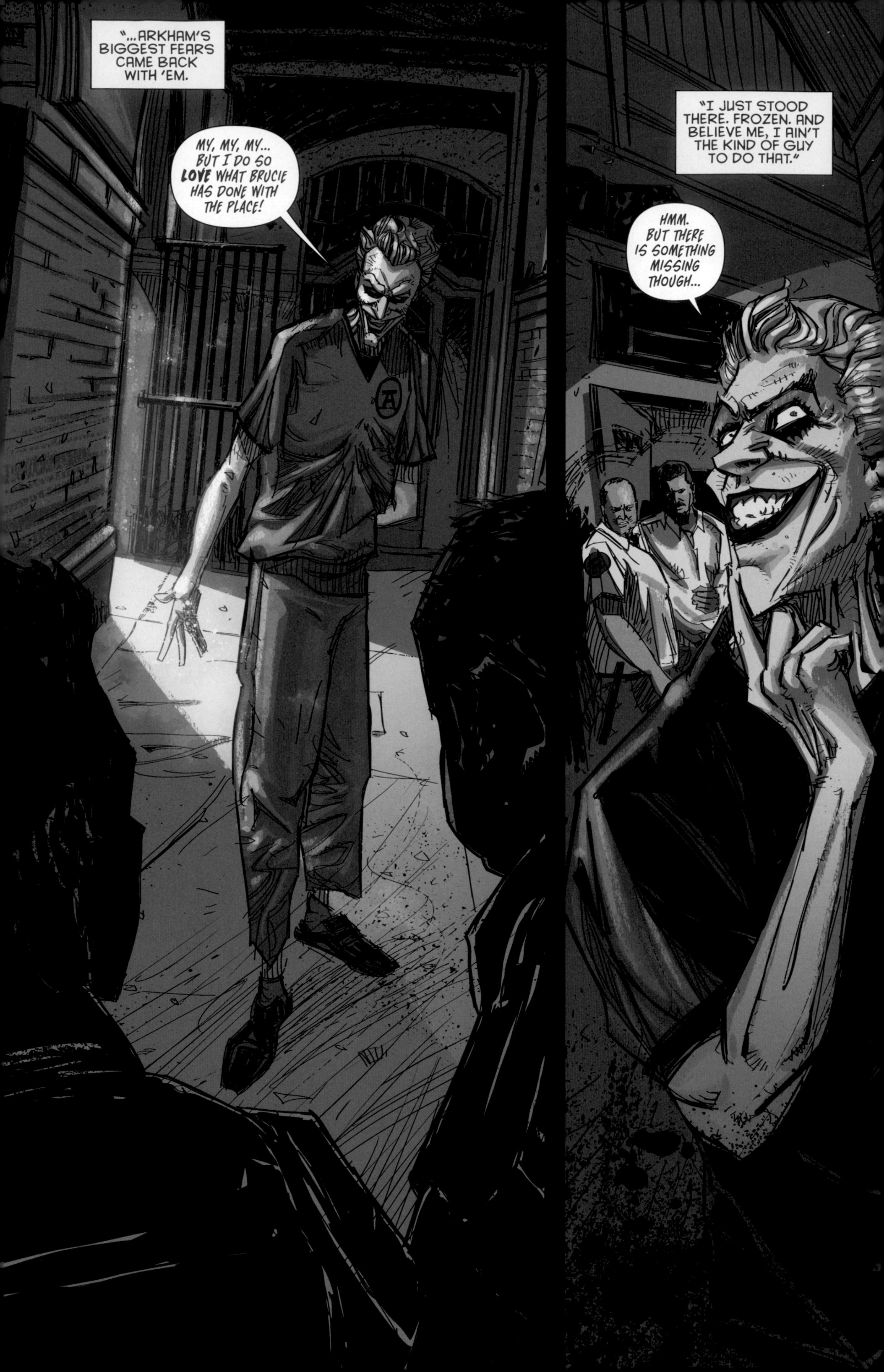
"...ARKHAM'S BIGGEST FEARS CAME BACK WITH 'EM.
MY, MY, MY... BUT I DO SO LOVE WHAT BRUCIE HAS DONE WITH THE PLACE!
"I JUST STOOD THERE. FROZEN. AND BELIEVE ME, I AIN'T THE KIND OF GUY TO DO THAT."
HMM. BUT THERE IS SOMETHING MISSING THOUGH...

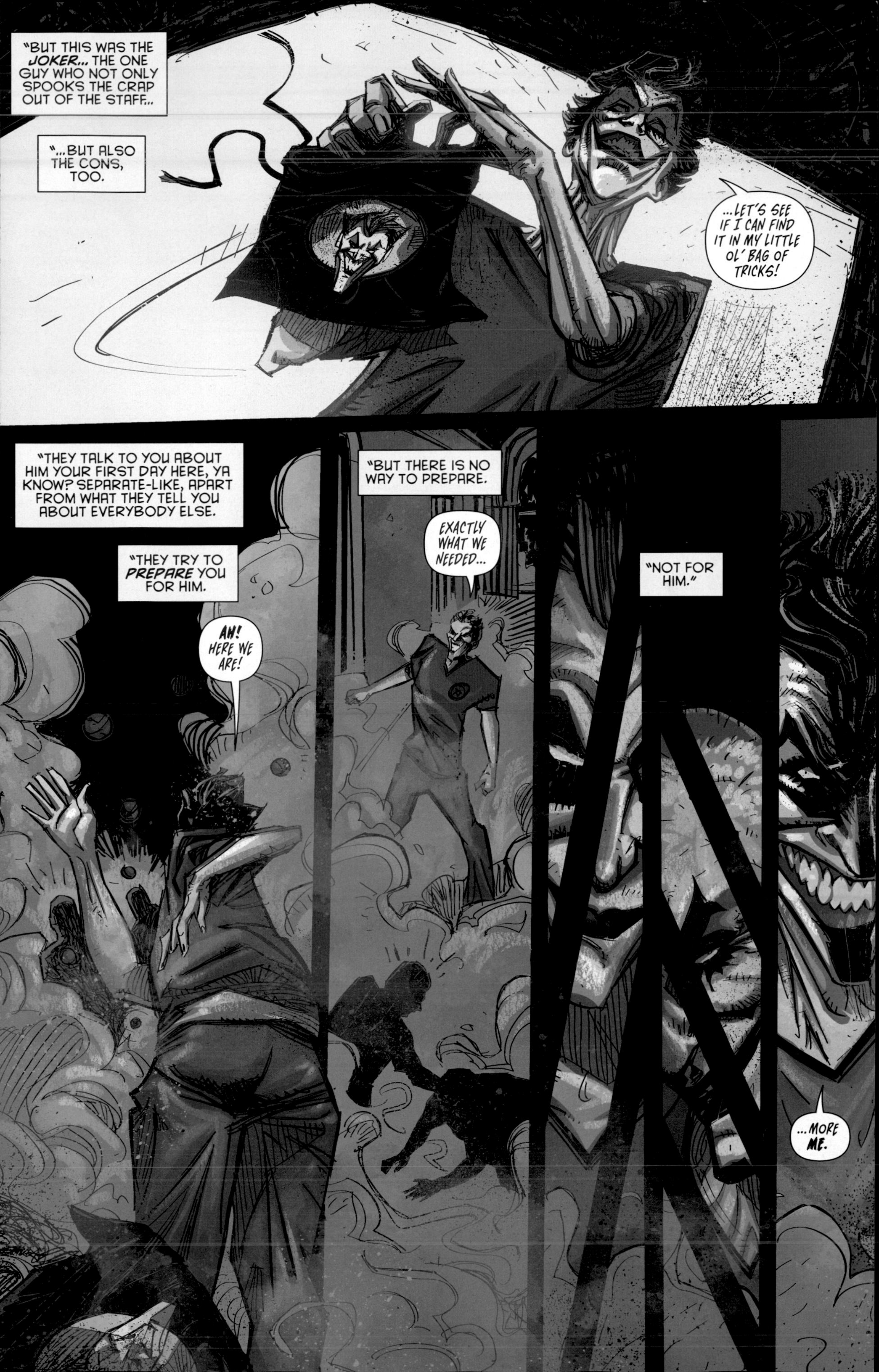
"BUT THIS WAS THE JOKER... THE ONE GUY WHO NOT ONLY SPOOKS THE CRAP OUT OF THE STAFF...
"...BUT ALSO THE CONS, TOO.
...LET'S SEE IF I CAN FIND IT IN MY LITTLE OL' BAG OF TRICKS!
"THEY TALK TO YOU ABOUT HIM YOUR FIRST DAY HERE, YA KNOW? SEPARATE-LIKE, APART FROM WHAT THEY TELL YOU ABOUT EVERYBODY ELSE.
"THEY TRY TO PREPARE YOU FOR HIM.
AH! HERE WE ARE!
"BUT THERE IS NO WAY TO PREPARE.
EXACTLY WHAT WE NEEDED...
"NOT FOR HIM."
...MORE ME.

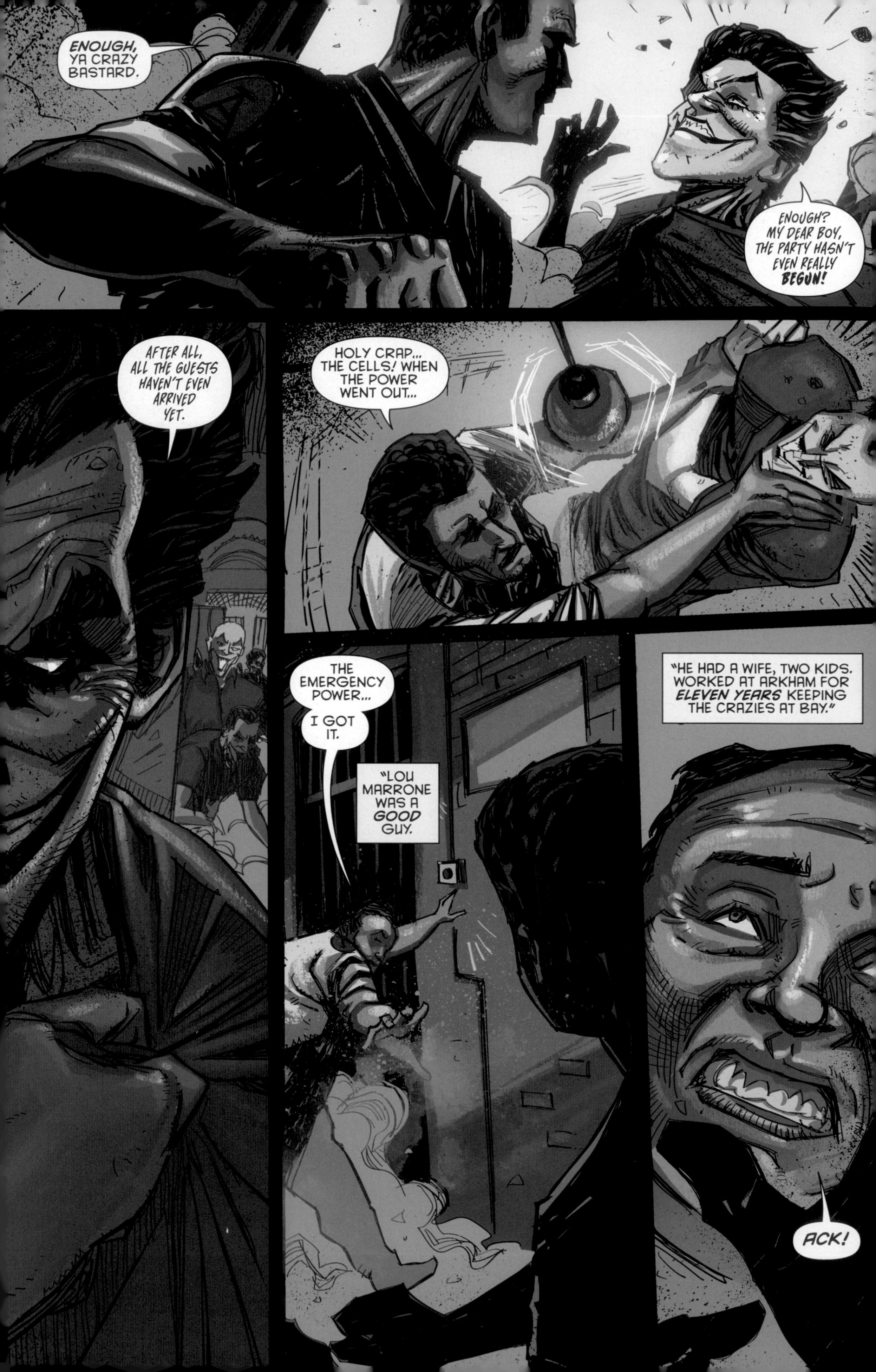
ENOUGH, YA CRAZY BASTARD.
ENOUGH? MY DEAR BOY, THE PARTY HASN'T EVEN REALLY BEGUN!
AFTER ALL, ALL THE GUESTS HAVEN'T EVEN ARRIVED YET.
HOLY CRAP... THE CELLS! WHEN THE POWER WENT OUT...
THE EMERGENCY POWER...
I GOT IT.
"LOU MARRONE WAS A GOOD GUY.
"HE HAD A WIFE, TWO KIDS. WORKED AT ARKHAM FOR ELEVEN YEARS KEEPING THE CRAZIES AT BAY."
ACK!

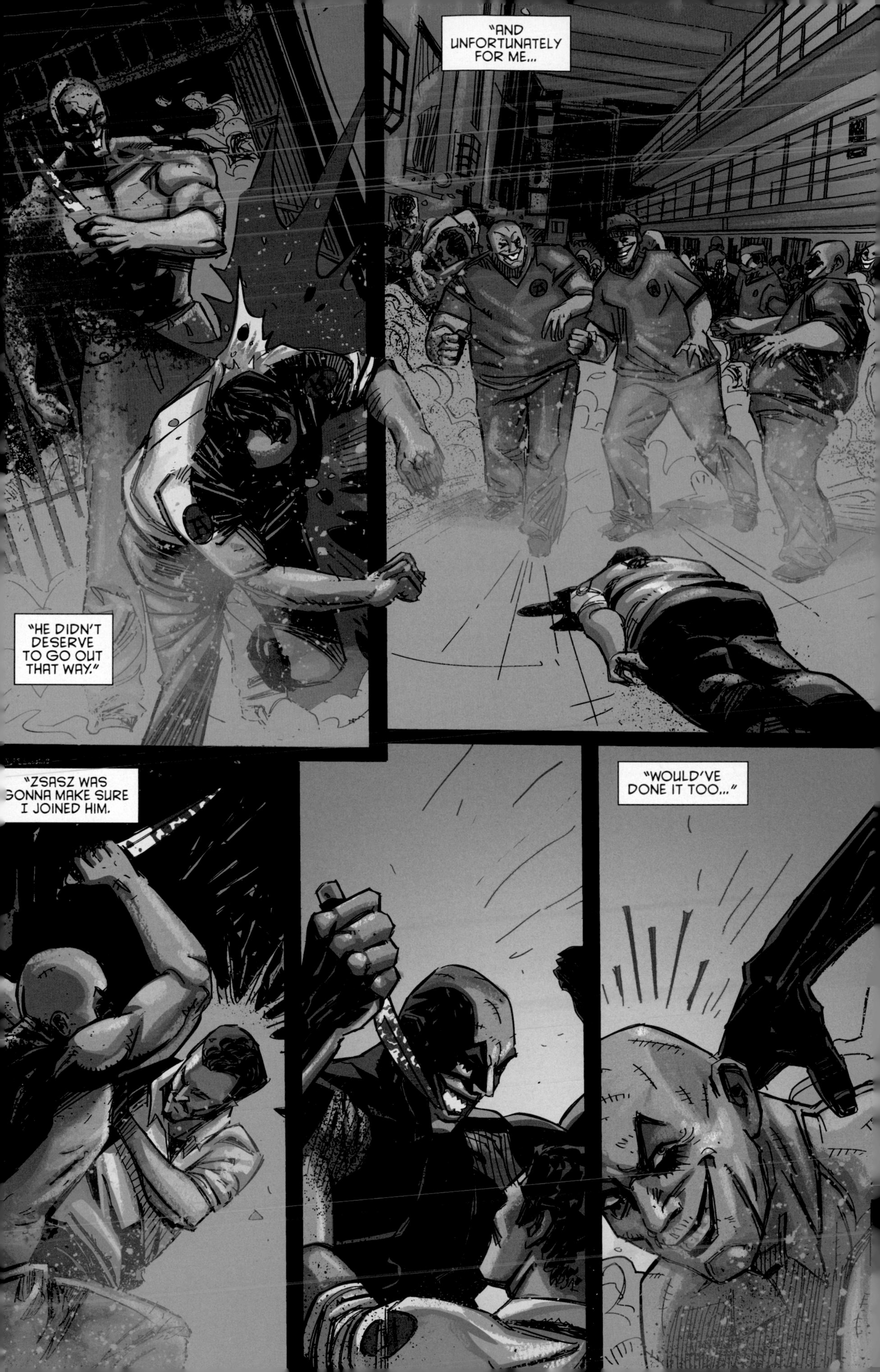
"HE DIDN'T DESERVE TO GO OUT THAT WAY."
"AND UNFORTUNATELY FOR ME...
"ZSASZ WAS GONNA MAKE SURE I JOINED HIM.
"WOULD'VE DONE IT TOO..."

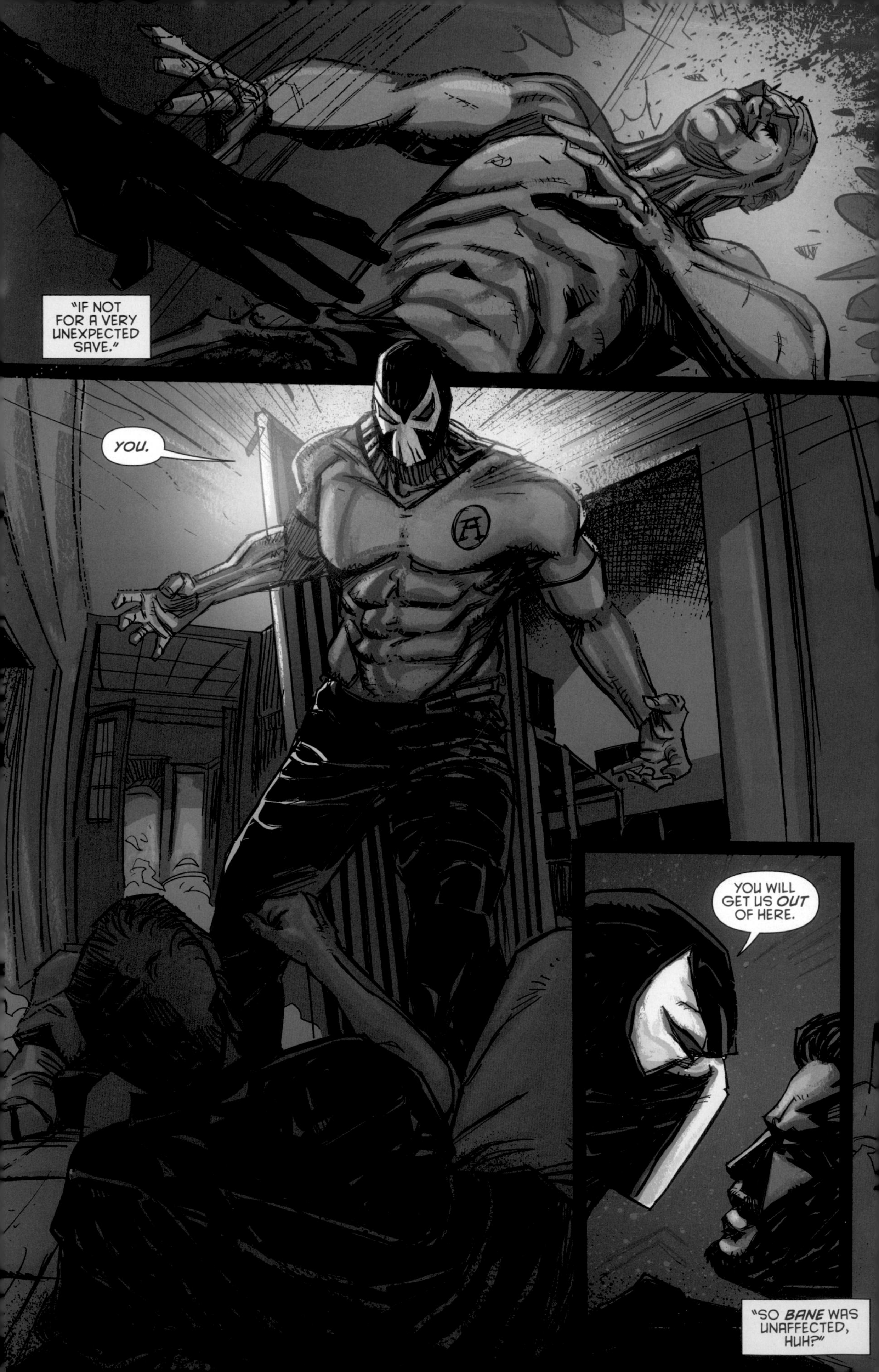
"IF NOT FOR A VERY UNEXPECTED SAVE."
YOU.
YOU WILL GET US OUT OF HERE.
"SO BANE WAS UNAFFECTED, HUH?"

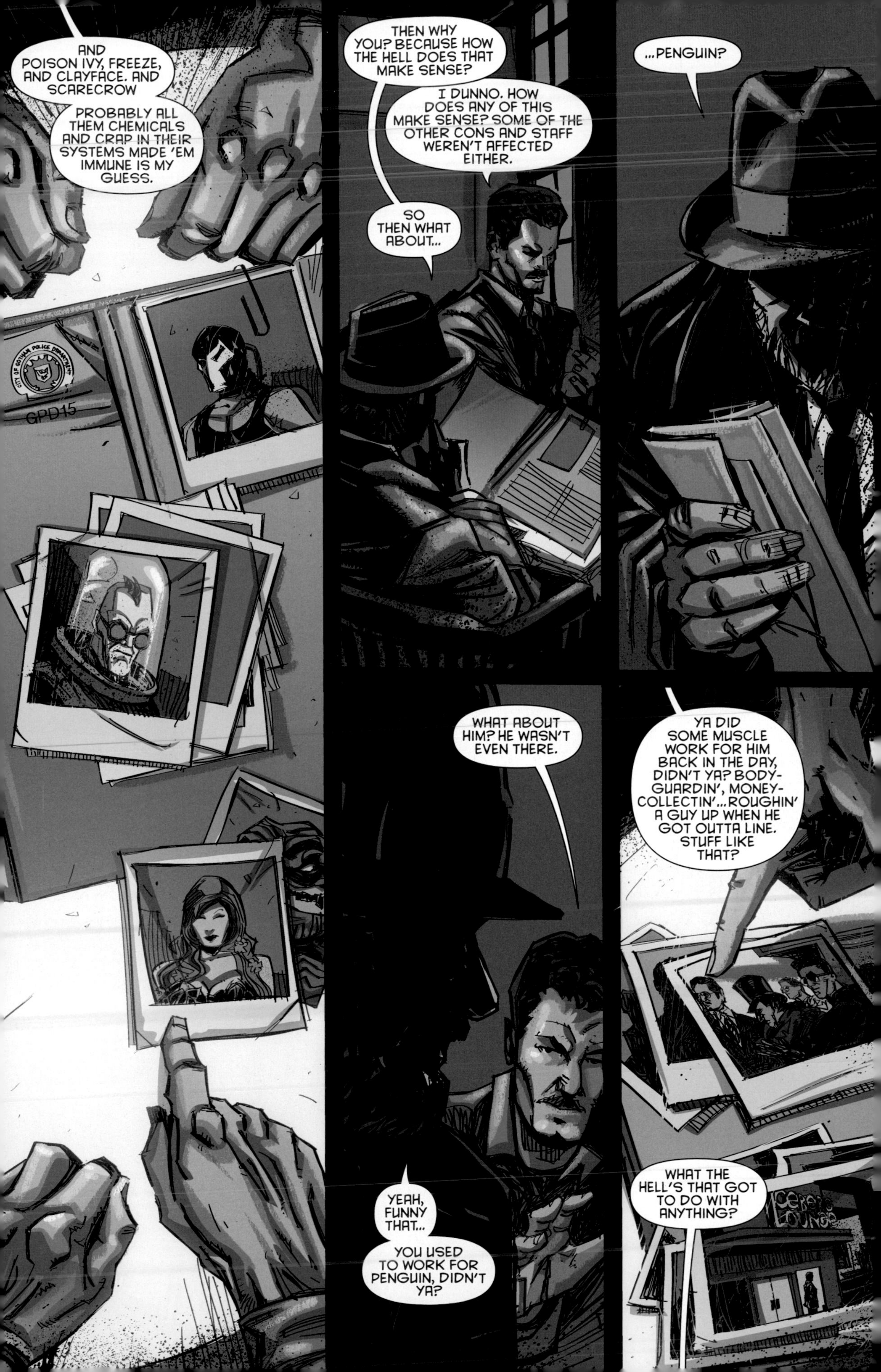
AND POISON IVY, FREEZE, AND CLAYFACE. AND SCARECROW
PROBABLY ALL THEM CHEMICALS AND CRAP IN THEIR SYSTEMS MADE 'EM IMMUNE IS MY GUESS.
GPD15
THEN WHY YOU? BECAUSE HOW THE HELL DOES THAT MAKE SENSE?
I DUNNO. HOW DOES ANY OF THIS MAKE SENSE? SOME OF THE OTHER CONS AND STAFF WEREN'T AFFECTED EITHER.
SO THEN WHAT ABOUT...
...PENGUIN?
WHAT ABOUT HIM? HE WASN'T EVEN THERE.
YEAH, FUNNY THAT...
YOU USED TO WORK FOR PENGUIN, DIDN'T YA?
YA DID SOME MUSCLE WORK FOR HIM BACK IN THE DAY, DIDN'T YA? BODY-GUARDIN', MONEY-COLLECTIN'...ROUGHIN' A GUY UP WHEN HE GOT OUTTA LINE. STUFF LIKE THAT?
WHAT THE HELL'S THAT GOT TO DO WITH ANYTHING?

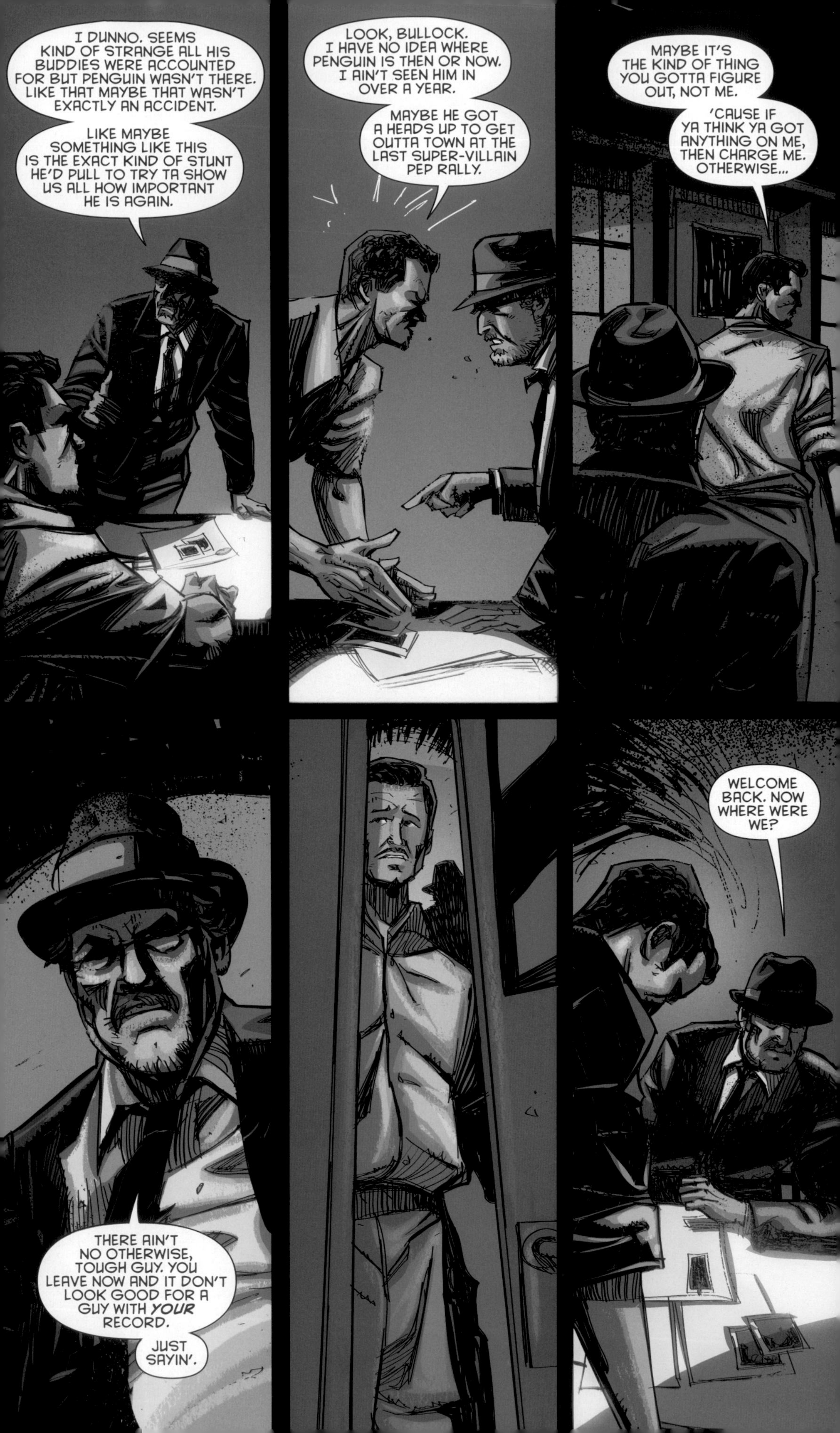
I DUNNO. SEEMS KIND OF STRANGE ALL HIS BUDDIES WERE ACCOUNTED FOR BUT PENGUIN WASN'T THERE. LIKE THAT MAYBE THAT WASN'T EXACTLY AN ACCIDENT.
LIKE MAYBE SOMETHING LIKE THIS IS THE EXACT KIND OF STUNT HE'D PULL TO TRY TA SHOW US ALL HOW IMPORTANT HE IS AGAIN.
LOOK, BULLOCK. I HAVE NO IDEA WHERE PENGUIN IS THEN OR NOW. I AIN'T SEEN HIM IN OVER A YEAR.
MAYBE HE GOT A HEADS UP TO GET OUTTA TOWN AT THE LAST SUPER-VILLAIN PEP RALLY.
MAYBE IT'S THE KIND OF THING YOU GOTTA FIGURE OUT, NOT ME.
'CAUSE IF YA THINK YA GOT ANYTHING ON ME, THEN CHARGE ME. OTHERWISE...
THERE AIN'T NO OTHERWISE, TOUGH GUY. YOU LEAVE NOW AND IT DON'T LOOK GOOD FOR A GUY WITH *YOUR* RECORD.
JUST SAYIN'.
WELCOME BACK. NOW WHERE WERE WE?

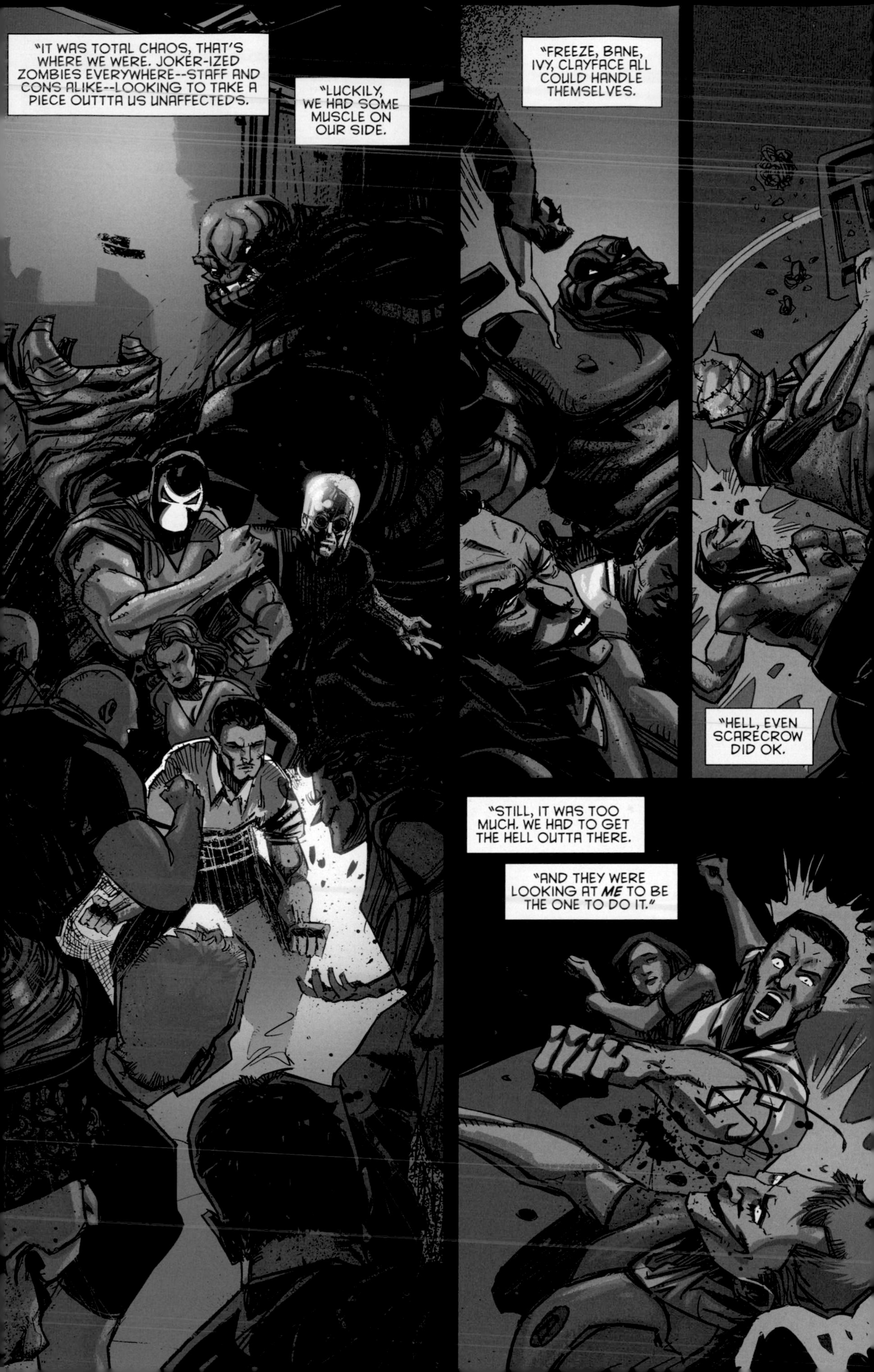
"IT WAS TOTAL CHAOS, THAT'S WHERE WE WERE. JOKER-IZED ZOMBIES EVERYWHERE--STAFF AND CONS ALIKE--LOOKING TO TAKE A PIECE OUTTTA US UNAFFECTEDS.
"LUCKILY, WE HAD SOME MUSCLE ON OUR SIDE.
"FREEZE, BANE, IVY, CLAYFACE ALL COULD HANDLE THEMSELVES.
"HELL, EVEN SCARECROW DID OK.
"STILL, IT WAS TOO MUCH. WE HAD TO GET THE HELL OUTTA THERE.
"AND THEY WERE LOOKING AT *ME* TO BE THE ONE TO DO IT."

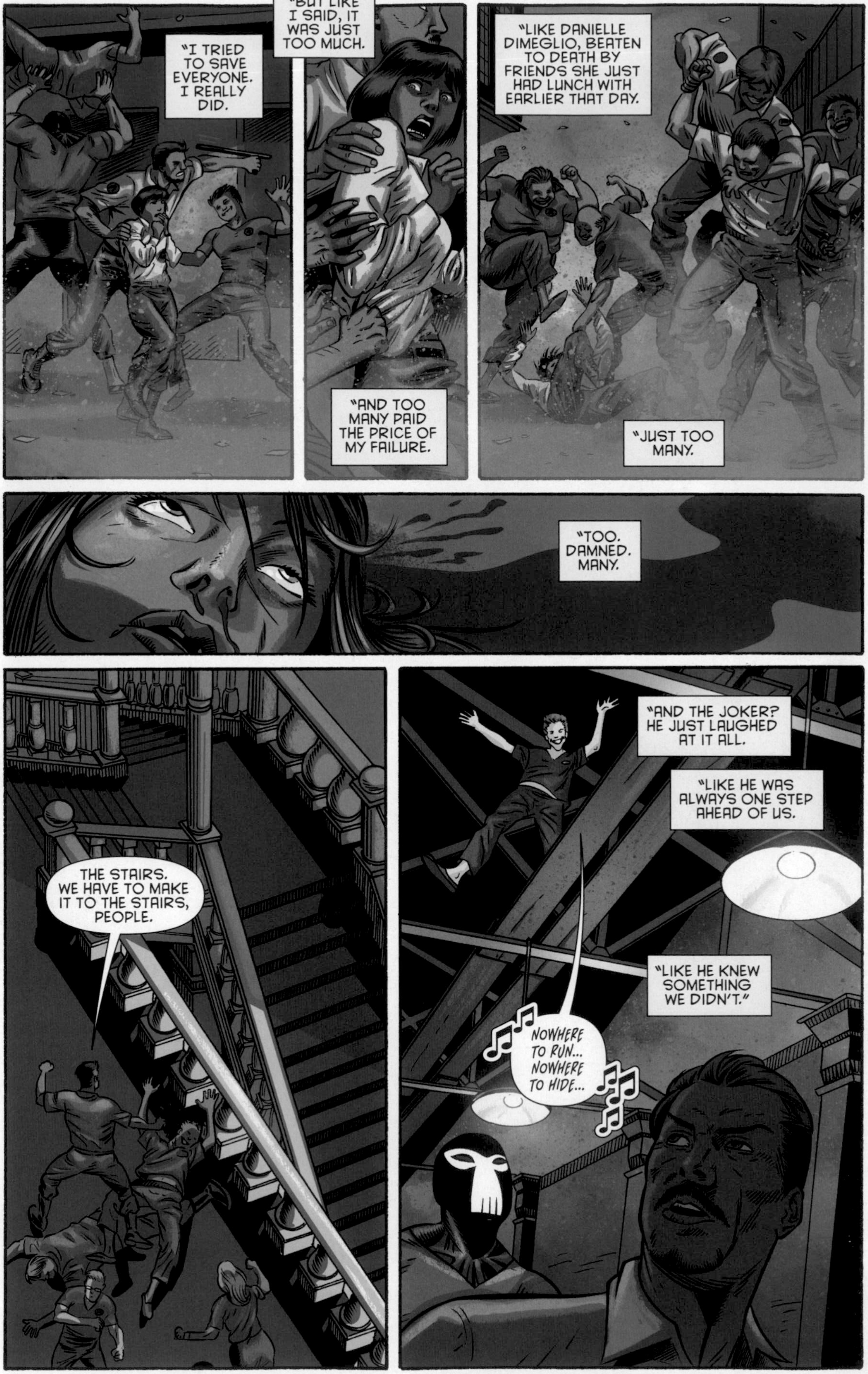
"I TRIED TO SAVE EVERYONE. I REALLY DID.
"BUT LIKE I SAID, IT WAS JUST TOO MUCH.
"AND TOO MANY PAID THE PRICE OF MY FAILURE.
"LIKE DANIELLE DIMEGLIO, BEATEN TO DEATH BY FRIENDS SHE JUST HAD LUNCH WITH EARLIER THAT DAY.
"JUST TOO MANY.
"TOO. DAMNED. MANY.
THE STAIRS. WE HAVE TO MAKE IT TO THE STAIRS, PEOPLE.
"AND THE JOKER? HE JUST LAUGHED AT IT ALL.
"LIKE HE WAS ALWAYS ONE STEP AHEAD OF US.
"LIKE HE KNEW SOMETHING WE DIDN'T."
NOWHERE TO RUN... NOWHERE TO HIDE...

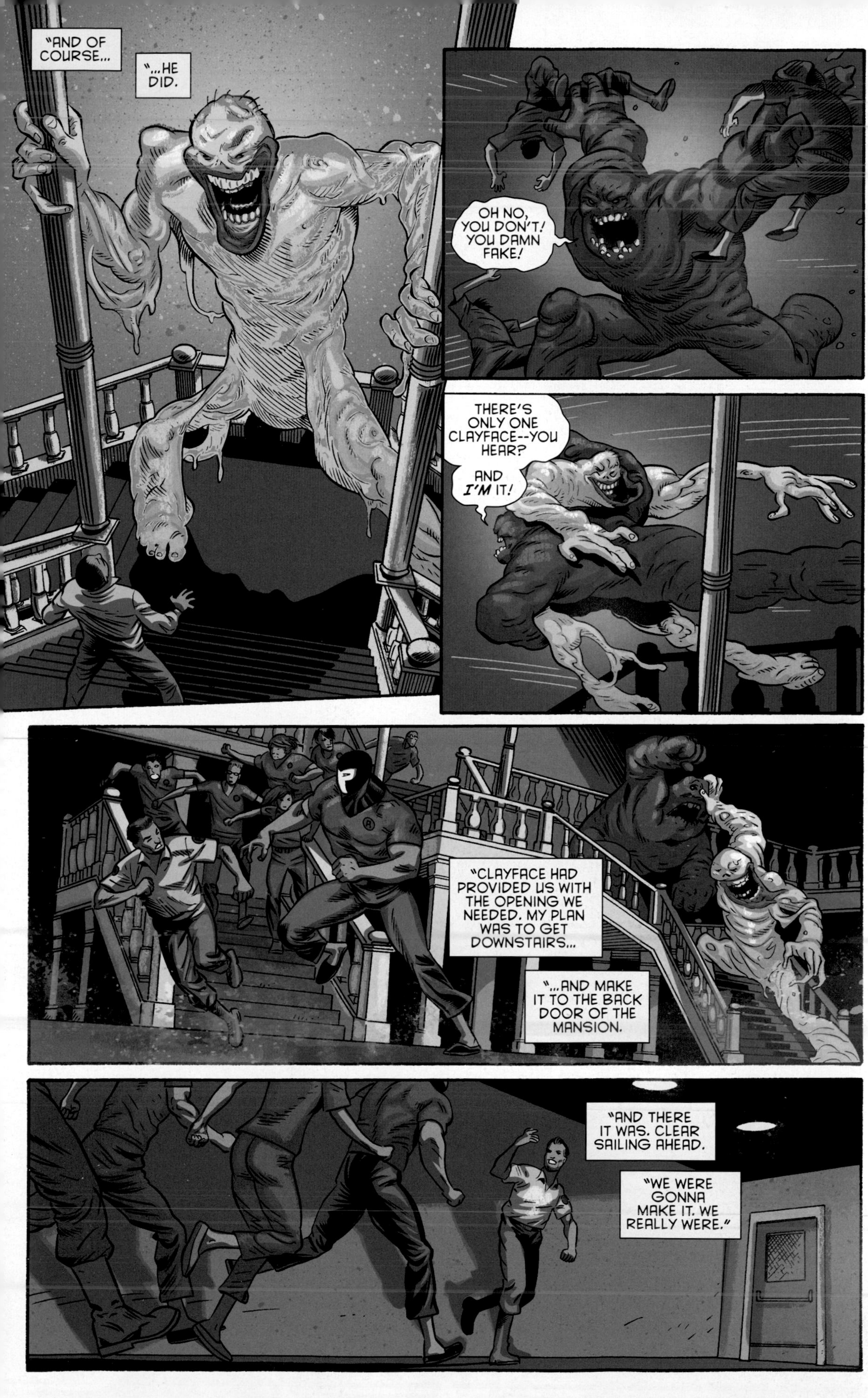
"AND OF COURSE...
"...HE DID.
OH NO, YOU DON'T! YOU DAMN FAKE!
THERE'S ONLY ONE CLAYFACE--YOU HEAR?
AND I'M IT!
"CLAYFACE HAD PROVIDED US WITH THE OPENING WE NEEDED. MY PLAN WAS TO GET DOWNSTAIRS...
"...AND MAKE IT TO THE BACK DOOR OF THE MANSION.
"AND THERE IT WAS. CLEAR SAILING AHEAD.
"WE WERE GONNA MAKE IT. WE REALLY WERE."

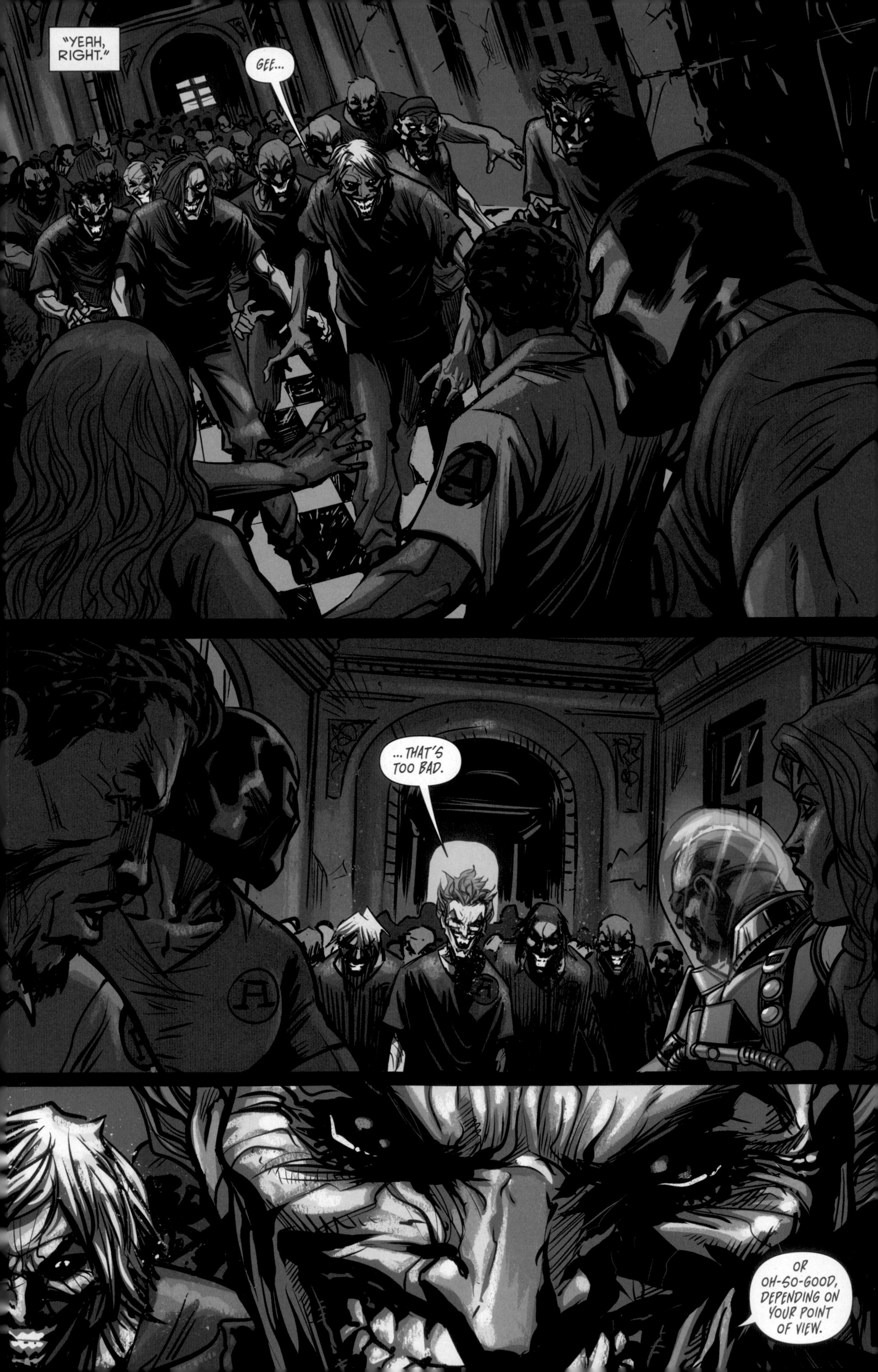
"YEAH, RIGHT."
GEE...
...THAT'S TOO BAD.
OR OH-SO-GOOD, DEPENDING ON YOUR POINT OF VIEW.

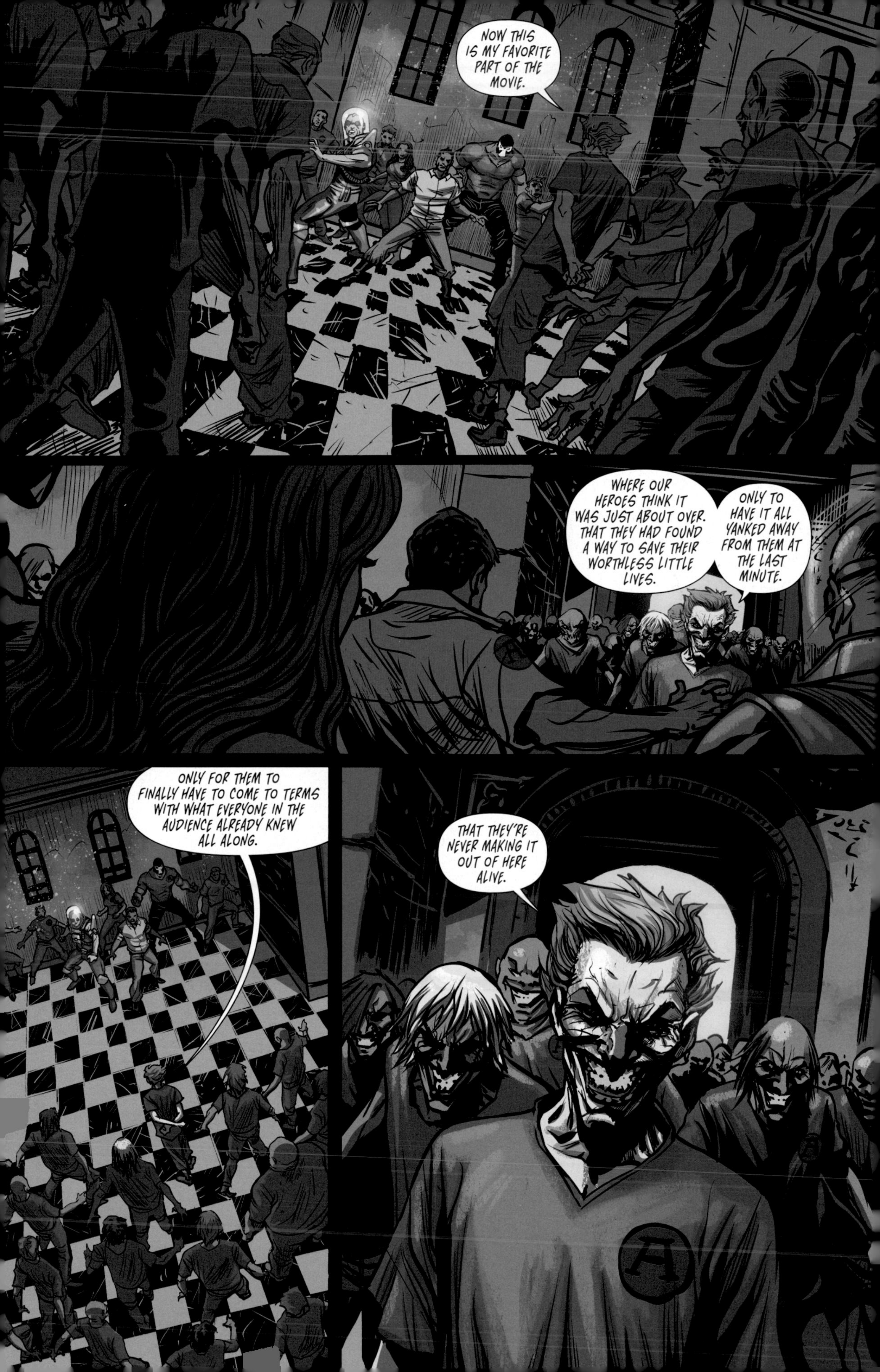
NOW THIS IS MY FAVORITE PART OF THE MOVIE.
WHERE OUR HEROES THINK IT WAS JUST ABOUT OVER. THAT THEY HAD FOUND A WAY TO SAVE THEIR WORTHLESS LITTLE LIVES.
ONLY TO HAVE IT ALL YANKED AWAY FROM THEM AT THE LAST MINUTE.
ONLY FOR THEM TO FINALLY HAVE TO COME TO TERMS WITH WHAT EVERYONE IN THE AUDIENCE ALREADY KNEW ALL ALONG.
THAT THEY'RE NEVER MAKING IT OUT OF HERE ALIVE.

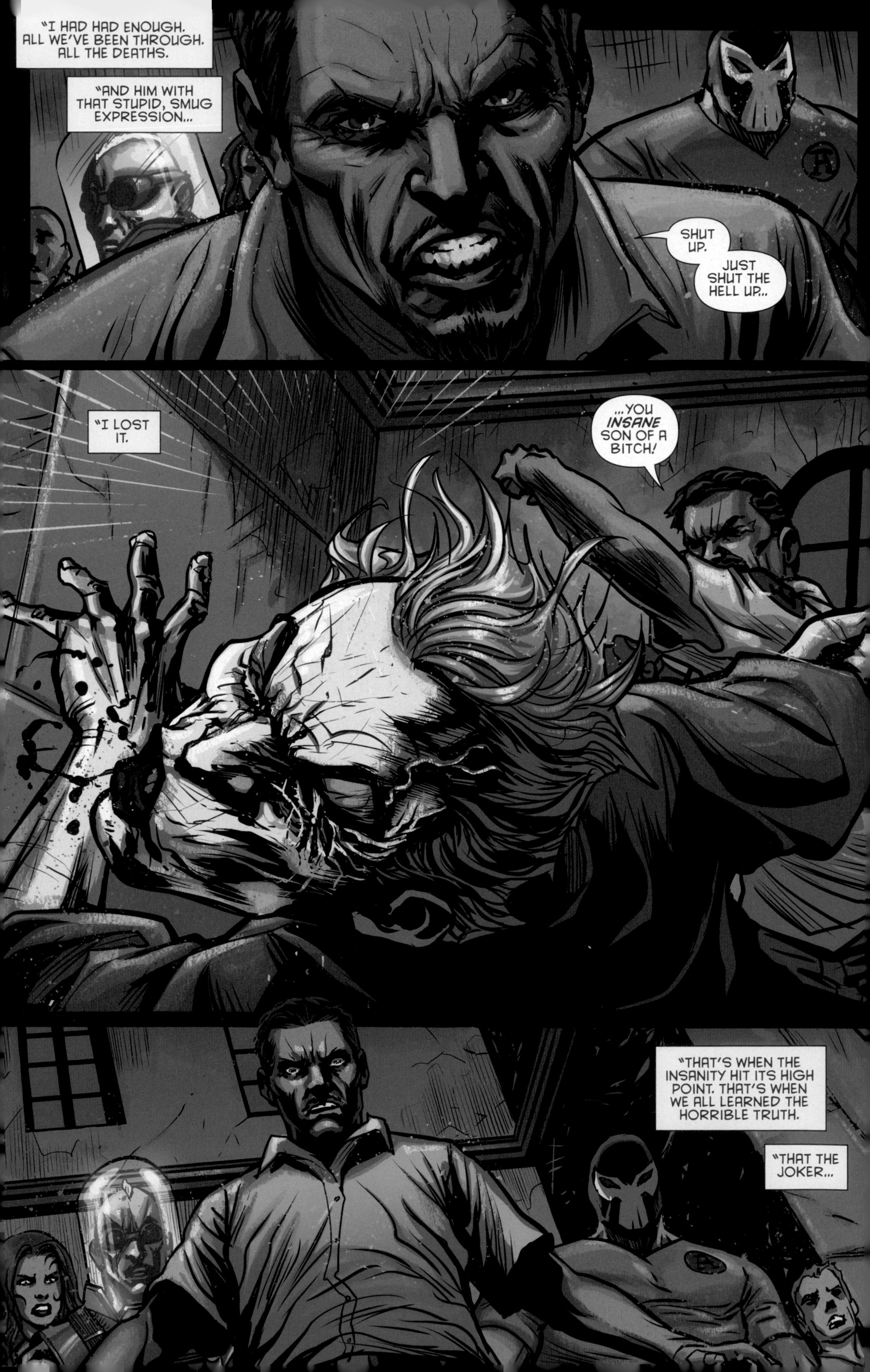
"I HAD HAD ENOUGH. ALL WE'VE BEEN THROUGH. ALL THE DEATHS.
"AND HIM WITH THAT STUPID, SMUG EXPRESSION...
SHUT UP.
JUST SHUT THE HELL UP...
"I LOST IT.
...YOU *INSANE* SON OF A BITCH!
"THAT'S WHEN THE INSANITY HIT ITS HIGH POINT. THAT'S WHEN WE ALL LEARNED THE HORRIBLE TRUTH.
"THAT THE JOKER...

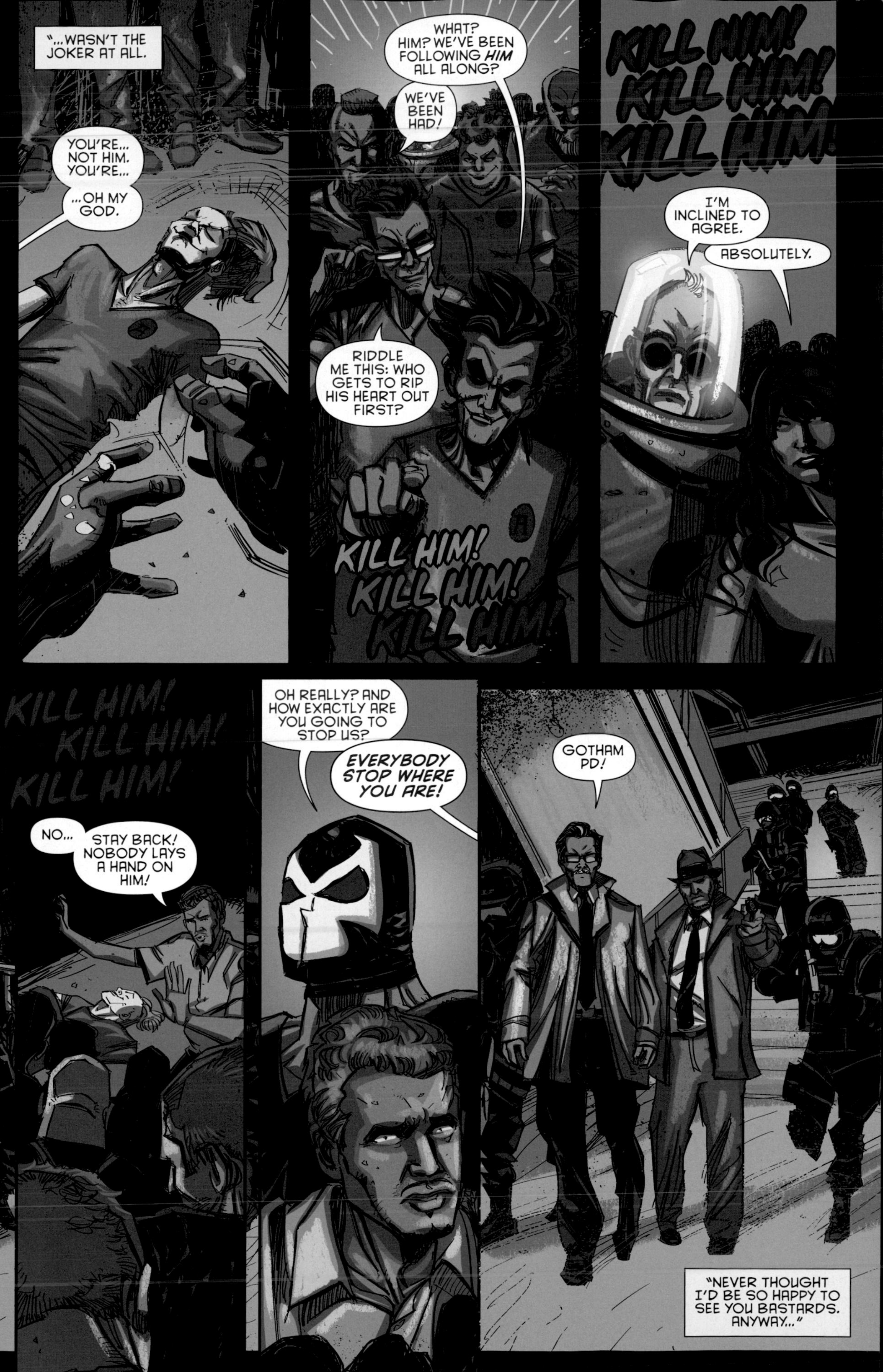
"...WASN'T THE JOKER AT ALL.
YOU'RE... NOT HIM. YOU'RE...
...OH MY GOD.
WHAT? HIM? WE'VE BEEN FOLLOWING HIM ALL ALONG?
WE'VE BEEN HAD!
RIDDLE ME THIS: WHO GETS TO RIP HIS HEART OUT FIRST?
KILL HIM! KILL HIM! KILL HIM!
KILL HIM! KILL HIM! KILL HIM!
I'M INCLINED TO AGREE.
ABSOLUTELY.
KILL HIM! KILL HIM! KILL HIM!
NO...
STAY BACK! NOBODY LAYS A HAND ON HIM!
OH REALLY? AND HOW EXACTLY ARE YOU GOING TO STOP US?
EVERYBODY STOP WHERE YOU ARE!
GOTHAM PD!
"NEVER THOUGHT I'D BE SO HAPPY TO SEE YOU BASTARDS. ANYWAY..."

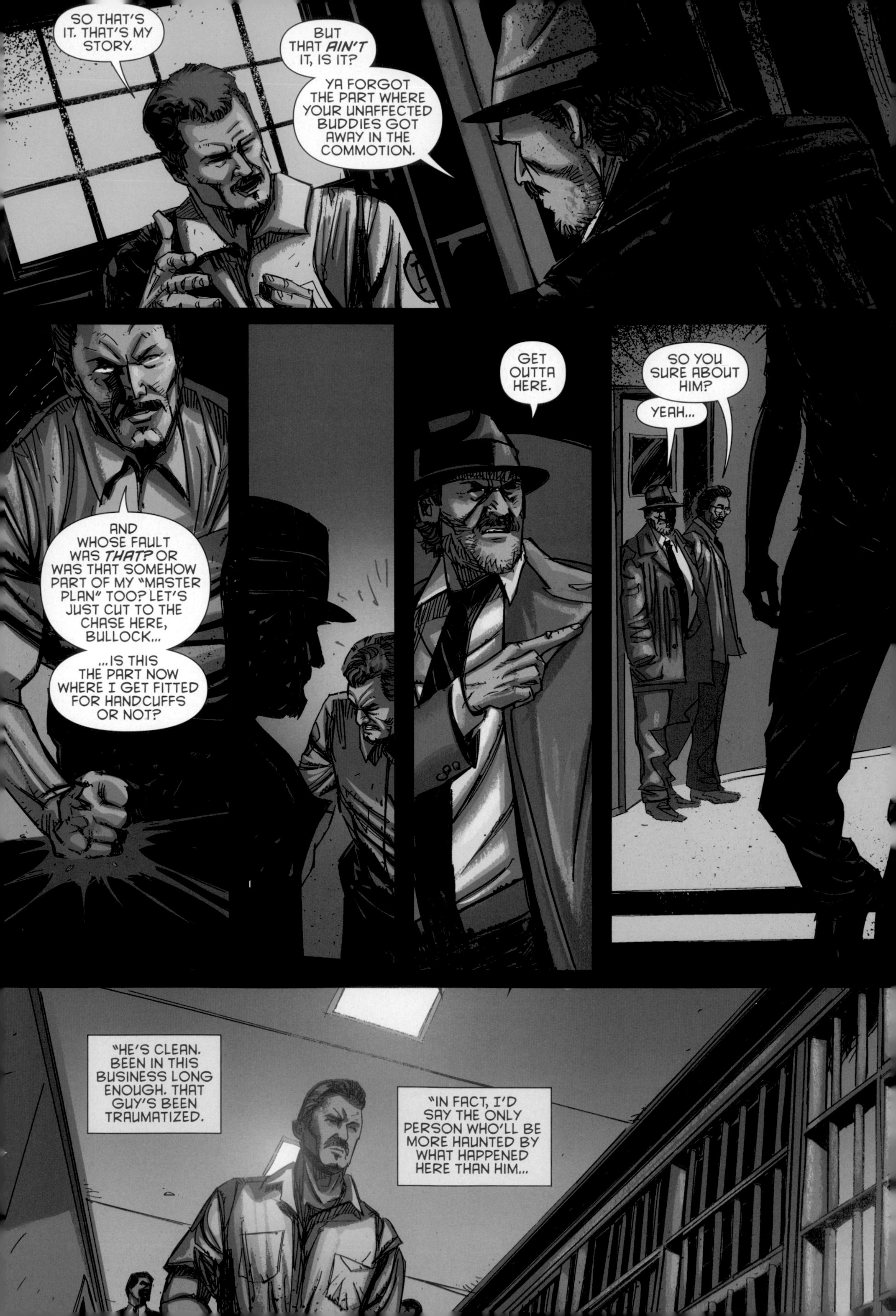

SO THAT'S IT. THAT'S MY STORY.
BUT THAT *AIN'T* IT, IS IT?
YA FORGOT THE PART WHERE YOUR UNAFFECTED BUDDIES GOT AWAY IN THE COMMOTION.
AND WHOSE FAULT WAS *THAT?* OR WAS THAT SOMEHOW PART OF MY "MASTER PLAN" TOO? LET'S JUST CUT TO THE CHASE HERE, BULLOCK...
...IS THIS THE PART NOW WHERE I GET FITTED FOR *HANDCUFFS* OR NOT?
GET OUTTA HERE.
SO YOU SURE ABOUT HIM?
YEAH...
"HE'S CLEAN. BEEN IN THIS BUSINESS LONG ENOUGH. THAT GUY'S BEEN TRAUMATIZED.
"IN FACT, I'D SAY THE ONLY PERSON WHO'LL BE MORE HAUNTED BY WHAT HAPPENED HERE THAN HIM...

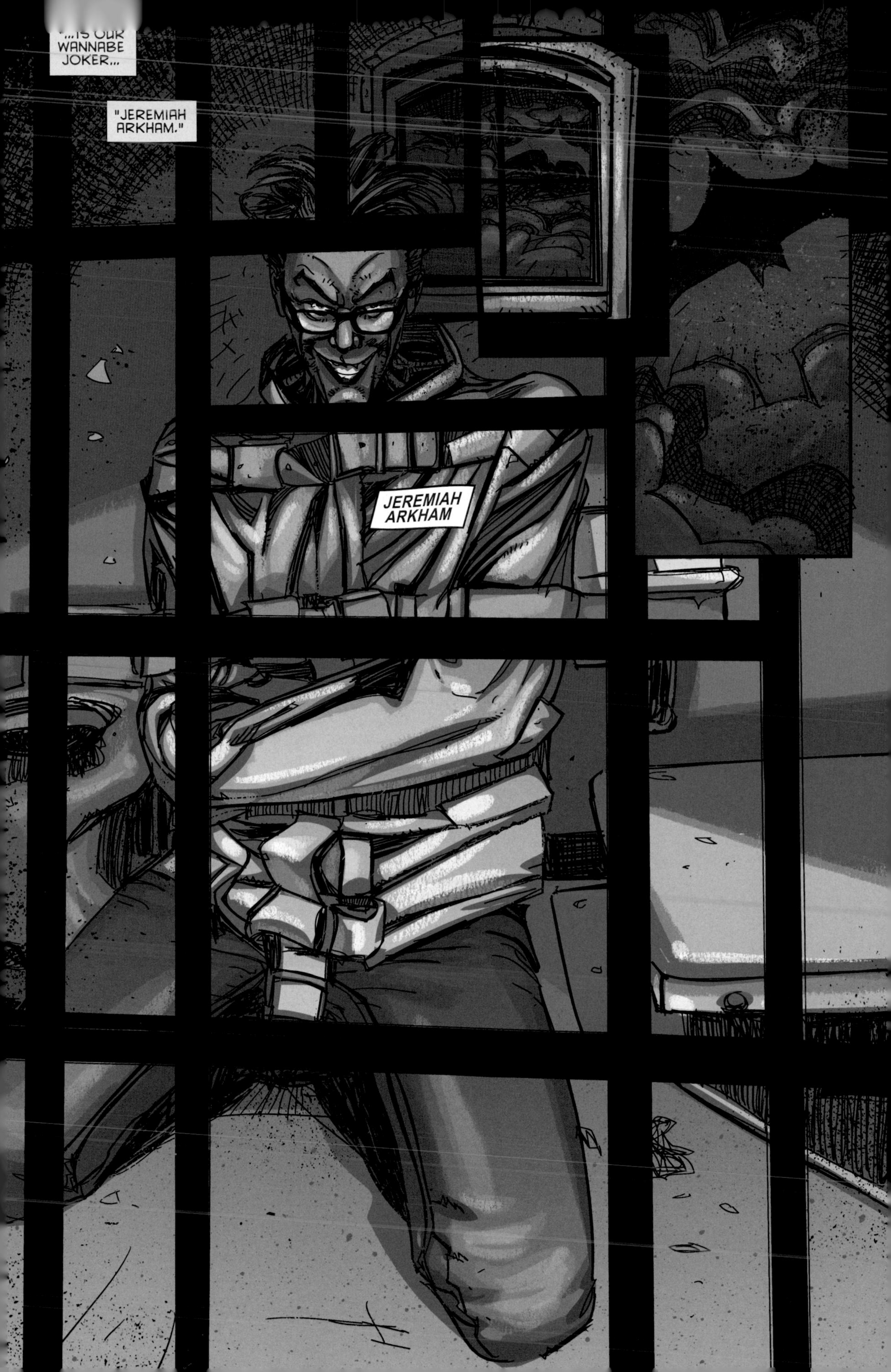
"...IS OUR WANNABE JOKER...
"JEREMIAH ARKHAM."
JEREMIAH ARKHAM

cover by GREG CAPULLO, DANNY MIKI & FCO PLASCENCIA

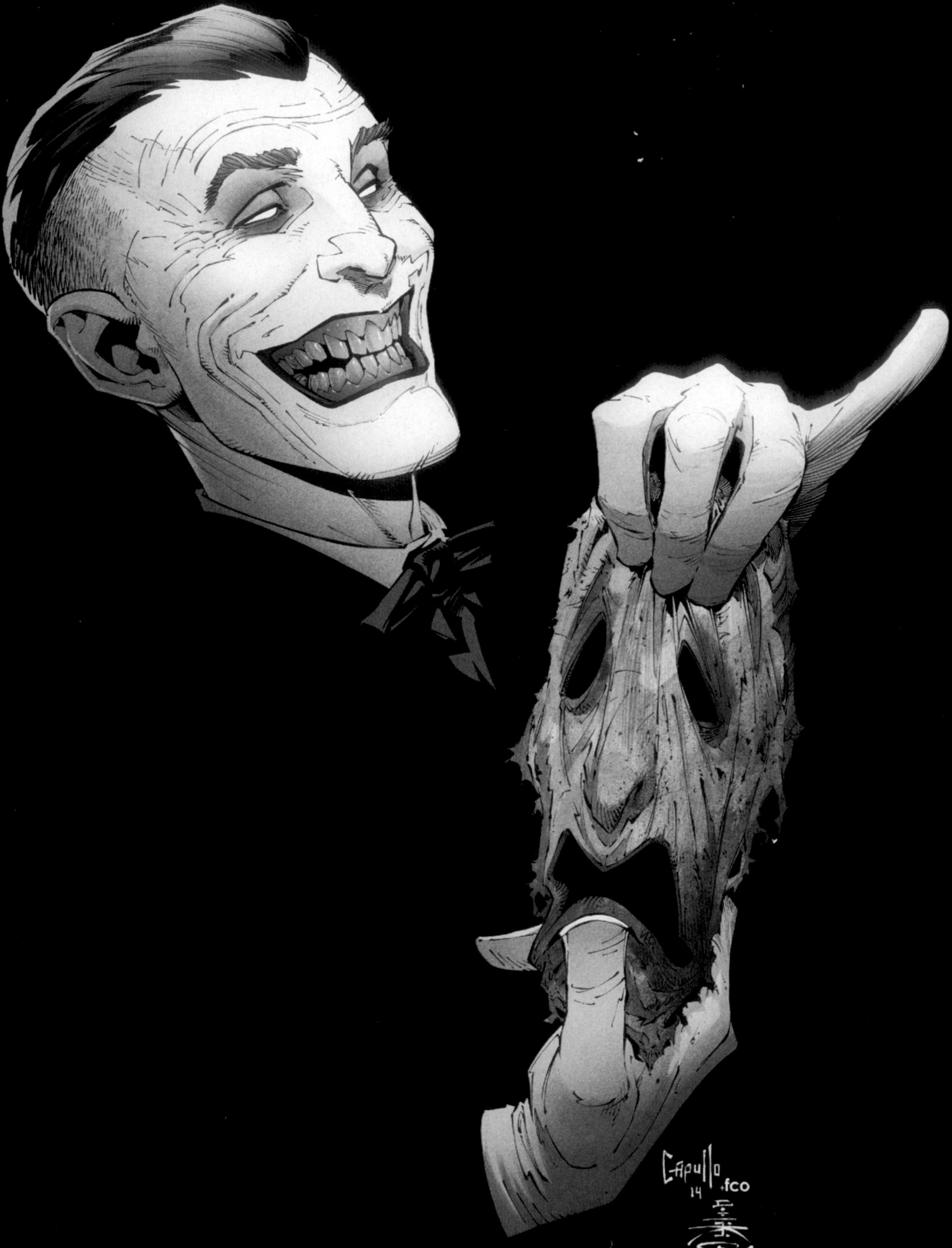

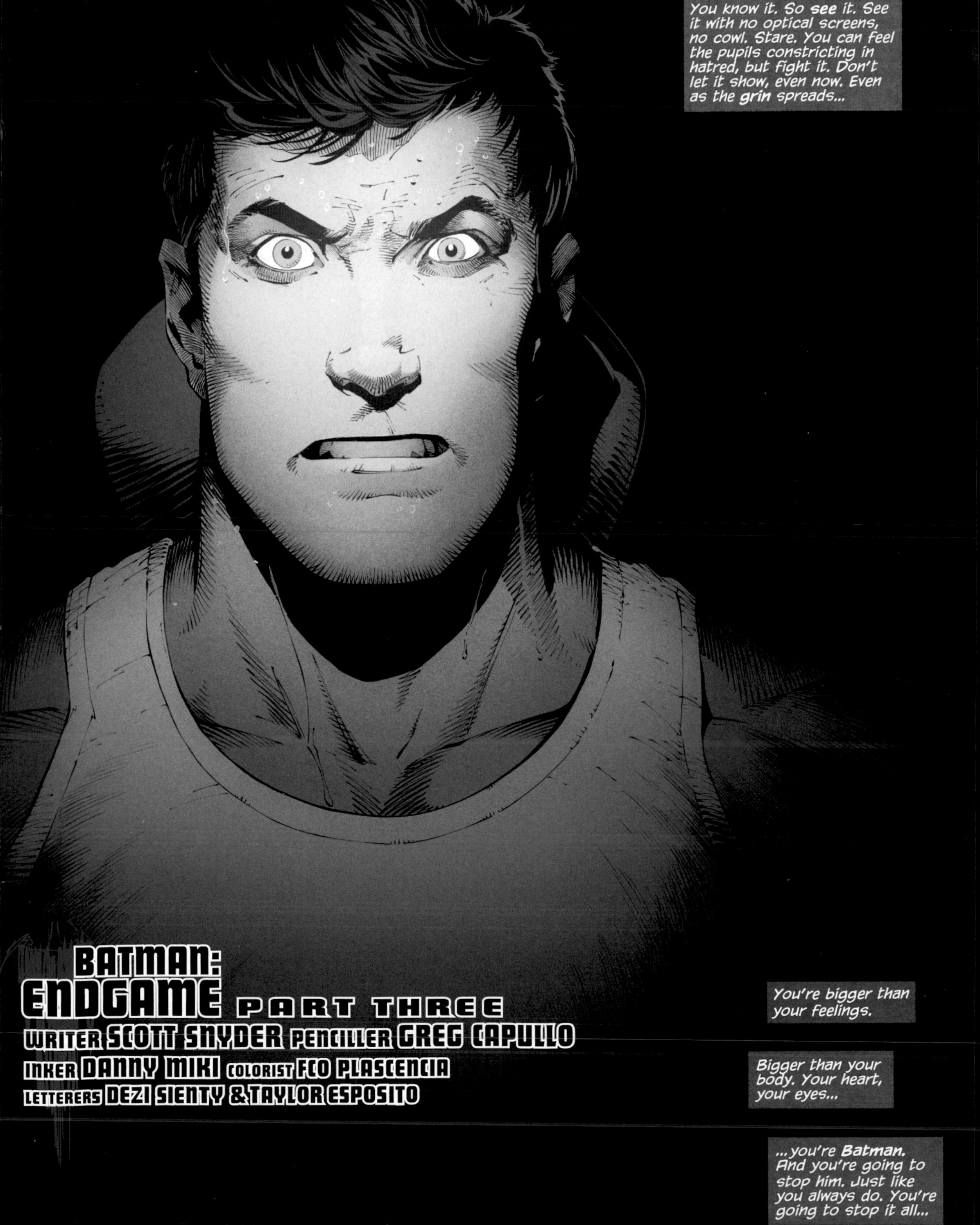

You know it. So **see** it. See it with no optical screens, no cowl. Stare. You can feel the pupils constricting in hatred, but fight it. Don't let it show, even now. Even as the **grin** spreads...
BATMAN: ENDGAME PART THREE
WRITER SCOTT SNYDER PENCILLER GREG CAPULLO
INKER DANNY MIKI COLORIST FCO PLASCENCIA
LETTERERS DEZI SIENTY & TAYLOR ESPOSITO
You're bigger than your feelings.
Bigger than your body. Your heart, your eyes...
...you're **Batman.** And you're going to stop him. Just like you always do. You're going to stop it all...

RAAHHH!

BRUCE!

SIR! YOU'VE COME OUT OF IT. ARE YOU--

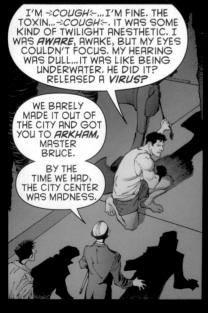

I'M ⤙COUGH⤚... I'M FINE. THE TOXIN... ⤙COUGH⤚. IT WAS SOME KIND OF TWILIGHT ANESTHETIC. I WAS *AWARE*, AWAKE, BUT MY EYES COULDN'T FOCUS. MY HEARING WAS DULL...IT WAS LIKE BEING UNDERWATER. HE DID IT? RELEASED A *VIRUS*?

WE BARELY MADE IT OUT OF THE CITY AND GOT YOU TO *ARKHAM*, MASTER BRUCE.

BY THE TIME WE HAD, THE CITY CENTER WAS MADNESS.

IT WAS BLOODY... UNBELIEVABLE. THE MILITARY AND THE CDC, THE POLICE, THEY'RE TRYING TO KEEP IT TO THESE *RED* AREAS, HOLD IT AT YELLOW.

BUT IT'S... I'VE NEVER SEEN ANYTHING LIKE IT.

I NEED TO SEE.

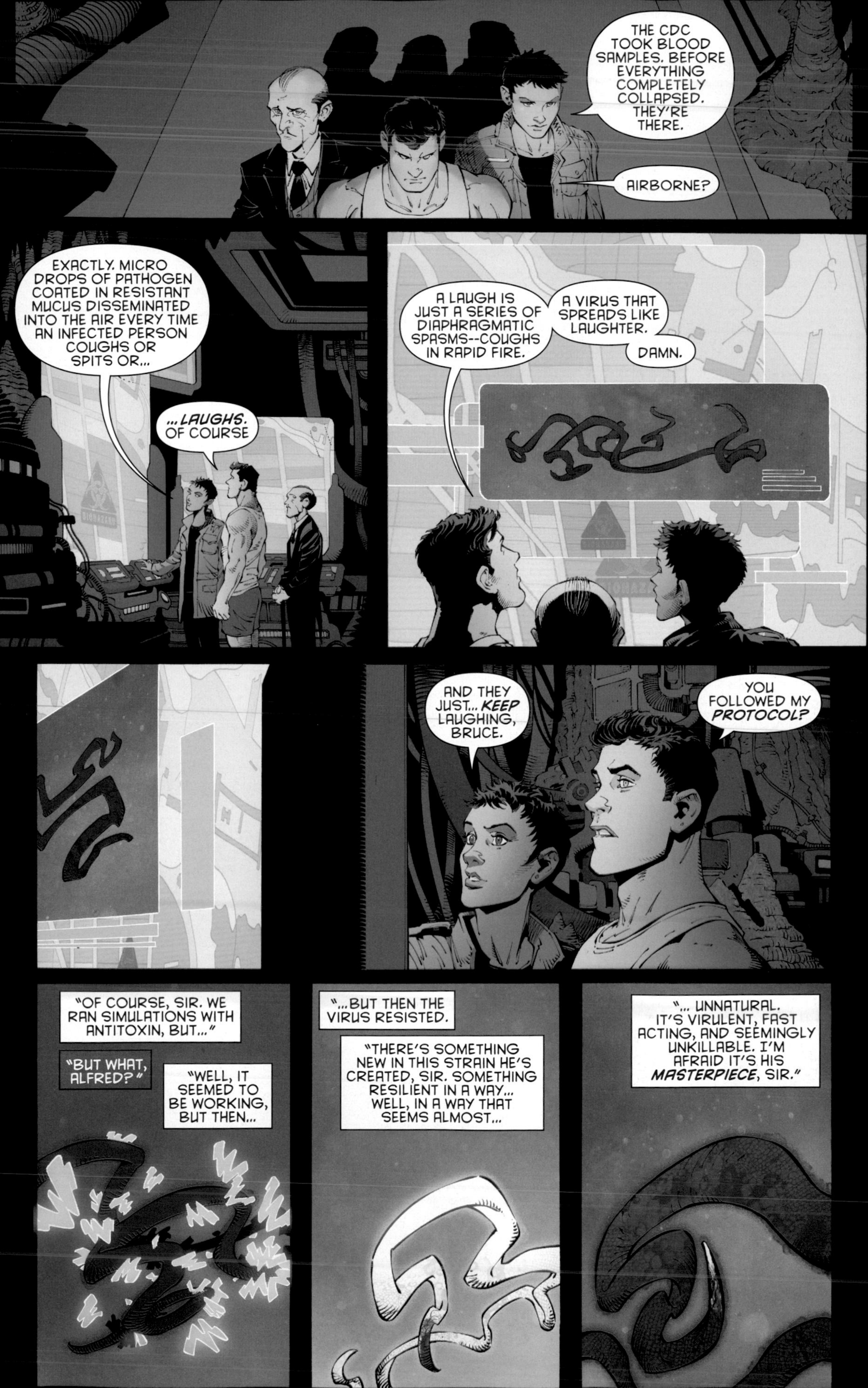
THE CDC TOOK BLOOD SAMPLES. BEFORE EVERYTHING COMPLETELY COLLAPSED. THEY'RE THERE.
AIRBORNE?
EXACTLY. MICRO DROPS OF PATHOGEN COATED IN RESISTANT MUCUS DISSEMINATED INTO THE AIR EVERY TIME AN INFECTED PERSON COUGHS OR SPITS OR...
...LAUGHS. OF COURSE
A LAUGH IS JUST A SERIES OF DIAPHRAGMATIC SPASMS--COUGHS IN RAPID FIRE.
A VIRUS THAT SPREADS LIKE LAUGHTER.
DAMN.
AND THEY JUST... KEEP LAUGHING, BRUCE.
YOU FOLLOWED MY PROTOCOL?
"OF COURSE, SIR. WE RAN SIMULATIONS WITH ANTITOXIN, BUT..."
"BUT WHAT, ALFRED?"
"WELL, IT SEEMED TO BE WORKING, BUT THEN...
"...BUT THEN THE VIRUS RESISTED.
"THERE'S SOMETHING NEW IN THIS STRAIN HE'S CREATED, SIR. SOMETHING RESILIENT IN A WAY... WELL, IN A WAY THAT SEEMS ALMOST...
"... UNNATURAL. IT'S VIRULENT, FAST ACTING, AND SEEMINGLY UNKILLABLE. I'M AFRAID IT'S HIS MASTERPIECE, SIR."

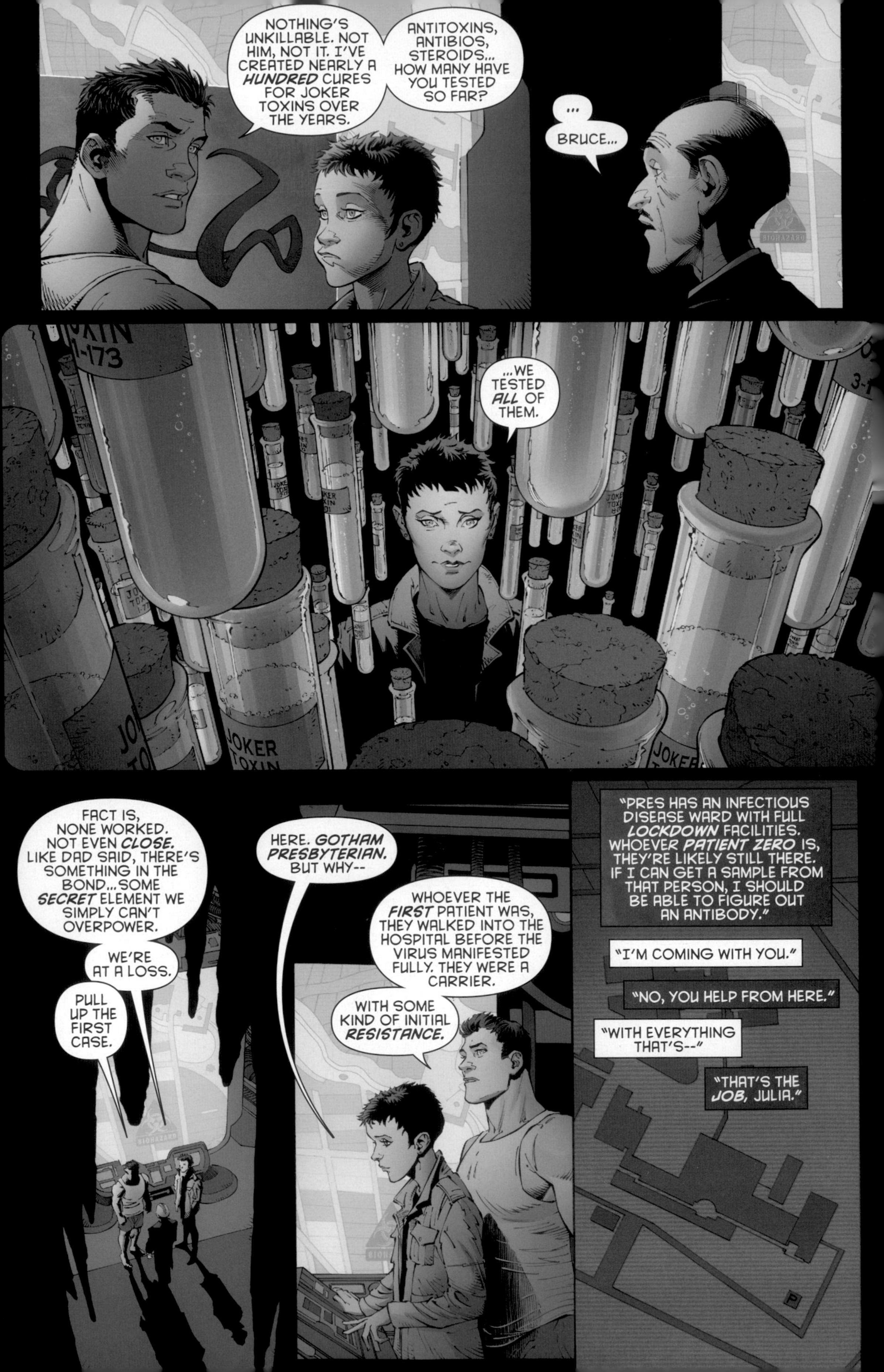
NOTHING'S UNKILLABLE. NOT HIM, NOT IT. I'VE CREATED NEARLY A HUNDRED CURES FOR JOKER TOXINS OVER THE YEARS.
ANTITOXINS, ANTIBIOS, STEROIDS... HOW MANY HAVE YOU TESTED SO FAR?
...
BRUCE...
BIOHAZARD
TOXIN
1-173
...WE TESTED ALL OF THEM.
JOKER TOXIN
FACT IS, NONE WORKED. NOT EVEN CLOSE. LIKE DAD SAID, THERE'S SOMETHING IN THE BOND...SOME SECRET ELEMENT WE SIMPLY CAN'T OVERPOWER.
WE'RE AT A LOSS.
PULL UP THE FIRST CASE.
HERE. GOTHAM PRESBYTERIAN. BUT WHY--
WHOEVER THE FIRST PATIENT WAS, THEY WALKED INTO THE HOSPITAL BEFORE THE VIRUS MANIFESTED FULLY. THEY WERE A CARRIER.
WITH SOME KIND OF INITIAL RESISTANCE.
"PRES HAS AN INFECTIOUS DISEASE WARD WITH FULL LOCKDOWN FACILITIES. WHOEVER PATIENT ZERO IS, THEY'RE LIKELY STILL THERE. IF I CAN GET A SAMPLE FROM THAT PERSON, I SHOULD BE ABLE TO FIGURE OUT AN ANTIBODY."
"I'M COMING WITH YOU."
"NO, YOU HELP FROM HERE."
"WITH EVERYTHING THAT'S--"
"THAT'S THE JOB, JULIA."

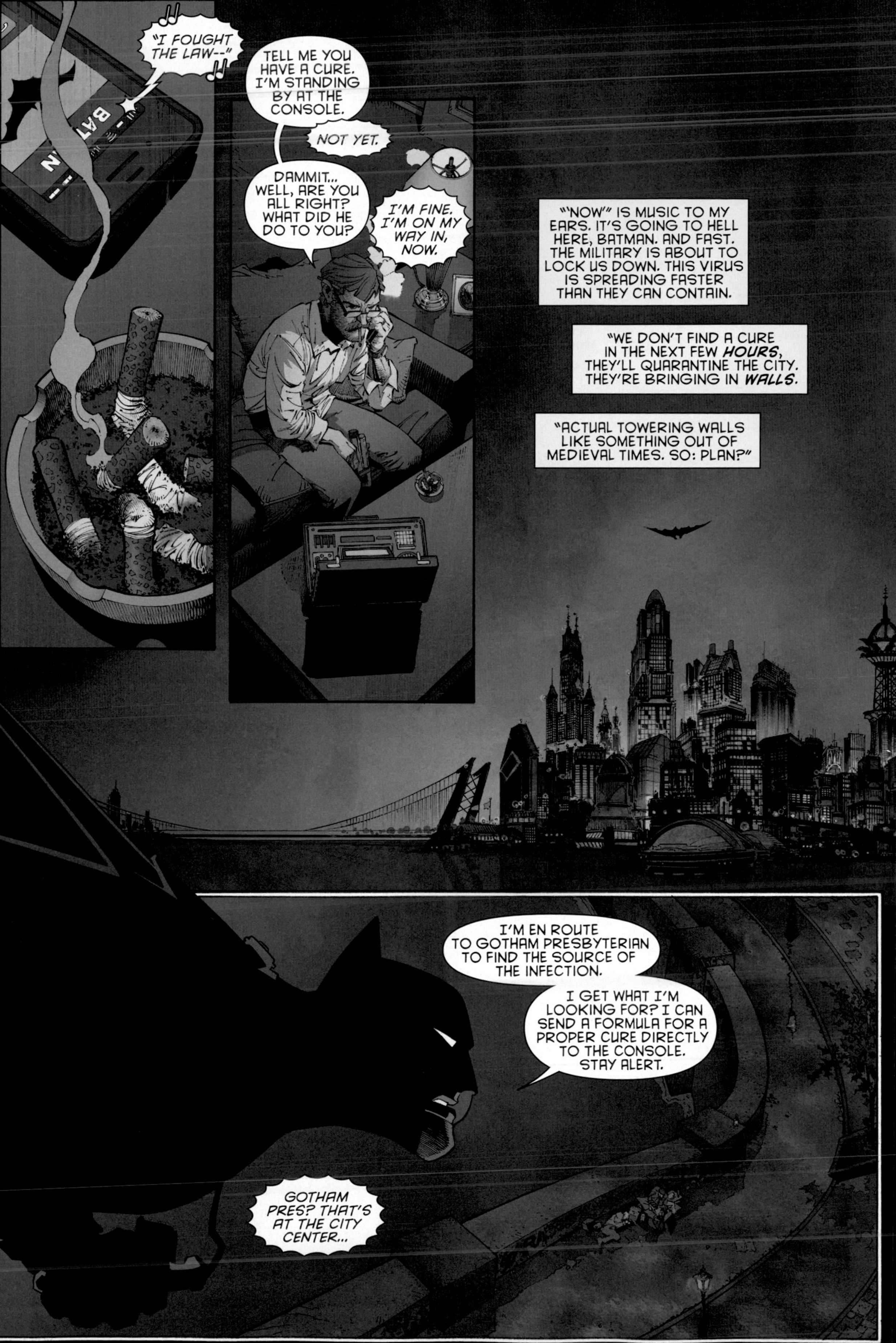
"I FOUGHT THE LAW--"
TELL ME YOU HAVE A CURE. I'M STANDING BY AT THE CONSOLE.
NOT YET.
DAMMIT... WELL, ARE YOU ALL RIGHT? WHAT DID HE DO TO YOU?
I'M FINE. I'M ON MY WAY IN, NOW.
"'NOW'" IS MUSIC TO MY EARS. IT'S GOING TO HELL HERE, BATMAN. AND FAST. THE MILITARY IS ABOUT TO LOCK US DOWN. THIS VIRUS IS SPREADING FASTER THAN THEY CAN CONTAIN.
"WE DON'T FIND A CURE IN THE NEXT FEW HOURS, THEY'LL QUARANTINE THE CITY. THEY'RE BRINGING IN WALLS.
"ACTUAL TOWERING WALLS LIKE SOMETHING OUT OF MEDIEVAL TIMES. SO: PLAN?"
I'M EN ROUTE TO GOTHAM PRESBYTERIAN TO FIND THE SOURCE OF THE INFECTION.
I GET WHAT I'M LOOKING FOR? I CAN SEND A FORMULA FOR A PROPER CURE DIRECTLY TO THE CONSOLE. STAY ALERT.
GOTHAM PRES? THAT'S AT THE CITY CENTER...

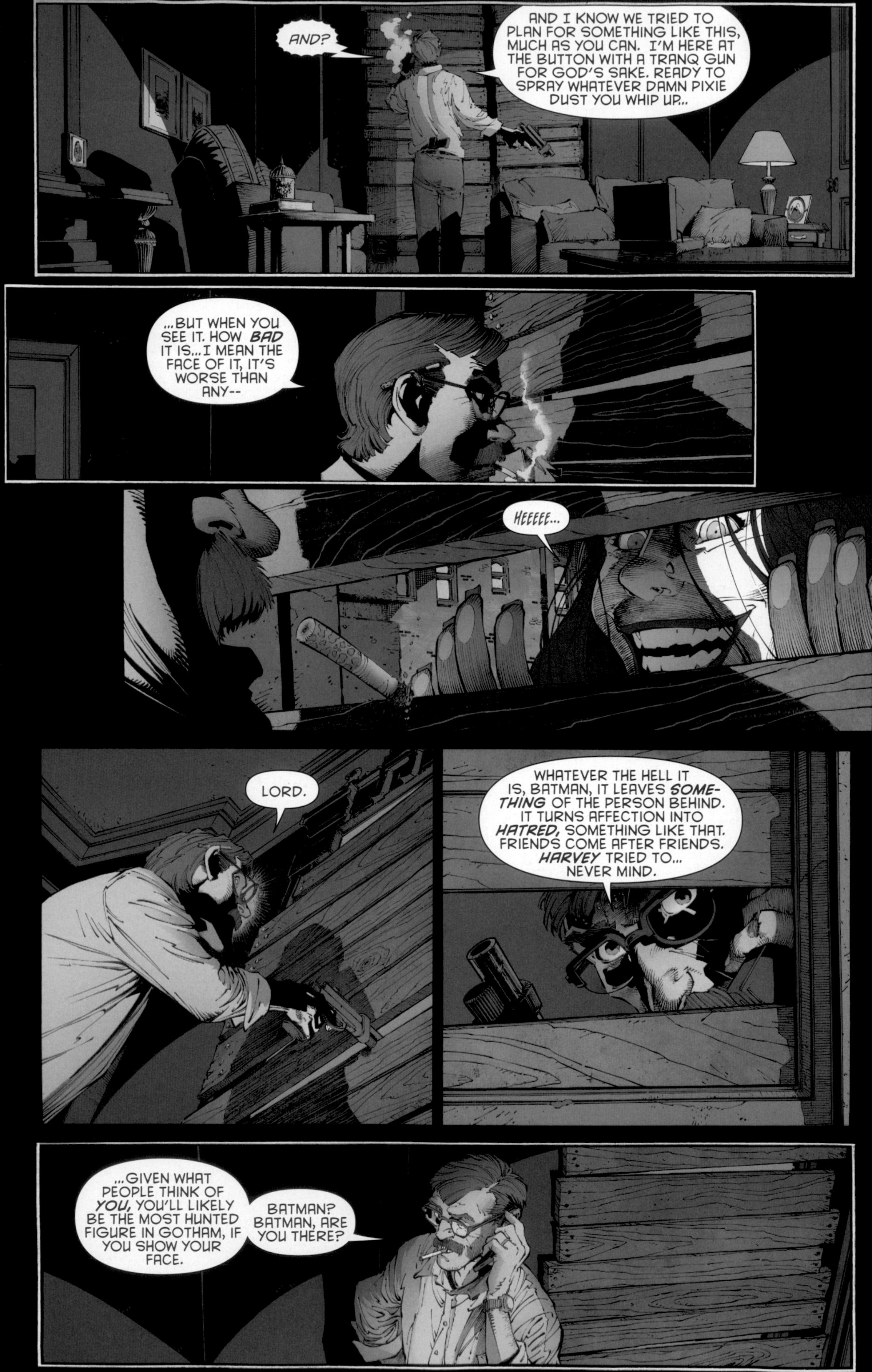
AND?
AND I KNOW WE TRIED TO PLAN FOR SOMETHING LIKE THIS, MUCH AS YOU CAN. I'M HERE AT THE BUTTON WITH A TRANQ GUN FOR GOD'S SAKE. READY TO SPRAY WHATEVER DAMN PIXIE DUST YOU WHIP UP...
...BUT WHEN YOU SEE IT. HOW BAD IT IS... I MEAN THE FACE OF IT, IT'S WORSE THAN ANY--
HEEEEE...
LORD.
WHATEVER THE HELL IT IS, BATMAN, IT LEAVES SOMETHING OF THE PERSON BEHIND. IT TURNS AFFECTION INTO HATRED, SOMETHING LIKE THAT. FRIENDS COME AFTER FRIENDS. HARVEY TRIED TO... NEVER MIND.
...GIVEN WHAT PEOPLE THINK OF YOU, YOU'LL LIKELY BE THE MOST HUNTED FIGURE IN GOTHAM, IF YOU SHOW YOUR FACE.
BATMAN? BATMAN, ARE YOU THERE?

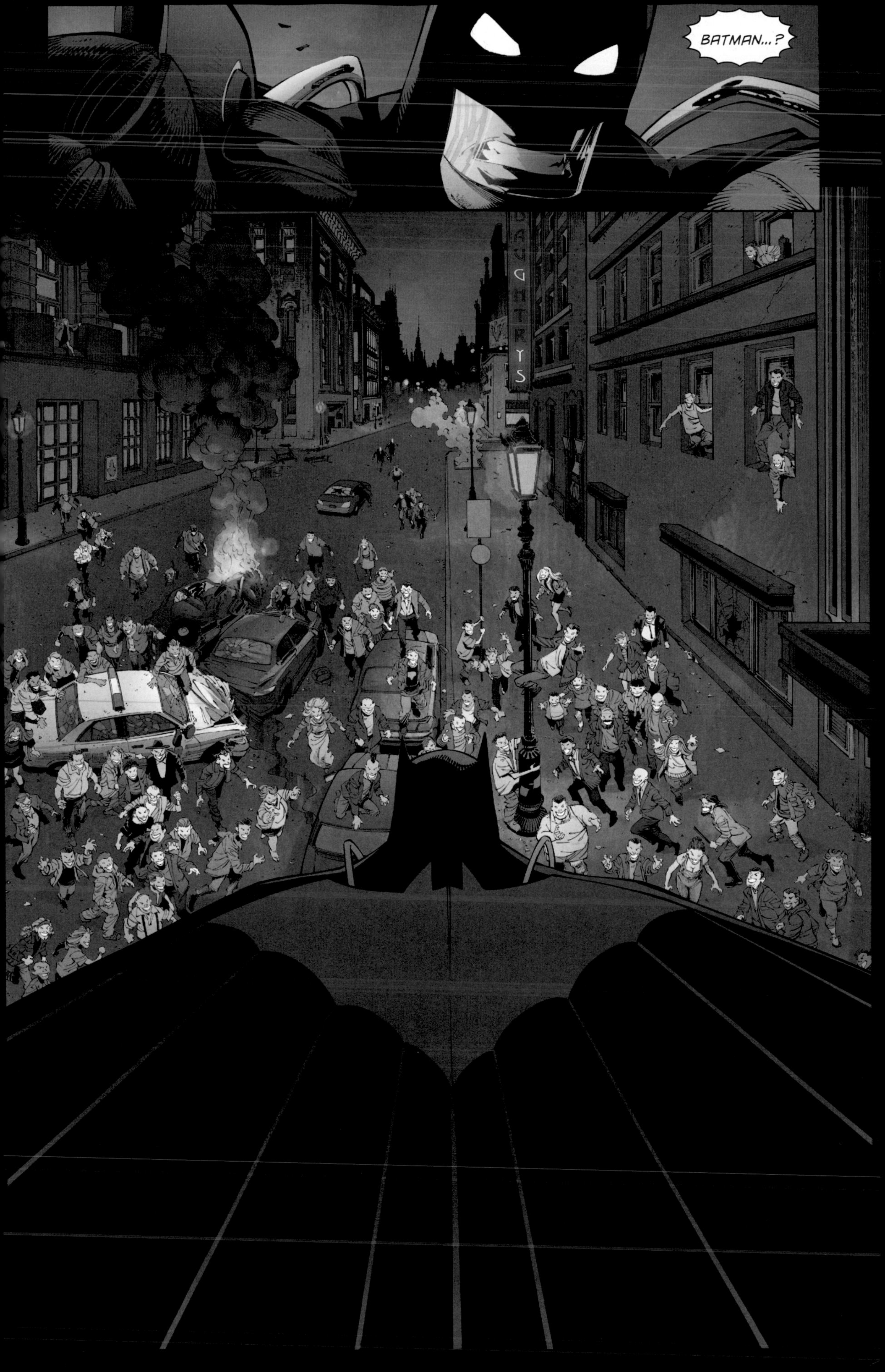
BATMAN...?

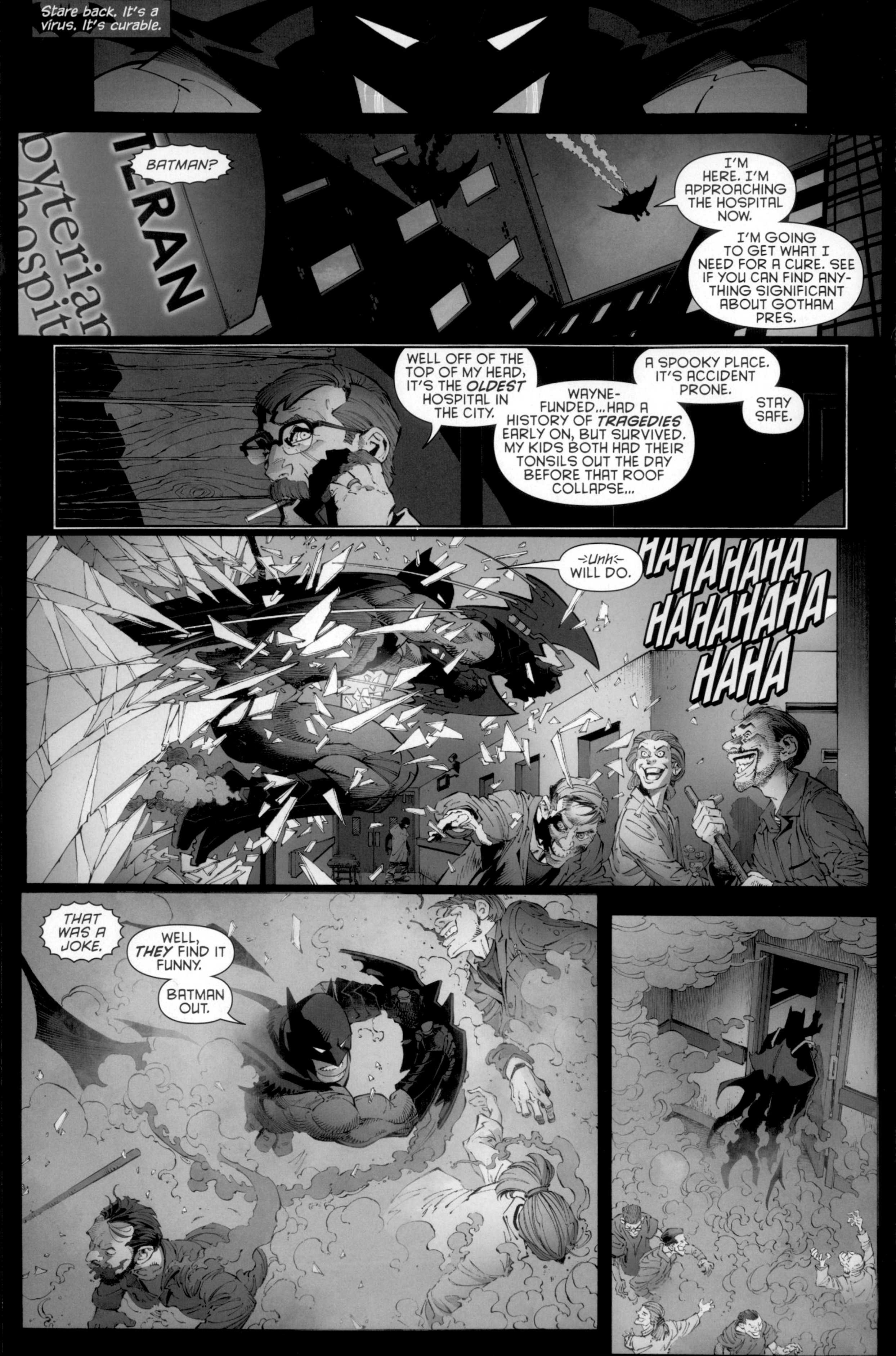
Stare back. It's a virus. It's curable.
BATMAN?
I'M HERE. I'M APPROACHING THE HOSPITAL NOW.
I'M GOING TO GET WHAT I NEED FOR A CURE. SEE IF YOU CAN FIND ANYTHING SIGNIFICANT ABOUT GOTHAM PRES.
WELL OFF OF THE TOP OF MY HEAD, IT'S THE OLDEST HOSPITAL IN THE CITY.
WAYNE-FUNDED...HAD A HISTORY OF TRAGEDIES EARLY ON, BUT SURVIVED. MY KIDS BOTH HAD THEIR TONSILS OUT THE DAY BEFORE THAT ROOF COLLAPSE...
A SPOOKY PLACE. IT'S ACCIDENT PRONE.
STAY SAFE.
-Unh- WILL DO.
HAHAHAHA HAHAHAHA HAHA
THAT WAS A JOKE.
WELL, THEY FIND IT FUNNY.
BATMAN OUT.

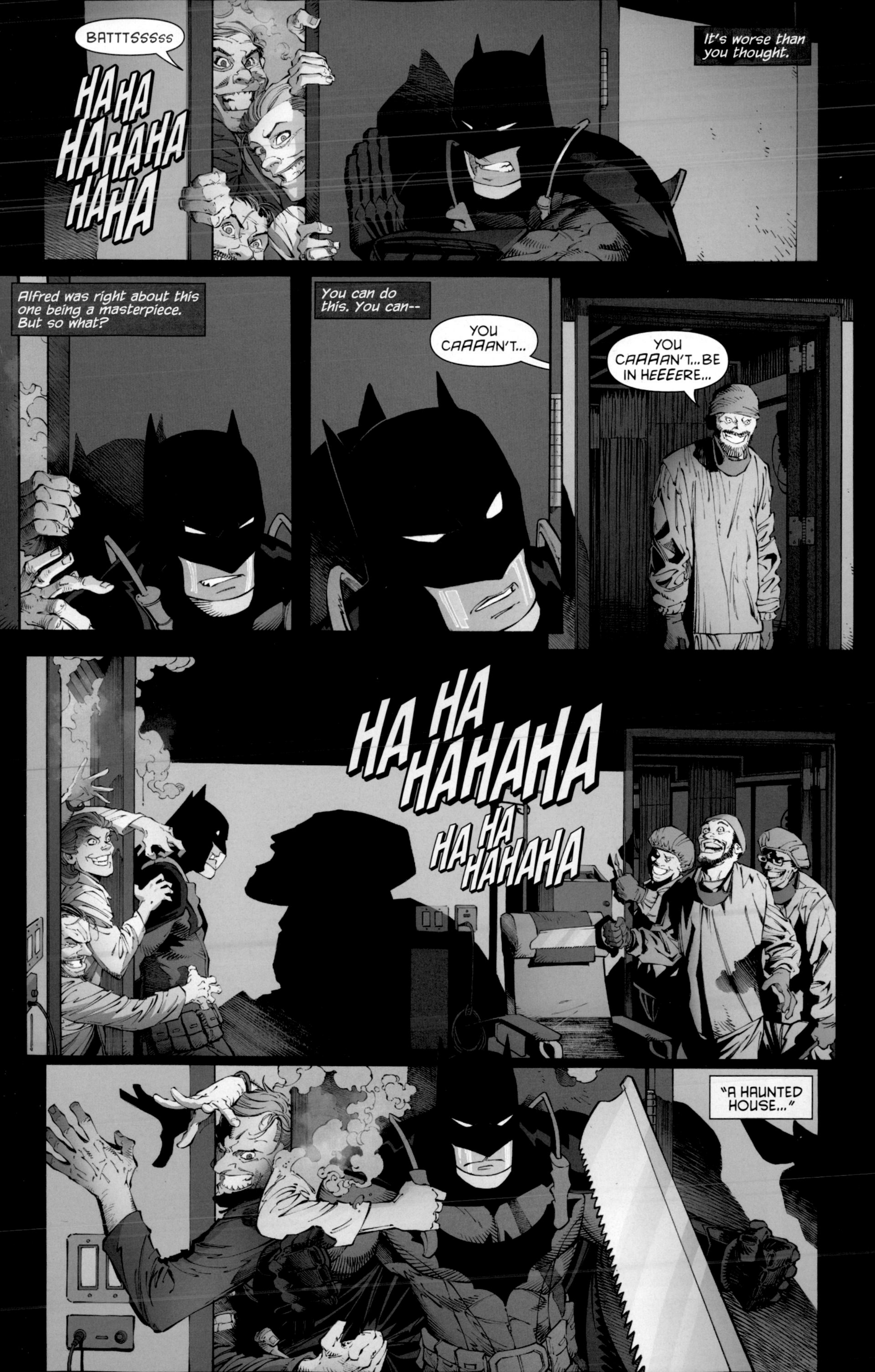
BATTTSSSSS
HA HA HAHAHA HAHA
It's worse than you thought.
Alfred was right about this one being a masterpiece. But so what?
You can do this. You can--
YOU CAAAAN'T...
YOU CAAAAN'T...BE IN HEEEERE...
HA HA HAHAHA HA HA HAHAHA
"A HAUNTED HOUSE..."

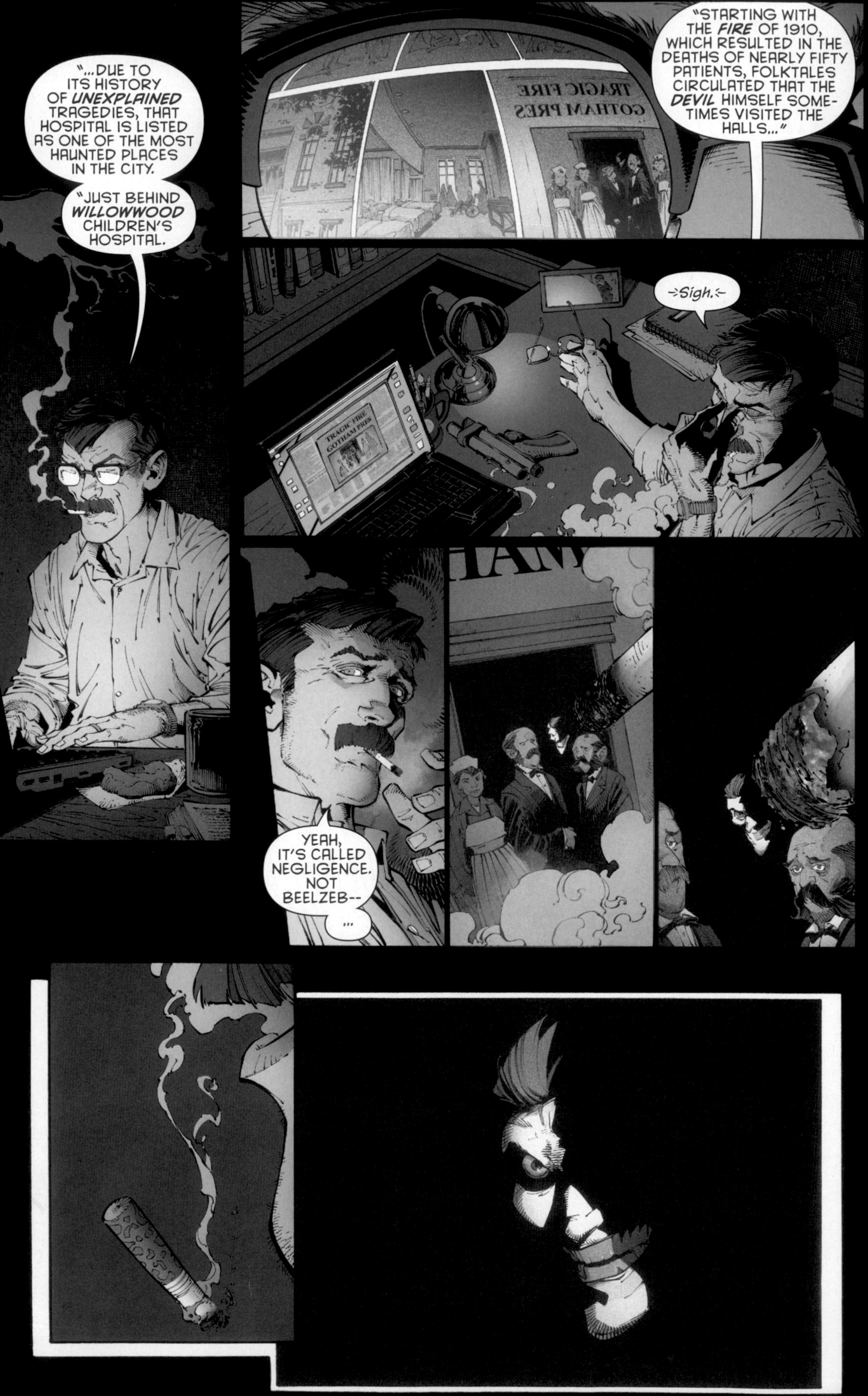

"...DUE TO ITS HISTORY OF *UNEXPLAINED* TRAGEDIES, THAT HOSPITAL IS LISTED AS ONE OF THE MOST HAUNTED PLACES IN THE CITY.
"JUST BEHIND *WILLOWWOOD* CHILDREN'S HOSPITAL.
TRAGIC FIRE
GOTHAM PRES
"STARTING WITH THE *FIRE* OF 1910, WHICH RESULTED IN THE DEATHS OF NEARLY FIFTY PATIENTS, FOLKTALES CIRCULATED THAT THE *DEVIL* HIMSELF SOMETIMES VISITED THE HALLS..."
-Sigh.-
YEAH, IT'S CALLED NEGLIGENCE. NOT BEELZEB--
...

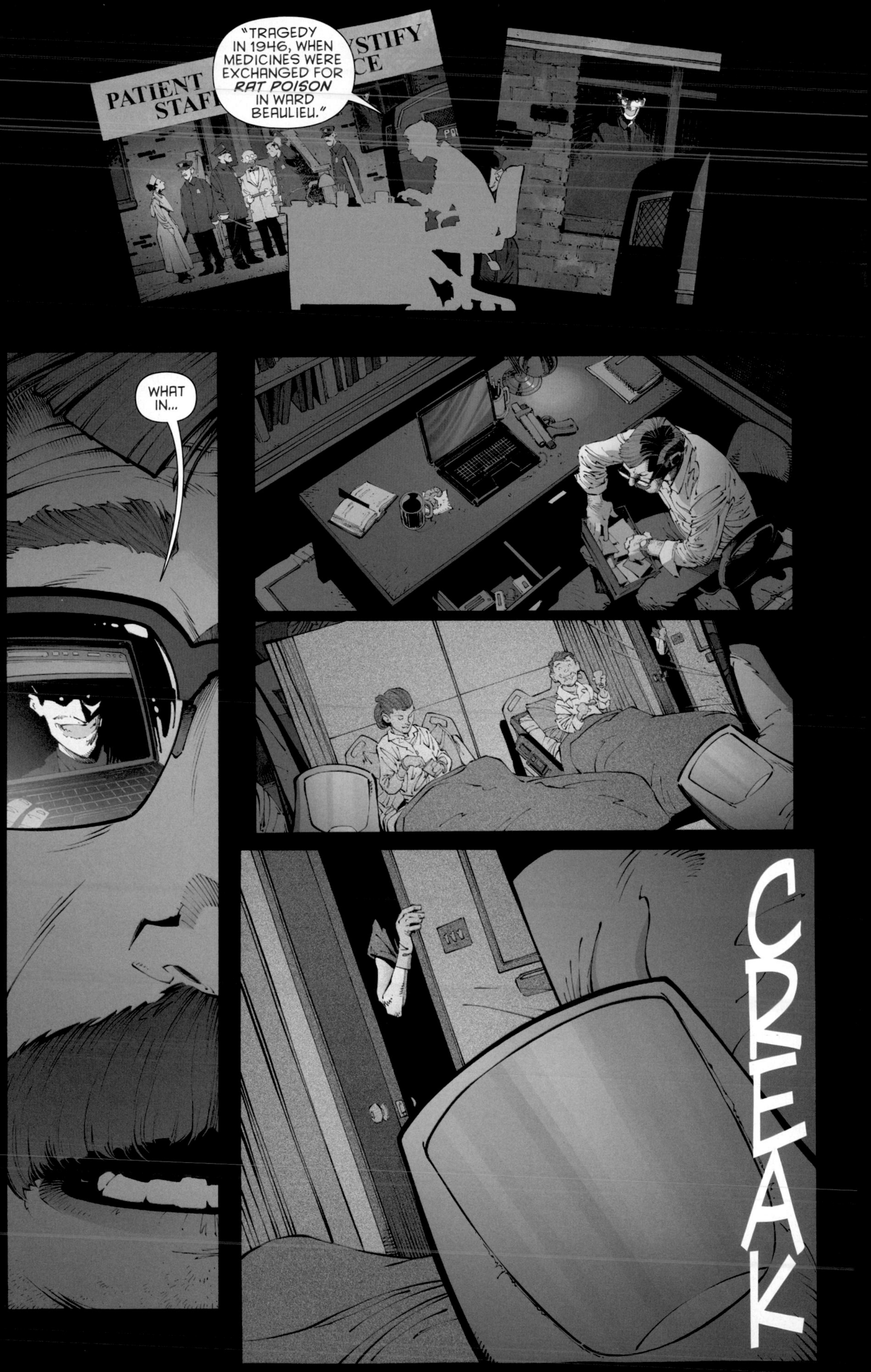
"TRAGEDY IN 1946, WHEN MEDICINES WERE EXCHANGED FOR *RAT POISON* IN WARD BEAULIEU."
WHAT IN...
CREAK

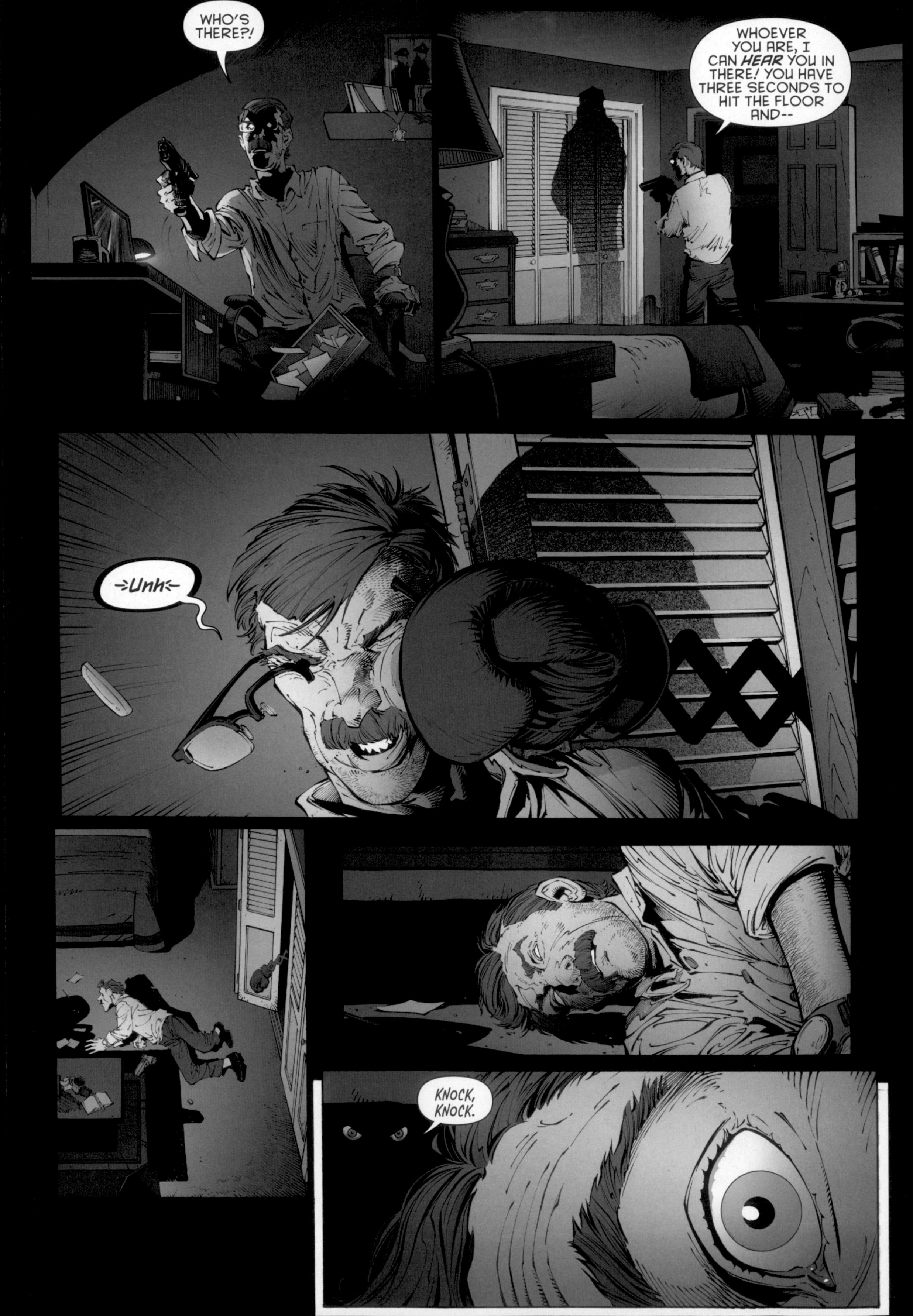
WHO'S THERE?!
WHOEVER YOU ARE, I CAN HEAR YOU IN THERE! YOU HAVE THREE SECONDS TO HIT THE FLOOR AND--
Unh
KNOCK, KNOCK.

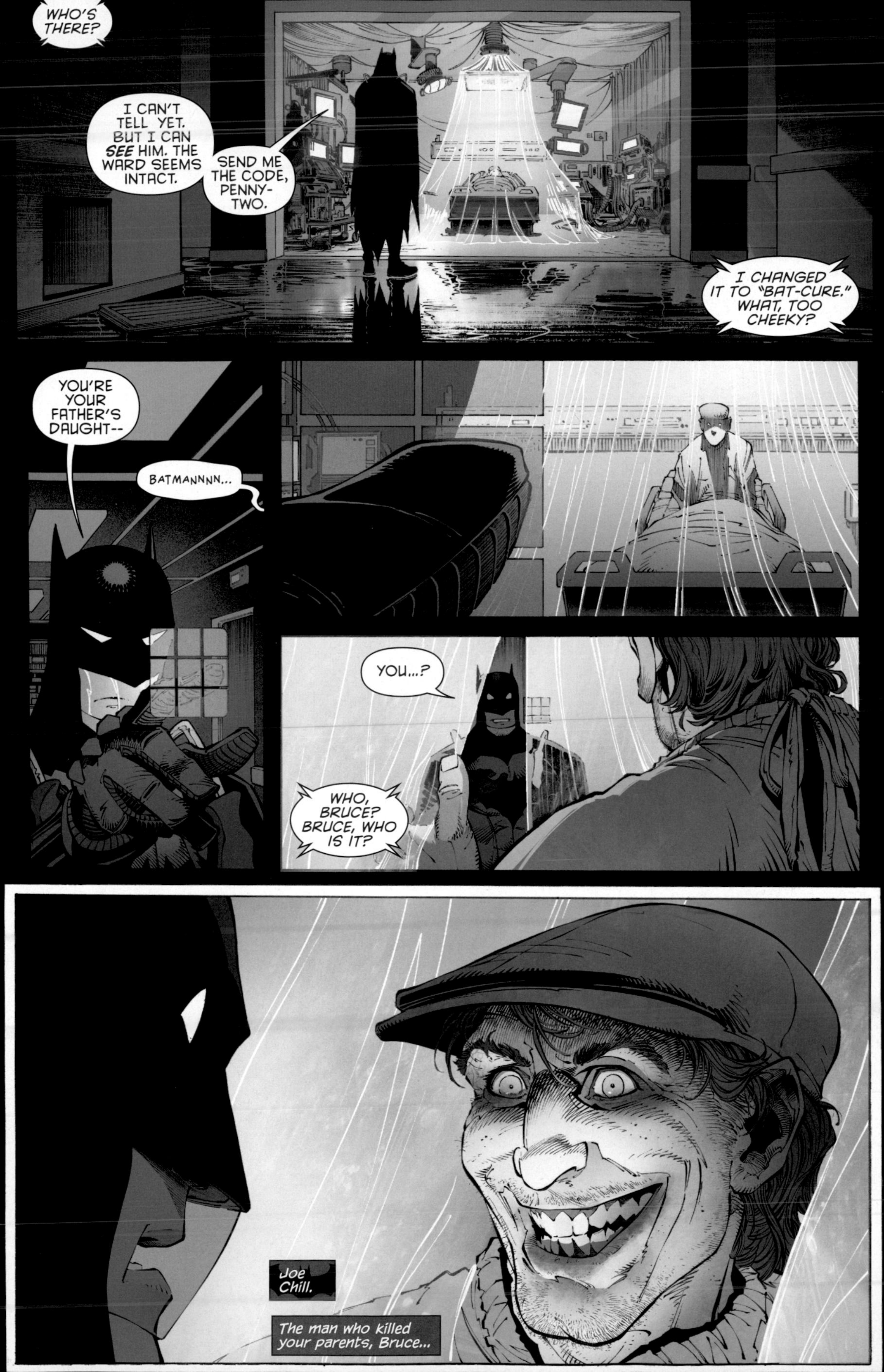
WHO'S THERE?
I CAN'T TELL YET. BUT I CAN SEE HIM. THE WARD SEEMS INTACT.
SEND ME THE CODE, PENNY-TWO.
I CHANGED IT TO "BAT-CURE." WHAT, TOO CHEEKY?
YOU'RE YOUR FATHER'S DAUGHT--
BATMANNNN...
YOU...?
WHO, BRUCE? BRUCE, WHO IS IT?
Joe Chill.
The man who killed your parents, Bruce...

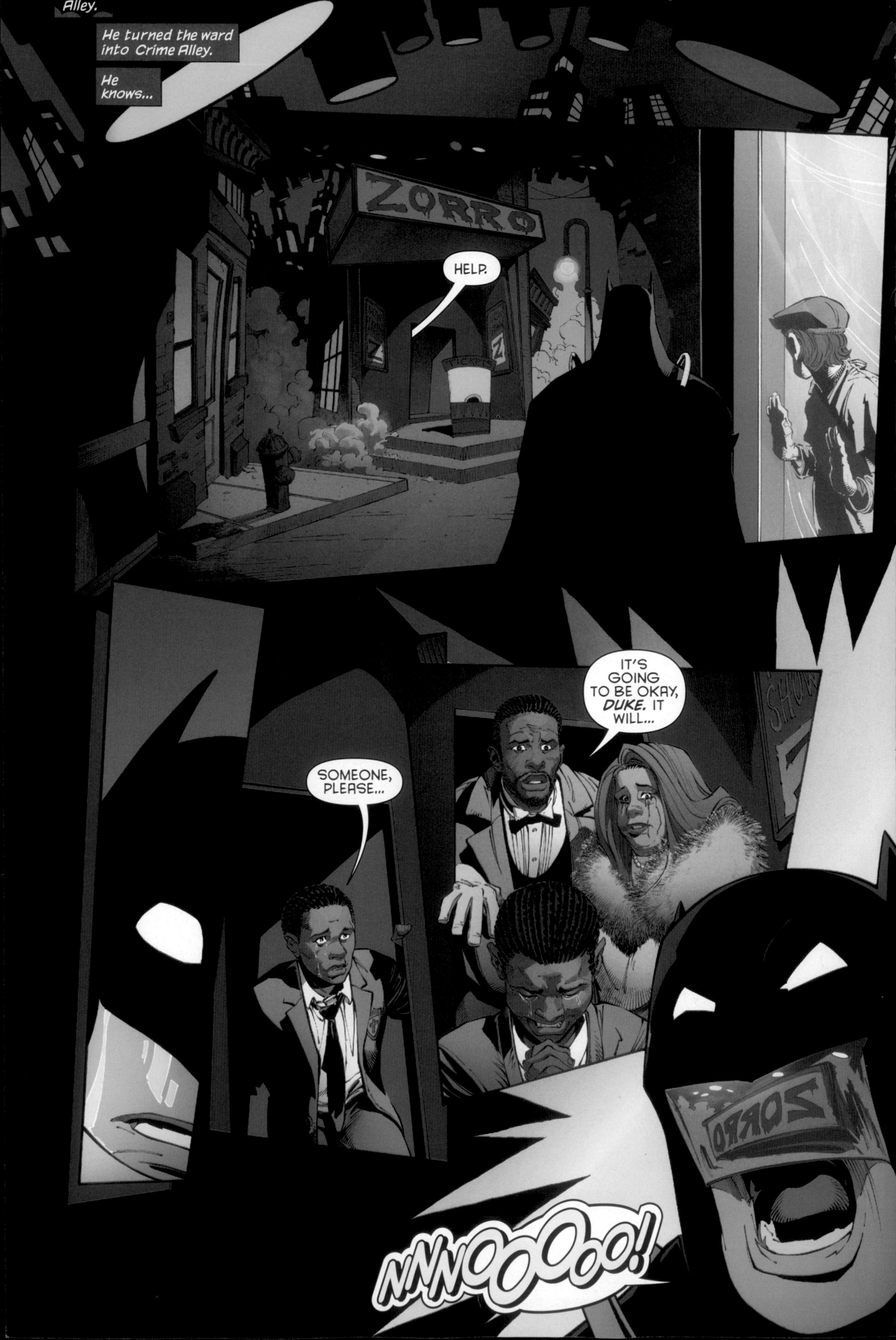
Alley.
He turned the ward into Crime Alley.
He knows...
ZORRO
HELP.
IT'S GOING TO BE OKAY, DUKE. IT WILL...
SOMEONE, PLEASE...
ZORRO
NNNOOOOoo!

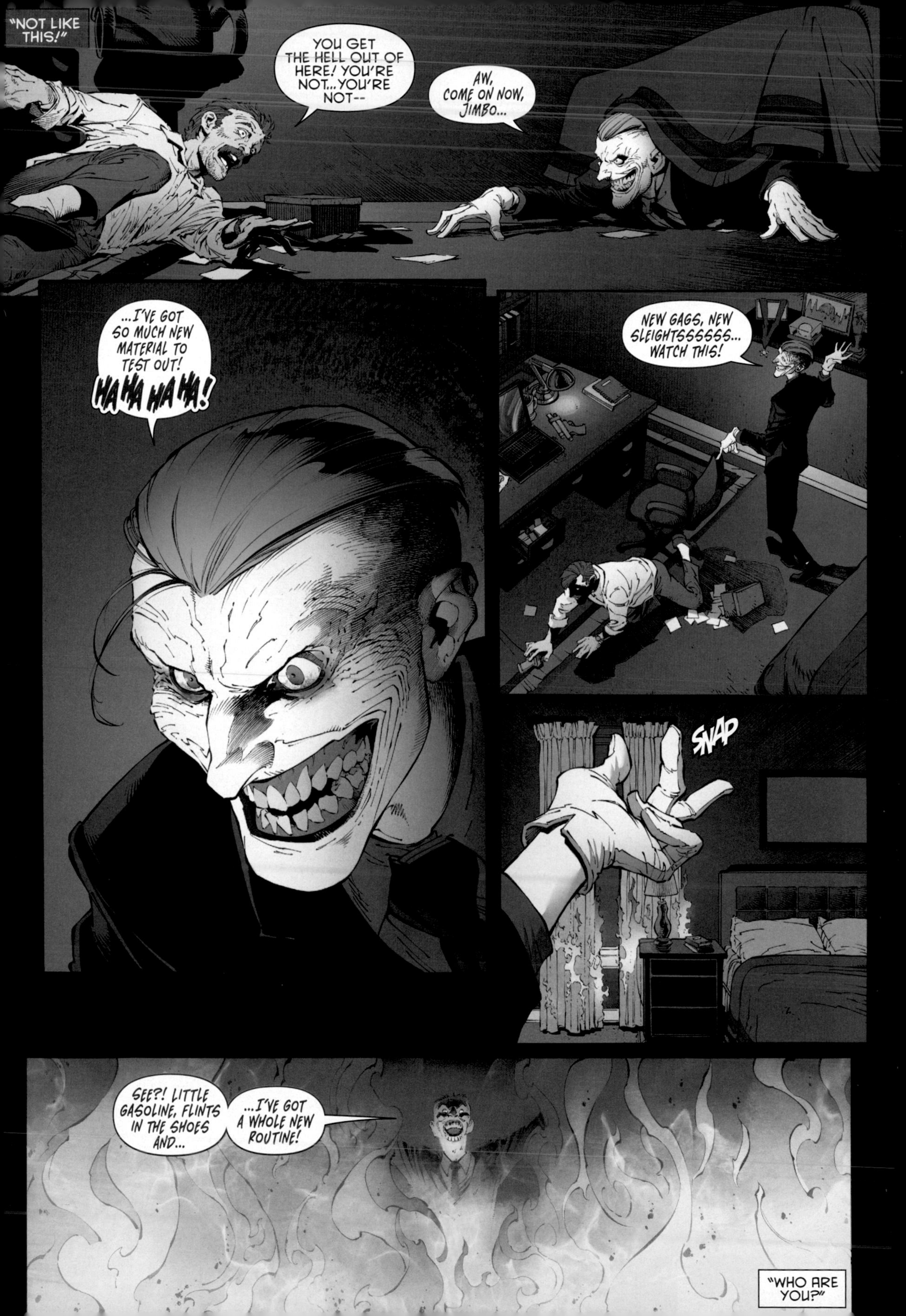

"NOT LIKE THIS!"
YOU GET THE HELL OUT OF HERE! YOU'RE NOT...YOU'RE NOT--
AW, COME ON NOW, JIMBO...
...I'VE GOT SO MUCH NEW MATERIAL TO TEST OUT! HA HA HA HA!
NEW GAGS, NEW SLEIGHTSSSSSS... WATCH THIS!
SNAP
SEE?! LITTLE GASOLINE, FLINTS IN THE SHOES AND...
...I'VE GOT A WHOLE NEW ROUTINE!
"WHO ARE YOU?"

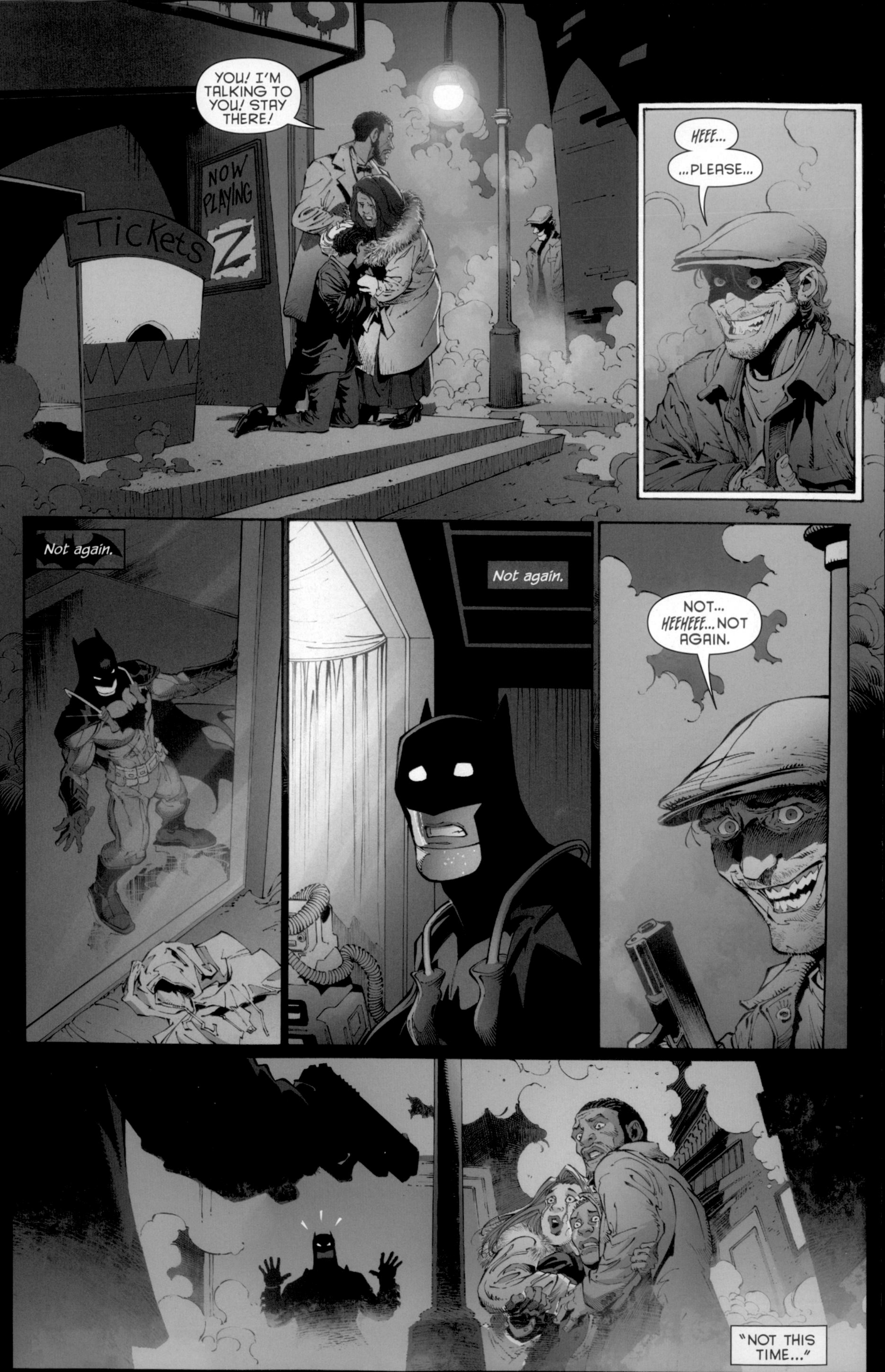

YOU! I'M TALKING TO YOU! STAY THERE!
NOW PLAYING
Z
Tickets
HEEE...
...PLEASE...
Not again.
Not again.
NOT... HEEHEEE...NOT AGAIN.
"NOT THIS TIME..."

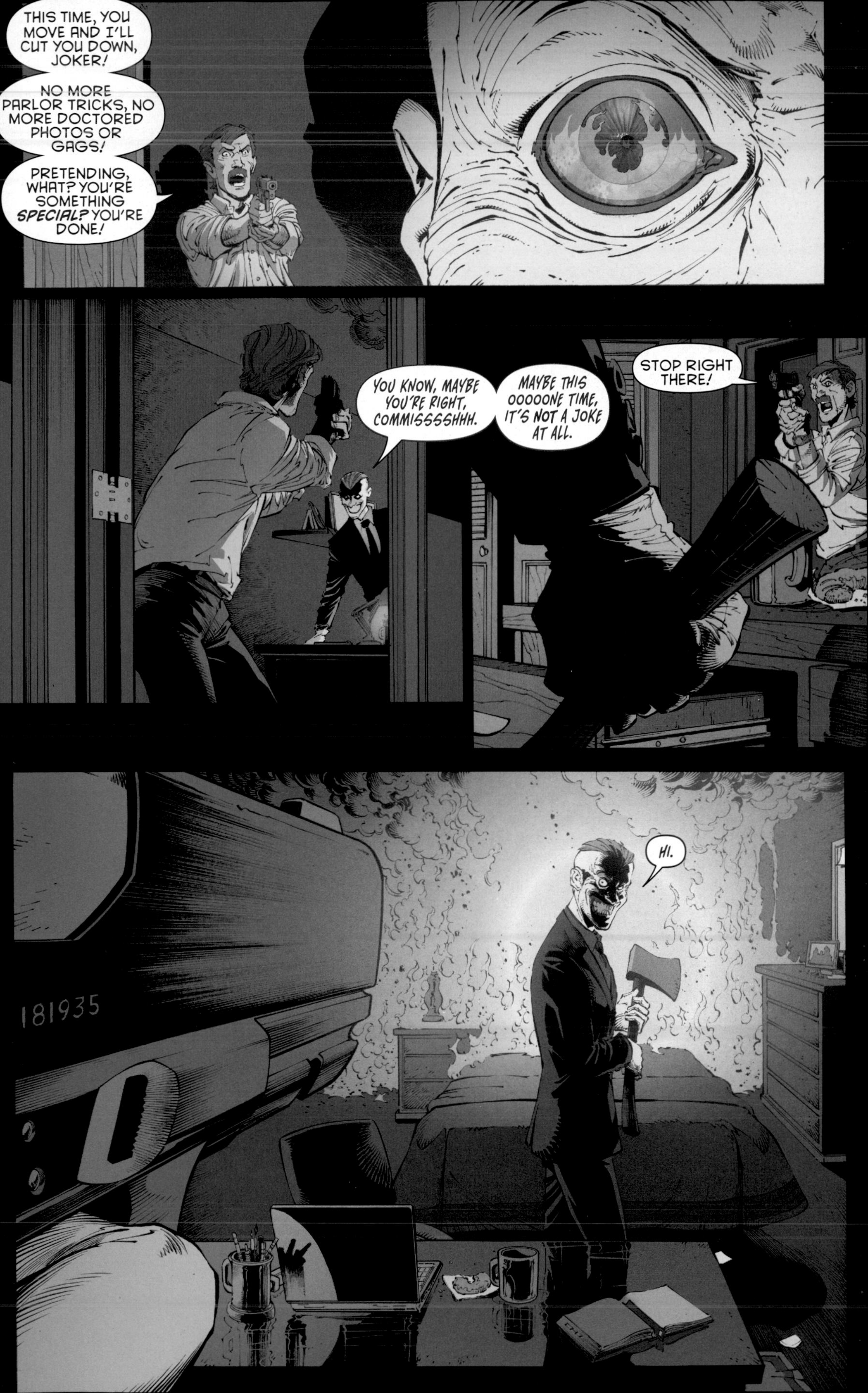
THIS TIME, YOU MOVE AND I'LL CUT YOU DOWN, JOKER!
NO MORE PARLOR TRICKS, NO MORE DOCTORED PHOTOS OR GAGS!
PRETENDING, WHAT? YOU'RE SOMETHING *SPECIAL*? YOU'RE DONE!
YOU KNOW, MAYBE YOU'RE RIGHT, COMMISSSSSHHH.
MAYBE THIS OOOOONE TIME, IT'S NOT A JOKE AT ALL.
STOP RIGHT THERE!
181935
HI.

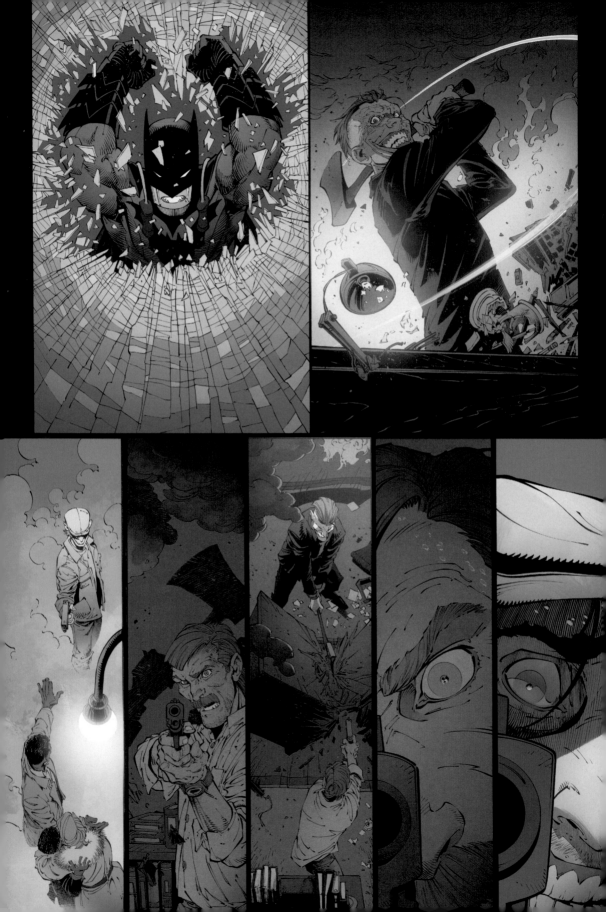

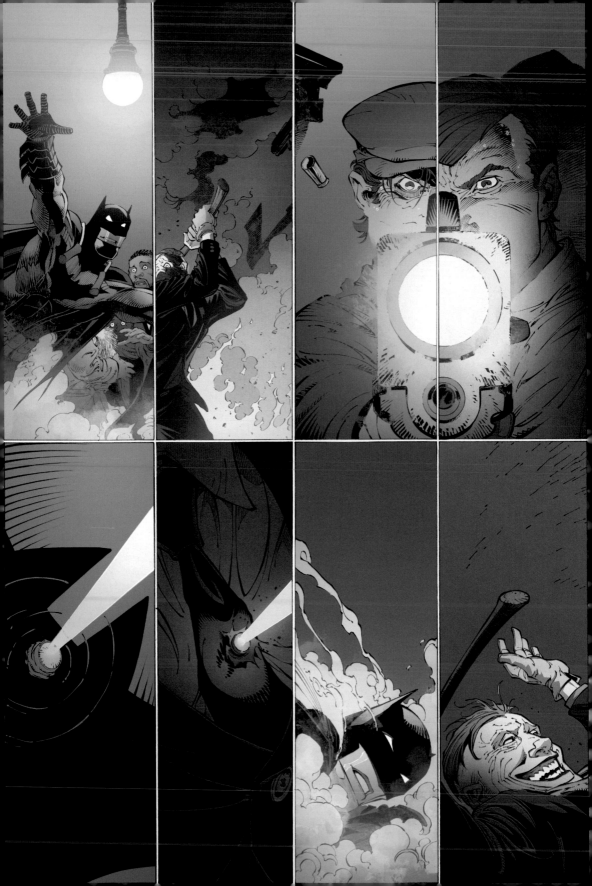

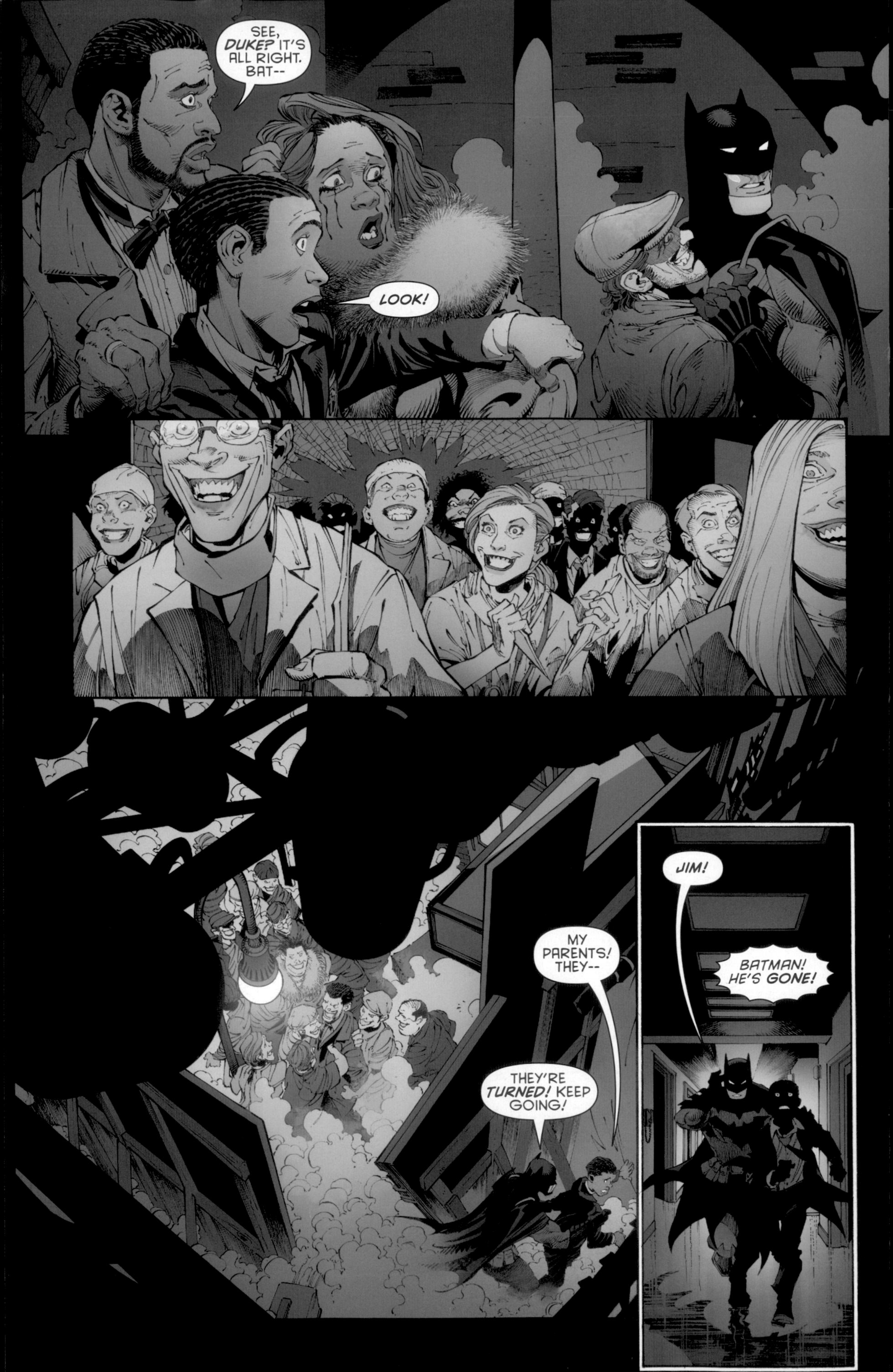
SEE, DUKE? IT'S ALL RIGHT. BAT--
LOOK!
JIM!
BATMAN! HE'S GONE!
MY PARENTS! THEY--
THEY'RE TURNED! KEEP GOING!

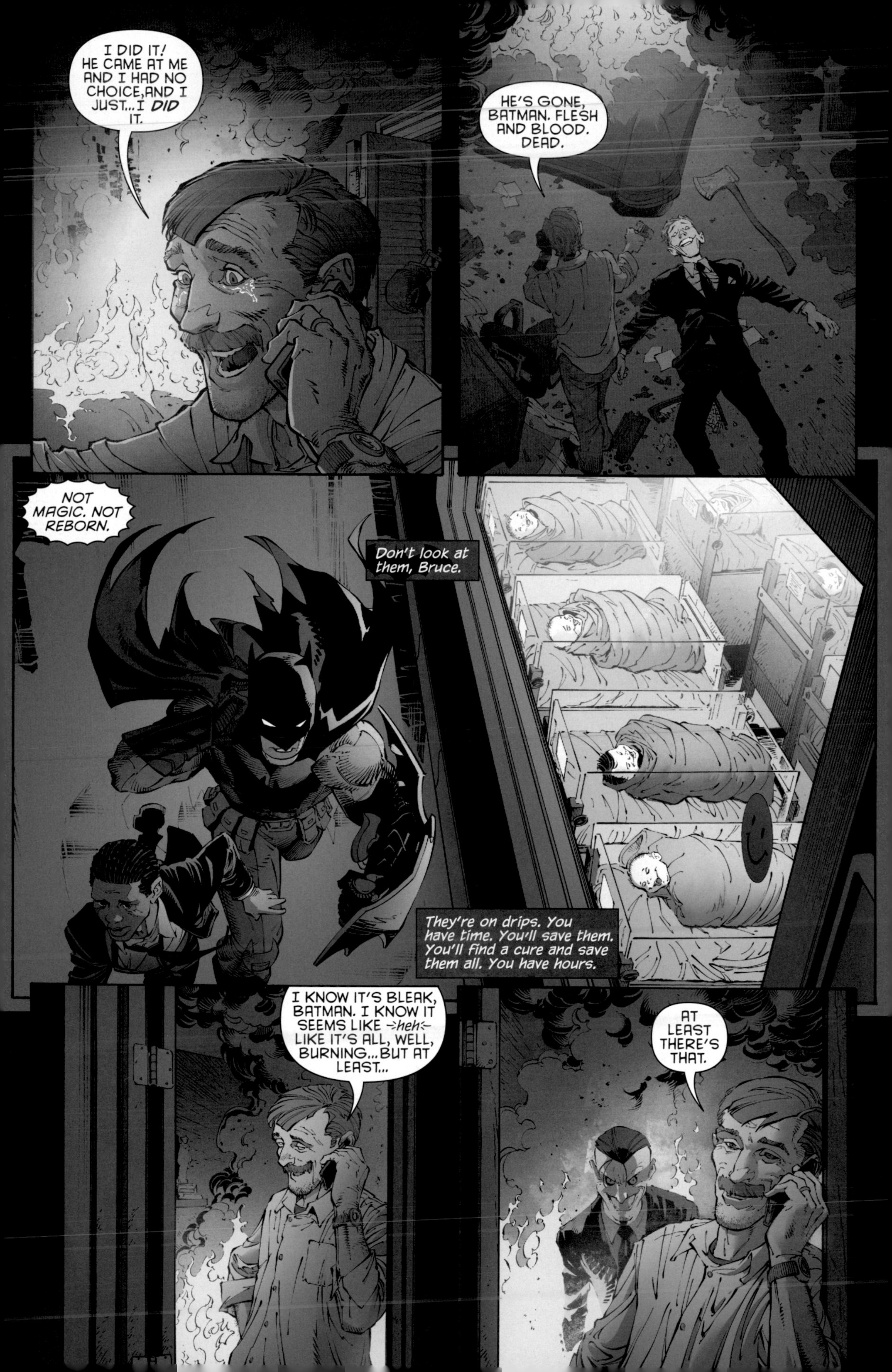
I DID IT! HE CAME AT ME AND I HAD NO CHOICE,AND I JUST...I *DID* IT.
HE'S GONE, BATMAN. FLESH AND BLOOD. DEAD.
NOT MAGIC. NOT REBORN.
Don't look at them, Bruce.
They're on drips. You have time. You'll save them. You'll find a cure and save them all. You have hours.
I KNOW IT'S BLEAK, BATMAN. I KNOW IT SEEMS LIKE *heh* LIKE IT'S ALL, WELL, BURNING...BUT AT LEAST...
AT LEAST THERE'S THAT.

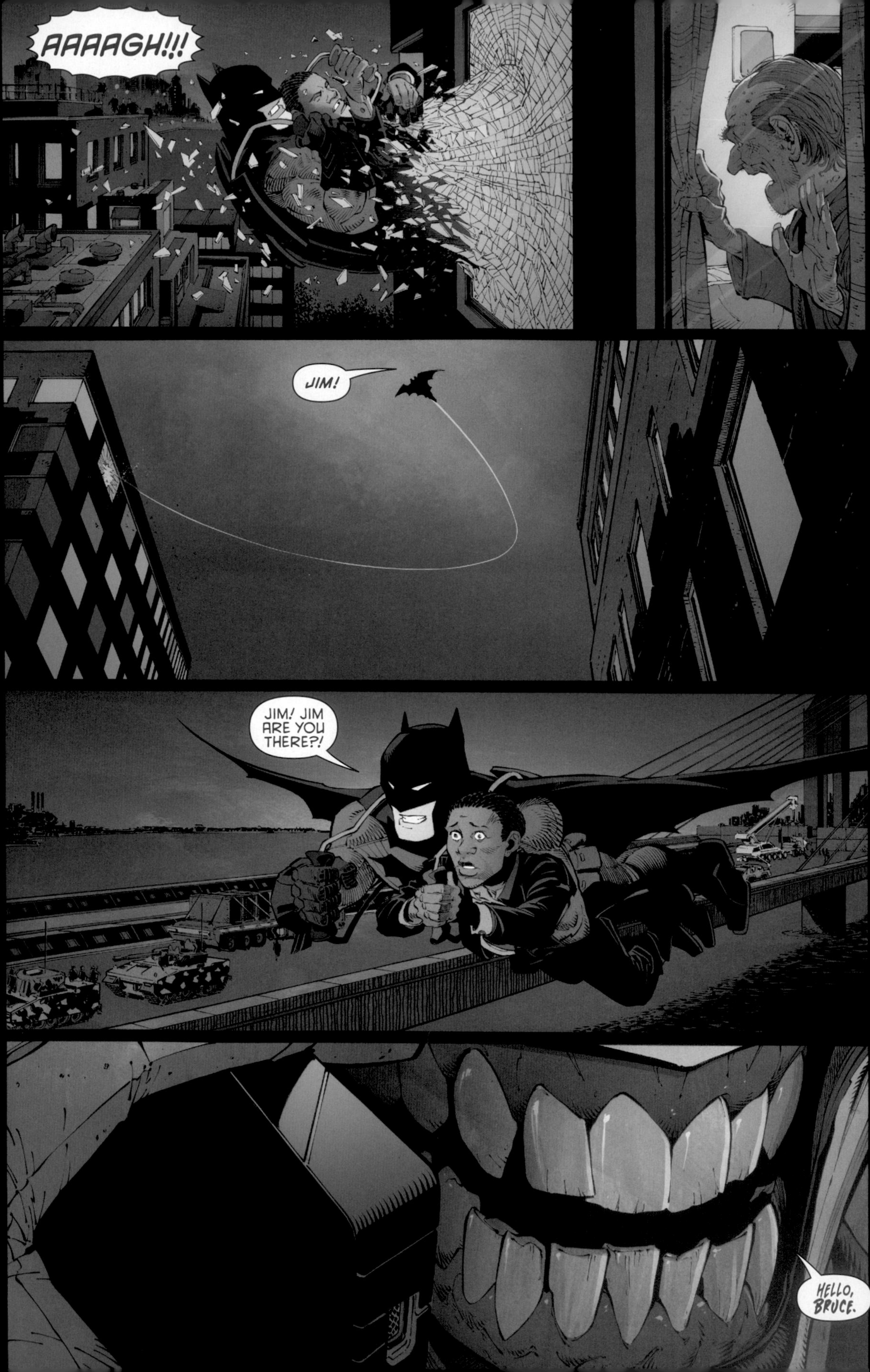
AAAAGH!!!
JIM!
JIM! JIM ARE YOU THERE?!
HELLO, BRUCE.

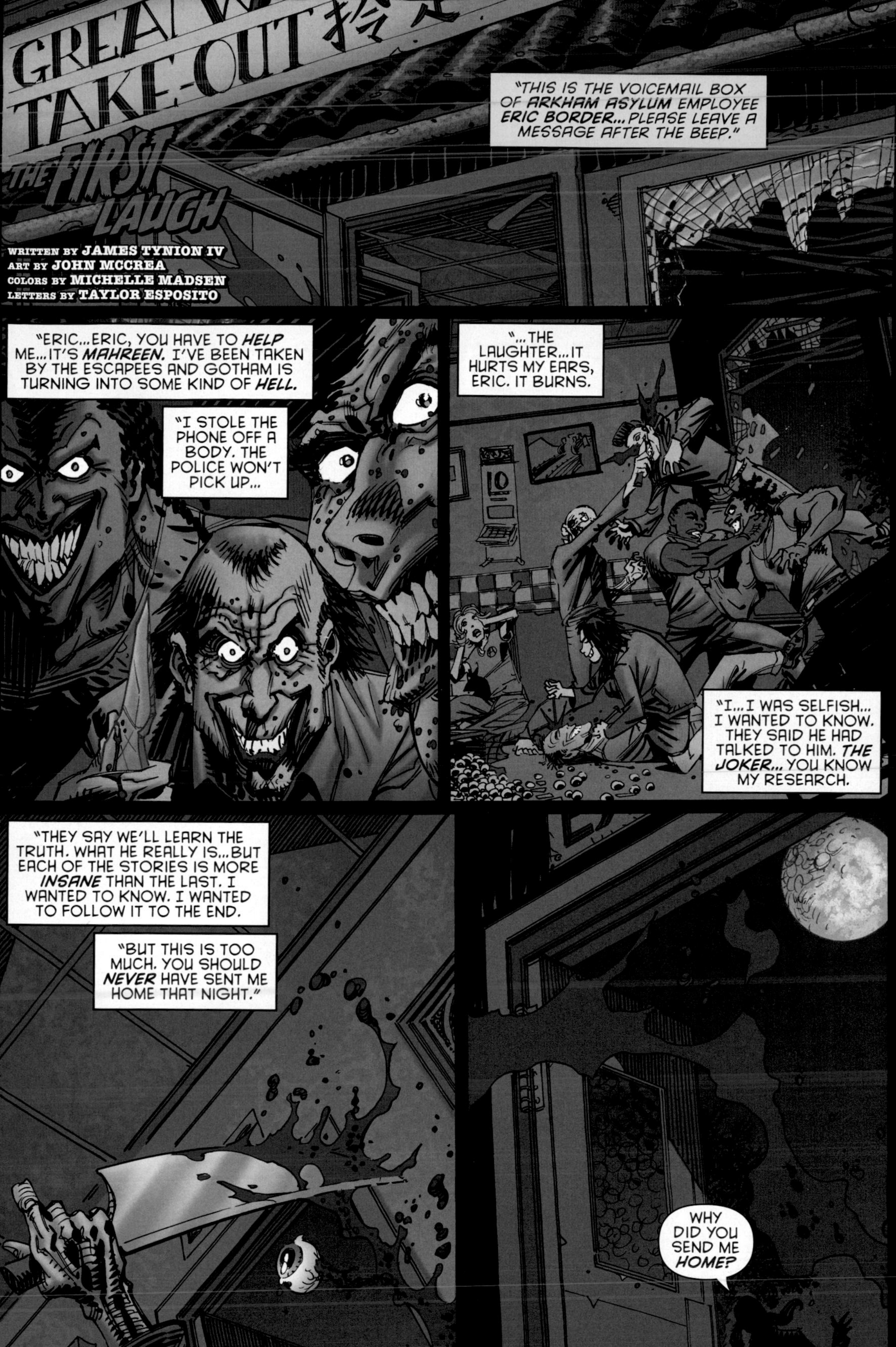
GREAT W
TAKE-OUT
THE FIRST LAUGH
WRITTEN BY JAMES TYNION IV
ART BY JOHN MCCREA
COLORS BY MICHELLE MADSEN
LETTERS BY TAYLOR ESPOSITO
"THIS IS THE VOICEMAIL BOX OF ARKHAM ASYLUM EMPLOYEE ERIC BORDER... PLEASE LEAVE A MESSAGE AFTER THE BEEP."
"ERIC... ERIC, YOU HAVE TO HELP ME... IT'S MAHREEN. I'VE BEEN TAKEN BY THE ESCAPEES AND GOTHAM IS TURNING INTO SOME KIND OF HELL.
"I STOLE THE PHONE OFF A BODY. THE POLICE WON'T PICK UP...
"...THE LAUGHTER... IT HURTS MY EARS, ERIC. IT BURNS.
"I... I WAS SELFISH... I WANTED TO KNOW. THEY SAID HE HAD TALKED TO HIM. THE JOKER... YOU KNOW MY RESEARCH.
"THEY SAY WE'LL LEARN THE TRUTH. WHAT HE REALLY IS... BUT EACH OF THE STORIES IS MORE INSANE THAN THE LAST. I WANTED TO KNOW. I WANTED TO FOLLOW IT TO THE END.
"BUT THIS IS TOO MUCH. YOU SHOULD NEVER HAVE SENT ME HOME THAT NIGHT."
WHY DID YOU SEND ME HOME?

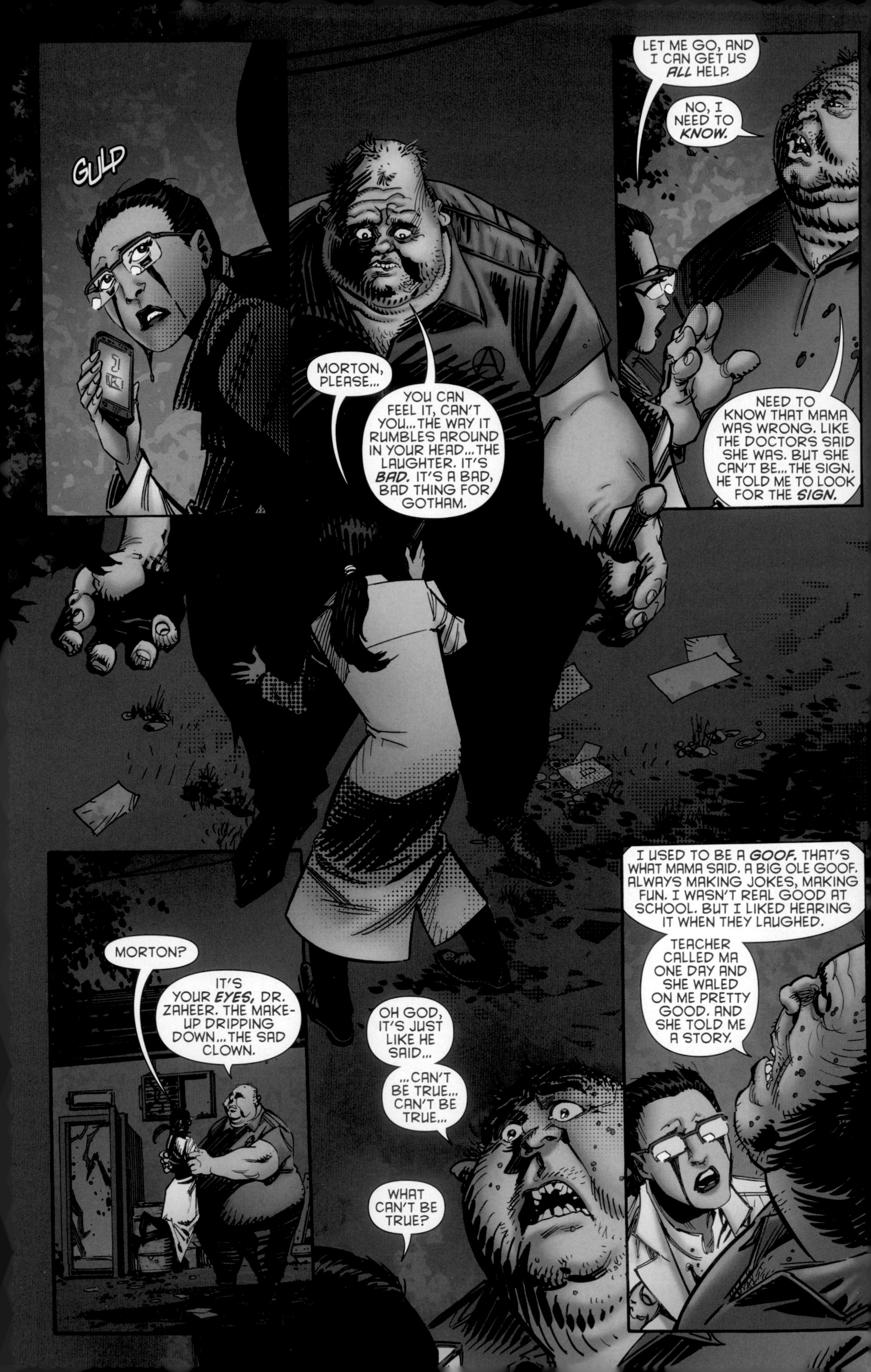
GULP
MORTON, PLEASE...
YOU CAN FEEL IT, CAN'T YOU...THE WAY IT RUMBLES AROUND IN YOUR HEAD...THE LAUGHTER. IT'S BAD. IT'S A BAD, BAD THING FOR GOTHAM.
LET ME GO, AND I CAN GET US ALL HELP.
NO, I NEED TO KNOW.
NEED TO KNOW THAT MAMA WAS WRONG. LIKE THE DOCTORS SAID SHE WAS. BUT SHE CAN'T BE...THE SIGN. HE TOLD ME TO LOOK FOR THE SIGN.
MORTON?
IT'S YOUR EYES, DR. ZAHEER. THE MAKE-UP DRIPPING DOWN...THE SAD CLOWN.
OH GOD, IT'S JUST LIKE HE SAID...
...CAN'T BE TRUE... CAN'T BE TRUE...
WHAT CAN'T BE TRUE?
I USED TO BE A GOOF. THAT'S WHAT MAMA SAID. A BIG OLE GOOF. ALWAYS MAKING JOKES, MAKING FUN. I WASN'T REAL GOOD AT SCHOOL. BUT I LIKED HEARING IT WHEN THEY LAUGHED.
TEACHER CALLED MA ONE DAY AND SHE WALED ON ME PRETTY GOOD. AND SHE TOLD ME A STORY.

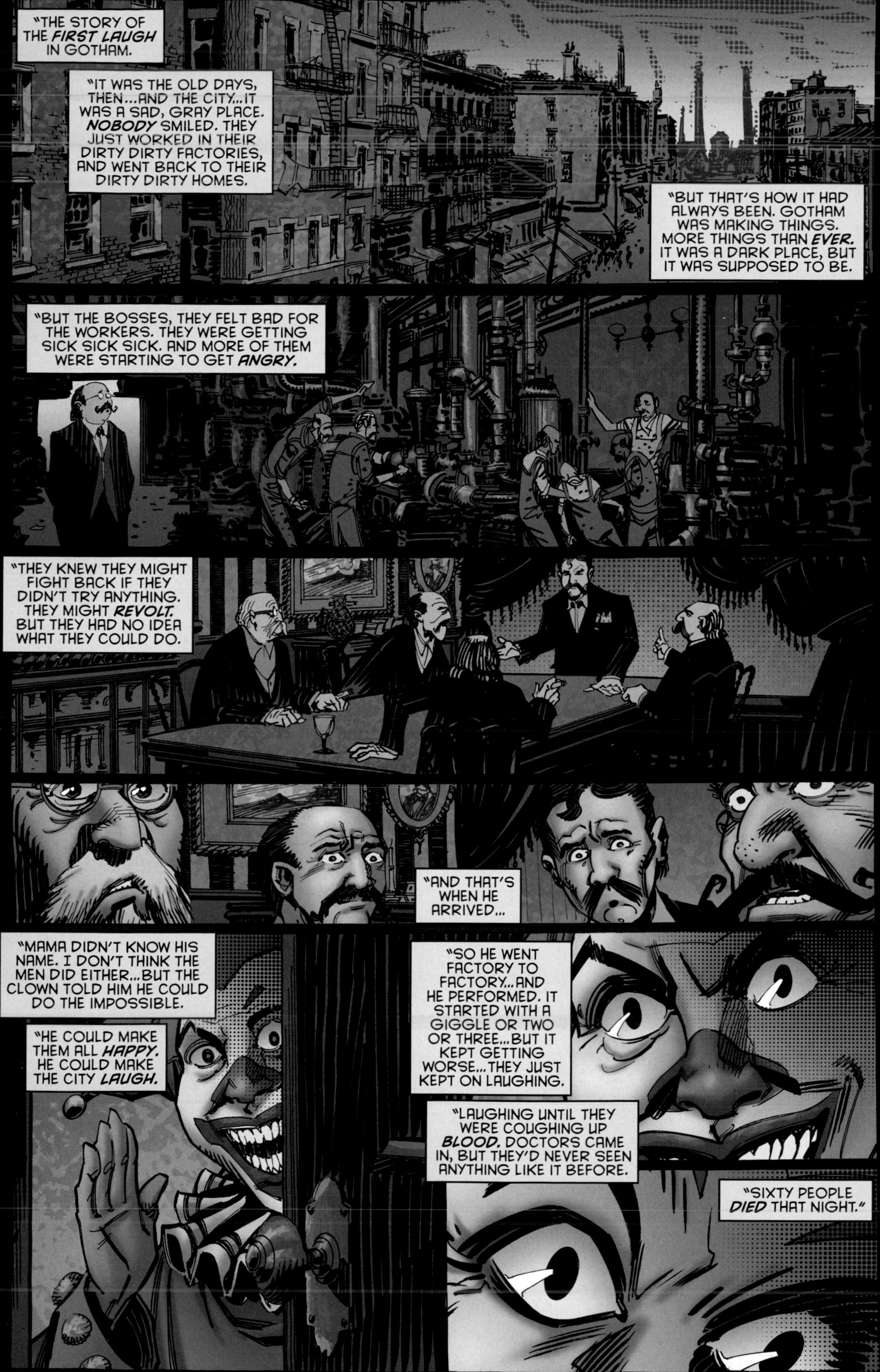
"THE STORY OF THE FIRST LAUGH IN GOTHAM.
"IT WAS THE OLD DAYS, THEN...AND THE CITY...IT WAS A SAD, GRAY PLACE. NOBODY SMILED. THEY JUST WORKED IN THEIR DIRTY DIRTY FACTORIES, AND WENT BACK TO THEIR DIRTY DIRTY HOMES.
"BUT THAT'S HOW IT HAD ALWAYS BEEN. GOTHAM WAS MAKING THINGS. MORE THINGS THAN EVER. IT WAS A DARK PLACE, BUT IT WAS SUPPOSED TO BE.
"BUT THE BOSSES, THEY FELT BAD FOR THE WORKERS. THEY WERE GETTING SICK SICK SICK. AND MORE OF THEM WERE STARTING TO GET ANGRY.
"THEY KNEW THEY MIGHT FIGHT BACK IF THEY DIDN'T TRY ANYTHING. THEY MIGHT REVOLT. BUT THEY HAD NO IDEA WHAT THEY COULD DO.
"AND THAT'S WHEN HE ARRIVED...
"MAMA DIDN'T KNOW HIS NAME. I DON'T THINK THE MEN DID EITHER...BUT THE CLOWN TOLD HIM HE COULD DO THE IMPOSSIBLE.
"HE COULD MAKE THEM ALL HAPPY. HE COULD MAKE THE CITY LAUGH.
"SO HE WENT FACTORY TO FACTORY...AND HE PERFORMED. IT STARTED WITH A GIGGLE OR TWO OR THREE...BUT IT KEPT GETTING WORSE...THEY JUST KEPT ON LAUGHING.
"LAUGHING UNTIL THEY WERE COUGHING UP BLOOD. DOCTORS CAME IN, BUT THEY'D NEVER SEEN ANYTHING LIKE IT BEFORE.
"SIXTY PEOPLE DIED THAT NIGHT."

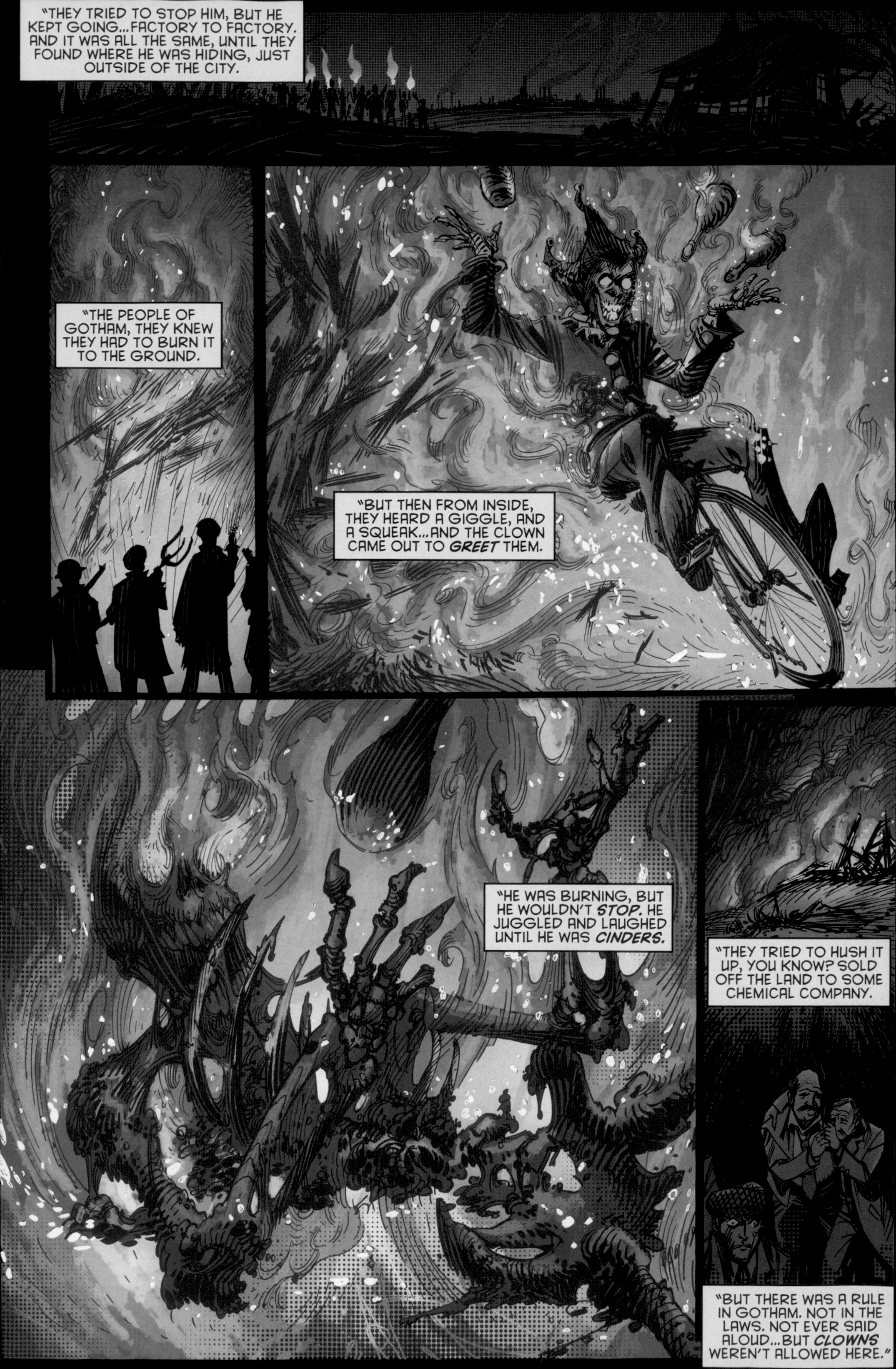
"THEY TRIED TO STOP HIM, BUT HE KEPT GOING...FACTORY TO FACTORY. AND IT WAS ALL THE SAME, UNTIL THEY FOUND WHERE HE WAS HIDING, JUST OUTSIDE OF THE CITY.
"THE PEOPLE OF GOTHAM, THEY KNEW THEY HAD TO BURN IT TO THE GROUND.
"BUT THEN FROM INSIDE, THEY HEARD A GIGGLE, AND A SQUEAK...AND THE CLOWN CAME OUT TO GREET THEM.
"HE WAS BURNING, BUT HE WOULDN'T STOP. HE JUGGLED AND LAUGHED UNTIL HE WAS CINDERS.
"THEY TRIED TO HUSH IT UP, YOU KNOW? SOLD OFF THE LAND TO SOME CHEMICAL COMPANY.
"BUT THERE WAS A RULE IN GOTHAM. NOT IN THE LAWS. NOT EVER SAID ALOUD...BUT CLOWNS WEREN'T ALLOWED HERE."

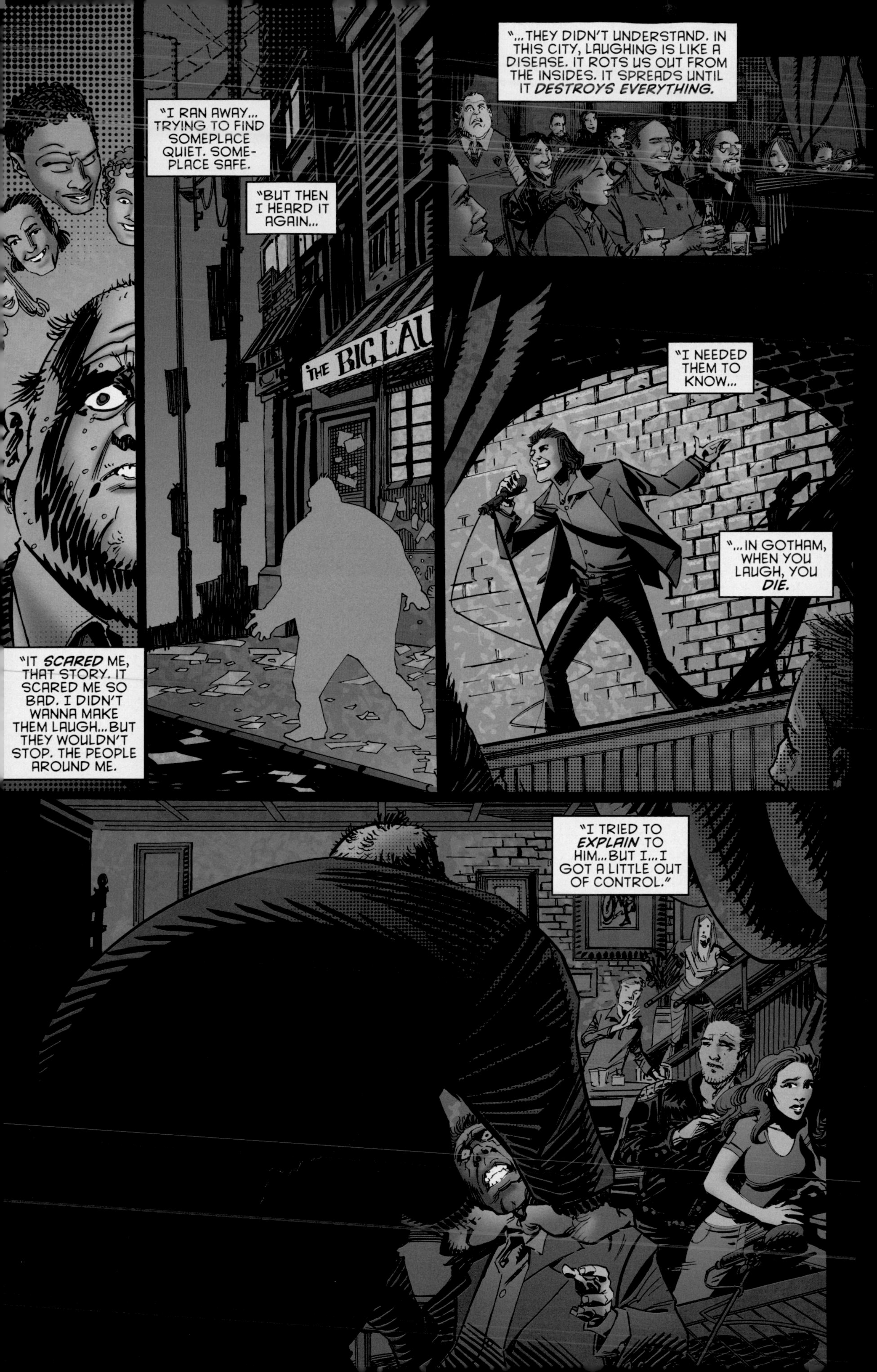
"IT SCARED ME, THAT STORY. IT SCARED ME SO BAD. I DIDN'T WANNA MAKE THEM LAUGH...BUT THEY WOULDN'T STOP. THE PEOPLE AROUND ME.
"I RAN AWAY... TRYING TO FIND SOMEPLACE QUIET. SOME-PLACE SAFE.
"BUT THEN I HEARD IT AGAIN...
THE BIG LAU
"...THEY DIDN'T UNDERSTAND. IN THIS CITY, LAUGHING IS LIKE A DISEASE. IT ROTS US OUT FROM THE INSIDES. IT SPREADS UNTIL IT DESTROYS EVERYTHING.
"I NEEDED THEM TO KNOW...
"...IN GOTHAM, WHEN YOU LAUGH, YOU DIE.
"I TRIED TO EXPLAIN TO HIM...BUT I...I GOT A LITTLE OUT OF CONTROL."

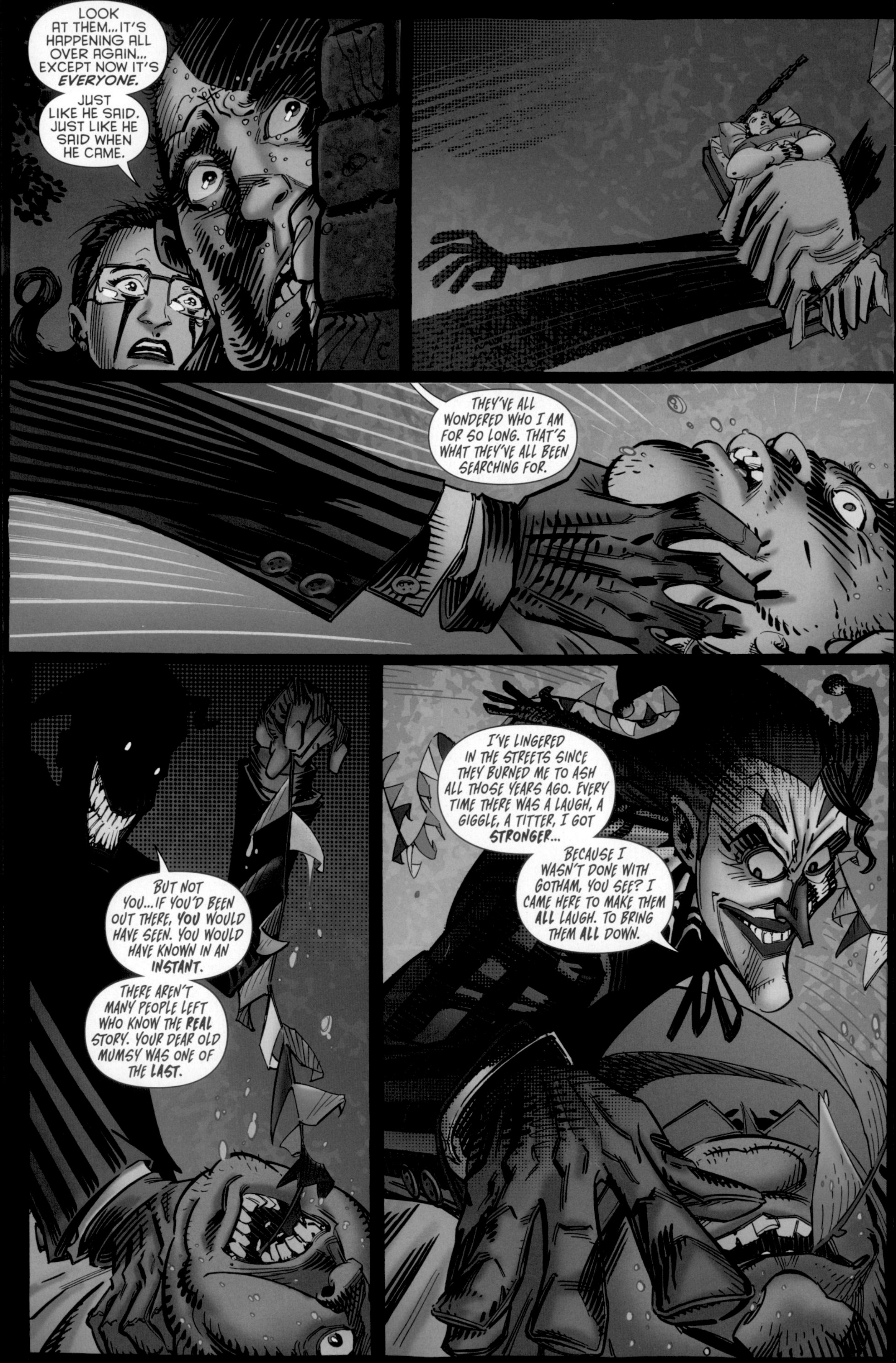
LOOK AT THEM...IT'S HAPPENING ALL OVER AGAIN... EXCEPT NOW IT'S EVERYONE.
JUST LIKE HE SAID. JUST LIKE HE SAID WHEN HE CAME.
THEY'VE ALL WONDERED WHO I AM FOR SO LONG. THAT'S WHAT THEY'VE ALL BEEN SEARCHING FOR.
BUT NOT YOU...IF YOU'D BEEN OUT THERE, YOU WOULD HAVE SEEN. YOU WOULD HAVE KNOWN IN AN INSTANT.
THERE AREN'T MANY PEOPLE LEFT WHO KNOW THE REAL STORY. YOUR DEAR OLD MUMSY WAS ONE OF THE LAST.
I'VE LINGERED IN THE STREETS SINCE THEY BURNED ME TO ASH ALL THOSE YEARS AGO. EVERY TIME THERE WAS A LAUGH, A GIGGLE, A TITTER, I GOT STRONGER...
BECAUSE I WASN'T DONE WITH GOTHAM, YOU SEE? I CAME HERE TO MAKE THEM ALL LAUGH. TO BRING THEM ALL DOWN.

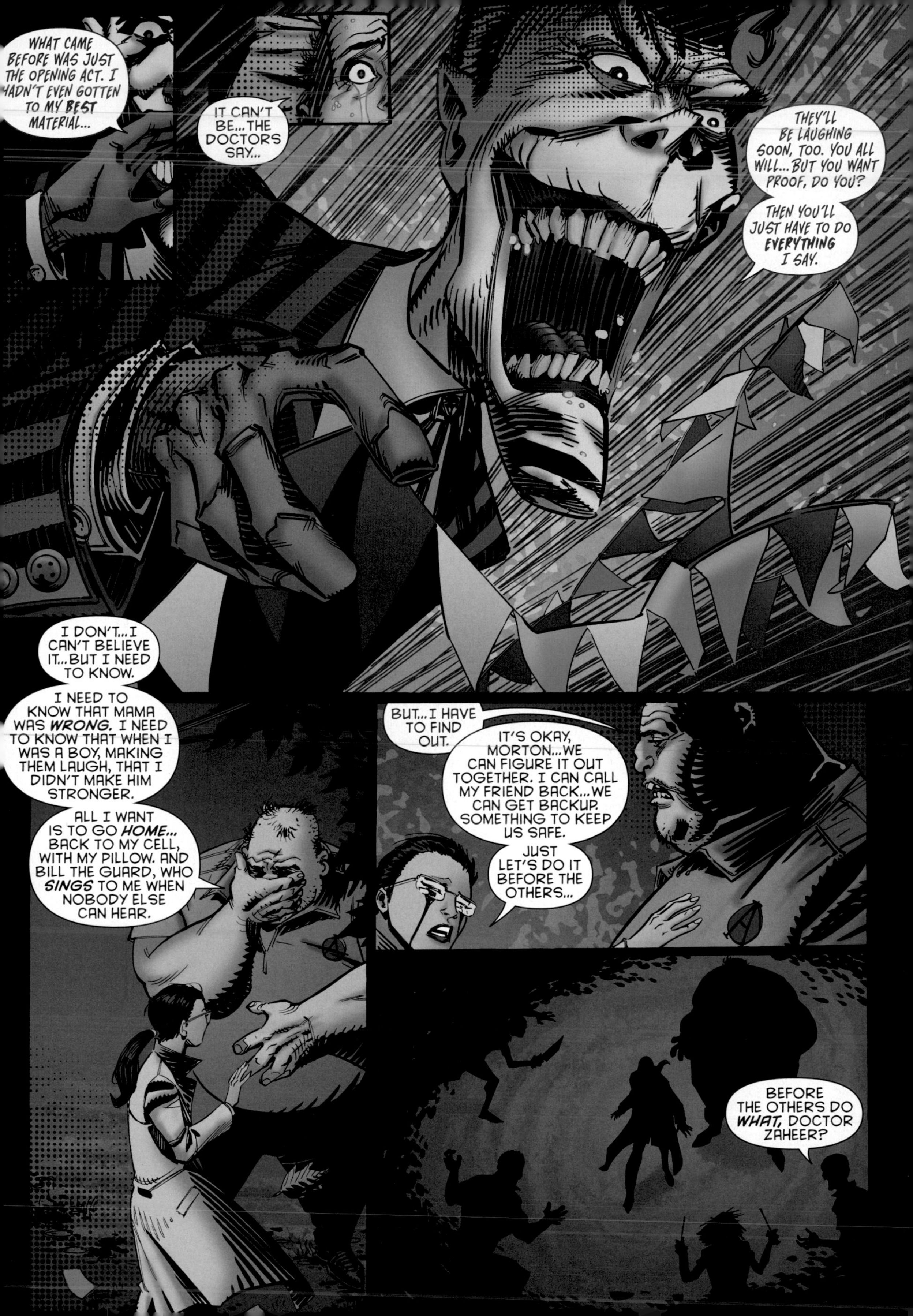
WHAT CAME BEFORE WAS JUST THE OPENING ACT. I HADN'T EVEN GOTTEN TO MY **BEST** MATERIAL...
IT CAN'T BE... THE DOCTORS SAY...
THEY'LL BE LAUGHING SOON, TOO. YOU ALL WILL... BUT YOU WANT PROOF, DO YOU?
THEN YOU'LL JUST HAVE TO DO **EVERYTHING** I SAY.
I DON'T... I CAN'T BELIEVE IT... BUT I NEED TO KNOW.
I NEED TO KNOW THAT MAMA WAS ***WRONG.*** I NEED TO KNOW THAT WHEN I WAS A BOY, MAKING THEM LAUGH, THAT I DIDN'T MAKE HIM STRONGER.
ALL I WANT IS TO GO ***HOME...*** BACK TO MY CELL, WITH MY PILLOW. AND BILL THE GUARD, WHO ***SINGS*** TO ME WHEN NOBODY ELSE CAN HEAR.
BUT... I HAVE TO FIND OUT.
IT'S OKAY, MORTON... WE CAN FIGURE IT OUT TOGETHER. I CAN CALL MY FRIEND BACK... WE CAN GET BACKUP. SOMETHING TO KEEP US SAFE.
JUST LET'S DO IT BEFORE THE OTHERS...
BEFORE THE OTHERS DO ***WHAT,*** DOCTOR ZAHEER?

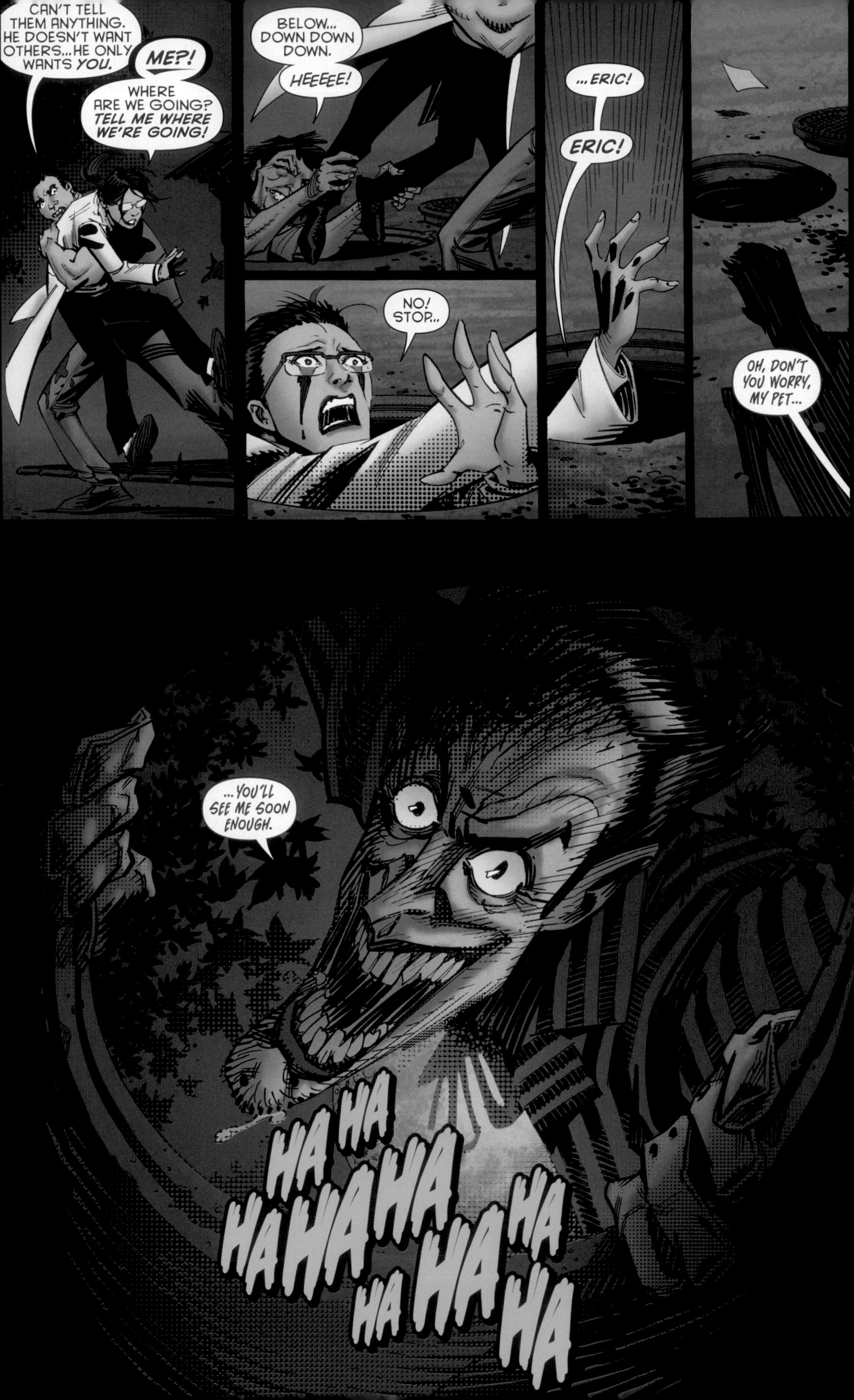
CAN'T TELL THEM ANYTHING. HE DOESN'T WANT OTHERS...HE ONLY WANTS YOU.
ME?!
WHERE ARE WE GOING? TELL ME WHERE WE'RE GOING!
BELOW... DOWN DOWN DOWN.
HEEEEE!
NO! STOP...
...ERIC!
ERIC!
OH, DON'T YOU WORRY, MY PET...
...YOU'LL SEE ME SOON ENOUGH.
HA HA HA HA HA HA HA HA HA HA HA HA

Cover by **MARCUS TO** & **GABE ELTAEB**

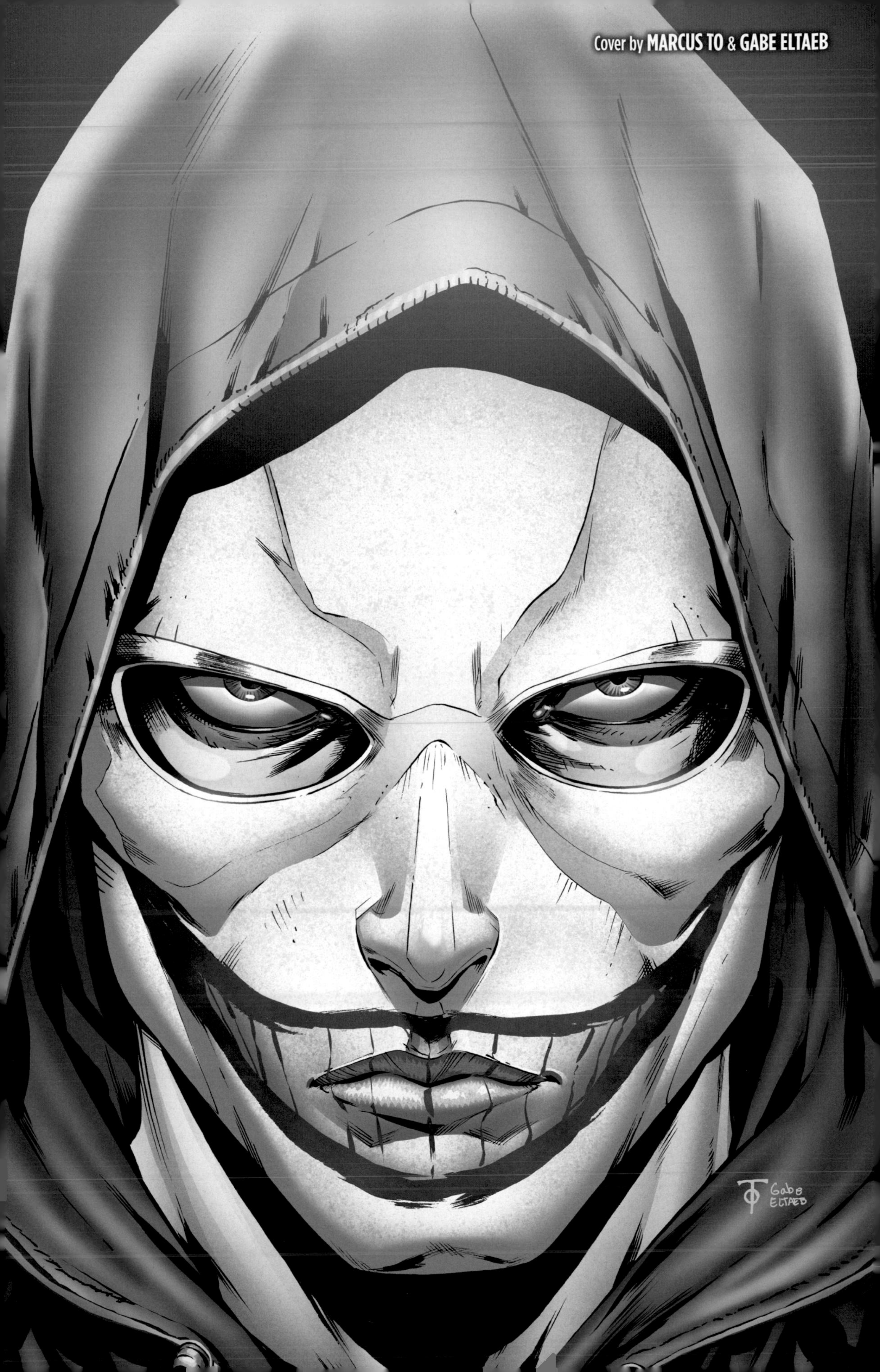
Gabe
ELTAEB

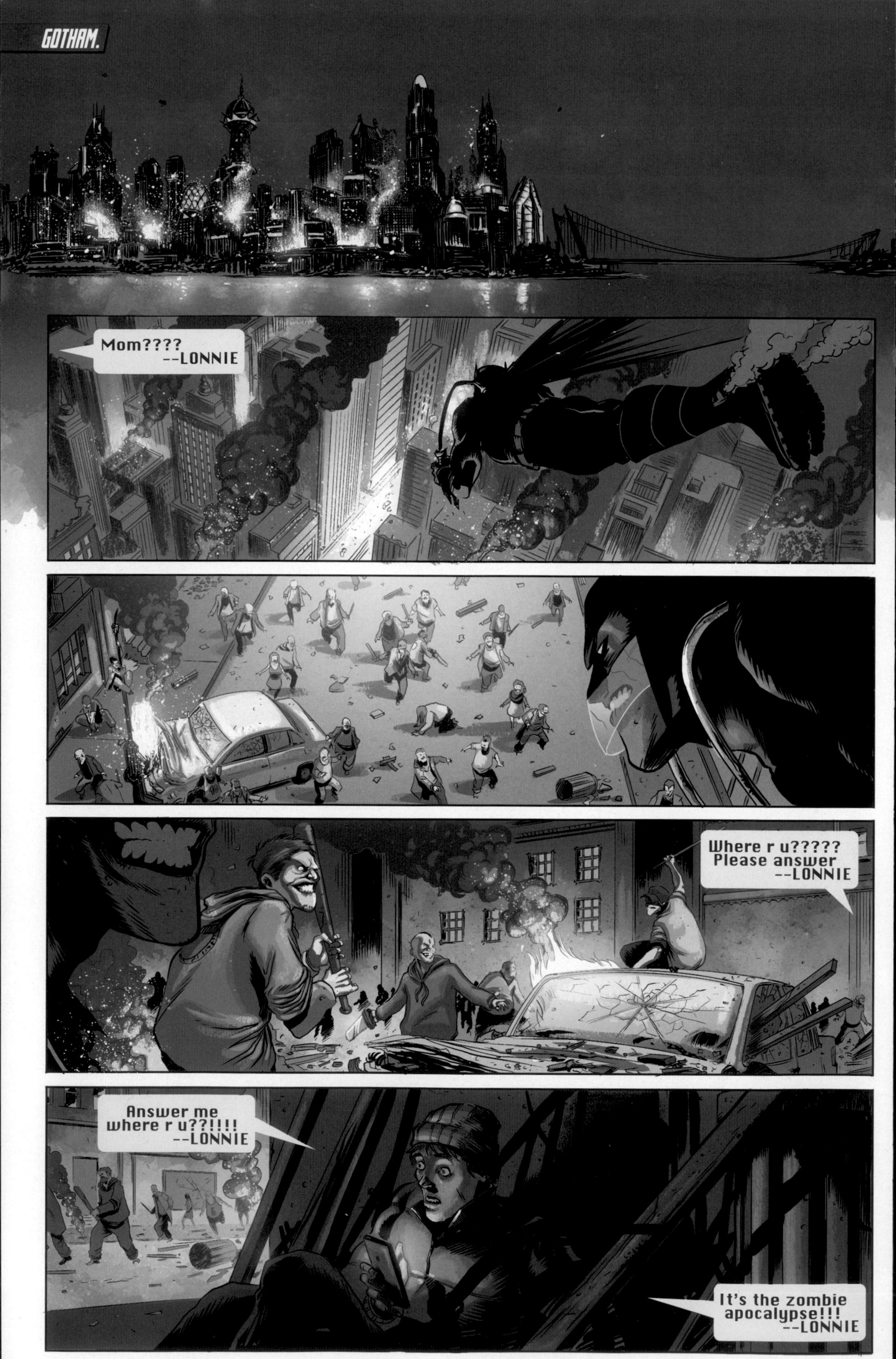
GOTHAM.
Mom???? --LONNIE
Where r u????? Please answer --LONNIE
Answer me where r u??!!!! --LONNIE
It's the zombie apocalypse!!! --LONNIE

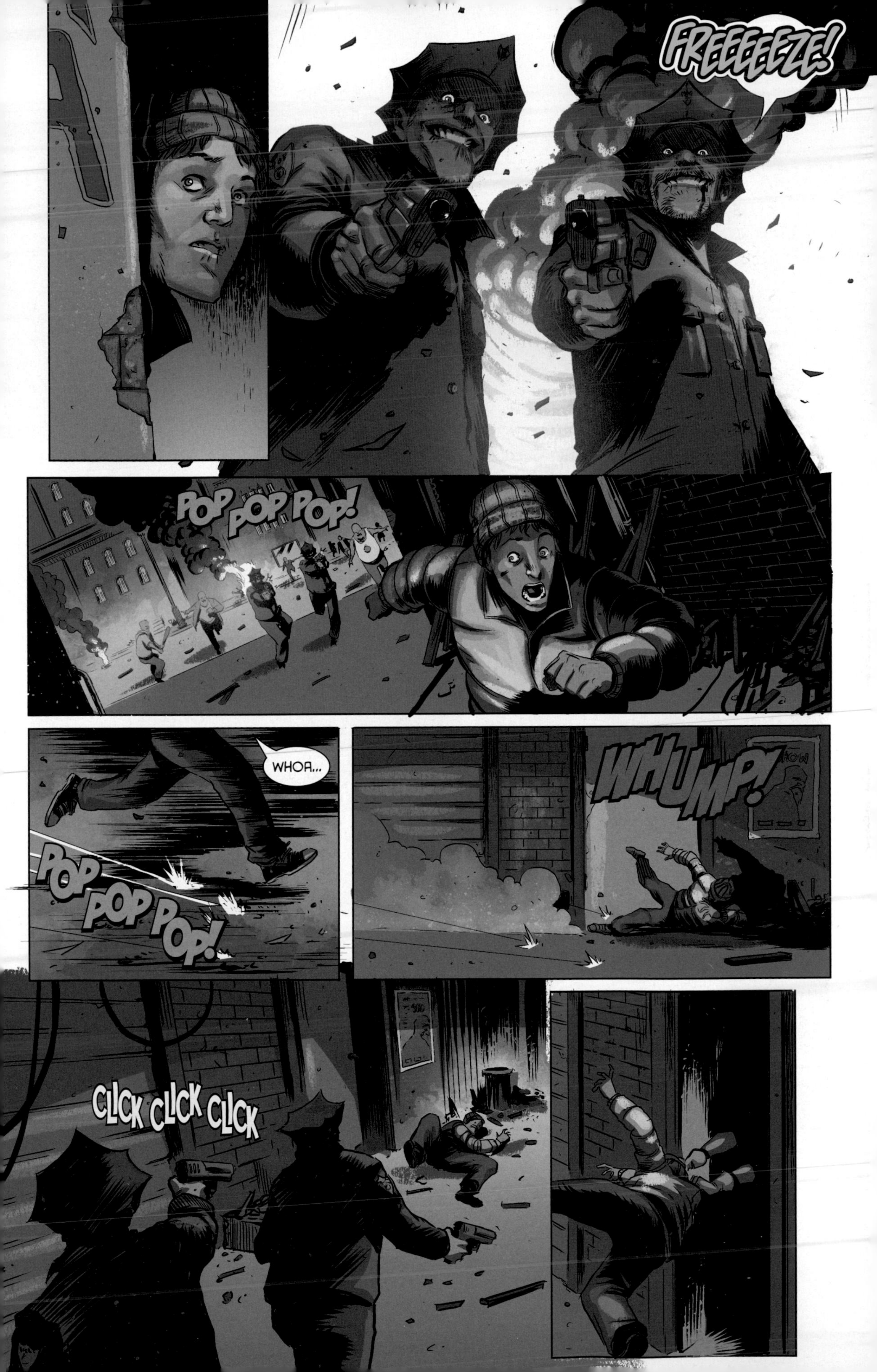
FREEEEEEZE!
POP POP POP!
WHOA...
POP POP POP!
WHUMP!
CLICK CLICK CLICK

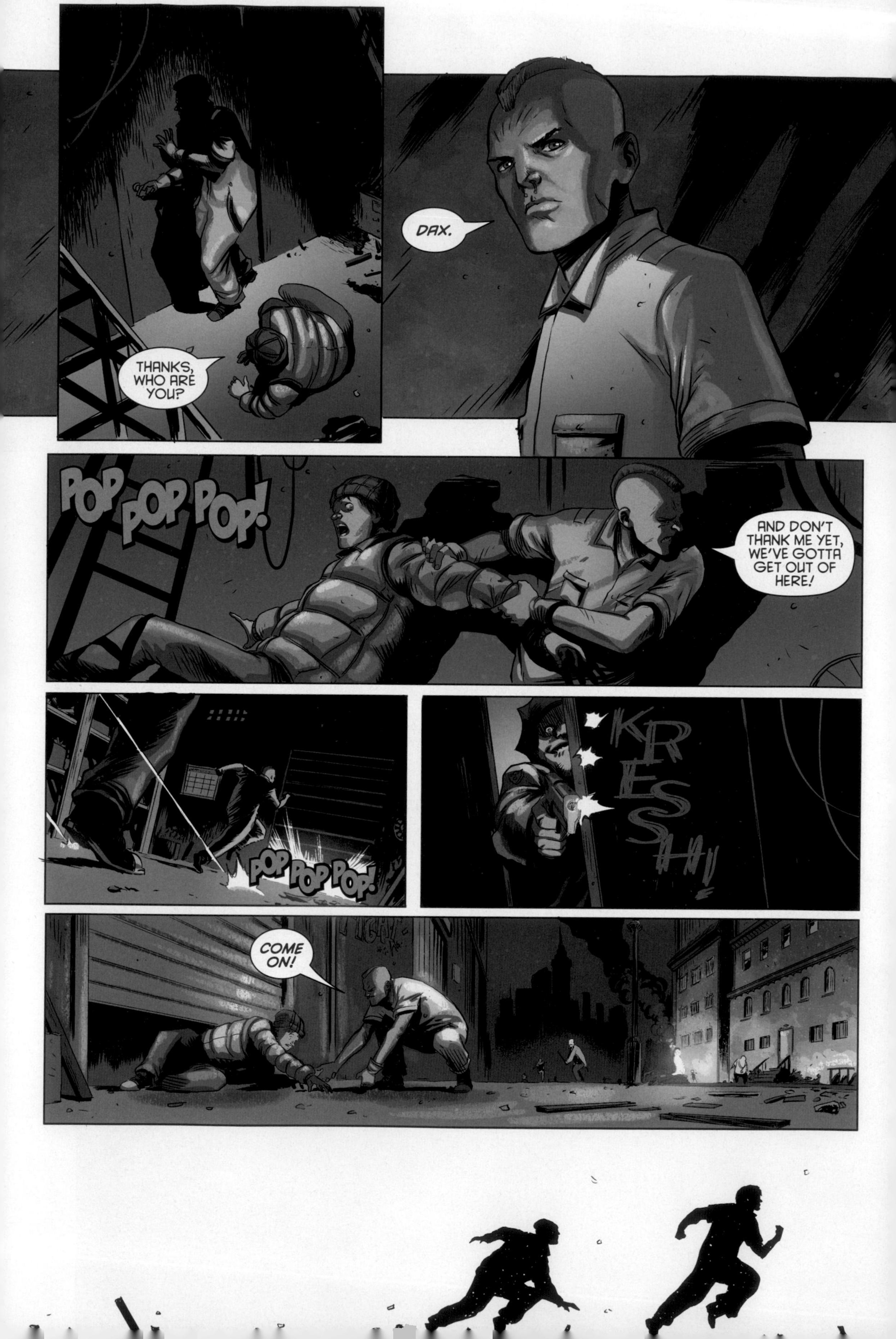
THANKS, WHO ARE YOU?
DAX.
POP POP POP!
AND DON'T THANK ME YET, WE'VE GOTTA GET OUT OF HERE!
POP POP POP!
KRESSH!
COME ON!

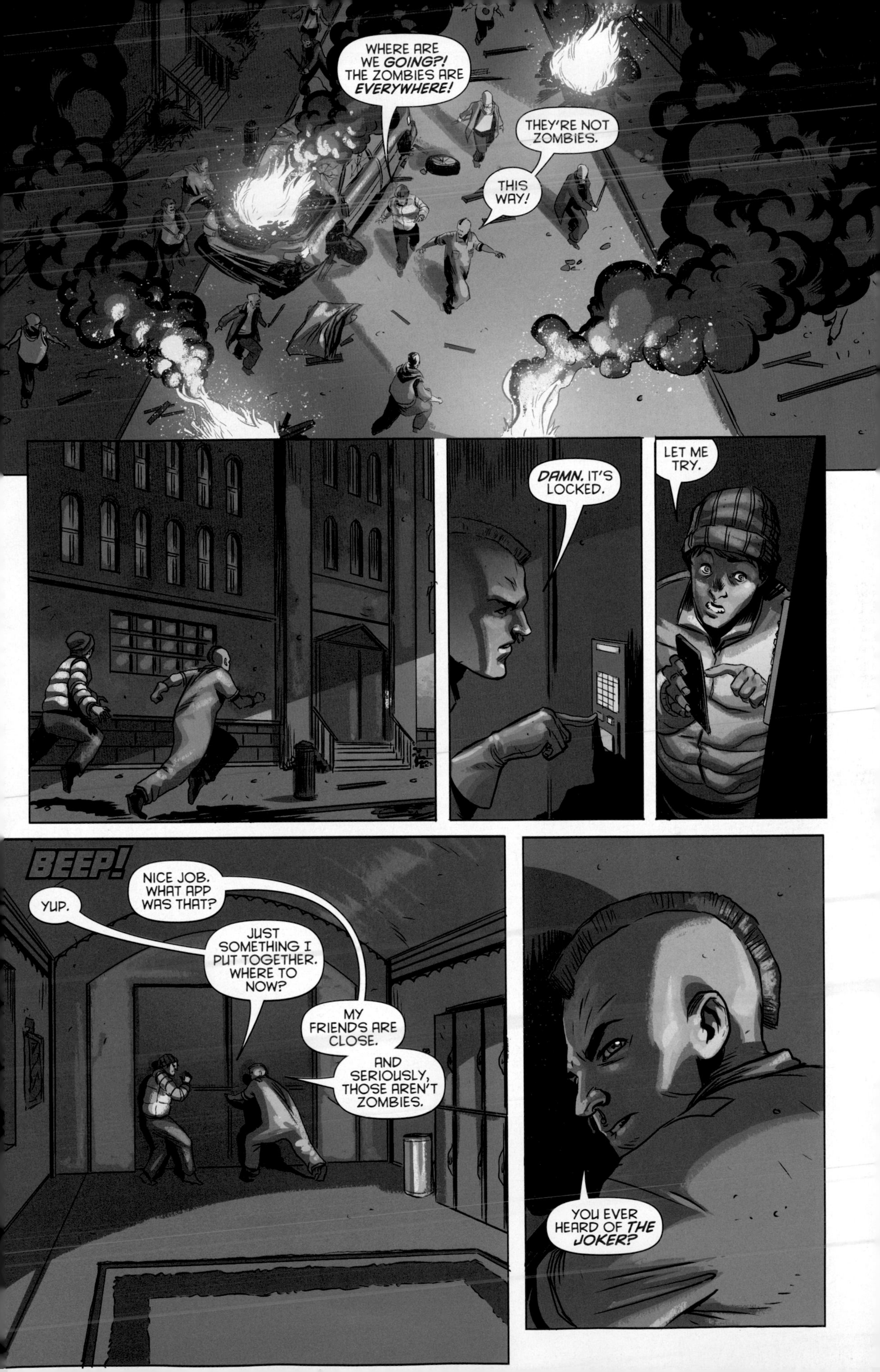
WHERE ARE WE GOING?! THE ZOMBIES ARE EVERYWHERE!
THEY'RE NOT ZOMBIES.
THIS WAY!
DAMN. IT'S LOCKED.
LET ME TRY.
BEEP!
NICE JOB. WHAT APP WAS THAT?
YUP.
JUST SOMETHING I PUT TOGETHER. WHERE TO NOW?
MY FRIENDS ARE CLOSE.
AND SERIOUSLY, THOSE AREN'T ZOMBIES.
YOU EVER HEARD OF THE JOKER?

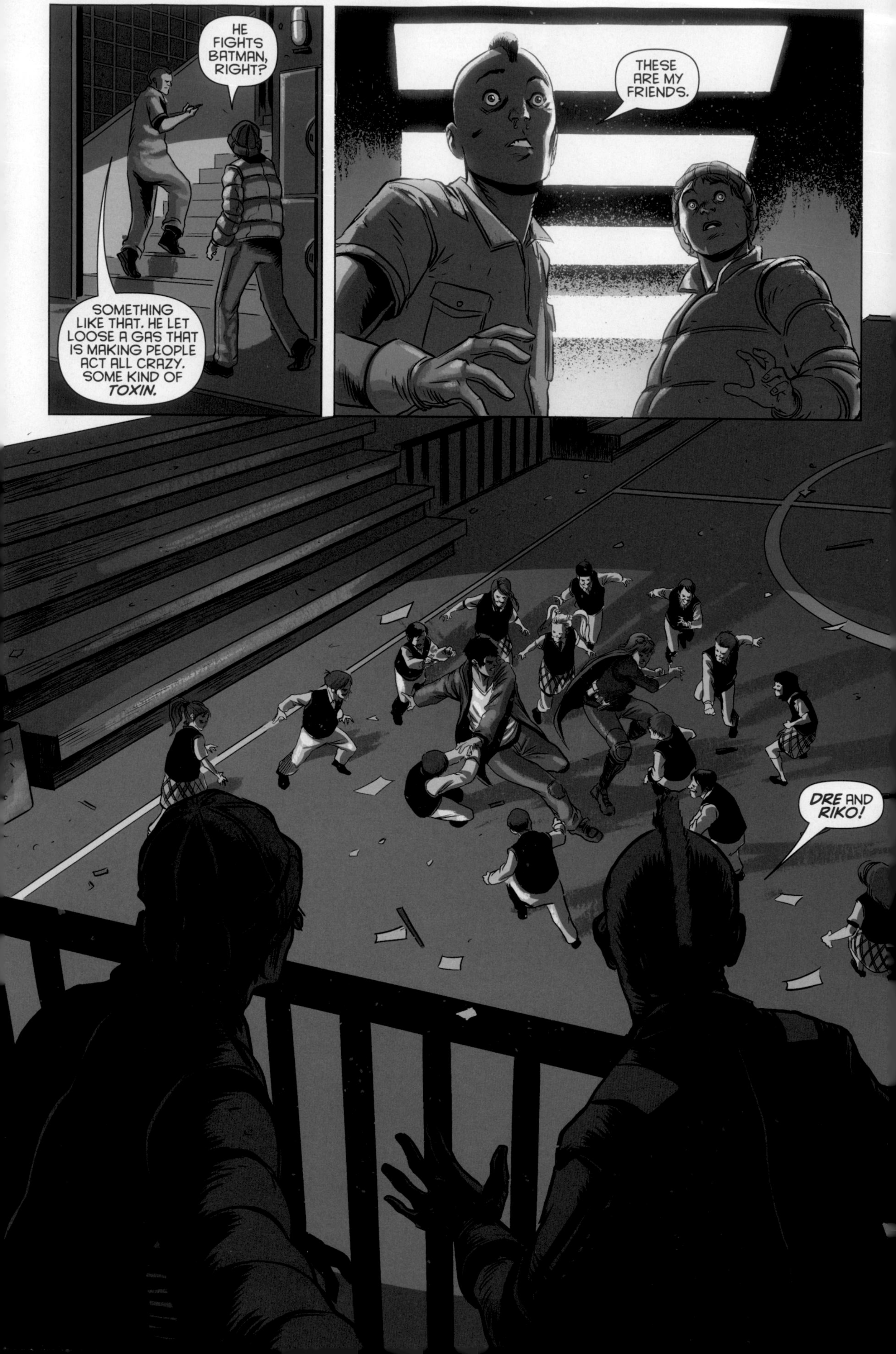
HE FIGHTS BATMAN, RIGHT?
SOMETHING LIKE THAT. HE LET LOOSE A GAS THAT IS MAKING PEOPLE ACT ALL CRAZY. SOME KIND OF *TOXIN.*
THESE ARE MY FRIENDS.
DRE AND *RIKO!*

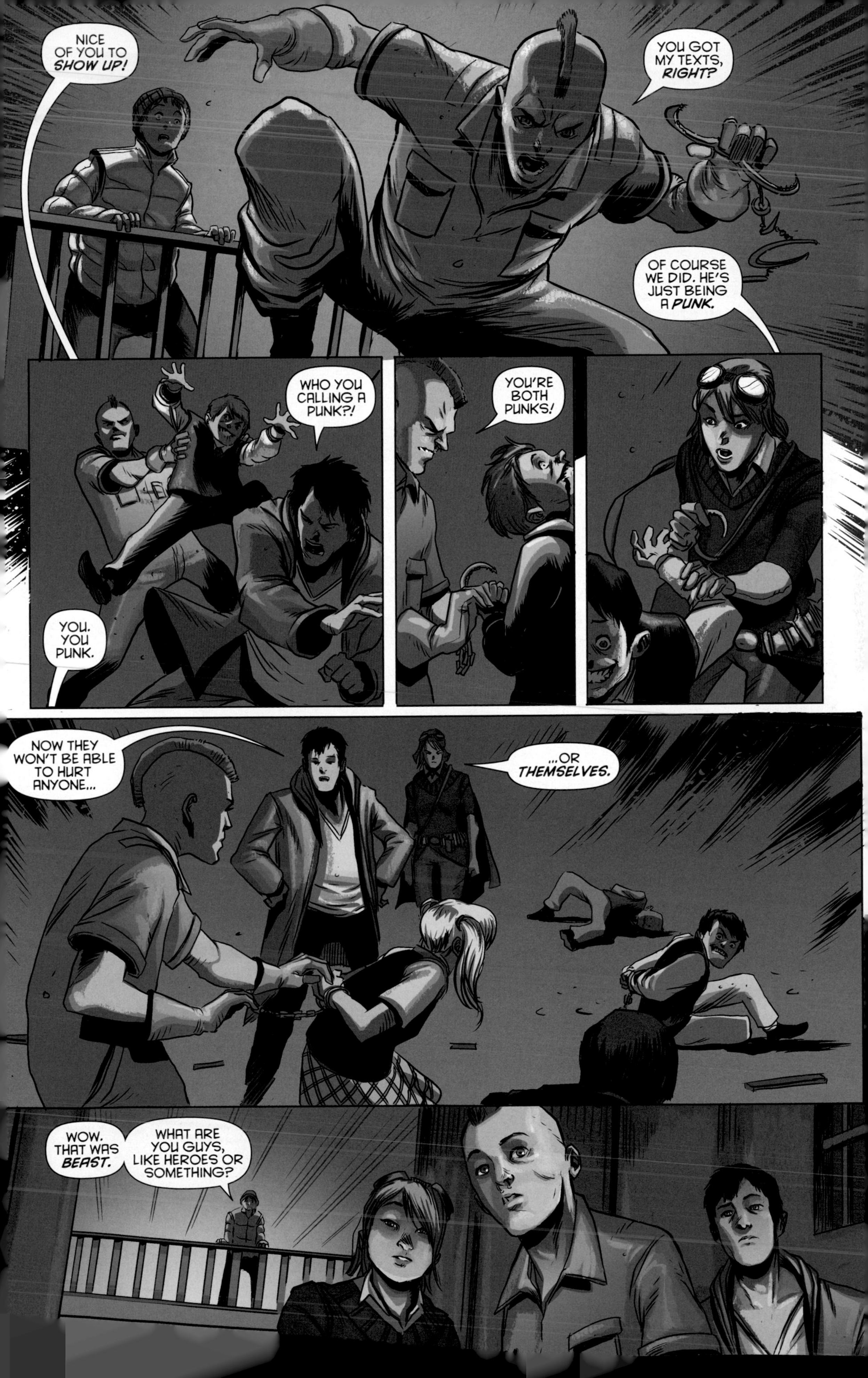
NICE OF YOU TO SHOW UP!
YOU GOT MY TEXTS, RIGHT?
OF COURSE WE DID. HE'S JUST BEING A PUNK.
WHO YOU CALLING A PUNK?!
YOU. YOU PUNK.
YOU'RE BOTH PUNKS!
NOW THEY WON'T BE ABLE TO HURT ANYONE...
...OR THEMSELVES.
WOW. THAT WAS BEAST.
WHAT ARE YOU GUYS, LIKE HEROES OR SOMETHING?

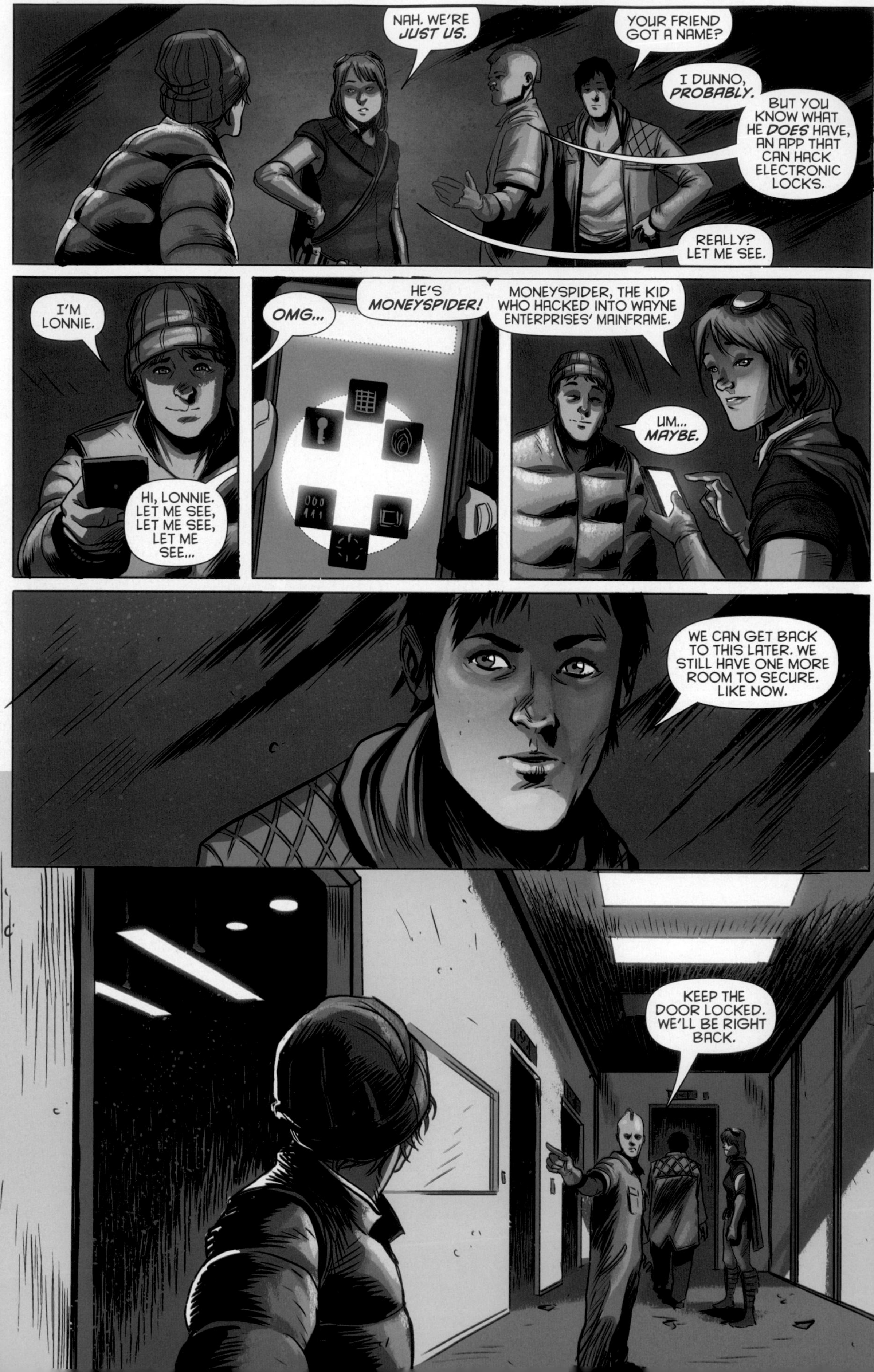
NAH. WE'RE JUST US.
YOUR FRIEND GOT A NAME?
I DUNNO, PROBABLY.
BUT YOU KNOW WHAT HE DOES HAVE, AN APP THAT CAN HACK ELECTRONIC LOCKS.
REALLY? LET ME SEE.
I'M LONNIE.
HI, LONNIE. LET ME SEE, LET ME SEE, LET ME SEE...
OMG...
HE'S MONEYSPIDER!
MONEYSPIDER, THE KID WHO HACKED INTO WAYNE ENTERPRISES' MAINFRAME.
UM... MAYBE.
WE CAN GET BACK TO THIS LATER. WE STILL HAVE ONE MORE ROOM TO SECURE. LIKE NOW.
KEEP THE DOOR LOCKED. WE'LL BE RIGHT BACK.

Mom????
--LONNIE

elivered

Where r u?????
Please answer
--LONNIE

elivered

Answ
where r u
--L

elivered

It's the zombie
apocalypse!!!
--LONNIE

elivered

OKAY.
YOUR PHONE IS
AT WORK.

NOW ALL
I GOTTA DO
IS TAP INTO THE
CLUB'S SECURITY
CAMERAS
AND--

--AND
SEE IF YOU'RE
THERE TOO.

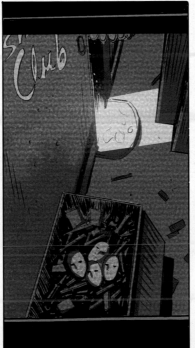

MOM!

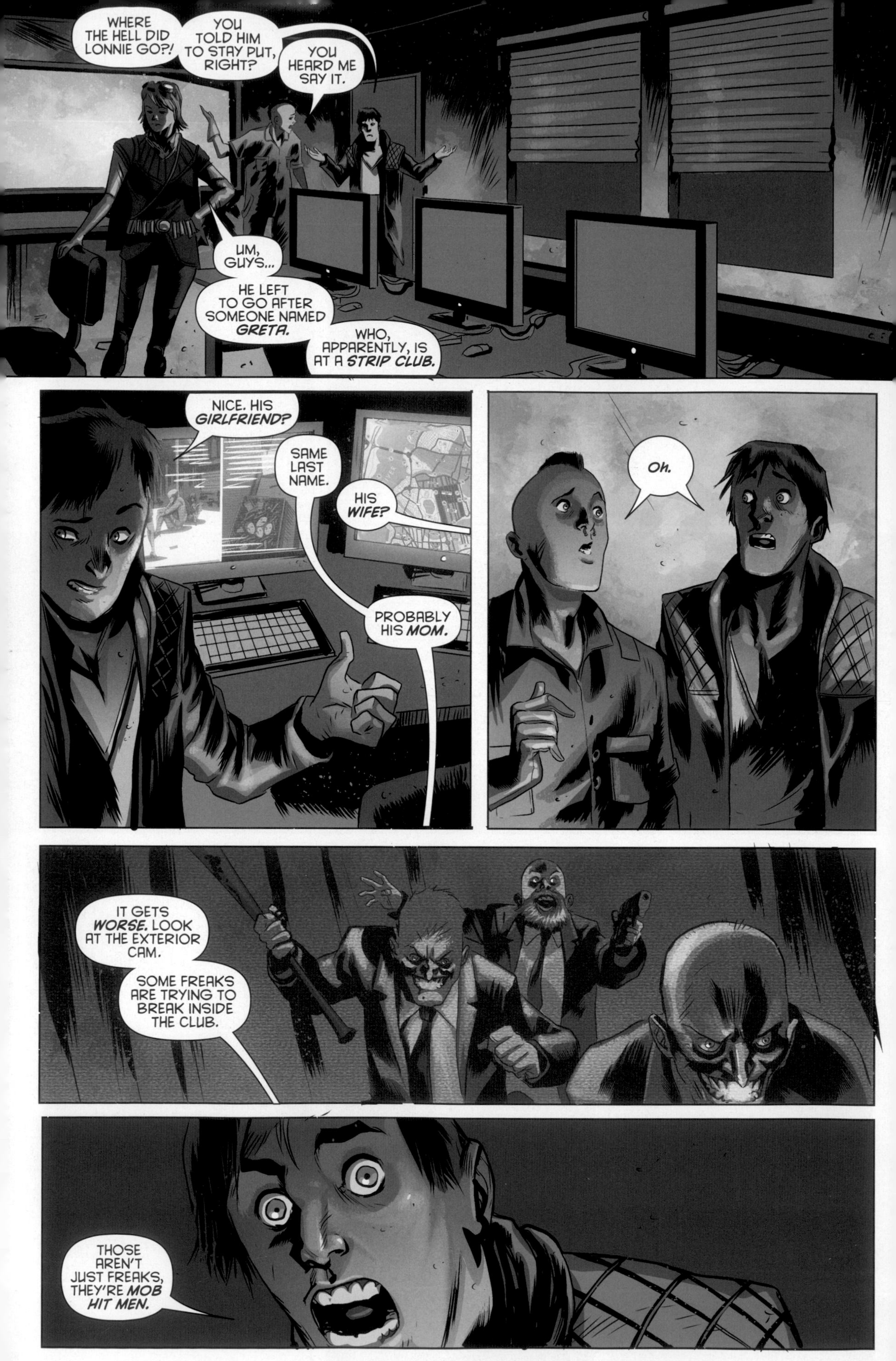
WHERE THE HELL DID LONNIE GO?!
YOU TOLD HIM TO STAY PUT, RIGHT?
YOU HEARD ME SAY IT.
UM, GUYS...
HE LEFT TO GO AFTER SOMEONE NAMED GRETA.
WHO, APPARENTLY, IS AT A STRIP CLUB.
NICE. HIS GIRLFRIEND?
SAME LAST NAME.
HIS WIFE?
PROBABLY HIS MOM.
Oh.
IT GETS WORSE. LOOK AT THE EXTERIOR CAM.
SOME FREAKS ARE TRYING TO BREAK INSIDE THE CLUB.
THOSE AREN'T JUST FREAKS, THEY'RE MOB HIT MEN.

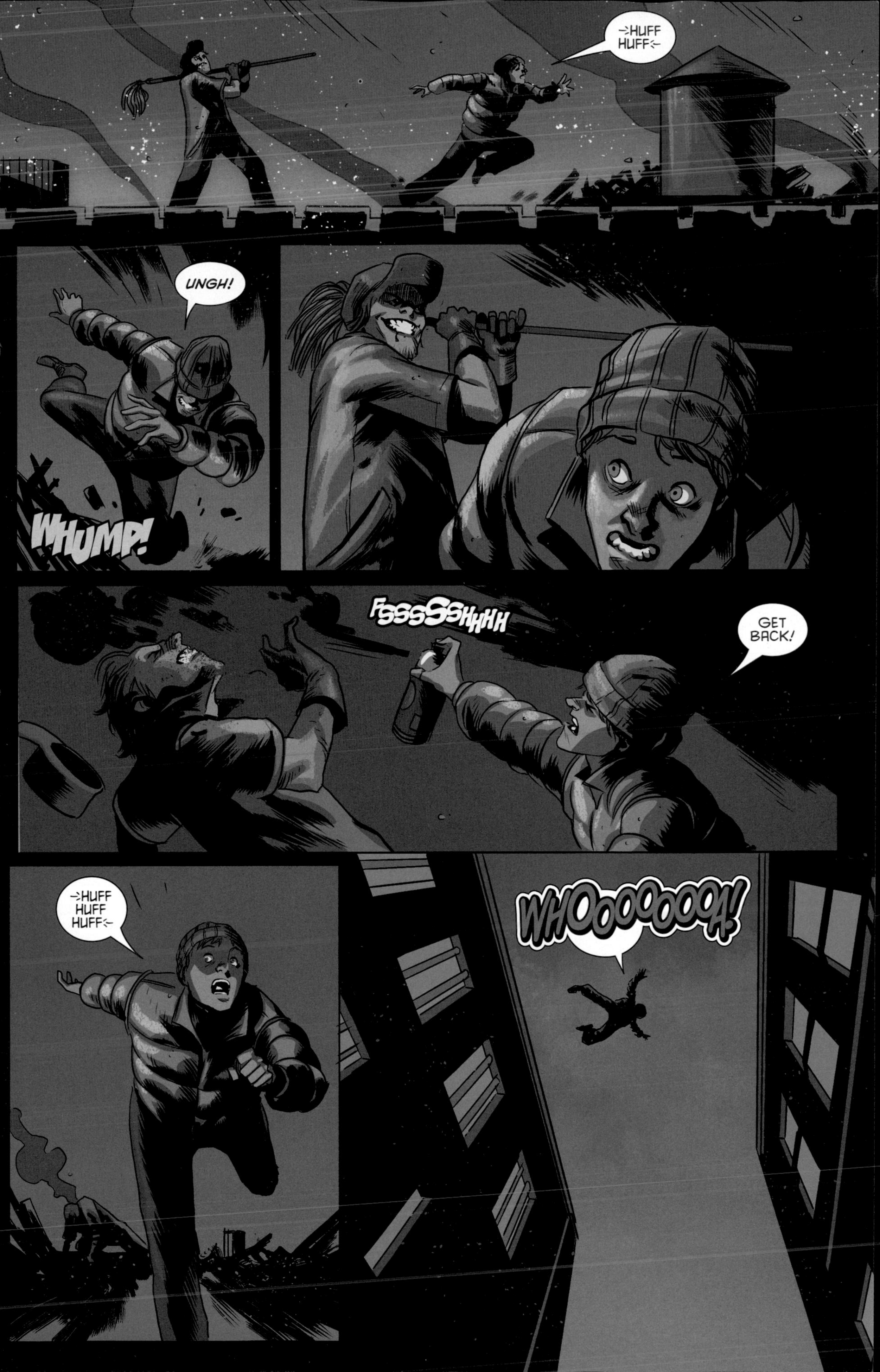

HUFF HUFF
UNGH!
WHUMP!
FSSSSSHHHH
GET BACK!
HUFF HUFF HUFF
WHOOOOOOOA!

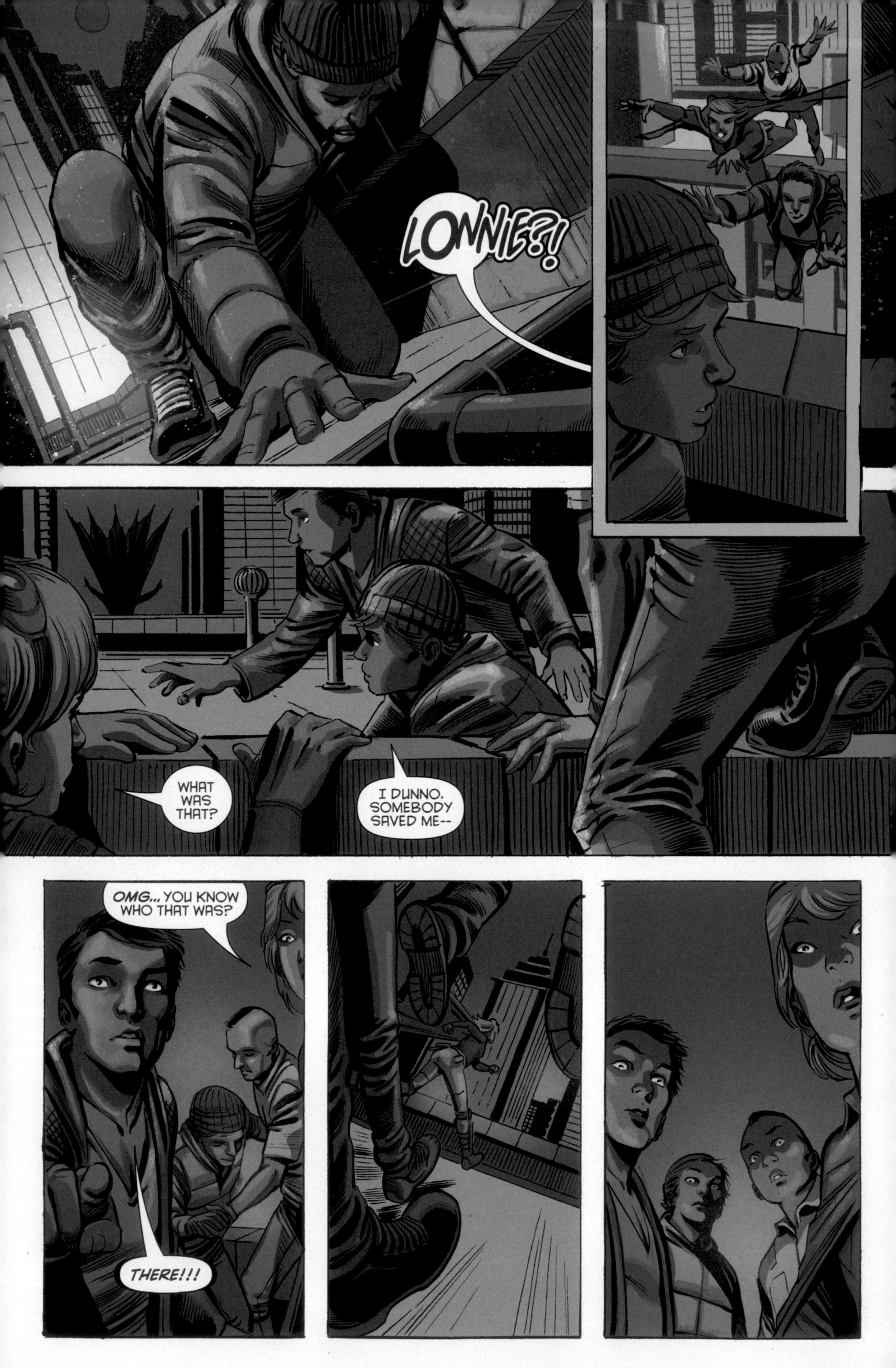
LONNIE?!
WHAT WAS THAT?
I DUNNO. SOMEBODY SAVED ME--
OMG... YOU KNOW WHO THAT WAS?
THERE!!!

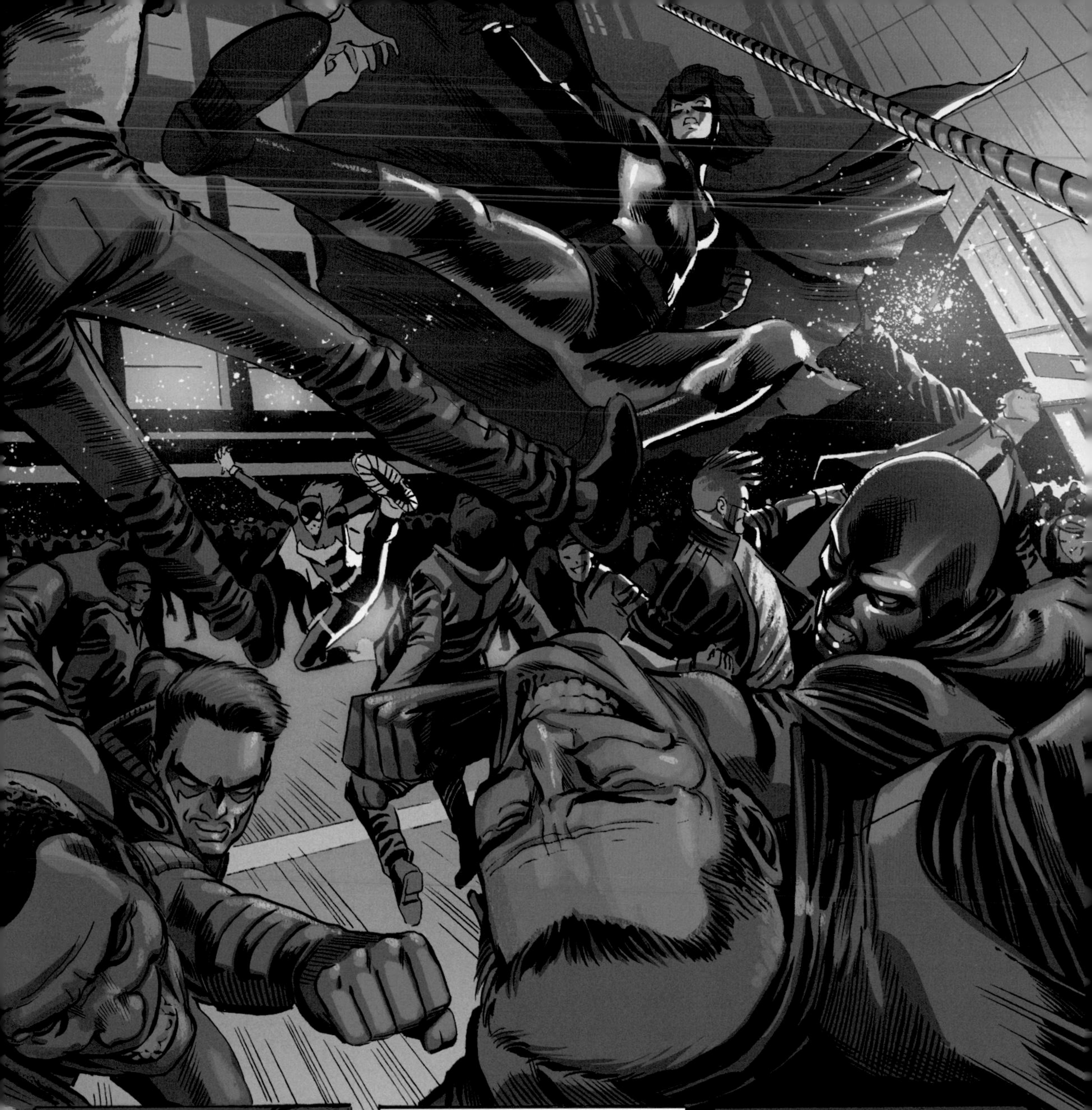

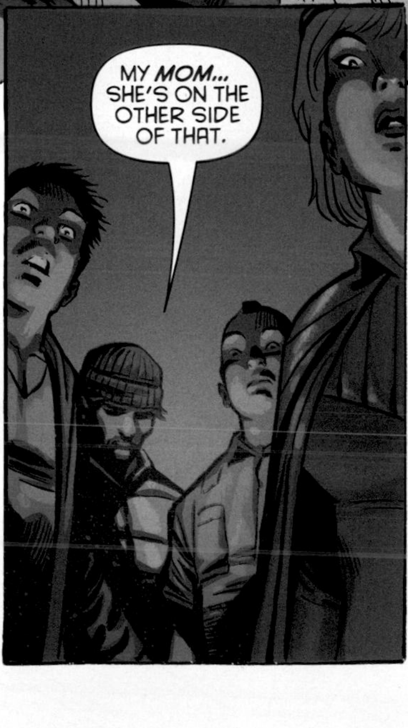
MY **MOM**... SHE'S ON THE OTHER SIDE OF THAT.

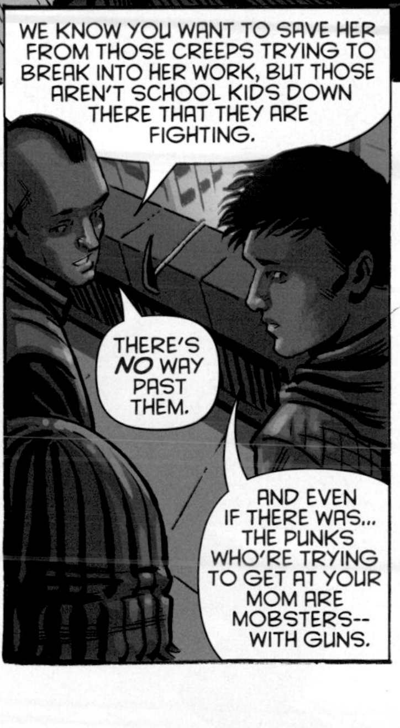
WE KNOW YOU WANT TO SAVE HER FROM THOSE CREEPS TRYING TO BREAK INTO HER WORK, BUT THOSE AREN'T SCHOOL KIDS DOWN THERE THAT THEY ARE FIGHTING.
THERE'S **NO** WAY PAST THEM.
AND EVEN IF THERE WAS... THE PUNKS WHO'RE TRYING TO GET AT YOUR MOM ARE MOBSTERS-- WITH GUNS.

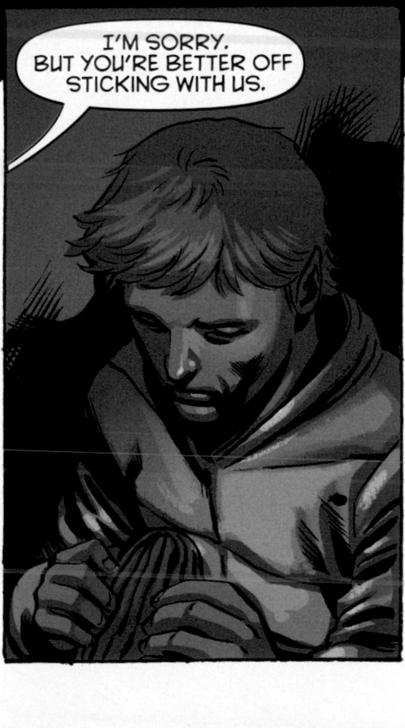
I'M SORRY. BUT YOU'RE BETTER OFF STICKING WITH US.

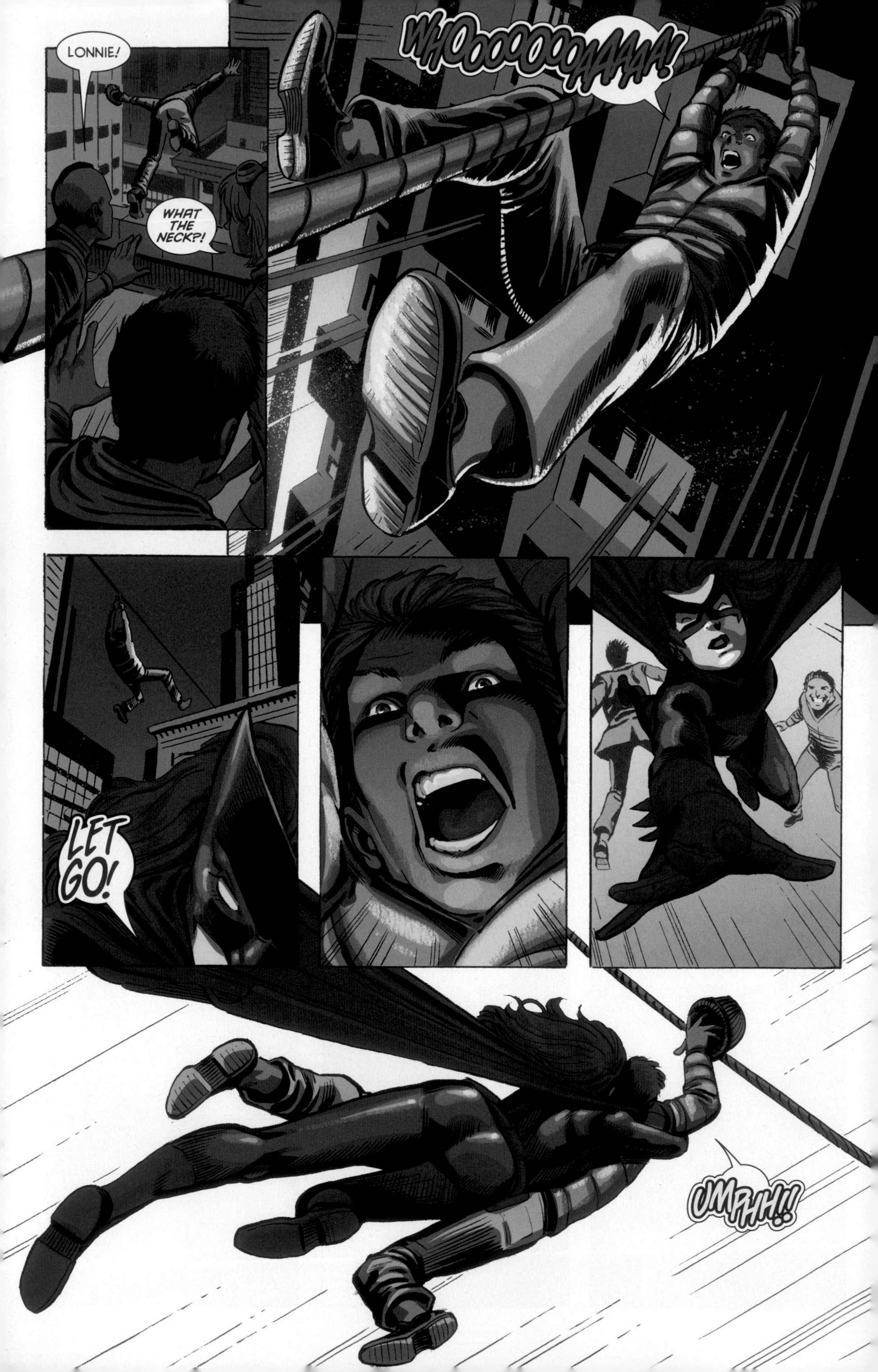
LONNIE!
WHAT THE NECK?!
WHOOOOOOOAAAAA!
LET GO!
UMPHH!!

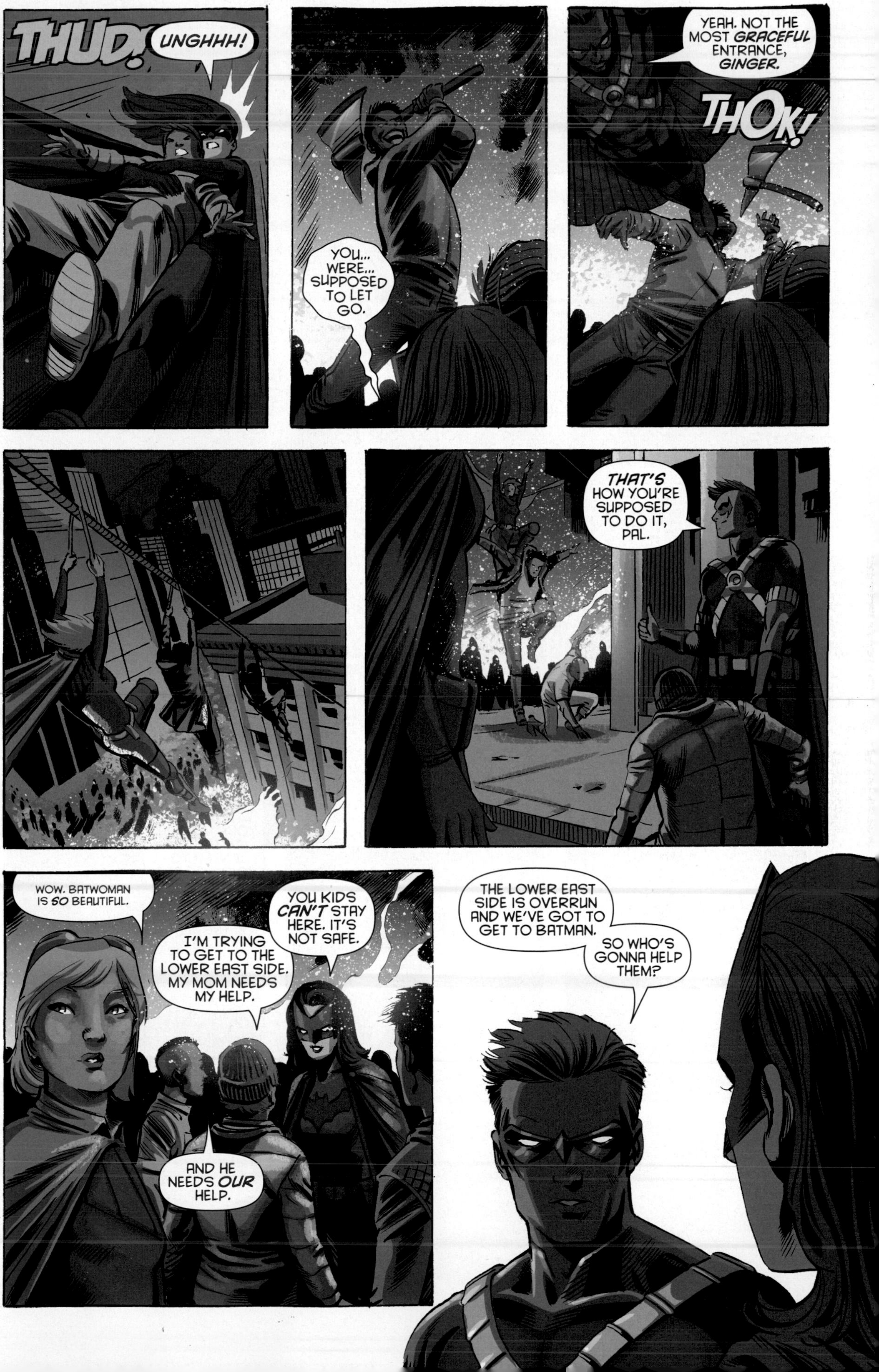
THUD!
UNGHHH!
YOU... WERE... SUPPOSED TO LET GO.
YEAH. NOT THE MOST GRACEFUL ENTRANCE, GINGER.
THOK!
THAT'S HOW YOU'RE SUPPOSED TO DO IT, PAL.
WOW. BATWOMAN IS SO BEAUTIFUL.
I'M TRYING TO GET TO THE LOWER EAST SIDE. MY MOM NEEDS MY HELP.
YOU KIDS CAN'T STAY HERE. IT'S NOT SAFE.
AND HE NEEDS OUR HELP.
THE LOWER EAST SIDE IS OVERRUN AND WE'VE GOT TO GET TO BATMAN.
SO WHO'S GONNA HELP THEM?

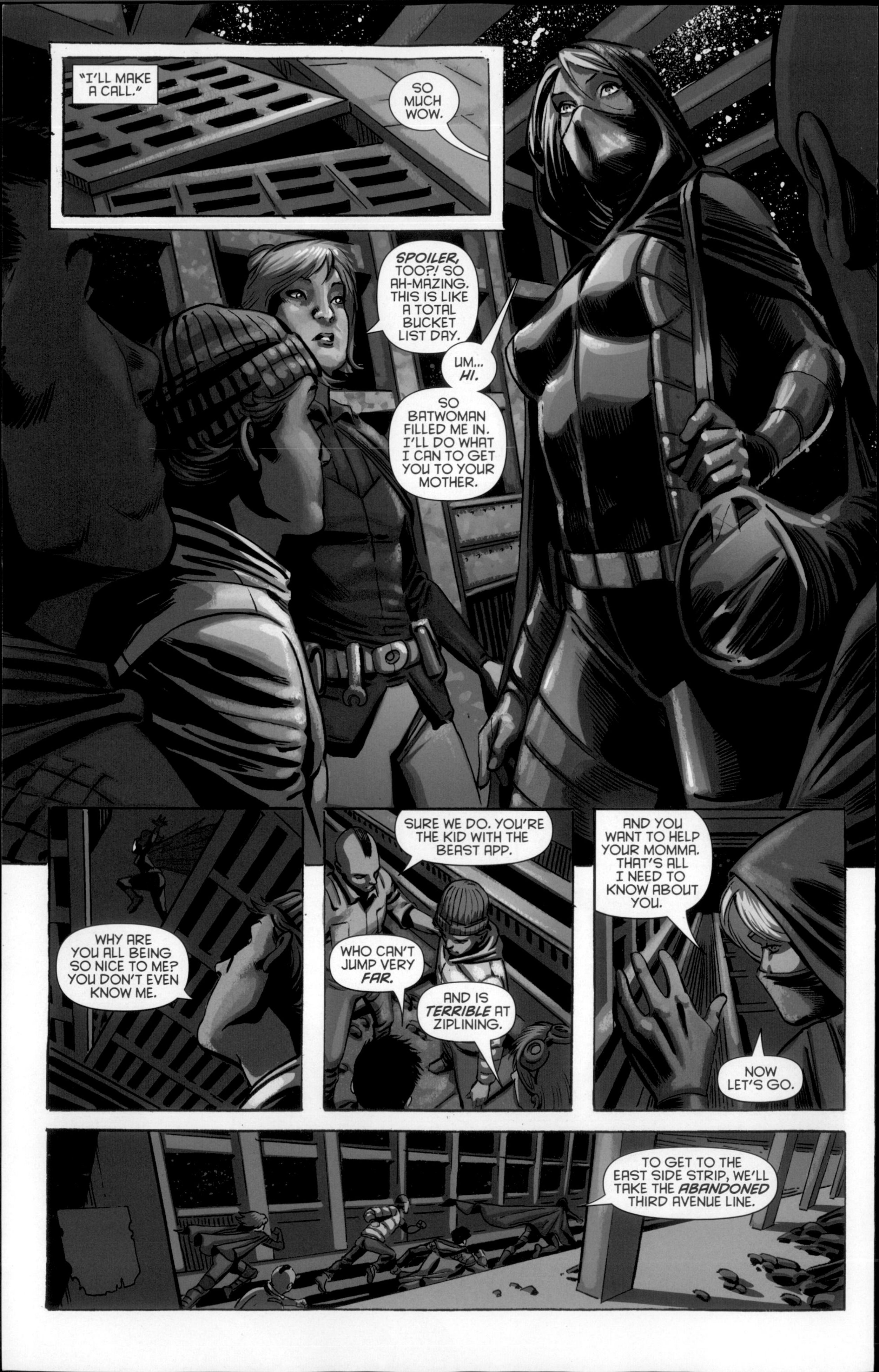
"I'LL MAKE A CALL."
SO MUCH WOW.
SPOILER, TOO?! SO AH-MAZING. THIS IS LIKE A TOTAL BUCKET LIST DAY.
UM... *HI.*
SO BATWOMAN FILLED ME IN. I'LL DO WHAT I CAN TO GET YOU TO YOUR MOTHER.
WHY ARE YOU ALL BEING SO NICE TO ME? YOU DON'T EVEN KNOW ME.
SURE WE DO. YOU'RE THE KID WITH THE BEAST APP.
WHO CAN'T JUMP VERY *FAR.*
AND IS *TERRIBLE* AT ZIPLINING.
AND YOU WANT TO HELP YOUR MOMMA. THAT'S ALL I NEED TO KNOW ABOUT YOU.
NOW LET'S GO.
TO GET TO THE EAST SIDE STRIP, WE'LL TAKE THE *ABANDONED* THIRD AVENUE LINE.

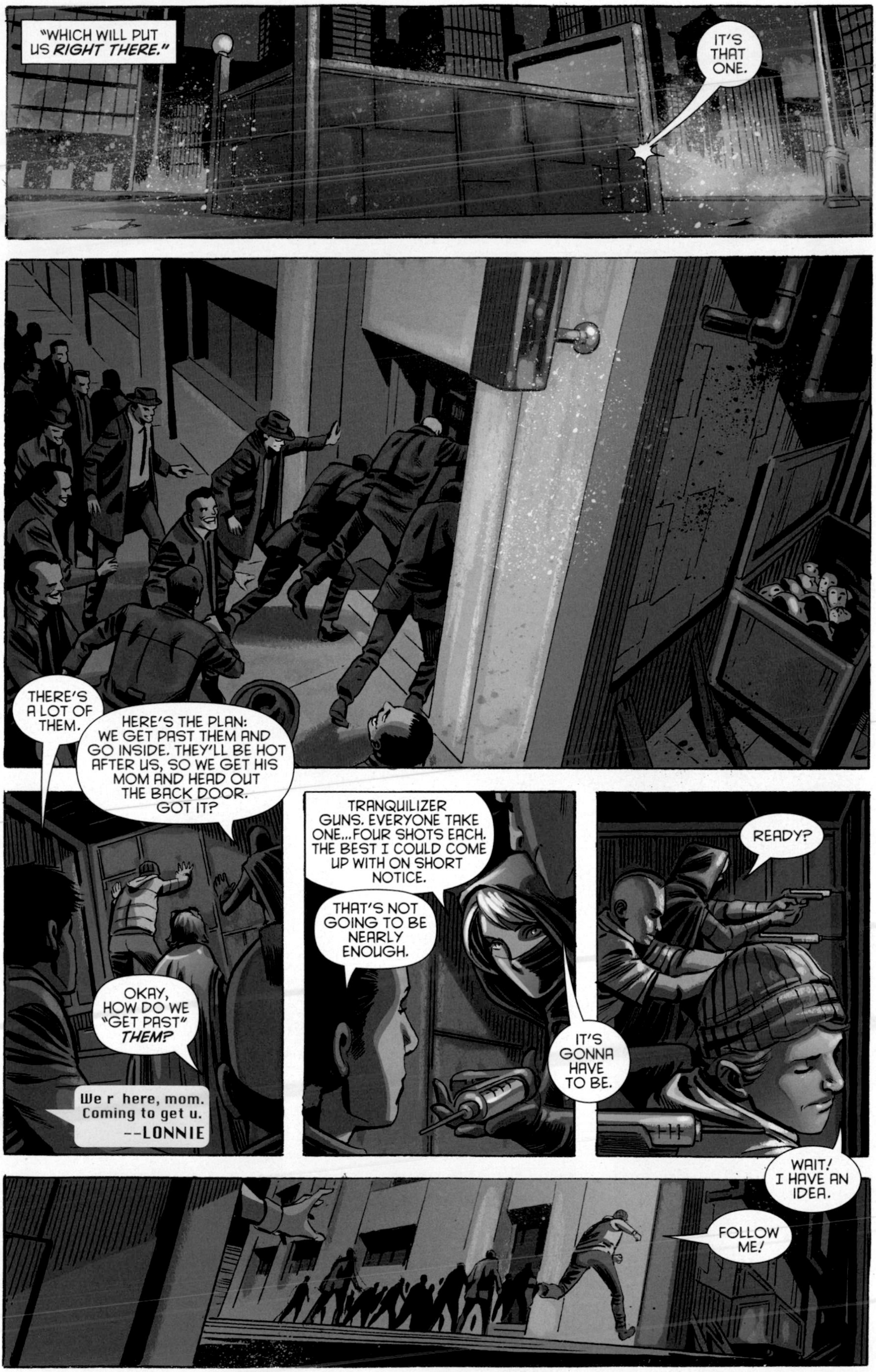

"WHICH WILL PUT US RIGHT THERE."
IT'S THAT ONE.
THERE'S A LOT OF THEM.
HERE'S THE PLAN: WE GET PAST THEM AND GO INSIDE. THEY'LL BE HOT AFTER US, SO WE GET HIS MOM AND HEAD OUT THE BACK DOOR. GOT IT?
OKAY, HOW DO WE "GET PAST" THEM?
We r here, mom. Coming to get u. --LONNIE
TRANQUILIZER GUNS. EVERYONE TAKE ONE...FOUR SHOTS EACH. THE BEST I COULD COME UP WITH ON SHORT NOTICE.
THAT'S NOT GOING TO BE NEARLY ENOUGH.
IT'S GONNA HAVE TO BE.
READY?
WAIT! I HAVE AN IDEA.
FOLLOW ME!

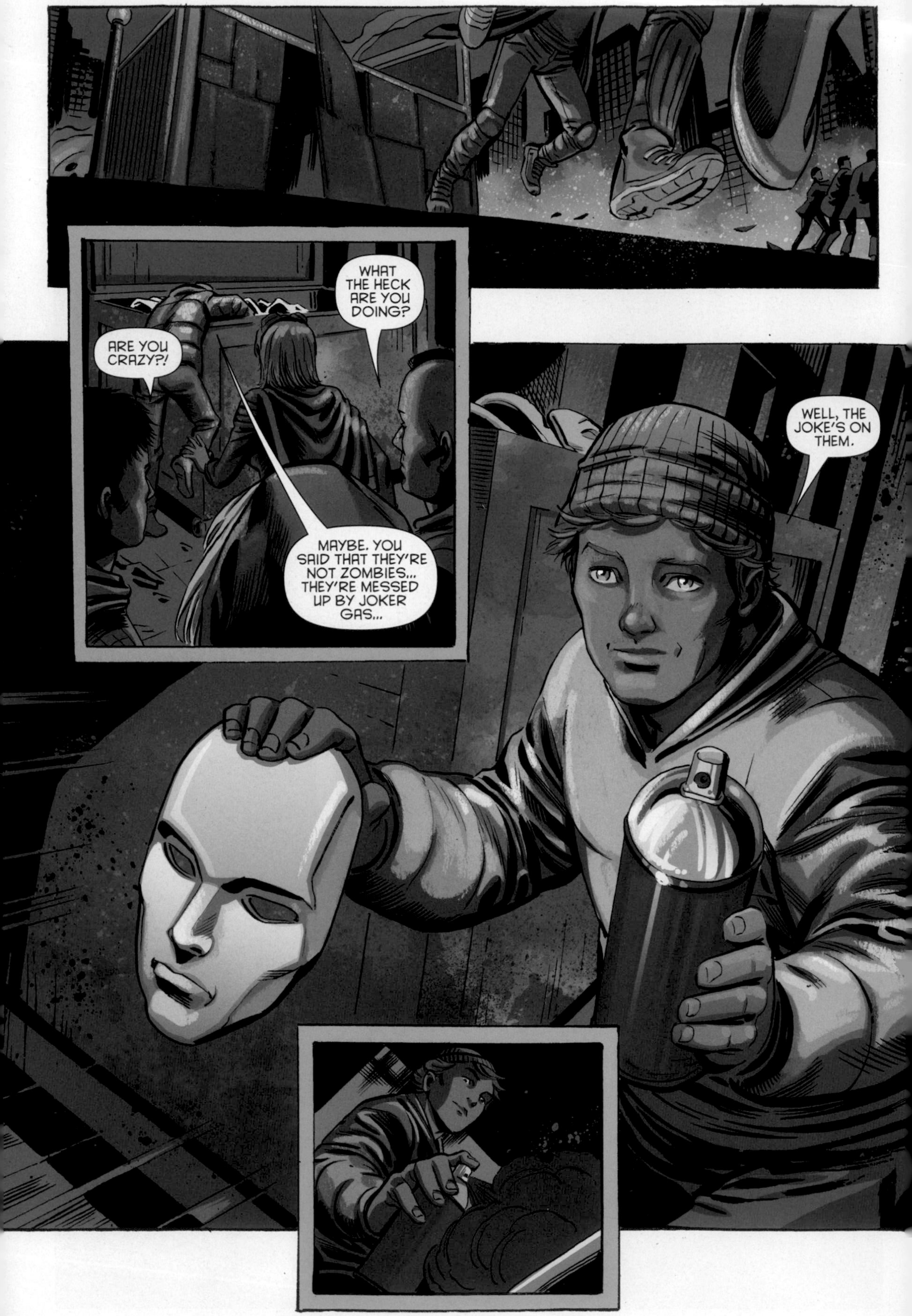
WHAT THE HECK ARE YOU DOING?
ARE YOU CRAZY?!
MAYBE. YOU SAID THAT THEY'RE NOT ZOMBIES... THEY'RE MESSED UP BY JOKER GAS...
WELL, THE JOKE'S ON THEM.

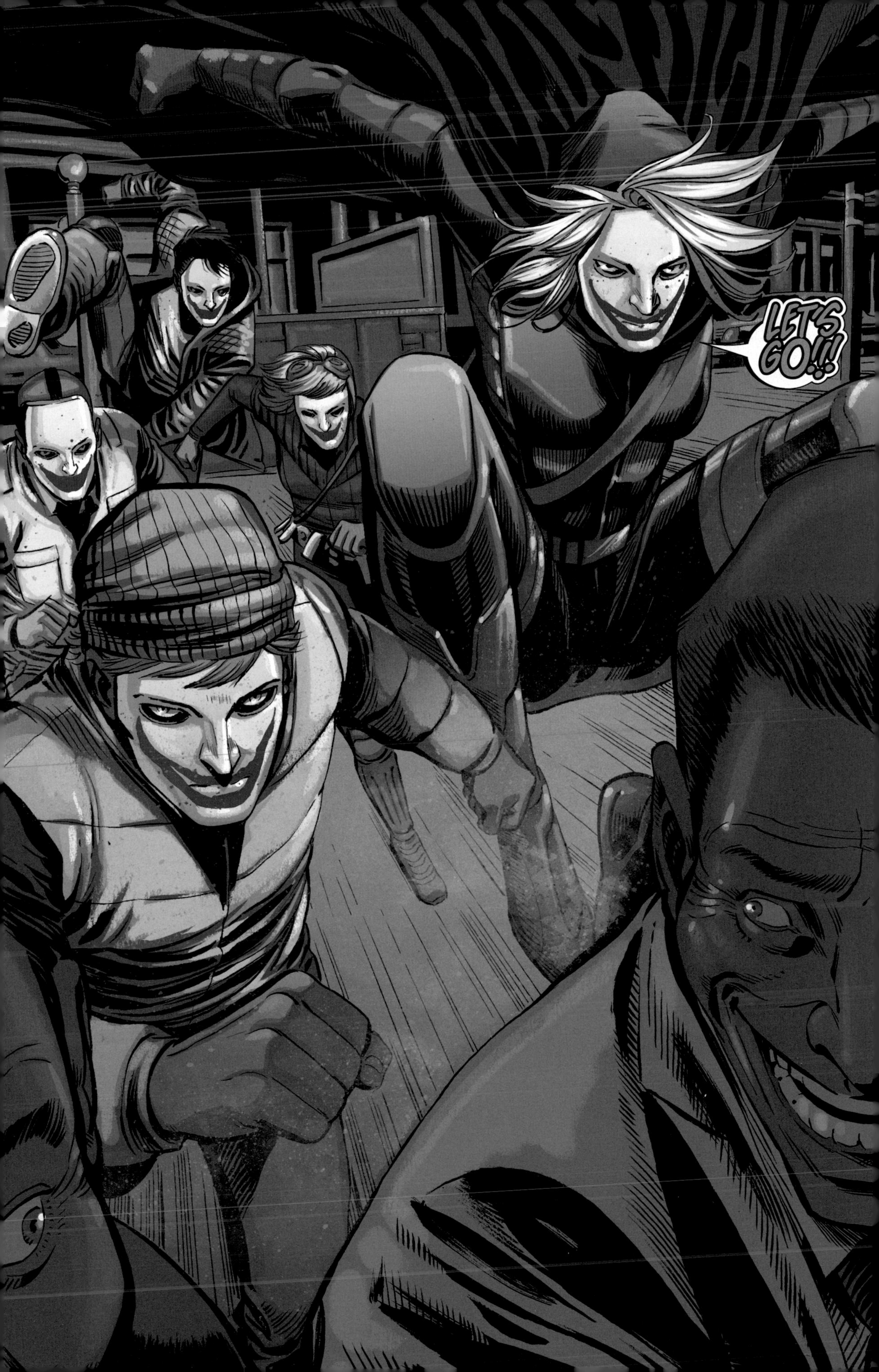
LET'S GO!!!

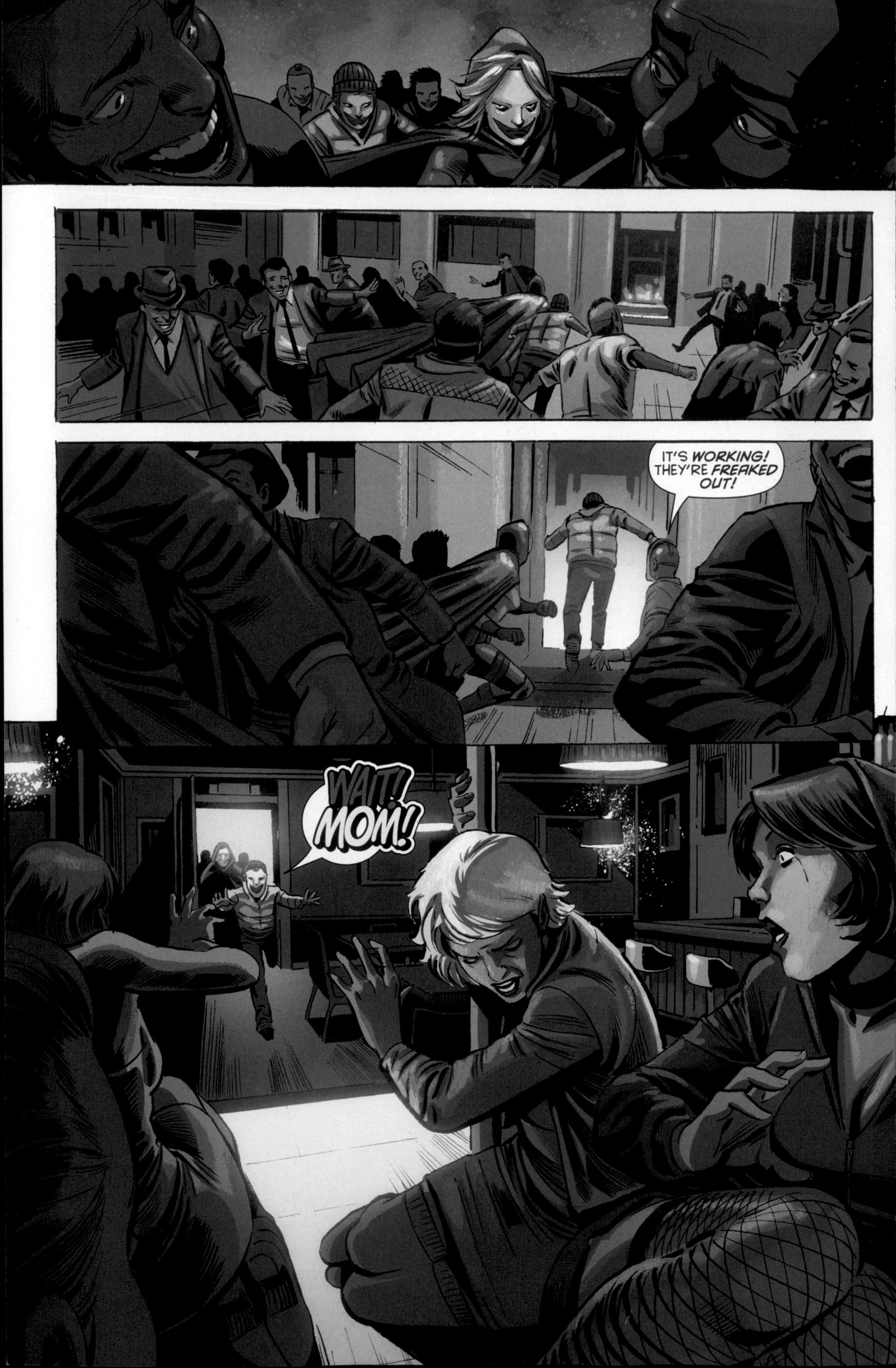
IT'S WORKING! THEY'RE FREAKED OUT!
WAIT! MOM!

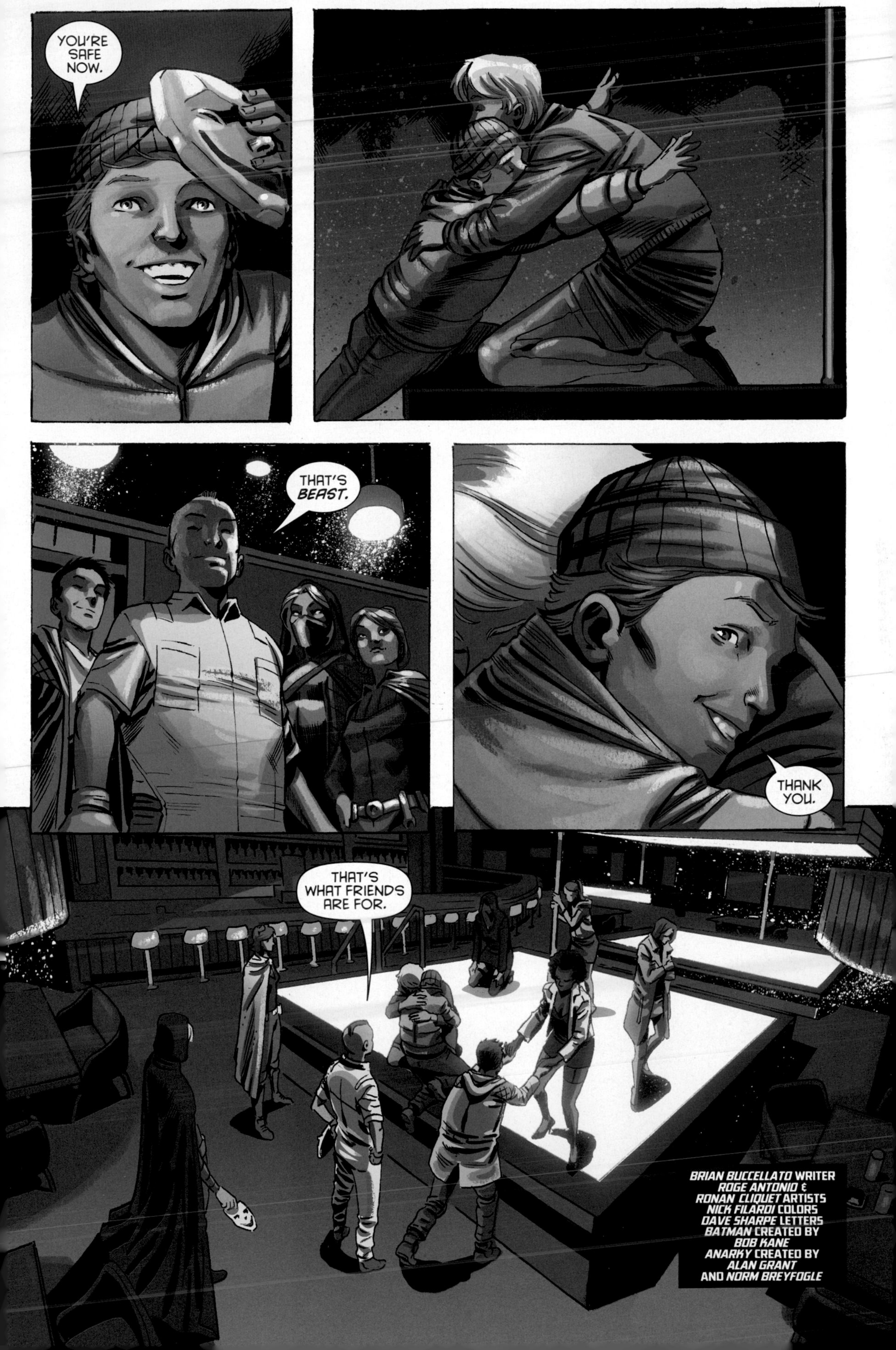
YOU'RE SAFE NOW.
THAT'S BEAST.
THANK YOU.
THAT'S WHAT FRIENDS ARE FOR.
BRIAN BUCCELLATO WRITER
ROGE ANTONIO & RONAN CLIQUET ARTISTS
NICK FILARDI COLORS
DAVE SHARPE LETTERS
BATMAN CREATED BY BOB KANE
ANARKY CREATED BY ALAN GRANT AND NORM BREYFOGLE

Cover by GREG CAPULLO, DANNY MIKI & FCO PLASCENCIA

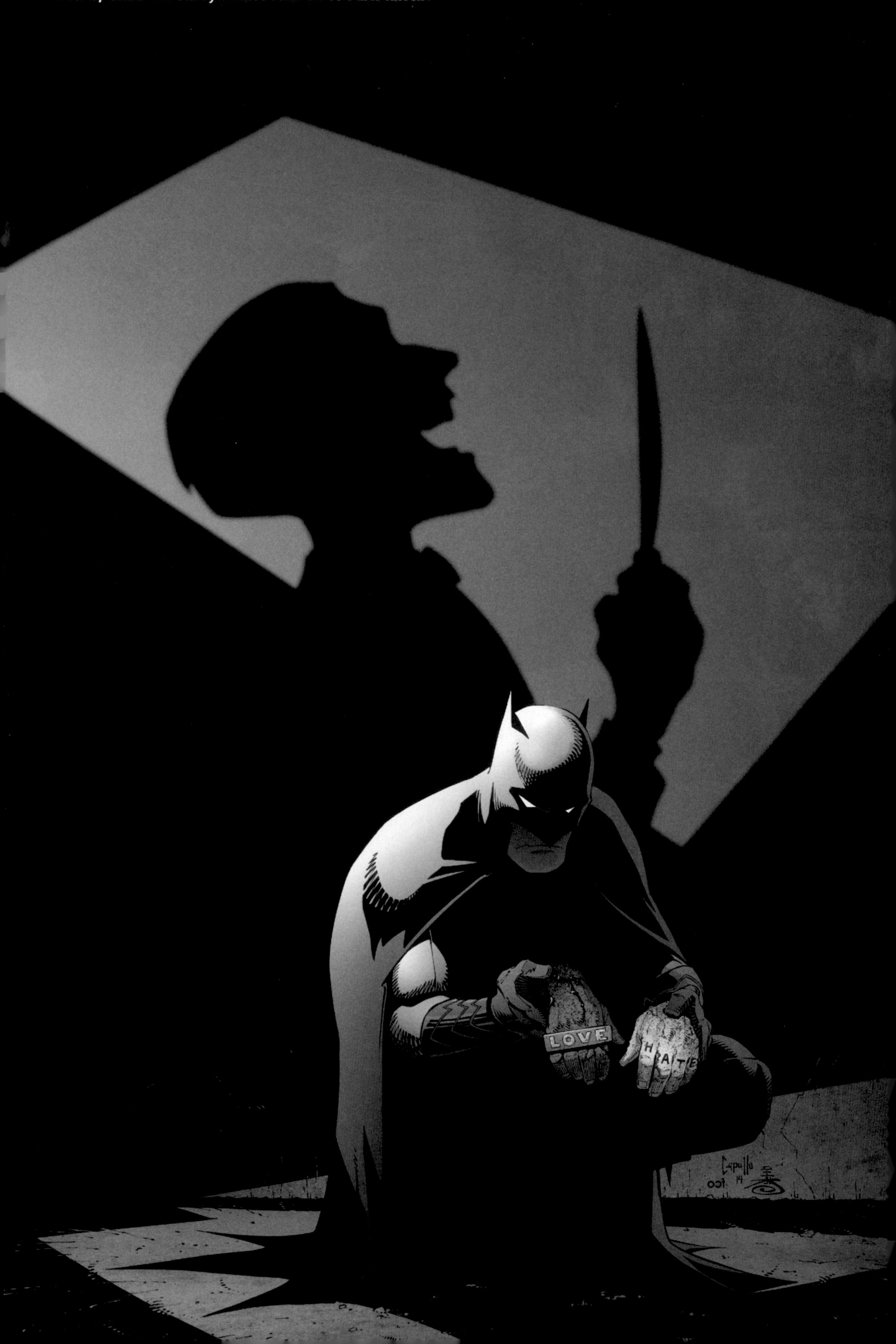
LOVE
HATE

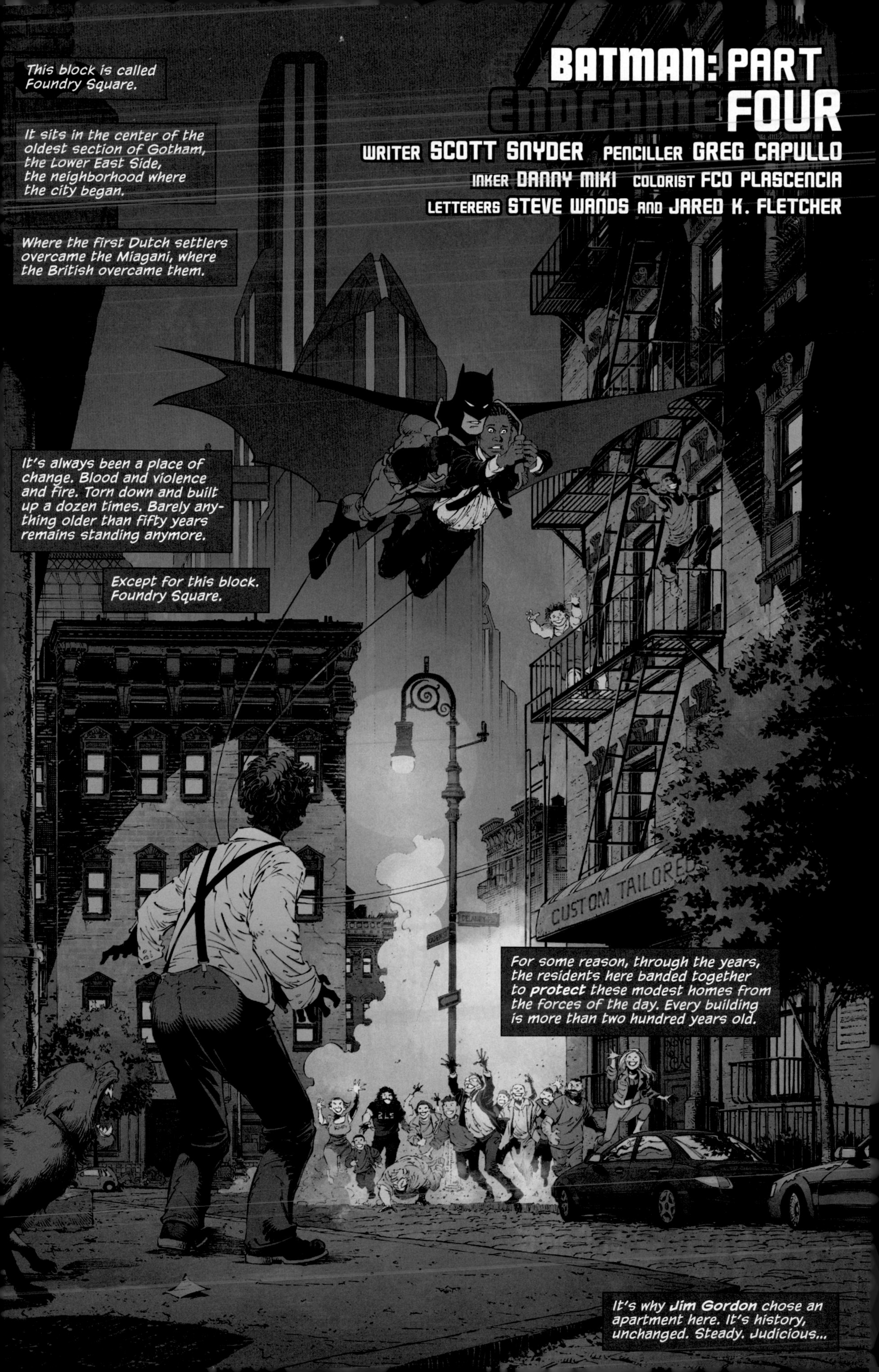

BATMAN: ENDGAME PART FOUR
WRITER SCOTT SNYDER PENCILLER GREG CAPULLO
INKER DANNY MIKI COLORIST FCO PLASCENCIA
LETTERERS STEVE WANDS AND JARED K. FLETCHER
This block is called Foundry Square.
It sits in the center of the oldest section of Gotham, the Lower East Side, the neighborhood where the city began.
Where the first Dutch settlers overcame the Miagani, where the British overcame them.
It's always been a place of change. Blood and violence and fire. Torn down and built up a dozen times. Barely anything older than fifty years remains standing anymore.
Except for this block. Foundry Square.
CUSTOM TAILORED
For some reason, through the years, the residents here banded together to protect these modest homes from the forces of the day. Every building is more than two hundred years old.
It's why Jim Gordon chose an apartment here. It's history, unchanged. Steady. Judicious...

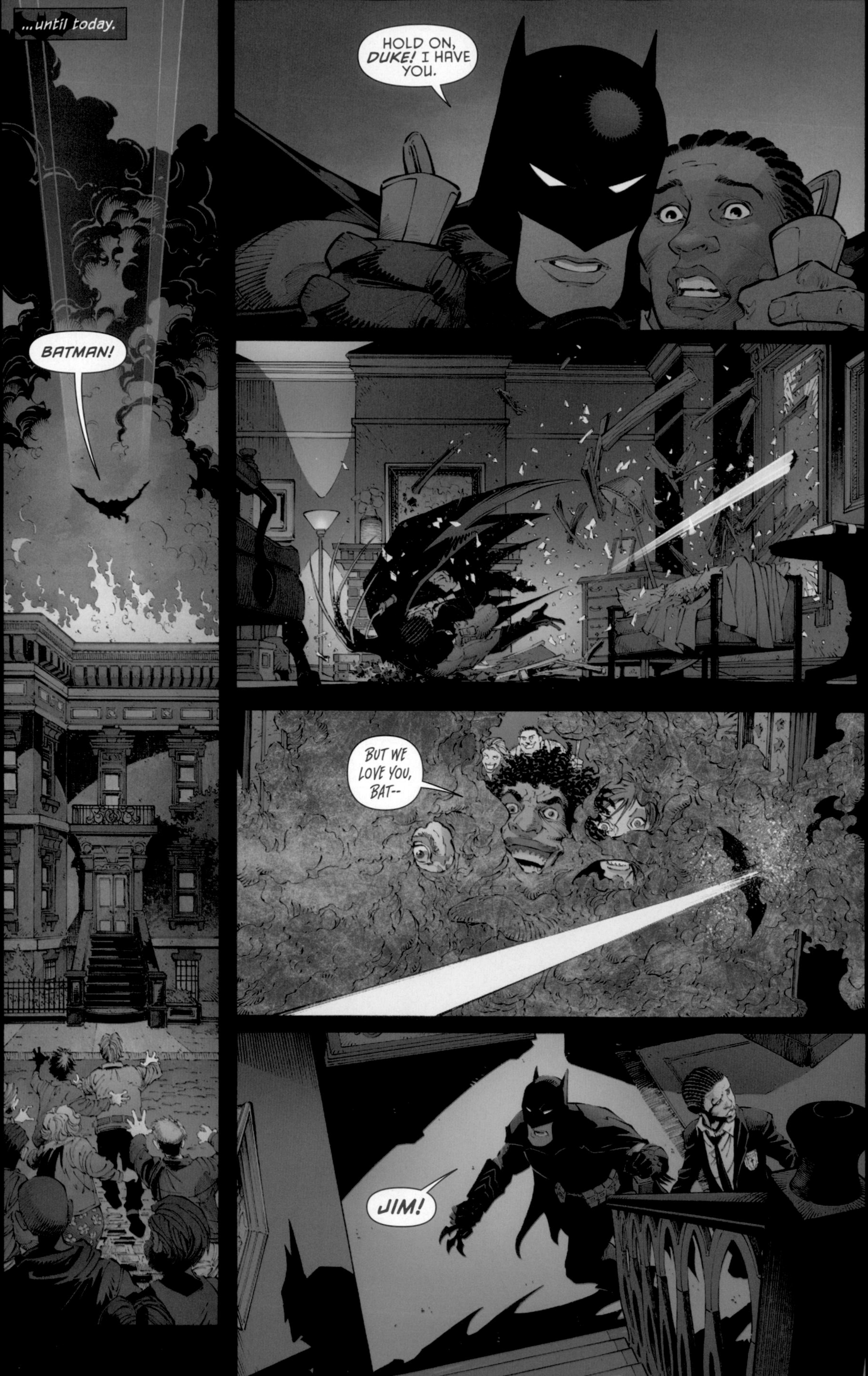
...until today.
HOLD ON, DUKE! I HAVE YOU.
BATMAN!
BUT WE LOVE YOU, BAT--
JIM!

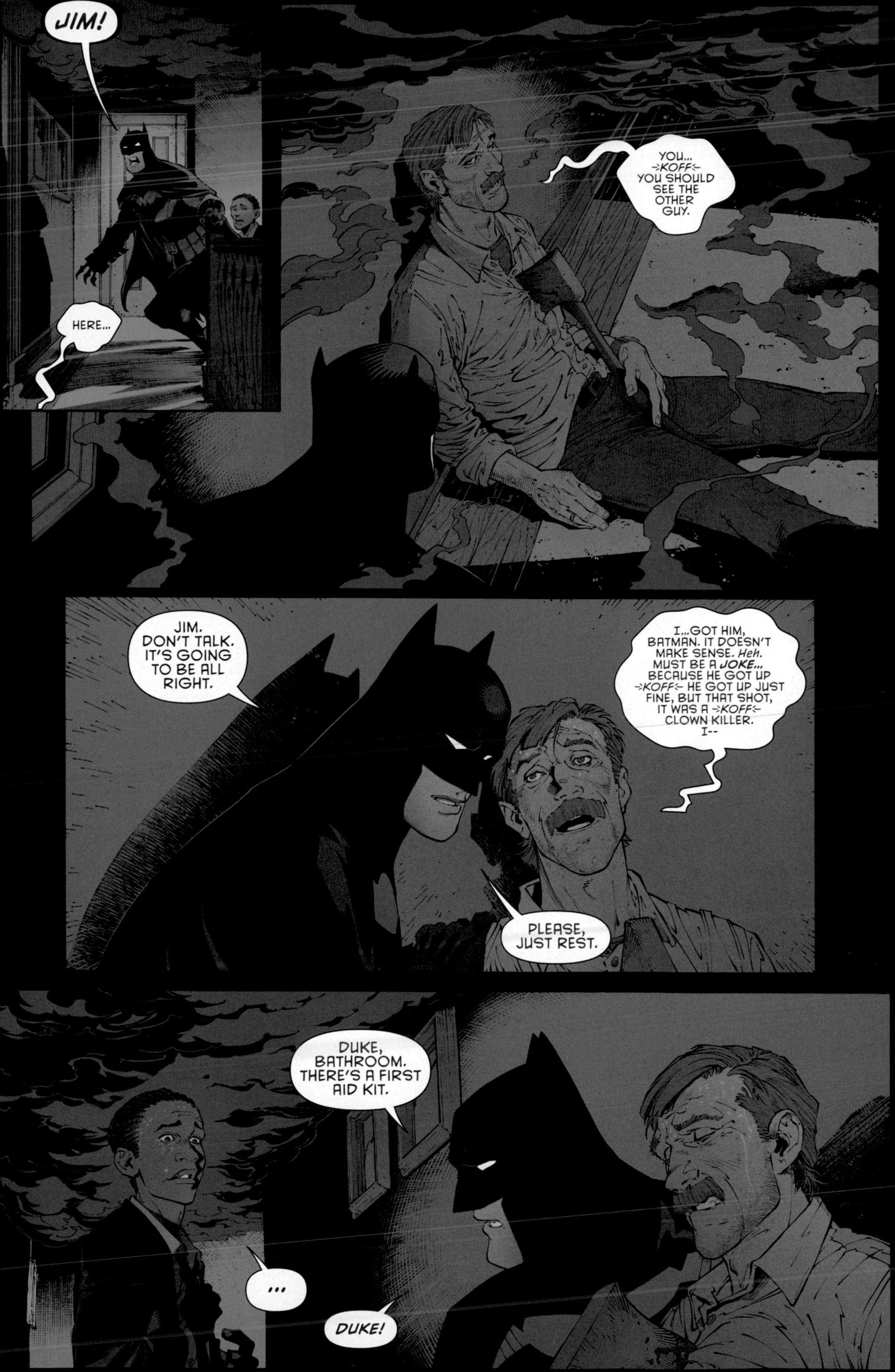
JIM!
HERE...
YOU... ⇝KOFF⇜ YOU SHOULD SEE THE OTHER GUY.
JIM. DON'T TALK. IT'S GOING TO BE ALL RIGHT.
I...GOT HIM, BATMAN. IT DOESN'T MAKE SENSE. *Heh.* MUST BE A *JOKE*... BECAUSE HE GOT UP ⇝KOFF⇜ HE GOT UP JUST FINE, BUT THAT SHOT, IT WAS A ⇝KOFF⇜ CLOWN KILLER. I--
PLEASE, JUST REST.
DUKE, BATHROOM. THERE'S A FIRST AID KIT.
...
DUKE!

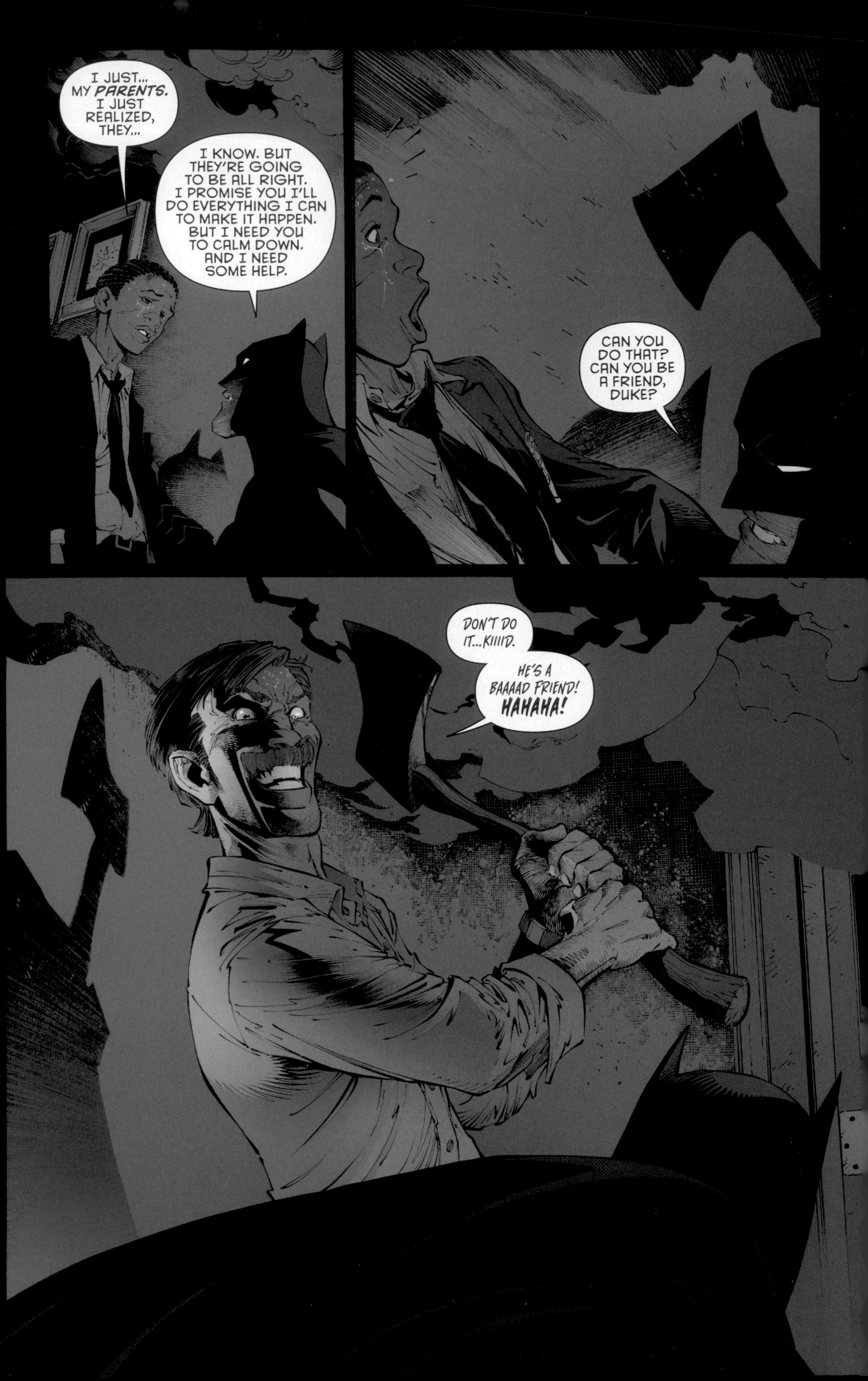
I JUST... MY PARENTS. I JUST REALIZED, THEY...
I KNOW. BUT THEY'RE GOING TO BE ALL RIGHT. I PROMISE YOU I'LL DO EVERYTHING I CAN TO MAKE IT HAPPEN. BUT I NEED YOU TO CALM DOWN. AND I NEED SOME HELP.
CAN YOU DO THAT? CAN YOU BE A FRIEND, DUKE?
DON'T DO IT...KIIIID.
HE'S A BAAAAD FRIEND! HAHAHA!

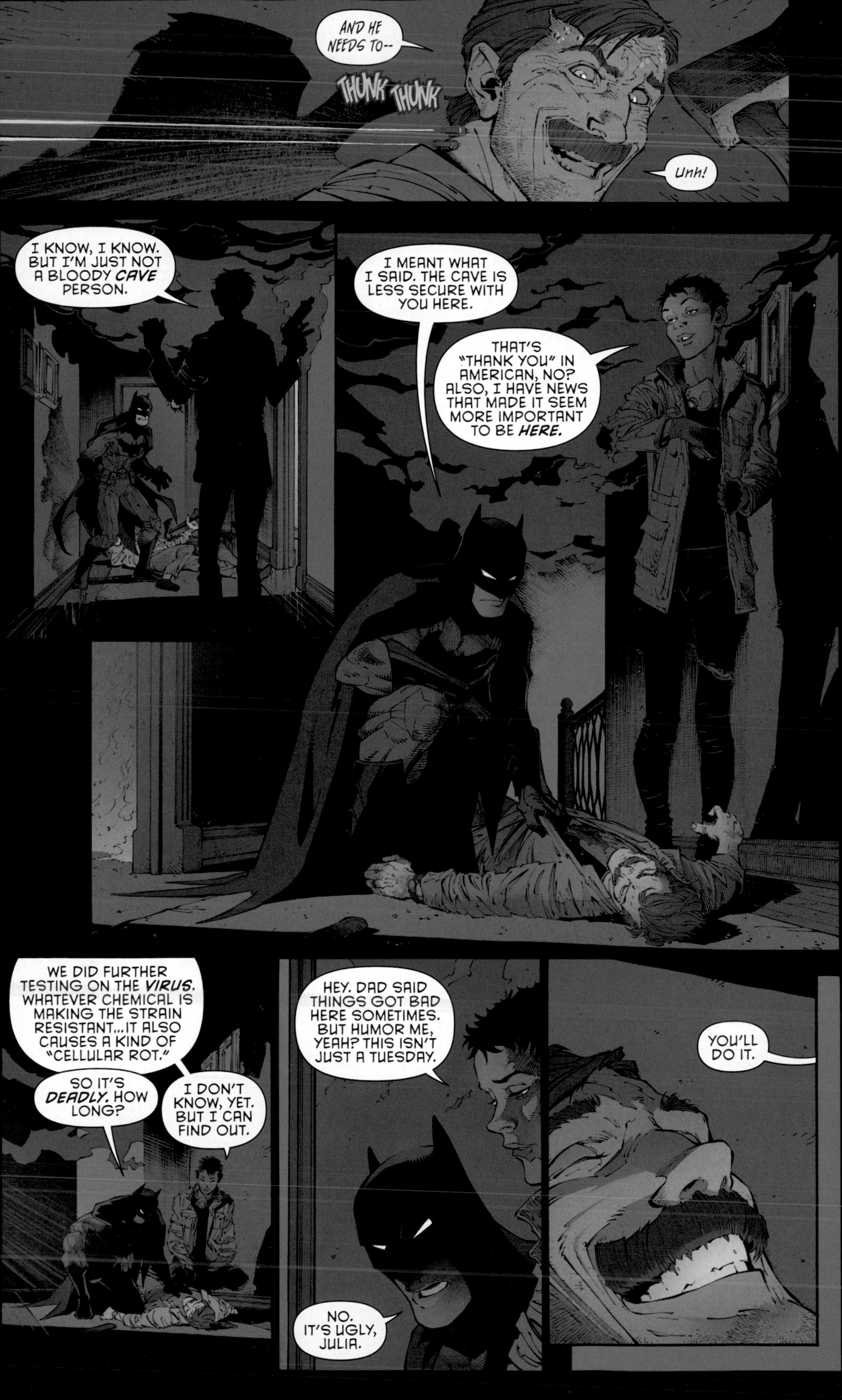

AND HE NEEDS TO--
THUNK THUNK
Unh!
I KNOW, I KNOW. BUT I'M JUST NOT A BLOODY CAVE PERSON.
I MEANT WHAT I SAID. THE CAVE IS LESS SECURE WITH YOU HERE.
THAT'S "THANK YOU" IN AMERICAN, NO? ALSO, I HAVE NEWS THAT MADE IT SEEM MORE IMPORTANT TO BE HERE.
WE DID FURTHER TESTING ON THE VIRUS. WHATEVER CHEMICAL IS MAKING THE STRAIN RESISTANT...IT ALSO CAUSES A KIND OF "CELLULAR ROT."
SO IT'S DEADLY. HOW LONG?
I DON'T KNOW, YET. BUT I CAN FIND OUT.
HEY. DAD SAID THINGS GOT BAD HERE SOMETIMES. BUT HUMOR ME, YEAH? THIS ISN'T JUST A TUESDAY.
NO. IT'S UGLY, JULIA.
YOU'LL DO IT.

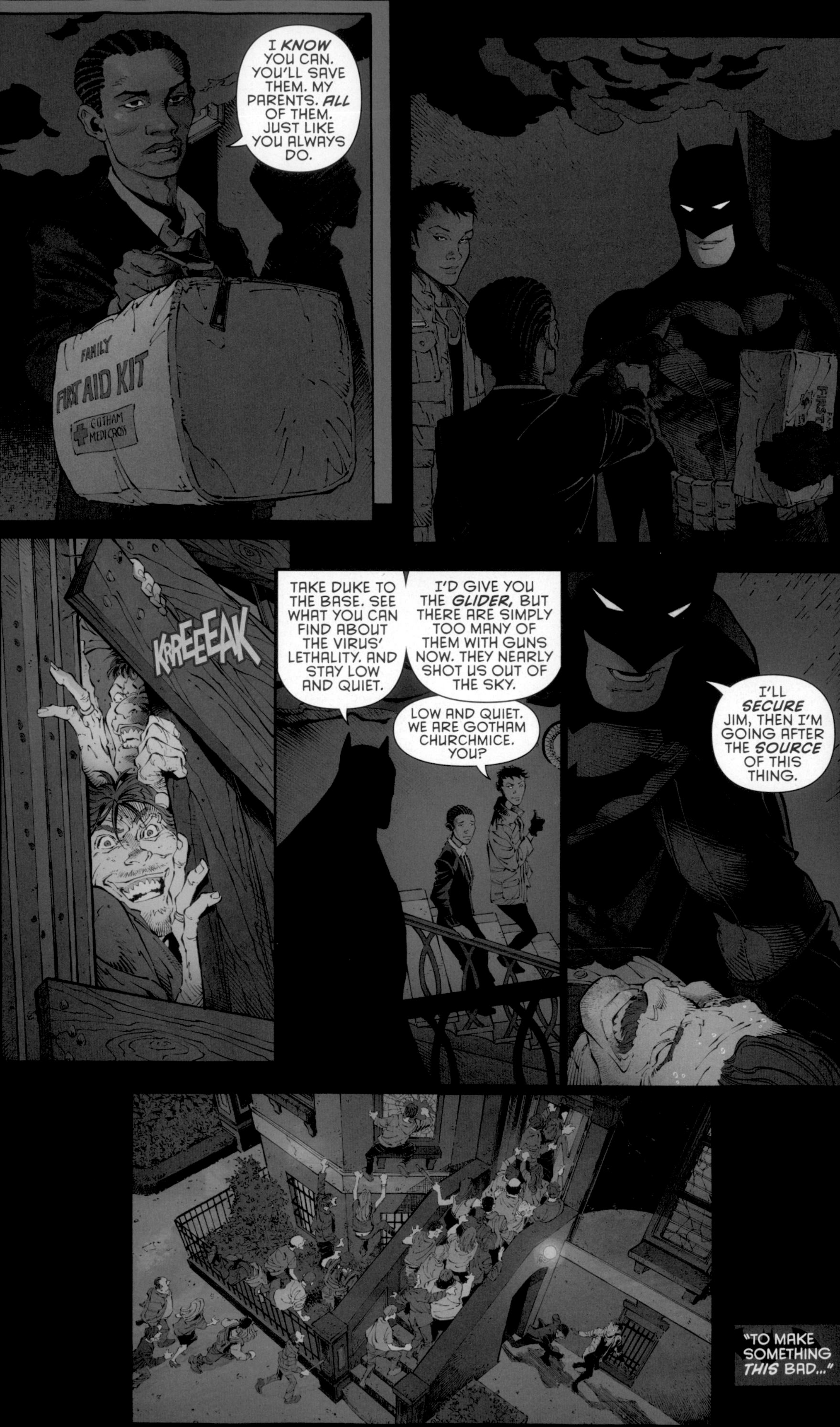
I KNOW YOU CAN. YOU'LL SAVE THEM. MY PARENTS. ALL OF THEM. JUST LIKE YOU ALWAYS DO.
FAMILY FIRST AID KIT GOTHAM MEDI CROSS
KRREEEAK
TAKE DUKE TO THE BASE. SEE WHAT YOU CAN FIND ABOUT THE VIRUS' LETHALITY. AND STAY LOW AND QUIET.
I'D GIVE YOU THE GLIDER, BUT THERE ARE SIMPLY TOO MANY OF THEM WITH GUNS NOW. THEY NEARLY SHOT US OUT OF THE SKY.
LOW AND QUIET. WE ARE GOTHAM CHURCHMICE. YOU?
I'LL SECURE JIM, THEN I'M GOING AFTER THE SOURCE OF THIS THING.
"TO MAKE SOMETHING THIS BAD..."

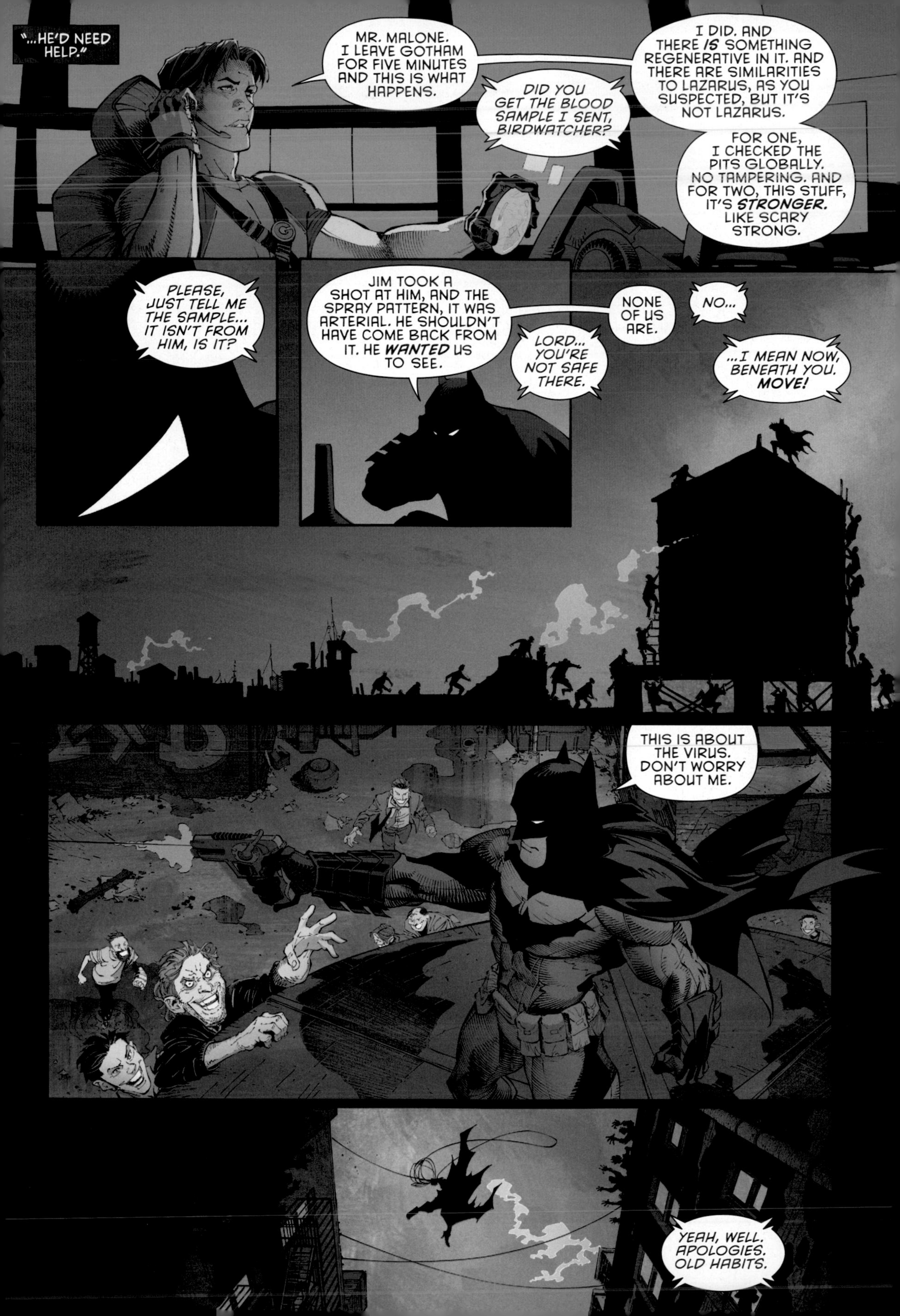
"...HE'D NEED HELP."
MR. MALONE. I LEAVE GOTHAM FOR FIVE MINUTES AND THIS IS WHAT HAPPENS.
DID YOU GET THE BLOOD SAMPLE I SENT, BIRDWATCHER?
I DID. AND THERE IS SOMETHING REGENERATIVE IN IT. AND THERE ARE SIMILARITIES TO LAZARUS, AS YOU SUSPECTED, BUT IT'S NOT LAZARUS.
FOR ONE, I CHECKED THE PITS GLOBALLY. NO TAMPERING. AND FOR TWO, THIS STUFF, IT'S STRONGER. LIKE SCARY STRONG.
PLEASE, JUST TELL ME THE SAMPLE... IT ISN'T FROM HIM, IS IT?
JIM TOOK A SHOT AT HIM, AND THE SPRAY PATTERN, IT WAS ARTERIAL. HE SHOULDN'T HAVE COME BACK FROM IT. HE WANTED US TO SEE.
LORD... YOU'RE NOT SAFE THERE.
NONE OF US ARE.
NO...
...I MEAN NOW, BENEATH YOU. MOVE!
THIS IS ABOUT THE VIRUS. DON'T WORRY ABOUT ME.
YEAH, WELL. APOLOGIES. OLD HABITS.

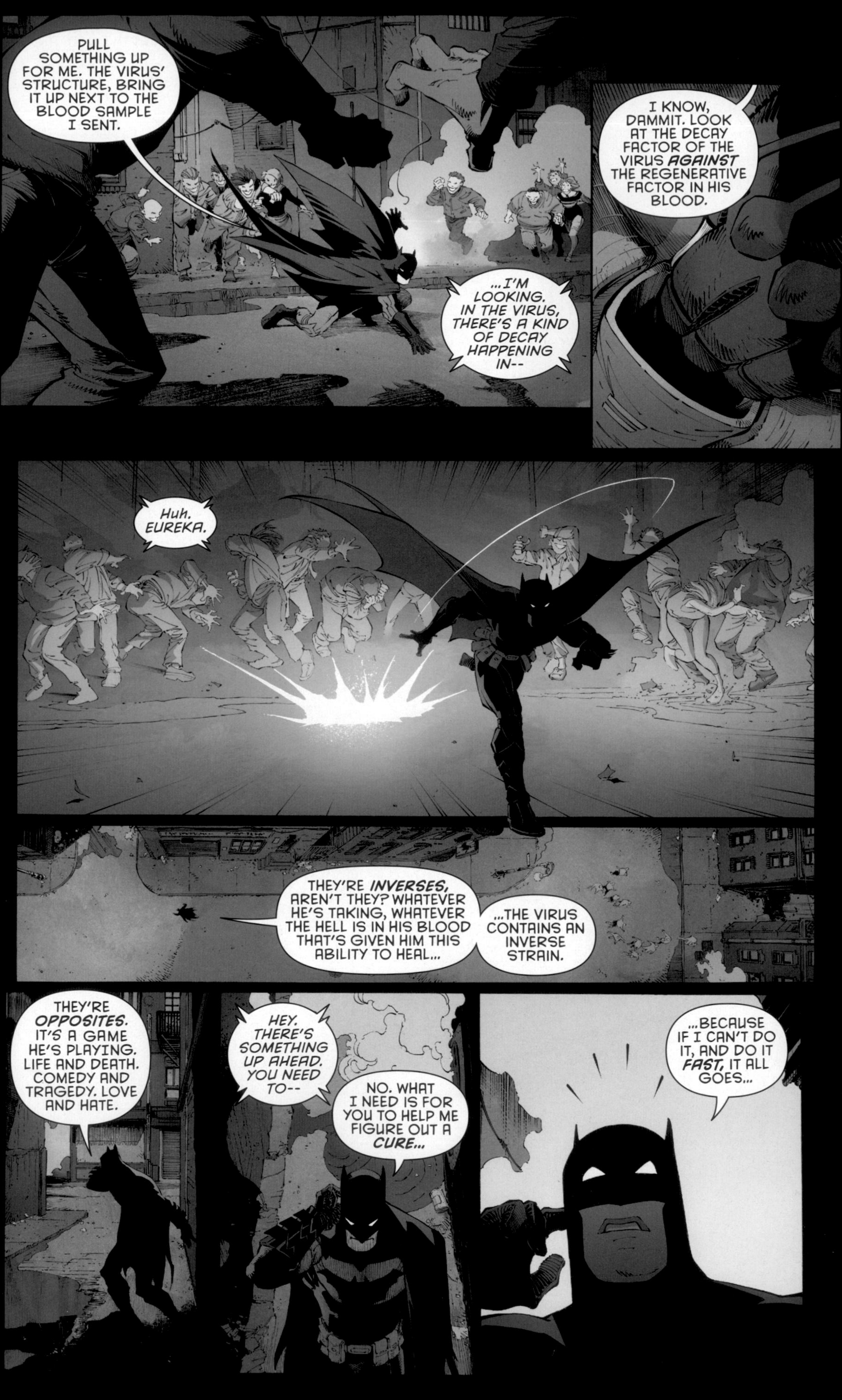
PULL SOMETHING UP FOR ME. THE VIRUS' STRUCTURE, BRING IT UP NEXT TO THE BLOOD SAMPLE I SENT.
...I'M LOOKING. IN THE VIRUS, THERE'S A KIND OF DECAY HAPPENING IN--
I KNOW, DAMMIT. LOOK AT THE DECAY FACTOR OF THE VIRUS AGAINST THE REGENERATIVE FACTOR IN HIS BLOOD.
Huh. EUREKA.
THEY'RE INVERSES, AREN'T THEY? WHATEVER HE'S TAKING, WHATEVER THE HELL IS IN HIS BLOOD THAT'S GIVEN HIM THIS ABILITY TO HEAL...
...THE VIRUS CONTAINS AN INVERSE STRAIN.
THEY'RE OPPOSITES. IT'S A GAME HE'S PLAYING. LIFE AND DEATH. COMEDY AND TRAGEDY. LOVE AND HATE.
HEY. THERE'S SOMETHING UP AHEAD. YOU NEED TO--
NO. WHAT I NEED IS FOR YOU TO HELP ME FIGURE OUT A CURE...
...BECAUSE IF I CAN'T DO IT, AND DO IT FAST, IT ALL GOES...

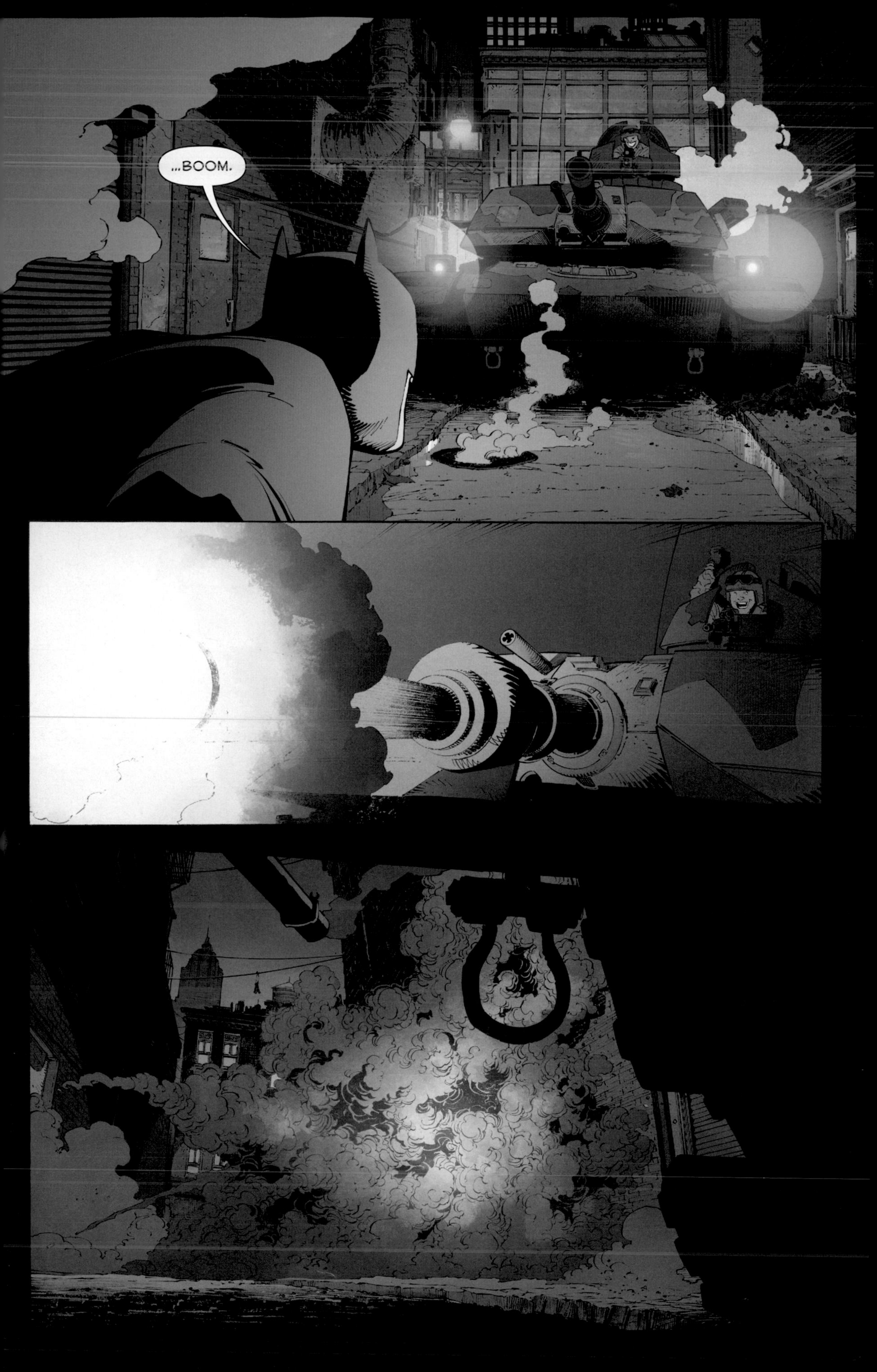
...BOOM.

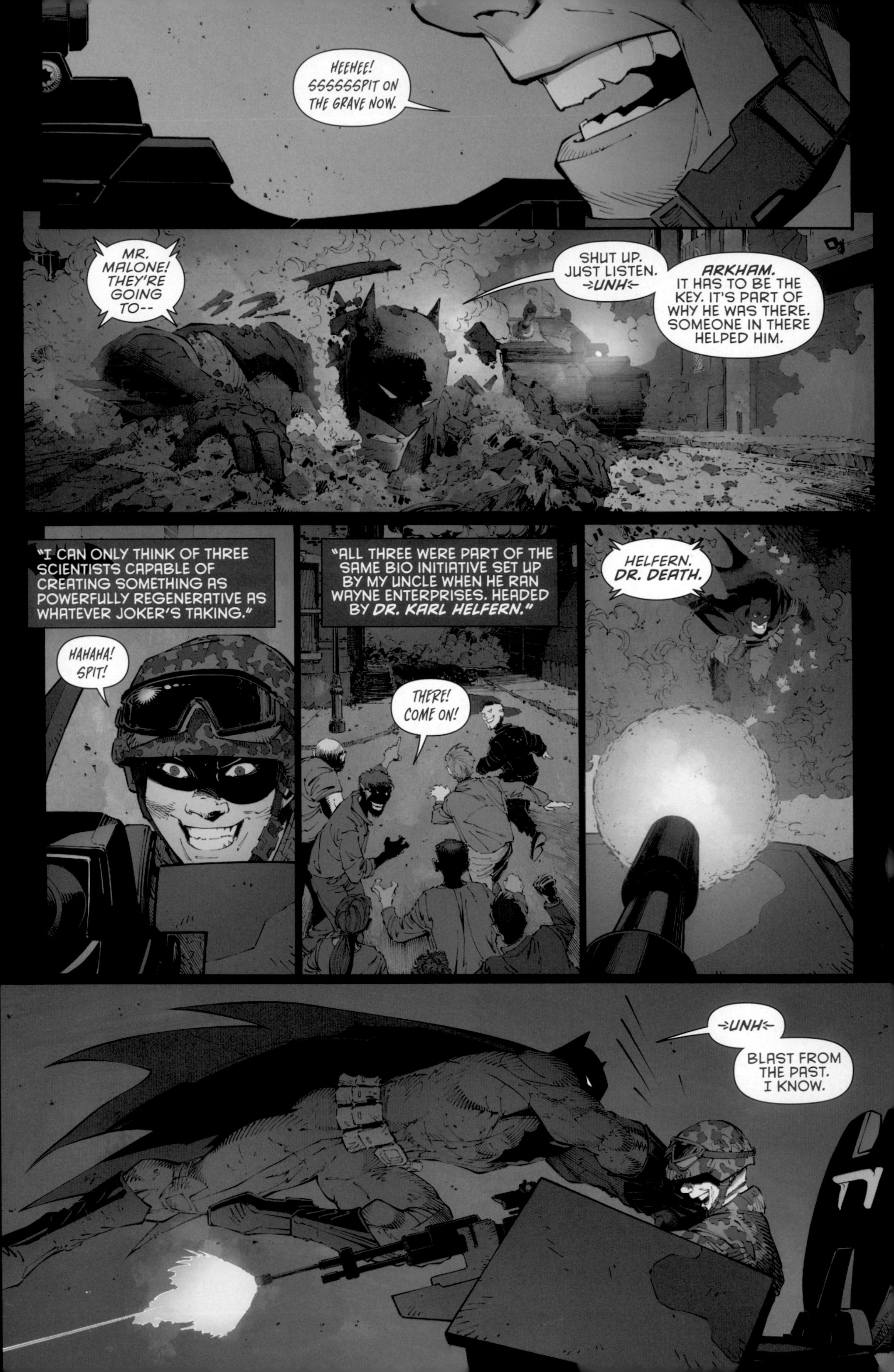

HEEHEE! SSSSSSPIT ON THE GRAVE NOW.
MR. MALONE! THEY'RE GOING TO--
SHUT UP. JUST LISTEN. -UNH-
ARKHAM. IT HAS TO BE THE KEY. IT'S PART OF WHY HE WAS THERE. SOMEONE IN THERE HELPED HIM.
"I CAN ONLY THINK OF THREE SCIENTISTS CAPABLE OF CREATING SOMETHING AS POWERFULLY REGENERATIVE AS WHATEVER JOKER'S TAKING."
HAHAHA! SPIT!
"ALL THREE WERE PART OF THE SAME BIO INITIATIVE SET UP BY MY UNCLE WHEN HE RAN WAYNE ENTERPRISES. HEADED BY DR. KARL HELFERN."
THERE! COME ON!
HELFERN. DR. DEATH.
-UNH-
BLAST FROM THE PAST. I KNOW.

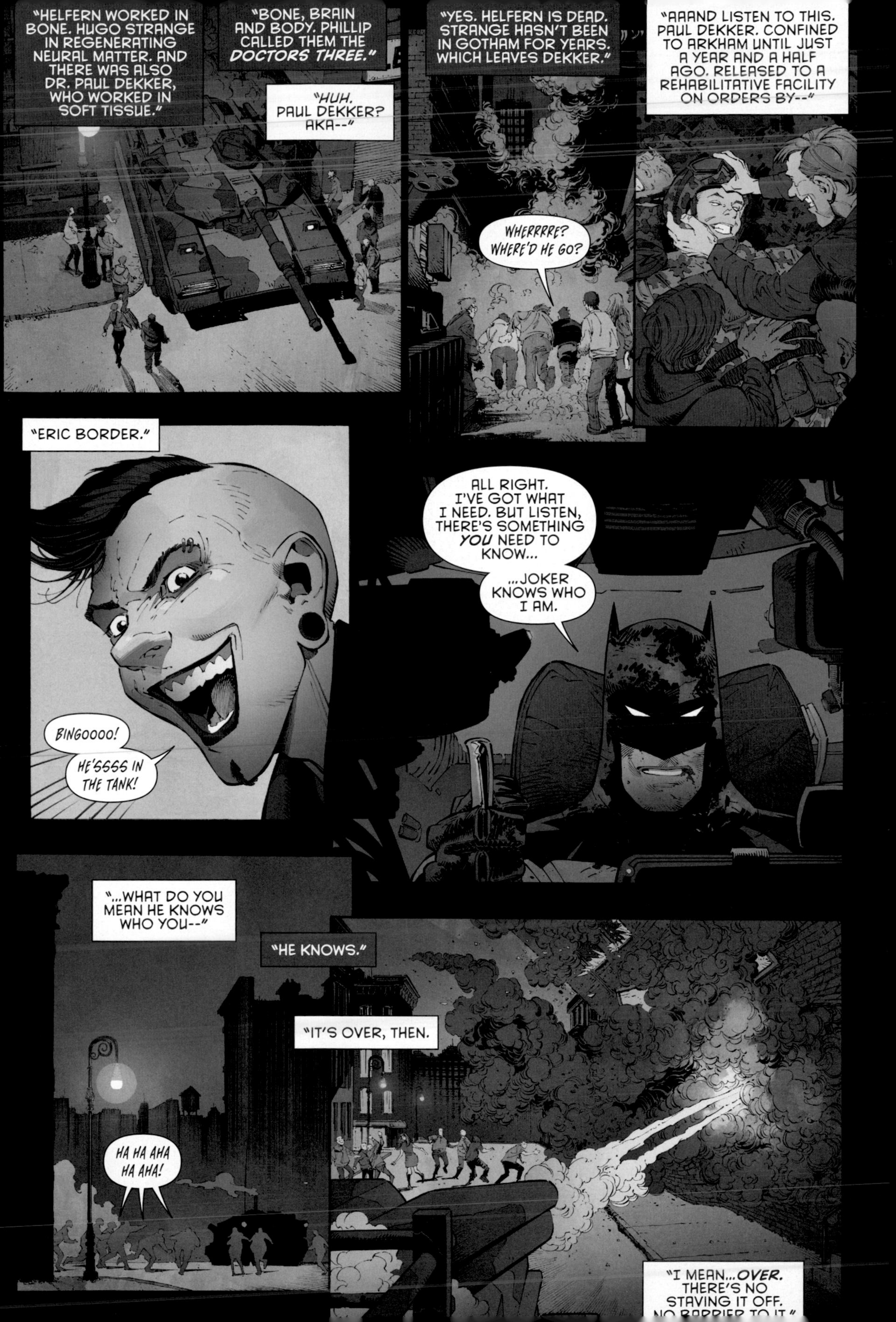
"HELFERN WORKED IN BONE. HUGO STRANGE IN REGENERATING NEURAL MATTER. AND THERE WAS ALSO DR. PAUL DEKKER, WHO WORKED IN SOFT TISSUE."
"BONE, BRAIN AND BODY. PHILLIP CALLED THEM THE *DOCTORS THREE.*"
"*HUH.* PAUL DEKKER? AKA--"
"YES. HELFERN IS DEAD. STRANGE HASN'T BEEN IN GOTHAM FOR YEARS. WHICH LEAVES DEKKER."
WHERRRRE? WHERE'D HE GO?
"AAAND LISTEN TO THIS. PAUL DEKKER. CONFINED TO ARKHAM UNTIL JUST A YEAR AND A HALF AGO. RELEASED TO A REHABILITATIVE FACILITY ON ORDERS BY--"
"ERIC BORDER."
BINGOOOO!
HE'SSSS IN THE TANK!
ALL RIGHT. I'VE GOT WHAT I NEED. BUT LISTEN, THERE'S SOMETHING *YOU* NEED TO KNOW...
...JOKER KNOWS WHO I AM.
"...WHAT DO YOU MEAN HE KNOWS WHO YOU--"
"HE KNOWS."
"IT'S OVER, THEN.
HA HA AHA HA AHA!
"I MEAN...*OVER.* THERE'S NO STAVING IT OFF.

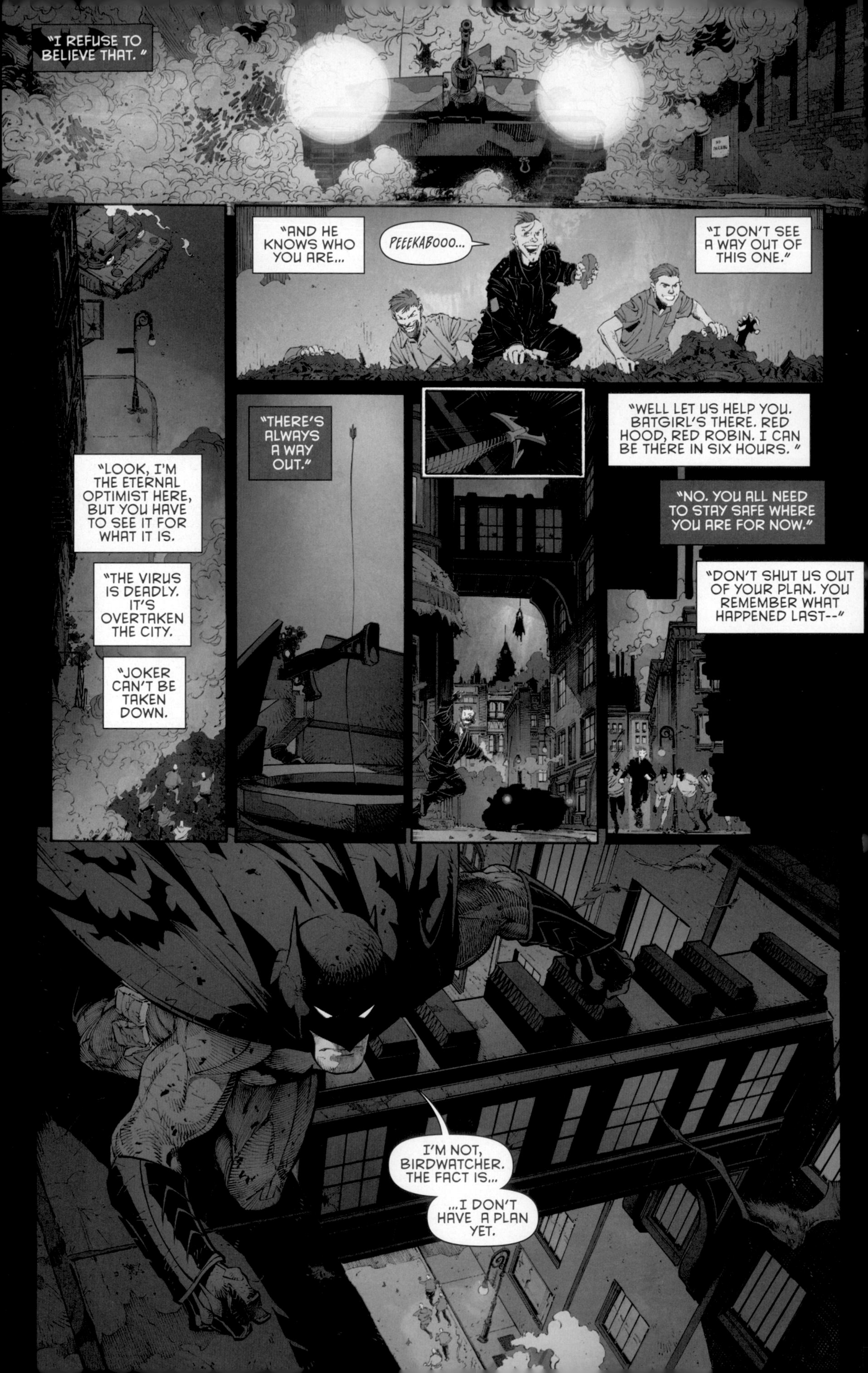
"I REFUSE TO BELIEVE THAT."
"AND HE KNOWS WHO YOU ARE...
PEEEKABOOO...
"I DON'T SEE A WAY OUT OF THIS ONE."
"LOOK, I'M THE ETERNAL OPTIMIST HERE, BUT YOU HAVE TO SEE IT FOR WHAT IT IS.
"THE VIRUS IS DEADLY. IT'S OVERTAKEN THE CITY.
"JOKER CAN'T BE TAKEN DOWN.
"THERE'S ALWAYS A WAY OUT."
"WELL LET US HELP YOU. BATGIRL'S THERE. RED HOOD, RED ROBIN. I CAN BE THERE IN SIX HOURS."
"NO. YOU ALL NEED TO STAY SAFE WHERE YOU ARE FOR NOW."
"DON'T SHUT US OUT OF YOUR PLAN. YOU REMEMBER WHAT HAPPENED LAST--"
I'M NOT, BIRDWATCHER. THE FACT IS...
...I DON'T HAVE A PLAN YET.

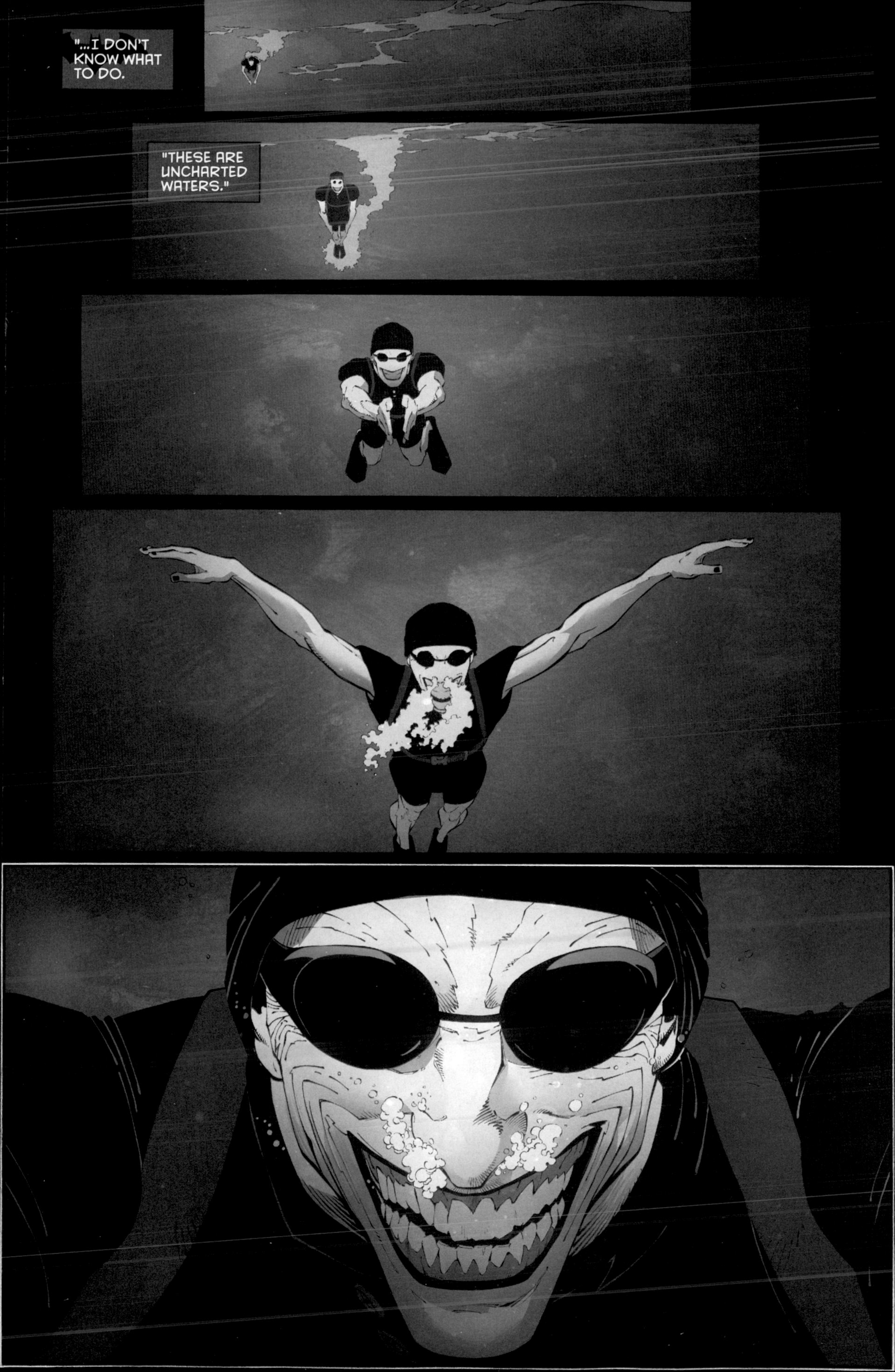
"...I DON'T KNOW WHAT TO DO.
"THESE ARE UNCHARTED WATERS."

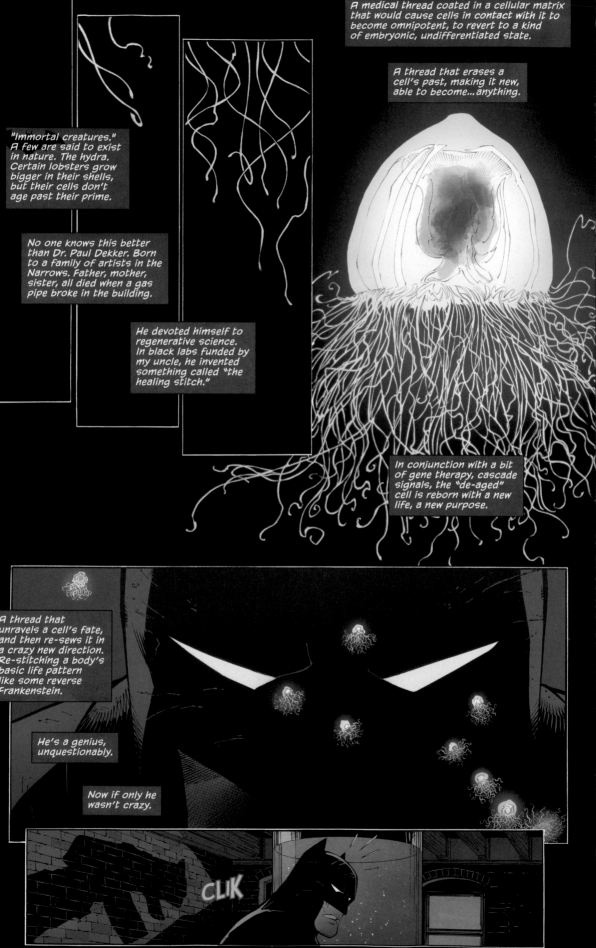

A medical thread coated in a cellular matrix that would cause cells in contact with it to become omnipotent, to revert to a kind of embryonic, undifferentiated state.

A thread that erases a cell's past, making it new, able to become...anything.

"Immortal creatures." A few are said to exist in nature. The hydra. Certain lobsters grow bigger in their shells, but their cells don't age past their prime.

No one knows this better than Dr. Paul Dekker. Born to a family of artists in the Narrows. Father, mother, sister, all died when a gas pipe broke in the building.

He devoted himself to regenerative science. In black labs funded by my uncle, he invented something called "the healing stitch."

In conjunction with a bit of gene therapy, cascade signals, the "de-aged" cell is reborn with a new life, a new purpose.

A thread that unravels a cell's fate, and then re-sews it in a crazy new direction. Re-stitching a body's basic life pattern like some reverse Frankenstein.

He's a genius, unquestionably.

Now if only he wasn't crazy.

CLIK

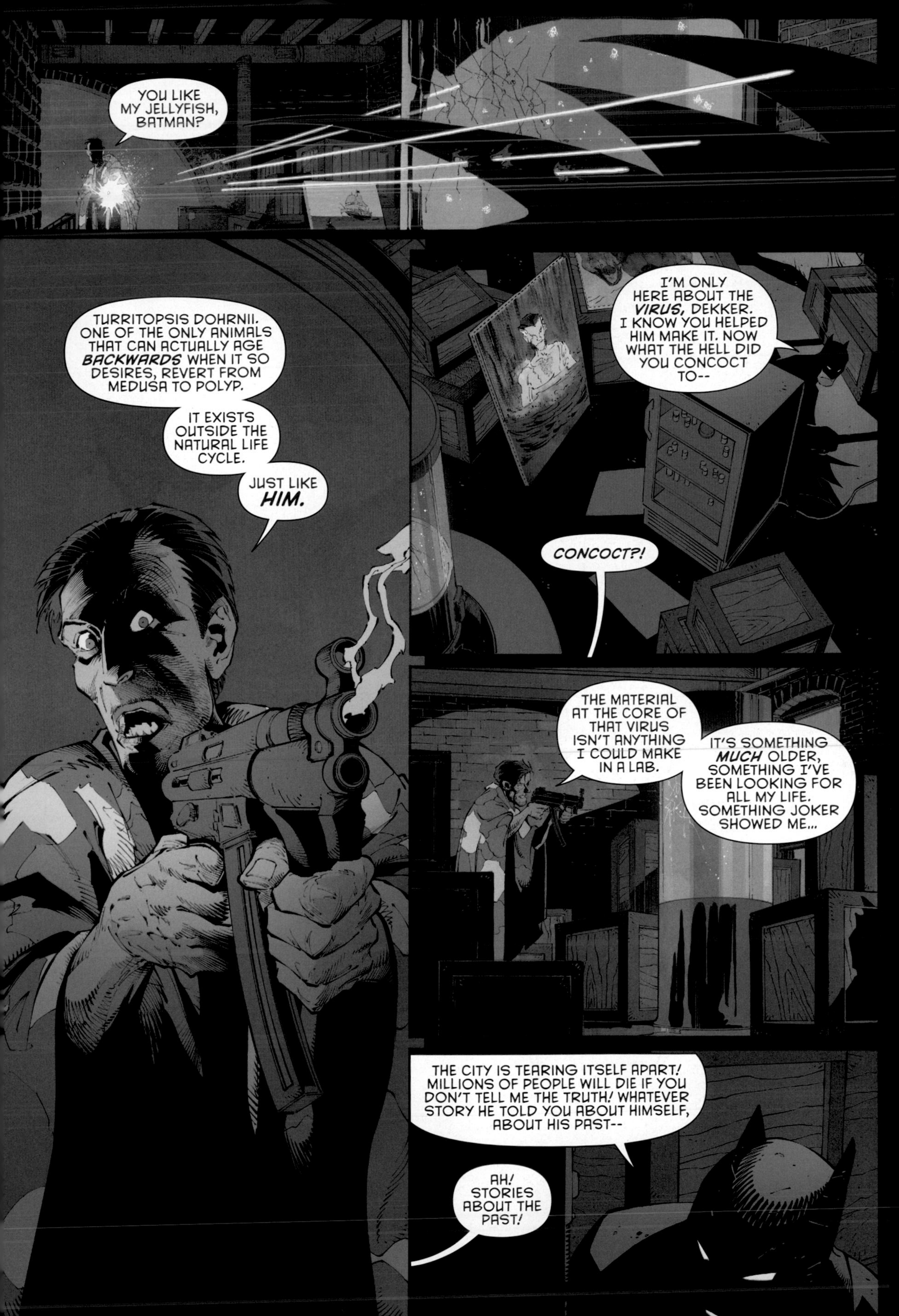
YOU LIKE MY JELLYFISH, BATMAN?
TURRITOPSIS DOHRNII. ONE OF THE ONLY ANIMALS THAT CAN ACTUALLY AGE BACKWARDS WHEN IT SO DESIRES, REVERT FROM MEDUSA TO POLYP.
IT EXISTS OUTSIDE THE NATURAL LIFE CYCLE.
JUST LIKE HIM.
I'M ONLY HERE ABOUT THE VIRUS, DEKKER. I KNOW YOU HELPED HIM MAKE IT. NOW WHAT THE HELL DID YOU CONCOCT TO--
CONCOCT?!
THE MATERIAL AT THE CORE OF THAT VIRUS ISN'T ANYTHING I COULD MAKE IN A LAB.
IT'S SOMETHING MUCH OLDER, SOMETHING I'VE BEEN LOOKING FOR ALL MY LIFE. SOMETHING JOKER SHOWED ME...
THE CITY IS TEARING ITSELF APART! MILLIONS OF PEOPLE WILL DIE IF YOU DON'T TELL ME THE TRUTH! WHATEVER STORY HE TOLD YOU ABOUT HIMSELF, ABOUT HIS PAST--
AH! STORIES ABOUT THE PAST!

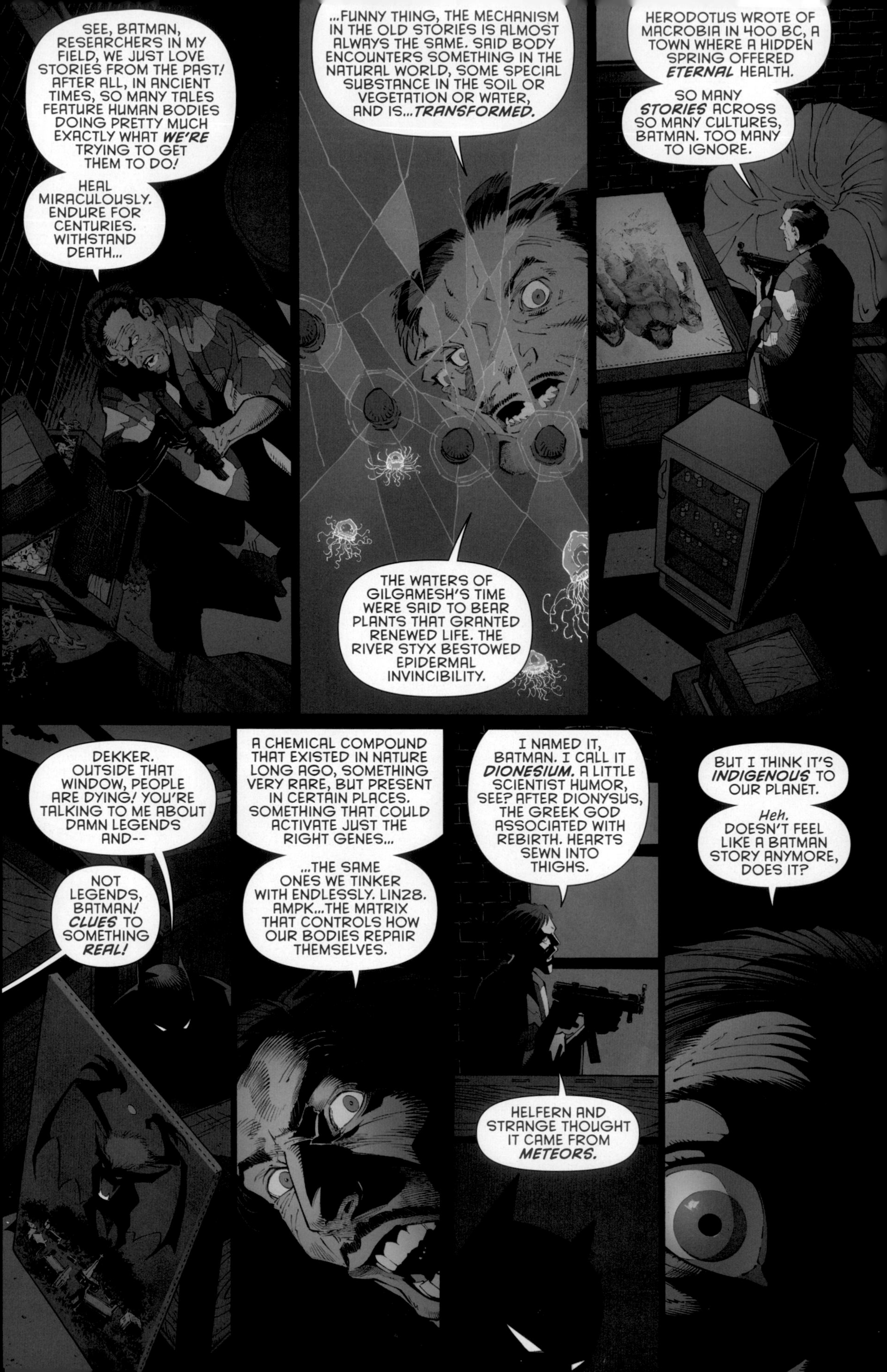
SEE, BATMAN, RESEARCHERS IN MY FIELD, WE JUST LOVE STORIES FROM THE PAST! AFTER ALL, IN ANCIENT TIMES, SO MANY TALES FEATURE HUMAN BODIES DOING PRETTY MUCH EXACTLY WHAT *WE'RE* TRYING TO GET THEM TO DO!
HEAL MIRACULOUSLY. ENDURE FOR CENTURIES. WITHSTAND DEATH...
...FUNNY THING, THE MECHANISM IN THE OLD STORIES IS ALMOST ALWAYS THE SAME. SAID BODY ENCOUNTERS SOMETHING IN THE NATURAL WORLD, SOME SPECIAL SUBSTANCE IN THE SOIL OR VEGETATION OR WATER, AND IS...*TRANSFORMED.*
THE WATERS OF GILGAMESH'S TIME WERE SAID TO BEAR PLANTS THAT GRANTED RENEWED LIFE. THE RIVER STYX BESTOWED EPIDERMAL INVINCIBILITY.
HERODOTUS WROTE OF MACROBIA IN 400 BC, A TOWN WHERE A HIDDEN SPRING OFFERED *ETERNAL* HEALTH.
SO MANY *STORIES* ACROSS SO MANY CULTURES, BATMAN. TOO MANY TO IGNORE.
DEKKER. OUTSIDE THAT WINDOW, PEOPLE ARE DYING! YOU'RE TALKING TO ME ABOUT DAMN LEGENDS AND--
NOT LEGENDS, BATMAN! *CLUES* TO SOMETHING *REAL!*
A CHEMICAL COMPOUND THAT EXISTED IN NATURE LONG AGO, SOMETHING VERY RARE, BUT PRESENT IN CERTAIN PLACES. SOMETHING THAT COULD ACTIVATE JUST THE RIGHT GENES...
...THE SAME ONES WE TINKER WITH ENDLESSLY. LIN28. AMPK...THE MATRIX THAT CONTROLS HOW OUR BODIES REPAIR THEMSELVES.
I NAMED IT, BATMAN. I CALL IT *DIONESIUM.* A LITTLE SCIENTIST HUMOR, SEE? AFTER DIONYSUS, THE GREEK GOD ASSOCIATED WITH REBIRTH. HEARTS SEWN INTO THIGHS.
HELFERN AND STRANGE THOUGHT IT CAME FROM *METEORS.*
BUT I THINK IT'S *INDIGENOUS* TO OUR PLANET.
Heh. DOESN'T FEEL LIKE A BATMAN STORY ANYMORE, DOES IT?

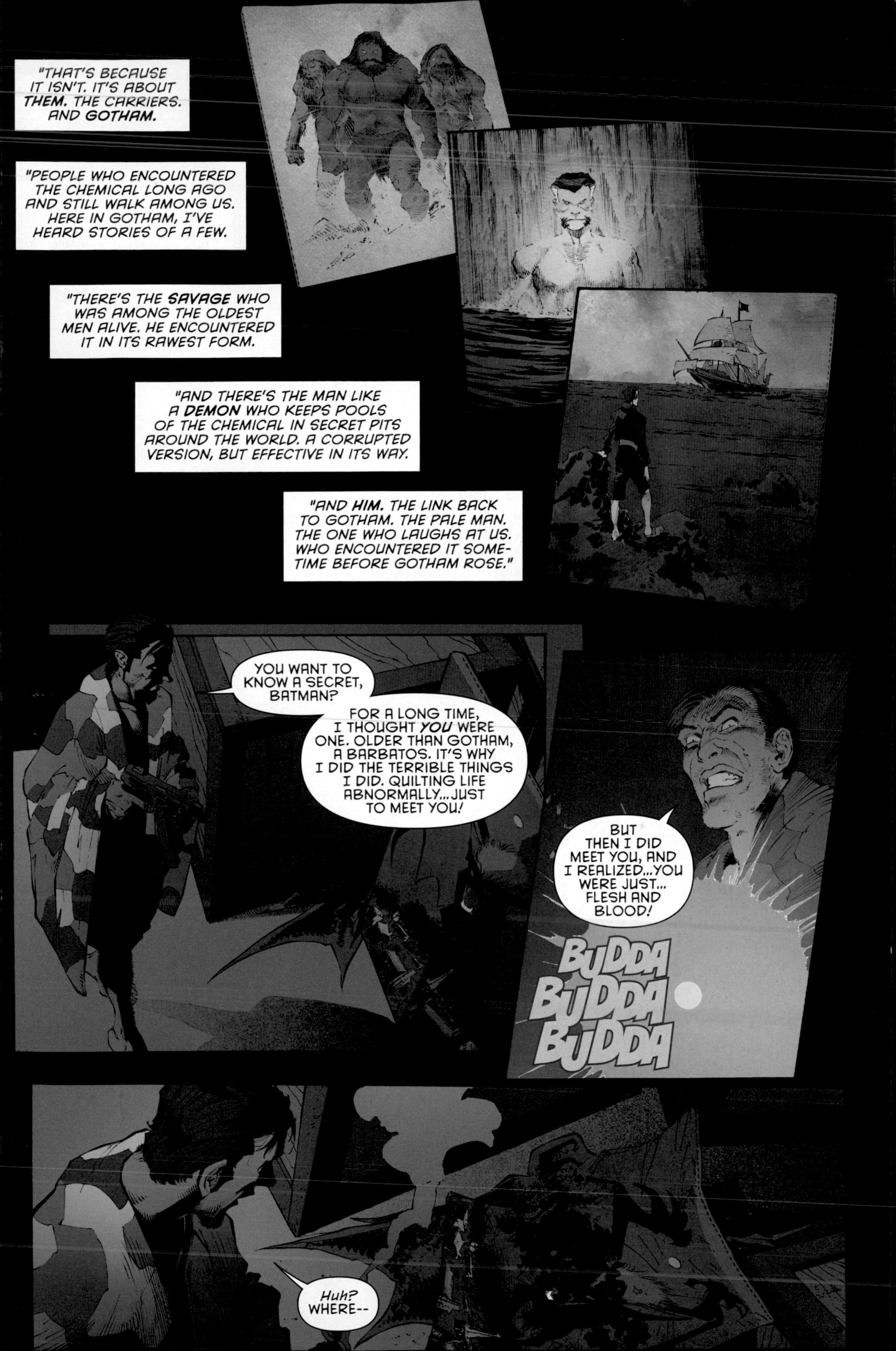
"THAT'S BECAUSE IT ISN'T. IT'S ABOUT THEM. THE CARRIERS. AND GOTHAM.
"PEOPLE WHO ENCOUNTERED THE CHEMICAL LONG AGO AND STILL WALK AMONG US. HERE IN GOTHAM, I'VE HEARD STORIES OF A FEW.
"THERE'S THE SAVAGE WHO WAS AMONG THE OLDEST MEN ALIVE. HE ENCOUNTERED IT IN ITS RAWEST FORM.
"AND THERE'S THE MAN LIKE A DEMON WHO KEEPS POOLS OF THE CHEMICAL IN SECRET PITS AROUND THE WORLD. A CORRUPTED VERSION, BUT EFFECTIVE IN ITS WAY.
"AND HIM. THE LINK BACK TO GOTHAM. THE PALE MAN. THE ONE WHO LAUGHS AT US. WHO ENCOUNTERED IT SOME-TIME BEFORE GOTHAM ROSE."
YOU WANT TO KNOW A SECRET, BATMAN?
FOR A LONG TIME, I THOUGHT YOU WERE ONE. OLDER THAN GOTHAM, A BARBATOS. IT'S WHY I DID THE TERRIBLE THINGS I DID. QUILTING LIFE ABNORMALLY... JUST TO MEET YOU!
BUT THEN I DID MEET YOU, AND I REALIZED... YOU WERE JUST... FLESH AND BLOOD!
BUDDA BUDDA BUDDA
Huh? WHERE--

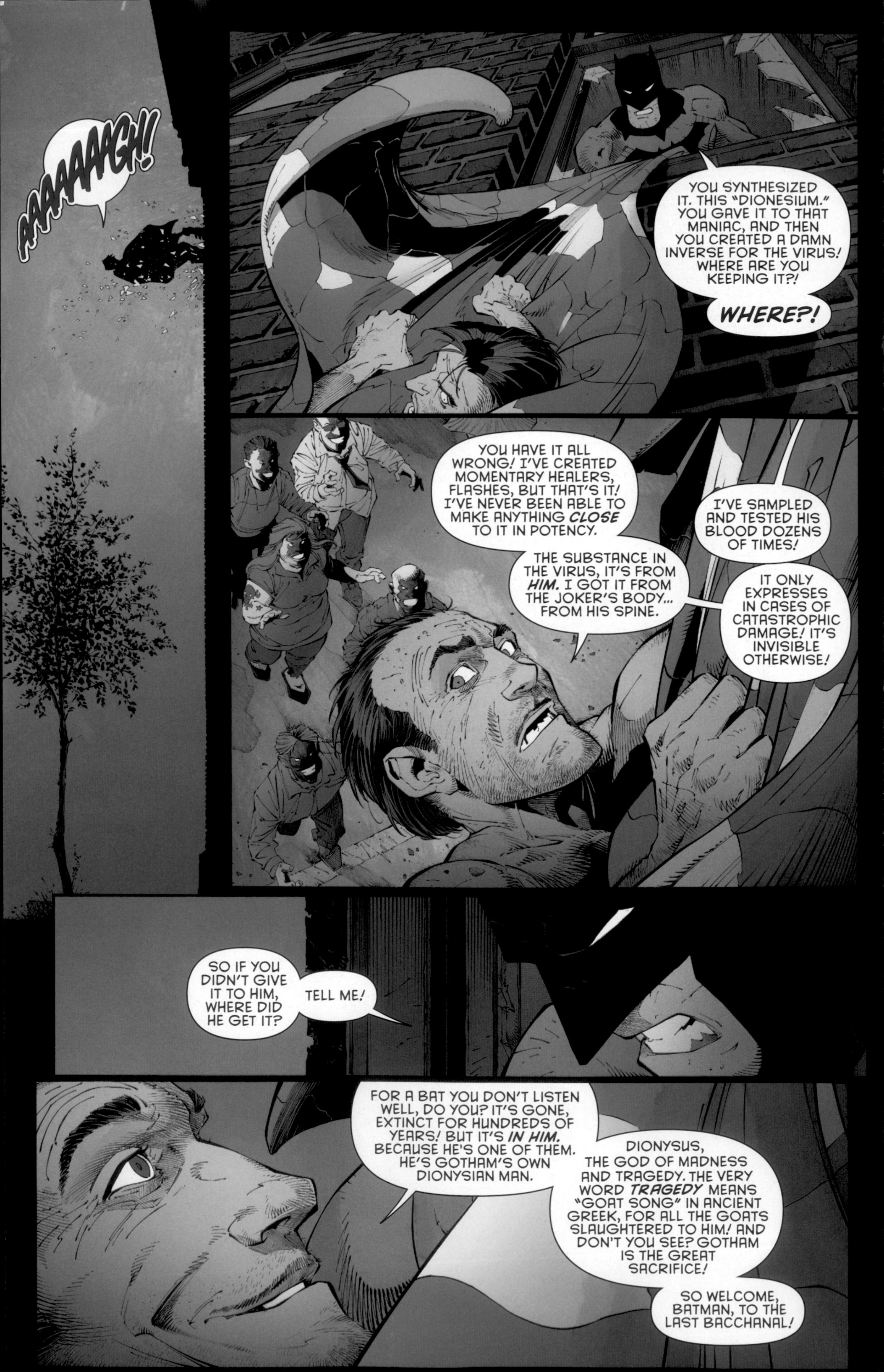
AAAAAAAGH!!
YOU SYNTHESIZED IT. THIS "DIONESIUM." YOU GAVE IT TO THAT MANIAC, AND THEN YOU CREATED A DAMN INVERSE FOR THE VIRUS! WHERE ARE YOU KEEPING IT?!
WHERE?!
YOU HAVE IT ALL WRONG! I'VE CREATED MOMENTARY HEALERS, FLASHES, BUT THAT'S IT! I'VE NEVER BEEN ABLE TO MAKE ANYTHING CLOSE TO IT IN POTENCY.
THE SUBSTANCE IN THE VIRUS, IT'S FROM HIM. I GOT IT FROM THE JOKER'S BODY... FROM HIS SPINE.
I'VE SAMPLED AND TESTED HIS BLOOD DOZENS OF TIMES!
IT ONLY EXPRESSES IN CASES OF CATASTROPHIC DAMAGE! IT'S INVISIBLE OTHERWISE!
SO IF YOU DIDN'T GIVE IT TO HIM, WHERE DID HE GET IT?
TELL ME!
FOR A BAT YOU DON'T LISTEN WELL, DO YOU? IT'S GONE, EXTINCT FOR HUNDREDS OF YEARS! BUT IT'S IN HIM. BECAUSE HE'S ONE OF THEM. HE'S GOTHAM'S OWN DIONYSIAN MAN.
DIONYSUS, THE GOD OF MADNESS AND TRAGEDY. THE VERY WORD TRAGEDY MEANS "GOAT SONG" IN ANCIENT GREEK, FOR ALL THE GOATS SLAUGHTERED TO HIM! AND DON'T YOU SEE? GOTHAM IS THE GREAT SACRIFICE!
SO WELCOME, BATMAN, TO THE LAST BACCHANAL!

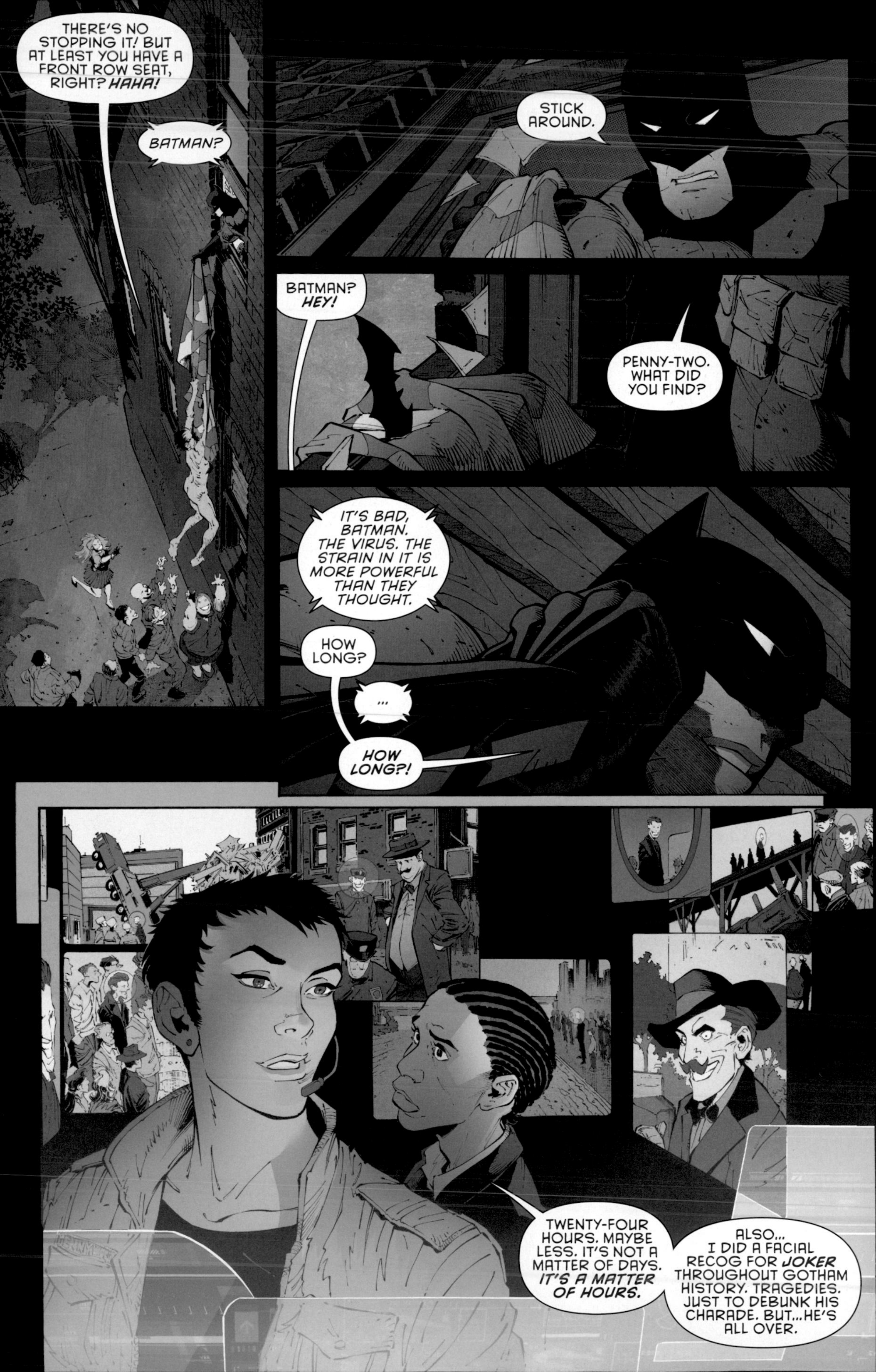
THERE'S NO STOPPING IT! BUT AT LEAST YOU HAVE A FRONT ROW SEAT, RIGHT? HAHA!
BATMAN?
STICK AROUND.
BATMAN? HEY!
PENNY-TWO. WHAT DID YOU FIND?
IT'S BAD, BATMAN. THE VIRUS. THE STRAIN IN IT IS MORE POWERFUL THAN THEY THOUGHT.
HOW LONG?
...
HOW LONG?!
TWENTY-FOUR HOURS. MAYBE LESS. IT'S NOT A MATTER OF DAYS. IT'S A MATTER OF HOURS.
ALSO... I DID A FACIAL RECOG FOR JOKER THROUGHOUT GOTHAM HISTORY. TRAGEDIES. JUST TO DEBUNK HIS CHARADE. BUT...HE'S ALL OVER.

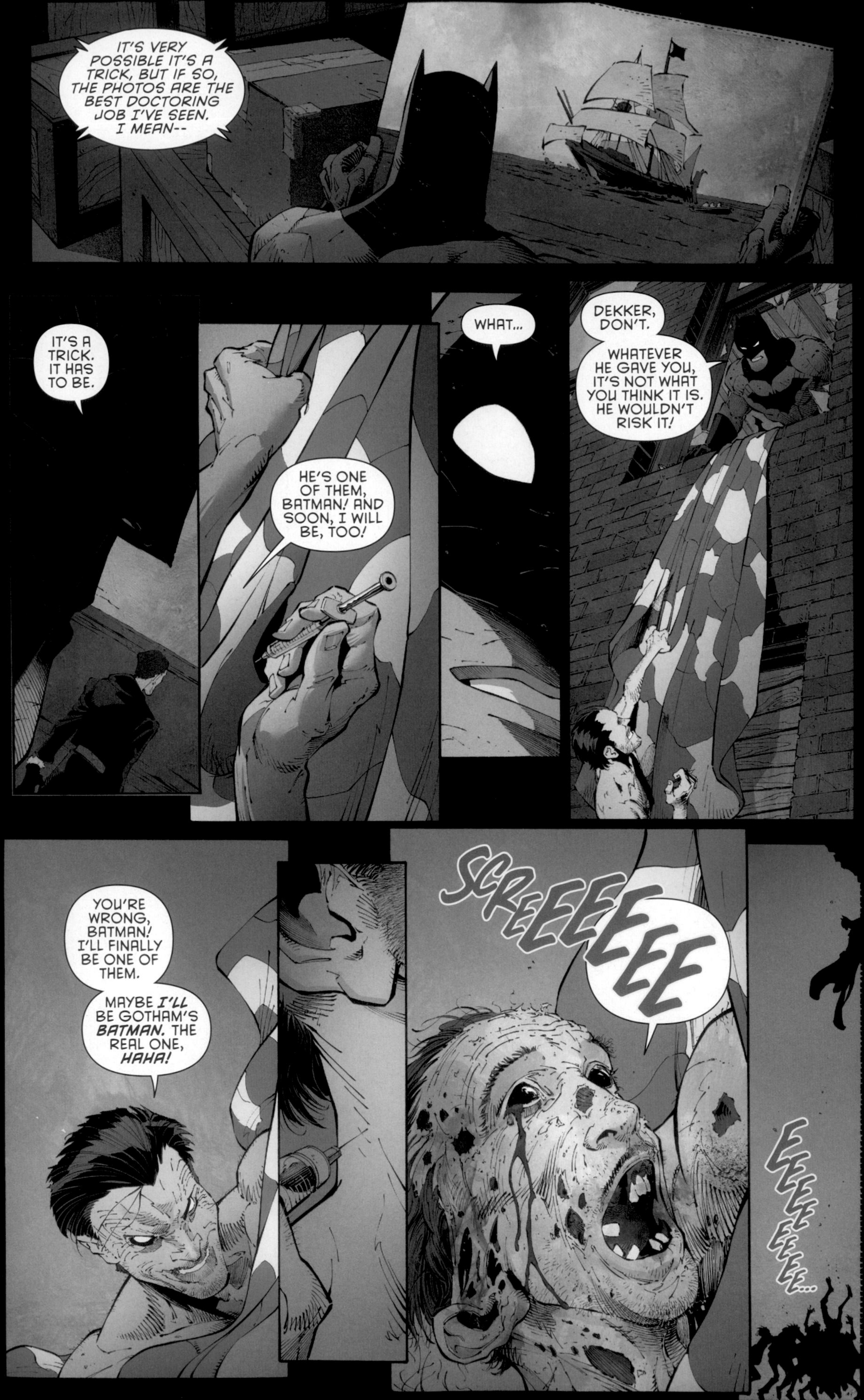
IT'S VERY POSSIBLE IT'S A TRICK, BUT IF SO, THE PHOTOS ARE THE BEST DOCTORING JOB I'VE SEEN. I MEAN--
IT'S A TRICK. IT HAS TO BE.
HE'S ONE OF THEM, BATMAN! AND SOON, I WILL BE, TOO!
WHAT...
DEKKER, DON'T.
WHATEVER HE GAVE YOU, IT'S NOT WHAT YOU THINK IT IS. HE WOULDN'T RISK IT!
YOU'RE WRONG, BATMAN! I'LL FINALLY BE ONE OF THEM.
MAYBE I'LL BE GOTHAM'S BATMAN. THE REAL ONE, HAHA!
SCREEEEEE
EEEEEEE...

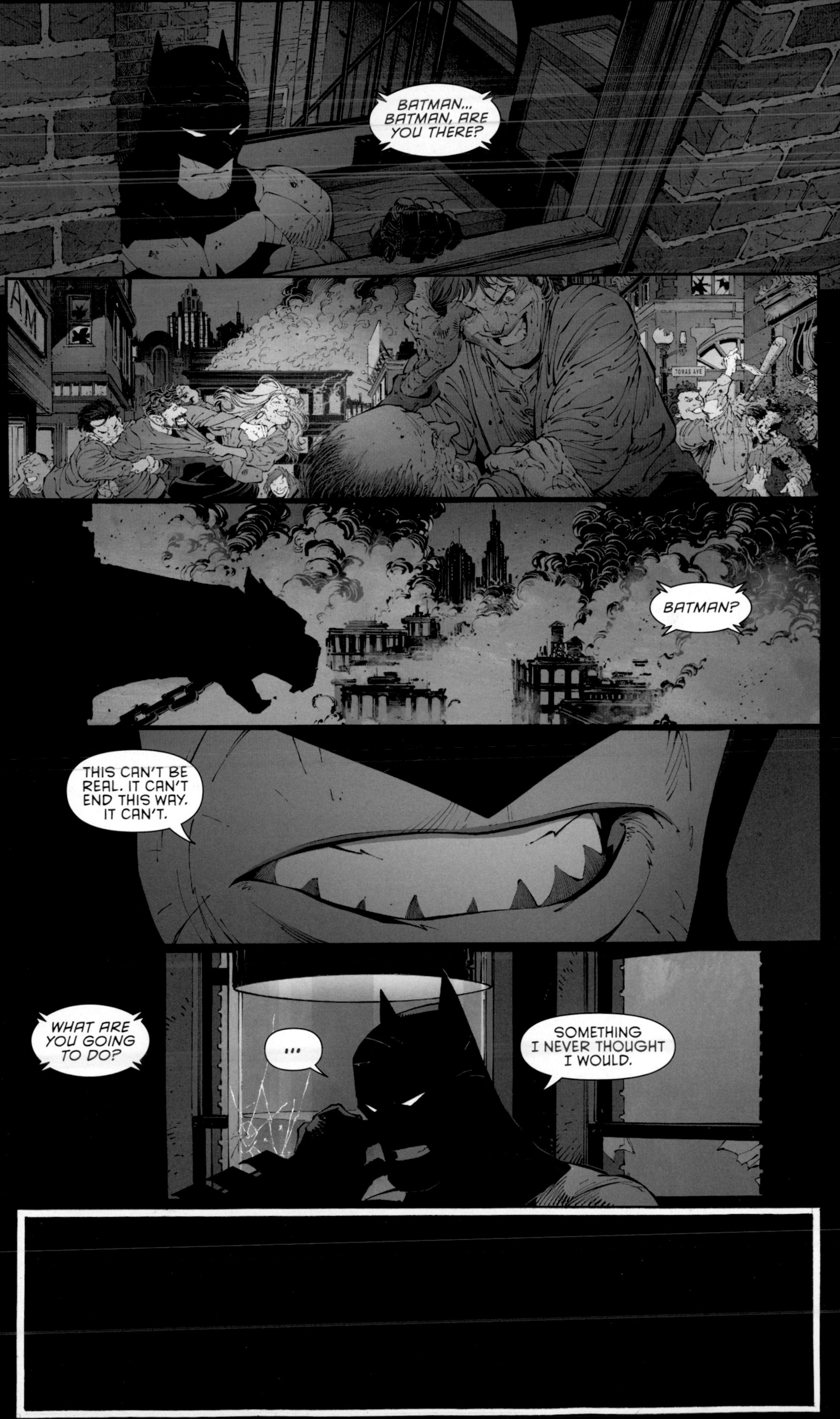
BATMAN... BATMAN, ARE YOU THERE?
TOMAS AVE
BATMAN?
THIS CAN'T BE REAL. IT CAN'T END THIS WAY. IT CAN'T.
WHAT ARE YOU GOING TO DO?
...
SOMETHING I NEVER THOUGHT I WOULD.

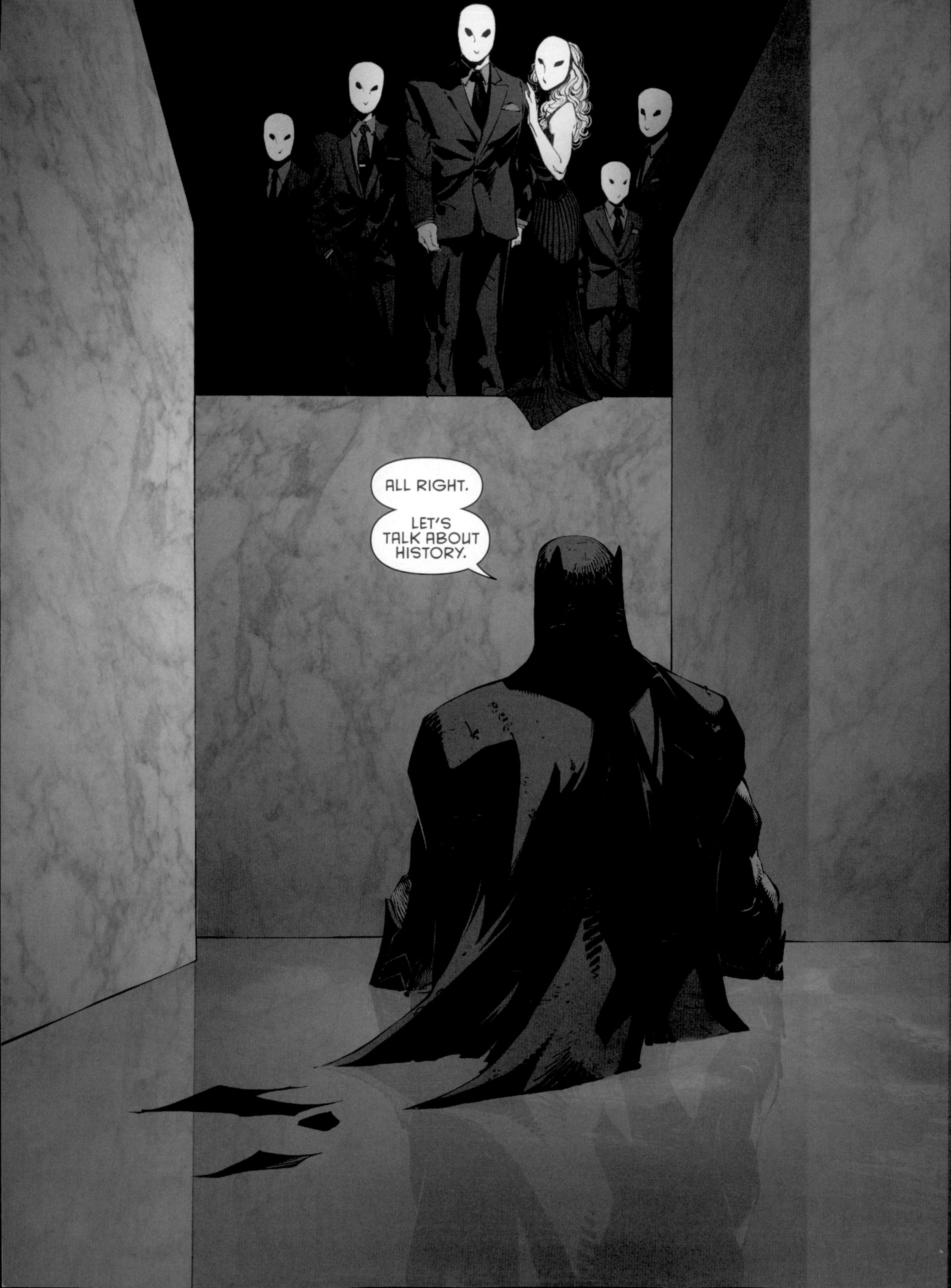
ALL RIGHT.
LET'S TALK ABOUT HISTORY.

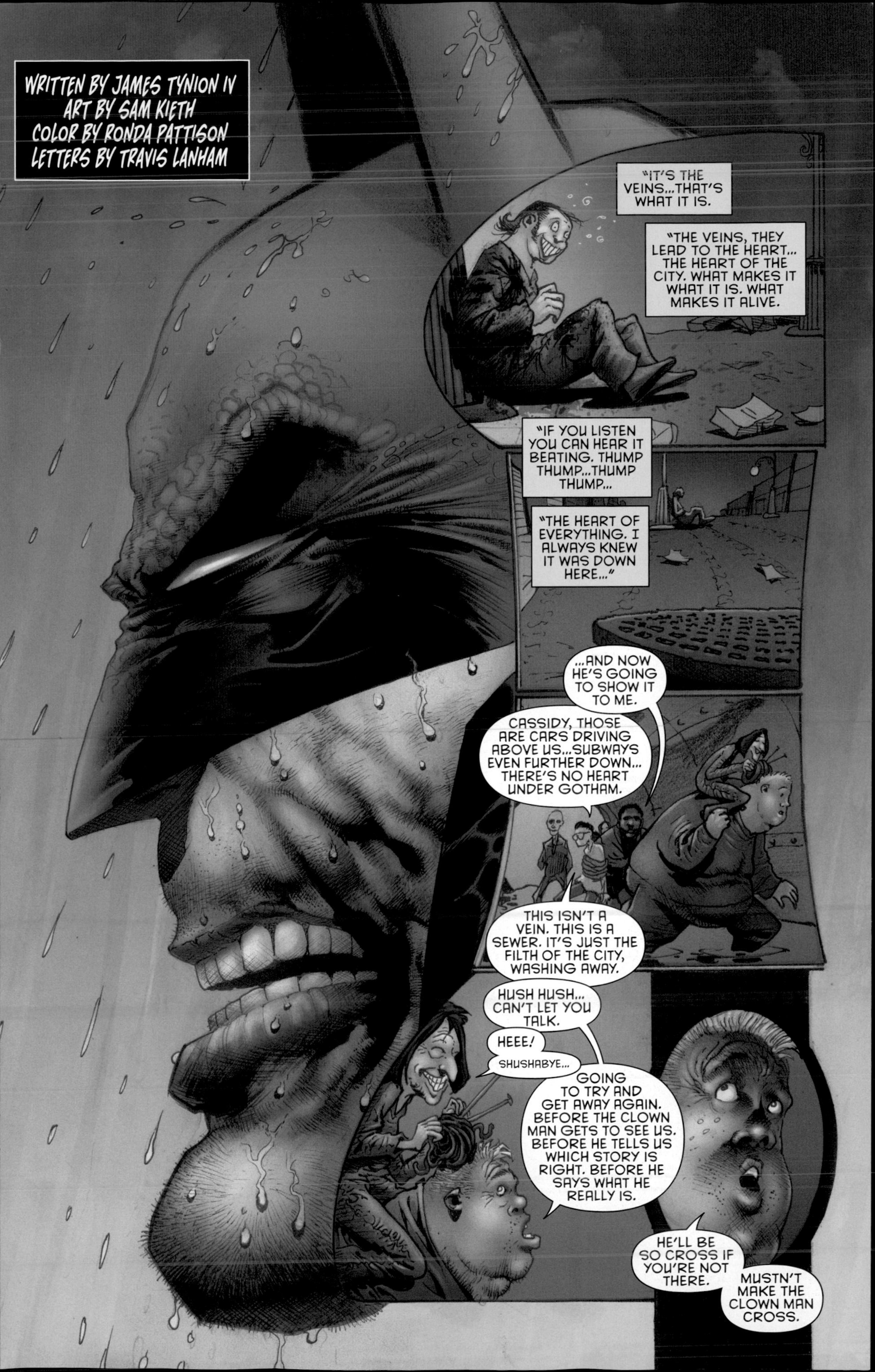
WRITTEN BY JAMES TYNION IV
ART BY SAM KIETH
COLOR BY RONDA PATTISON
LETTERS BY TRAVIS LANHAM
"IT'S THE VEINS...THAT'S WHAT IT IS.
"THE VEINS, THEY LEAD TO THE HEART... THE HEART OF THE CITY. WHAT MAKES IT WHAT IT IS. WHAT MAKES IT ALIVE.
"IF YOU LISTEN YOU CAN HEAR IT BEATING. THUMP THUMP...THUMP THUMP...
"THE HEART OF EVERYTHING. I ALWAYS KNEW IT WAS DOWN HERE..."
...AND NOW HE'S GOING TO SHOW IT TO ME.
CASSIDY, THOSE ARE CARS DRIVING ABOVE US...SUBWAYS EVEN FURTHER DOWN... THERE'S NO HEART UNDER GOTHAM.
THIS ISN'T A VEIN. THIS IS A SEWER. IT'S JUST THE FILTH OF THE CITY, WASHING AWAY.
HUSH HUSH... CAN'T LET YOU TALK.
HEEE!
SHUSHABYE...
GOING TO TRY AND GET AWAY AGAIN. BEFORE THE CLOWN MAN GETS TO SEE US. BEFORE HE TELLS US WHICH STORY IS RIGHT. BEFORE HE SAYS WHAT HE REALLY IS.
HE'LL BE SO CROSS IF YOU'RE NOT THERE.
MUSTN'T MAKE THE CLOWN MAN CROSS.

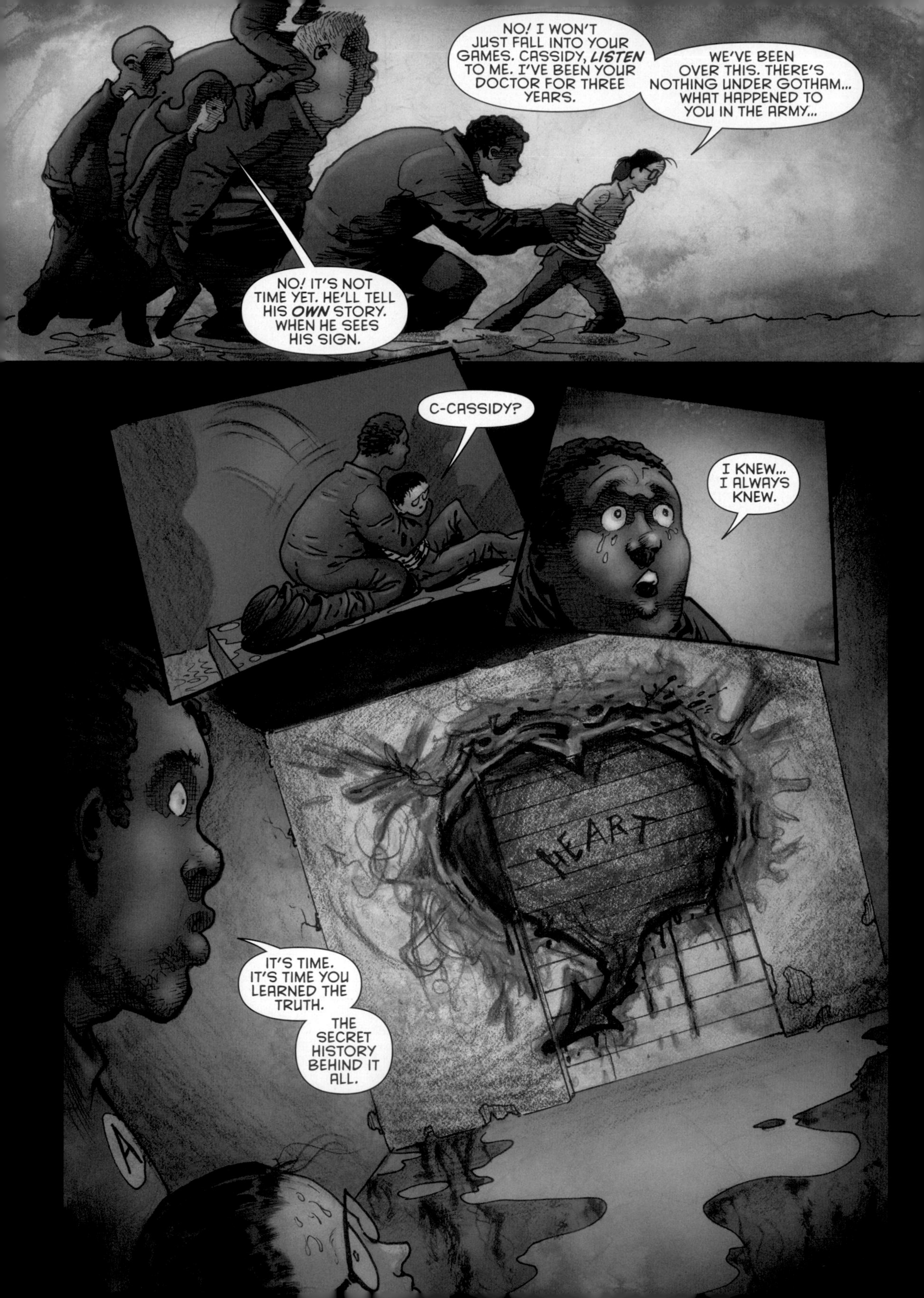

NO! I WON'T JUST FALL INTO YOUR GAMES. CASSIDY, LISTEN TO ME. I'VE BEEN YOUR DOCTOR FOR THREE YEARS.
WE'VE BEEN OVER THIS. THERE'S NOTHING UNDER GOTHAM... WHAT HAPPENED TO YOU IN THE ARMY...
NO! IT'S NOT TIME YET. HE'LL TELL HIS OWN STORY. WHEN HE SEES HIS SIGN.
C-CASSIDY?
I KNEW... I ALWAYS KNEW.
HEART
IT'S TIME. IT'S TIME YOU LEARNED THE TRUTH.
THE SECRET HISTORY BEHIND IT ALL.

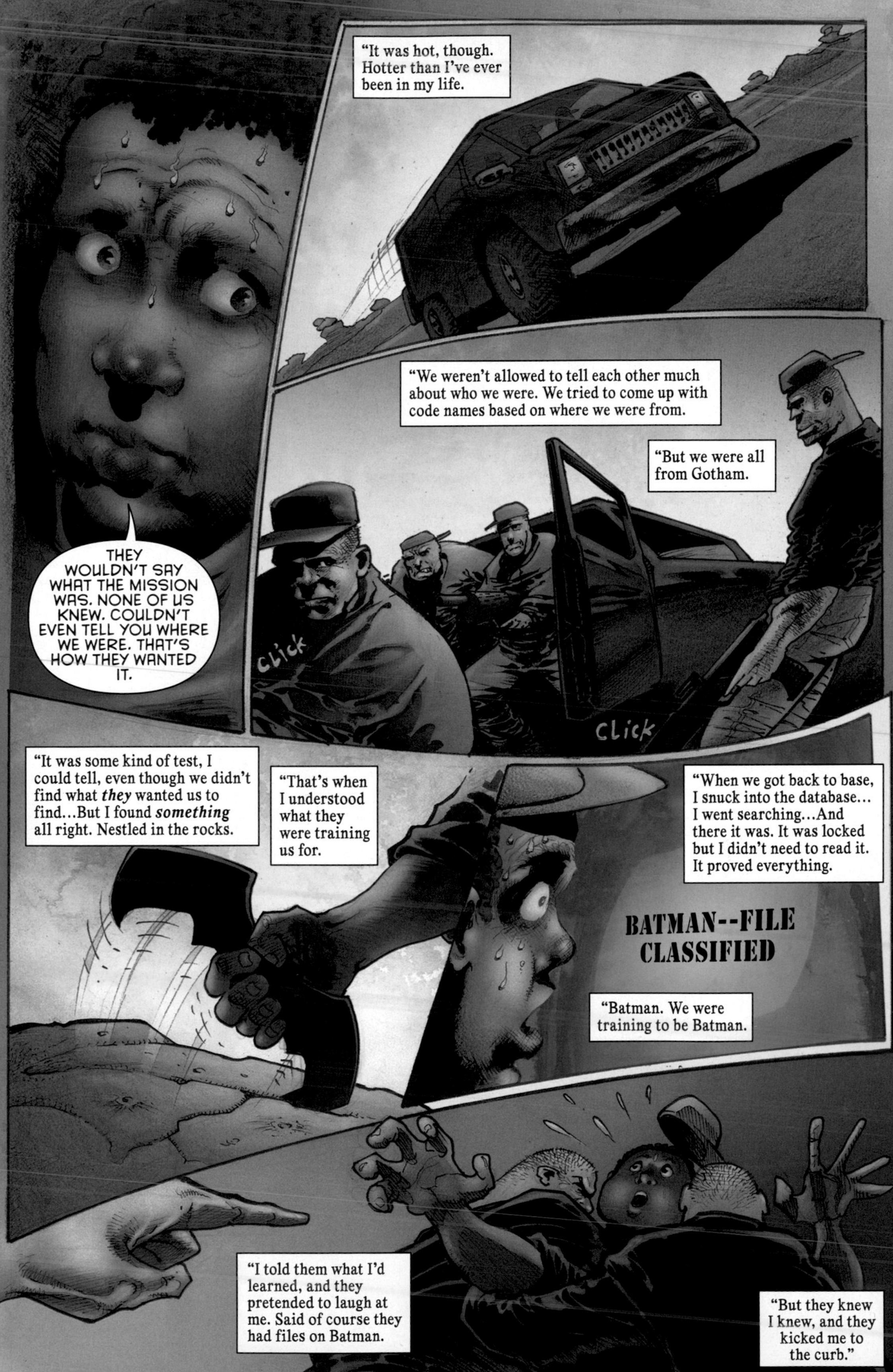
"It was hot, though. Hotter than I've ever been in my life.
THEY WOULDN'T SAY WHAT THE MISSION WAS. NONE OF US KNEW. COULDN'T EVEN TELL YOU WHERE WE WERE. THAT'S HOW THEY WANTED IT.
"We weren't allowed to tell each other much about who we were. We tried to come up with code names based on where we were from.
"But we were all from Gotham.
CLICK
CLICK
"It was some kind of test, I could tell, even though we didn't find what *they* wanted us to find...But I found *something* all right. Nestled in the rocks.
"That's when I understood what they were training us for.
"When we got back to base, I snuck into the database... I went searching...And there it was. It was locked but I didn't need to read it. It proved everything.
BATMAN--FILE CLASSIFIED
"Batman. We were training to be Batman.
"I told them what I'd learned, and they pretended to laugh at me. Said of course they had files on Batman.
"But they knew I knew, and they kicked me to the curb."

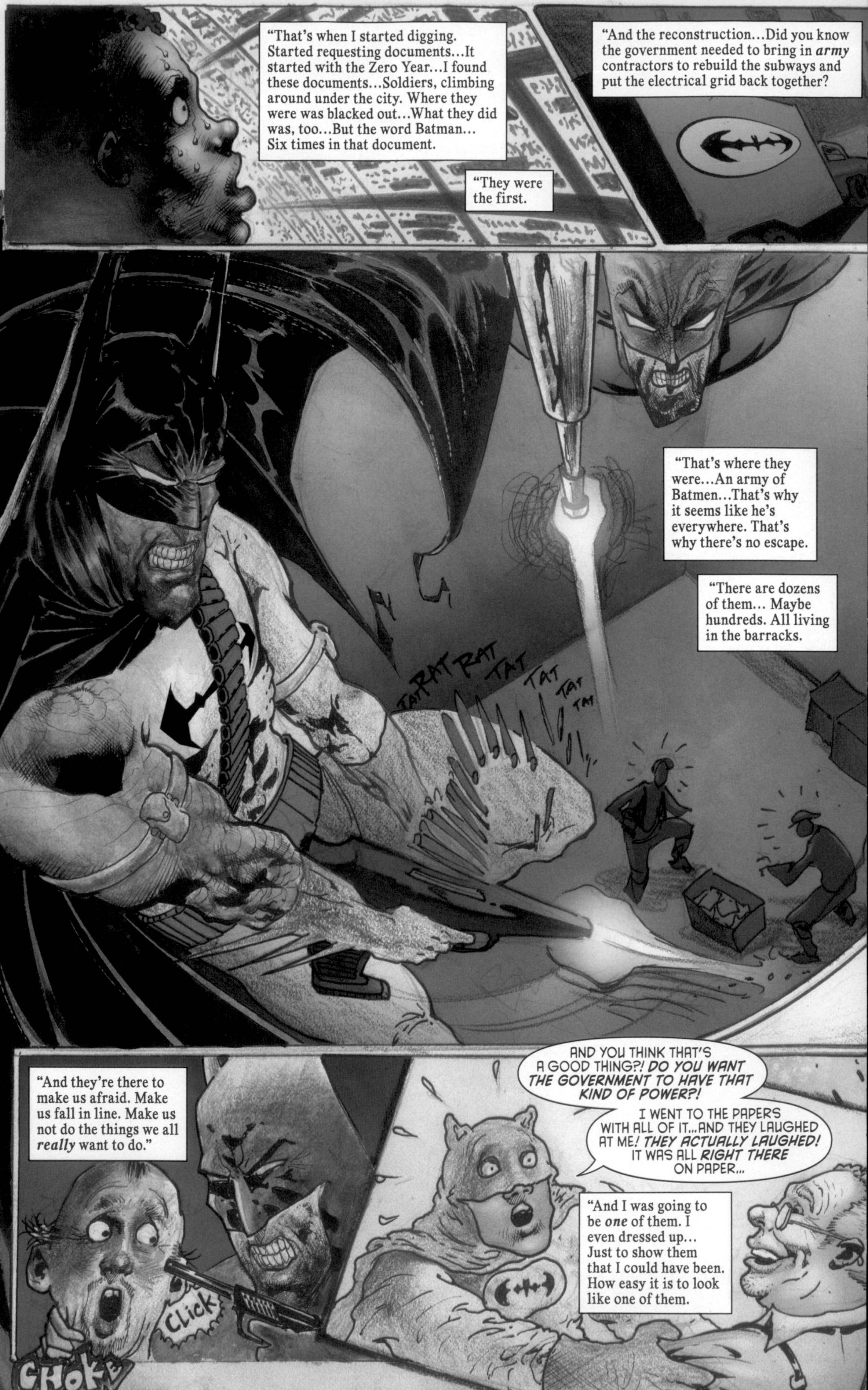
"That's when I started digging. Started requesting documents...It started with the Zero Year...I found these documents...Soldiers, climbing around under the city. Where they were was blacked out...What they did was, too...But the word Batman... Six times in that document.
"They were the first.
"And the reconstruction...Did you know the government needed to bring in *army* contractors to rebuild the subways and put the electrical grid back together?
"That's where they were...An army of Batmen...That's why it seems like he's everywhere. That's why there's no escape.
"There are dozens of them... Maybe hundreds. All living in the barracks.
TAT RAT RAT TAT TAT TAT TAT
"And they're there to make us afraid. Make us fall in line. Make us not do the things we all *really* want to do."
AND YOU THINK THAT'S A GOOD THING?! *DO YOU WANT THE GOVERNMENT TO HAVE THAT KIND OF POWER?!*
I WENT TO THE PAPERS WITH ALL OF IT...AND THEY LAUGHED AT ME! *THEY ACTUALLY LAUGHED!* IT WAS ALL *RIGHT THERE* ON PAPER...
"And I was going to be *one* of them. I even dressed up... Just to show them that I could have been. How easy it is to look like one of them.
CLICK
CHOKE

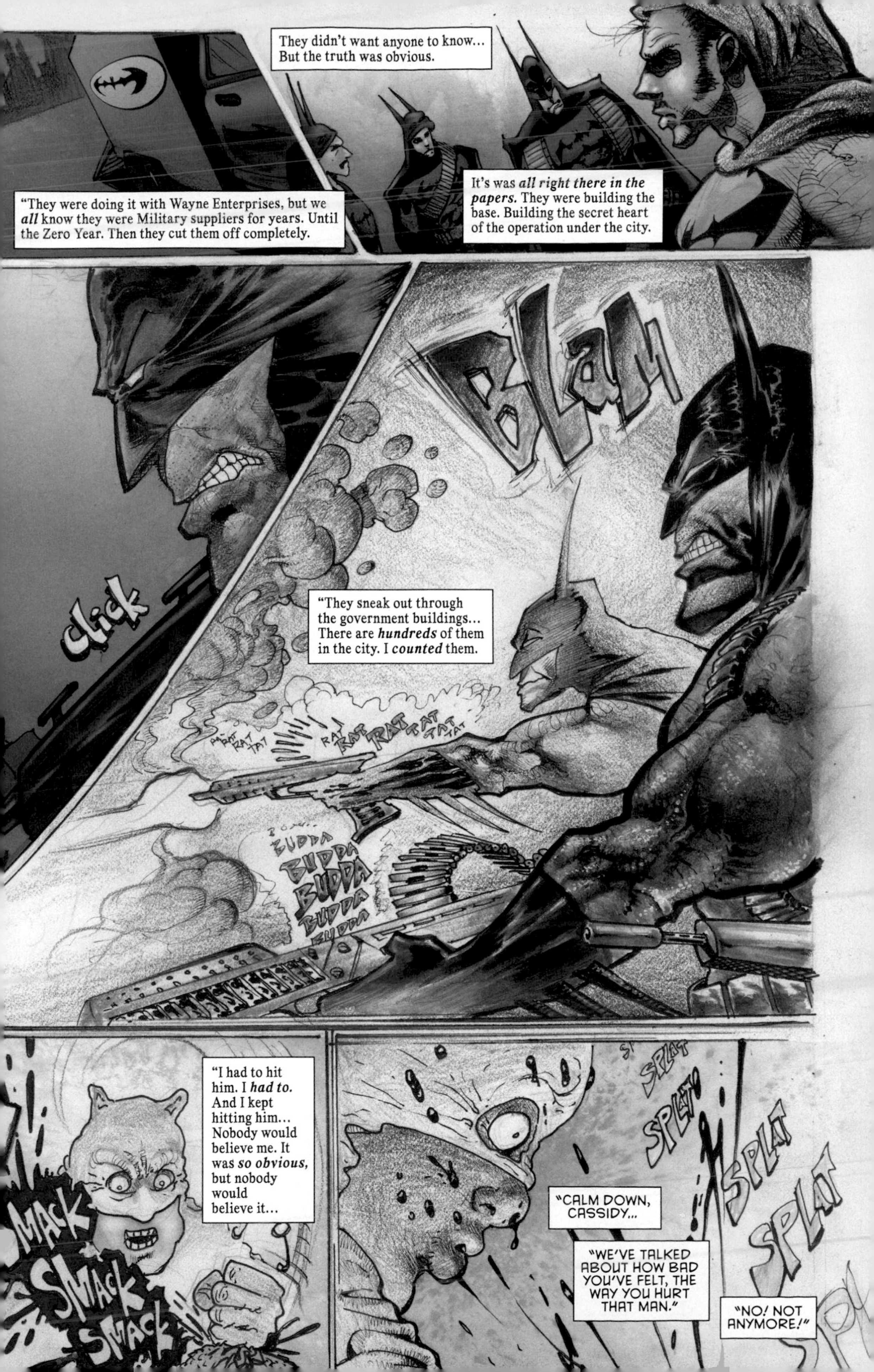

They didn't want anyone to know…
But the truth was obvious.
"They were doing it with Wayne Enterprises, but we *all* know they were Military suppliers for years. Until the Zero Year. Then they cut them off completely.
It's was ***all right there in the papers.*** They were building the base. Building the secret heart of the operation under the city.
BLAM
click
"They sneak out through the government buildings… There are ***hundreds*** of them in the city. I *counted* them.
RAT RAT RAT TAT TAT TAT
BUDDA BUDDA BUDDA BUDDA
"I had to hit him. I ***had to.*** And I kept hitting him… Nobody would believe me. It was *so obvious,* but nobody would believe it…
SMACK SMACK SMACK
SPLAT SPLAT SPLAT SPLAT
"CALM DOWN, CASSIDY…
"WE'VE TALKED ABOUT HOW BAD YOU'VE FELT, THE WAY YOU HURT THAT MAN."
"NO! NOT ANYMORE!"

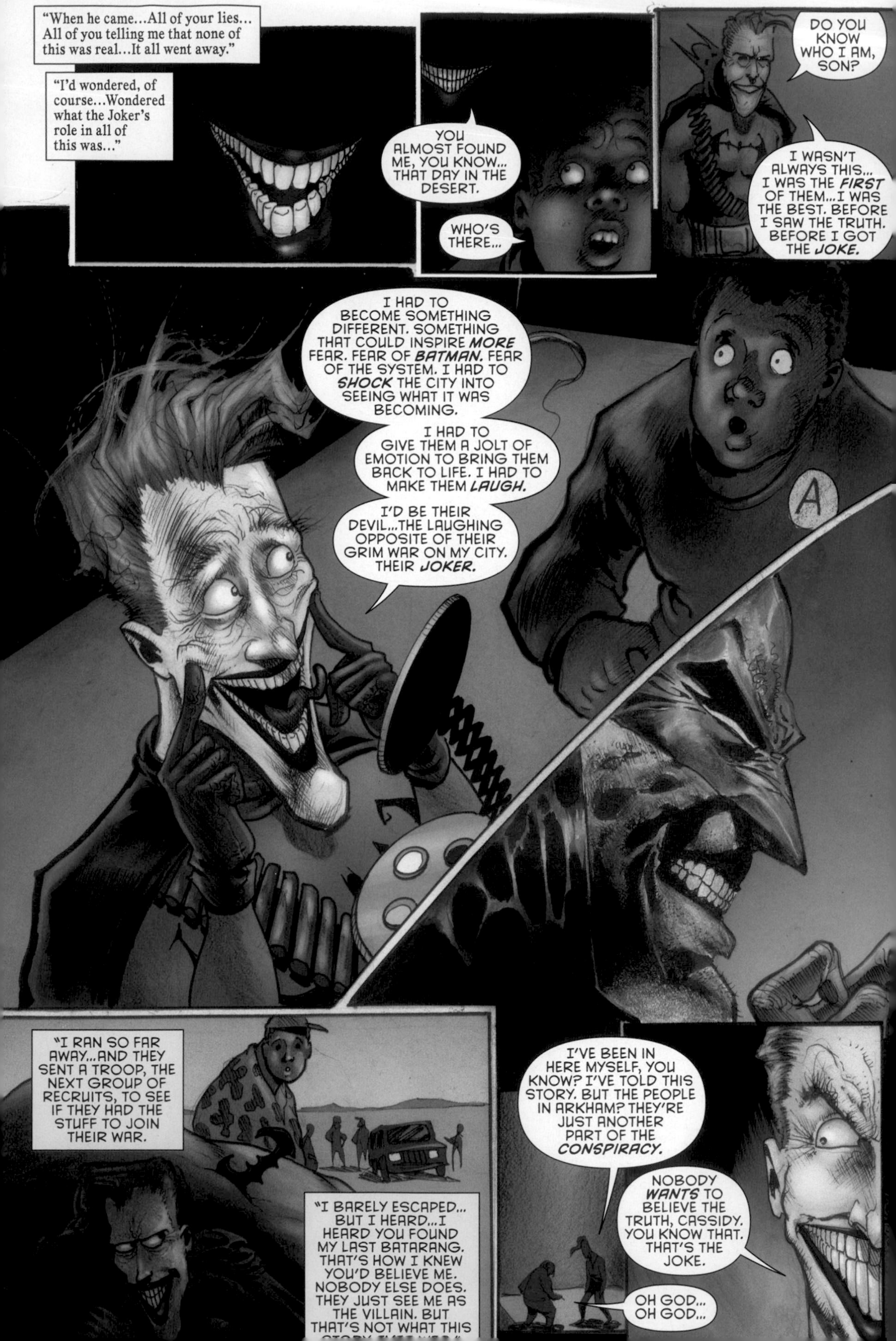

"When he came...All of your lies... All of you telling me that none of this was real...It all went away."
"I'd wondered, of course...Wondered what the Joker's role in all of this was..."
YOU ALMOST FOUND ME, YOU KNOW... THAT DAY IN THE DESERT.
WHO'S THERE...
DO YOU KNOW WHO I AM, SON?
I WASN'T ALWAYS THIS... I WAS THE FIRST OF THEM...I WAS THE BEST. BEFORE I SAW THE TRUTH. BEFORE I GOT THE JOKE.
I HAD TO BECOME SOMETHING DIFFERENT. SOMETHING THAT COULD INSPIRE MORE FEAR. FEAR OF BATMAN. FEAR OF THE SYSTEM. I HAD TO SHOCK THE CITY INTO SEEING WHAT IT WAS BECOMING.
I HAD TO GIVE THEM A JOLT OF EMOTION TO BRING THEM BACK TO LIFE. I HAD TO MAKE THEM LAUGH.
I'D BE THEIR DEVIL...THE LAUGHING OPPOSITE OF THEIR GRIM WAR ON MY CITY. THEIR JOKER.
A
"I RAN SO FAR AWAY...AND THEY SENT A TROOP, THE NEXT GROUP OF RECRUITS, TO SEE IF THEY HAD THE STUFF TO JOIN THEIR WAR.
"I BARELY ESCAPED... BUT I HEARD...I HEARD YOU FOUND MY LAST BATARANG. THAT'S HOW I KNEW YOU'D BELIEVE ME. NOBODY ELSE DOES. THEY JUST SEE ME AS THE VILLAIN. BUT THAT'S NOT WHAT THIS
I'VE BEEN IN HERE MYSELF, YOU KNOW? I'VE TOLD THIS STORY. BUT THE PEOPLE IN ARKHAM? THEY'RE JUST ANOTHER PART OF THE CONSPIRACY.
NOBODY WANTS TO BELIEVE THE TRUTH, CASSIDY. YOU KNOW THAT. THAT'S THE JOKE.
OH GOD... OH GOD...

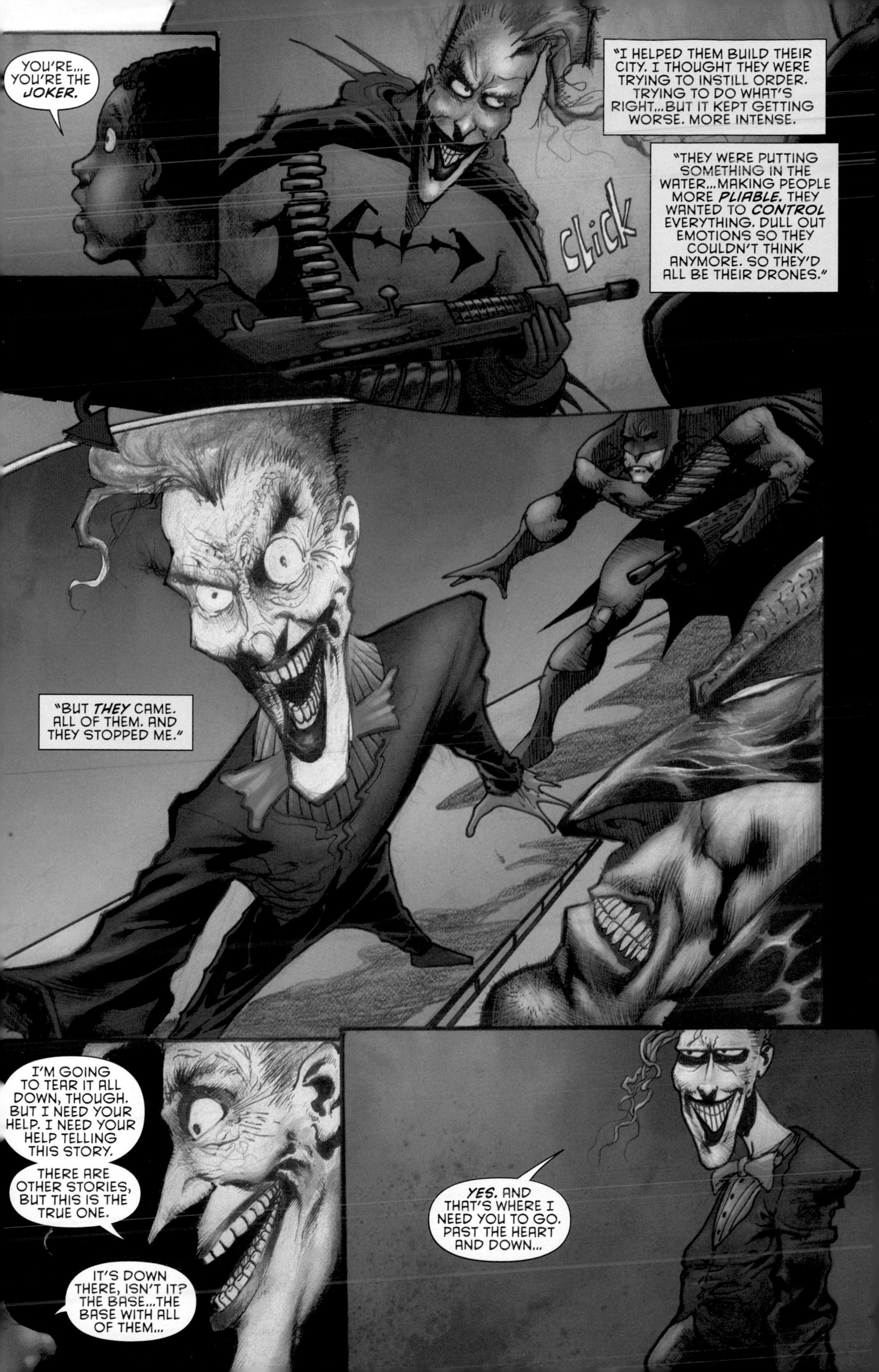

YOU'RE... YOU'RE THE JOKER.
"I HELPED THEM BUILD THEIR CITY. I THOUGHT THEY WERE TRYING TO INSTILL ORDER. TRYING TO DO WHAT'S RIGHT...BUT IT KEPT GETTING WORSE. MORE INTENSE.
"THEY WERE PUTTING SOMETHING IN THE WATER...MAKING PEOPLE MORE PLIABLE. THEY WANTED TO CONTROL EVERYTHING. DULL OUT EMOTIONS SO THEY COULDN'T THINK ANYMORE. SO THEY'D ALL BE THEIR DRONES."
CLICK
"BUT THEY CAME. ALL OF THEM. AND THEY STOPPED ME."
I'M GOING TO TEAR IT ALL DOWN, THOUGH. BUT I NEED YOUR HELP. I NEED YOUR HELP TELLING THIS STORY.
THERE ARE OTHER STORIES, BUT THIS IS THE TRUE ONE.
IT'S DOWN THERE, ISN'T IT? THE BASE...THE BASE WITH ALL OF THEM...
YES. AND THAT'S WHERE I NEED YOU TO GO. PAST THE HEART AND DOWN...

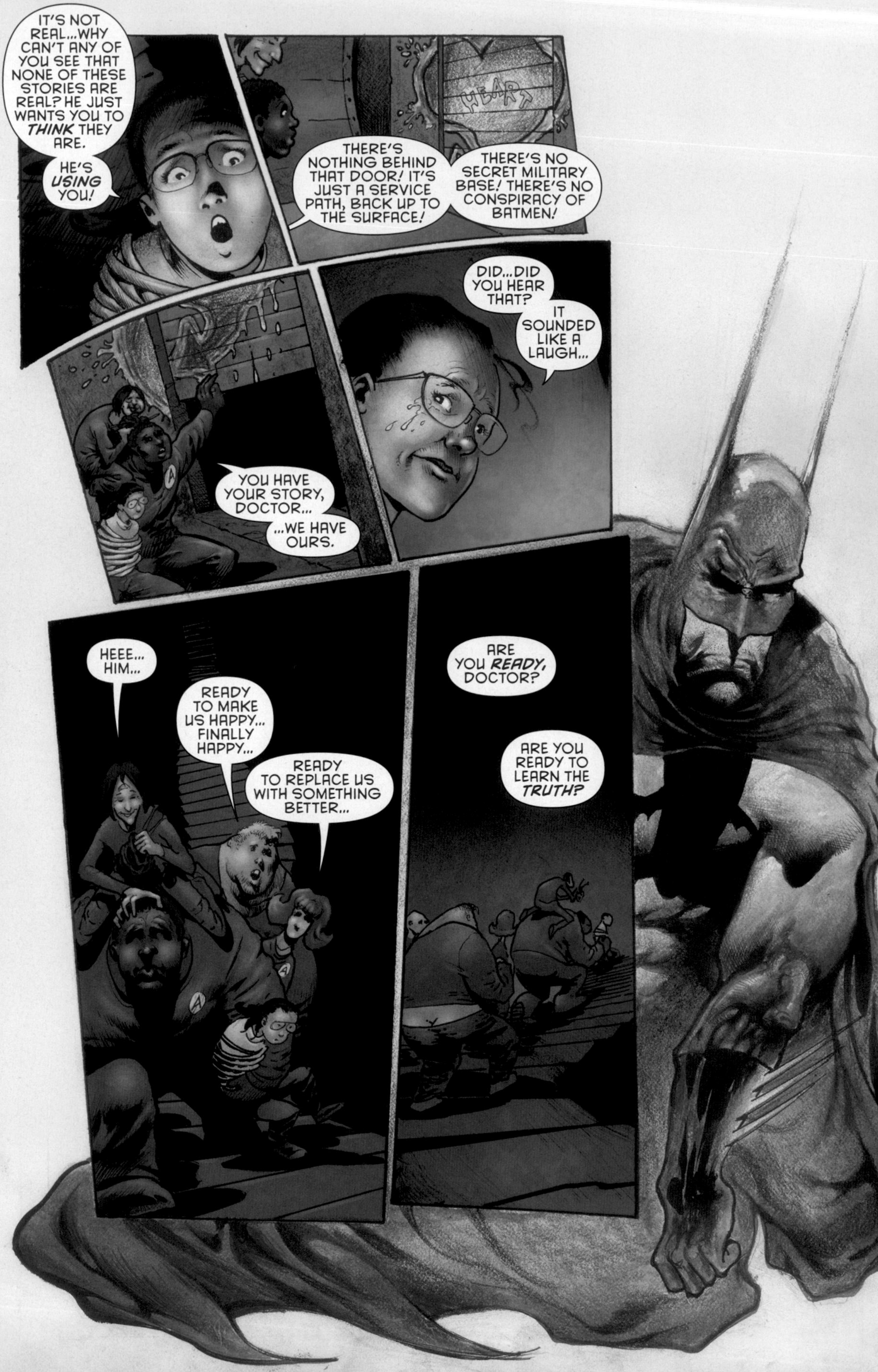
IT'S NOT REAL...WHY CAN'T ANY OF YOU SEE THAT NONE OF THESE STORIES ARE REAL? HE JUST WANTS YOU TO *THINK* THEY ARE.
HE'S *USING* YOU!
HEART
THERE'S NOTHING BEHIND THAT DOOR! IT'S JUST A SERVICE PATH, BACK UP TO THE SURFACE!
THERE'S NO SECRET MILITARY BASE! THERE'S NO CONSPIRACY OF BATMEN!
YOU HAVE YOUR STORY, DOCTOR...
...WE HAVE OURS.
DID...DID YOU HEAR THAT?
IT SOUNDED LIKE A LAUGH...
HEEE... HIM...
READY TO MAKE US HAPPY... FINALLY HAPPY...
READY TO REPLACE US WITH SOMETHING BETTER...
ARE YOU *READY,* DOCTOR?
ARE YOU READY TO LEARN THE *TRUTH?*

Cover by **JOY ANG**

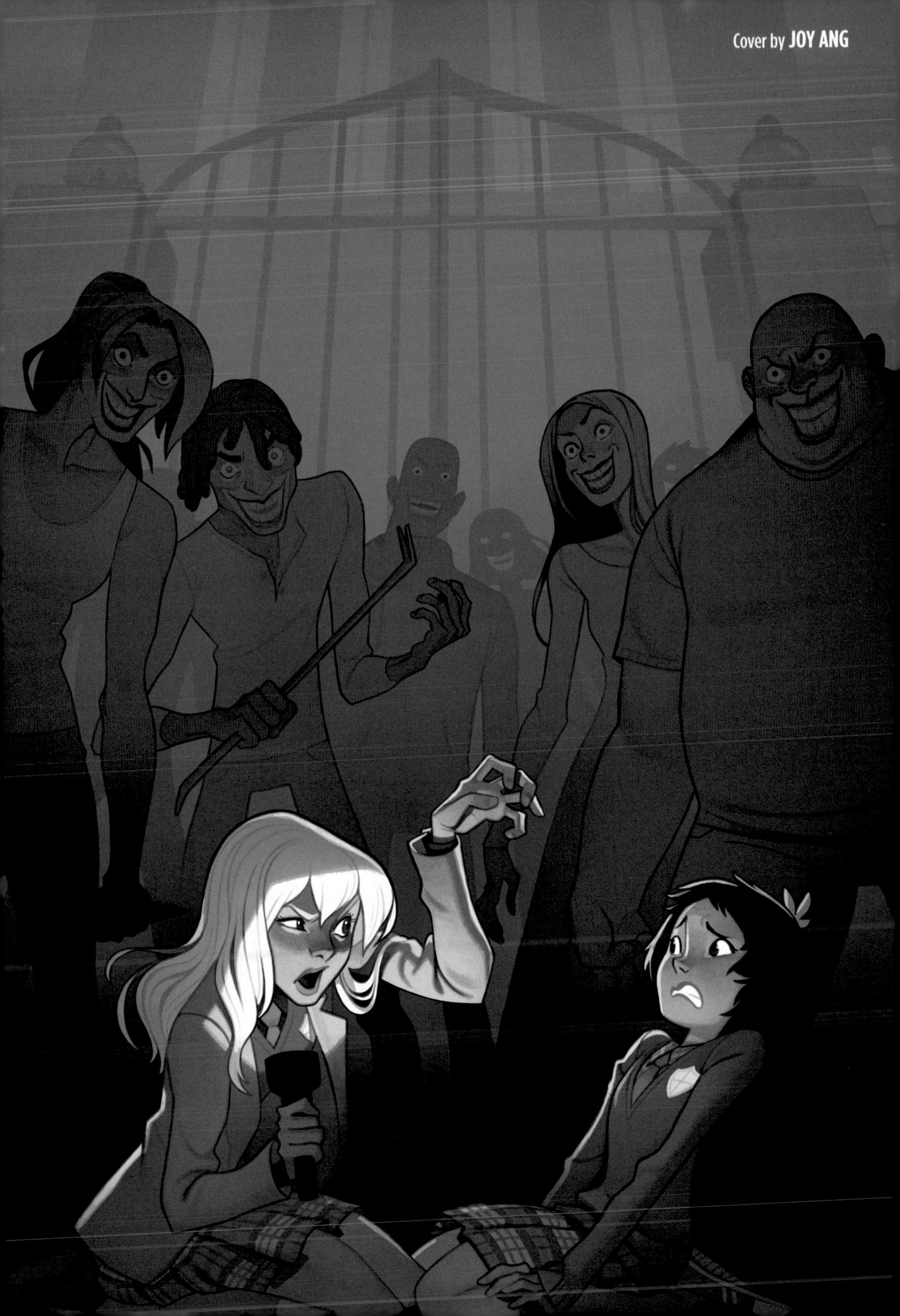

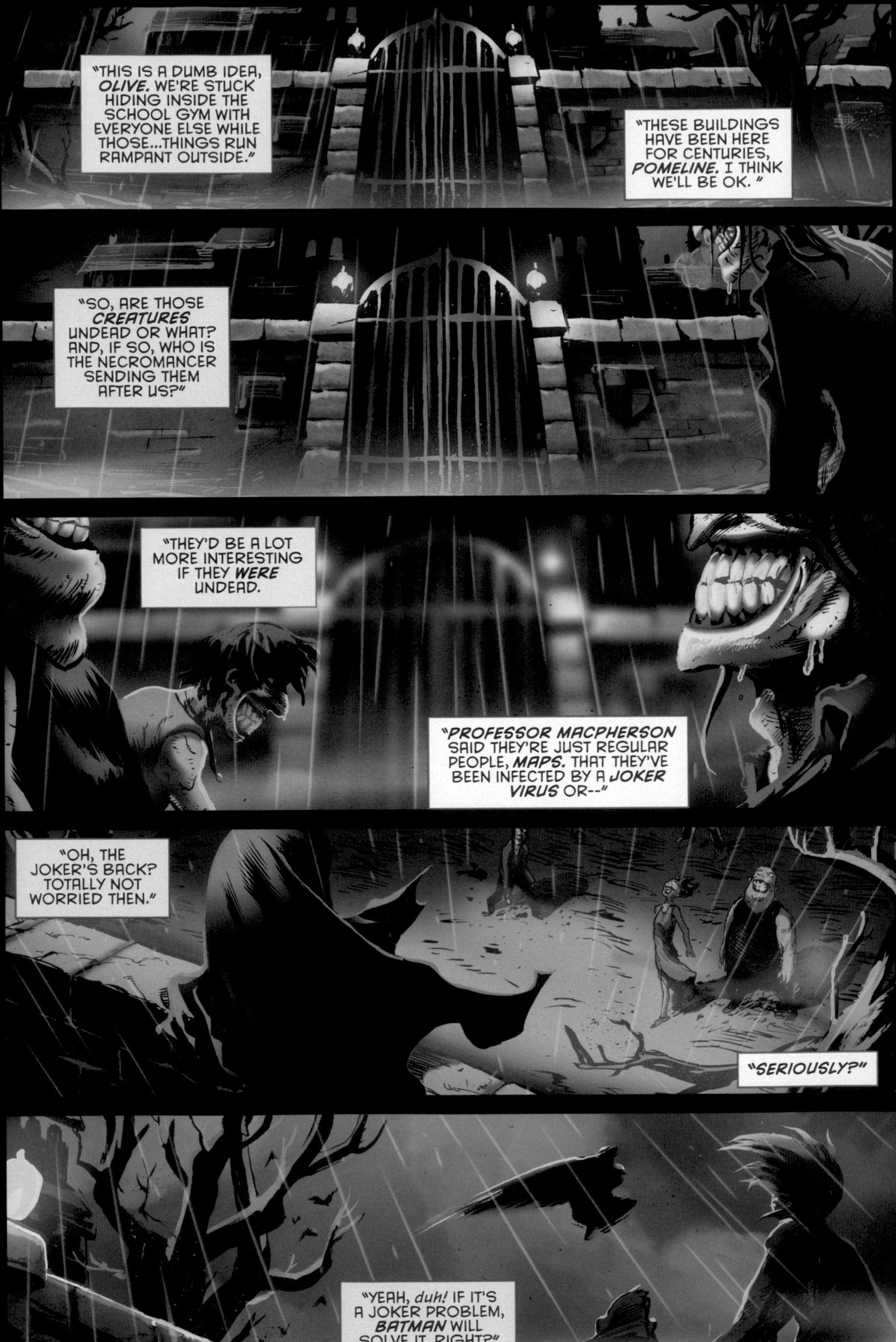
"THIS IS A DUMB IDEA, OLIVE. WE'RE STUCK HIDING INSIDE THE SCHOOL GYM WITH EVERYONE ELSE WHILE THOSE...THINGS RUN RAMPANT OUTSIDE."
"THESE BUILDINGS HAVE BEEN HERE FOR CENTURIES, POMELINE. I THINK WE'LL BE OK."
"SO, ARE THOSE CREATURES UNDEAD OR WHAT? AND, IF SO, WHO IS THE NECROMANCER SENDING THEM AFTER US?"
"THEY'D BE A LOT MORE INTERESTING IF THEY WERE UNDEAD.
"PROFESSOR MACPHERSON SAID THEY'RE JUST REGULAR PEOPLE, MAPS. THAT THEY'VE BEEN INFECTED BY A JOKER VIRUS OR--"
"OH, THE JOKER'S BACK? TOTALLY NOT WORRIED THEN."
"SERIOUSLY?"
"YEAH, duh! IF IT'S A JOKER PROBLEM, BATMAN WILL SOLVE IT, RIGHT?"

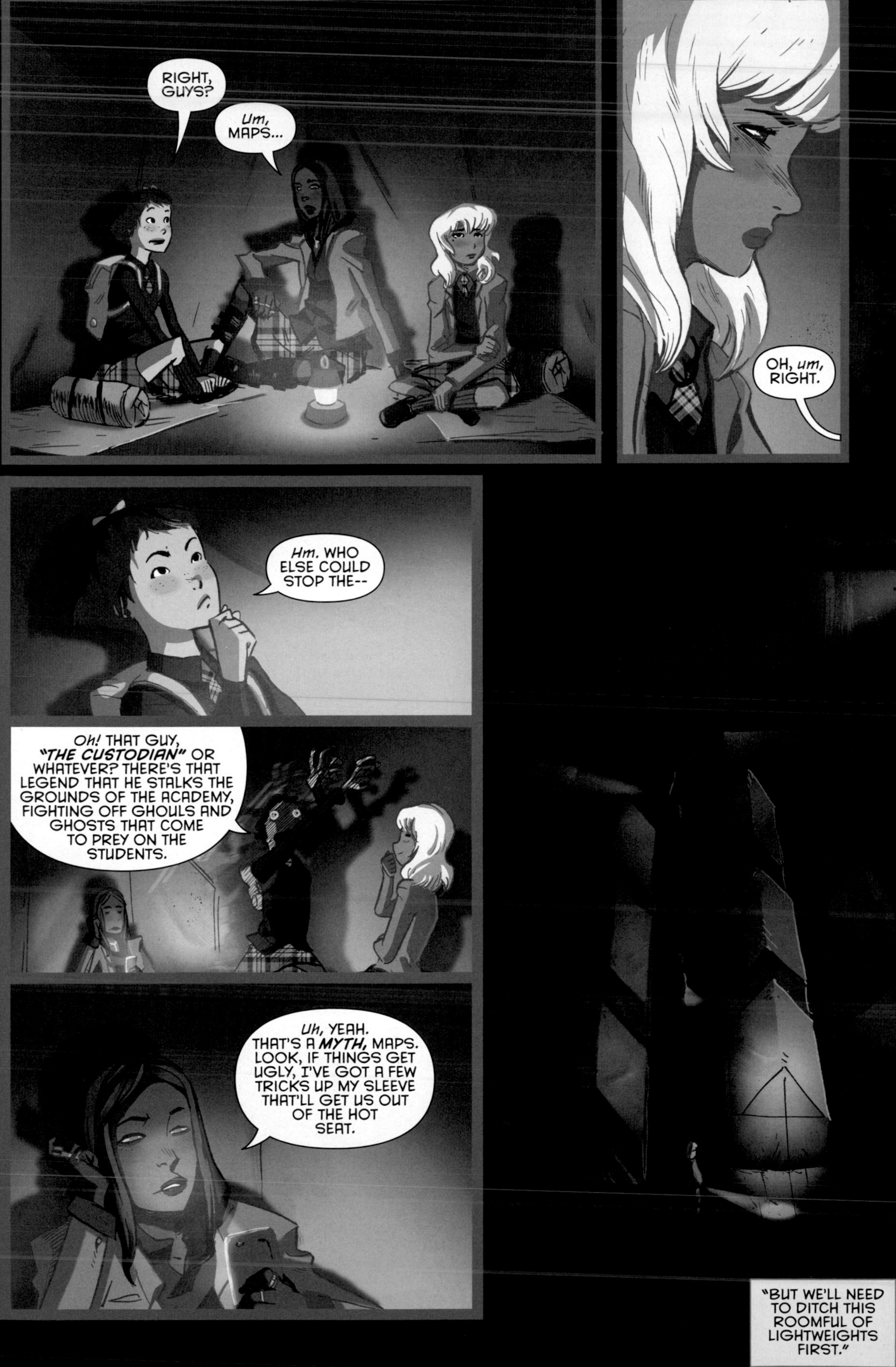
RIGHT, GUYS?
Um, MAPS...
OH, um, RIGHT.
Hm. WHO ELSE COULD STOP THE--
Oh! THAT GUY, "THE CUSTODIAN" OR WHATEVER? THERE'S THAT LEGEND THAT HE STALKS THE GROUNDS OF THE ACADEMY, FIGHTING OFF GHOULS AND GHOSTS THAT COME TO PREY ON THE STUDENTS.
Uh, YEAH. THAT'S A MYTH, MAPS. LOOK, IF THINGS GET UGLY, I'VE GOT A FEW TRICKS UP MY SLEEVE THAT'LL GET US OUT OF THE HOT SEAT.
"BUT WE'LL NEED TO DITCH THIS ROOMFUL OF LIGHTWEIGHTS FIRST."

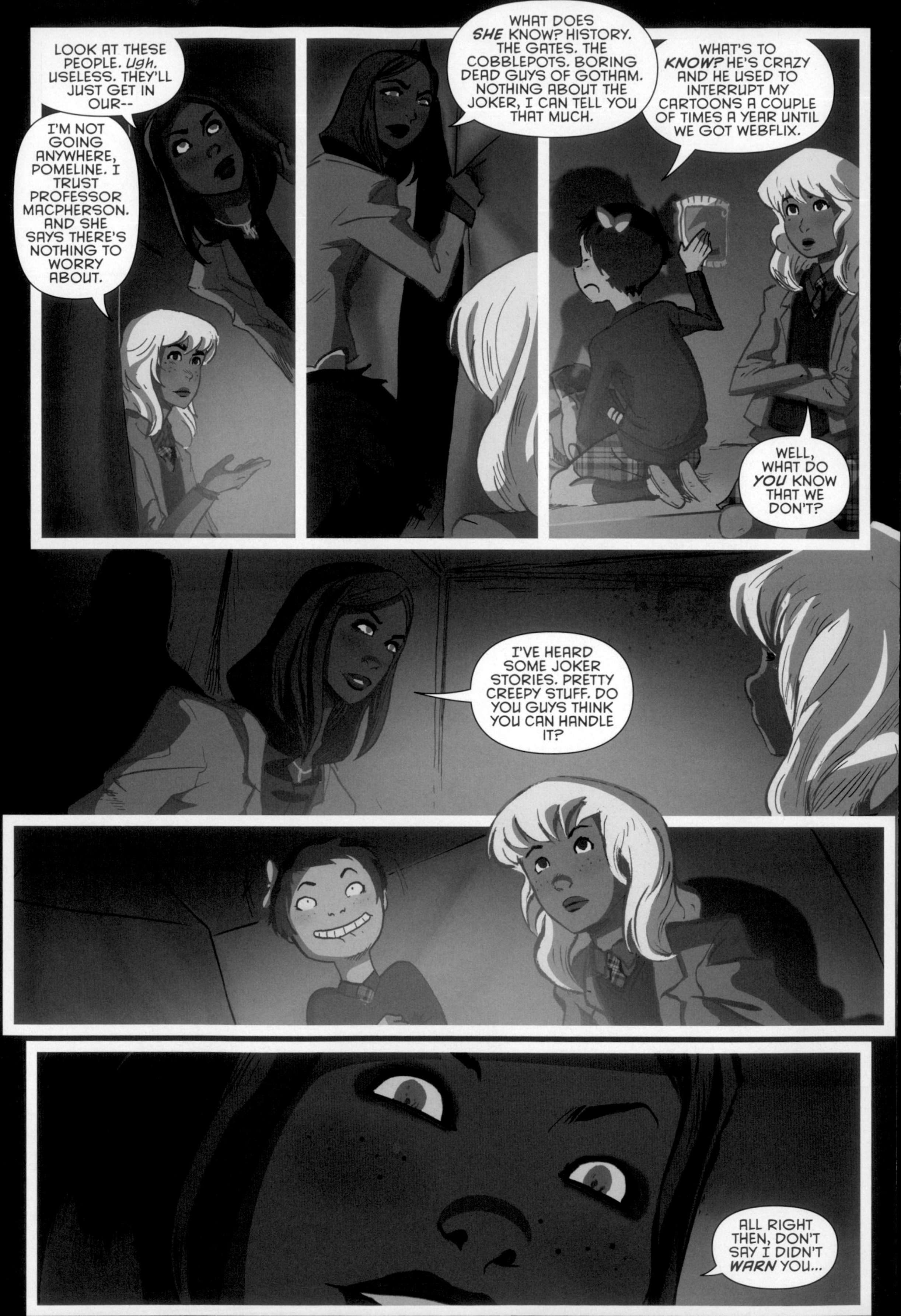
LOOK AT THESE PEOPLE. *Ugh.* USELESS. THEY'LL JUST GET IN OUR--
I'M NOT GOING ANYWHERE, POMELINE. I TRUST PROFESSOR MACPHERSON. AND SHE SAYS THERE'S NOTHING TO WORRY ABOUT.
WHAT DOES *SHE* KNOW? HISTORY. THE GATES. THE COBBLEPOTS. BORING DEAD GUYS OF GOTHAM. NOTHING ABOUT THE JOKER, I CAN TELL YOU THAT MUCH.
WHAT'S TO *KNOW?* HE'S CRAZY AND HE USED TO INTERRUPT MY CARTOONS A COUPLE OF TIMES A YEAR UNTIL WE GOT WEBFLIX.
WELL, WHAT DO *YOU* KNOW THAT WE DON'T?
I'VE HEARD SOME JOKER STORIES. PRETTY CREEPY STUFF. DO YOU GUYS THINK YOU CAN HANDLE IT?
ALL RIGHT THEN, DON'T SAY I DIDN'T *WARN* YOU...

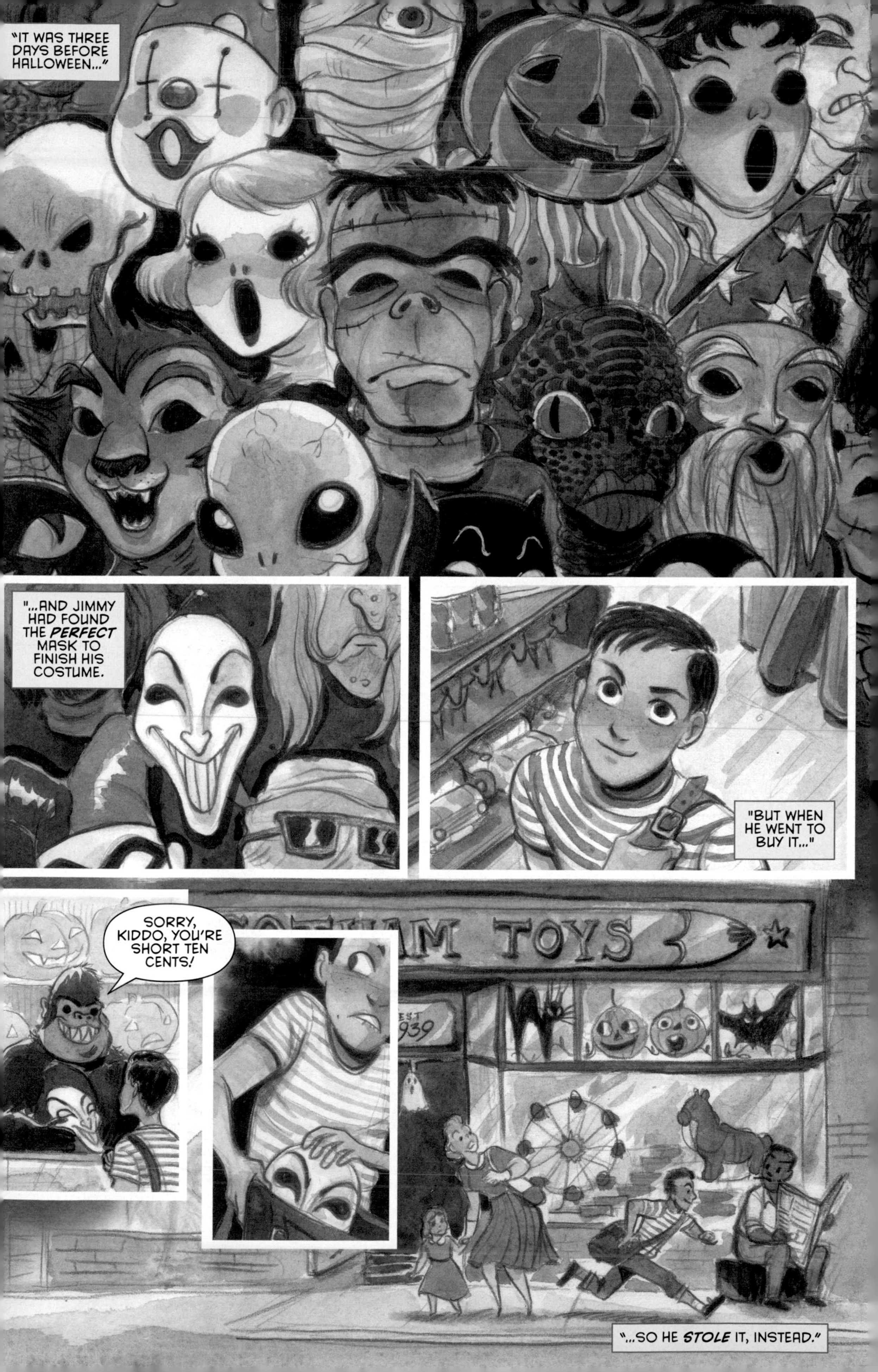
"IT WAS THREE DAYS BEFORE HALLOWEEN..."
"...AND JIMMY HAD FOUND THE *PERFECT* MASK TO FINISH HIS COSTUME.
"BUT WHEN HE WENT TO BUY IT..."
SORRY, KIDDO, YOU'RE SHORT TEN CENTS!
TOYS
EST 1939
"...SO HE *STOLE* IT, INSTEAD."

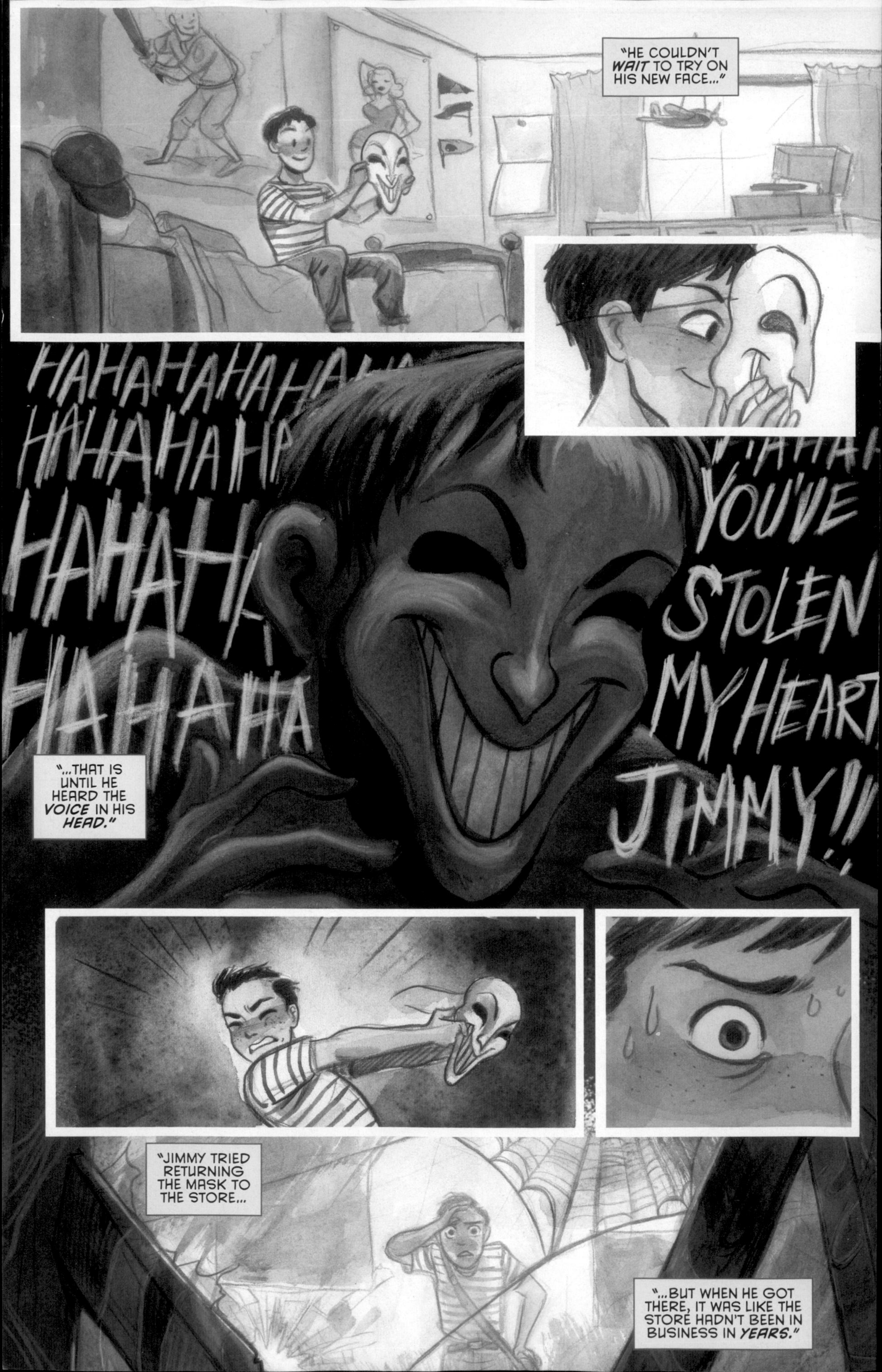
"HE COULDN'T *WAIT* TO TRY ON HIS NEW FACE..."
HAHAHAHAHAHA
HAHAHAHA
HAHAH
HAHAHAHA
"...THAT IS UNTIL HE HEARD THE *VOICE* IN HIS *HEAD*."
YOU'VE STOLEN MY HEART JIMMY!!
"JIMMY TRIED RETURNING THE MASK TO THE STORE...
"...BUT WHEN HE GOT THERE, IT WAS LIKE THE STORE HADN'T BEEN IN BUSINESS IN *YEARS*."

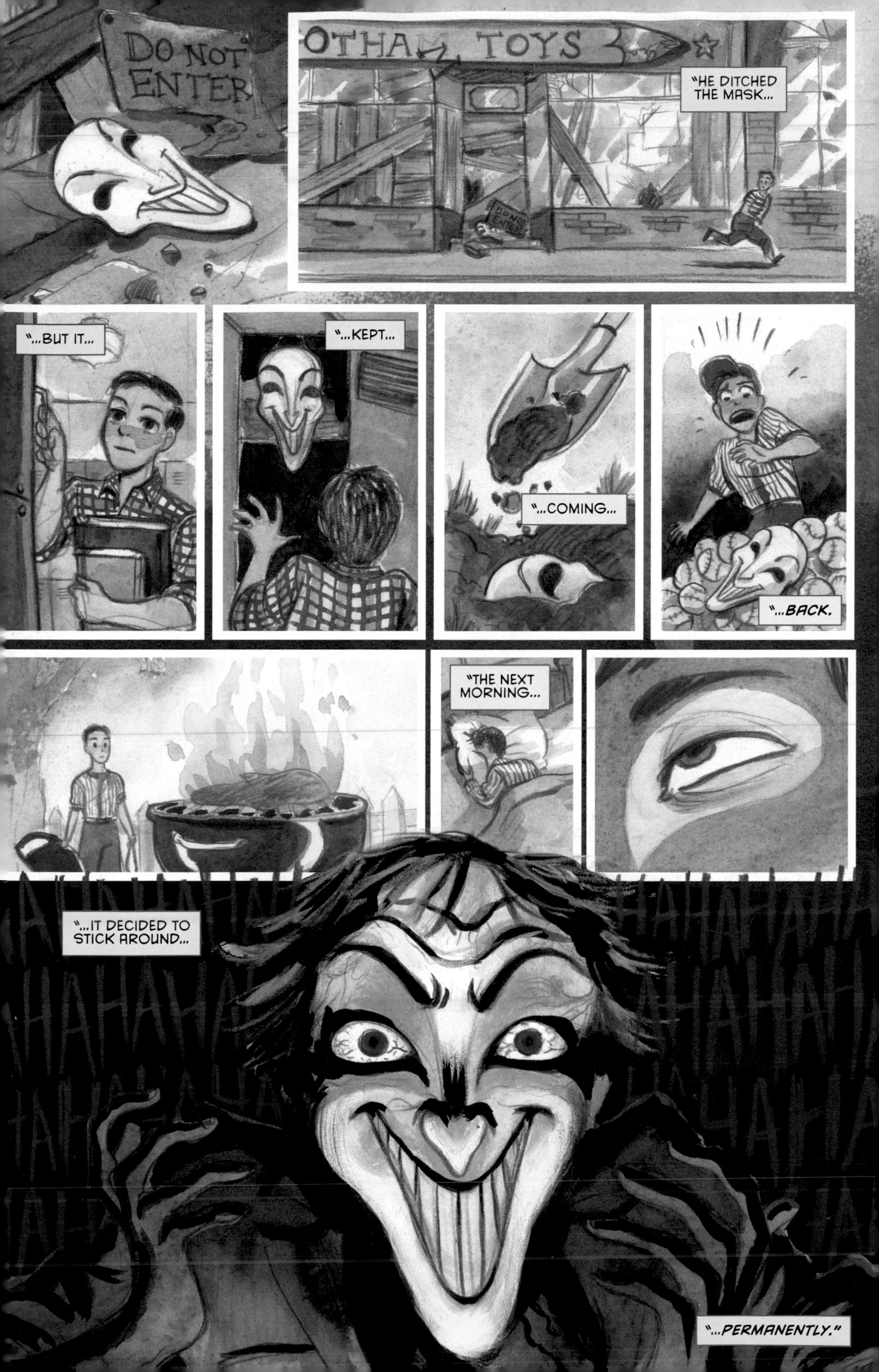
DO NOT ENTER
OTHAM TOYS
"HE DITCHED THE MASK...
"...BUT IT...
"...KEPT...
"...COMING...
"...BACK.
"THE NEXT MORNING...
"...IT DECIDED TO STICK AROUND...
"...PERMANENTLY."

"POOR JIMMY.

"NOWADAYS HE ONLY SHOWS HIS FACE AROUND *HALLOWEEN.*

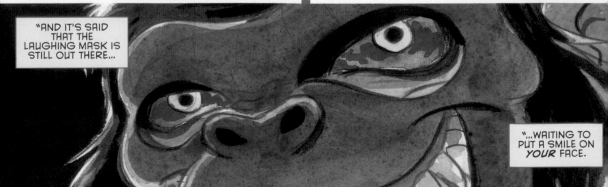

"AND IT'S SAID THAT THE LAUGHING MASK IS STILL OUT THERE...

"...WAITING TO PUT A SMILE ON *YOUR* FACE.

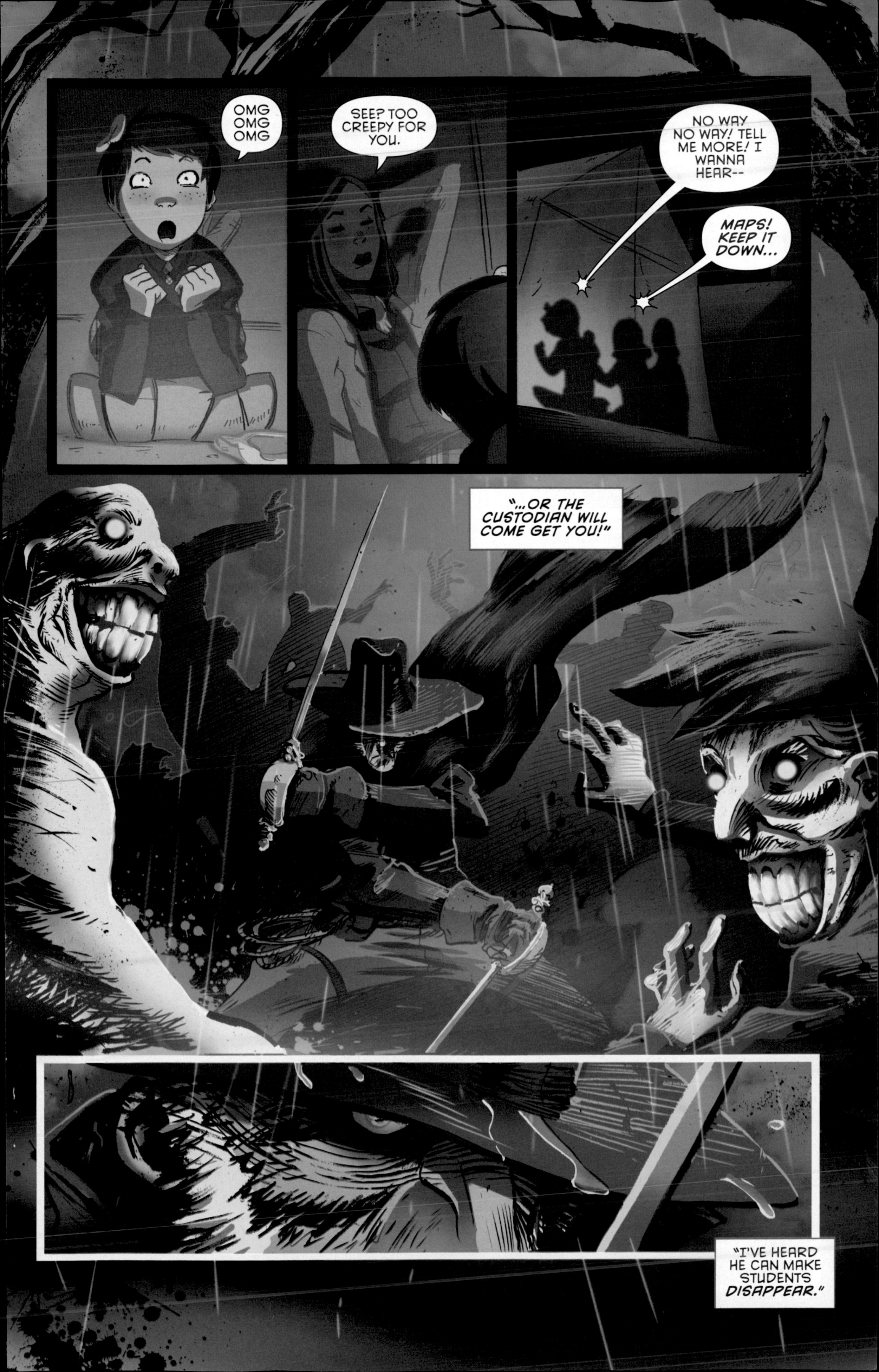
OMG OMG OMG
SEE? TOO CREEPY FOR YOU.
NO WAY NO WAY! TELL ME MORE! I WANNA HEAR--
MAPS! KEEP IT DOWN...
"...OR THE CUSTODIAN WILL COME GET YOU!"
"I'VE HEARD HE CAN MAKE STUDENTS DISAPPEAR."

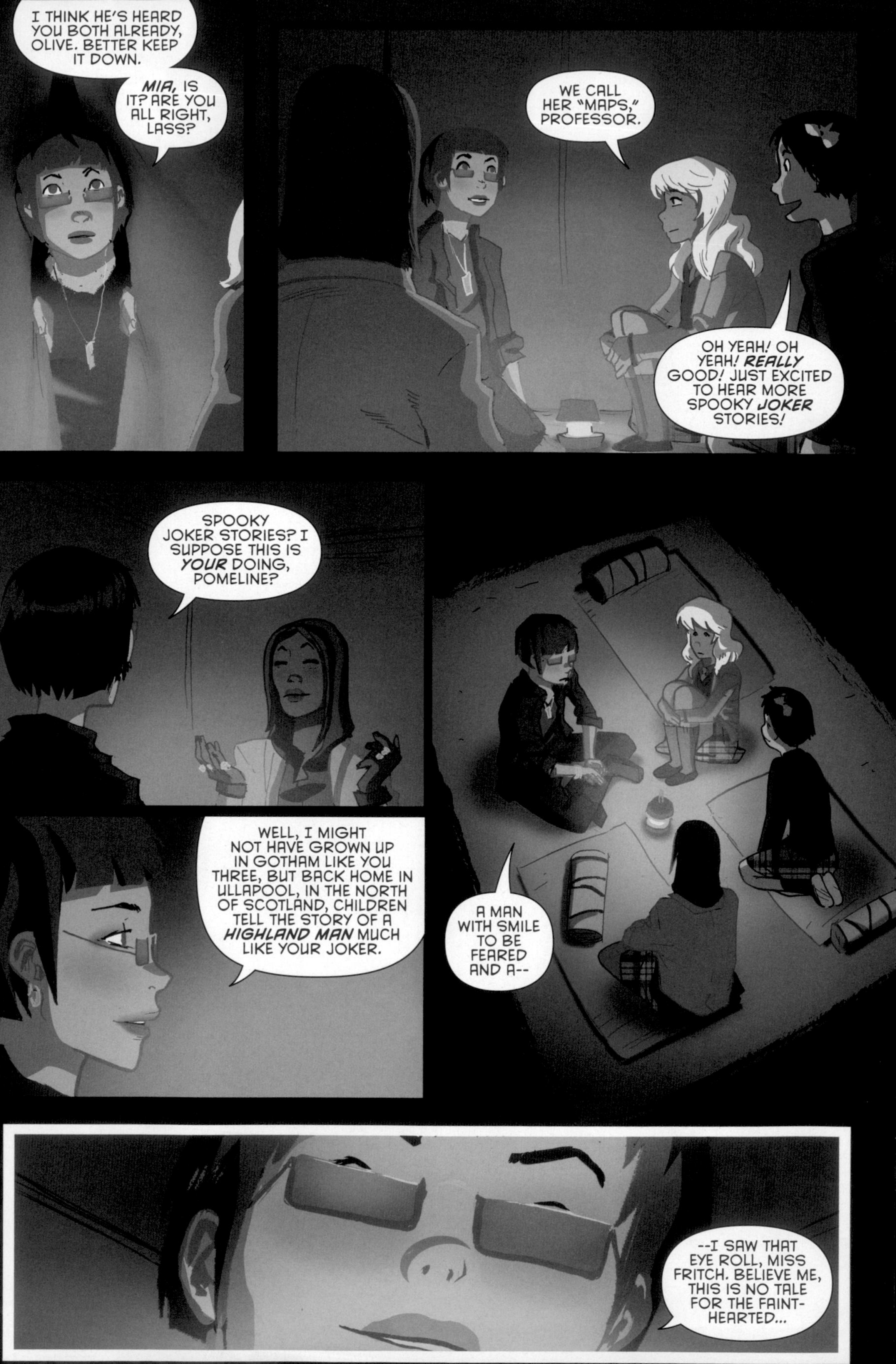
I THINK HE'S HEARD YOU BOTH ALREADY, OLIVE. BETTER KEEP IT DOWN.
MIA, IS IT? ARE YOU ALL RIGHT, LASS?
WE CALL HER "MAPS," PROFESSOR.
OH YEAH! OH YEAH! REALLY GOOD! JUST EXCITED TO HEAR MORE SPOOKY JOKER STORIES!
SPOOKY JOKER STORIES? I SUPPOSE THIS IS YOUR DOING, POMELINE?
WELL, I MIGHT NOT HAVE GROWN UP IN GOTHAM LIKE YOU THREE, BUT BACK HOME IN ULLAPOOL, IN THE NORTH OF SCOTLAND, CHILDREN TELL THE STORY OF A HIGHLAND MAN MUCH LIKE YOUR JOKER.
A MAN WITH SMILE TO BE FEARED AND A--
--I SAW THAT EYE ROLL, MISS FRITCH. BELIEVE ME, THIS IS NO TALE FOR THE FAINT-HEARTED...

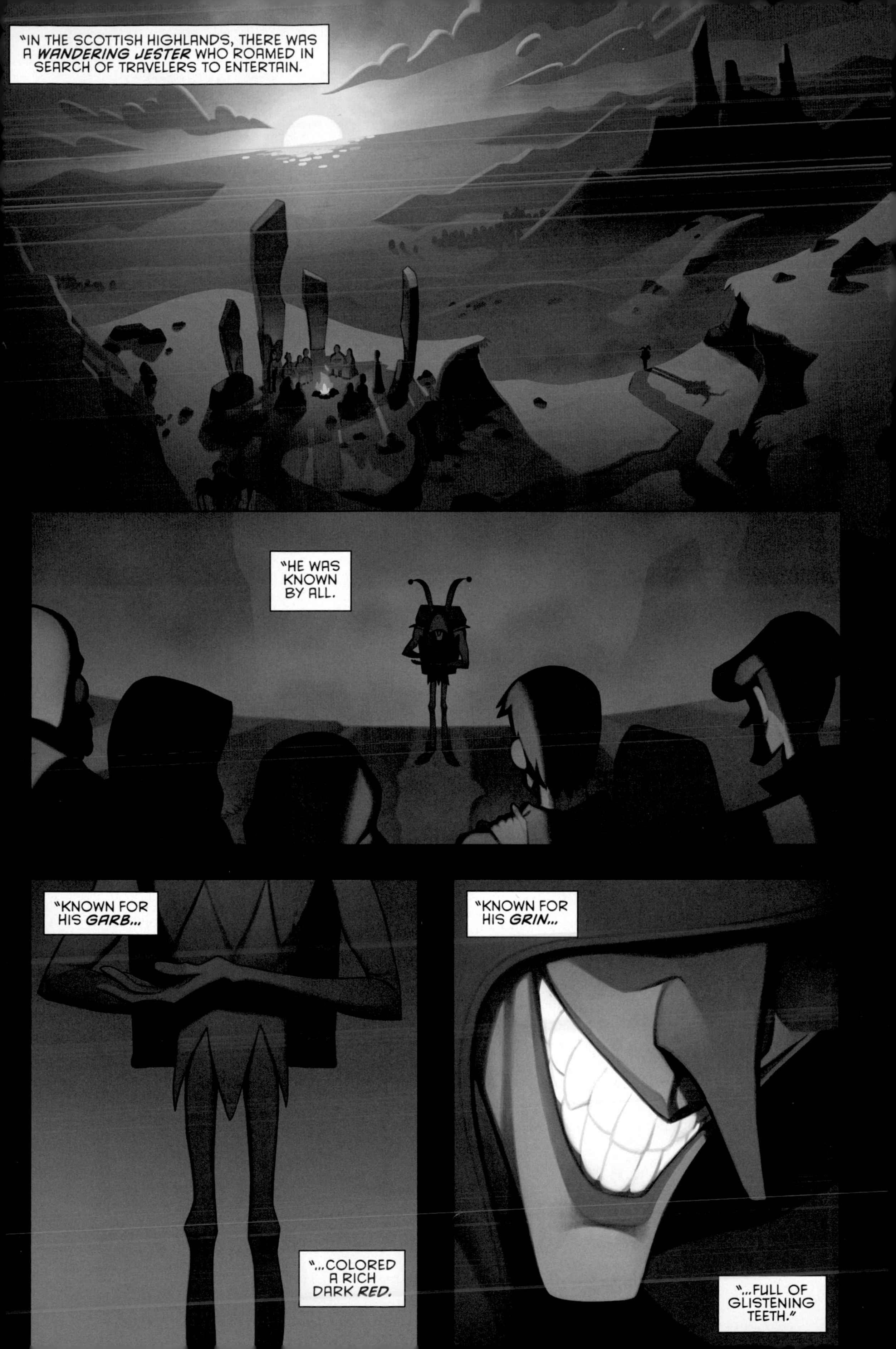
"IN THE SCOTTISH HIGHLANDS, THERE WAS A *WANDERING JESTER* WHO ROAMED IN SEARCH OF TRAVELERS TO ENTERTAIN.
"HE WAS KNOWN BY ALL.
"KNOWN FOR HIS *GARB*...
"...COLORED A RICH DARK *RED*.
"KNOWN FOR HIS *GRIN*...
"...FULL OF GLISTENING TEETH."

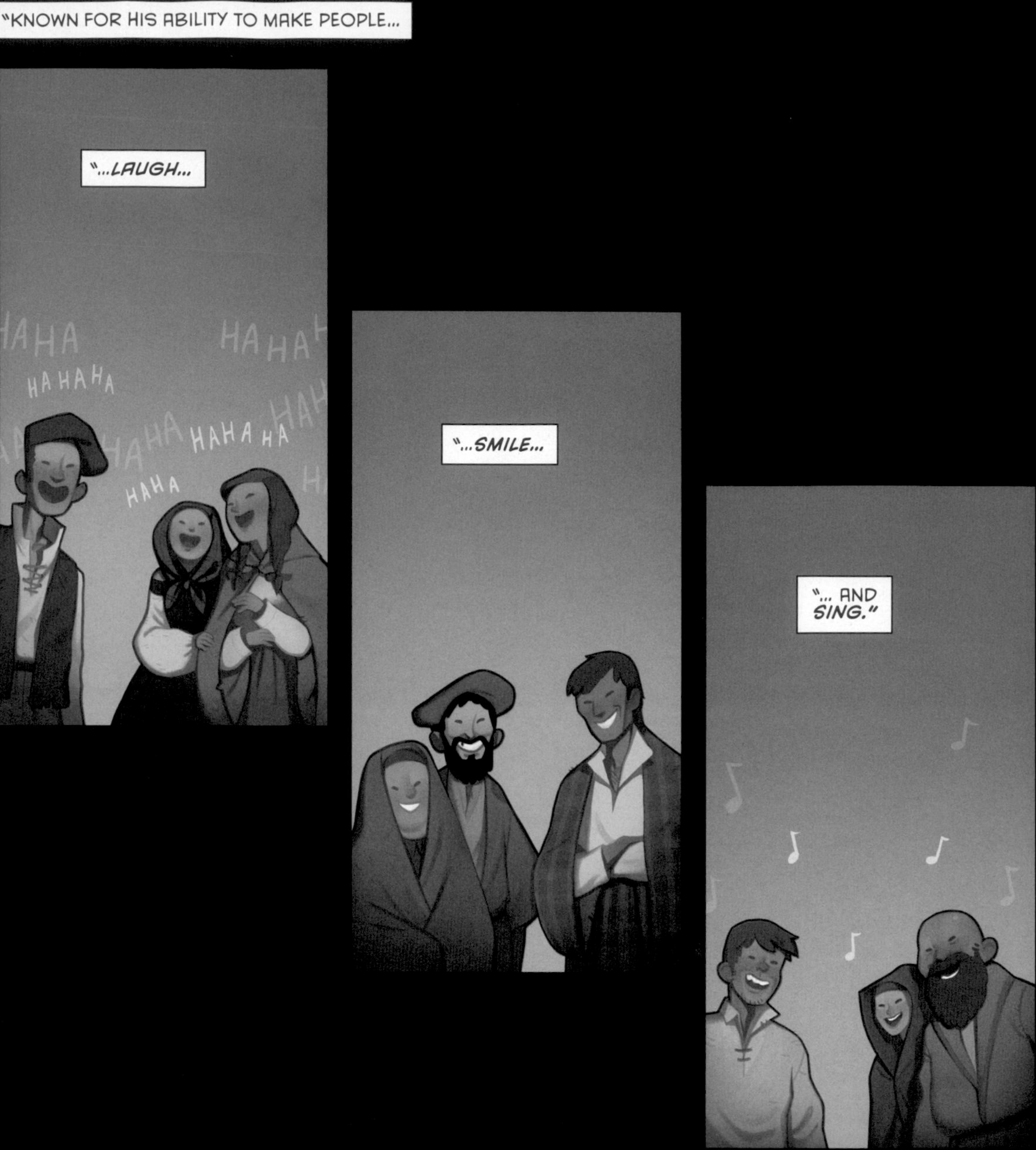
"KNOWN FOR HIS ABILITY TO MAKE PEOPLE...
"...LAUGH...
HAHA
HAHAHA
HAHAHA
HAHA
"...SMILE...
"... AND SING."

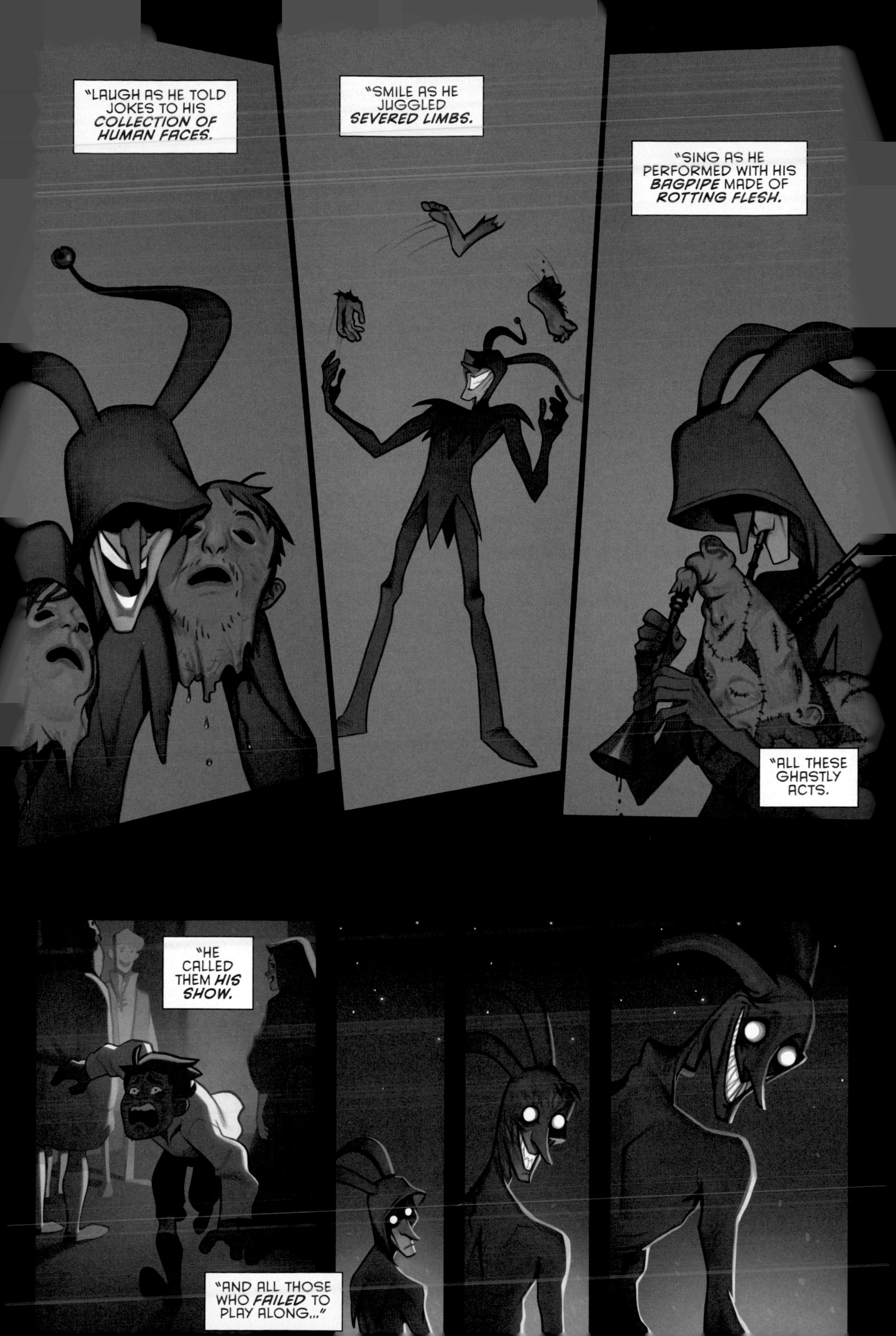
"LAUGH AS HE TOLD JOKES TO HIS COLLECTION OF HUMAN FACES.
"SMILE AS HE JUGGLED SEVERED LIMBS.
"SING AS HE PERFORMED WITH HIS BAGPIPE MADE OF ROTTING FLESH.
"ALL THESE GHASTLY ACTS.
"HE CALLED THEM HIS SHOW.
"AND ALL THOSE WHO FAILED TO PLAY ALONG..."

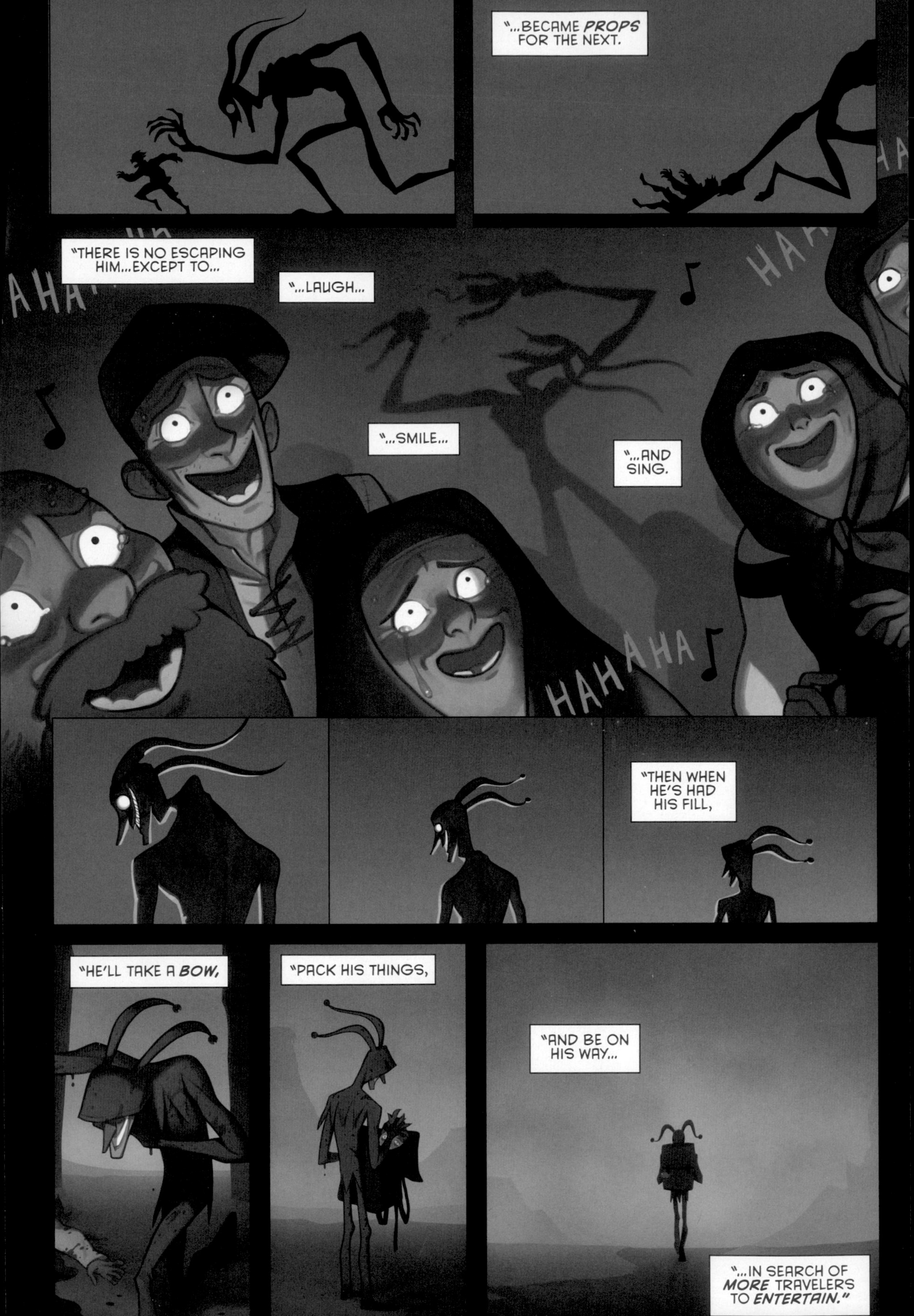
"...BECAME *PROPS* FOR THE NEXT.
HA
"THERE IS NO ESCAPING HIM...EXCEPT TO...
HAHA
"...LAUGH...
HA HA
"...SMILE...
"...AND SING.
HAHAHA
"THEN WHEN HE'S HAD HIS FILL,
"HE'LL TAKE A *BOW,*
"PACK HIS THINGS,
"AND BE ON HIS WAY...
"...IN SEARCH OF *MORE* TRAVELERS TO *ENTERTAIN.*"

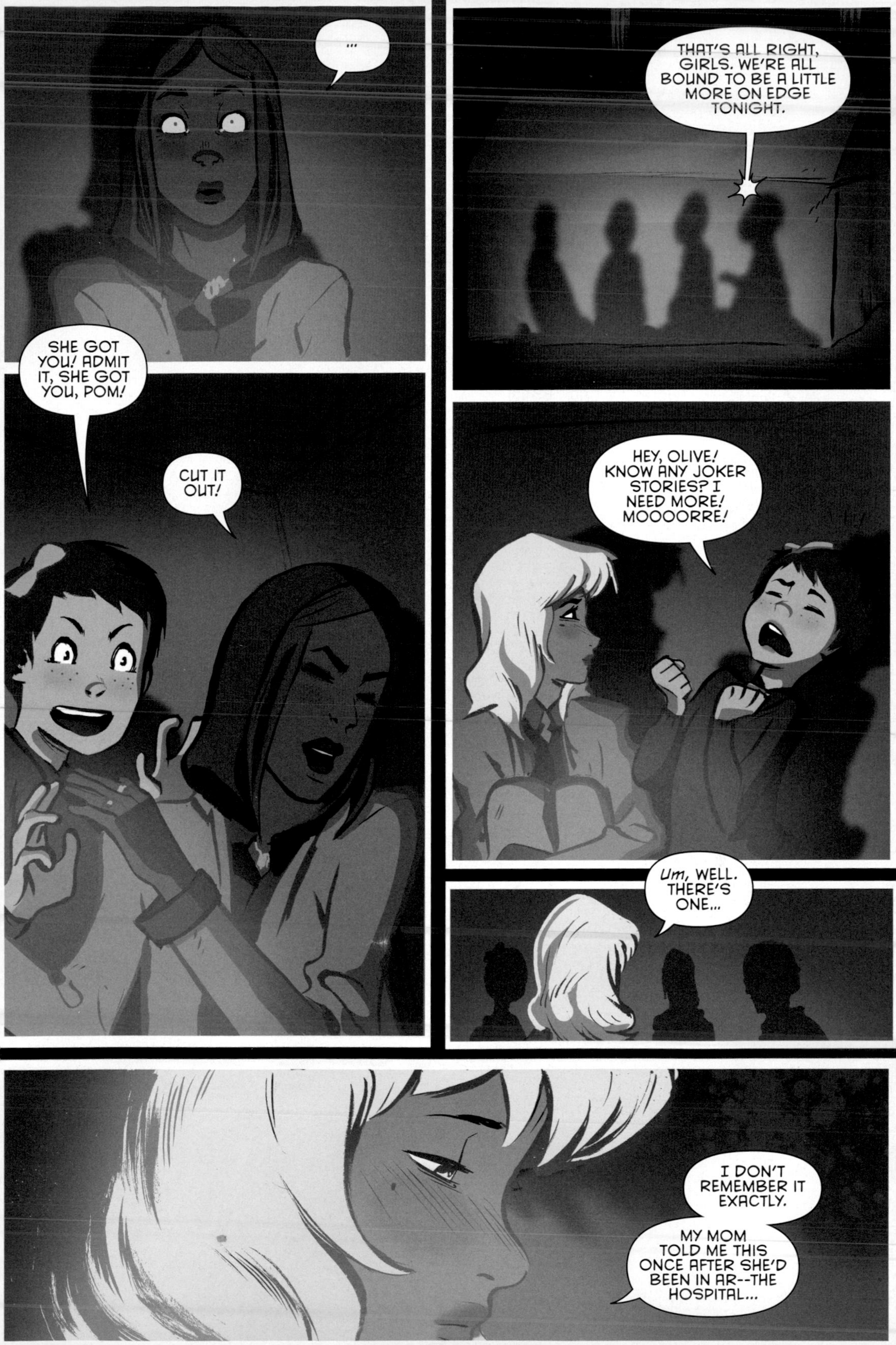
...
THAT'S ALL RIGHT, GIRLS. WE'RE ALL BOUND TO BE A LITTLE MORE ON EDGE TONIGHT.
SHE GOT YOU! ADMIT IT, SHE GOT YOU, POM!
CUT IT OUT!
HEY, OLIVE! KNOW ANY JOKER STORIES? I NEED MORE! MOOOORRE!
Um, WELL. THERE'S ONE...
I DON'T REMEMBER IT EXACTLY.
MY MOM TOLD ME THIS ONCE AFTER SHE'D BEEN IN AR--THE HOSPITAL...

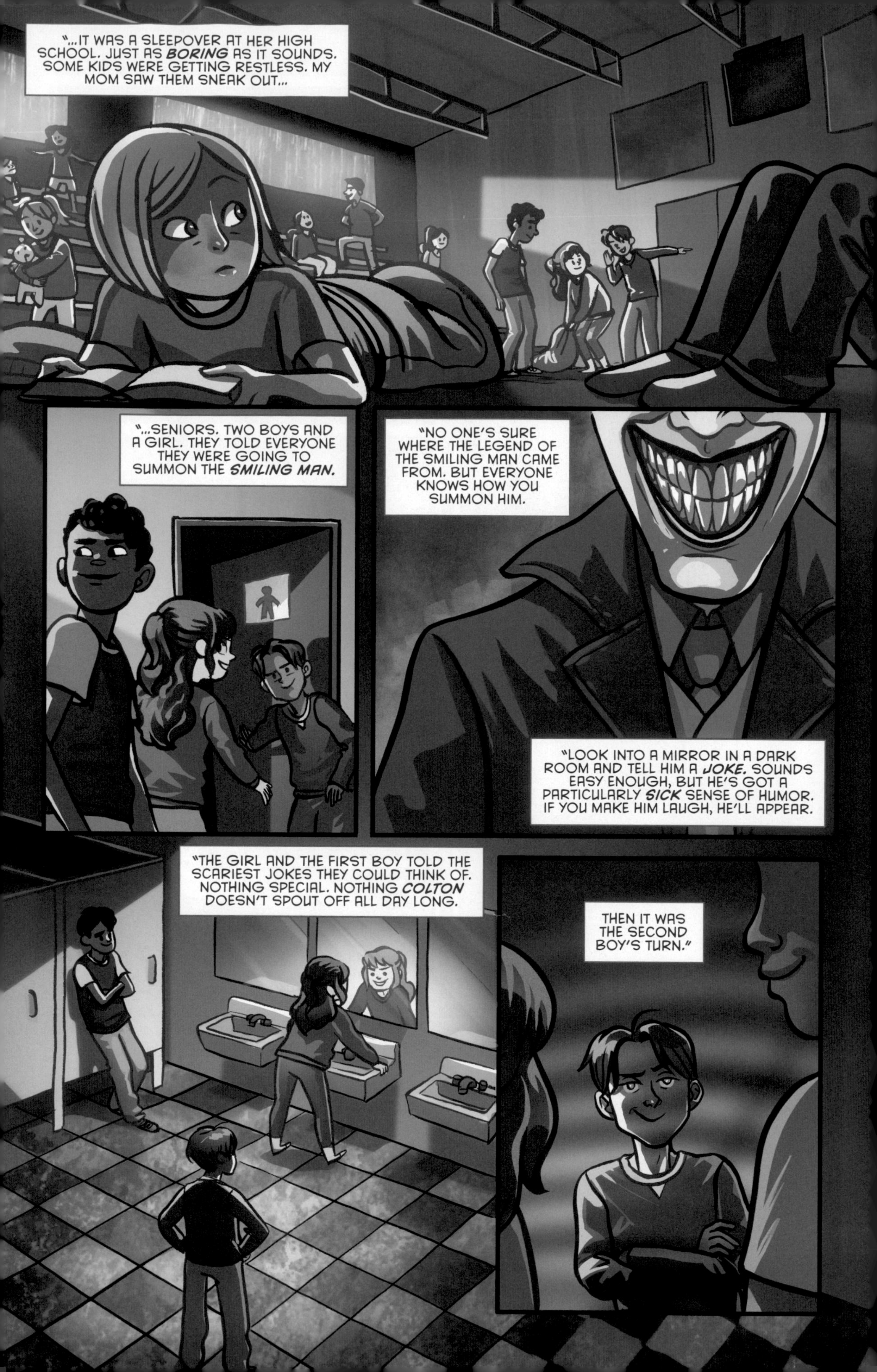
"...IT WAS A SLEEPOVER AT HER HIGH SCHOOL. JUST AS *BORING* AS IT SOUNDS. SOME KIDS WERE GETTING RESTLESS. MY MOM SAW THEM SNEAK OUT...
"...SENIORS. TWO BOYS AND A GIRL. THEY TOLD EVERYONE THEY WERE GOING TO SUMMON THE *SMILING MAN.*
"NO ONE'S SURE WHERE THE LEGEND OF THE SMILING MAN CAME FROM. BUT EVERYONE KNOWS HOW YOU SUMMON HIM.
"LOOK INTO A MIRROR IN A DARK ROOM AND TELL HIM A *JOKE.* SOUNDS EASY ENOUGH, BUT HE'S GOT A PARTICULARLY *SICK* SENSE OF HUMOR. IF YOU MAKE HIM LAUGH, HE'LL APPEAR.
"THE GIRL AND THE FIRST BOY TOLD THE SCARIEST JOKES THEY COULD THINK OF. NOTHING SPECIAL. NOTHING *COLTON* DOESN'T SPOUT OFF ALL DAY LONG.
THEN IT WAS THE SECOND BOY'S TURN."

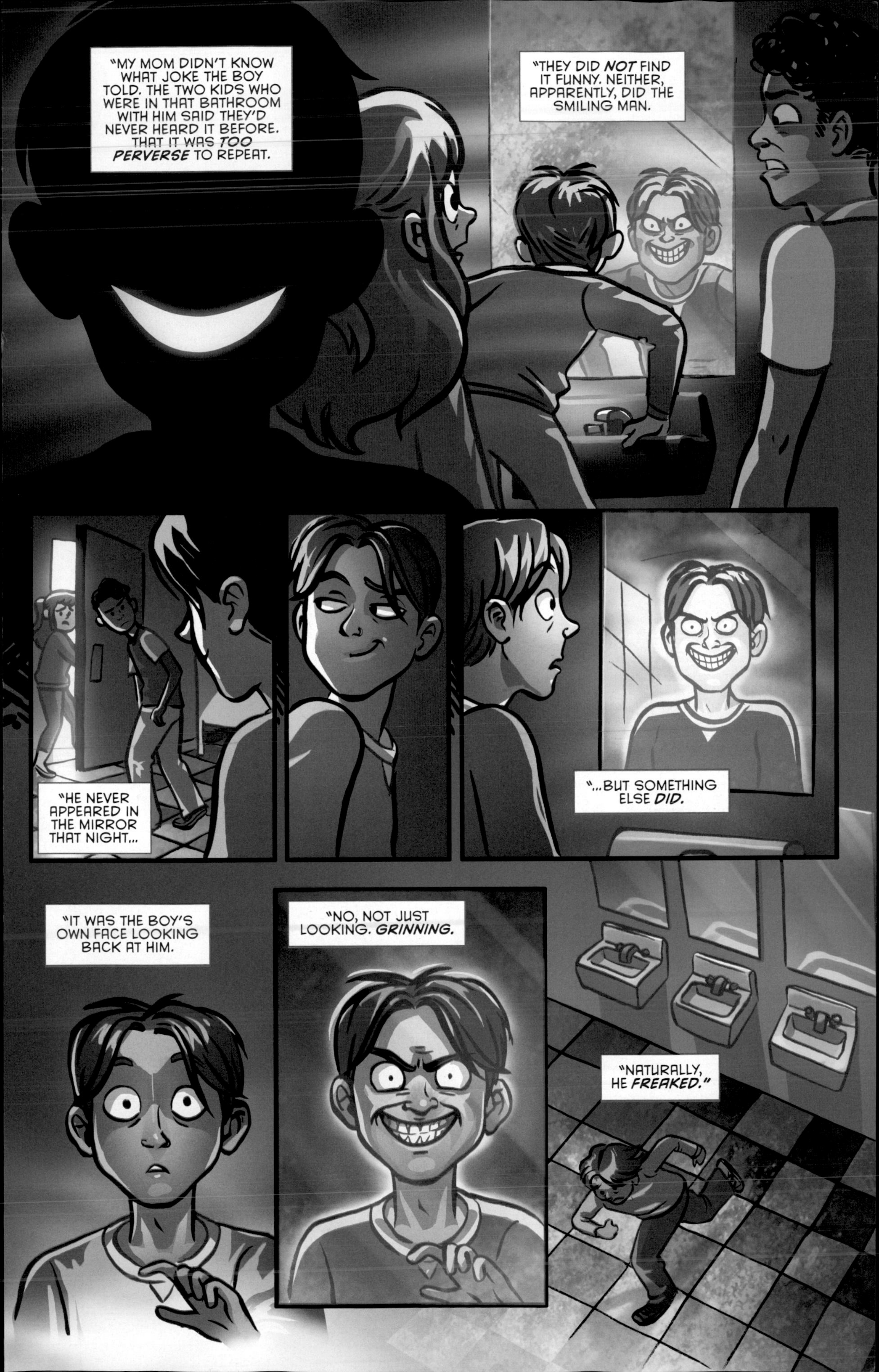
"MY MOM DIDN'T KNOW WHAT JOKE THE BOY TOLD. THE TWO KIDS WHO WERE IN THAT BATHROOM WITH HIM SAID THEY'D NEVER HEARD IT BEFORE. THAT IT WAS *TOO PERVERSE* TO REPEAT.
"THEY DID *NOT* FIND IT FUNNY. NEITHER, APPARENTLY, DID THE SMILING MAN.
"HE NEVER APPEARED IN THE MIRROR THAT NIGHT...
"...BUT SOMETHING ELSE *DID.*
"IT WAS THE BOY'S OWN FACE LOOKING BACK AT HIM.
"NO, NOT JUST LOOKING. *GRINNING.*
"NATURALLY, HE *FREAKED.*"

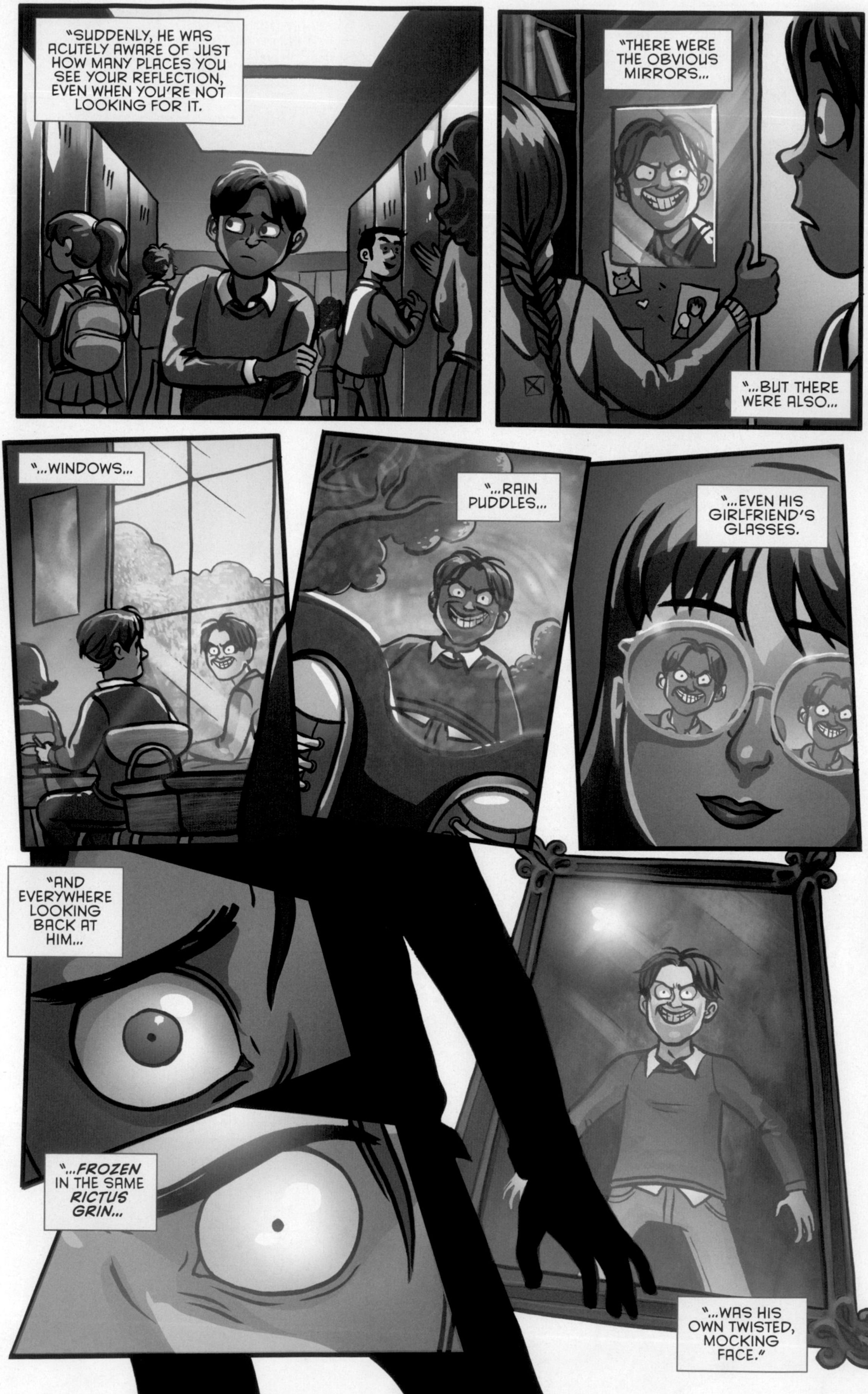
"SUDDENLY, HE WAS ACUTELY AWARE OF JUST HOW MANY PLACES YOU SEE YOUR REFLECTION, EVEN WHEN YOU'RE NOT LOOKING FOR IT.
"THERE WERE THE OBVIOUS MIRRORS...
"...BUT THERE WERE ALSO...
"...WINDOWS...
"...RAIN PUDDLES...
"...EVEN HIS GIRLFRIEND'S GLASSES.
"AND EVERYWHERE LOOKING BACK AT HIM...
"...*FROZEN* IN THE SAME *RICTUS GRIN*...
"...WAS HIS OWN TWISTED, MOCKING FACE."

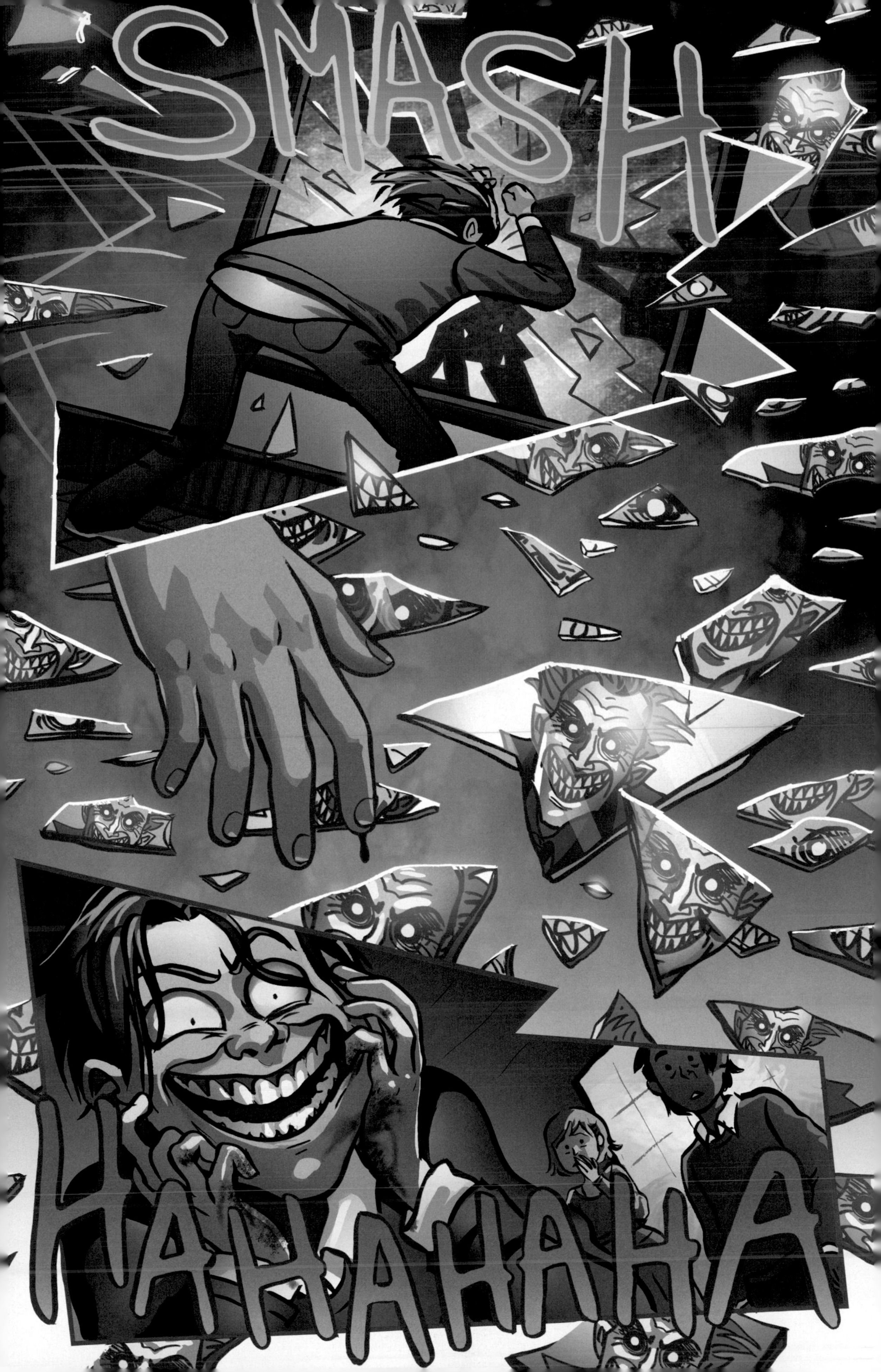
SMASH
HAHAHAHA

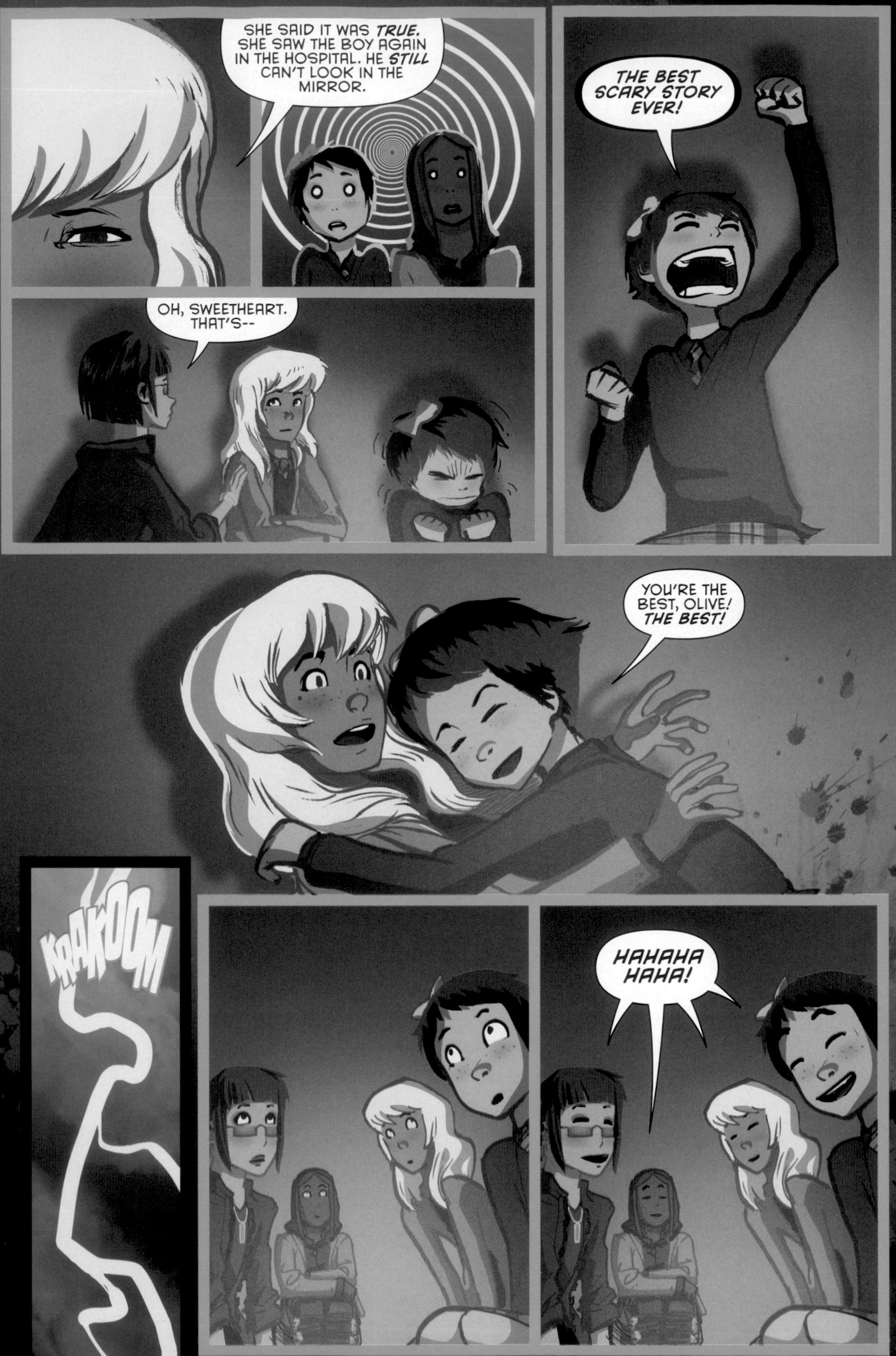
SHE SAID IT WAS TRUE. SHE SAW THE BOY AGAIN IN THE HOSPITAL. HE STILL CAN'T LOOK IN THE MIRROR.
THE BEST SCARY STORY EVER!
OH, SWEETHEART. THAT'S--
YOU'RE THE BEST, OLIVE! THE BEST!
KRAKOOM
HAHAHA HAHA!

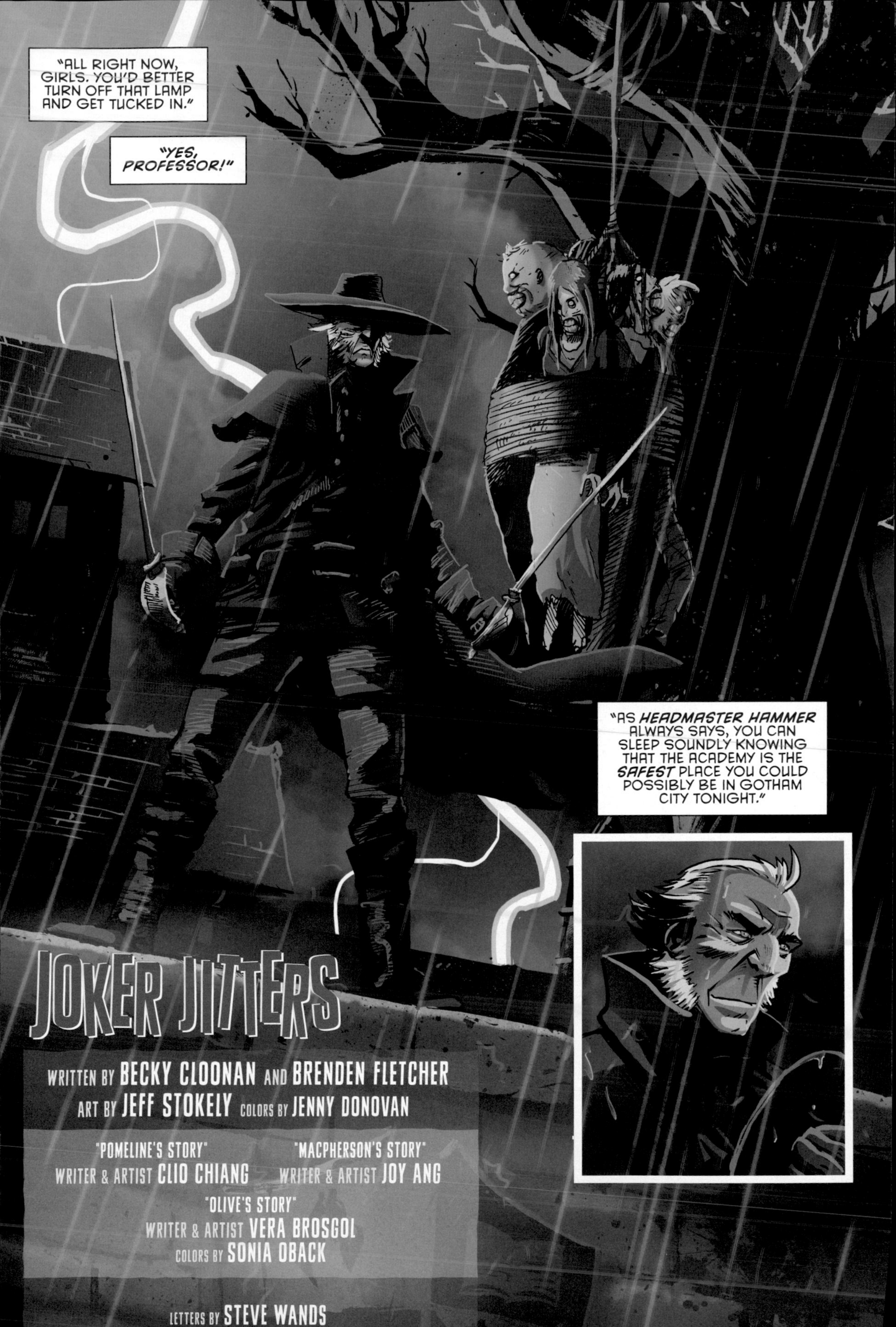
"ALL RIGHT NOW, GIRLS. YOU'D BETTER TURN OFF THAT LAMP AND GET TUCKED IN."
"YES, PROFESSOR!"
"AS HEADMASTER HAMMER ALWAYS SAYS, YOU CAN SLEEP SOUNDLY KNOWING THAT THE ACADEMY IS THE SAFEST PLACE YOU COULD POSSIBLY BE IN GOTHAM CITY TONIGHT."
JOKER JITTERS
WRITTEN BY BECKY CLOONAN AND BRENDEN FLETCHER
ART BY JEFF STOKELY COLORS BY JENNY DONOVAN
"POMELINE'S STORY" WRITER & ARTIST CLIO CHIANG
"MACPHERSON'S STORY" WRITER & ARTIST JOY ANG
"OLIVE'S STORY" WRITER & ARTIST VERA BROSGOL COLORS BY SONIA OBACK
LETTERS BY STEVE WANDS

Cover by **RAFAEL ALBUQUERQUE**

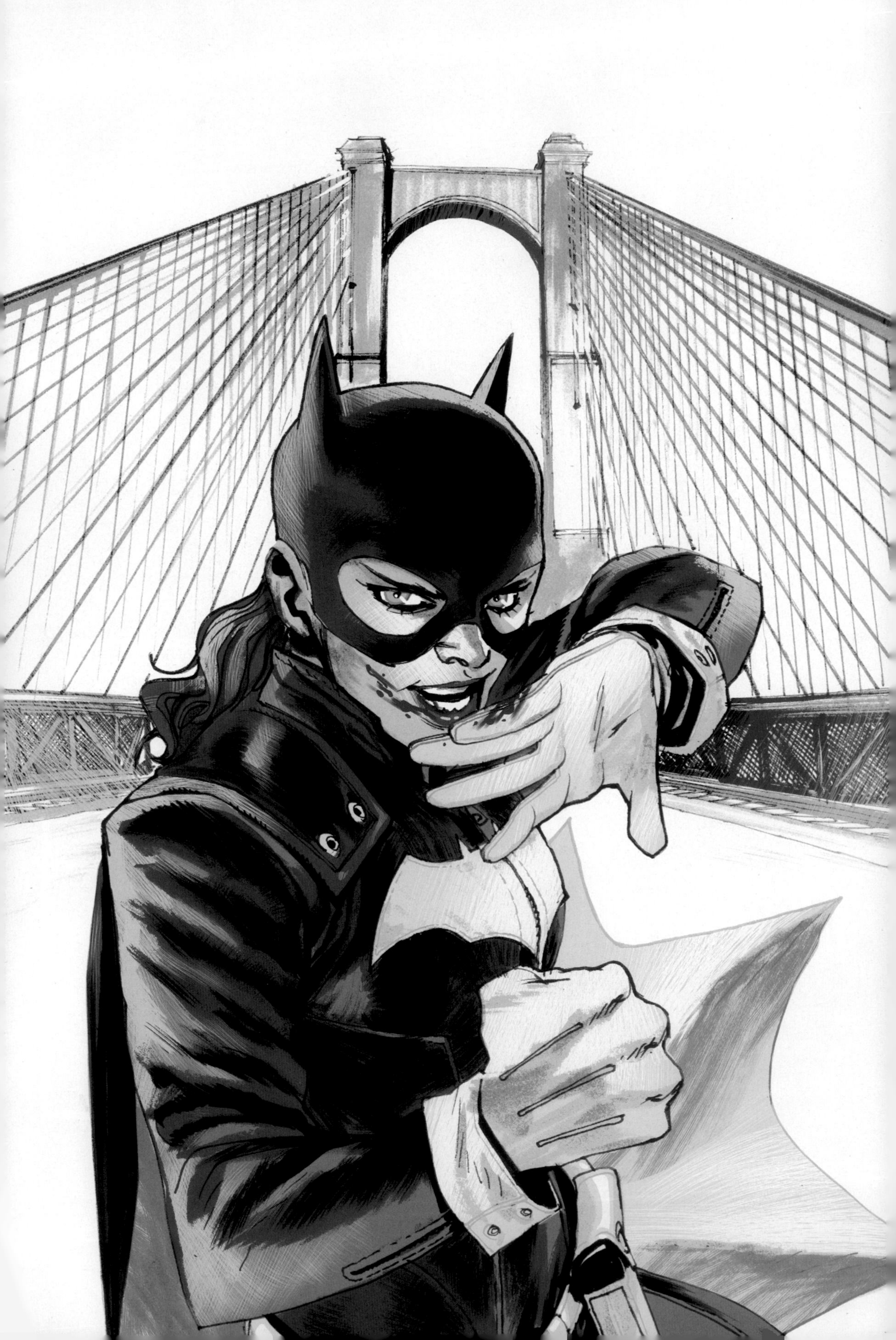

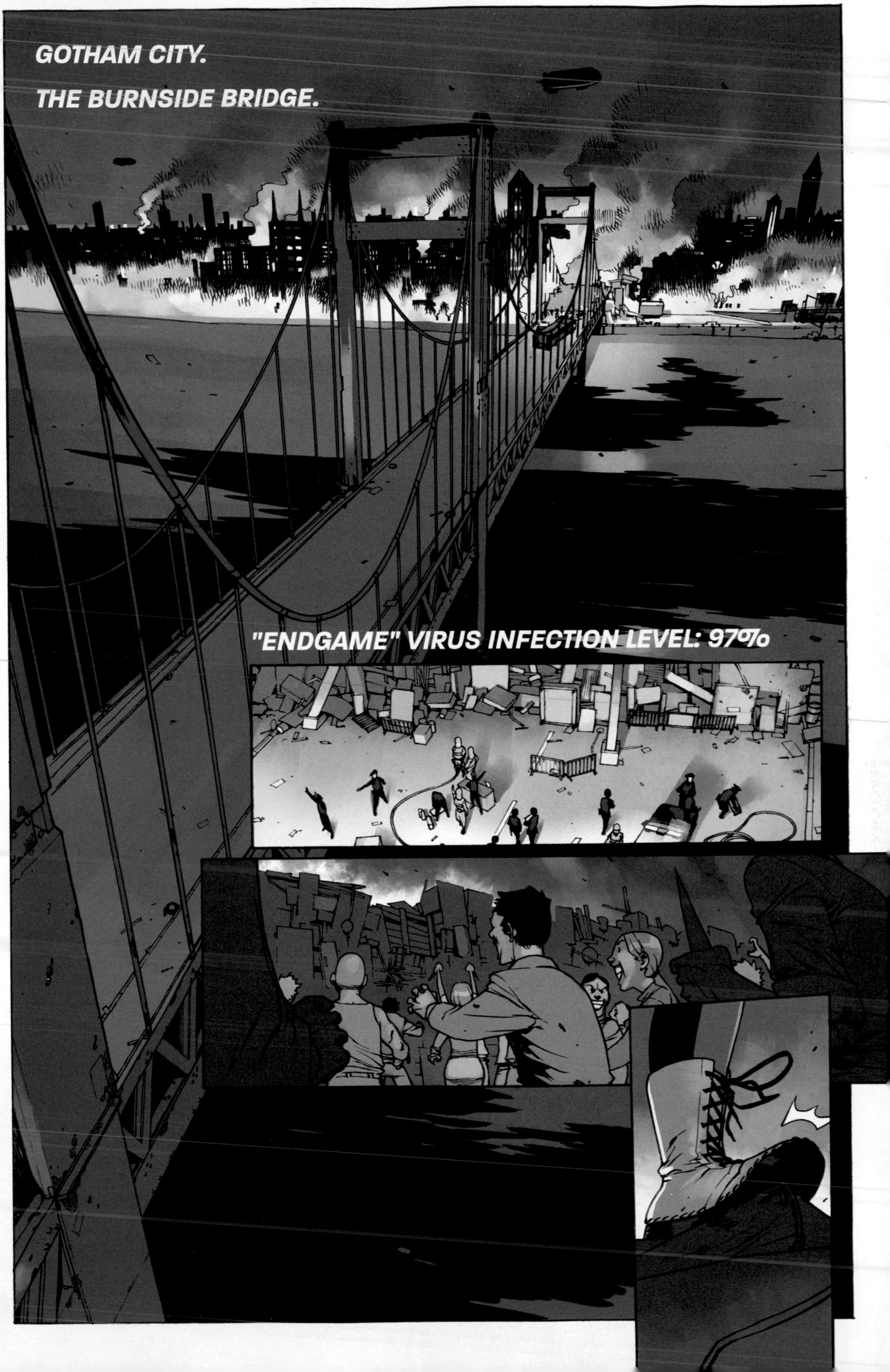
GOTHAM CITY.
THE BURNSIDE BRIDGE.
"ENDGAME" VIRUS INFECTION LEVEL: 97%

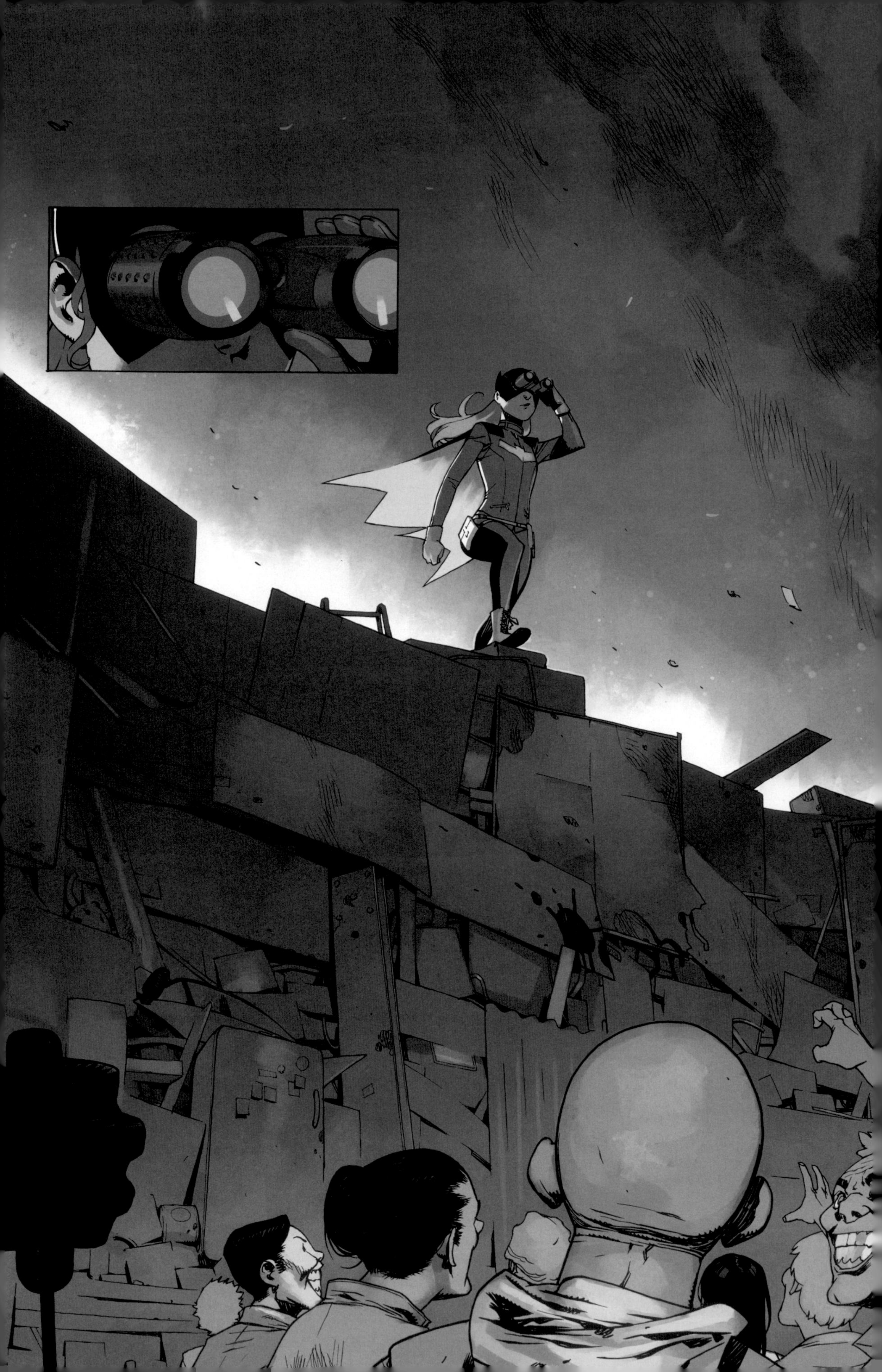

CAMERON STEWART &
BRENDEN FLETCHER writers
BENGAL art & color

JARED K. FLETCHER letters
RAFAEL ALBUQUERQUE cover

THE BATTLE FOR THE BURNSIDE BRIDGE

Frankie
NEW MESSAGE

VIP ON BO

Lucius Fox
Tanya Fox
Tiffany Fox
Ar...e Cro
Han...
Sebastian
Malcolm Po
aggie Saw

Frankie: Evacuate
VIP bus to Burnsid
safe zone! Avoid
nfected citizens!

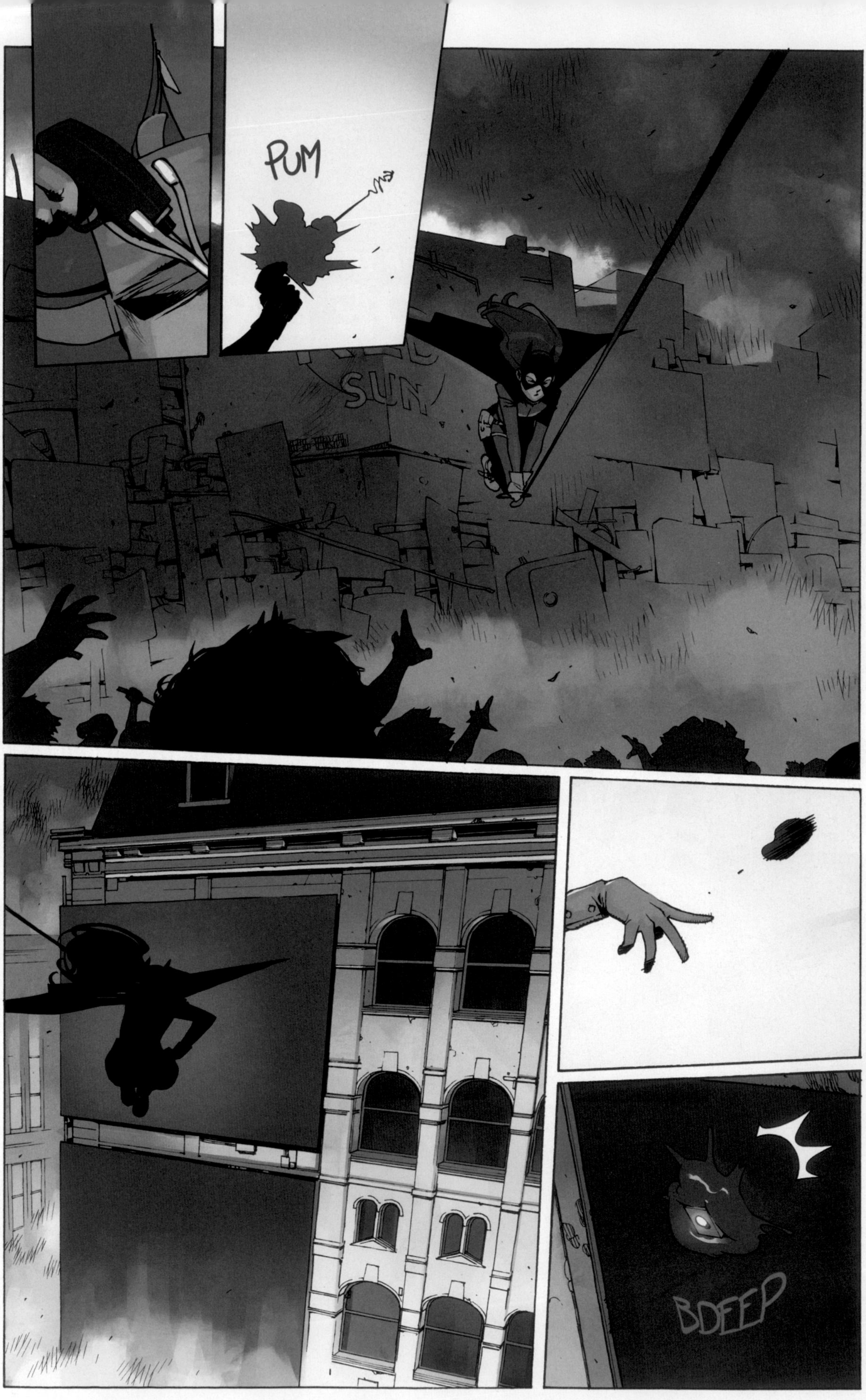
PUM
SUN
BDEEP

THOOM

CONTROL
ROOM

CONTROL
ROOM

BILLBOARD
ACTIVATION

UPLOADING

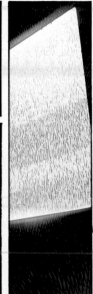

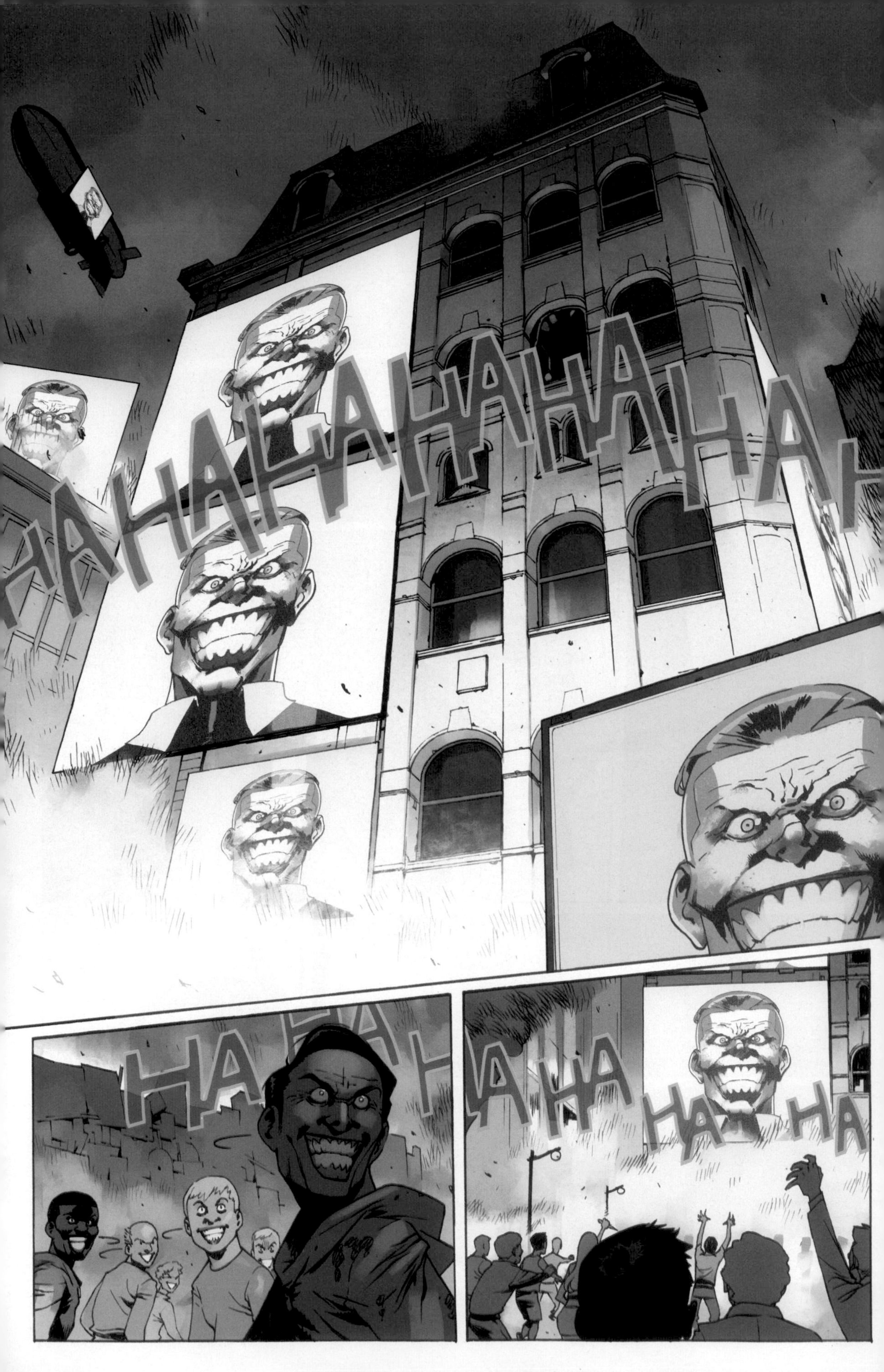
HAHAHAHAHAHAHAHA
HAHAHA
HAHAHA
HAHAHA

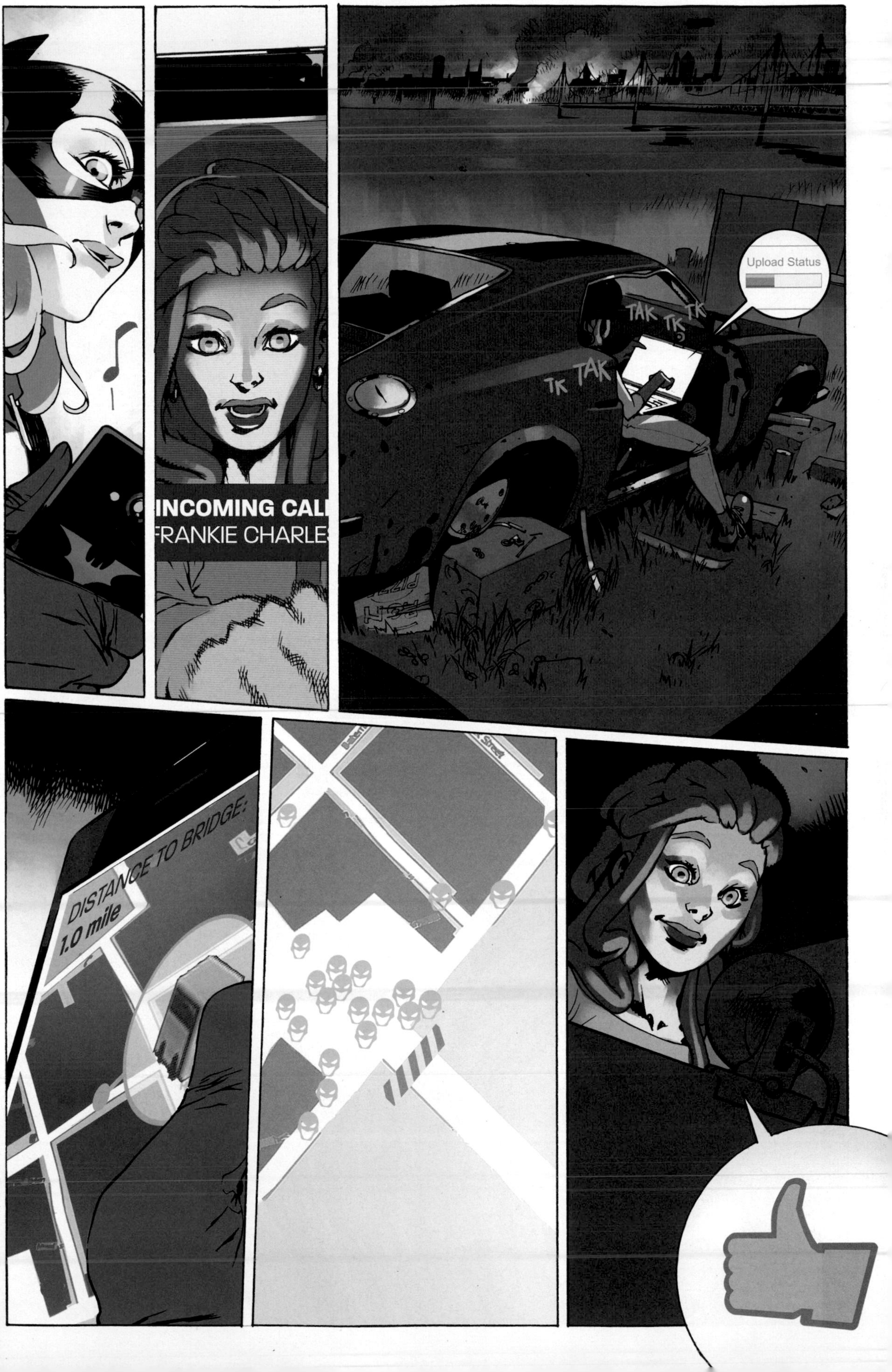
INCOMING CALL
FRANKIE CHARLES
Upload Status
TAK TK TK
TK TAK
DISTANCE TO BRIDGE:
1.0 mile

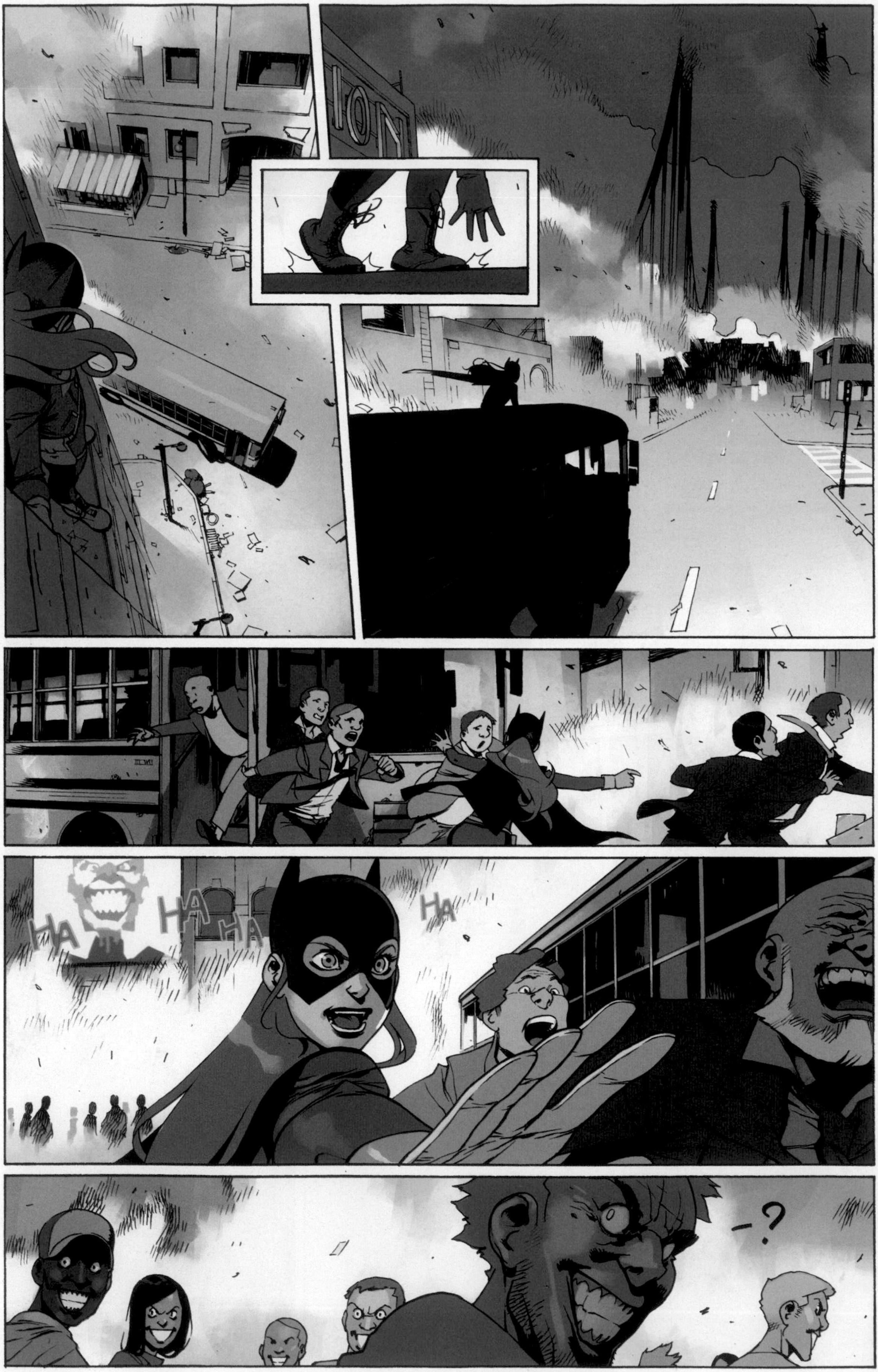
HA
HA
HA
HA
–?

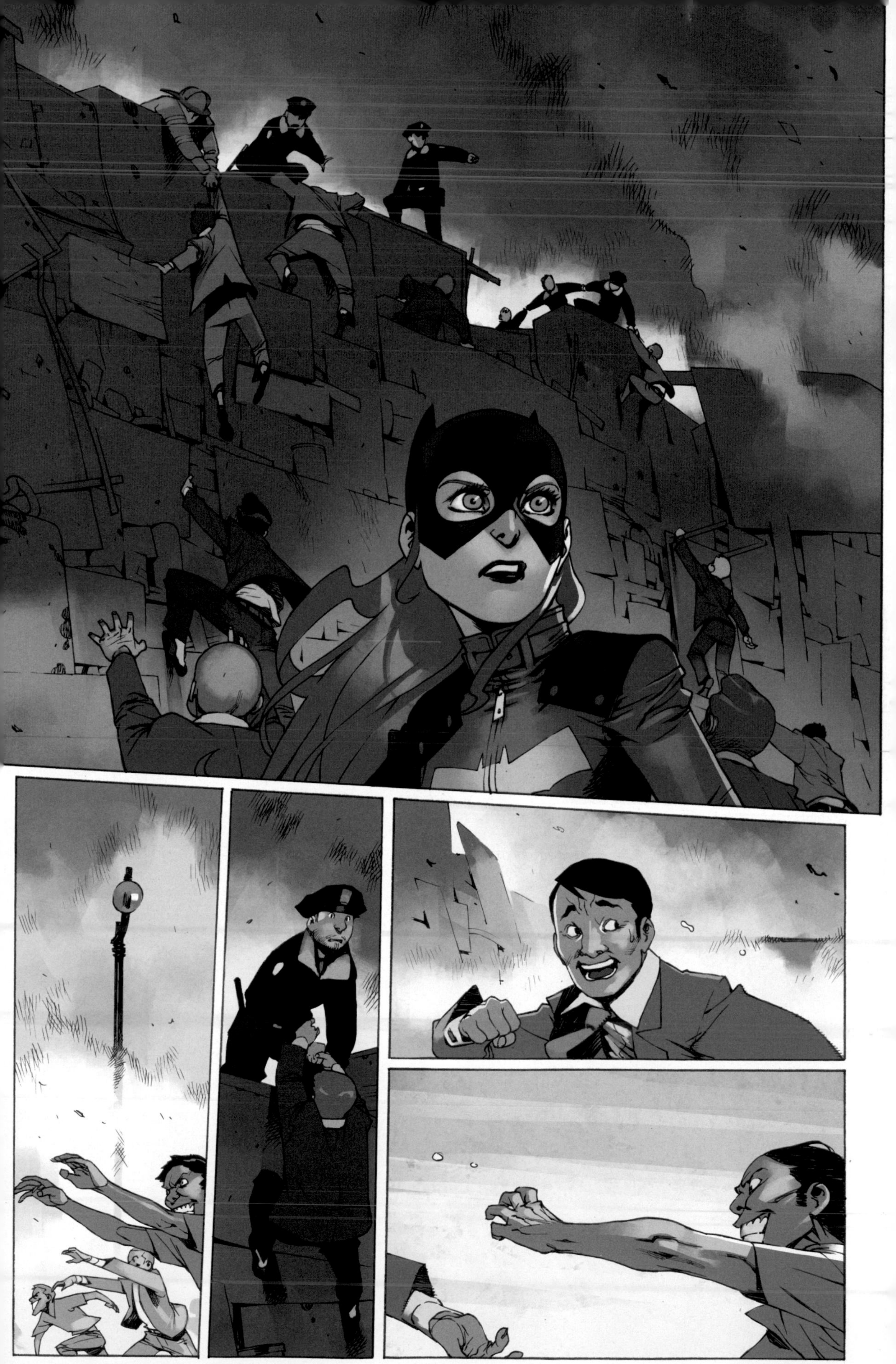

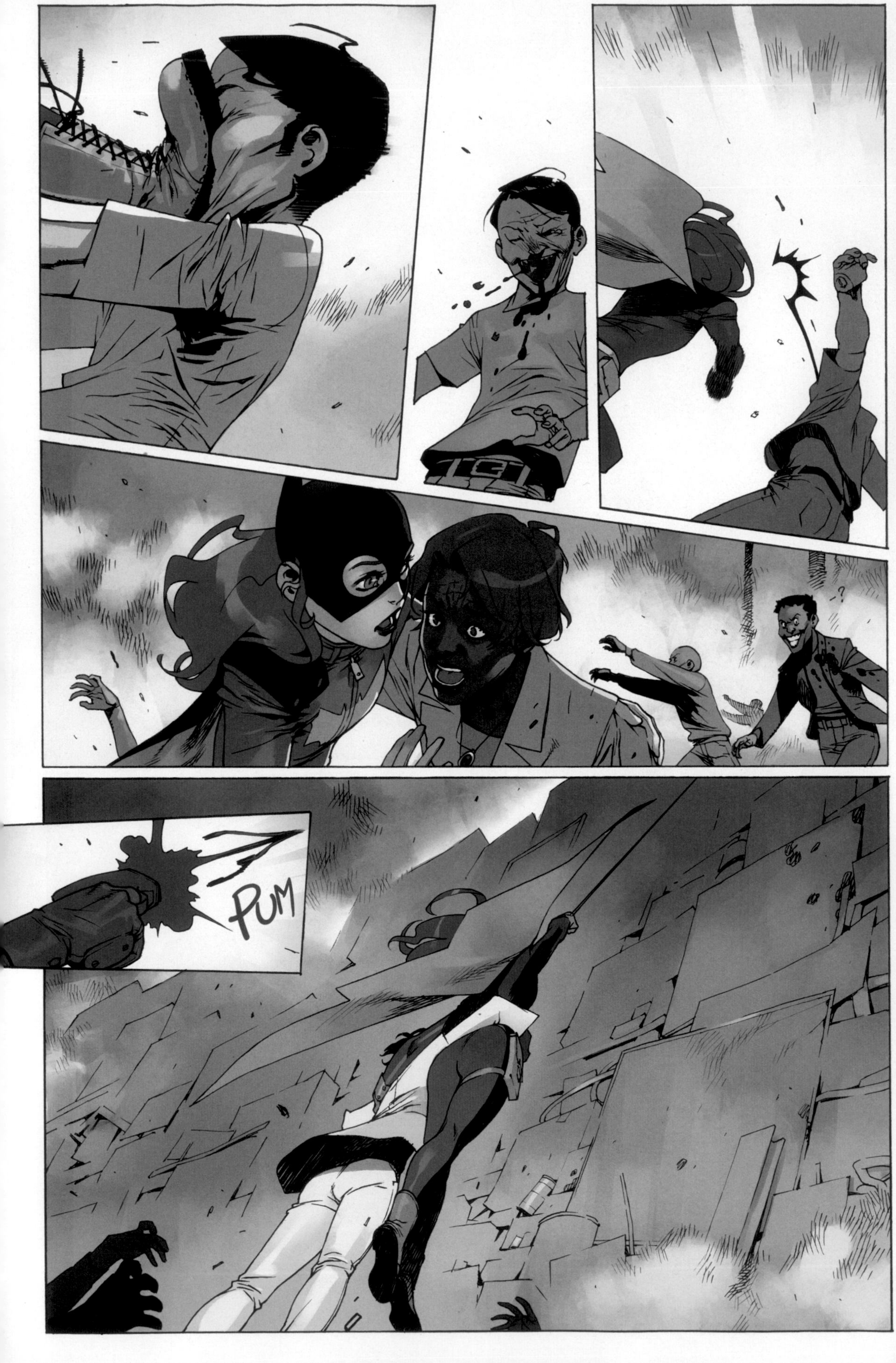
?
PUM

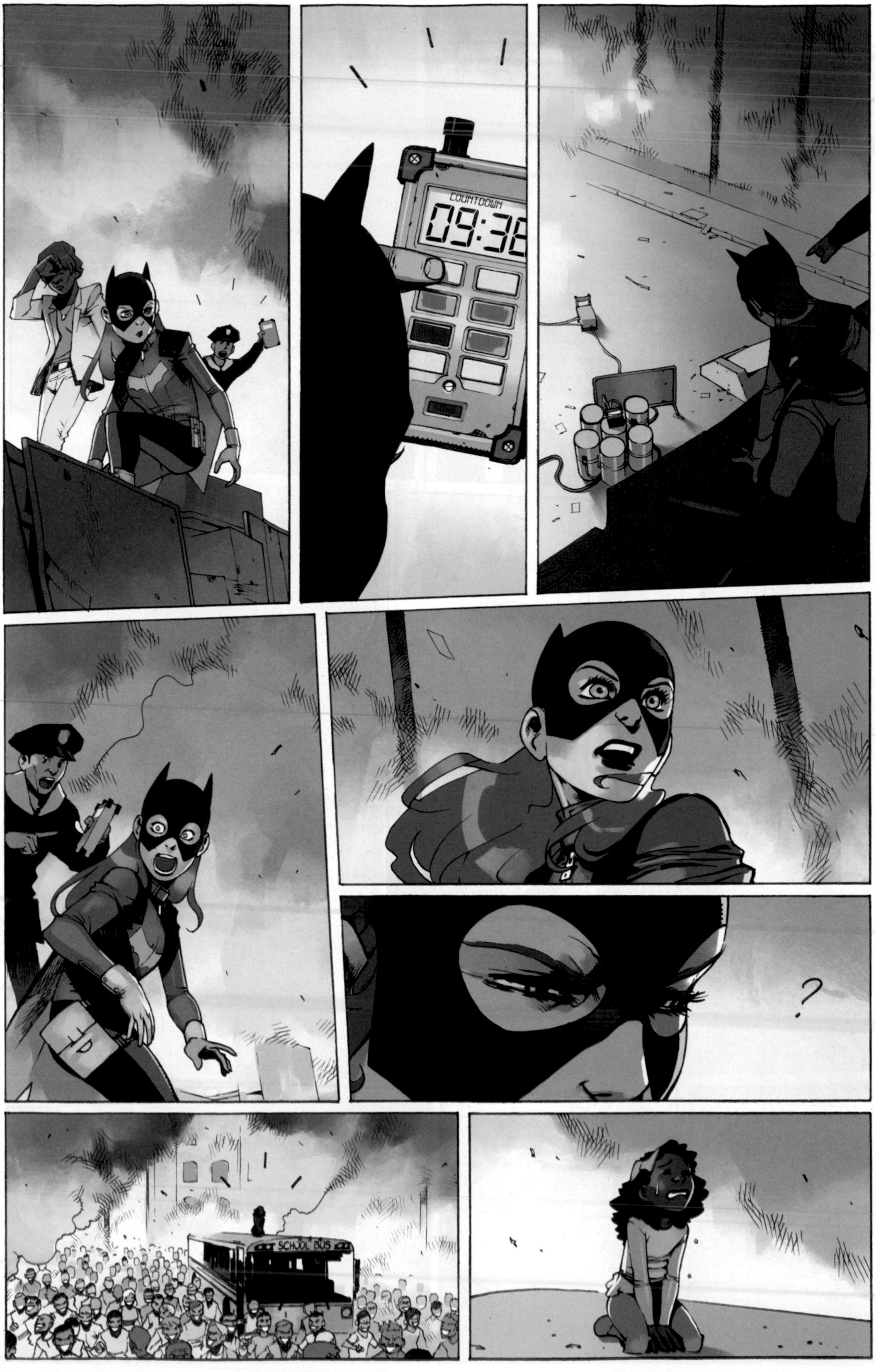
COUNTDOWN
09:3
SCHOOL BUS
?

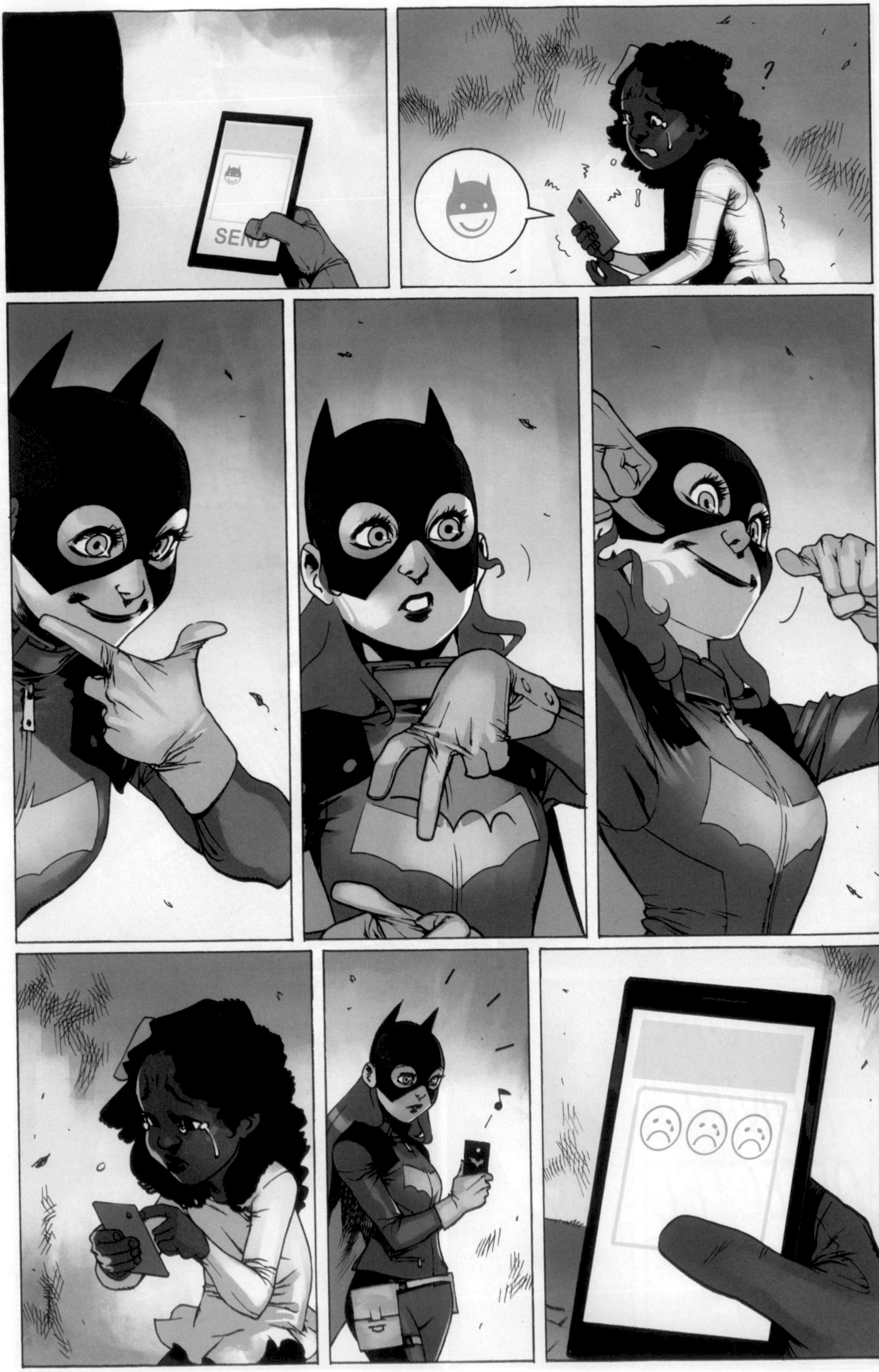
SEND

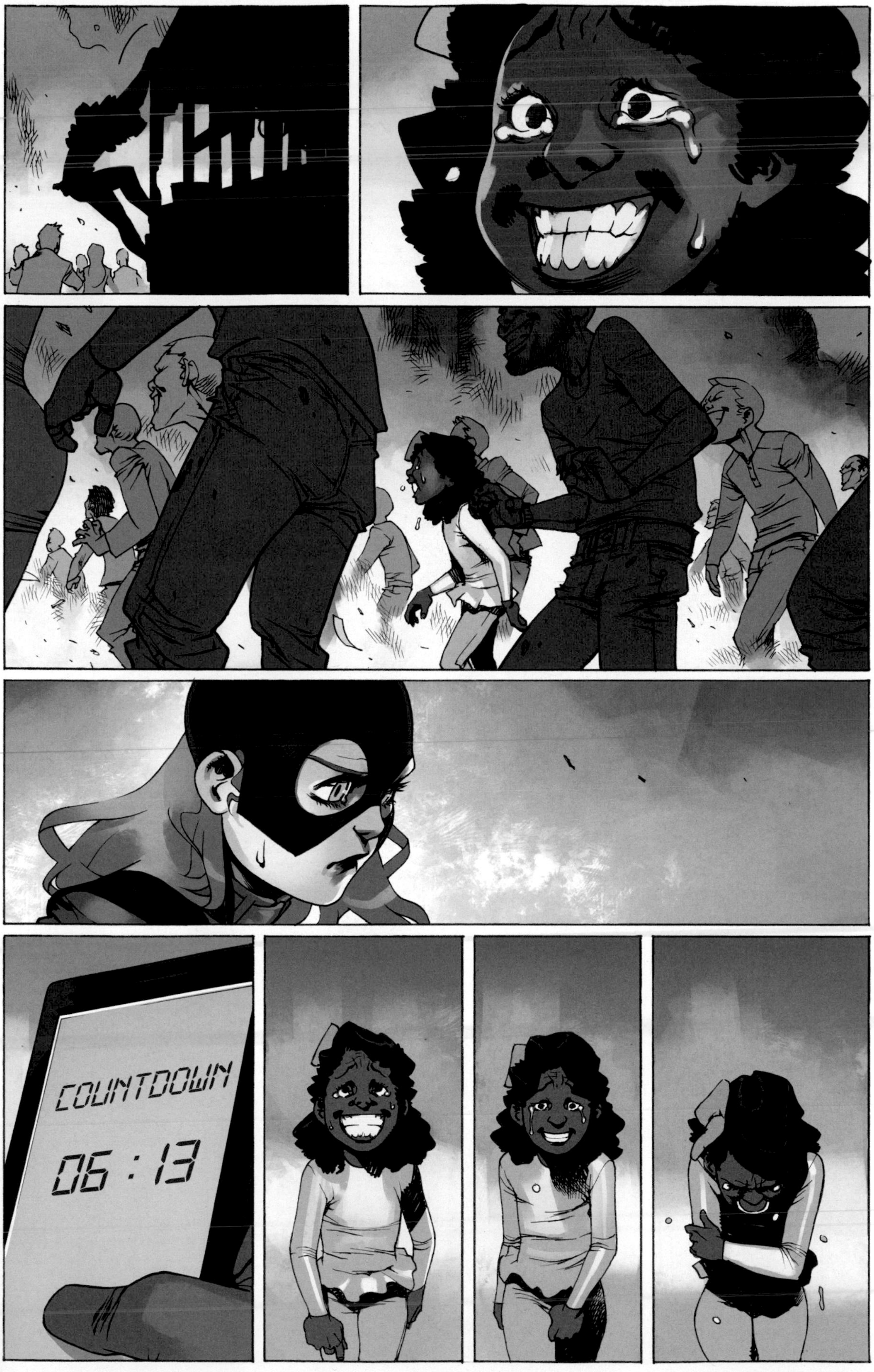
COUNTDOWN
06 : 13

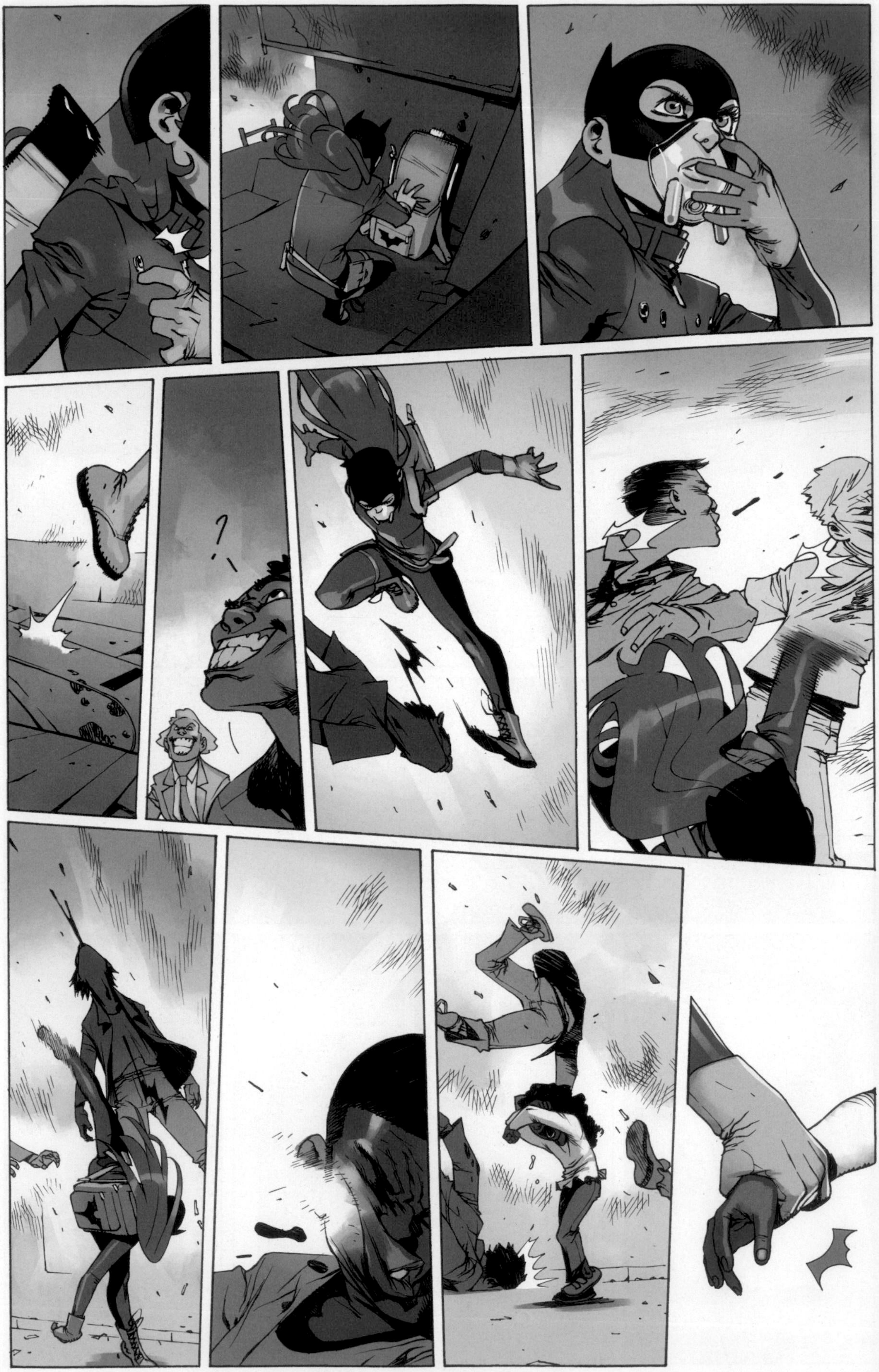

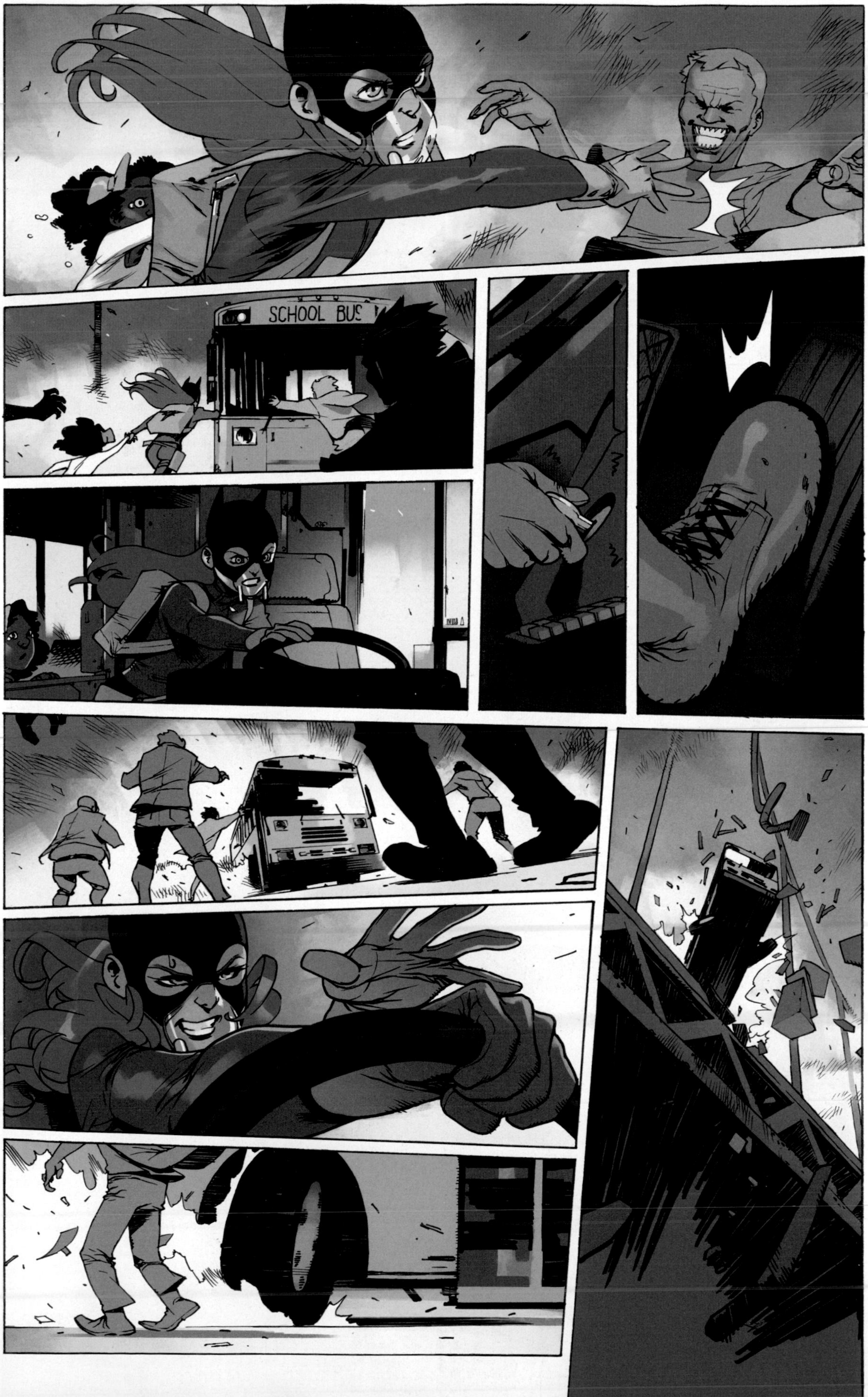
SCHOOL BUS

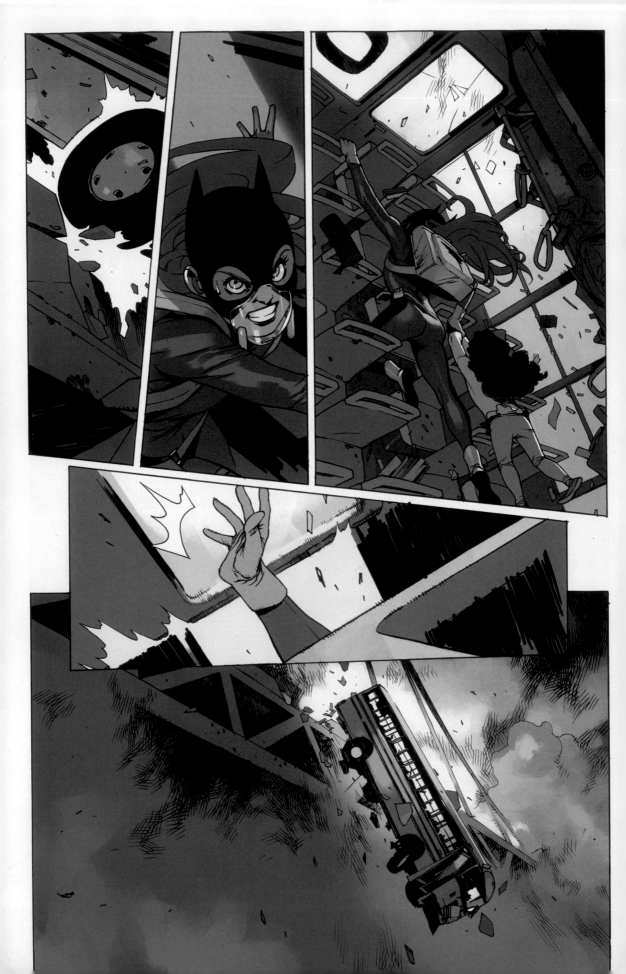

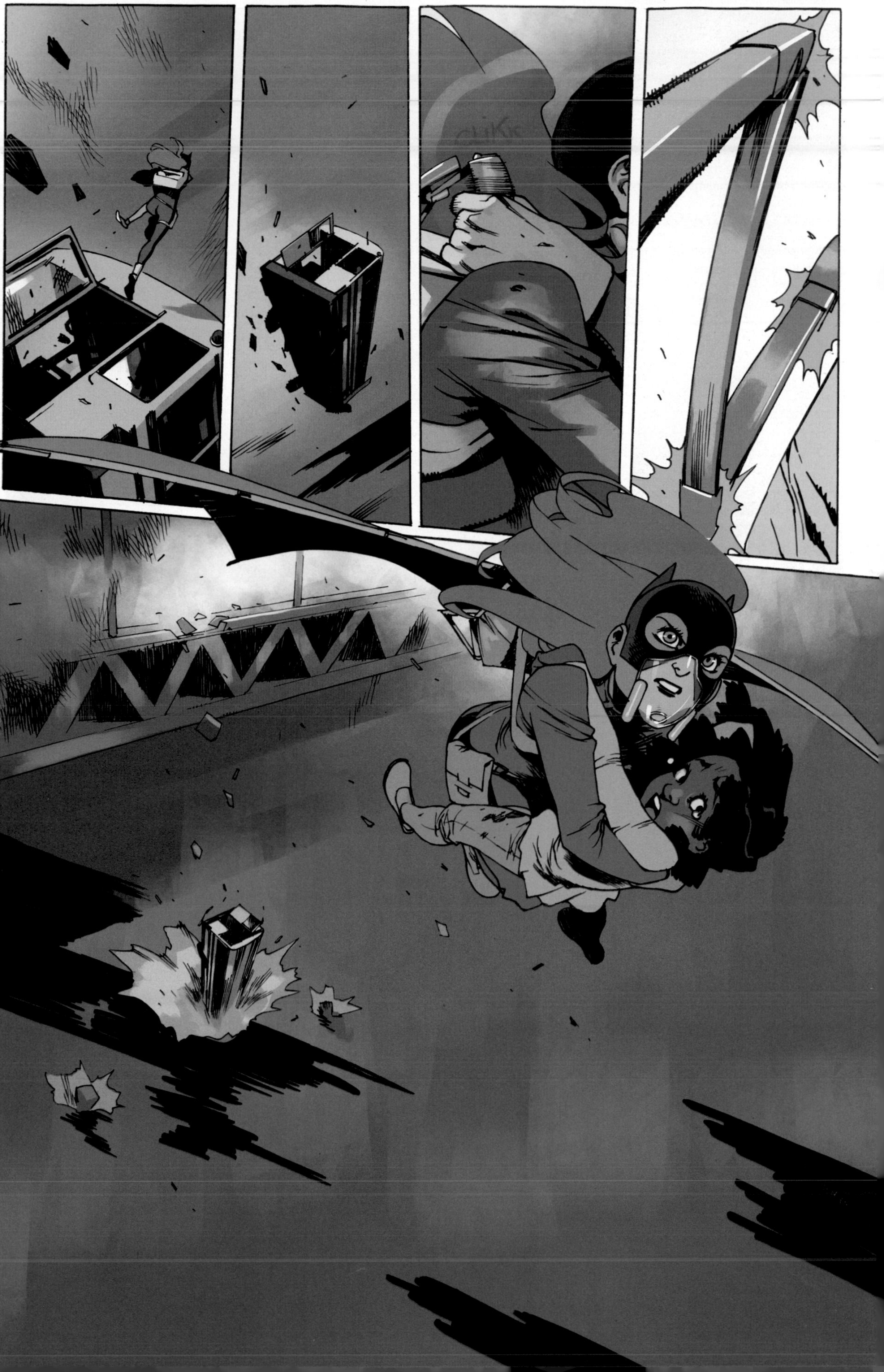
CLIKC

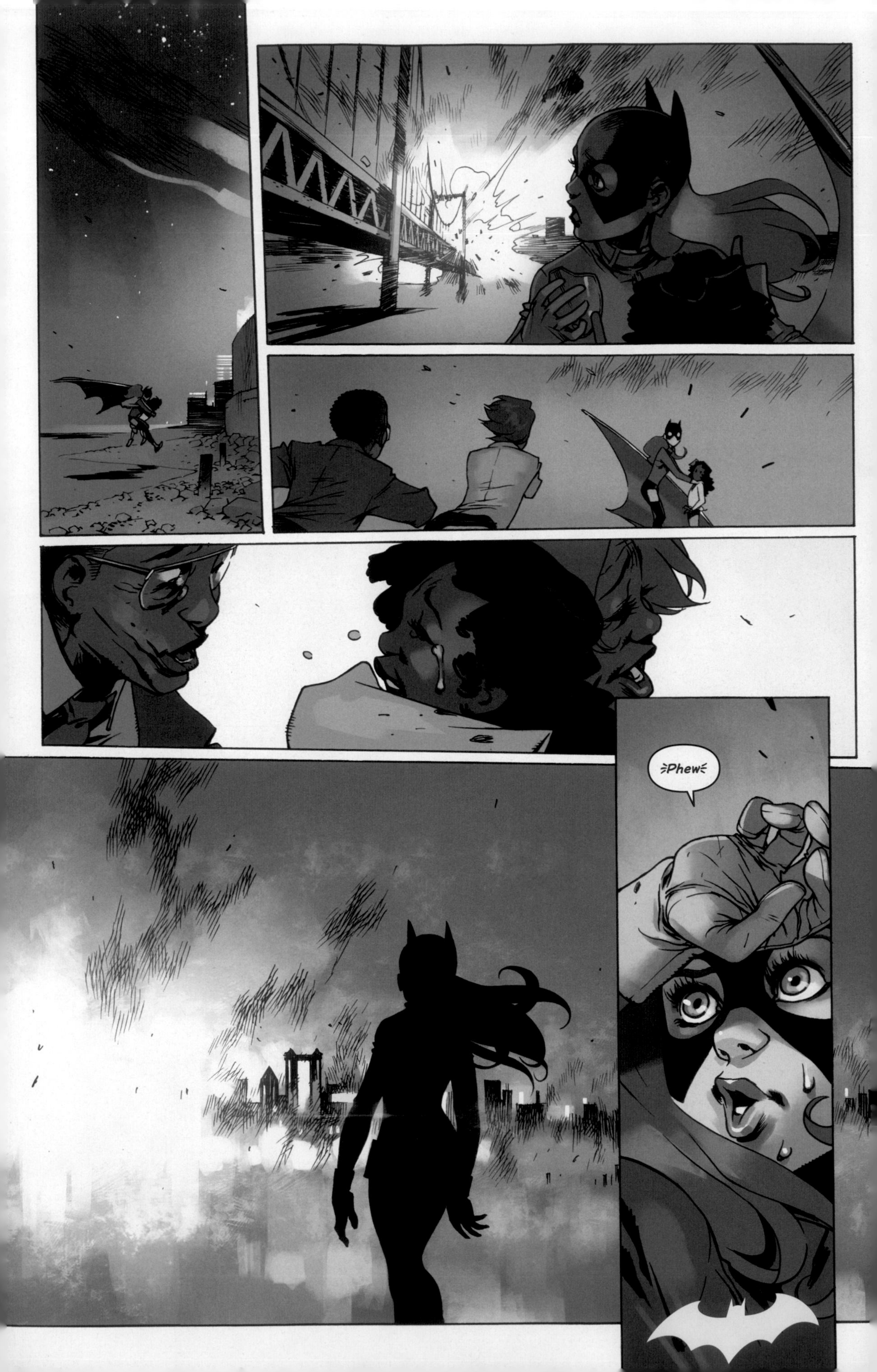
Phew

Cover by **GREG CAPULLO, DANNY MIKI** & **FCO PLASCENCIA**

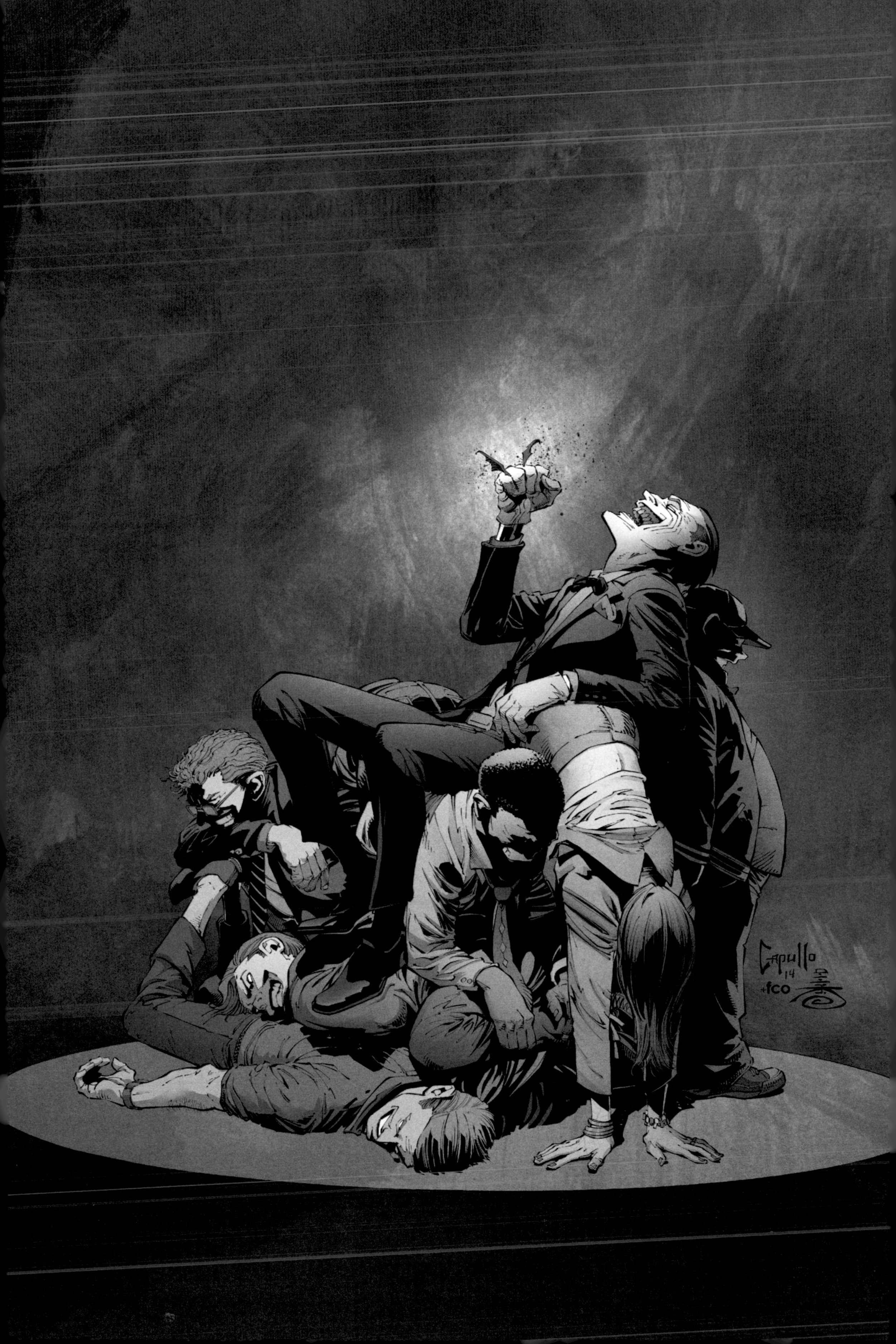

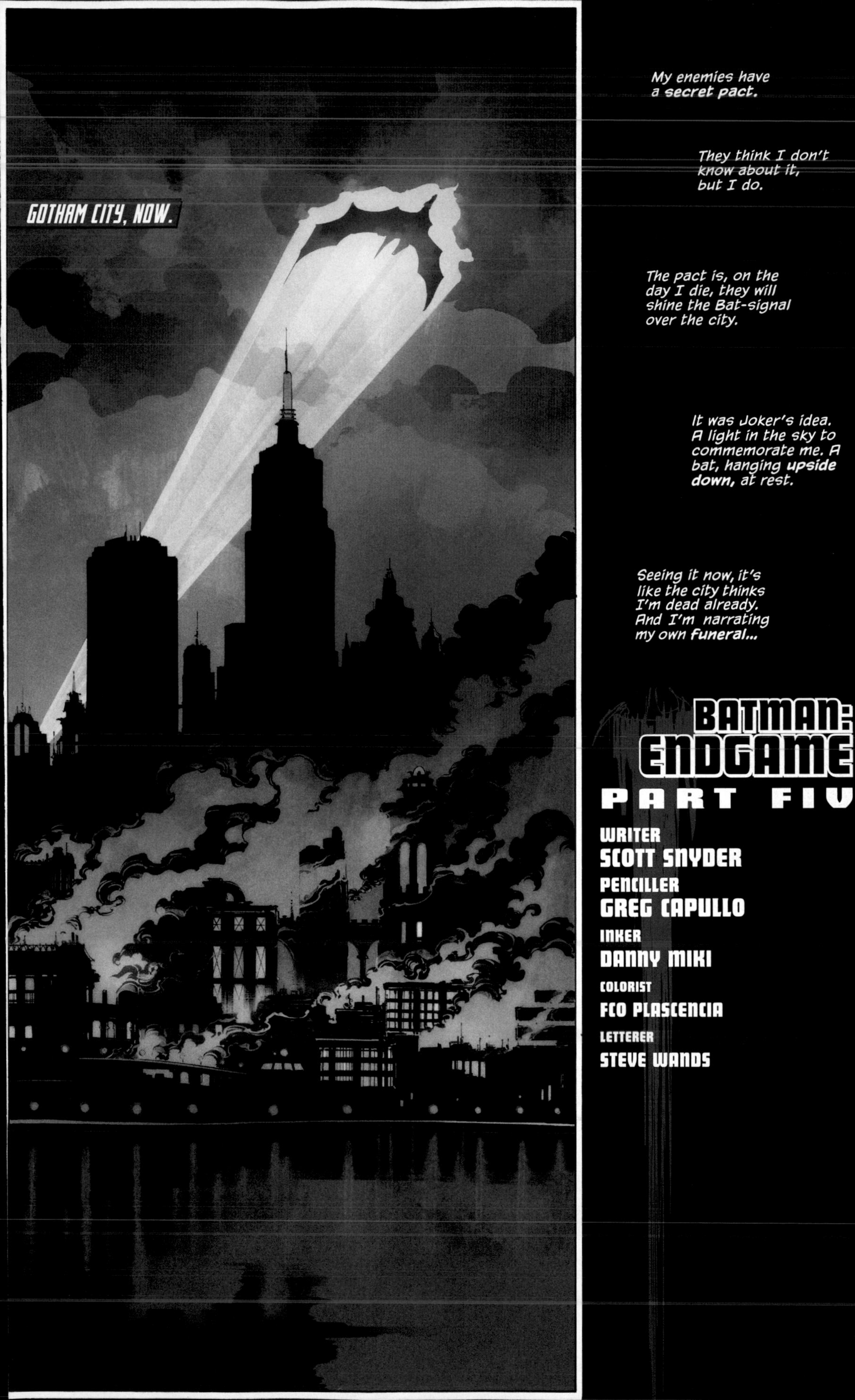
GOTHAM CITY, NOW.
My enemies have a secret pact.
They think I don't know about it, but I do.
The pact is, on the day I die, they will shine the Bat-signal over the city.
It was Joker's idea. A light in the sky to commemorate me. A bat, hanging upside down, at rest.
Seeing it now, it's like the city thinks I'm dead already. And I'm narrating my own funeral...
BATMAN: ENDGAME
PART FIV
WRITER
SCOTT SNYDER
PENCILLER
GREG CAPULLO
INKER
DANNY MIKI
COLORIST
FCO PLASCENCIA
LETTERER
STEVE WANDS

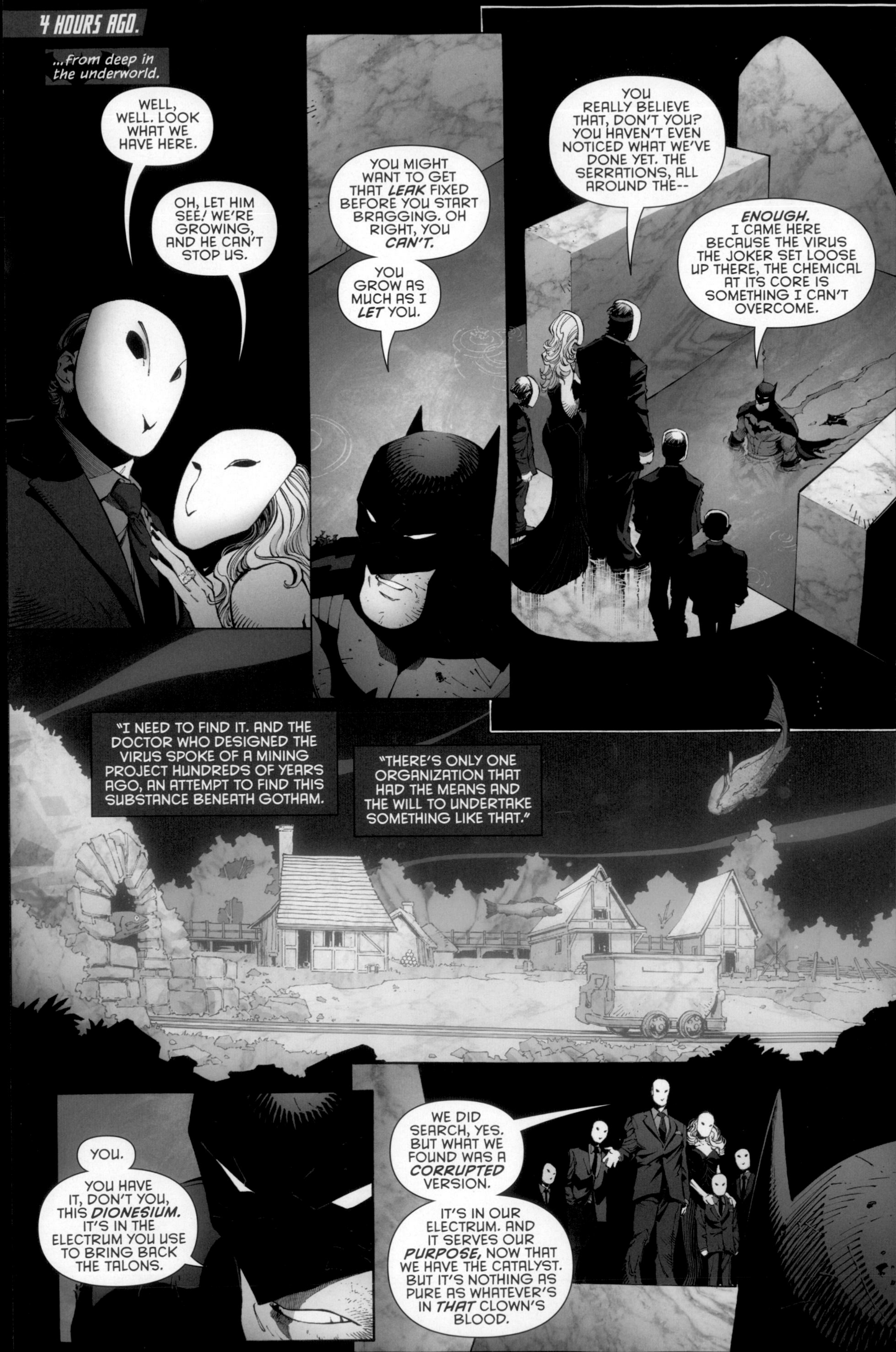

4 HOURS AGO.
...from deep in the underworld.
WELL, WELL. LOOK WHAT WE HAVE HERE.
OH, LET HIM SEE! WE'RE GROWING, AND HE CAN'T STOP US.
YOU MIGHT WANT TO GET THAT LEAK FIXED BEFORE YOU START BRAGGING. OH RIGHT, YOU CAN'T.
YOU GROW AS MUCH AS I LET YOU.
YOU REALLY BELIEVE THAT, DON'T YOU? YOU HAVEN'T EVEN NOTICED WHAT WE'VE DONE YET. THE SERRATIONS, ALL AROUND THE--
ENOUGH. I CAME HERE BECAUSE THE VIRUS THE JOKER SET LOOSE UP THERE, THE CHEMICAL AT ITS CORE IS SOMETHING I CAN'T OVERCOME.
"I NEED TO FIND IT. AND THE DOCTOR WHO DESIGNED THE VIRUS SPOKE OF A MINING PROJECT HUNDREDS OF YEARS AGO, AN ATTEMPT TO FIND THIS SUBSTANCE BENEATH GOTHAM.
"THERE'S ONLY ONE ORGANIZATION THAT HAD THE MEANS AND THE WILL TO UNDERTAKE SOMETHING LIKE THAT."
YOU.
YOU HAVE IT, DON'T YOU, THIS DIONESIUM. IT'S IN THE ELECTRUM YOU USE TO BRING BACK THE TALONS.
WE DID SEARCH, YES. BUT WHAT WE FOUND WAS A CORRUPTED VERSION.
IT'S IN OUR ELECTRUM. AND IT SERVES OUR PURPOSE, NOW THAT WE HAVE THE CATALYST. BUT IT'S NOTHING AS PURE AS WHATEVER'S IN THAT CLOWN'S BLOOD.

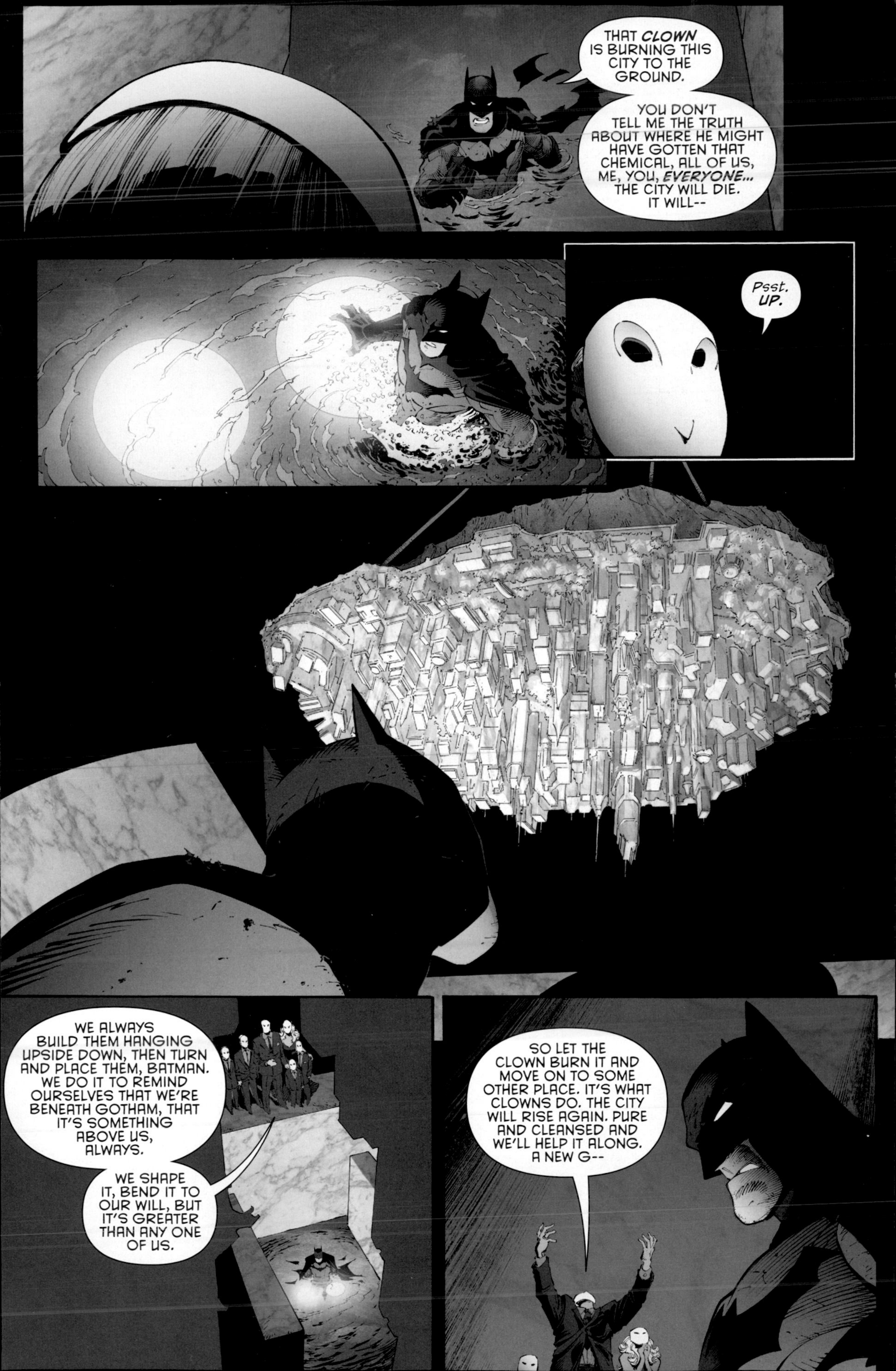

THAT CLOWN IS BURNING THIS CITY TO THE GROUND.
YOU DON'T TELL ME THE TRUTH ABOUT WHERE HE MIGHT HAVE GOTTEN THAT CHEMICAL, ALL OF US, ME, YOU, EVERYONE... THE CITY WILL DIE. IT WILL--
Psst. UP.
WE ALWAYS BUILD THEM HANGING UPSIDE DOWN, THEN TURN AND PLACE THEM, BATMAN. WE DO IT TO REMIND OURSELVES THAT WE'RE BENEATH GOTHAM, THAT IT'S SOMETHING ABOVE US, ALWAYS.
WE SHAPE IT, BEND IT TO OUR WILL, BUT IT'S GREATER THAN ANY ONE OF US.
SO LET THE CLOWN BURN IT AND MOVE ON TO SOME OTHER PLACE. IT'S WHAT CLOWNS DO. THE CITY WILL RISE AGAIN. PURE AND CLEANSED AND WE'LL HELP IT ALONG. A NEW G--

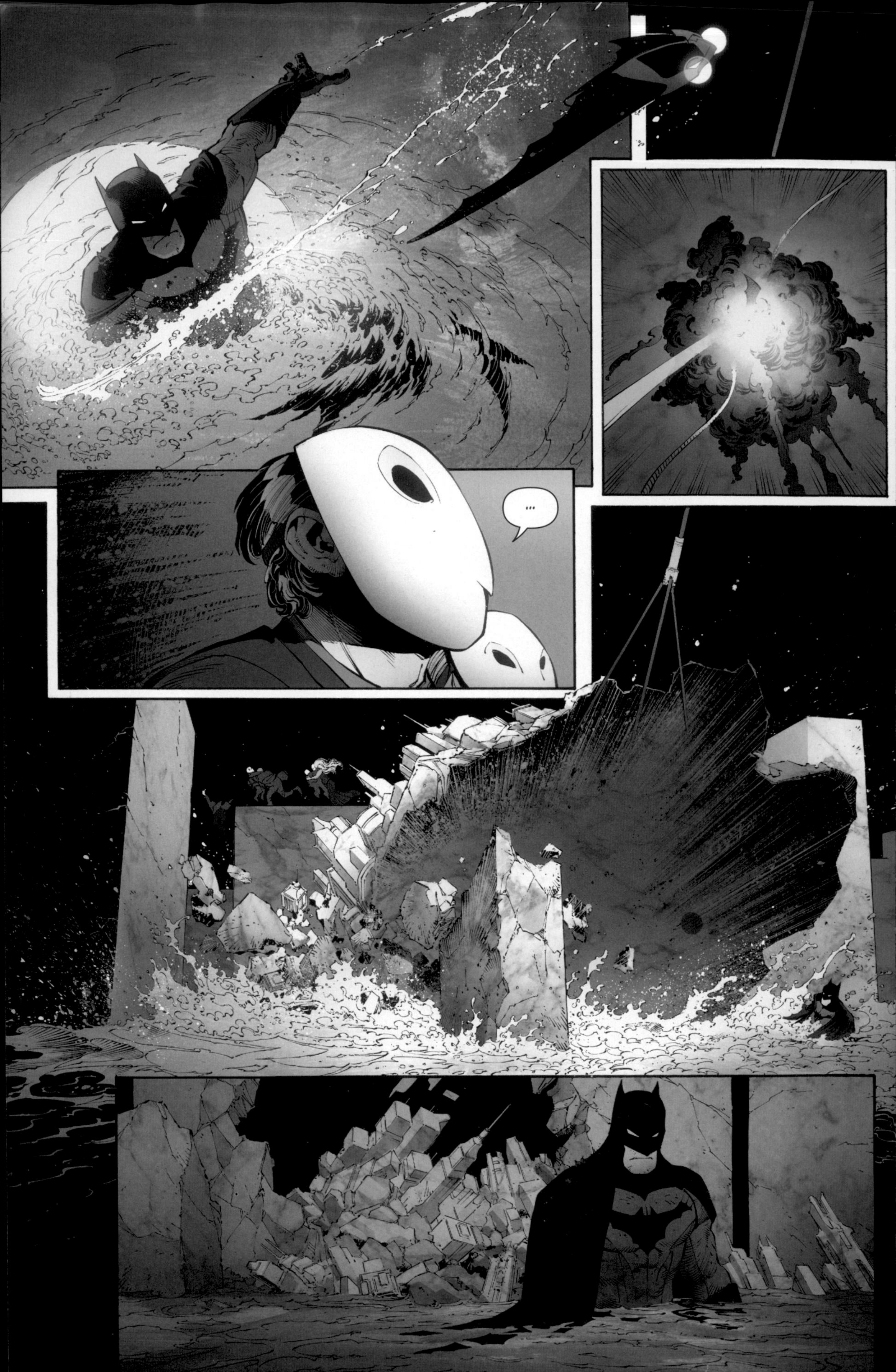
...

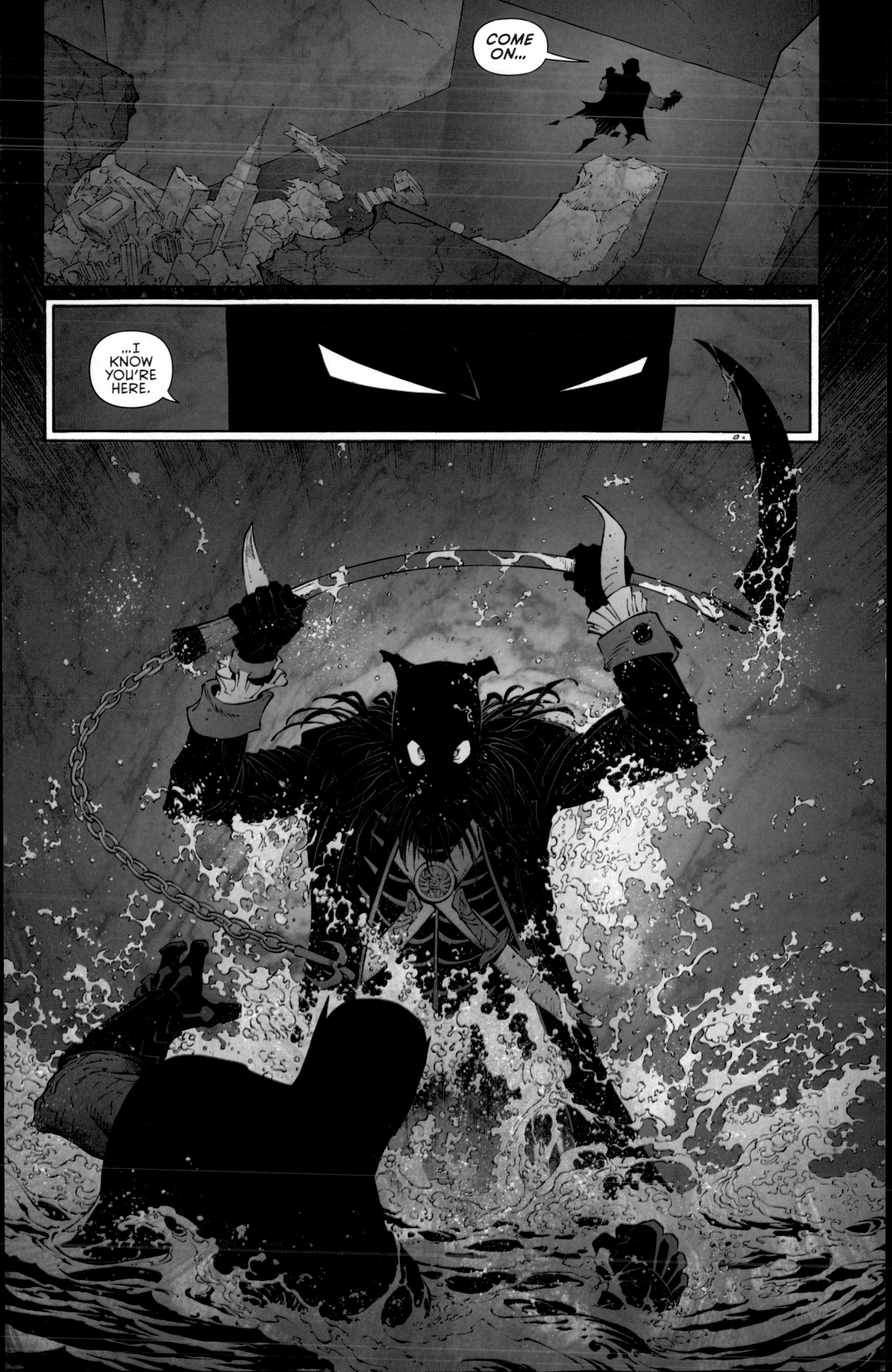
COME ON...
...I KNOW YOU'RE HERE.

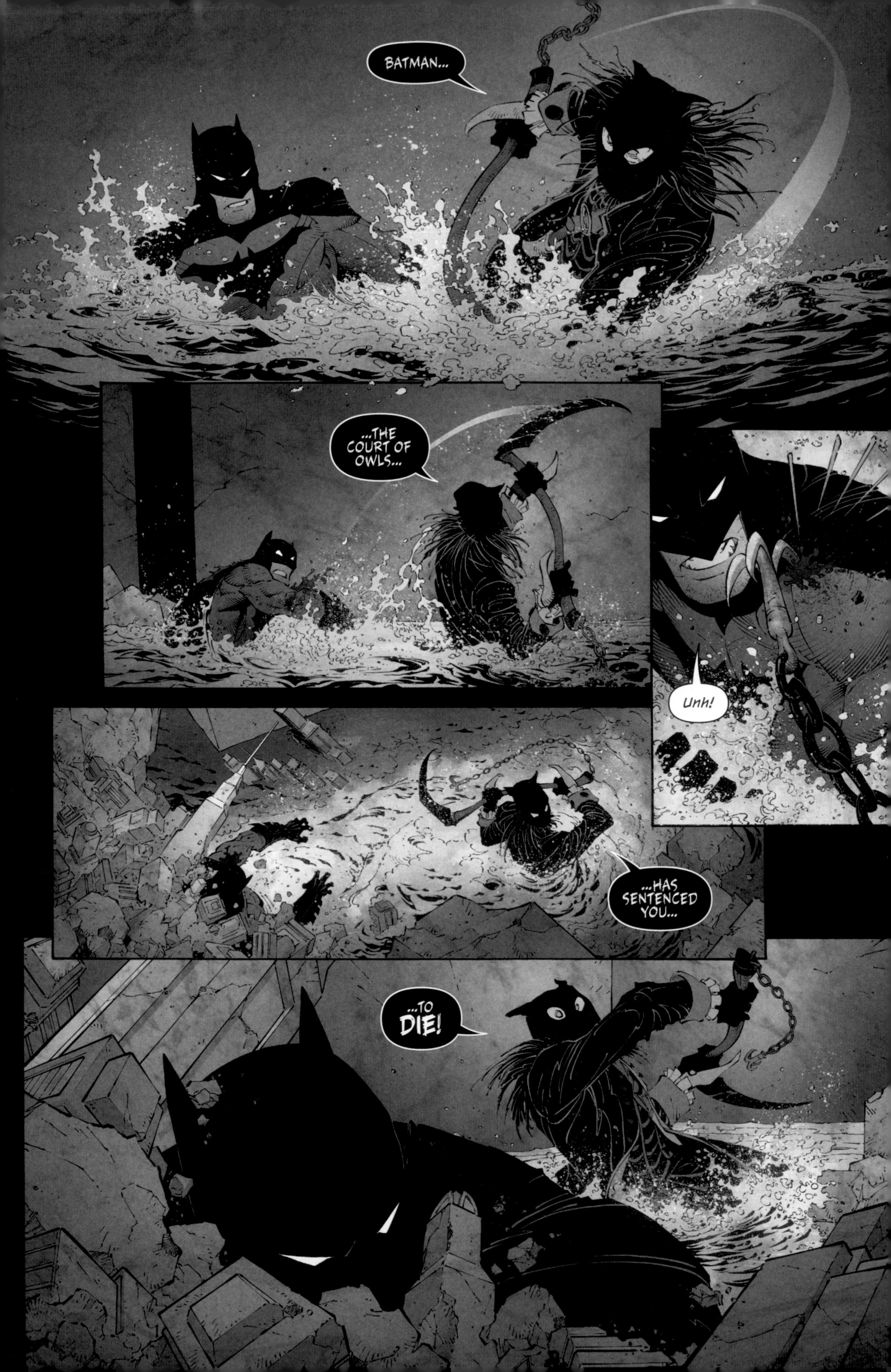
BATMAN...
...THE COURT OF OWLS...
Unh!
...HAS SENTENCED YOU...
...TO DIE!

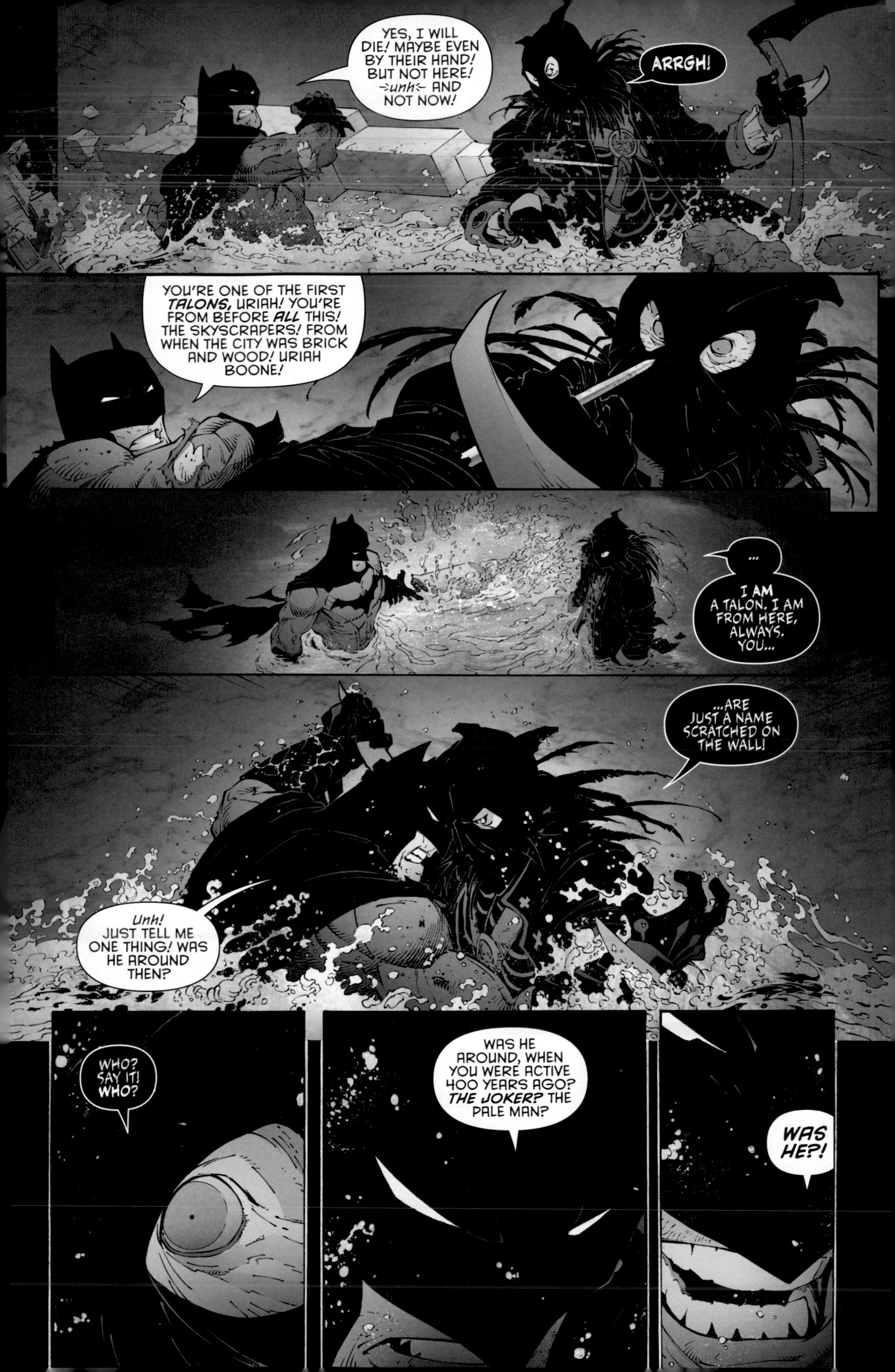

YES, I WILL DIE! MAYBE EVEN BY THEIR HAND! BUT NOT HERE! -unh- AND NOT NOW!
ARRGH!
YOU'RE ONE OF THE FIRST TALONS, URIAH! YOU'RE FROM BEFORE ALL THIS! THE SKYSCRAPERS! FROM WHEN THE CITY WAS BRICK AND WOOD! URIAH BOONE!
...
I AM A TALON. I AM FROM HERE, ALWAYS. YOU...
...ARE JUST A NAME SCRATCHED ON THE WALL!
Unh! JUST TELL ME ONE THING! WAS HE AROUND THEN?
WHO? SAY IT! WHO?
WAS HE AROUND, WHEN YOU WERE ACTIVE 400 YEARS AGO? THE JOKER? THE PALE MAN?
WAS HE?!

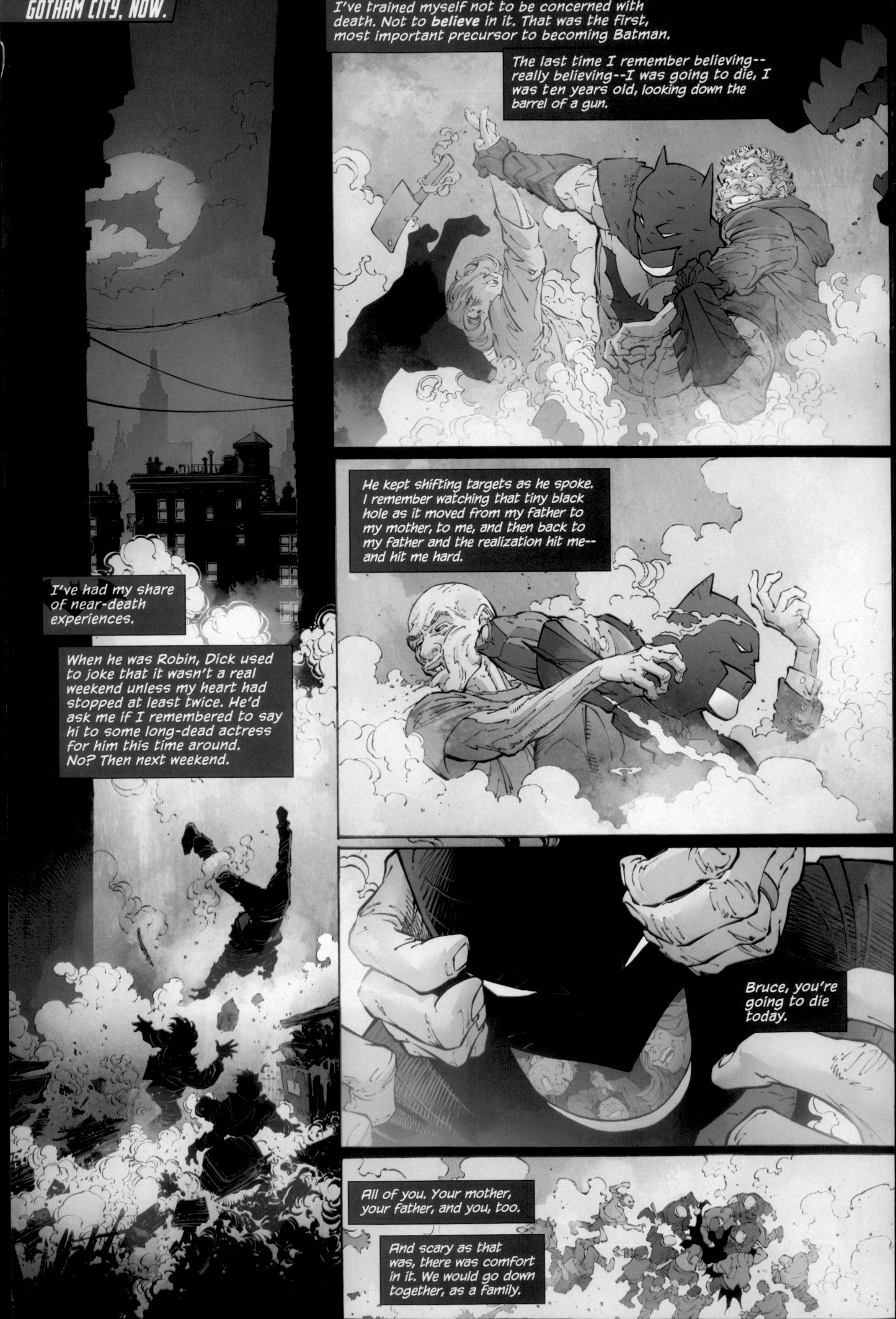
GOTHAM CITY, NOW.
I've trained myself not to be concerned with death. Not to believe in it. That was the first, most important precursor to becoming Batman.
The last time I remember believing--really believing--I was going to die, I was ten years old, looking down the barrel of a gun.
I've had my share of near-death experiences.
When he was Robin, Dick used to joke that it wasn't a real weekend unless my heart had stopped at least twice. He'd ask me if I remembered to say hi to some long-dead actress for him this time around. No? Then next weekend.
He kept shifting targets as he spoke. I remember watching that tiny black hole as it moved from my father to my mother, to me, and then back to my father and the realization hit me--and hit me hard.
Bruce, you're going to die today.
All of you. Your mother, your father, and you, too.
And scary as that was, there was comfort in it. We would go down together, as a family.

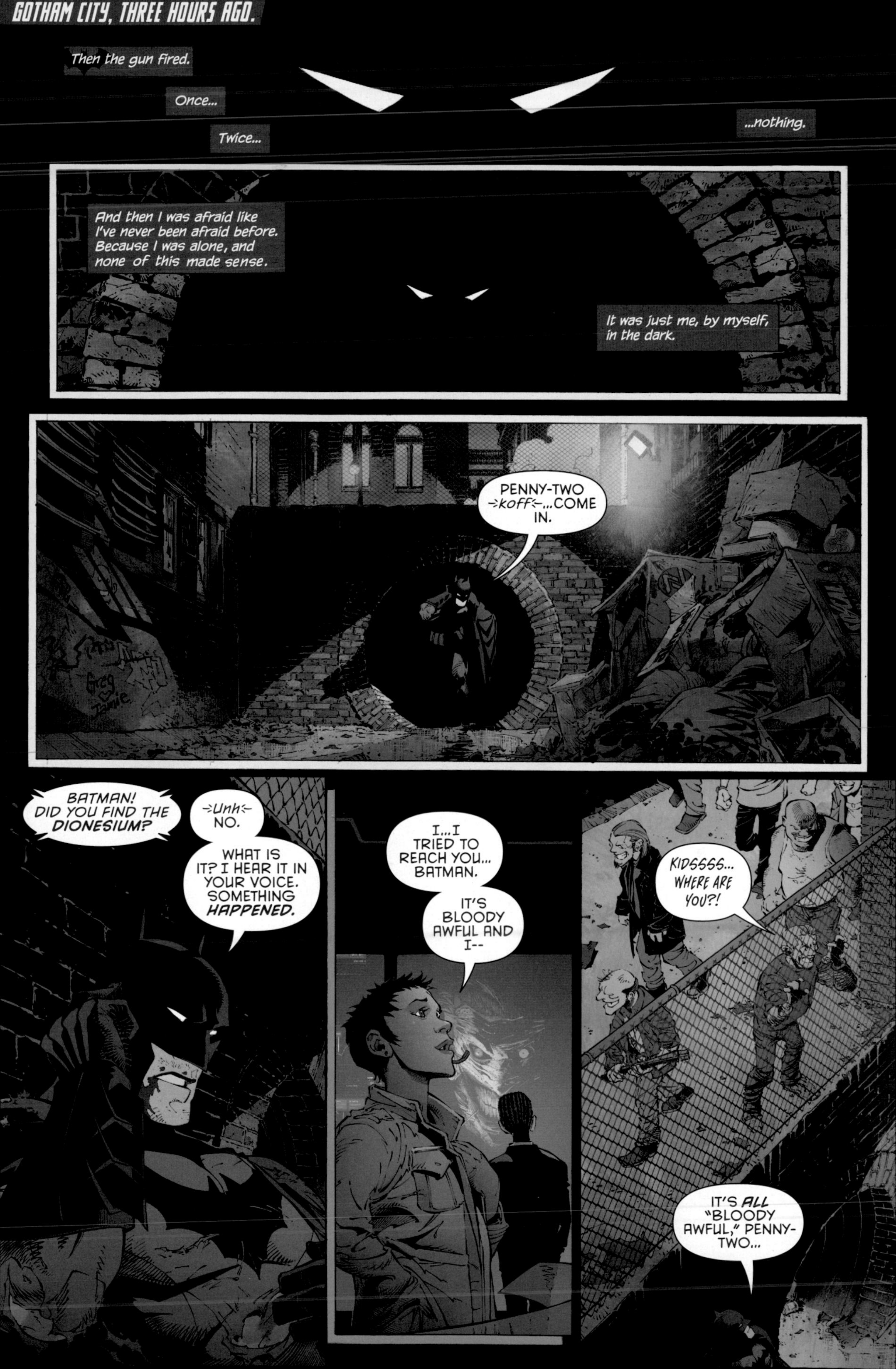
GOTHAM CITY, THREE HOURS AGO.
Then the gun fired.
Once...
Twice...
...nothing.
And then I was afraid like I've never been afraid before. Because I was alone, and none of this made sense.
It was just me, by myself, in the dark.
PENNY-TWO —koff—...COME IN.
BATMAN! DID YOU FIND THE DIONESIUM?
—Unh— NO.
WHAT IS IT? I HEAR IT IN YOUR VOICE. SOMETHING HAPPENED.
I...I TRIED TO REACH YOU... BATMAN.
IT'S BLOODY AWFUL AND I--
KIDSSSS... WHERE ARE YOU?!
IT'S ALL "BLOODY AWFUL," PENNY-TWO...

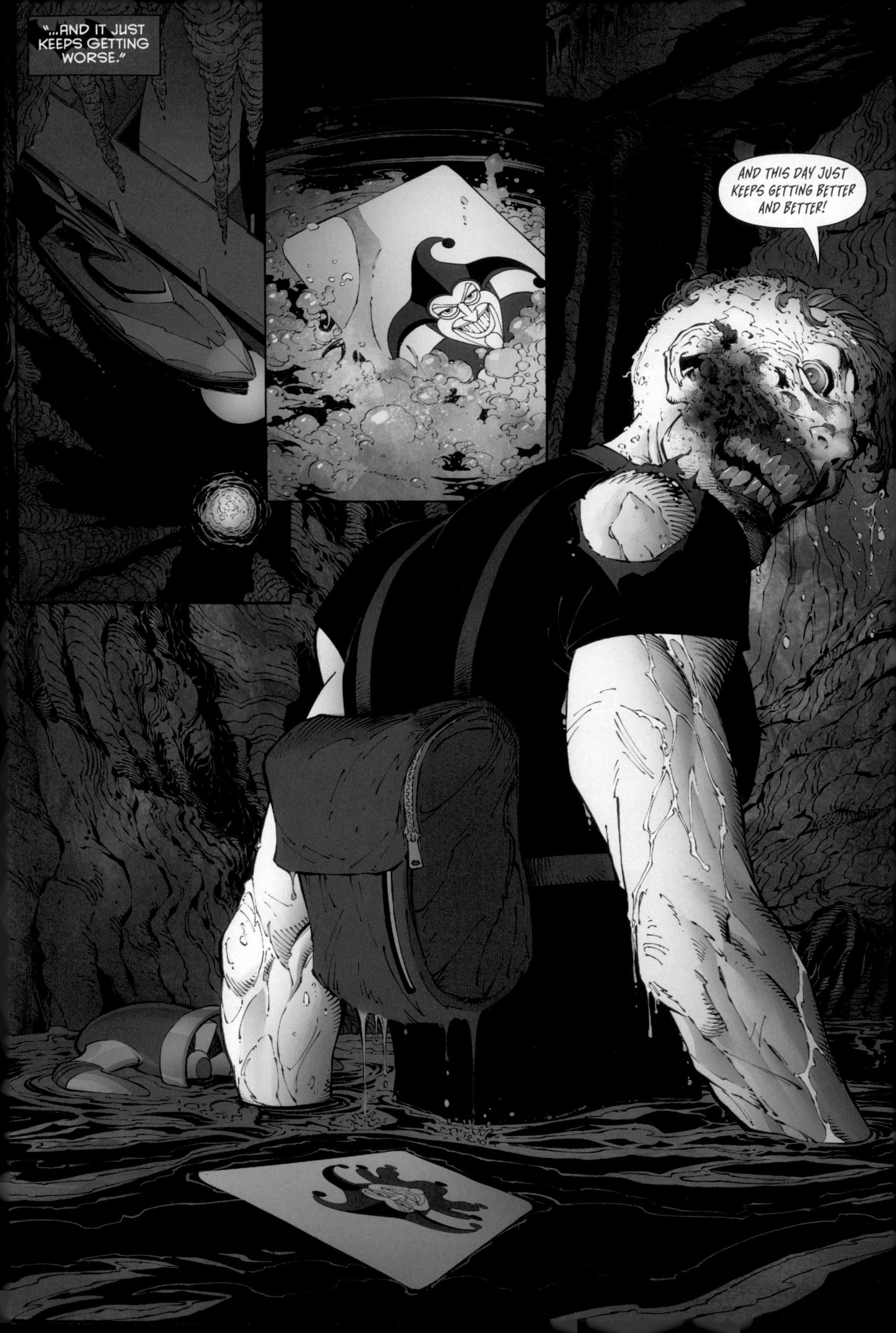
"...AND IT JUST KEEPS GETTING WORSE."
AND THIS DAY JUST KEEPS GETTING BETTER AND BETTER!

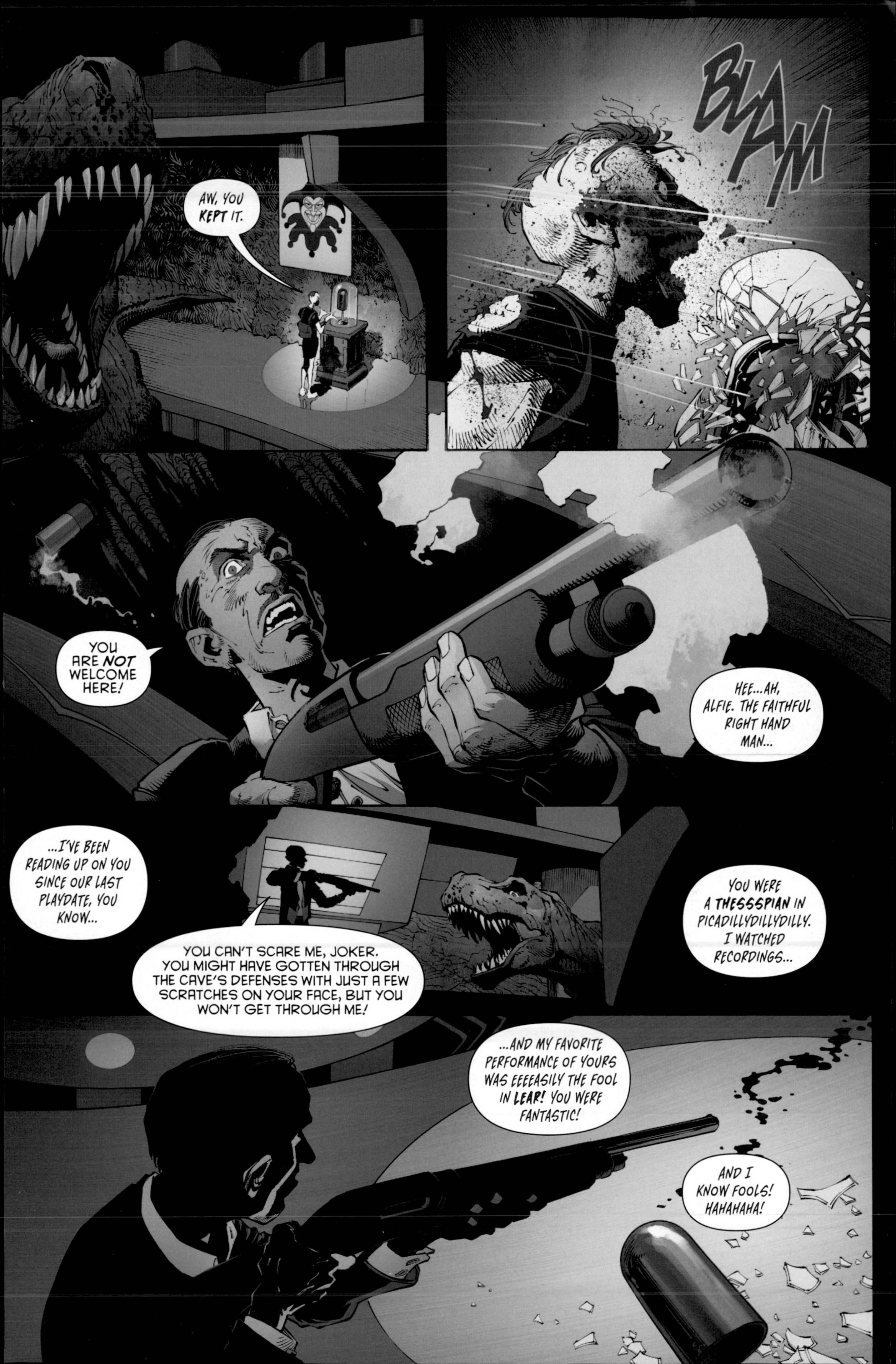
AW, YOU KEPT IT.
BLAM
YOU ARE NOT WELCOME HERE!
HEE...AH, ALFIE. THE FAITHFUL RIGHT HAND MAN...
...I'VE BEEN READING UP ON YOU SINCE OUR LAST PLAYDATE, YOU KNOW...
YOU CAN'T SCARE ME, JOKER. YOU MIGHT HAVE GOTTEN THROUGH THE CAVE'S DEFENSES WITH JUST A FEW SCRATCHES ON YOUR FACE, BUT YOU WON'T GET THROUGH ME!
YOU WERE A THESSSPIAN IN PICADILLYDILLYDILLY. I WATCHED RECORDINGS...
...AND MY FAVORITE PERFORMANCE OF YOURS WAS EEEEASILY THE FOOL IN LEAR! YOU WERE FANTASTIC!
AND I KNOW FOOLS! HAHAHAHA!

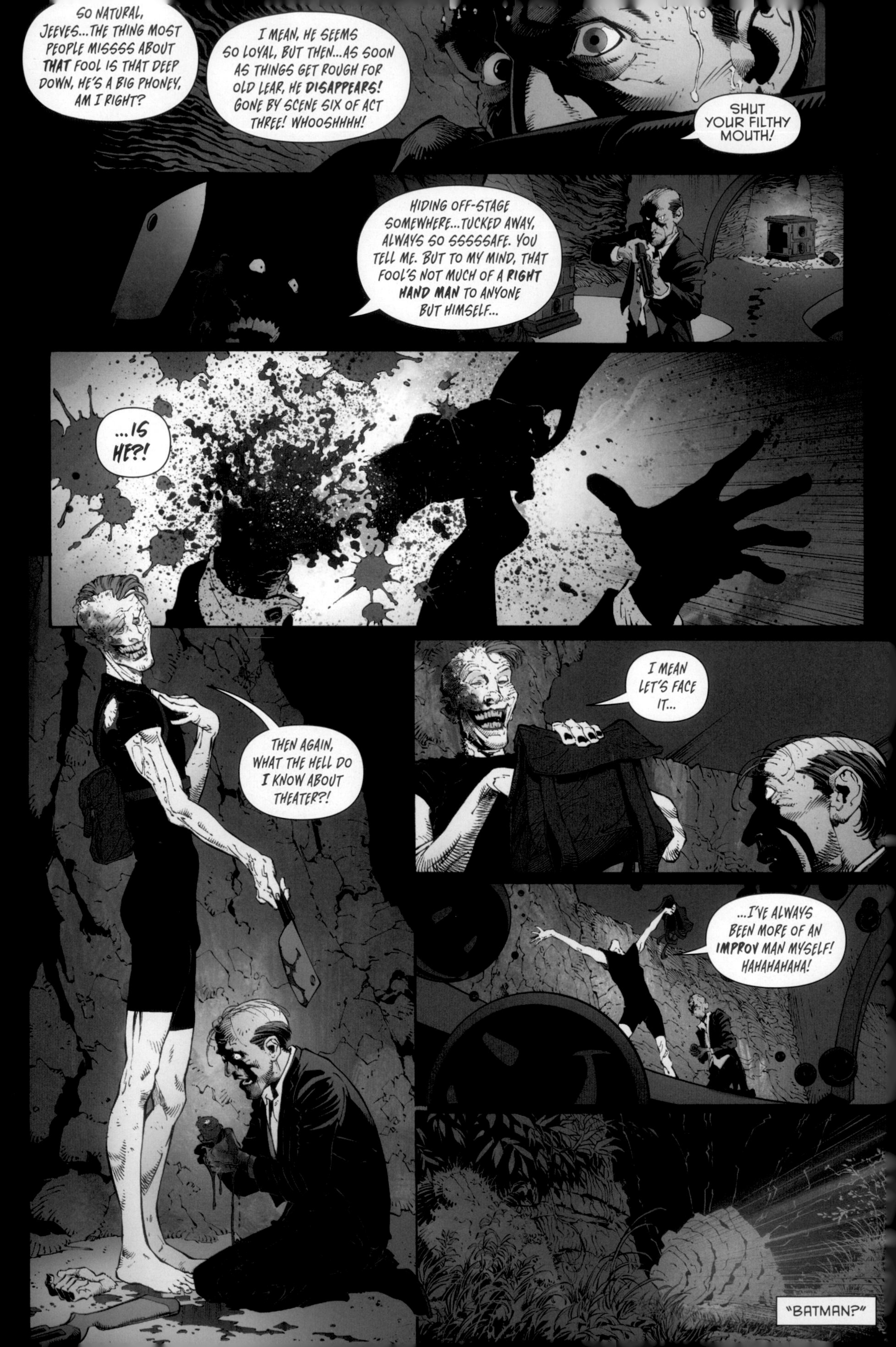
SO NATURAL, JEEVES...THE THING MOST PEOPLE MISSSS ABOUT **THAT** FOOL IS THAT DEEP DOWN, HE'S A BIG PHONEY, AM I RIGHT?
I MEAN, HE SEEMS SO LOYAL, BUT THEN...AS SOON AS THINGS GET ROUGH FOR OLD LEAR, HE **DISAPPEARS!** GONE BY SCENE SIX OF ACT THREE! WHOOSHHHH!
SHUT YOUR FILTHY MOUTH!
HIDING OFF-STAGE SOMEWHERE...TUCKED AWAY, ALWAYS SO SSSSSAFE. YOU TELL ME. BUT TO MY MIND, THAT FOOL'S NOT MUCH OF A **RIGHT HAND MAN** TO ANYONE BUT HIMSELF...
...IS HE?!
THEN AGAIN, WHAT THE HELL DO I KNOW ABOUT THEATER?!
I MEAN LET'S FACE IT...
...I'VE ALWAYS BEEN MORE OF AN **IMPROV** MAN MYSELF! HAHAHAHAHA!
"BATMAN?"

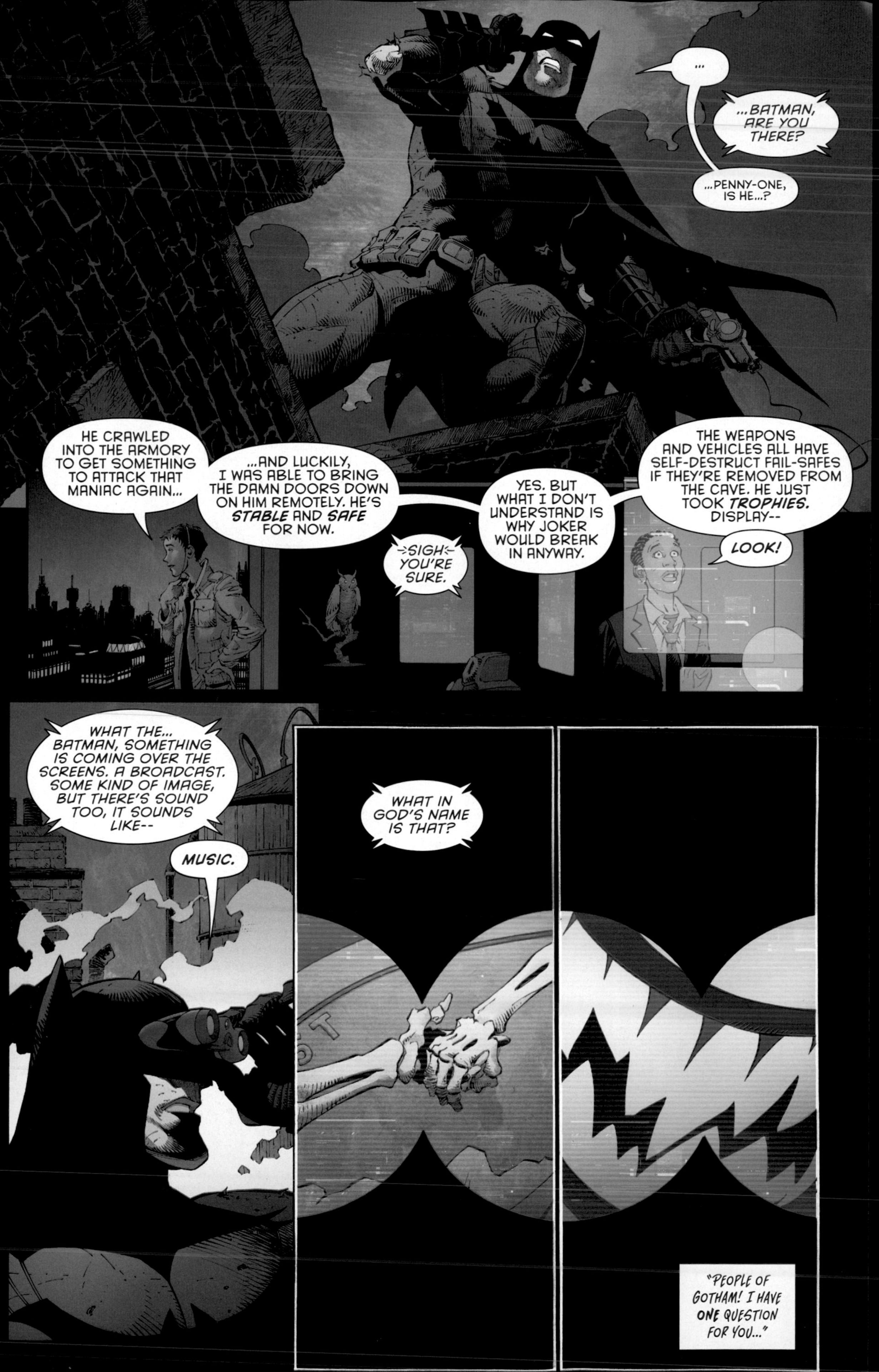
...
...BATMAN, ARE YOU THERE?
...PENNY-ONE, IS HE...?
HE CRAWLED INTO THE ARMORY TO GET SOMETHING TO ATTACK THAT MANIAC AGAIN...
...AND LUCKILY, I WAS ABLE TO BRING THE DAMN DOORS DOWN ON HIM REMOTELY. HE'S STABLE AND SAFE FOR NOW.
SIGH YOU'RE SURE.
YES. BUT WHAT I DON'T UNDERSTAND IS WHY JOKER WOULD BREAK IN ANYWAY.
THE WEAPONS AND VEHICLES ALL HAVE SELF-DESTRUCT FAIL-SAFES IF THEY'RE REMOVED FROM THE CAVE. HE JUST TOOK TROPHIES. DISPLAY--
LOOK!
WHAT THE... BATMAN, SOMETHING IS COMING OVER THE SCREENS. A BROADCAST. SOME KIND OF IMAGE, BUT THERE'S SOUND TOO, IT SOUNDS LIKE--
MUSIC.
WHAT IN GOD'S NAME IS THAT?
"PEOPLE OF GOTHAM! I HAVE ONE QUESTION FOR YOU..."

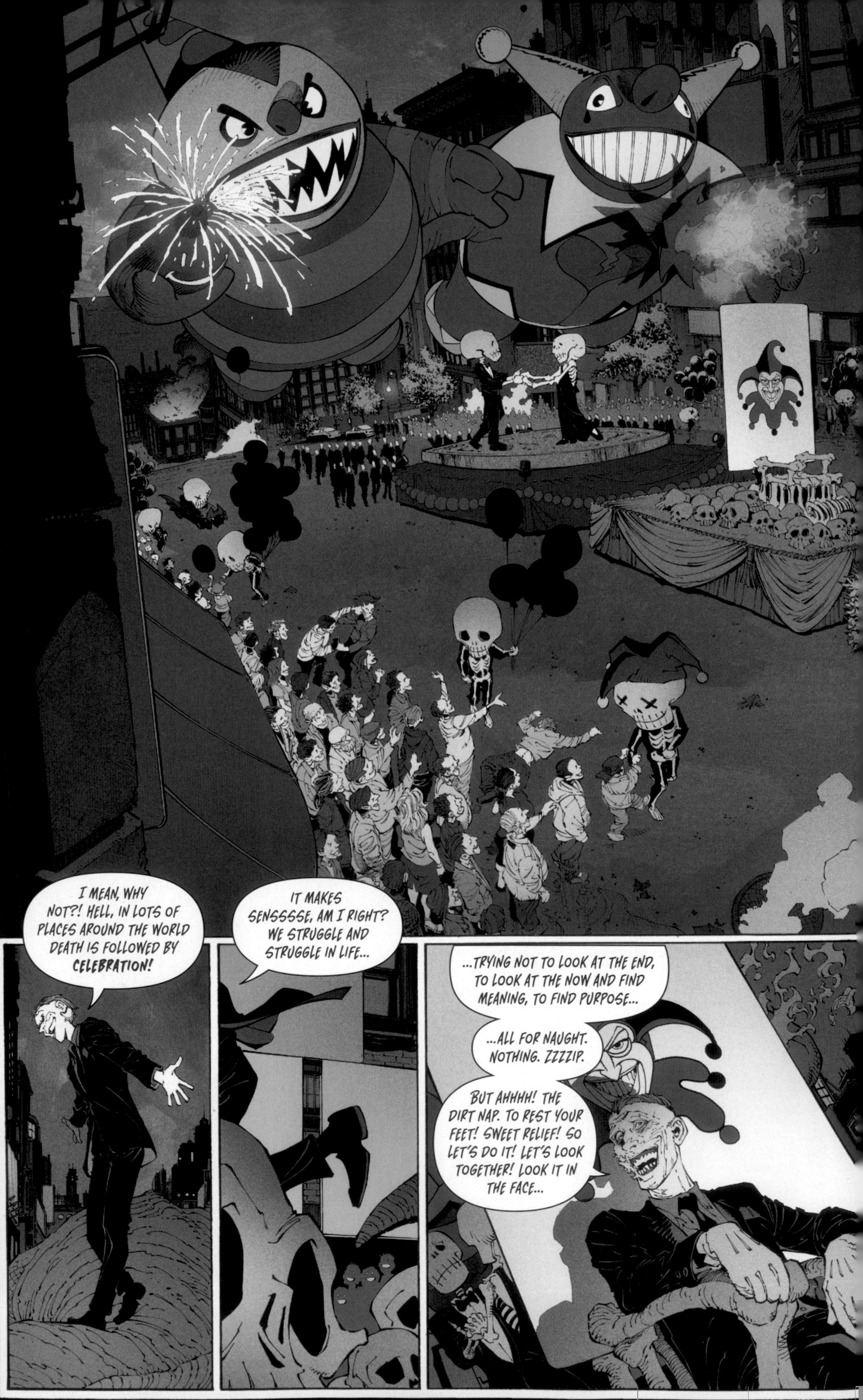

I MEAN, WHY NOT?! HELL, IN LOTS OF PLACES AROUND THE WORLD DEATH IS FOLLOWED BY **CELEBRATION!**
IT MAKES SENSSSSE, AM I RIGHT? WE STRUGGLE AND STRUGGLE IN LIFE...
...TRYING NOT TO LOOK AT THE END, TO LOOK AT THE NOW AND FIND MEANING, TO FIND PURPOSE...
...ALL FOR NAUGHT. NOTHING. ZZZZIP.
BUT AHHHH! THE DIRT NAP. TO REST YOUR FEET! SWEET RELIEF! SO LET'S DO IT! LET'S LOOK TOGETHER! LOOK IT IN THE FACE...

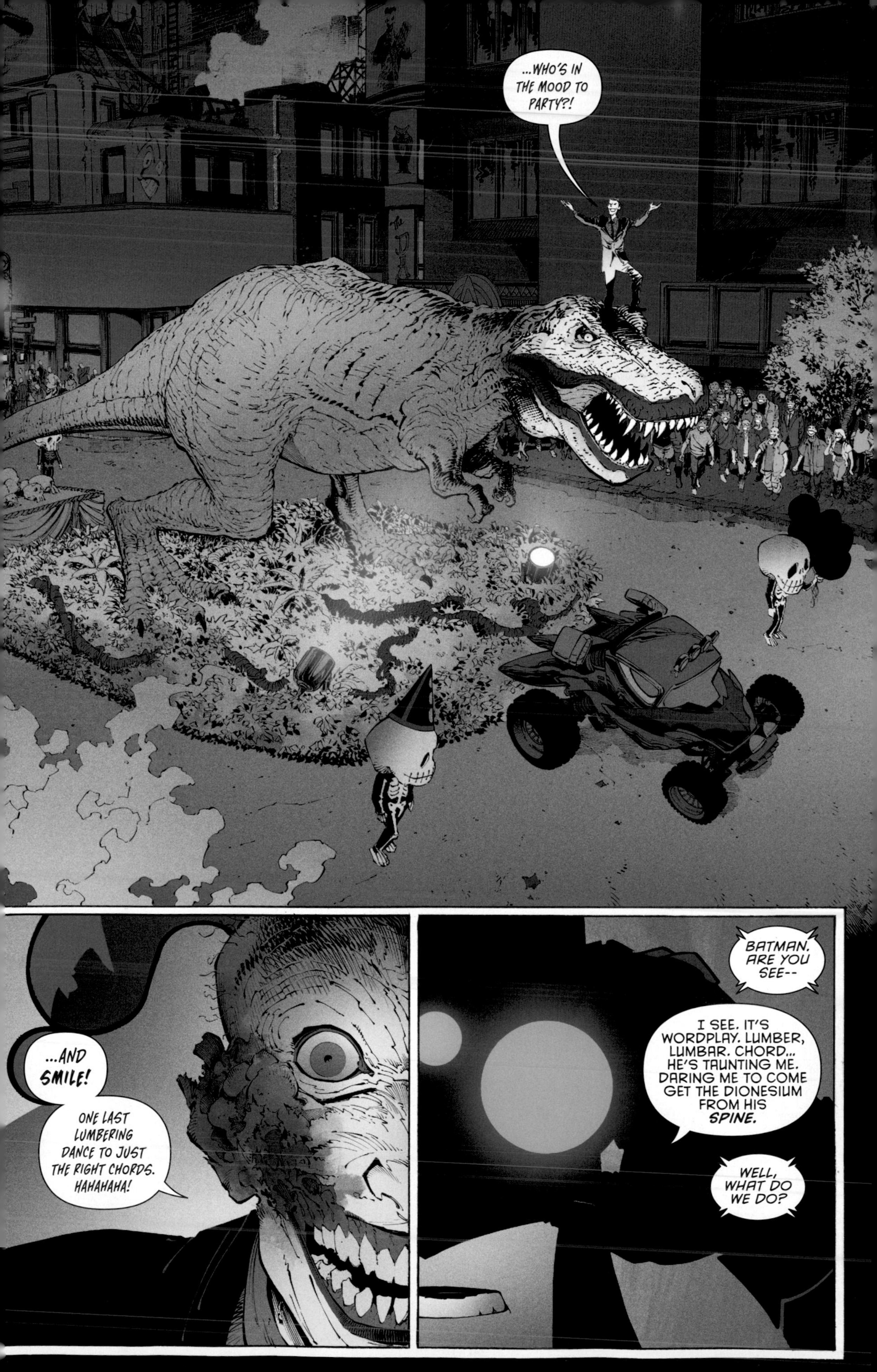
...WHO'S IN THE MOOD TO PARTY?!
...AND SMILE!
ONE LAST LUMBERING DANCE TO JUST THE RIGHT CHORDS. HAHAHAHA!
BATMAN, ARE YOU SEE--
I SEE. IT'S WORDPLAY. LUMBER, LUMBAR. CHORD... HE'S TAUNTING ME. DARING ME TO COME GET THE DIONESIUM FROM HIS SPINE.
WELL, WHAT DO WE DO?

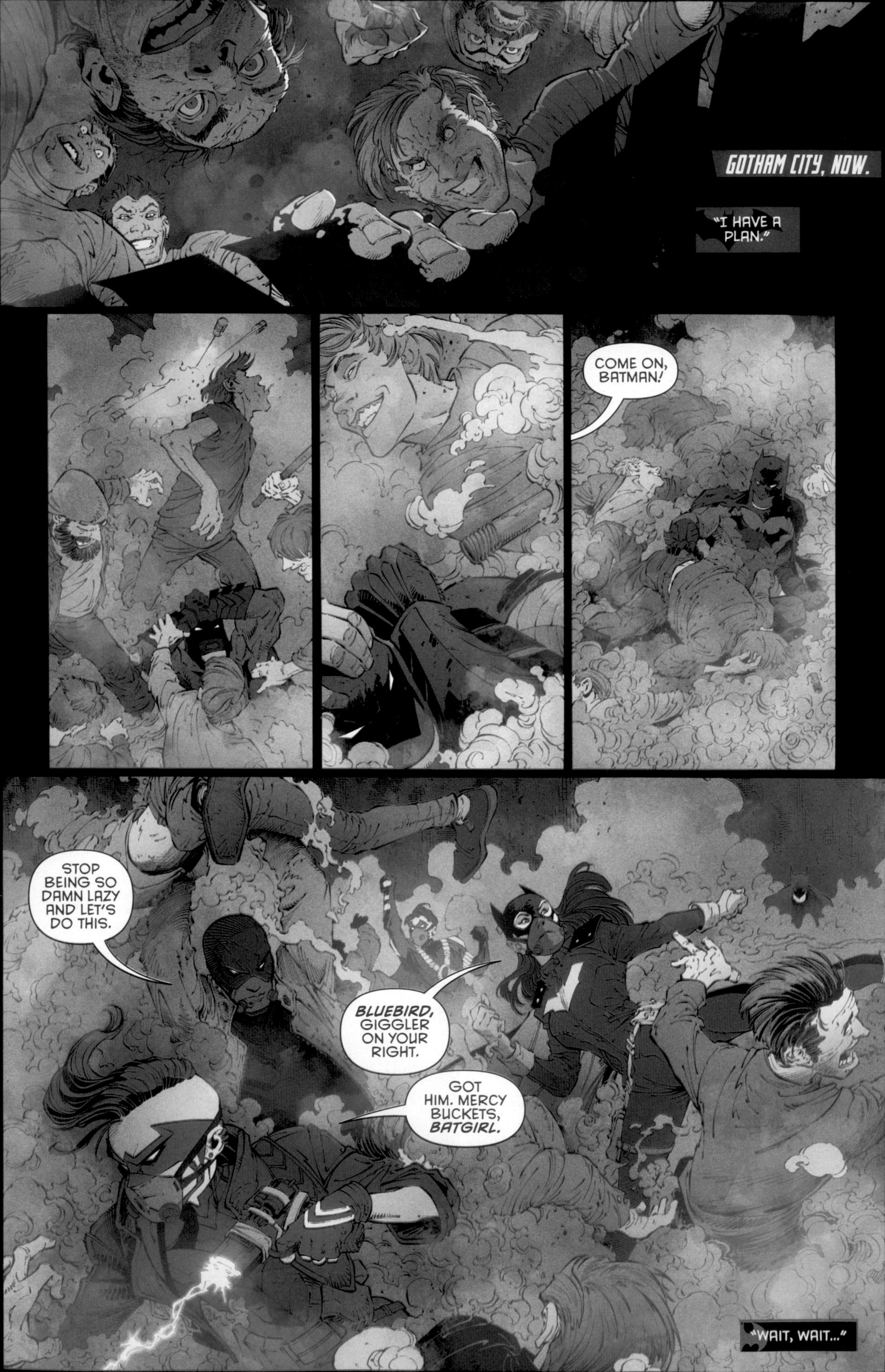
GOTHAM CITY, NOW.
"I HAVE A PLAN."
COME ON, BATMAN!
STOP BEING SO DAMN LAZY AND LET'S DO THIS.
BLUEBIRD, GIGGLER ON YOUR RIGHT.
GOT HIM. MERCY BUCKETS, BATGIRL.
"WAIT, WAIT..."

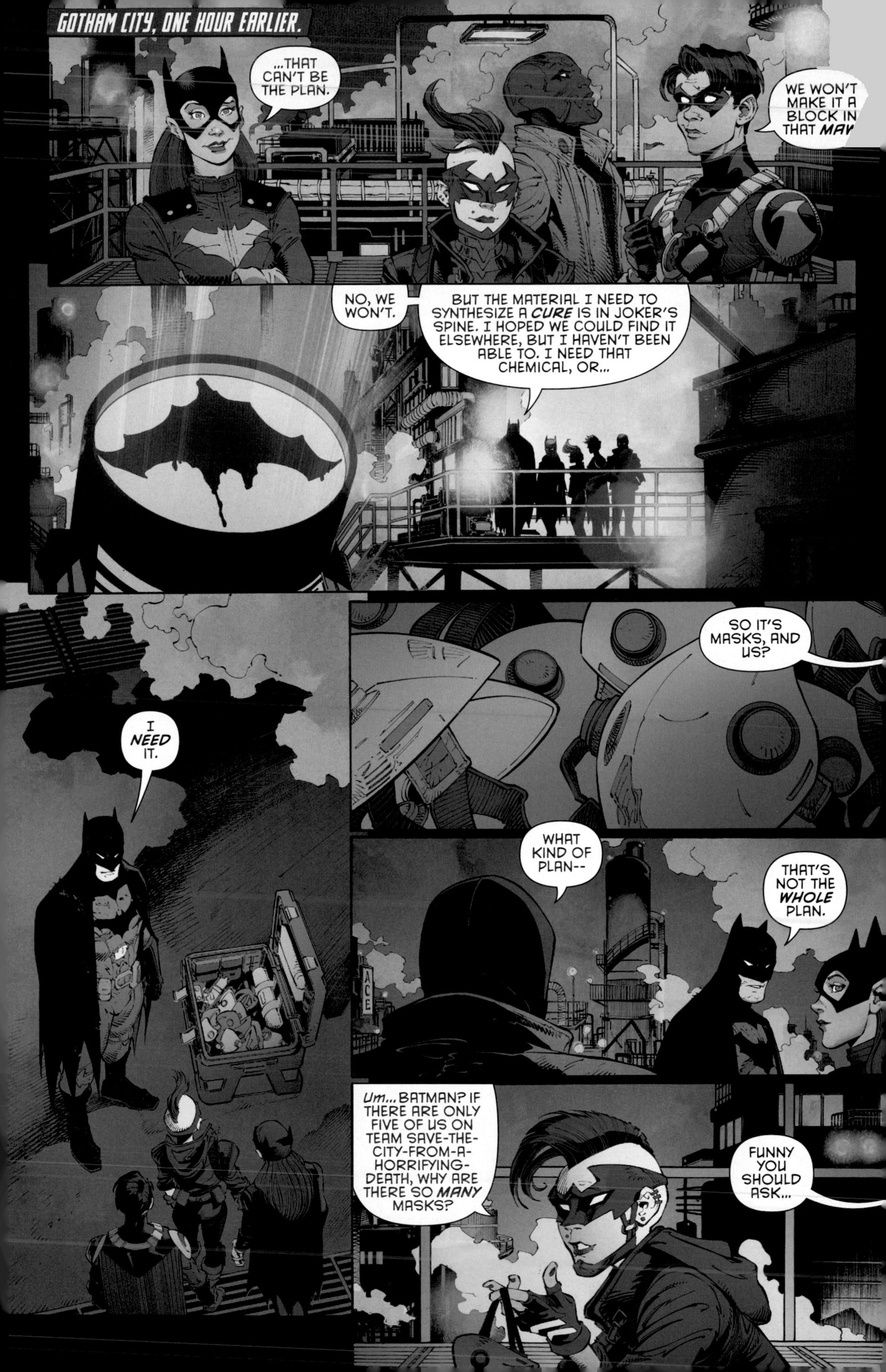
GOTHAM CITY, ONE HOUR EARLIER.
...THAT CAN'T BE THE PLAN.
WE WON'T MAKE IT A BLOCK IN THAT MA
NO, WE WON'T.
BUT THE MATERIAL I NEED TO SYNTHESIZE A CURE IS IN JOKER'S SPINE. I HOPED WE COULD FIND IT ELSEWHERE, BUT I HAVEN'T BEEN ABLE TO. I NEED THAT CHEMICAL, OR...
I NEED IT.
SO IT'S MASKS, AND US?
WHAT KIND OF PLAN--
THAT'S NOT THE WHOLE PLAN.
Um... BATMAN? IF THERE ARE ONLY FIVE OF US ON TEAM SAVE-THE-CITY-FROM-A-HORRIFYING-DEATH, WHY ARE THERE SO MANY MASKS?
FUNNY YOU SHOULD ASK...

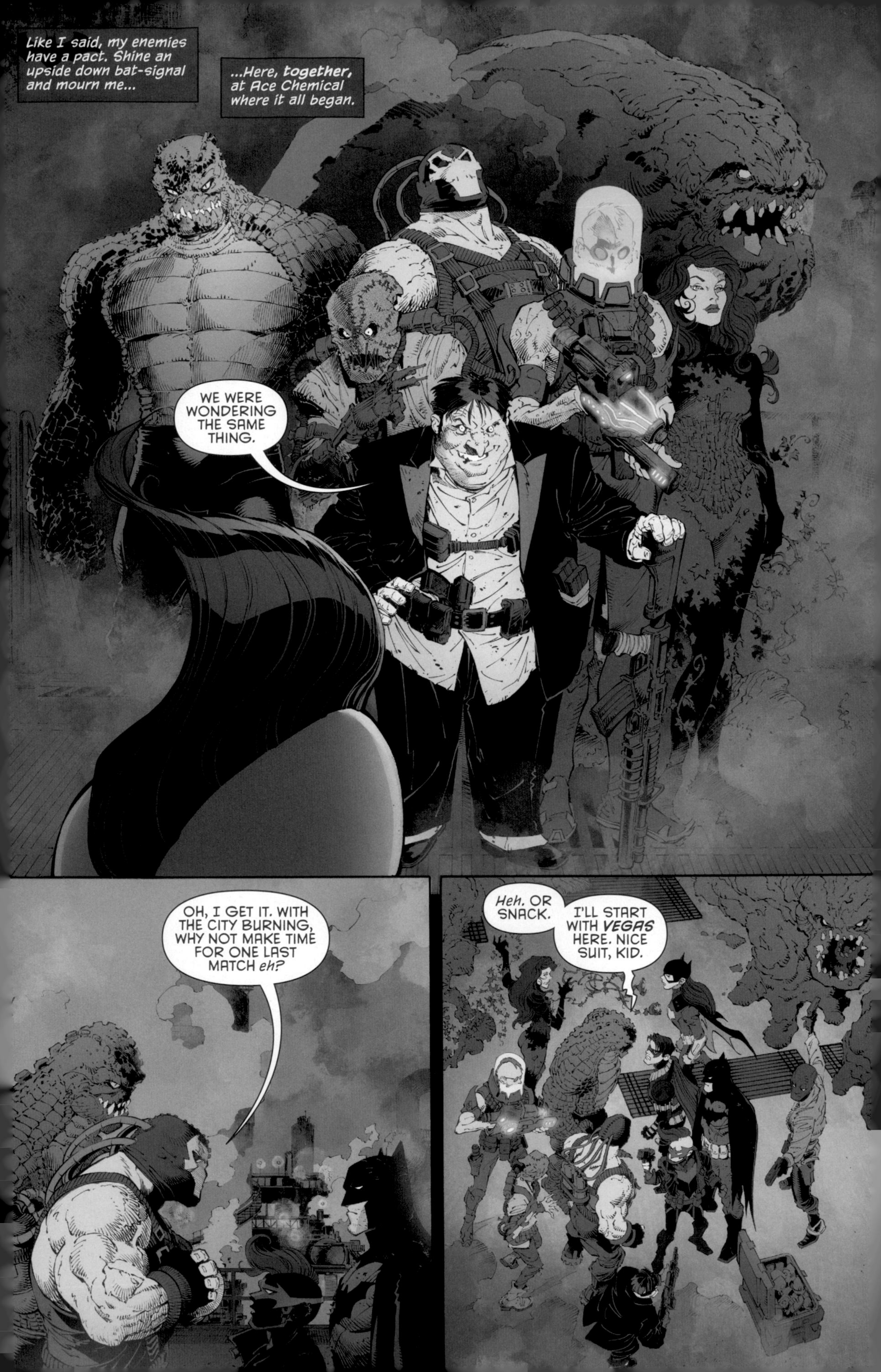
Like I said, my enemies have a pact. Shine an upside down bat-signal and mourn me...
...Here, together, at Ace Chemical where it all began.
WE WERE WONDERING THE SAME THING.
OH, I GET IT. WITH THE CITY BURNING, WHY NOT MAKE TIME FOR ONE LAST MATCH eh?
Heh. OR SNACK.
I'LL START WITH VEGAS HERE. NICE SUIT, KID.

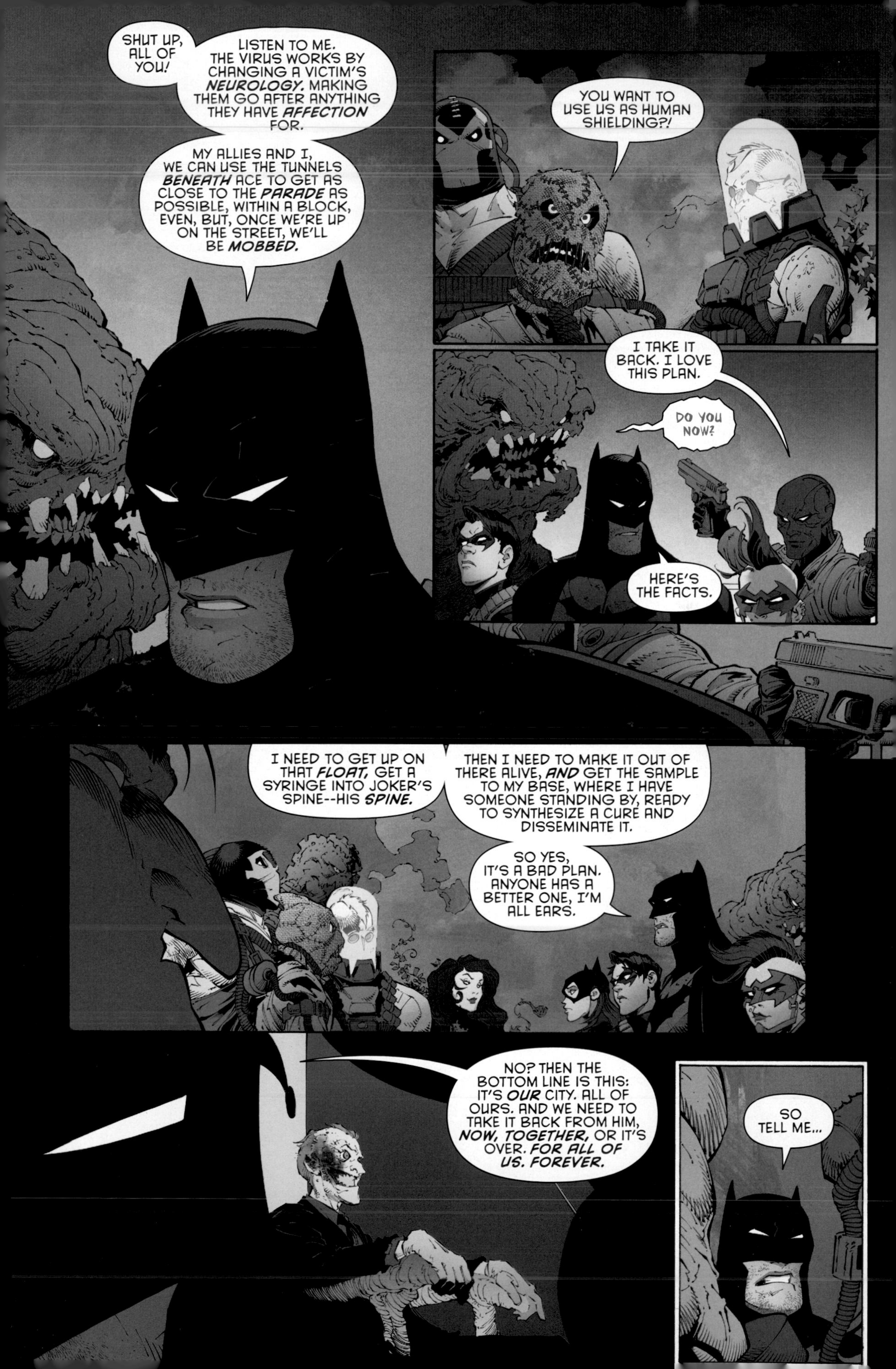
SHUT UP, ALL OF YOU!
LISTEN TO ME. THE VIRUS WORKS BY CHANGING A VICTIM'S NEUROLOGY, MAKING THEM GO AFTER ANYTHING THEY HAVE AFFECTION FOR.
MY ALLIES AND I, WE CAN USE THE TUNNELS BENEATH ACE TO GET AS CLOSE TO THE PARADE AS POSSIBLE, WITHIN A BLOCK, EVEN, BUT, ONCE WE'RE UP ON THE STREET, WE'LL BE MOBBED.
YOU WANT TO USE US AS HUMAN SHIELDING?!
I TAKE IT BACK. I LOVE THIS PLAN.
DO YOU NOW?
HERE'S THE FACTS.
I NEED TO GET UP ON THAT FLOAT, GET A SYRINGE INTO JOKER'S SPINE--HIS SPINE.
THEN I NEED TO MAKE IT OUT OF THERE ALIVE, AND GET THE SAMPLE TO MY BASE, WHERE I HAVE SOMEONE STANDING BY, READY TO SYNTHESIZE A CURE AND DISSEMINATE IT.
SO YES, IT'S A BAD PLAN. ANYONE HAS A BETTER ONE, I'M ALL EARS.
NO? THEN THE BOTTOM LINE IS THIS: IT'S OUR CITY. ALL OF OURS. AND WE NEED TO TAKE IT BACK FROM HIM, NOW, TOGETHER, OR IT'S OVER. FOR ALL OF US. FOREVER.
SO TELL ME...

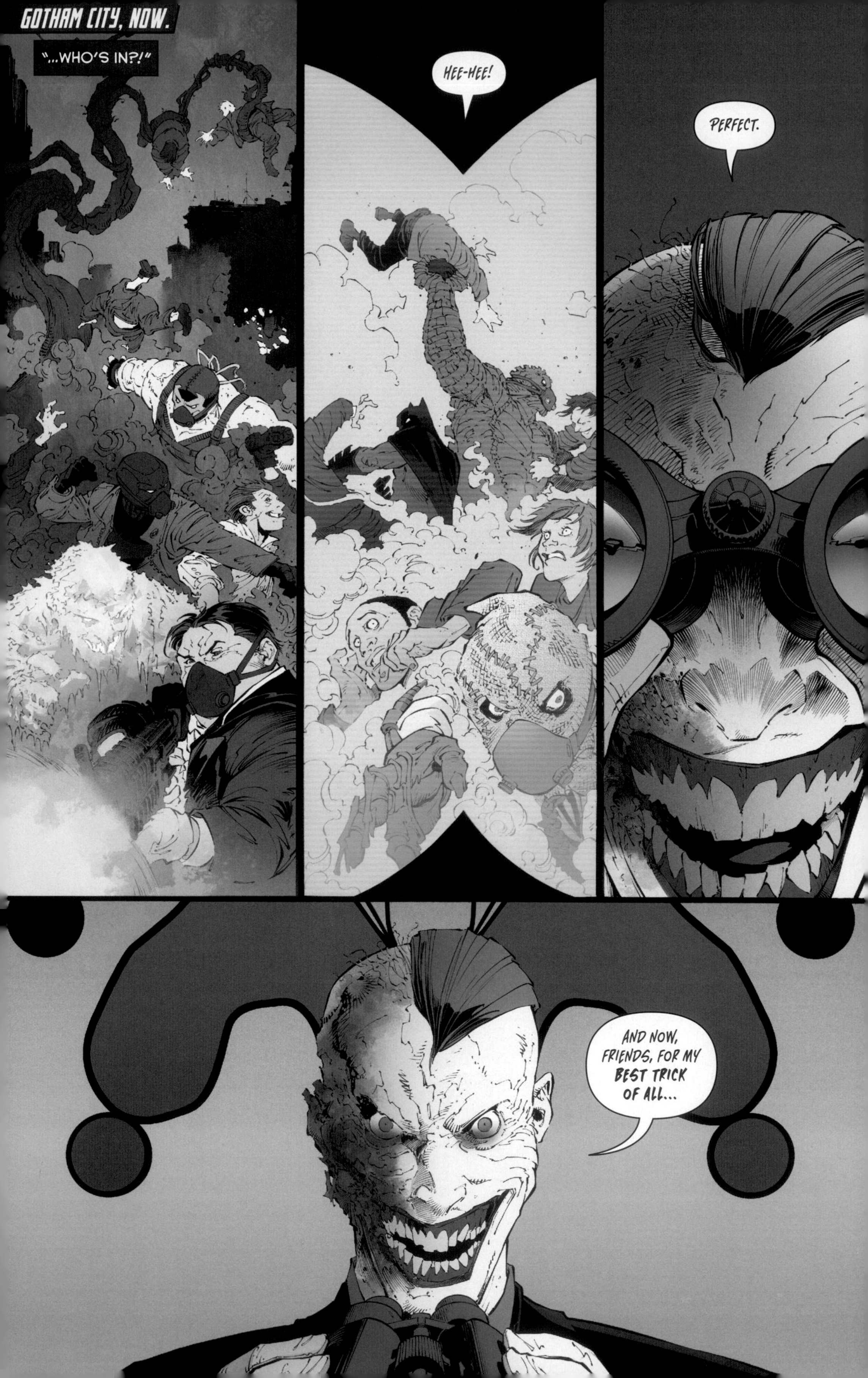
GOTHAM CITY, NOW.
"...WHO'S IN?!"
HEE-HEE!
PERFECT.
AND NOW, FRIENDS, FOR MY BEST TRICK OF ALL...

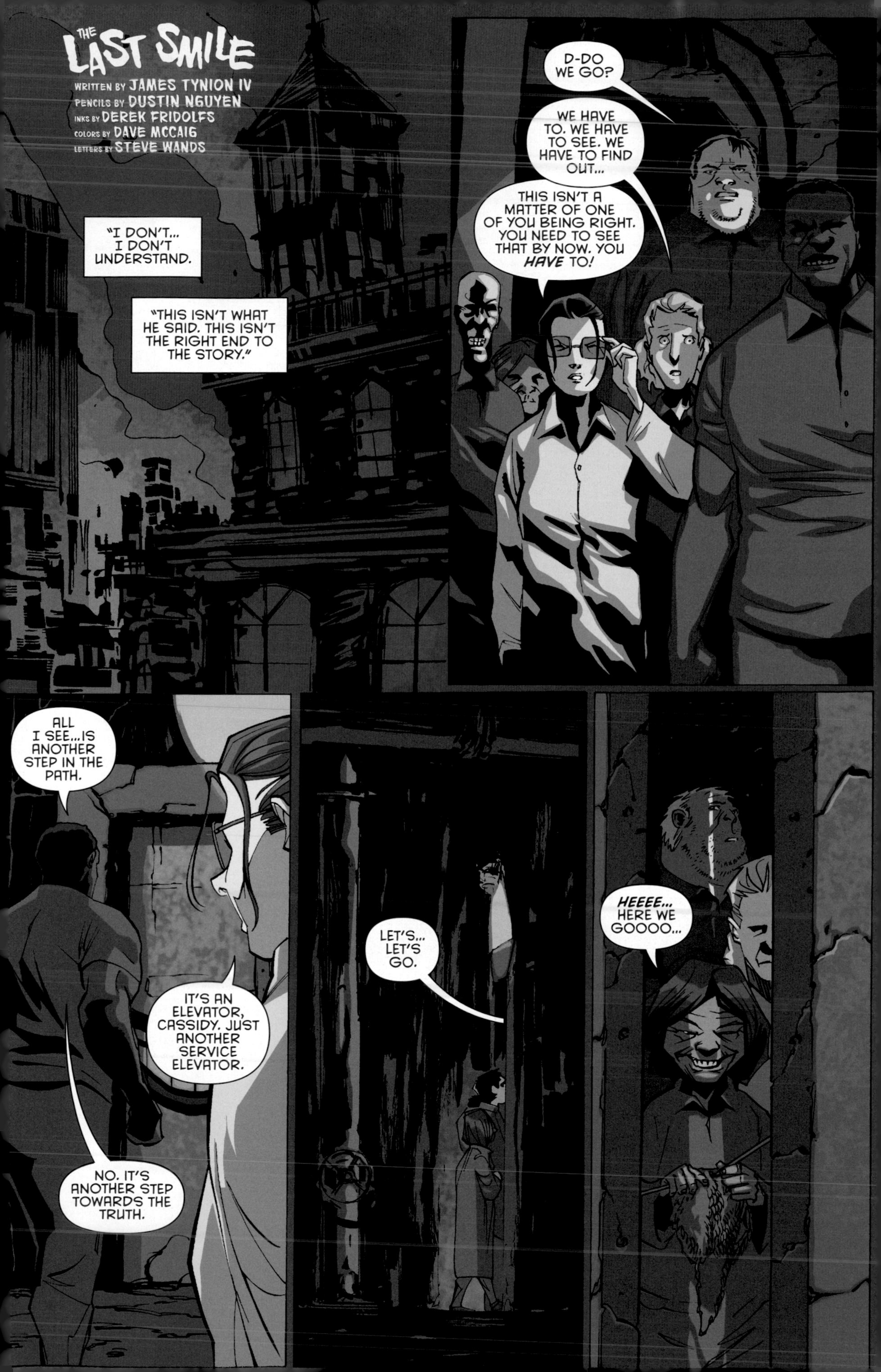

THE LAST SMILE
WRITTEN BY JAMES TYNION IV
PENCILS BY DUSTIN NGUYEN
INKS BY DEREK FRIDOLFS
COLORS BY DAVE MCCAIG
LETTERS BY STEVE WANDS
"I DON'T... I DON'T UNDERSTAND.
"THIS ISN'T WHAT HE SAID. THIS ISN'T THE RIGHT END TO THE STORY."
D-DO WE GO?
WE HAVE TO. WE HAVE TO SEE. WE HAVE TO FIND OUT...
THIS ISN'T A MATTER OF ONE OF YOU BEING RIGHT. YOU NEED TO SEE THAT BY NOW. YOU *HAVE* TO!
ALL I SEE...IS ANOTHER STEP IN THE PATH.
IT'S AN ELEVATOR, CASSIDY. JUST ANOTHER SERVICE ELEVATOR.
NO. IT'S ANOTHER STEP TOWARDS THE TRUTH.
LET'S... LET'S GO.
HEEEE... HERE WE GOOOO...

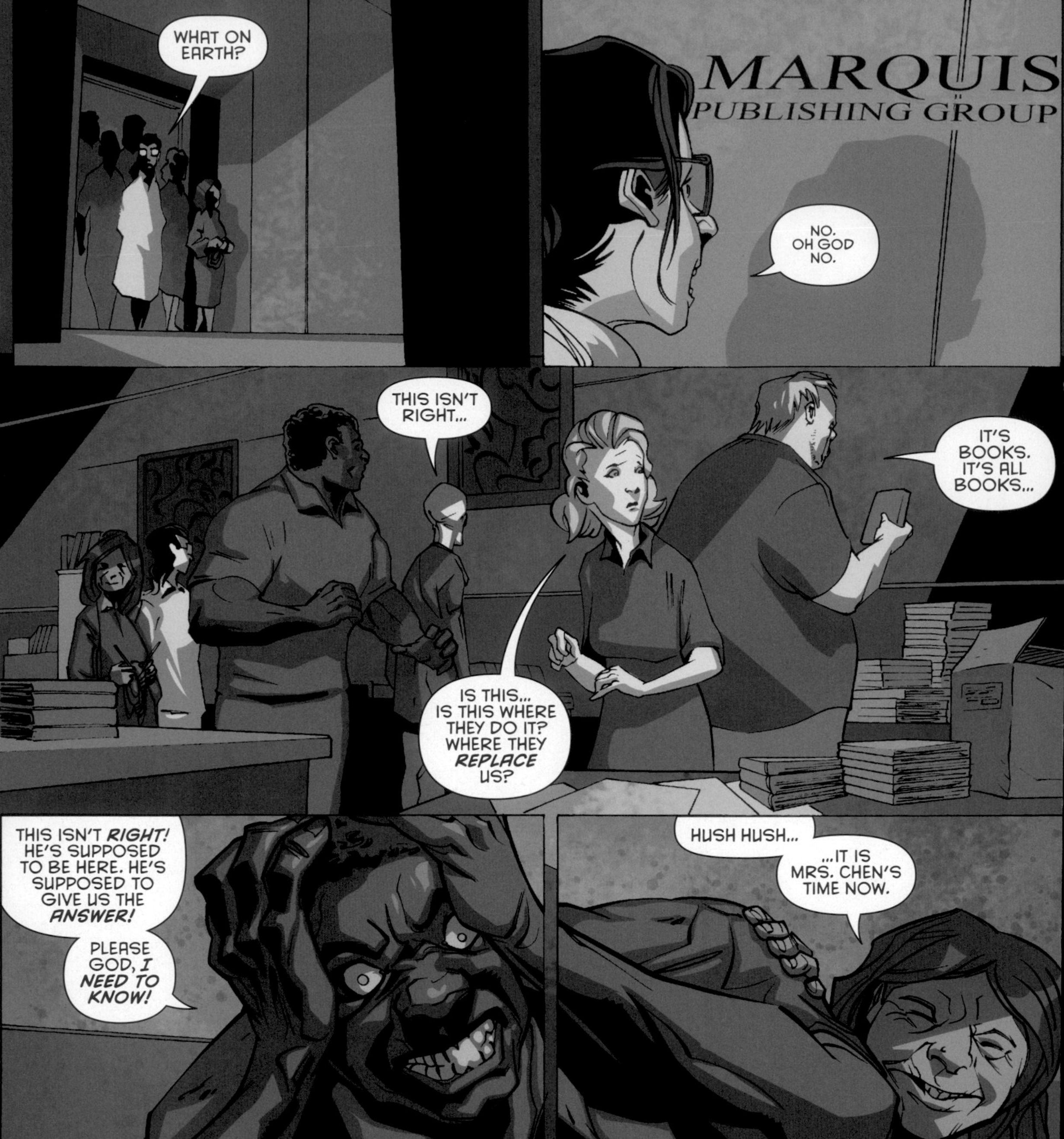

WHAT ON EARTH?
MARQUIS PUBLISHING GROUP
NO. OH GOD NO.
THIS ISN'T RIGHT...
IT'S BOOKS. IT'S ALL BOOKS...
IS THIS... IS THIS WHERE THEY DO IT? WHERE THEY *REPLACE* US?
THIS ISN'T *RIGHT*! HE'S SUPPOSED TO BE HERE. HE'S SUPPOSED TO GIVE US THE *ANSWER*!
PLEASE GOD, *I NEED TO KNOW!*
HUSH HUSH...
...IT IS MRS. CHEN'S TIME NOW.

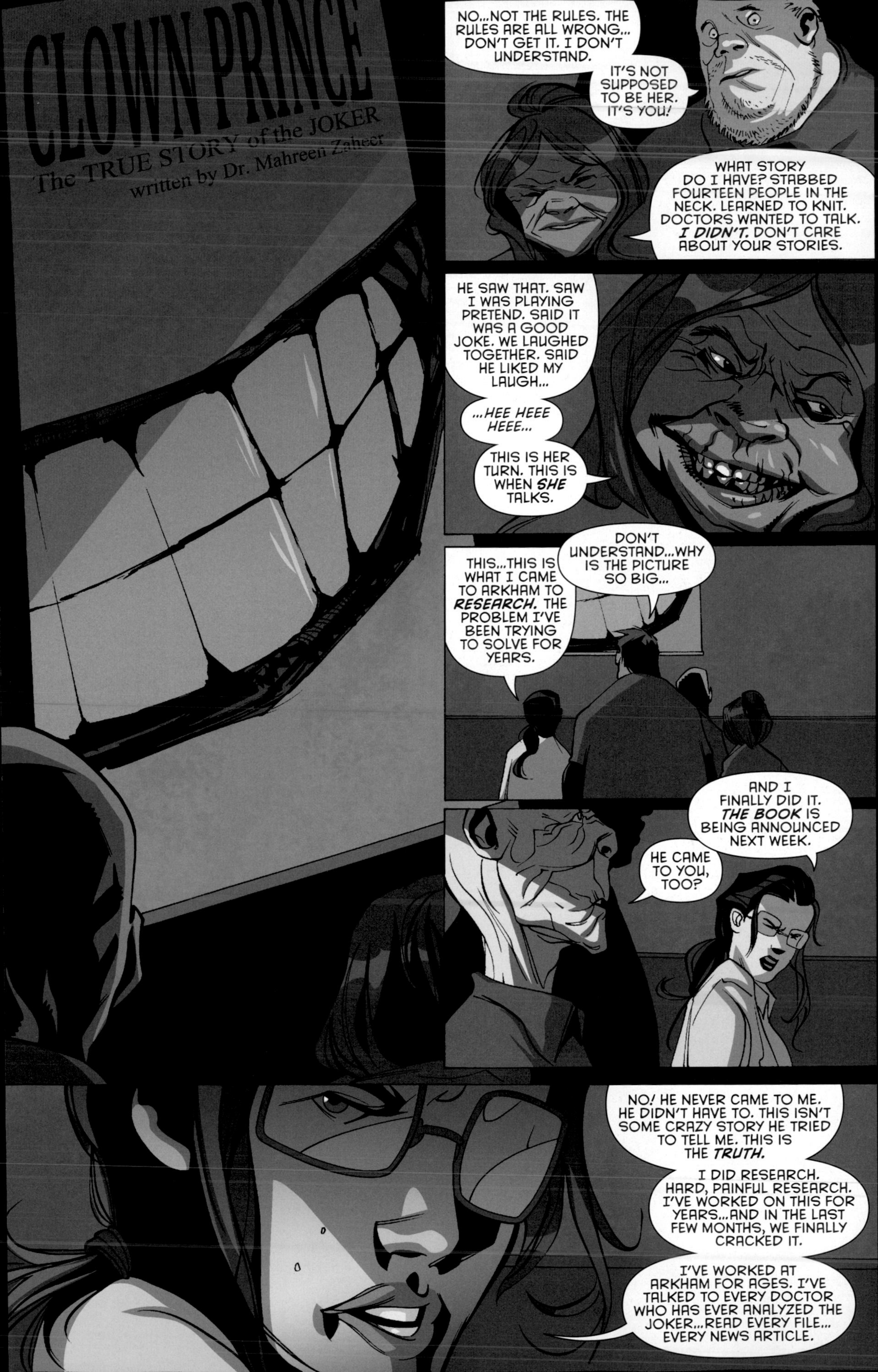
CLOWN PRINCE
The TRUE STORY of the JOKER
written by Dr. Mahreen Zaheer
NO...NOT THE RULES. THE RULES ARE ALL WRONG... DON'T GET IT. I DON'T UNDERSTAND.
IT'S NOT SUPPOSED TO BE HER. IT'S YOU!
WHAT STORY DO I HAVE? STABBED FOURTEEN PEOPLE IN THE NECK. LEARNED TO KNIT. DOCTORS WANTED TO TALK. I DIDN'T. DON'T CARE ABOUT YOUR STORIES.
HE SAW THAT. SAW I WAS PLAYING PRETEND. SAID IT WAS A GOOD JOKE. WE LAUGHED TOGETHER. SAID HE LIKED MY LAUGH...
...HEE HEEE HEEE...
THIS IS HER TURN. THIS IS WHEN SHE TALKS.
THIS...THIS IS WHAT I CAME TO ARKHAM TO RESEARCH. THE PROBLEM I'VE BEEN TRYING TO SOLVE FOR YEARS.
DON'T UNDERSTAND...WHY IS THE PICTURE SO BIG...
AND I FINALLY DID IT. THE BOOK IS BEING ANNOUNCED NEXT WEEK.
HE CAME TO YOU, TOO?
NO! HE NEVER CAME TO ME. HE DIDN'T HAVE TO. THIS ISN'T SOME CRAZY STORY HE TRIED TO TELL ME. THIS IS THE TRUTH.
I DID RESEARCH. HARD, PAINFUL RESEARCH. I'VE WORKED ON THIS FOR YEARS...AND IN THE LAST FEW MONTHS, WE FINALLY CRACKED IT.
I'VE WORKED AT ARKHAM FOR AGES. I'VE TALKED TO EVERY DOCTOR WHO HAS EVER ANALYZED THE JOKER...READ EVERY FILE... EVERY NEWS ARTICLE.

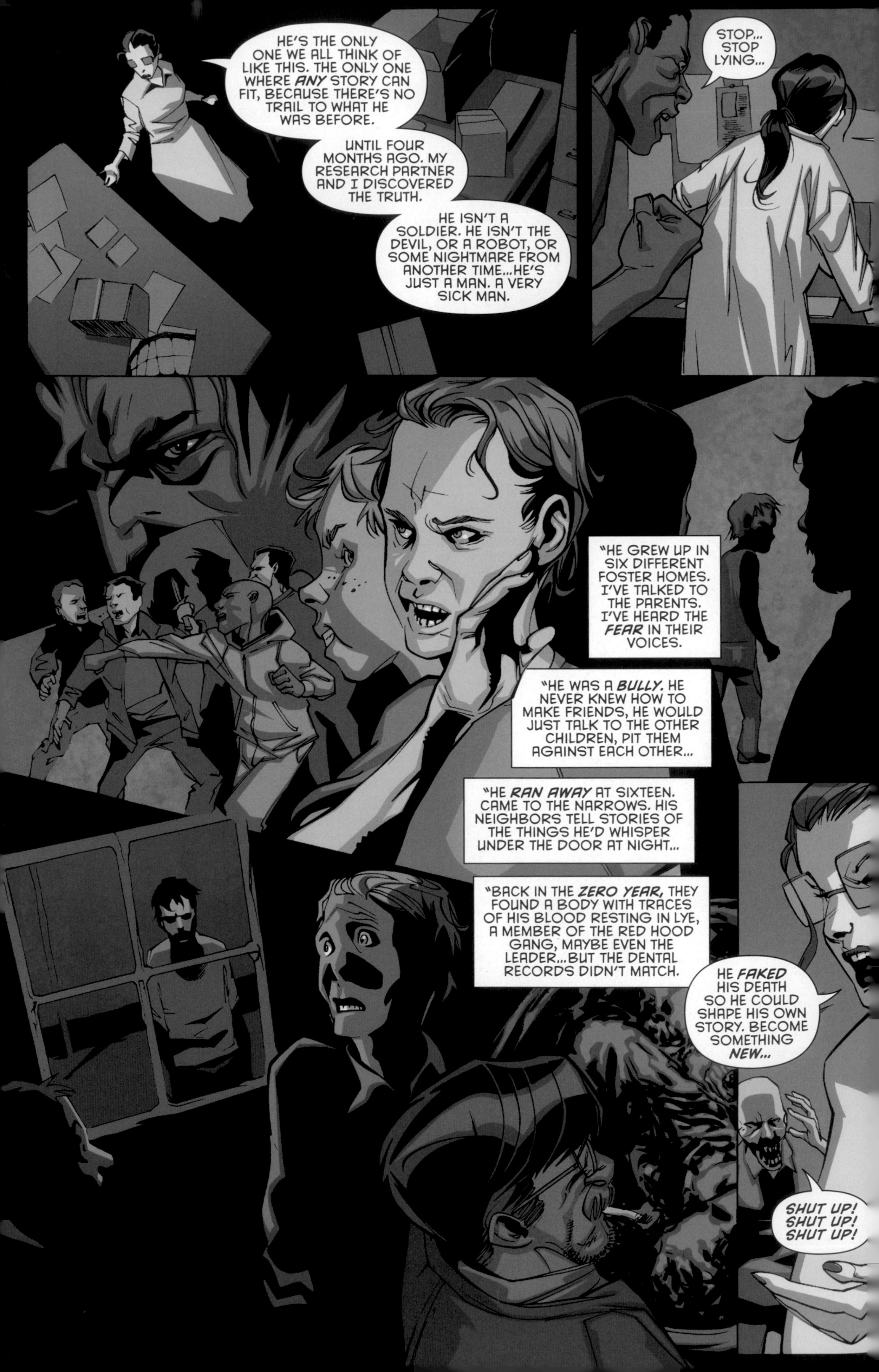
HE'S THE ONLY ONE WE ALL THINK OF LIKE THIS. THE ONLY ONE WHERE *ANY* STORY CAN FIT, BECAUSE THERE'S NO TRAIL TO WHAT HE WAS BEFORE.
UNTIL FOUR MONTHS AGO. MY RESEARCH PARTNER AND I DISCOVERED THE TRUTH.
HE ISN'T A SOLDIER. HE ISN'T THE DEVIL, OR A ROBOT, OR SOME NIGHTMARE FROM ANOTHER TIME...HE'S JUST A MAN. A VERY SICK MAN.
STOP... STOP LYING...
"HE GREW UP IN SIX DIFFERENT FOSTER HOMES. I'VE TALKED TO THE PARENTS. I'VE HEARD THE *FEAR* IN THEIR VOICES.
"HE WAS A *BULLY.* HE NEVER KNEW HOW TO MAKE FRIENDS, HE WOULD JUST TALK TO THE OTHER CHILDREN, PIT THEM AGAINST EACH OTHER...
"HE *RAN AWAY* AT SIXTEEN. CAME TO THE NARROWS. HIS NEIGHBORS TELL STORIES OF THE THINGS HE'D WHISPER UNDER THE DOOR AT NIGHT...
"BACK IN THE *ZERO YEAR,* THEY FOUND A BODY WITH TRACES OF HIS BLOOD RESTING IN LYE, A MEMBER OF THE RED HOOD GANG, MAYBE EVEN THE LEADER...BUT THE DENTAL RECORDS DIDN'T MATCH.
HE *FAKED* HIS DEATH SO HE COULD SHAPE HIS OWN STORY. BECOME SOMETHING *NEW...*
SHUT UP! SHUT UP! SHUT UP!

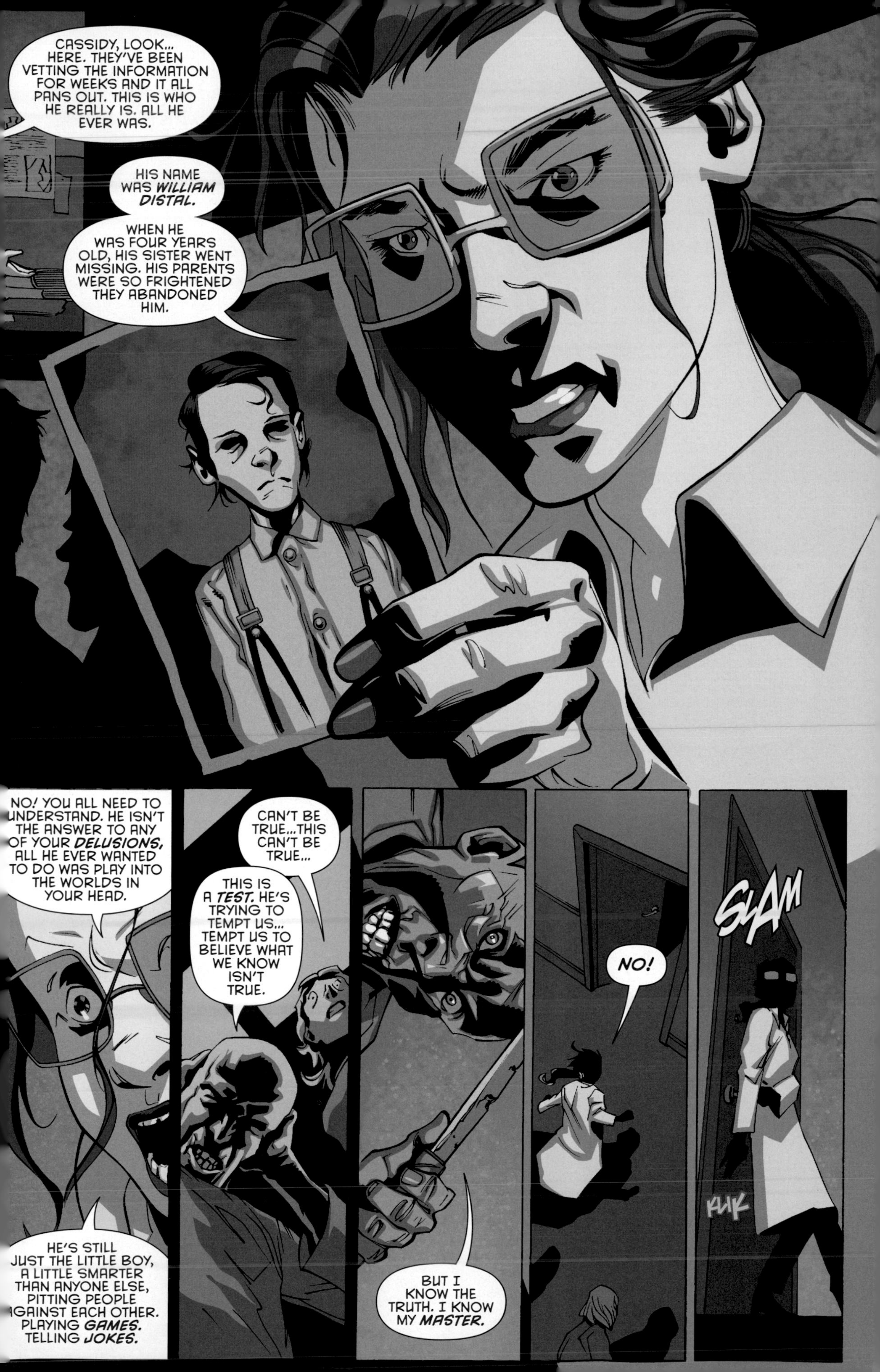
CASSIDY, LOOK... HERE. THEY'VE BEEN VETTING THE INFORMATION FOR WEEKS AND IT ALL PANS OUT. THIS IS WHO HE REALLY IS. ALL HE EVER WAS.
HIS NAME WAS *WILLIAM DISTAL.*
WHEN HE WAS FOUR YEARS OLD, HIS SISTER WENT MISSING. HIS PARENTS WERE SO FRIGHTENED THEY ABANDONED HIM.
NO! YOU ALL NEED TO UNDERSTAND. HE ISN'T THE ANSWER TO ANY OF YOUR *DELUSIONS,* ALL HE EVER WANTED TO DO WAS PLAY INTO THE WORLDS IN YOUR HEAD.
HE'S STILL JUST THE LITTLE BOY, A LITTLE SMARTER THAN ANYONE ELSE, PITTING PEOPLE AGAINST EACH OTHER. PLAYING *GAMES.* TELLING *JOKES.*
CAN'T BE TRUE...THIS CAN'T BE TRUE...
THIS IS A *TEST.* HE'S TRYING TO TEMPT US... TEMPT US TO BELIEVE WHAT WE KNOW ISN'T TRUE.
BUT I KNOW THE TRUTH. I KNOW MY *MASTER.*
NO!
SLAM
KLIK

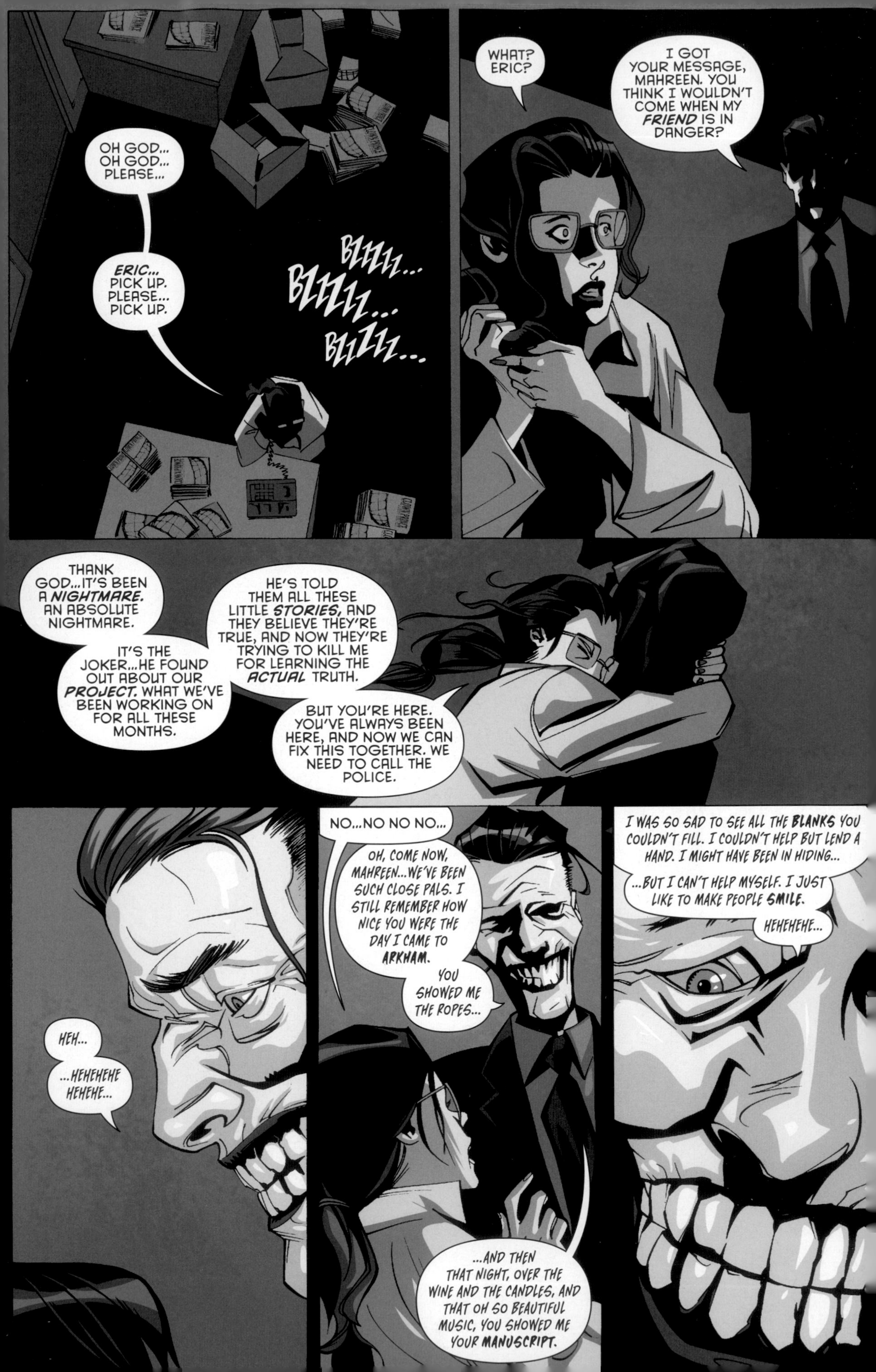
OH GOD... OH GOD... PLEASE...
ERIC... PICK UP. PLEASE... PICK UP.
BZZZZZ... BZZZZZ... BZZZZZ...
WHAT? ERIC?
I GOT YOUR MESSAGE, MAHREEN. YOU THINK I WOULDN'T COME WHEN MY FRIEND IS IN DANGER?
THANK GOD...IT'S BEEN A NIGHTMARE. AN ABSOLUTE NIGHTMARE.
IT'S THE JOKER...HE FOUND OUT ABOUT OUR PROJECT. WHAT WE'VE BEEN WORKING ON FOR ALL THESE MONTHS.
HE'S TOLD THEM ALL THESE LITTLE STORIES, AND THEY BELIEVE THEY'RE TRUE, AND NOW THEY'RE TRYING TO KILL ME FOR LEARNING THE ACTUAL TRUTH.
BUT YOU'RE HERE. YOU'VE ALWAYS BEEN HERE, AND NOW WE CAN FIX THIS TOGETHER. WE NEED TO CALL THE POLICE.
HEH...
...HEHEHEHE HEHEHE...
NO...NO NO NO...
OH, COME NOW, MAHREEN...WE'VE BEEN SUCH CLOSE PALS. I STILL REMEMBER HOW NICE YOU WERE THE DAY I CAME TO ARKHAM.
YOU SHOWED ME THE ROPES...
...AND THEN THAT NIGHT, OVER THE WINE AND THE CANDLES, AND THAT OH SO BEAUTIFUL MUSIC, YOU SHOWED ME YOUR MANUSCRIPT.
I WAS SO SAD TO SEE ALL THE BLANKS YOU COULDN'T FILL. I COULDN'T HELP BUT LEND A HAND. I MIGHT HAVE BEEN IN HIDING...
...BUT I CAN'T HELP MYSELF. I JUST LIKE TO MAKE PEOPLE SMILE.
HEHEHEHE...

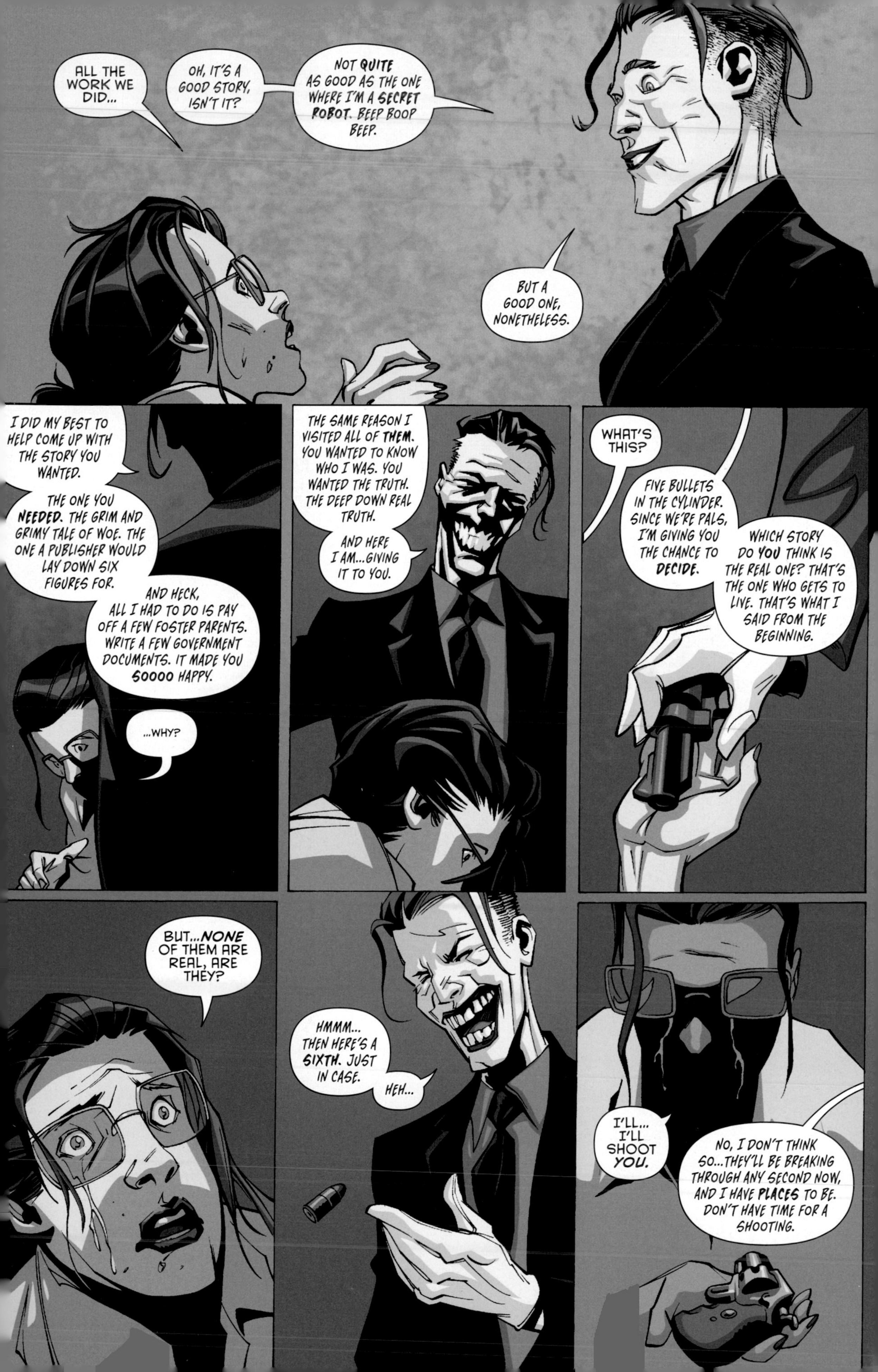
ALL THE WORK WE DID...
OH, IT'S A GOOD STORY, ISN'T IT?
NOT QUITE AS GOOD AS THE ONE WHERE I'M A SECRET ROBOT. BEEP BOOP BEEP.
BUT A GOOD ONE, NONETHELESS.
I DID MY BEST TO HELP COME UP WITH THE STORY YOU WANTED.
THE ONE YOU NEEDED. THE GRIM AND GRIMY TALE OF WOE. THE ONE A PUBLISHER WOULD LAY DOWN SIX FIGURES FOR.
AND HECK, ALL I HAD TO DO IS PAY OFF A FEW FOSTER PARENTS. WRITE A FEW GOVERNMENT DOCUMENTS. IT MADE YOU SOOOO HAPPY.
...WHY?
THE SAME REASON I VISITED ALL OF THEM. YOU WANTED TO KNOW WHO I WAS. YOU WANTED THE TRUTH. THE DEEP DOWN REAL TRUTH.
AND HERE I AM...GIVING IT TO YOU.
WHAT'S THIS?
FIVE BULLETS IN THE CYLINDER. SINCE WE'RE PALS, I'M GIVING YOU THE CHANCE TO DECIDE.
WHICH STORY DO YOU THINK IS THE REAL ONE? THAT'S THE ONE WHO GETS TO LIVE. THAT'S WHAT I SAID FROM THE BEGINNING.
BUT...NONE OF THEM ARE REAL, ARE THEY?
HMMM... THEN HERE'S A SIXTH. JUST IN CASE.
HEH...
I'LL... I'LL SHOOT YOU.
NO, I DON'T THINK SO...THEY'LL BE BREAKING THROUGH ANY SECOND NOW, AND I HAVE PLACES TO BE. DON'T HAVE TIME FOR A SHOOTING.

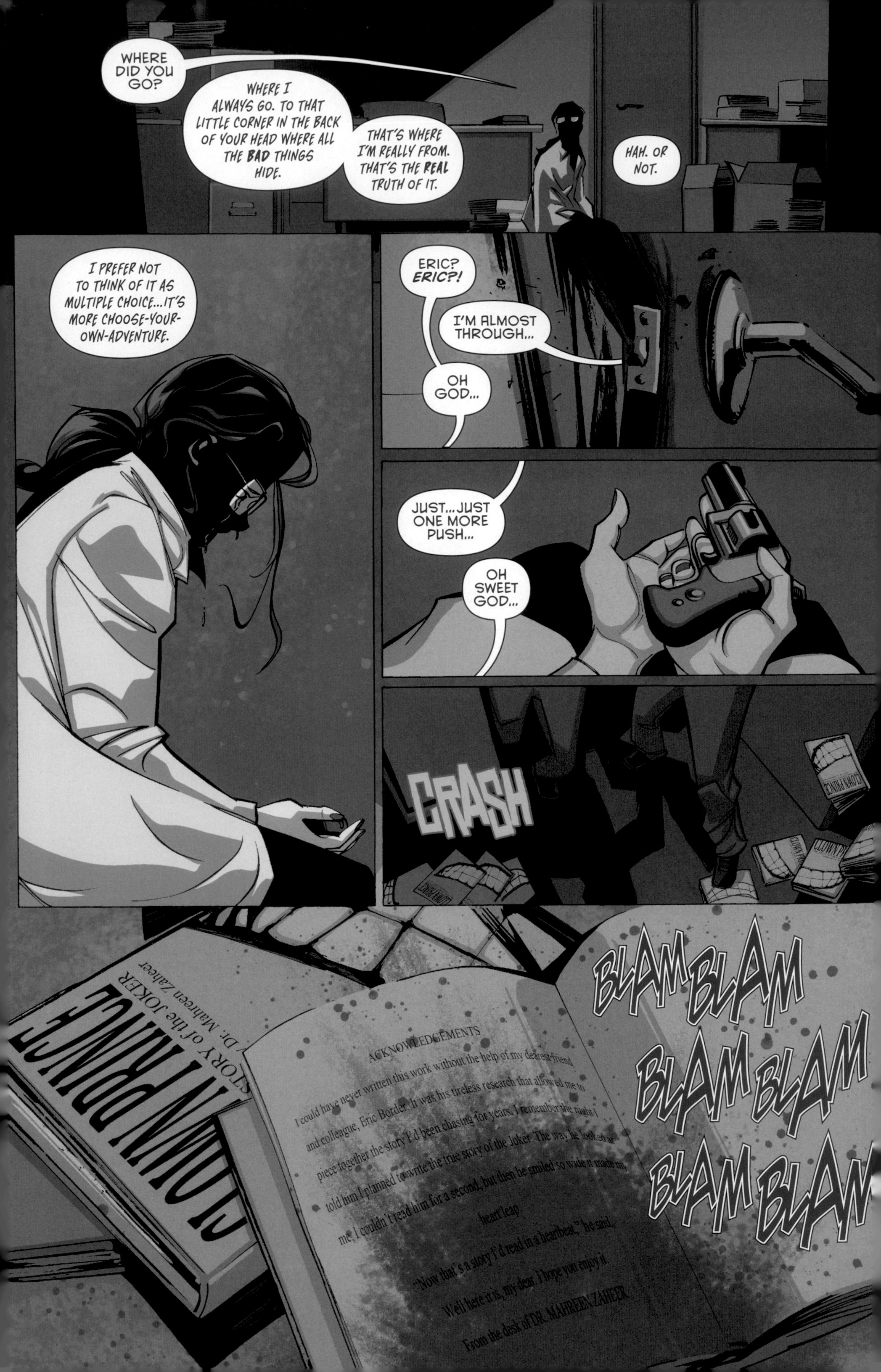
WHERE DID YOU GO?
WHERE I ALWAYS GO. TO THAT LITTLE CORNER IN THE BACK OF YOUR HEAD WHERE ALL THE BAD THINGS HIDE.
THAT'S WHERE I'M REALLY FROM. THAT'S THE REAL TRUTH OF IT.
HAH. OR NOT.
I PREFER NOT TO THINK OF IT AS MULTIPLE CHOICE...IT'S MORE CHOOSE-YOUR-OWN-ADVENTURE.
ERIC? ERIC?!
I'M ALMOST THROUGH...
OH GOD...
JUST...JUST ONE MORE PUSH...
OH SWEET GOD...
CRASH
ACKNOWLEDGEMENTS
I could have never written this work without the help of my dearest friend and colleague, Eric Border. It was his tireless research that allowed me to piece together the story I'd been chasing for years. I remember the night I told him I planned to write the true story of the Joker. The way he looked at me, I couldn't read him for a second, but then he smiled so wide it made my heart leap.
"Now that's a story I'd read in a heartbeat," he said.
Well here it is, my dear. I hope you enjoy it.
From the desk of DR. MAHREEN ZAHEER
BLAM BLAM
BLAM BLAM
BLAM BLAM

Cover by **GREG CAPULLO, DANNY MIKI** & **FCO PLASCENCIA**

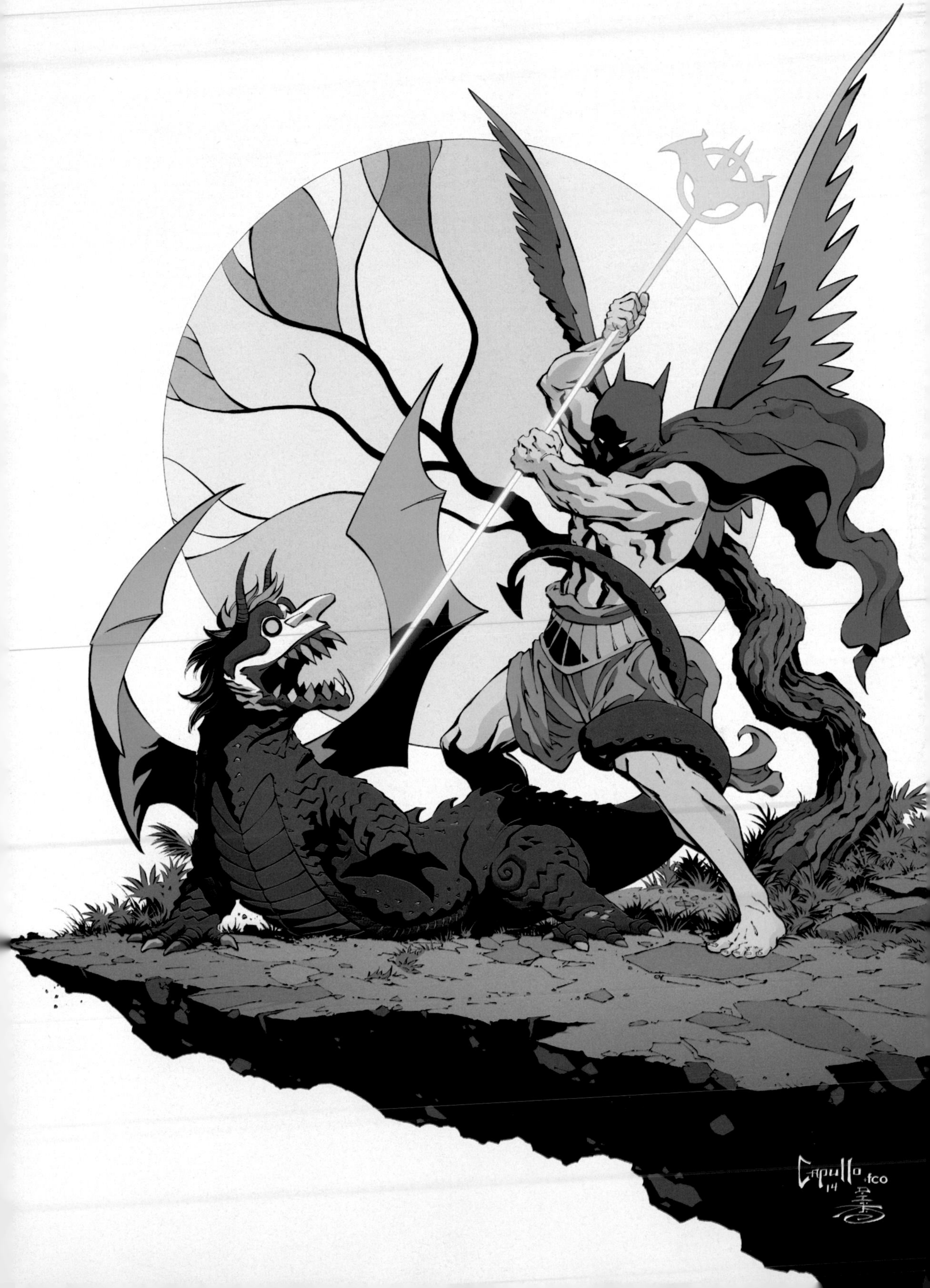

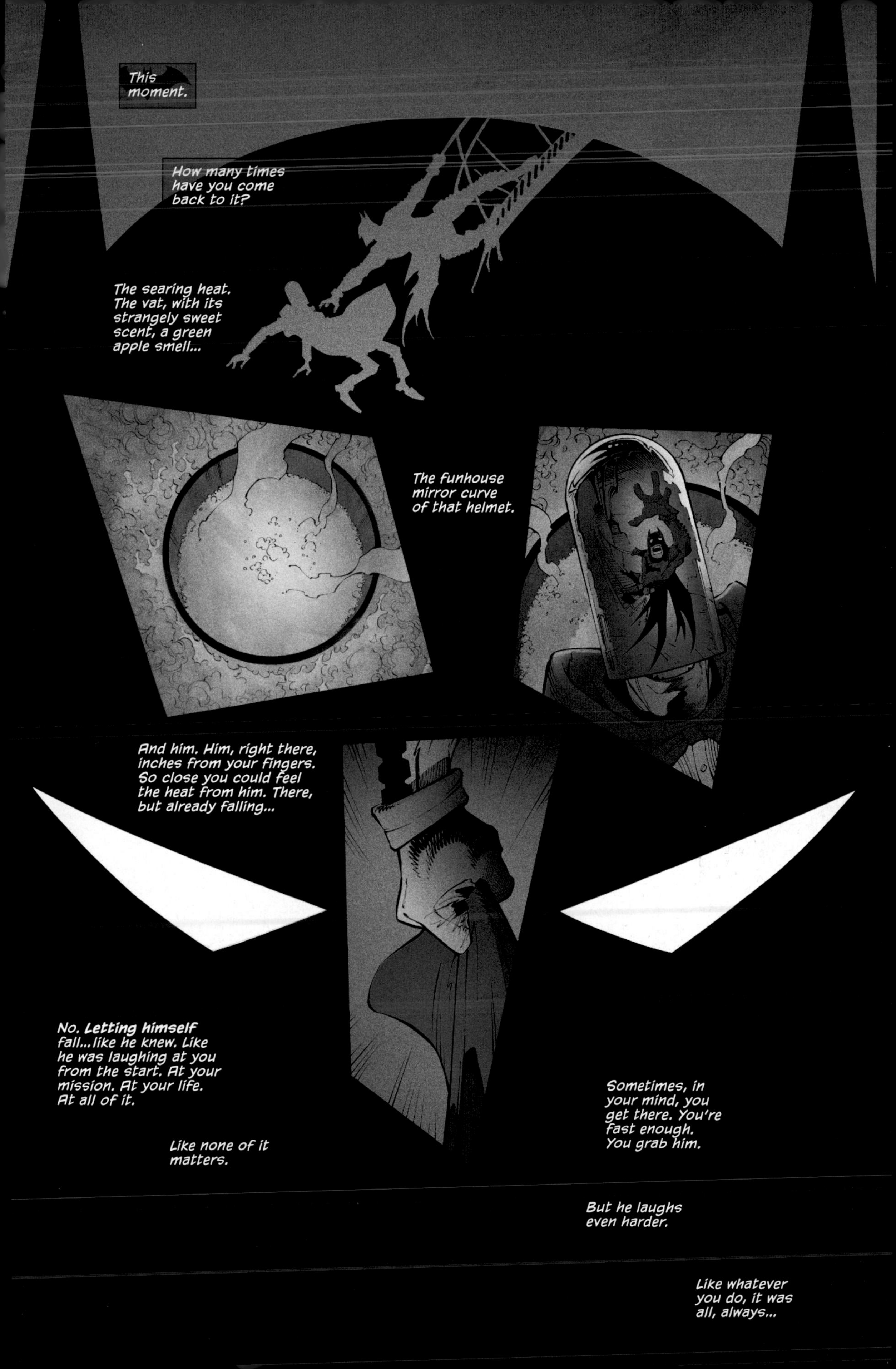
This moment.
How many times have you come back to it?
The searing heat. The vat, with its strangely sweet scent, a green apple smell...
The funhouse mirror curve of that helmet.
And him. Him, right there, inches from your fingers. So close you could feel the heat from him. There, but already falling...
No. **Letting himself** fall... like he knew. Like he was laughing at you from the start. At your mission. At your life. At all of it.
Like none of it matters.
Sometimes, in your mind, you get there. You're fast enough. You grab him.
But he laughs even harder.
Like whatever you do, it was all, always...

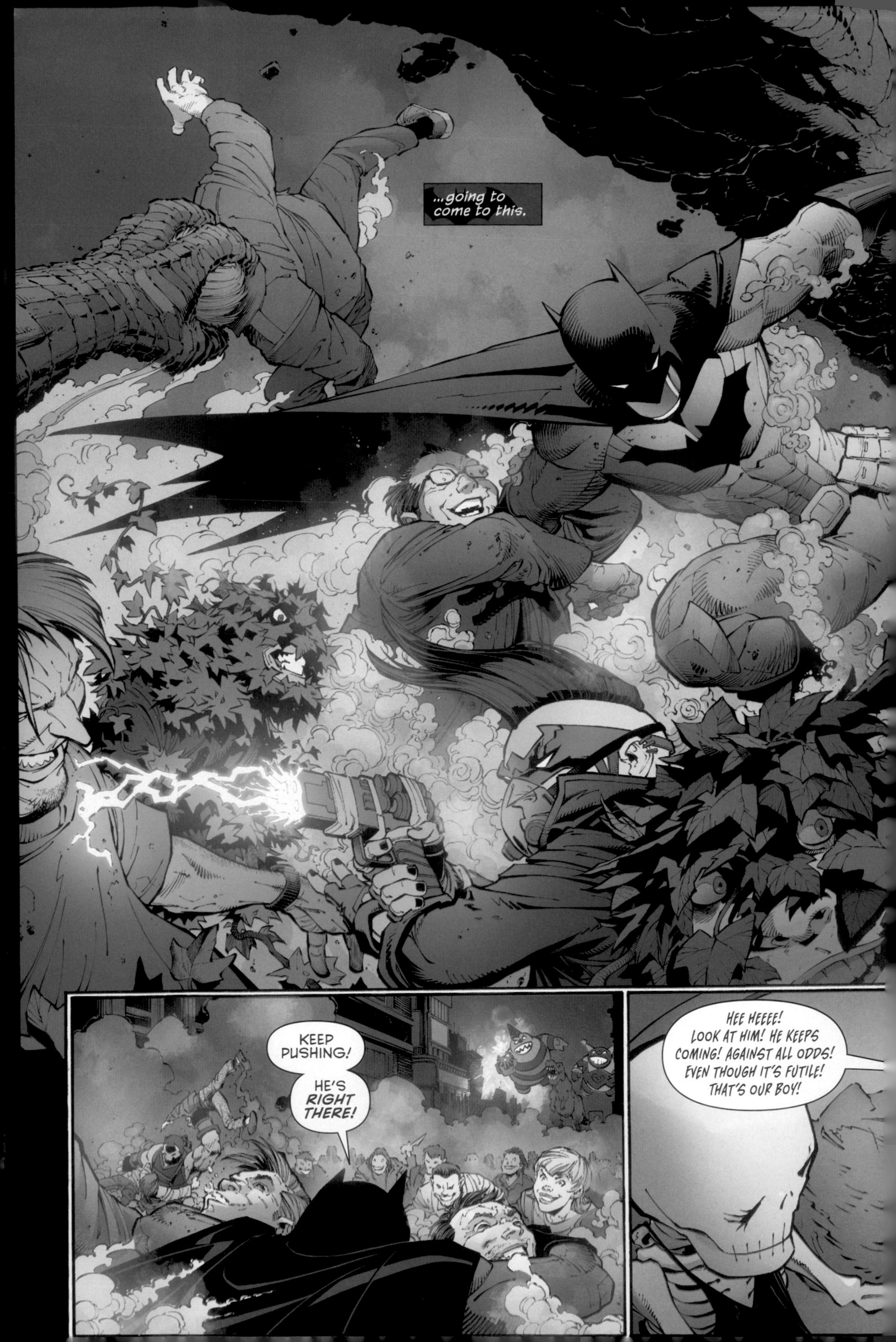
...going to come to this.
KEEP PUSHING!
HE'S RIGHT THERE!
HEE HEEEE! LOOK AT HIM! HE KEEPS COMING! AGAINST ALL ODDS! EVEN THOUGH IT'S FUTILE! THAT'S OUR BOY!

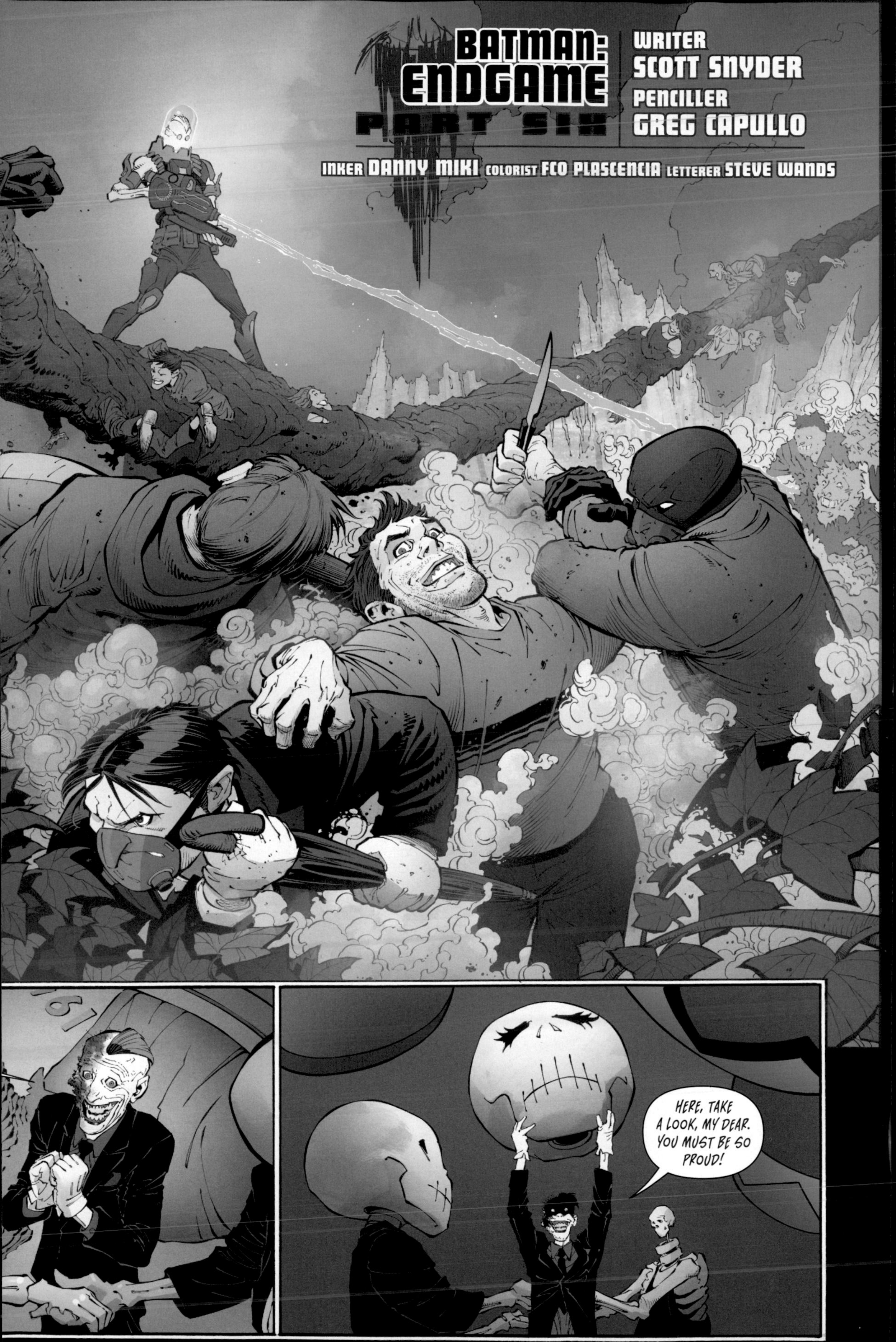
BATMAN: ENDGAME
PART SIX
WRITER SCOTT SNYDER
PENCILLER GREG CAPULLO
INKER DANNY MIKI COLORIST FCO PLASCENCIA LETTERER STEVE WANDS
HERE, TAKE A LOOK, MY DEAR. YOU MUST BE SO PROUD!

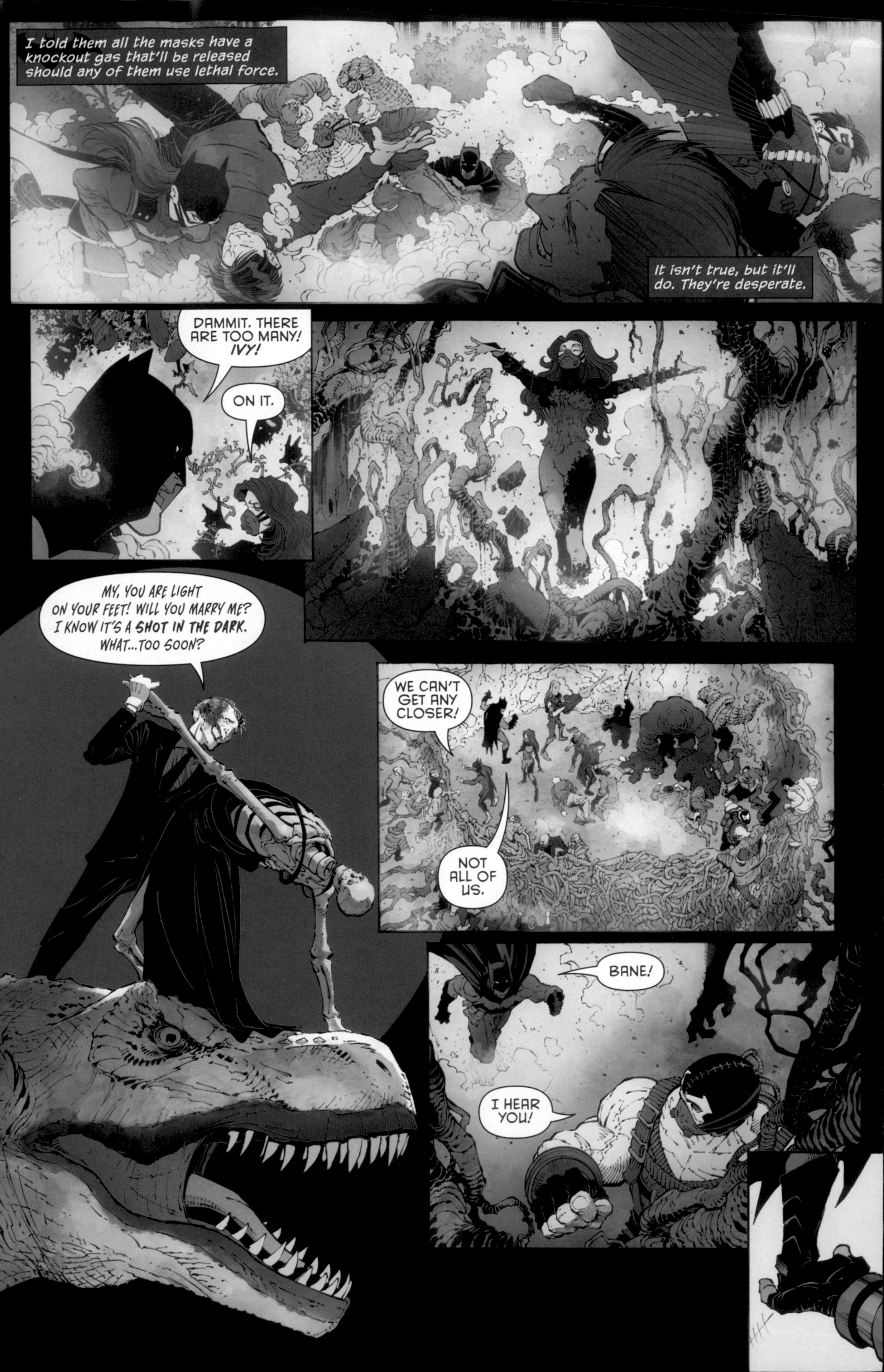
I told them all the masks have a knockout gas that'll be released should any of them use lethal force.
It isn't true, but it'll do. They're desperate.
DAMMIT. THERE ARE TOO MANY! IVY!
ON IT.
MY, YOU ARE LIGHT ON YOUR FEET! WILL YOU MARRY ME? I KNOW IT'S A SHOT IN THE DARK. WHAT...TOO SOON?
WE CAN'T GET ANY CLOSER!
NOT ALL OF US.
BANE!
I HEAR YOU!

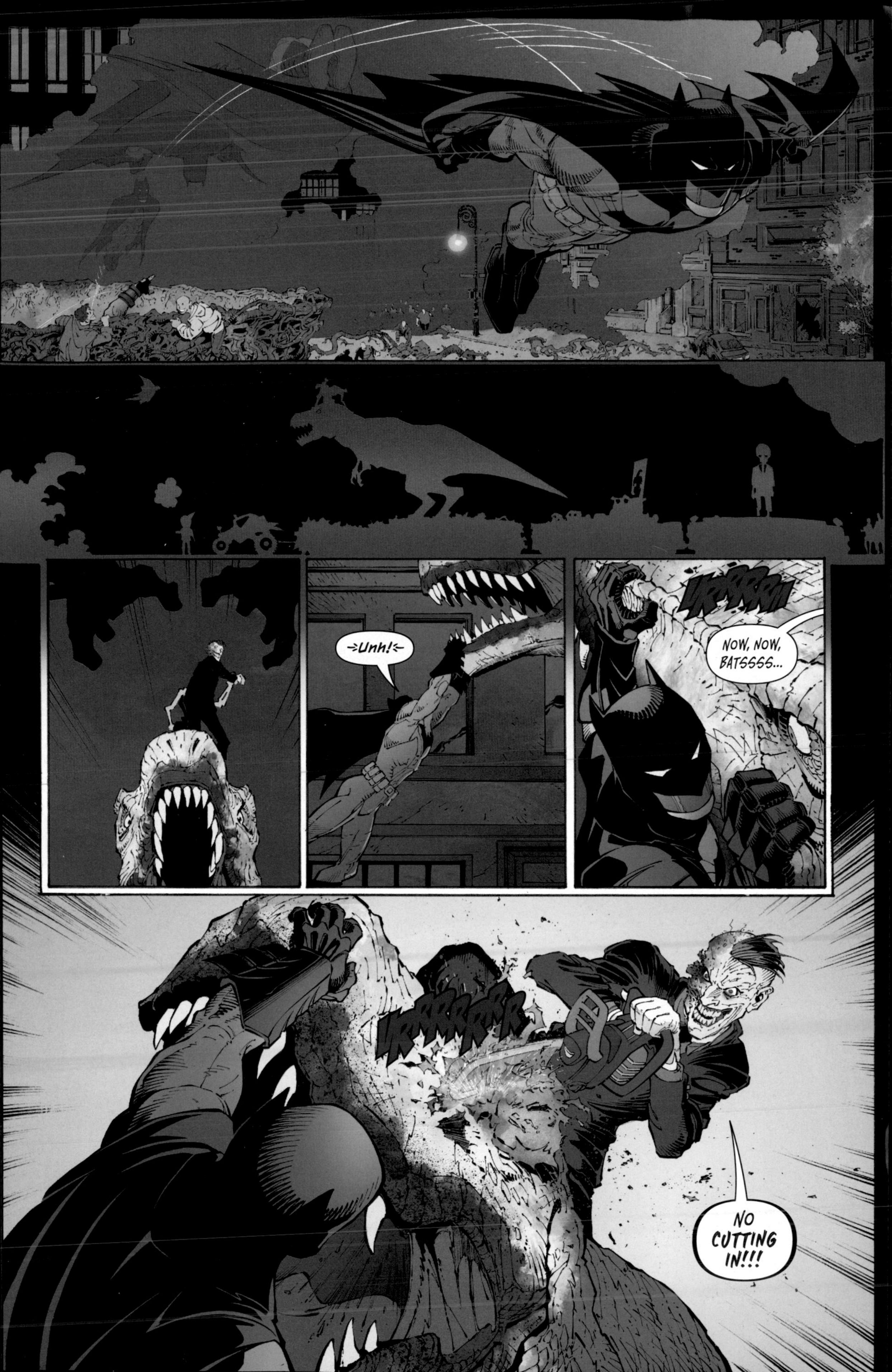

Unh!
URRRRRM
NOW, NOW, BATSSSS...
URRRRRRR
NO CUTTING IN!!!

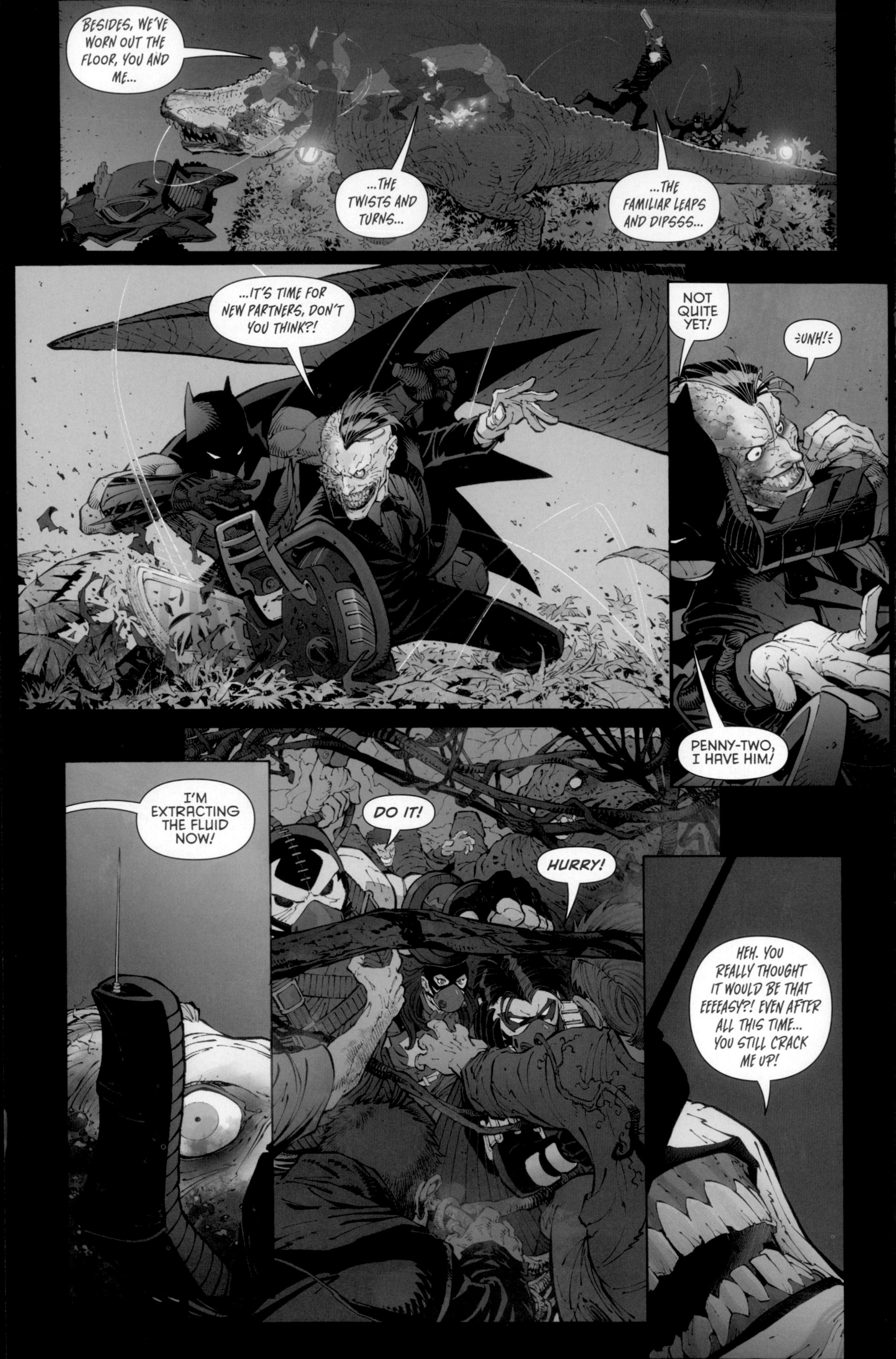
BESIDES, WE'VE WORN OUT THE FLOOR, YOU AND ME...
...THE TWISTS AND TURNS...
...THE FAMILIAR LEAPS AND DIPSSS...
...IT'S TIME FOR NEW PARTNERS, DON'T YOU THINK?!
NOT QUITE YET!
UNH!
PENNY-TWO, I HAVE HIM!
I'M EXTRACTING THE FLUID NOW!
DO IT!
HURRY!
HEH. YOU REALLY THOUGHT IT WOULD BE THAT EEEEASY?! EVEN AFTER ALL THIS TIME... YOU STILL CRACK ME UP!

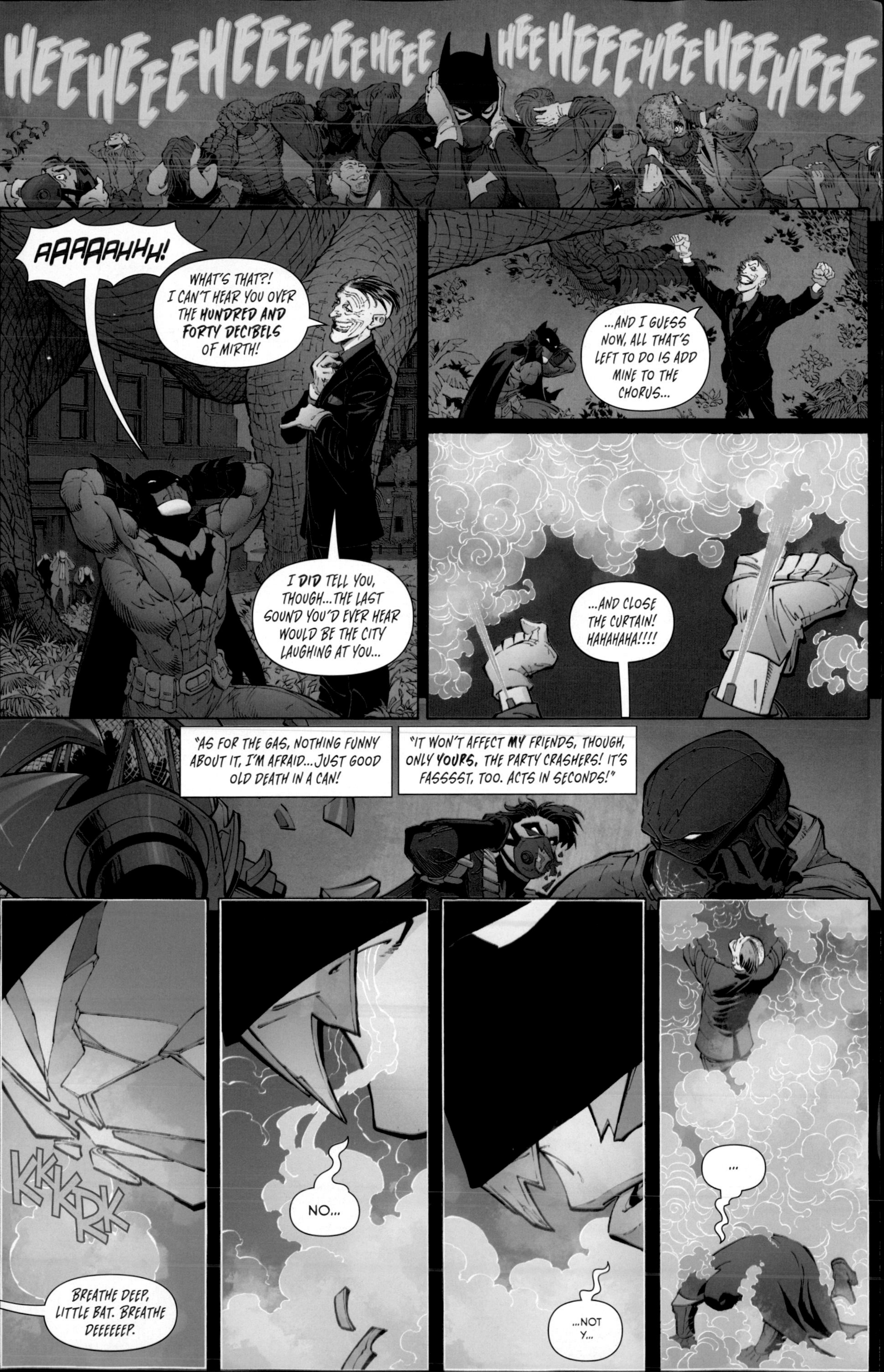
HEEHEEEHEEEHEEHEEE HEEHEEEHEEHEEEHEEE
AAAAAHHH!
WHAT'S THAT?! I CAN'T HEAR YOU OVER THE HUNDRED AND FORTY DECIBELS OF MIRTH!
I DID TELL YOU, THOUGH...THE LAST SOUND YOU'D EVER HEAR WOULD BE THE CITY LAUGHING AT YOU...
...AND I GUESS NOW, ALL THAT'S LEFT TO DO IS ADD MINE TO THE CHORUS...
...AND CLOSE THE CURTAIN! HAHAHAHA!!!!
"AS FOR THE GAS, NOTHING FUNNY ABOUT IT, I'M AFRAID...JUST GOOD OLD DEATH IN A CAN!
"IT WON'T AFFECT MY FRIENDS, THOUGH, ONLY YOURS, THE PARTY CRASHERS! IT'S FASSSST, TOO. ACTS IN SECONDS!"
KKKRK
BREATHE DEEP, LITTLE BAT. BREATHE DEEEEEEP.
NO...
...NOT Y...
...

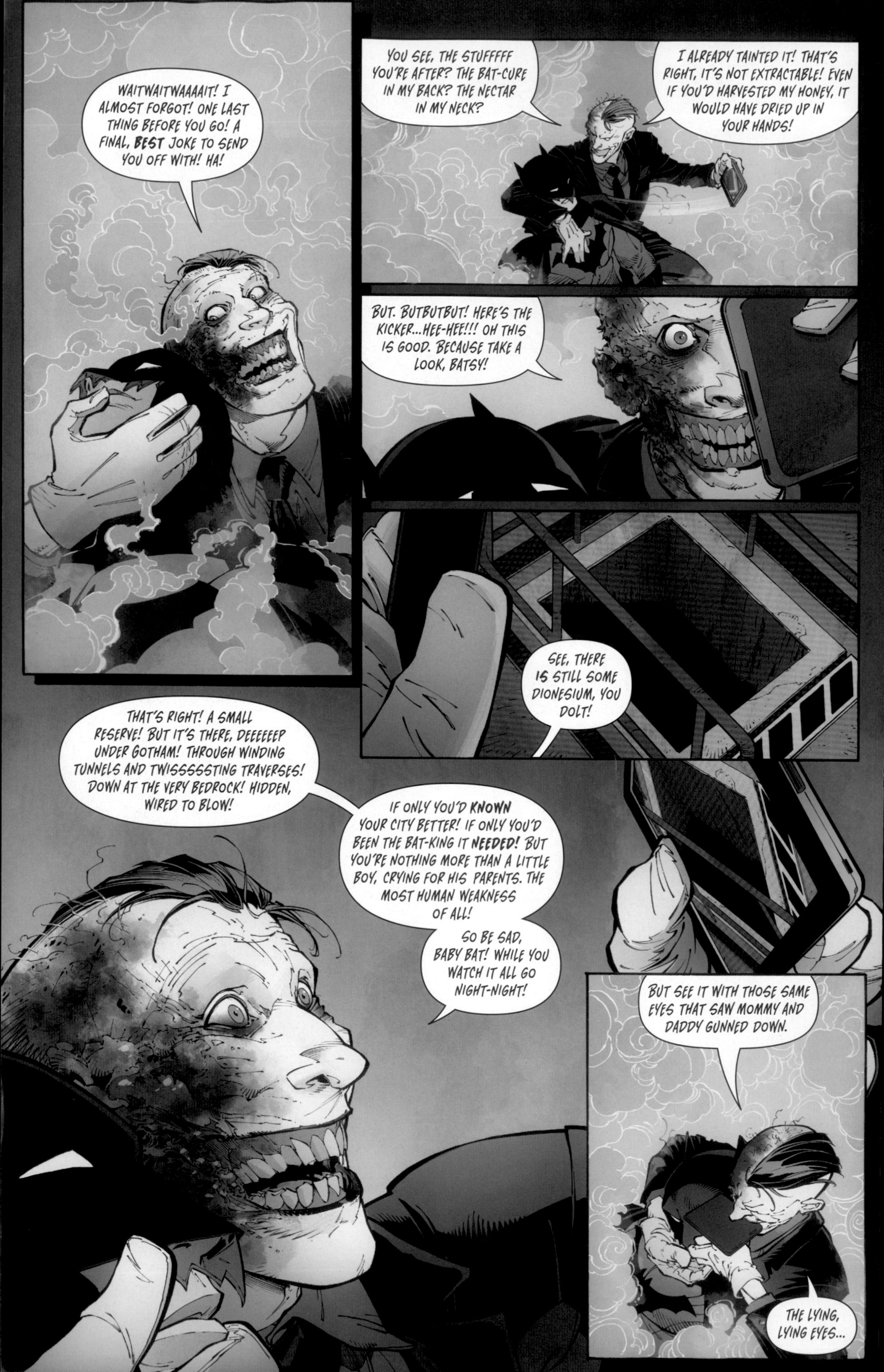
WAITWAITWAAAAIT! I ALMOST FORGOT! ONE LAST THING BEFORE YOU GO! A FINAL, BEST JOKE TO SEND YOU OFF WITH! HA!
YOU SEE, THE STUFFFFF YOU'RE AFTER? THE BAT-CURE IN MY BACK? THE NECTAR IN MY NECK?
I ALREADY TAINTED IT! THAT'S RIGHT, IT'S NOT EXTRACTABLE! EVEN IF YOU'D HARVESTED MY HONEY, IT WOULD HAVE DRIED UP IN YOUR HANDS!
BUT. BUTBUTBUT! HERE'S THE KICKER...HEE-HEE!!! OH THIS IS GOOD. BECAUSE TAKE A LOOK, BATSY!
SEE, THERE IS STILL SOME DIONESIUM, YOU DOLT!
THAT'S RIGHT! A SMALL RESERVE! BUT IT'S THERE, DEEEEEEP UNDER GOTHAM! THROUGH WINDING TUNNELS AND TWISSSSSTING TRAVERSES! DOWN AT THE VERY BEDROCK! HIDDEN, WIRED TO BLOW!
IF ONLY YOU'D KNOWN YOUR CITY BETTER! IF ONLY YOU'D BEEN THE BAT-KING IT NEEDED! BUT YOU'RE NOTHING MORE THAN A LITTLE BOY, CRYING FOR HIS PARENTS. THE MOST HUMAN WEAKNESS OF ALL!
SO BE SAD, BABY BAT! WHILE YOU WATCH IT ALL GO NIGHT-NIGHT!
BUT SEE IT WITH THOSE SAME EYES THAT SAW MOMMY AND DADDY GUNNED DOWN.
THE LYING, LYING EYES...

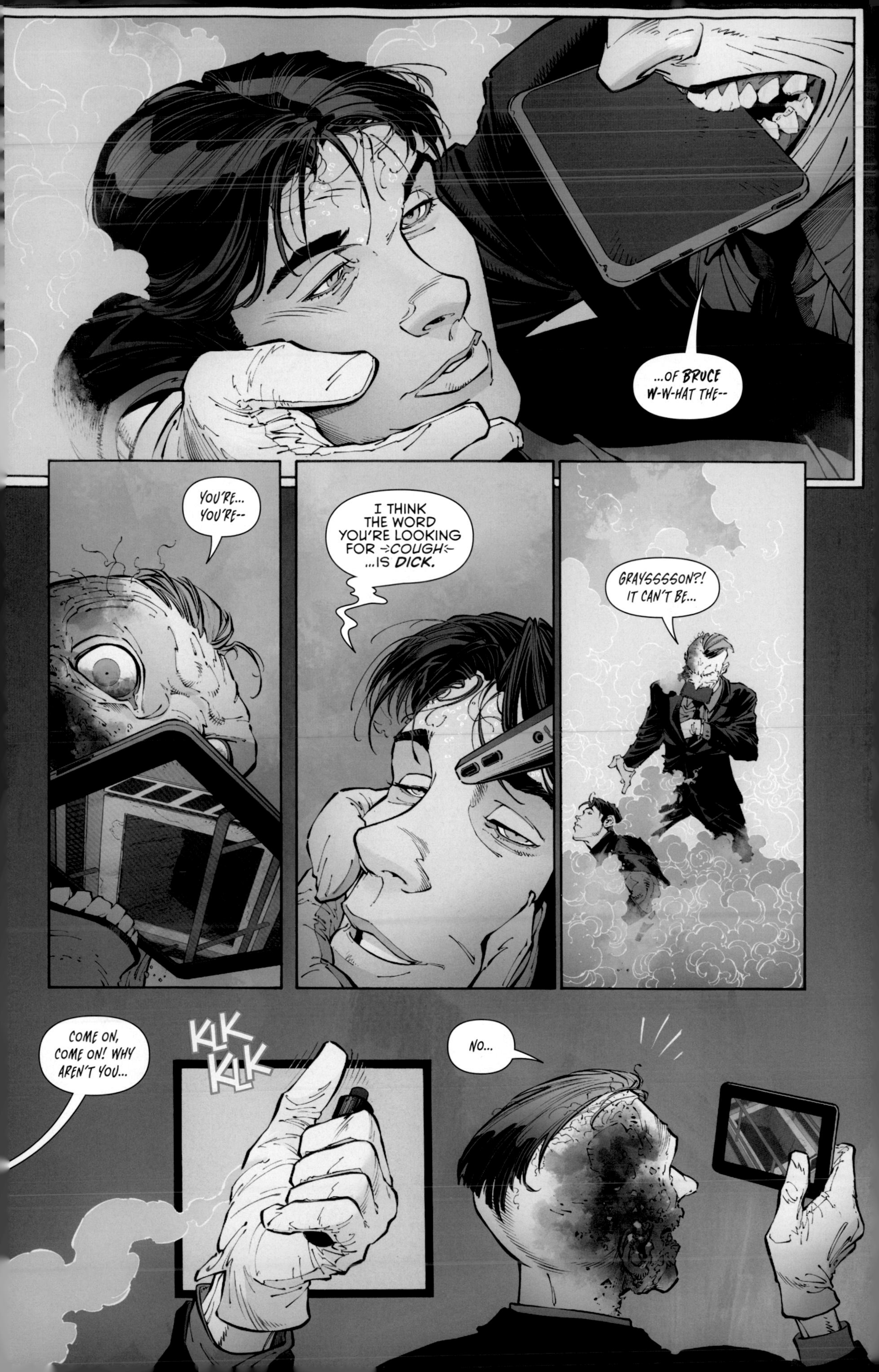
...OF BRUCE
W-W-HAT THE--
YOU'RE... YOU'RE--
I THINK THE WORD YOU'RE LOOKING FOR -COUGH- ...IS DICK.
GRAYSSSSON?! IT CAN'T BE...
COME ON, COME ON! WHY AREN'T YOU...
KLIK KLIK
NO...

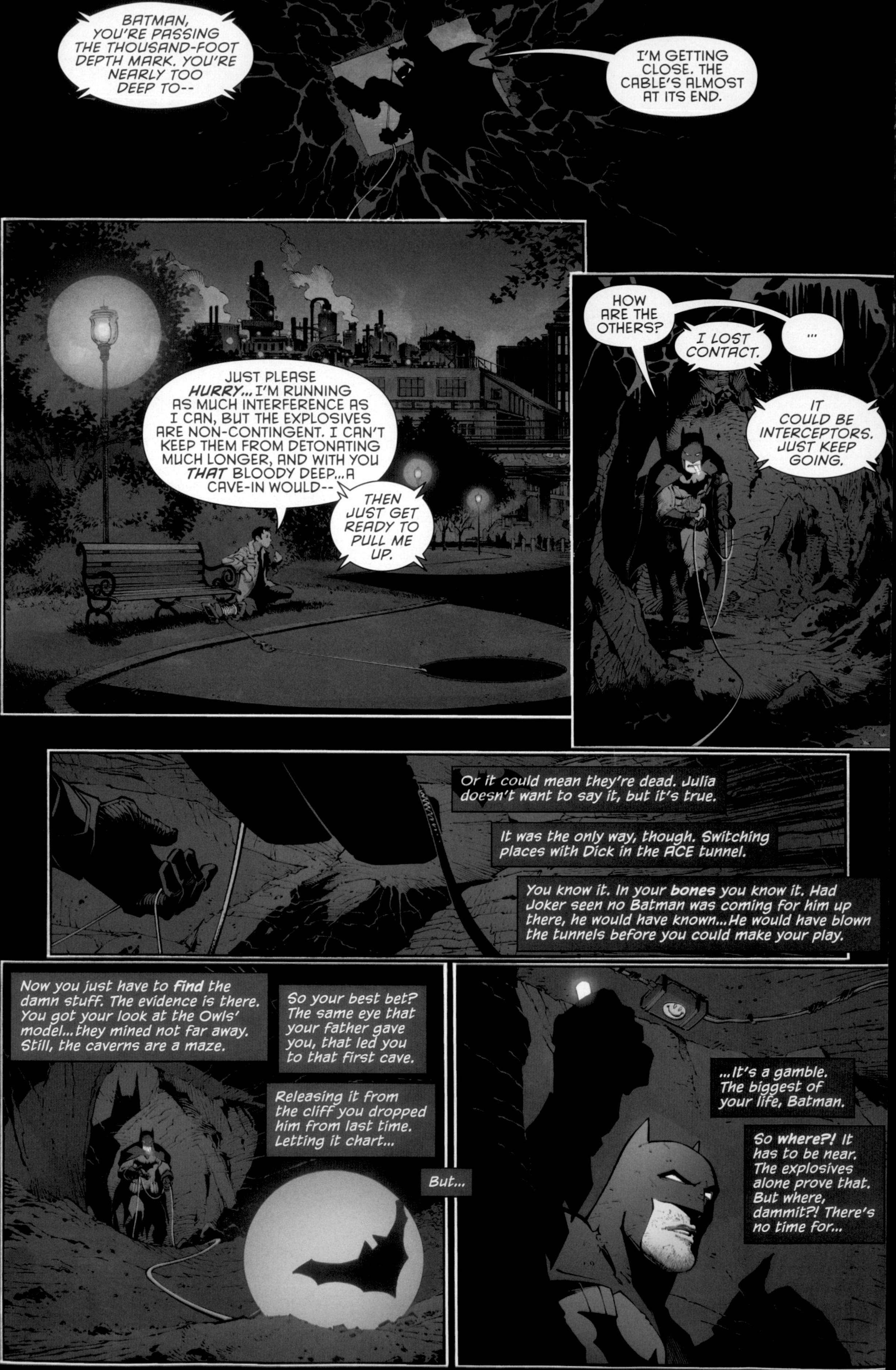
BATMAN, YOU'RE PASSING THE THOUSAND-FOOT DEPTH MARK. YOU'RE NEARLY TOO DEEP TO--
I'M GETTING CLOSE. THE CABLE'S ALMOST AT ITS END.
JUST PLEASE HURRY... I'M RUNNING AS MUCH INTERFERENCE AS I CAN, BUT THE EXPLOSIVES ARE NON-CONTINGENT. I CAN'T KEEP THEM FROM DETONATING MUCH LONGER, AND WITH YOU THAT BLOODY DEEP...A CAVE-IN WOULD--
THEN JUST GET READY TO PULL ME UP.
HOW ARE THE OTHERS?
I LOST CONTACT.
...
IT COULD BE INTERCEPTORS. JUST KEEP GOING.
Or it could mean they're dead. Julia doesn't want to say it, but it's true.
It was the only way, though. Switching places with Dick in the ACE tunnel.
You know it. In your bones you know it. Had Joker seen no Batman was coming for him up there, he would have known...He would have blown the tunnels before you could make your play.
Now you just have to find the damn stuff. The evidence is there. You got your look at the Owls' model...they mined not far away. Still, the caverns are a maze.
So your best bet? The same eye that your father gave you, that led you to that first cave.
Releasing it from the cliff you dropped him from last time. Letting it chart...
But...
...It's a gamble. The biggest of your life, Batman.
So where?! It has to be near. The explosives alone prove that. But where, dammit?! There's no time for...

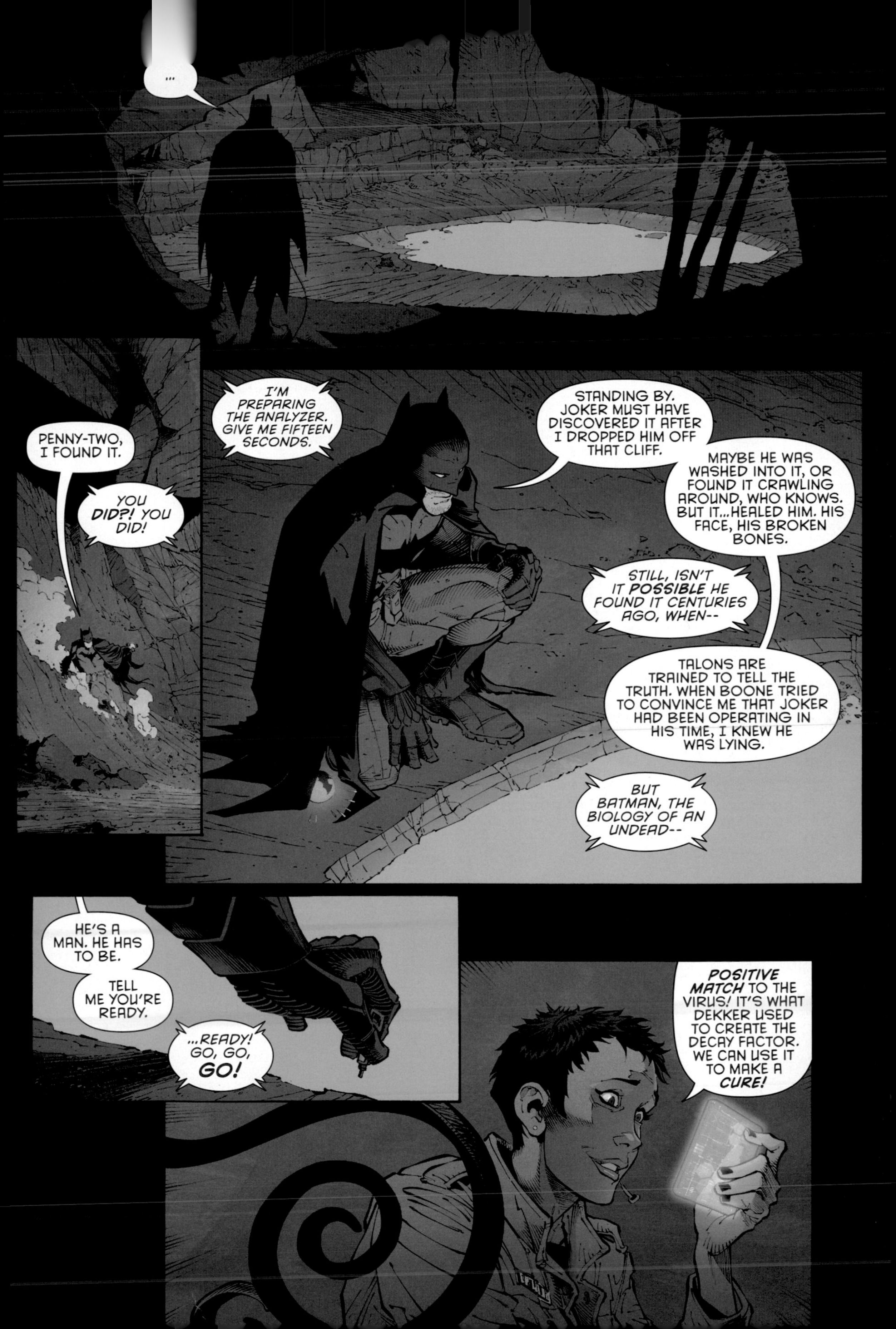
...
PENNY-TWO, I FOUND IT.
YOU DID?! YOU DID!
I'M PREPARING THE ANALYZER. GIVE ME FIFTEEN SECONDS.
STANDING BY. JOKER MUST HAVE DISCOVERED IT AFTER I DROPPED HIM OFF THAT CLIFF.
MAYBE HE WAS WASHED INTO IT, OR FOUND IT CRAWLING AROUND, WHO KNOWS. BUT IT...HEALED HIM. HIS FACE, HIS BROKEN BONES.
STILL, ISN'T IT POSSIBLE HE FOUND IT CENTURIES AGO, WHEN--
TALONS ARE TRAINED TO TELL THE TRUTH. WHEN BOONE TRIED TO CONVINCE ME THAT JOKER HAD BEEN OPERATING IN HIS TIME, I KNEW HE WAS LYING.
BUT BATMAN, THE BIOLOGY OF AN UNDEAD--
HE'S A MAN. HE HAS TO BE.
TELL ME YOU'RE READY.
...READY! GO, GO, GO!
POSITIVE MATCH TO THE VIRUS! IT'S WHAT DEKKER USED TO CREATE THE DECAY FACTOR. WE CAN USE IT TO MAKE A CURE!

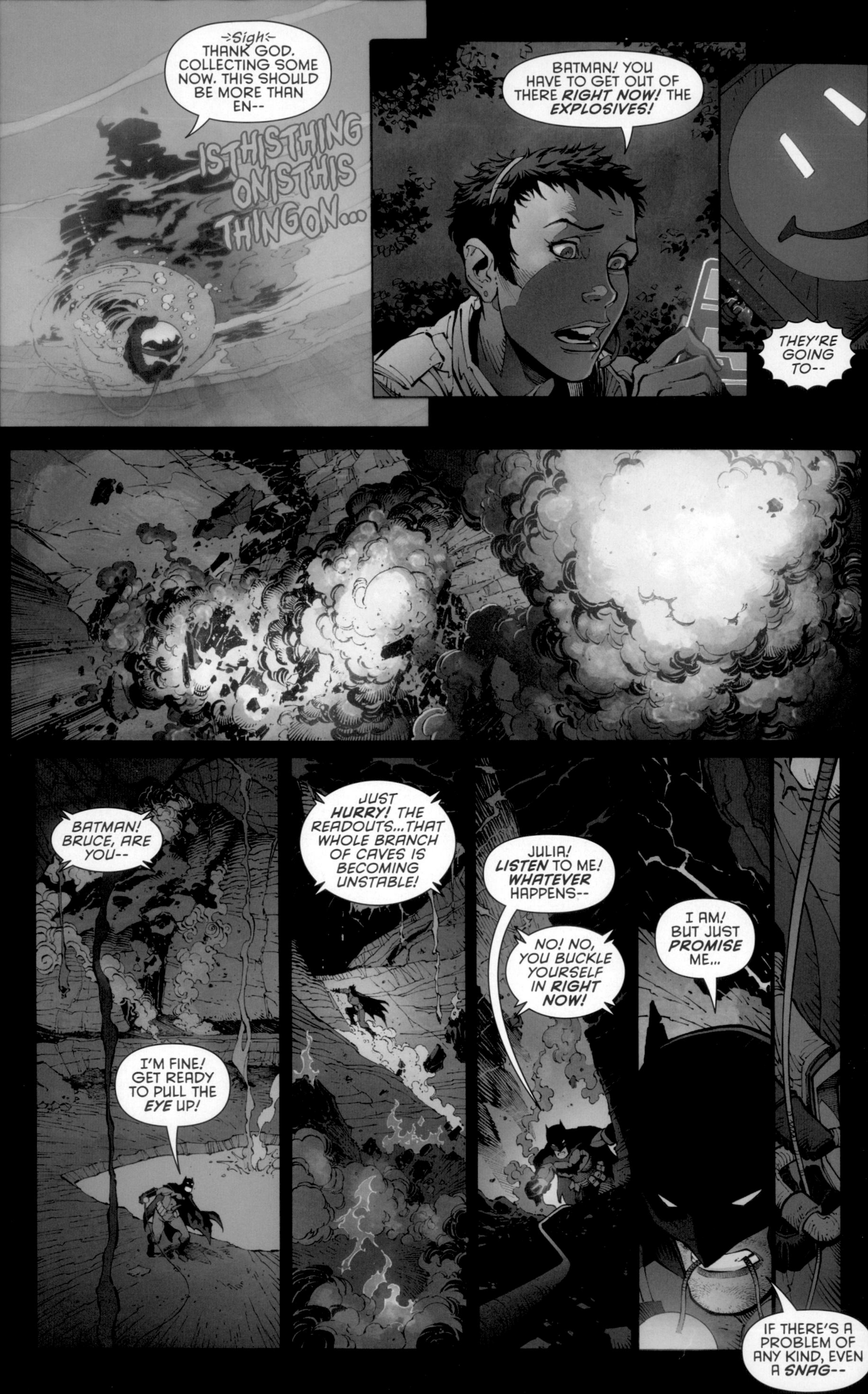

-Sigh- THANK GOD. COLLECTING SOME NOW. THIS SHOULD BE MORE THAN EN--
ISTHISTHING ONISTHIS THINGON...
BATMAN! YOU HAVE TO GET OUT OF THERE RIGHT NOW! THE EXPLOSIVES!
THEY'RE GOING TO--
BATMAN! BRUCE, ARE YOU--
I'M FINE! GET READY TO PULL THE EYE UP!
JUST HURRY! THE READOUTS...THAT WHOLE BRANCH OF CAVES IS BECOMING UNSTABLE!
JULIA! LISTEN TO ME! WHATEVER HAPPENS--
NO! NO, YOU BUCKLE YOURSELF IN RIGHT NOW!
I AM! BUT JUST PROMISE ME...
IF THERE'S A PROBLEM OF ANY KIND, EVEN A SNAG--

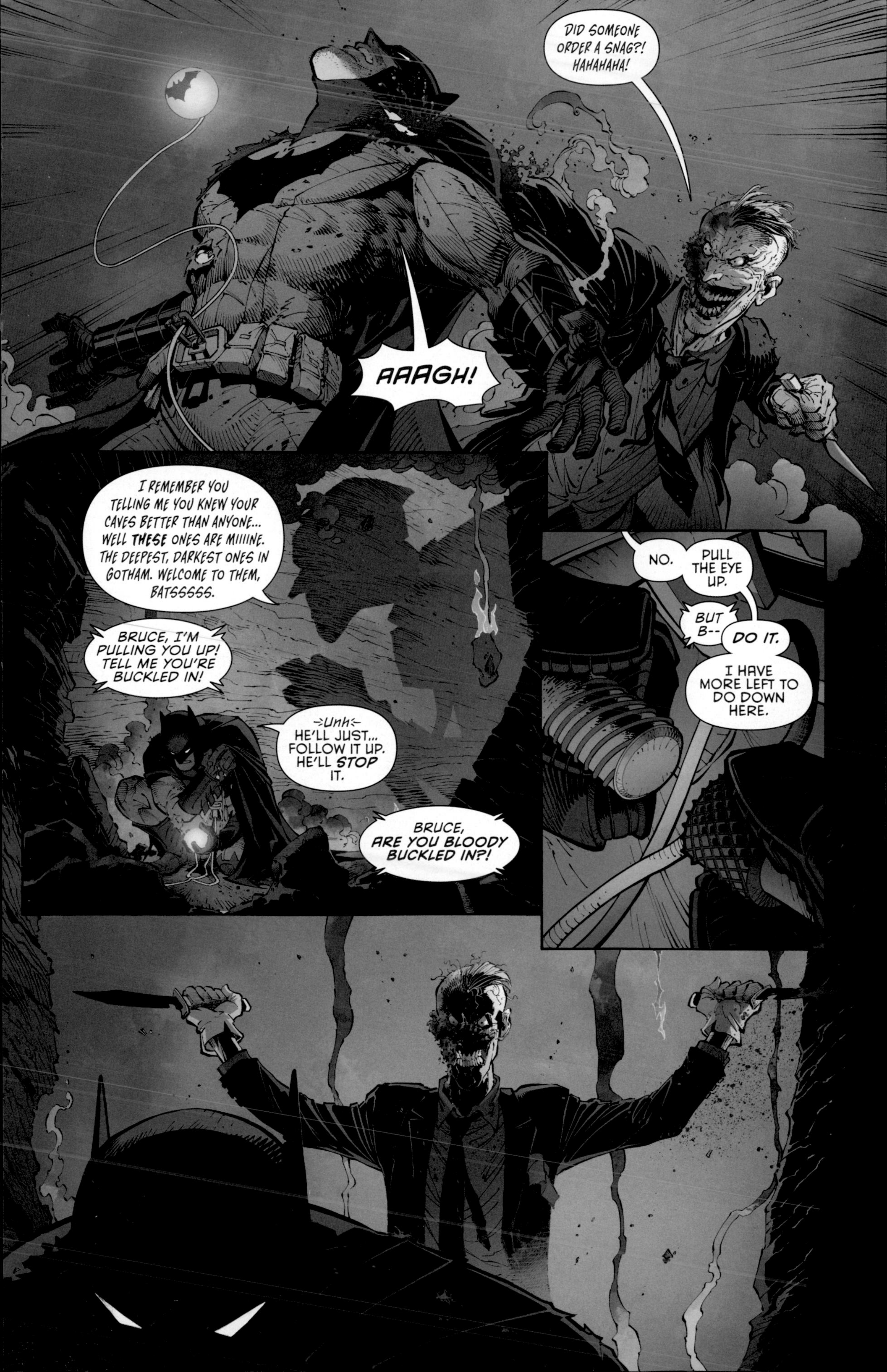
DID SOMEONE ORDER A SNAG?! HAHAHAHA!
AAAGH!
I REMEMBER YOU TELLING ME YOU KNEW YOUR CAVES BETTER THAN ANYONE... WELL THESE ONES ARE MIIIINE. THE DEEPEST, DARKEST ONES IN GOTHAM. WELCOME TO THEM, BATSSSSS.
BRUCE, I'M PULLING YOU UP! TELL ME YOU'RE BUCKLED IN!
Unh
HE'LL JUST... FOLLOW IT UP. HE'LL STOP IT.
BRUCE, ARE YOU BLOODY BUCKLED IN?!
NO.
PULL THE EYE UP.
BUT B--
DO IT.
I HAVE MORE LEFT TO DO DOWN HERE.

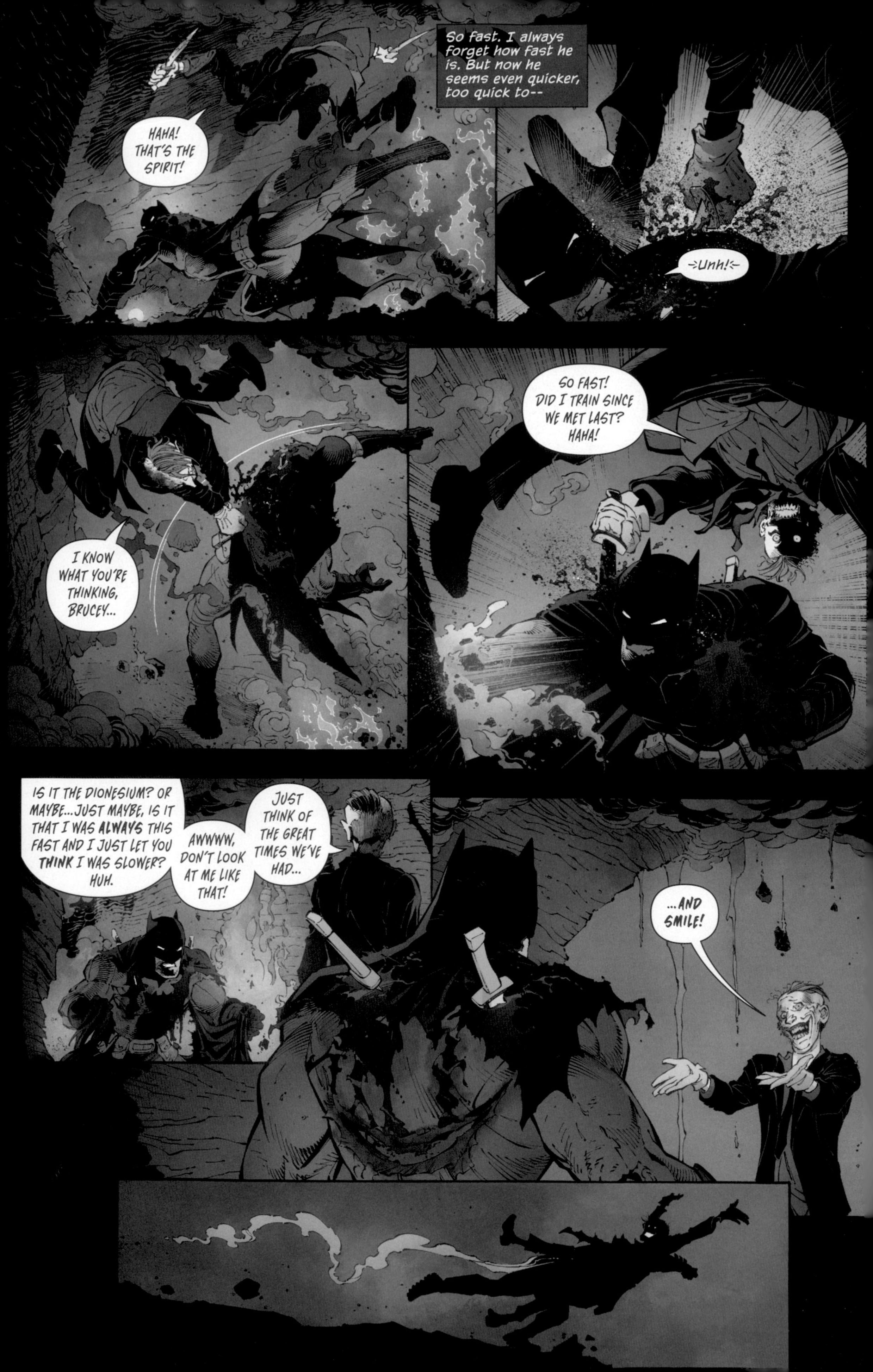
So fast. I always forget how fast he is. But now he seems even quicker, too quick to--
HAHA! THAT'S THE SPIRIT!
Unh!
I KNOW WHAT YOU'RE THINKING, BRUCEY...
SO FAST! DID I TRAIN SINCE WE MET LAST? HAHA!
IS IT THE DIONESIUM? OR MAYBE...JUST MAYBE, IS IT THAT I WAS ALWAYS THIS FAST AND I JUST LET YOU THINK I WAS SLOWER? HUH.
AWWWW, DON'T LOOK AT ME LIKE THAT!
JUST THINK OF THE GREAT TIMES WE'VE HAD...
...AND SMILE!

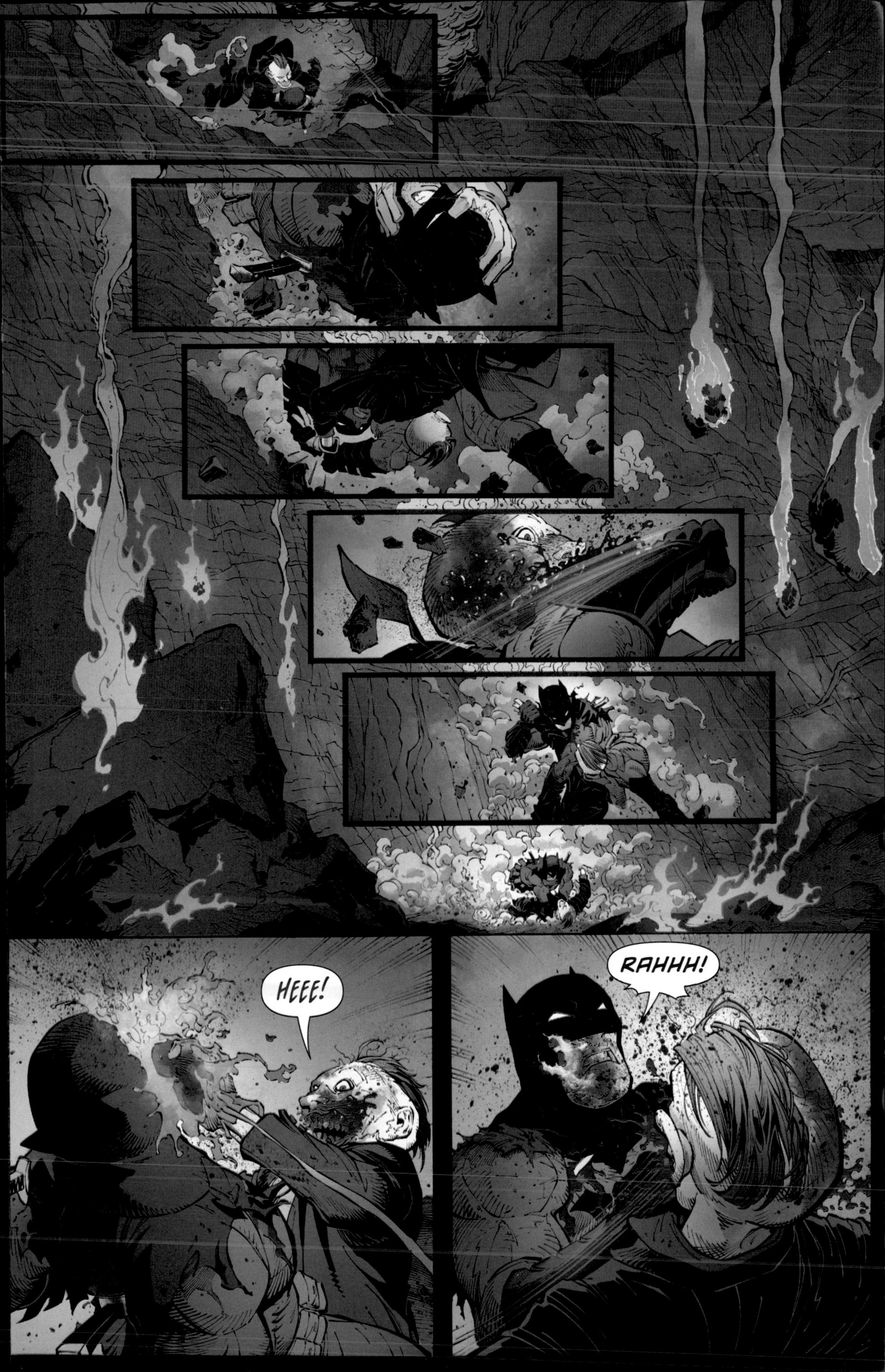
HEEE!
RAHHH!

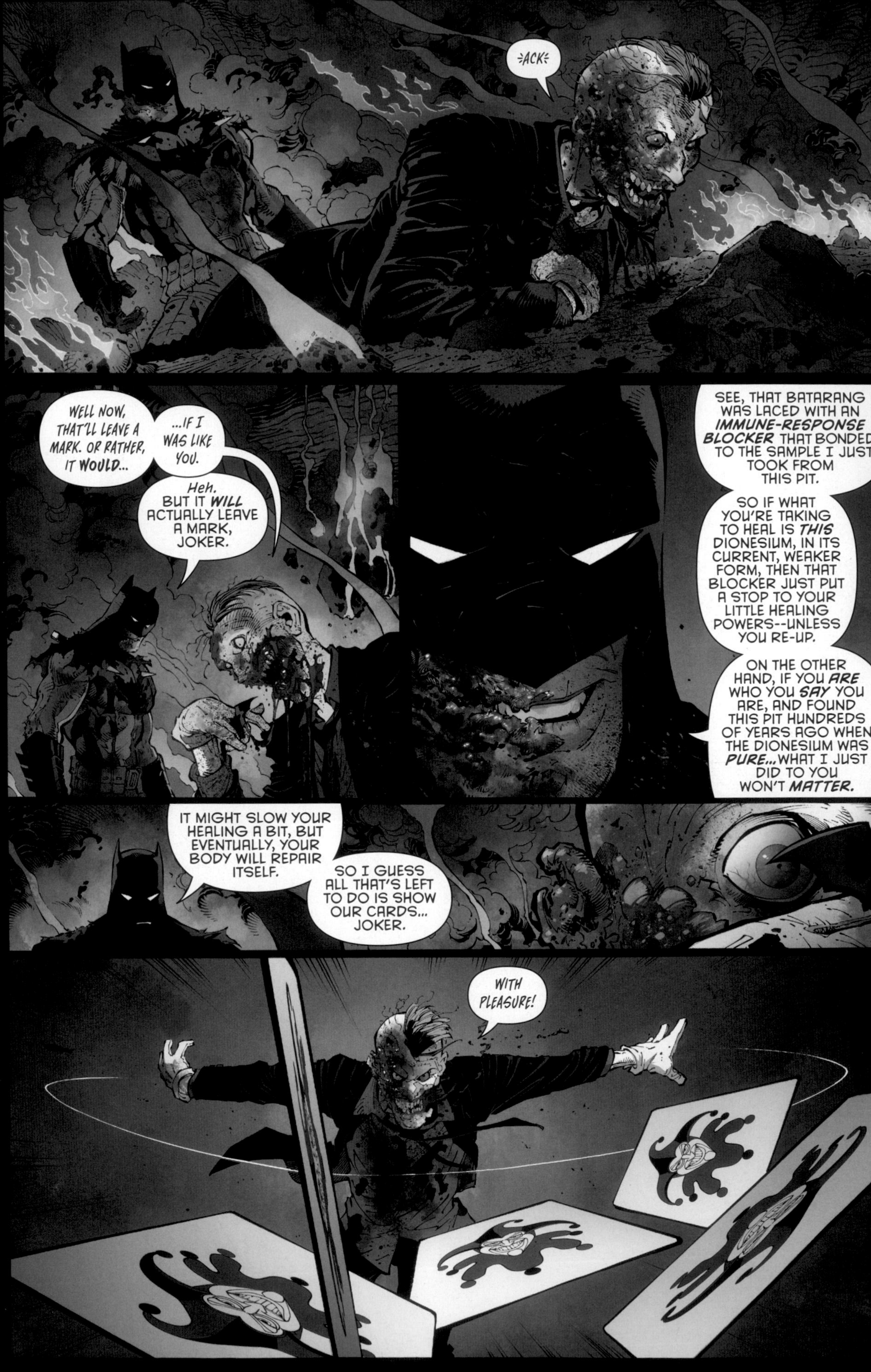

ACK
WELL NOW, THAT'LL LEAVE A MARK. OR RATHER, IT WOULD...
...IF I WAS LIKE YOU.
Heh. BUT IT WILL ACTUALLY LEAVE A MARK, JOKER.
SEE, THAT BATARANG WAS LACED WITH AN IMMUNE-RESPONSE BLOCKER THAT BONDED TO THE SAMPLE I JUST TOOK FROM THIS PIT.
SO IF WHAT YOU'RE TAKING TO HEAL IS THIS DIONESIUM, IN ITS CURRENT, WEAKER FORM, THEN THAT BLOCKER JUST PUT A STOP TO YOUR LITTLE HEALING POWERS--UNLESS YOU RE-UP.
ON THE OTHER HAND, IF YOU ARE WHO YOU SAY YOU ARE, AND FOUND THIS PIT HUNDREDS OF YEARS AGO WHEN THE DIONESIUM WAS PURE...WHAT I JUST DID TO YOU WON'T MATTER.
IT MIGHT SLOW YOUR HEALING A BIT, BUT EVENTUALLY, YOUR BODY WILL REPAIR ITSELF.
SO I GUESS ALL THAT'S LEFT TO DO IS SHOW OUR CARDS... JOKER.
WITH PLEASURE!

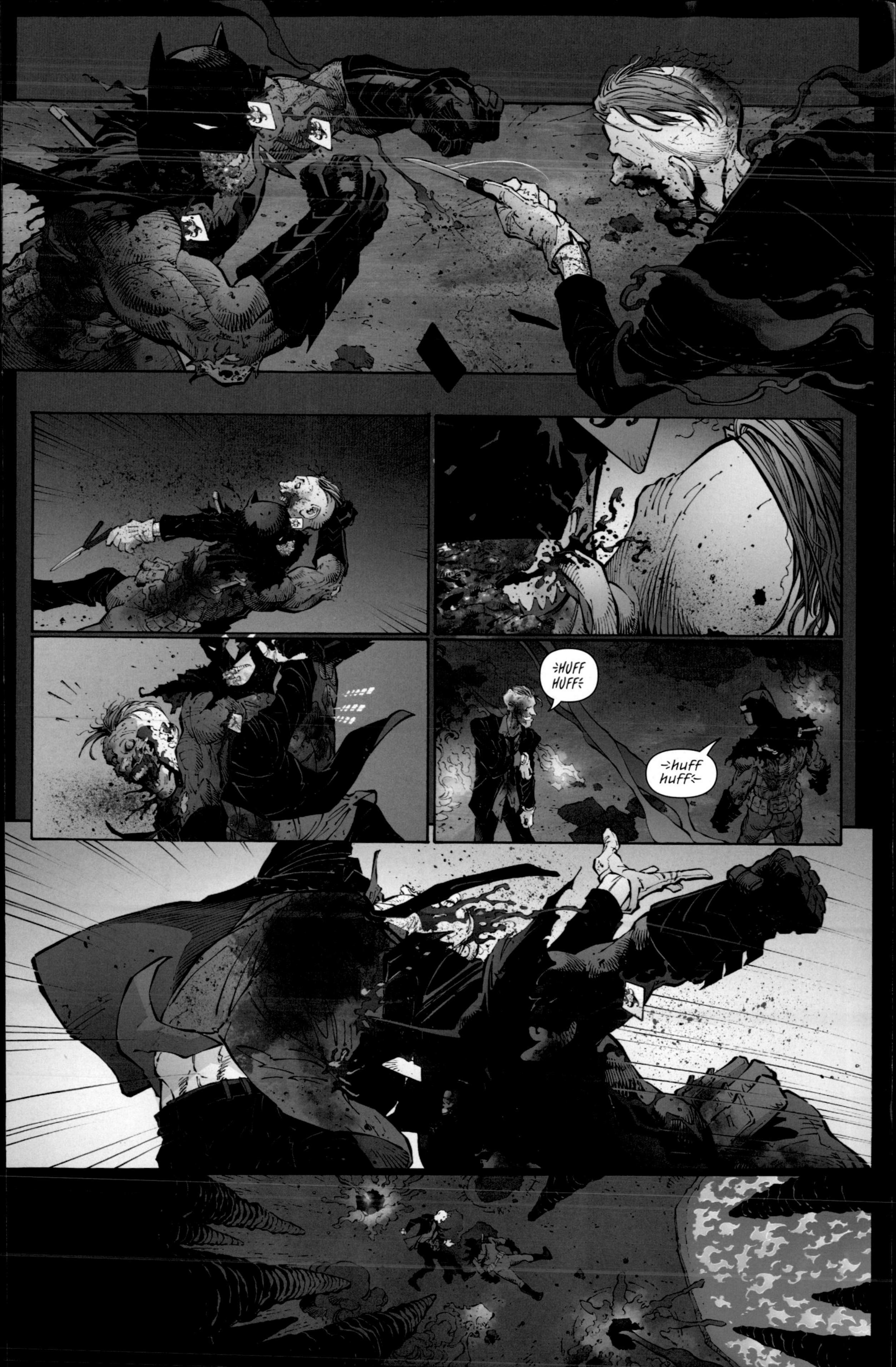

HUFF HUFF
huff huff

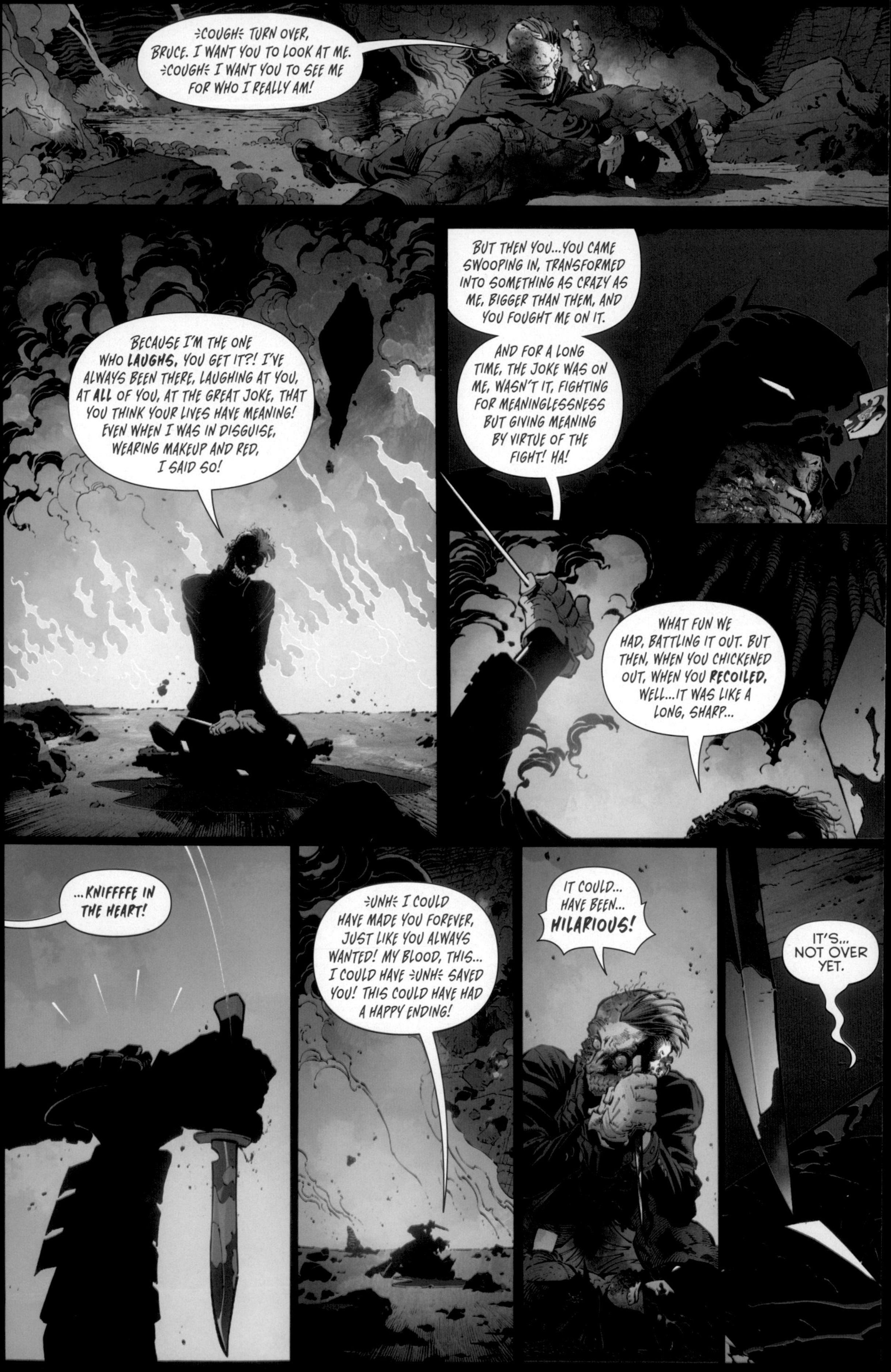

COUGH TURN OVER, BRUCE. I WANT YOU TO LOOK AT ME. COUGH I WANT YOU TO SEE ME FOR WHO I REALLY AM!
BECAUSE I'M THE ONE WHO LAUGHS, YOU GET IT?! I'VE ALWAYS BEEN THERE, LAUGHING AT YOU, AT ALL OF YOU, AT THE GREAT JOKE, THAT YOU THINK YOUR LIVES HAVE MEANING! EVEN WHEN I WAS IN DISGUISE, WEARING MAKEUP AND RED, I SAID SO!
BUT THEN YOU...YOU CAME SWOOPING IN, TRANSFORMED INTO SOMETHING AS CRAZY AS ME, BIGGER THAN THEM, AND YOU FOUGHT ME ON IT.
AND FOR A LONG TIME, THE JOKE WAS ON ME, WASN'T IT, FIGHTING FOR MEANINGLESSNESS BUT GIVING MEANING BY VIRTUE OF THE FIGHT! HA!
WHAT FUN WE HAD, BATTLING IT OUT. BUT THEN, WHEN YOU CHICKENED OUT, WHEN YOU RECOILED, WELL...IT WAS LIKE A LONG, SHARP...
...KNIFFFFE IN THE HEART!
UNH I COULD HAVE MADE YOU FOREVER, JUST LIKE YOU ALWAYS WANTED! MY BLOOD, THIS... I COULD HAVE UNH SAVED YOU! THIS COULD HAVE HAD A HAPPY ENDING!
IT COULD... HAVE BEEN... HILARIOUS!
IT'S... NOT OVER YET.

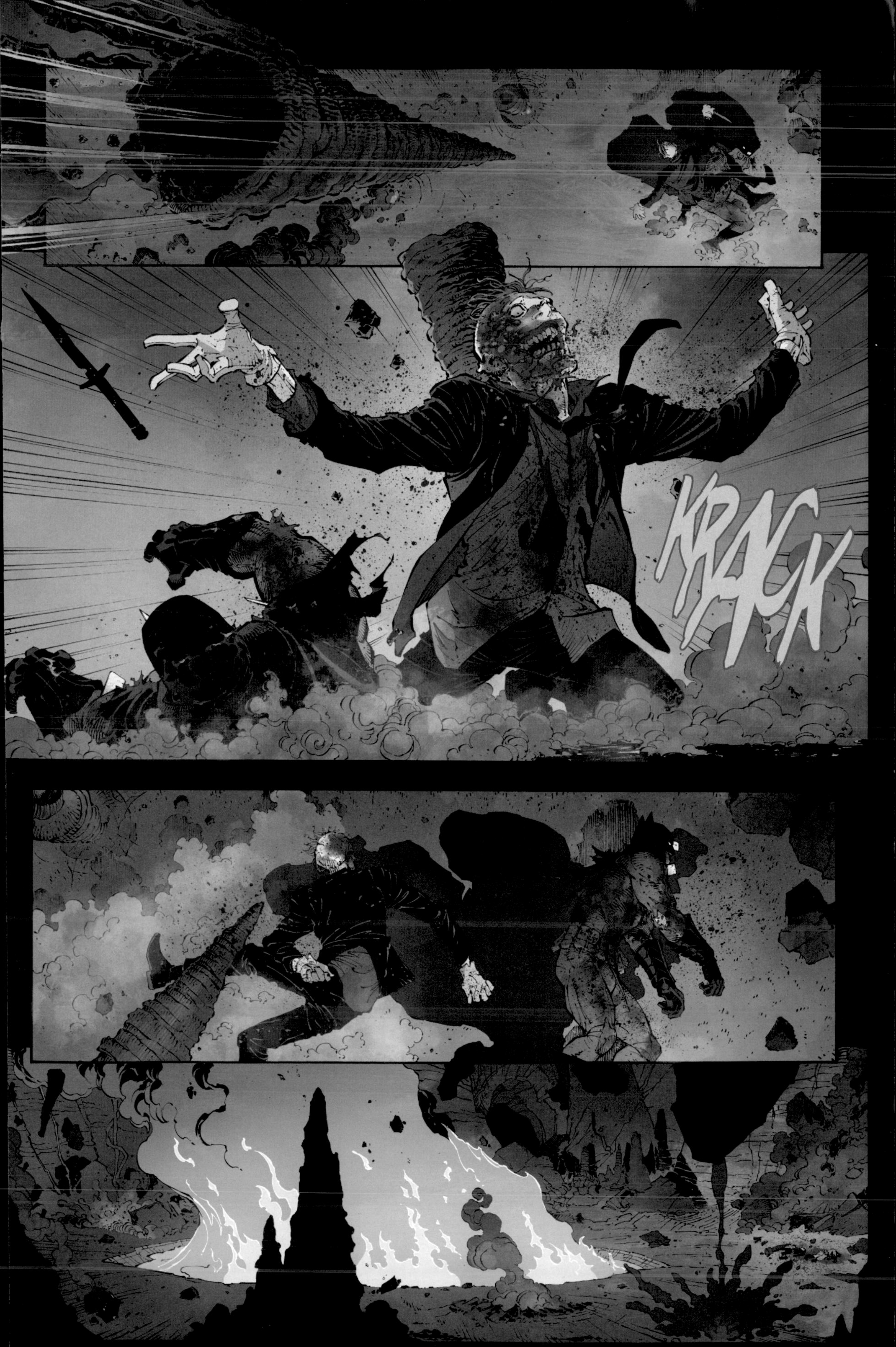
KRACK

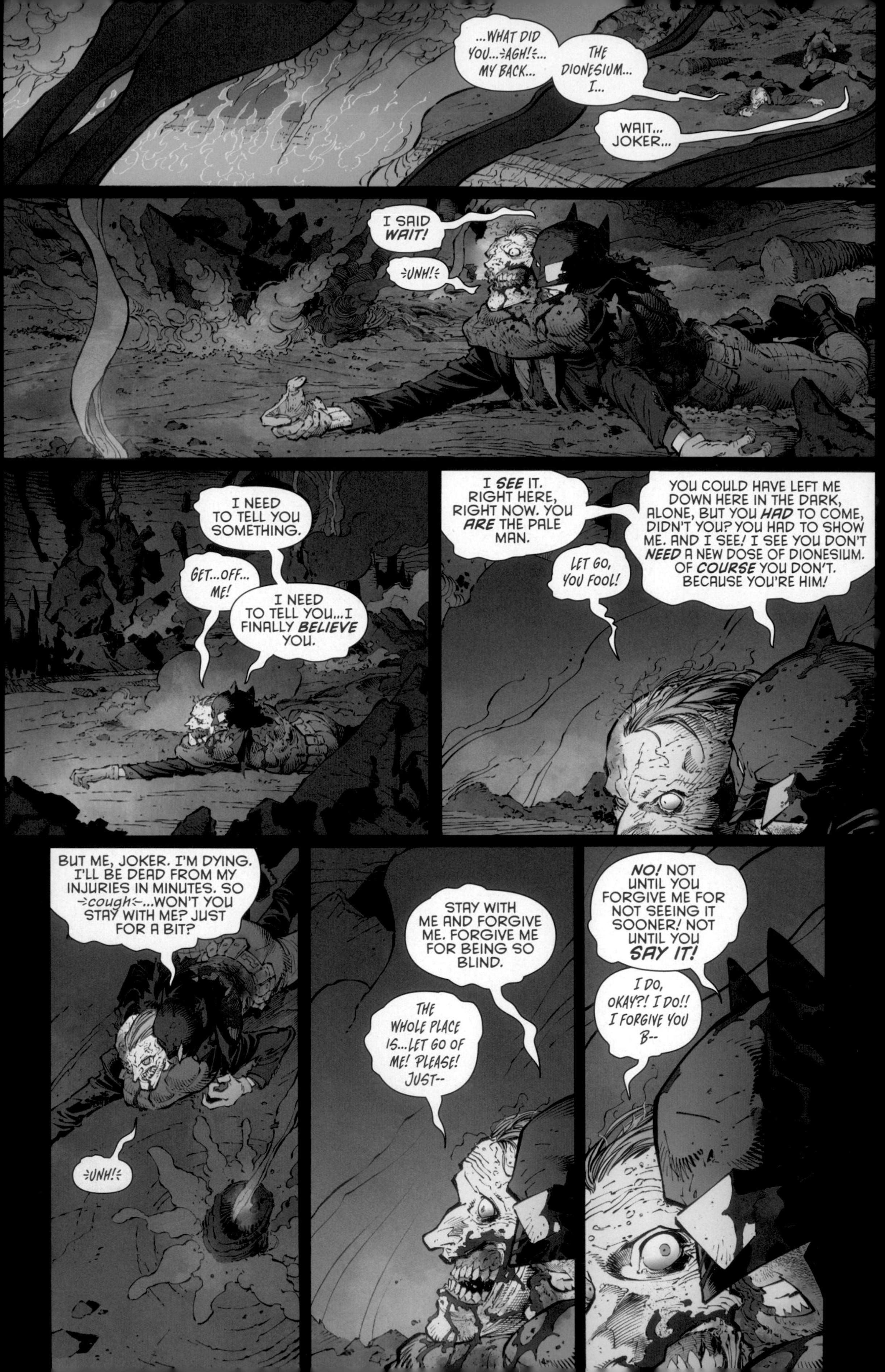
...WHAT DID YOU... ⇝AGH!⇜... MY BACK...
THE DIONESIUM... I...
WAIT... JOKER...
I SAID WAIT!
⇝UNH!⇜
I NEED TO TELL YOU SOMETHING.
GET...OFF... ME!
I NEED TO TELL YOU...I FINALLY BELIEVE YOU.
I SEE IT. RIGHT HERE, RIGHT NOW. YOU ARE THE PALE MAN.
YOU COULD HAVE LEFT ME DOWN HERE IN THE DARK, ALONE, BUT YOU HAD TO COME, DIDN'T YOU? YOU HAD TO SHOW ME. AND I SEE! I SEE YOU DON'T NEED A NEW DOSE OF DIONESIUM. OF COURSE YOU DON'T. BECAUSE YOU'RE HIM!
LET GO, YOU FOOL!
BUT ME, JOKER. I'M DYING. I'LL BE DEAD FROM MY INJURIES IN MINUTES. SO ⇝cough⇜...WON'T YOU STAY WITH ME? JUST FOR A BIT?
⇝UNH!⇜
STAY WITH ME AND FORGIVE ME. FORGIVE ME FOR BEING SO BLIND.
THE WHOLE PLACE IS...LET GO OF ME! PLEASE! JUST--
NO! NOT UNTIL YOU FORGIVE ME FOR NOT SEEING IT SOONER! NOT UNTIL YOU SAY IT!
I DO, OKAY?! I DO!! I FORGIVE YOU B--

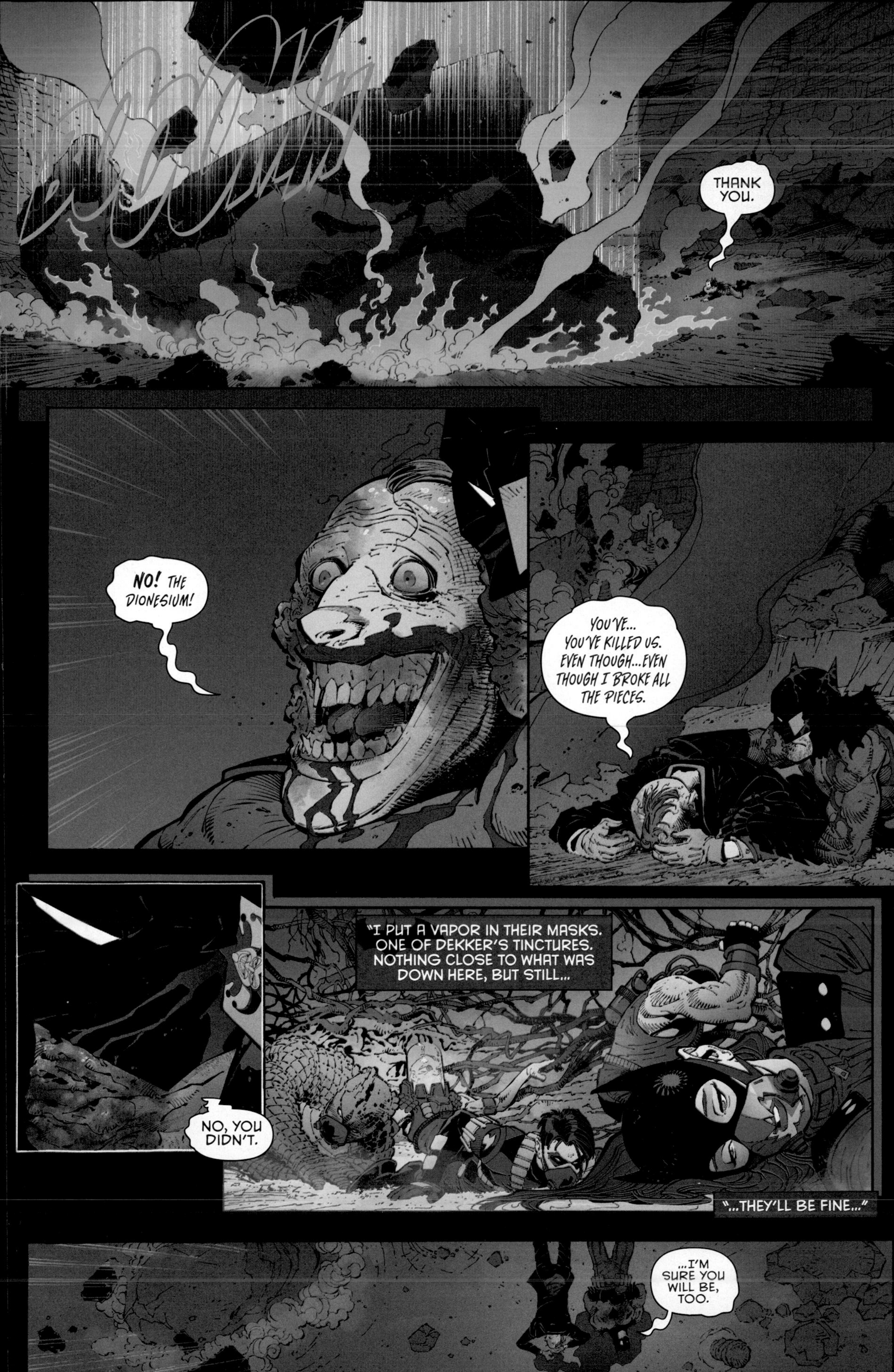
THANK YOU.
NO! THE DIONESIUM!
YOU'VE... YOU'VE KILLED US. EVEN THOUGH...EVEN THOUGH I BROKE ALL THE PIECES.
NO, YOU DIDN'T.
"I PUT A VAPOR IN THEIR MASKS. ONE OF DEKKER'S TINCTURES. NOTHING CLOSE TO WHAT WAS DOWN HERE, BUT STILL...
"...THEY'LL BE FINE..."
...I'M SURE YOU WILL BE, TOO.

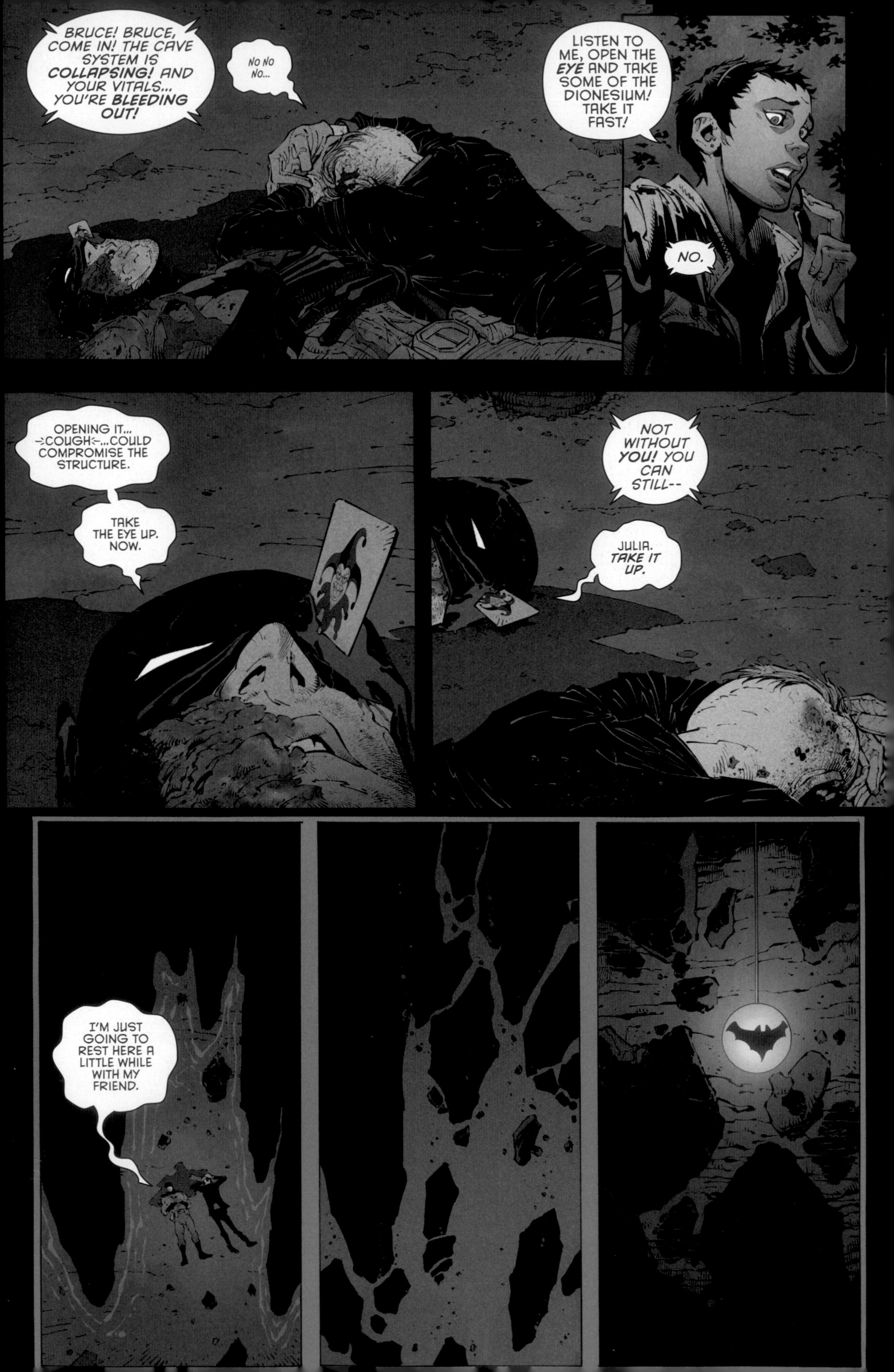
BRUCE! BRUCE, COME IN! THE CAVE SYSTEM IS COLLAPSING! AND YOUR VITALS... YOU'RE BLEEDING OUT!
NO NO NO...
LISTEN TO ME, OPEN THE EYE AND TAKE SOME OF THE DIONESIUM! TAKE IT FAST!
NO.
OPENING IT... -COUGH-...COULD COMPROMISE THE STRUCTURE.
TAKE THE EYE UP. NOW.
NOT WITHOUT YOU! YOU CAN STILL--
JULIA. TAKE IT UP.
I'M JUST GOING TO REST HERE A LITTLE WHILE WITH MY FRIEND.

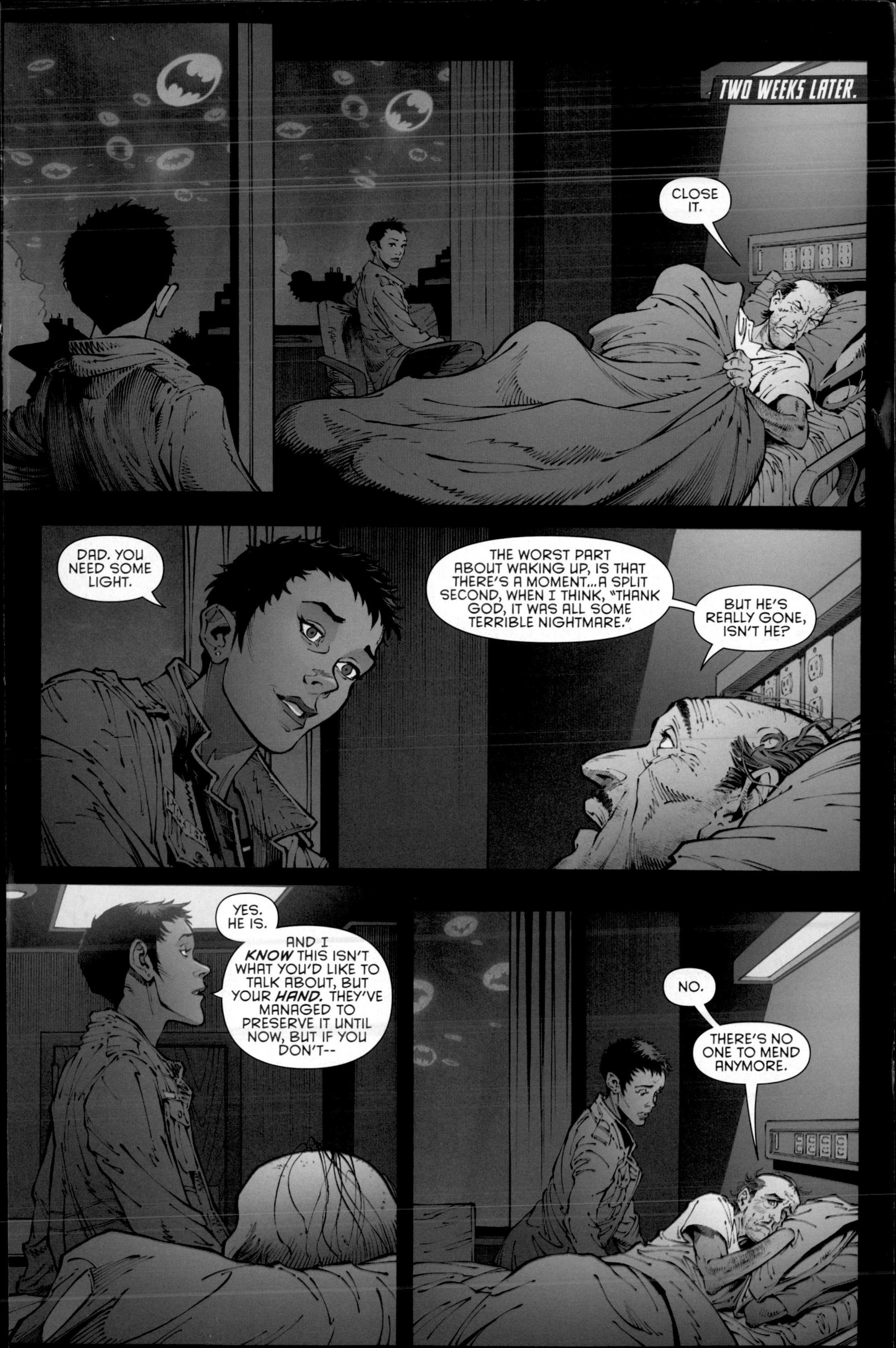
TWO WEEKS LATER.
CLOSE IT.
DAD. YOU NEED SOME LIGHT.
THE WORST PART ABOUT WAKING UP, IS THAT THERE'S A MOMENT...A SPLIT SECOND, WHEN I THINK, "THANK GOD, IT WAS ALL SOME TERRIBLE NIGHTMARE."
BUT HE'S REALLY GONE, ISN'T HE?
YES. HE IS.
AND I KNOW THIS ISN'T WHAT YOU'D LIKE TO TALK ABOUT, BUT YOUR HAND. THEY'VE MANAGED TO PRESERVE IT UNTIL NOW, BUT IF YOU DON'T--
NO.
THERE'S NO ONE TO MEND ANYMORE.

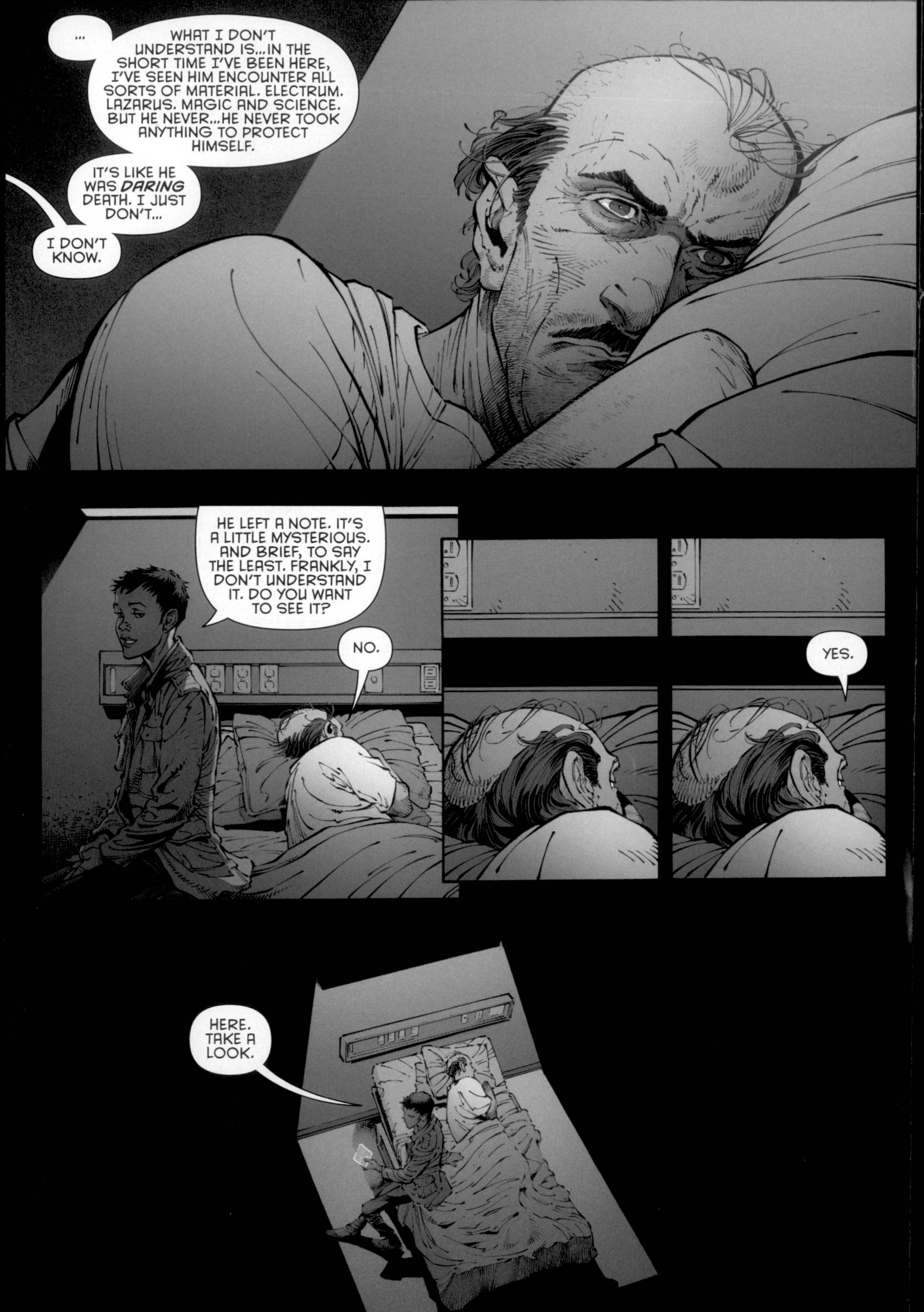
...
WHAT I DON'T UNDERSTAND IS...IN THE SHORT TIME I'VE BEEN HERE, I'VE SEEN HIM ENCOUNTER ALL SORTS OF MATERIAL. ELECTRUM. LAZARUS. MAGIC AND SCIENCE. BUT HE NEVER...HE NEVER TOOK ANYTHING TO PROTECT HIMSELF.
IT'S LIKE HE WAS *DARING* DEATH. I JUST DON'T...
I DON'T KNOW.
HE LEFT A NOTE. IT'S A LITTLE MYSTERIOUS. AND BRIEF, TO SAY THE LEAST. FRANKLY, I DON'T UNDERSTAND IT. DO YOU WANT TO SEE IT?
NO.
YES.
HERE. TAKE A LOOK.

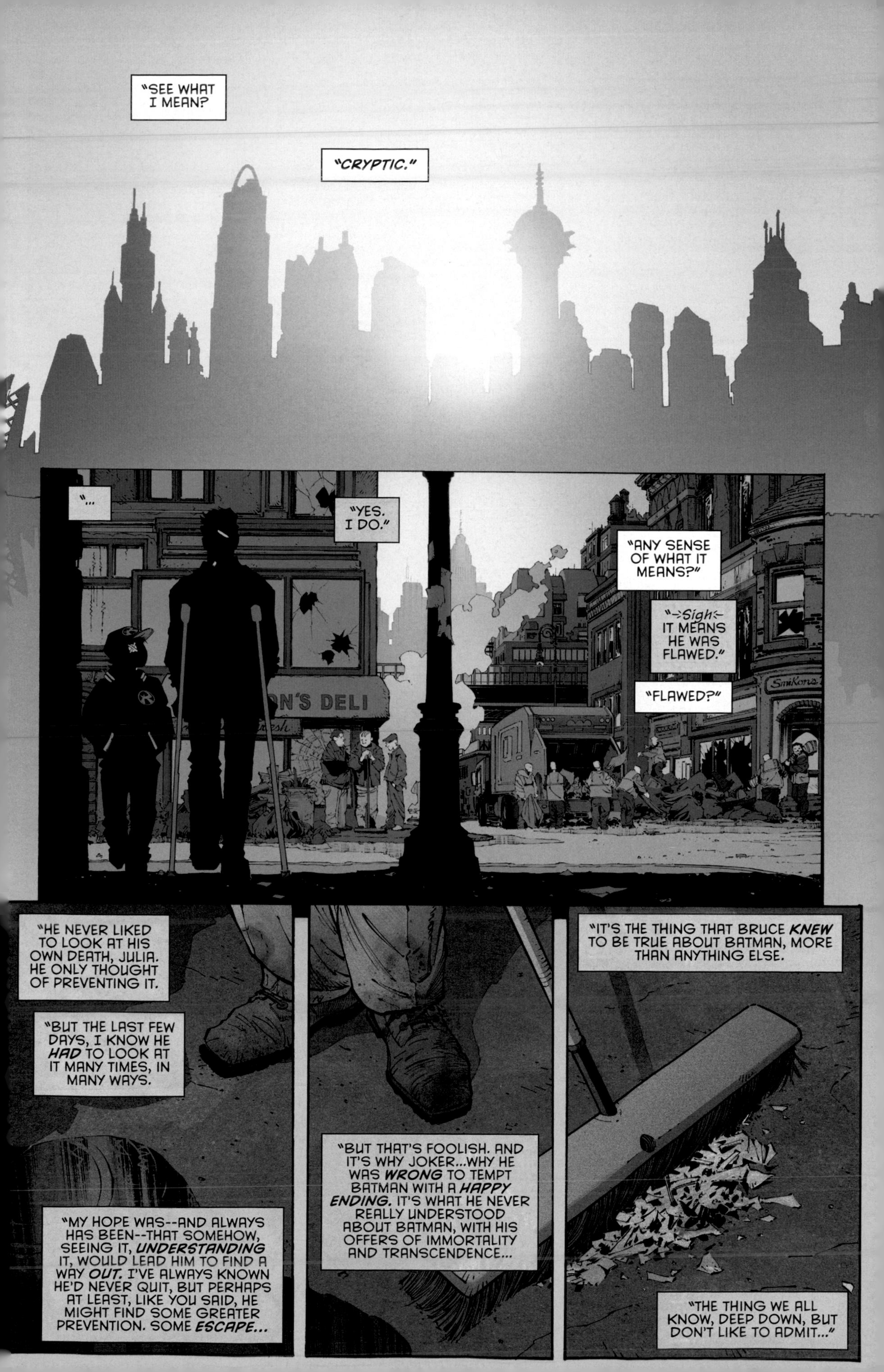
"SEE WHAT I MEAN?
"CRYPTIC."
"...
"YES. I DO."
"ANY SENSE OF WHAT IT MEANS?"
"-›Sigh‹- IT MEANS HE WAS FLAWED."
"FLAWED?"
'S DELI
"HE NEVER LIKED TO LOOK AT HIS OWN DEATH, JULIA. HE ONLY THOUGHT OF PREVENTING IT.
"BUT THE LAST FEW DAYS, I KNOW HE *HAD* TO LOOK AT IT MANY TIMES, IN MANY WAYS.
"MY HOPE WAS--AND ALWAYS HAS BEEN--THAT SOMEHOW, SEEING IT, *UNDERSTANDING* IT, WOULD LEAD HIM TO FIND A WAY *OUT*. I'VE ALWAYS KNOWN HE'D NEVER QUIT, BUT PERHAPS AT LEAST, LIKE YOU SAID, HE MIGHT FIND SOME GREATER PREVENTION. SOME *ESCAPE...*
"BUT THAT'S FOOLISH. AND IT'S WHY JOKER...WHY HE WAS *WRONG* TO TEMPT BATMAN WITH A *HAPPY ENDING.* IT'S WHAT HE NEVER REALLY UNDERSTOOD ABOUT BATMAN, WITH HIS OFFERS OF IMMORTALITY AND TRANSCENDENCE...
"IT'S THE THING THAT BRUCE *KNEW* TO BE TRUE ABOUT BATMAN, MORE THAN ANYTHING ELSE.
"THE THING WE ALL KNOW, DEEP DOWN, BUT DON'T LIKE TO ADMIT..."

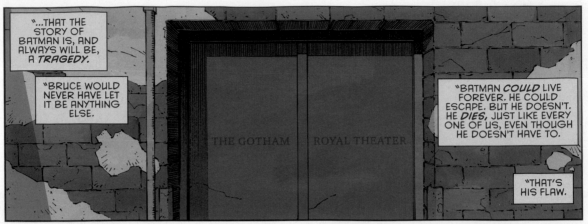

"...THAT THE STORY OF BATMAN IS, AND ALWAYS WILL BE, A *TRAGEDY.*

"BRUCE WOULD NEVER HAVE LET IT BE ANYTHING ELSE.

THE GOTHAM ROYAL THEATER

"BATMAN *COULD* LIVE FOREVER. HE COULD ESCAPE. BUT HE DOESN'T. HE *DIES*, JUST LIKE EVERY ONE OF US, EVEN THOUGH HE DOESN'T HAVE TO.

"THAT'S HIS FLAW.

"BUT IT'S ALSO HIS GREATEST STRENGTH. THE VERY THING THAT MAKES HIM IMMORTAL.

"HE SAYS, WE'RE IN THIS TOGETHER. HE SAYS, LIVE BRAVELY IN THE TIME YOU HAVE AND SMILE AT THE VOID.

"THAT'S WHY THE NOTE SAYS WHAT IT DOES. WHY IT'S ONLY ONE WORD.

"WHY BATMAN'S LAST MESSAGE IS, AND WILL ALWAYS BE...

HA.